THIRD YEAR

LATIN

ROBERT J. HENLE, S.J.

LOYOLAPRESS.
CHICAGO

LOYOLA PRESS.
3441 N. Ashland Avenue
Chicago, Illinois 60657
(800) 621-1008
www.loyolapress.com

Library of Congress Catalog Card Number: 59-5027

ISBN 13: 978-0-8294-1028-0
ISBN 10: 0-8294-1028-7

Printed in the United States of America.
16 17 18 TS 10 9 8 7 6 5 4 3

PREFACE

This edition of selected speeches of Cicero constitutes the third volume in the four-year high-school Latin course by Reverend Robert J. Henle, S. J. The first and third Catilinarians, together with generous selections from the Verrines, will give the student an ample acquaintance with the finest in Roman oratory. Selections from the philosophical works and the letters of Cicero were not included because of a desire to secure for the students a rather thorough acquaintance with that which constituted the strongest element in the education of the Romans.

In accordance with this concentration on the oratory of Cicero, and because of the suggestions of teachers using the series, we have included, for theirs and the students' convenience, a brief description of the salient features of Roman oratory. Outlines of the various speeches have been included to help the student master the sequence of ideas and appreciate the cogency of Cicero's arguments. As a help toward securing an appreciation of Cicero's style a somewhat lengthy list of stylistic devices has also been included.

Acknowledgment is due to Reverend Gilbert C. Peterson, S. J., for permission to use his sense-line arrangement of the *First Oration against Catiline,* published by the *Classical Bulletin,* and to the Harvard University Press for permission to quote passages from L. H. G. Greenwood's *Cicero: The Verrine Orations* (the Loeb Classical Library), as well as to M. L. Clarke of University College of North Wales for permission to use a quotation from his book, *Rhetoric at Rome.* Very special thanks are due to Reverend Charles T. Hunter, S. J., who was responsible for a revision of the first printing of the book.

CONTENTS

ROMAN ORATORY

Even a superficial study of ancient history reveals the Romans as great soldiers whose conquests embraced the then known world. A closer scrutiny, however, shows them to be no less great as politicians and orators. Caesar we have followed in his extension and consolidation of the Roman Empire. Now, in this the third year of Latin, we turn our attention to Roman politics and law, in which oratory played such a great part. But before plunging into the finished masterpieces of Cicero, we will take a brief look at some of the elements that helped to fashion Roman oratory.

History of Roman Oratory

We can distinguish four great periods in the development of oratory at Rome. Cato the censor (d. 194 B. C.) may be considered the model in the earlier period which was characterized by communication of ideas rather than fineness of expression. Actual practice was the mother of eloquence, and she made little use of artificial adornment.

Tiberius Gracchus, who was tribune in 133 B. C. and his brother Gaius, who was tribune in 123 B. C., both of them strong proponents of agrarian and other reforms, were prominent in the Greek period. Due in large part to Greek influence and the rhetorical treatises that had been published, the orators began to aim at beauty of expression as well as effectiveness. The orators of this period exhibited a freedom and ease of composition that reflected the influence of the Greek masters like Lysias, who used the plain style, Isocrates, who used an ornate style, and Demosthenes, who more or less combined the good features of both styles.

Marcus Antonius (d. 87 B. C.) and Lucius Crassus (d. 91 B. C.) ushered in the Ciceronian period. Both were outstanding orators and exerted a marked influence on Cicero (d. December 7,

43 B. C.). Quintus Hortensius (d. 50 B. C.) was the *rex judiciorum* for thirteen years until Cicero bested him at the trial of Verres and took over the position of leading orator at Rome. Both men, however, remained friends and took many cases together.

After Cicero we have the imperial period, which spelled the death of oratory since the form of government no longer allowed such a wide scope for the orator's powers, nor was oratory any longer the steppingstone to the highest offices of the state. Oratory became more or less academic; one might say, art for art's sake. This period is noteworthy because Marcus Fabius Quintilian (d. cir. A. D. 97), the renowned rhetorician, wrote his famous work *Dē Institūtiōne Ōrātōriā,* which together with Cicero's work *Dē Ōrātōre* give us most of the theory of Roman oratory.

Oratorical Styles in the Ciceronian Period

During the Ciceronian period there were two styles of oratory. Hortensius represented the Asiatic school, which delighted in display and emotional affectation both in composition and delivery, even to the extent of subordinating content to it. Cicero professed to be an adherent of the Attic school, which was characterized by directness, simplicity, and naturalness. But in view of Cicero's training at Rhodes under the famous rhetorician Molo, it seems more correct to say that he achieved the ideal combination of both schools of oratory.

Types of Orations

Roman rhetoricians mention three types of orations. The *genus jūdiciāle* was used in civil and criminal actions in court, whether in defense or prosecution. Cicero's *Prō Archiā* is an example of this type, even though the last two thirds of this oration might be considered as belonging to the *genus dēmōnstrātīvum.*

The *genus dēlīberātīvum* was used in the Senate or before the popular assembly when discussing some public question. The speeches of Cicero against Catiline are excellent examples of this second type.

The *genus dēmōnstrātīvum* was used when the orator wished

to praise or censure someone. Cicero's *Prō Mārcellō,* in which he praised both Caesar and Marcellus, may be considered fairly exemplary of this type. The Catilinarians, insofar as they censure Catiline, belong also to this type.

Outline of an Oration

The *genus jūdiciāle* was the most important type and set the pattern for the oration in general. In this pattern we can distinguish six main elements, though not all six are to be found in every oration.

Exordium, the introduction. Its purpose was to render the audience well disposed, attentive, and willing to be persuaded *(reddere audītōrēs benevolōs, attentōs, docilēs).* Roman rhetoricians distinguished two main types, that of the *principium* or direct approach, and the *insinuātiō* or indirect approach. This last was used when for some reason the speaker found himself in an unfavorable position with the audience.

Nārrātiō, the statement of the facts in the case. Such a narration provided the foundation upon which the speaker would rely to prove his case. It provided a summary that was helpful to the jury in following the argument. Toward the close of the *nārrātiō* the orator gave the *prōpositiō* or statement of the main theme.

Partītiō, or *dīvīsiō,*[1] the outline of the proof that is to follow. Here the orator indicated what points he would consider and the order in which he will take them.

Cōnfirmātiō, the affirmative proofs. This, the most important part of the speech, was sometimes divided into the *dē causā* and the *extrā causam.* The former embraced the proofs that pertained strictly to the legal aspect of the case, while the latter dealt with things that had a bearing on the case but were not part of the strictly legal proof.

Refūtātiō, or *reprehensiō,* the rebuttal of the arguments advanced by the opposition. Here the orator had not only to point

---

[1] Cicero in the *Prō Archiā* does not follow the order given here. He gives first the *prōpositiō* and *dīvīsiō* and then follows with the *nārrātiō.*

out the faulty arguments advanced by the opposition, but had to clearly demonstrate their falsity.

Perōrātiō or *conclūsiō*, the conclusion of the speech. Several types of conclusion are listed by Roman rhetoricians. There was the *ēnumerātiō*, or orderly summary such as that had in the conclusion of the *Prō Archiā*. The *indignātiō* was a strong outcry against the position held by the opponent. The *conquestiō* or *commiserātiō* was an appeal to the sympathies of those with whom the decision of the case rested. The final few lines of the *Prō Archiā* are just such a conclusion.

Since among the Romans the study of oratory was an important element in their education, it is not surprising to find their rhetoricians giving detailed instructions for the preparation of a speech as well as for its delivery. The gathering of the materials was called *inventiō*. *Dispositiō* dealt with the proper and effective arrangement of the material. *Ēlocūtiō* concerned itself with the suitable and effective expression in language. Under this heading we find an enumeration of the ornaments of style *(lūmina)* which dealt with the figures of speech and rhetoric. There was, too, the memorization of the speech *(memoria)* and finally the *actiō* or delivery. This last included the use of the voice, facial expressions, and gestures. Roman orators had to be not only good speakers but good actors as well.

"Such was the Art of Rhetoric. It bears all the marks of its Greek origin. It was the creation of the Greek intellect, with its intellectual subtlety and its love of logic and fine distinctions, but of the Greek intellect in its decline, no longer adventurous and creative, but confined within professional and pedagogic bounds. It was open to criticism, and it was sometimes criticised, for its pedantry and remoteness from life. But on the whole the Romans took to it with surprising readiness. From its first introduction to the end of Roman civilisation it was part of the intellectual background of the educated Roman."[2]

---

[2] M. L. Clarke, *Rhetoric at Rome, A Historical Survey*, pp. 36-37. London: Cohen and West, 1953.

DIGEST OF THE FIRST ORATION AGAINST CATILINE

Prōpositiō

Precautions have been taken because your plans are known (1-20),
  yet Senate and consul do not order your execution (21-31)
    in accord with ample precedent in Roman history (32-44)
    and the decree of the Senate (45-48).
  Therefore the consuls are at fault (49).

Formerly such decrees brought instant execution (50-63),
  yet we have delayed the execution of this decree for twenty days (64-69),
  and this our clemency but emboldens you (70-74).
  Therefore I am at fault (75).

My negligence allows you openly to continue your nefarious plans (76-81),
  yet delay in arresting you and ordering your execution is necessary until such time as everyone is convinced of its legality (82-93).
  Meanwhile I shall counteract all your plans (94-98).

Nārrātiō

Your plans are and will be known (99-112); witness our knowledge of:
  the exact date on which Manlius would raise the standard of revolt (113-122),
  the exact date you had set for our slaughter (123-135),
  your designs on Praeneste, which were foiled (136-141).
  Therefore secrecy is impossible (142-147).

We know also of your meeting the night before last at Laeca's house (148-157).
  I even see in this august gathering of senators some of those who were there with you (158-170).
  I know who is to remain in the city and who is to leave, and that my being alive keeps you here (171-179).
  I know that two Roman knights promised to take care of my removal (180-183),
    which of course I foiled (184-191).
  Therefore leave the city, and take your henchmen with you, and free me from fear (192-203).

Hortātiō

You cannot be allowed to remain (204-207),
- even though, thanks to Jupiter, as consul-elect and as consul I successfully foiled your plots against me (208-228),
- since now universal anarchy is your aim (229-234).

Your death is no solution because the conspiracy would not be crushed, but your voluntary departure would be (235-243).

I encourage your departure into exile (244-251) because
- everyone hates and fears you (252-257),
- your influence is unsavory (258-266),
- your private life is a disgrace (267-272),
- you are a bankrupt (273-274),
- the national welfare demands it (275-278), since everyone knows
  - your nefarious plans in the consulship of Lepidus and Tullus (279-289) and
  - your attempts against me as consul-elect and consul (290-298),
    - all of which were foiled (299-306).

Your own happiness demands that you go into exile (307-310), since
- no one greeted you upon your arrival here in the Senate (311-316), and
- the seats around you were vacated (317-322).

Such an open display of fear and hatred would force me to depart whether it were displayed by
- my slaves (323-326),
- my fellow citizens (327-334), or
- my parents (335-337).
- Therefore all the more would I depart if my fatherland feared and hated me (338-344).

Our native land, though silent, pleads with you to depart (345) because
- you have openly flouted her laws (346-351),
- and this she can no longer tolerate (352-359).
- Therefore depart as is your duty, and free her from fear (359-367).

Your failure to achieve legal custody (368-369) from
- Manius Lepidus (370),
- me, the consul (371-377),
- Quintus Metellus (378-379), and
- Marcus Metellus (380-384)
  - should persuade you to depart (385-391).

A possible appeal to the Senate would urge you to depart (392), since
my words to you to depart bring no protest from them (393-406),
as they surely would do if I addressed similar words to Sestius or Marcellus (407-410).
The actions of the citizens should urge you to depart (411-422),
and they can be easily persuaded to accompany you to the city gates (423-426).
But may the gods help us, since
it is too much to expect you to heed my words (427-432),
even though your exile would raise a storm against me (433-441), and
it is too much to ask that you reform (442-449).
Therefore depart into exile (450-452)
if not upon command (453-457),
then at my invitation (458-467), since
your cohorts and standard have already been sent ahead (468-475),
you chafe at being separated from them (476-479),
you anticipate with joy your reunion with them (480-484),
you are prone by nature to rebellion (485-489), and
you have gathered together a band of depraved men (490-493),
with whom you will rejoice (494-499),
and share a common life of hardship (500-502)
in what may be called open war (503-507).

Perōrātiō

Our native land can now bring this just complaint against me (508-516):
Will you allow this man to depart and thereby actually send him against the city (517-526)?
What hindered your ordering his arrest and death (527-530)?
Precedent?—but this is against you (531-533).
Citizenship rights?—but traitors have no rights (534-536).
Fear of unpopularity (537)?
That would be fine gratitude to the country which has so favored you (538-544).
Moreover, the unpopularity arising from negligence and civil war is the more to be feared (545-551).
My hesitation in ordering his arrest and death (552-557) was not due to fear of unpopularity, since
in accord with precedent (558-565)
such action would rather gain true popularity (566-569).

It was due rather to a lack of conviction on the part of the Senate of Catiline's intent (570-578),

which could be made manifest only by his departure (579-583).

Moreover, Catiline's death offers no permanent solution (584-586), because

the conspirators are numerous (587-592) and

the conspiracy is of long standing (593-597).

In fact, Catiline's death would make the conspiracy harder to suppress (598-602),

just as a fever, temporarily relieved by a glass of cold water, later becomes worse (603-610).

Therefore let Catiline and his men depart in order that

men's loyalties may be made clear to everyone (611-620) and that

consuls, Senate, and knights may see the conspiracy fully revealed (621-627).

Let Catiline, then, go forth into open war (628-633), and

may Jupiter protect us (634-640)

and punish them (641-645).

DIGEST OF THE THIRD ORATION AGAINST CATILINE

Exordium

The state has been saved by my efforts because of the love of the gods for you (1-7).

The founder of the state had been deified; therefore
its savior should be honored (8-14),
since I kept you and the state from destruction (15-18).

The Senate has been fully informed about the conspiracy. It now remains for me to give you the facts also (19-22).

Nārrātiō

Precautions were continued after Catiline's departure (23-26),
even though I thought his followers would be ineffective without him (27-31).

I made every effort to learn their plans here at Rome in order to secure unimpeachable evidence of the conspiracy (32-38).

When I learned that
Publius Lentulus had contacted the envoys of the Allobroges,
letters inciting to rebellion had been entrusted to them,
Titus Volturcius would accompany them (39-44),
I realized that I had the opportunity of securing concrete evidence of the conspiracy (44-47).

The conspirators were captured:

At my instructions my agents quickly laid the trap at the Mulvian Bridge (48-55), reinforced by a number of chosen young men from Reate (56-59).

About three in the morning my agents surprised and attacked the Gauls and Volturcius as they were crossing the bridge (60-63).

After a brief encounter the letters to Catiline and others were seized intact and the group was brought to me (64-67).

Suspects in the city were arrested and brought to me, including Cimber Gabinius, Lucius Statilius, Gaius Cethegus, and Lentulus (68-72).

Despite the fact that many influential men urged the opening of the letters to make sure they contained real evidence, I kept them intact (73-78), since I felt that too much care could not be exercised in this matter (79-81).

An investigation was conducted:

- The Senate was summoned and the house of Cethegus was raided for further evidence (82-86).
- Volturcius, apart from the Gauls, was the first to be questioned; he turned state's evidence (87-96).
- Then the Gallic ambassadors gave their testimony (97-110).
- The letters were produced:
  - Those of Cethegus were opened and read (111-116), and after that he made no further alibis (117-120).
  - Then those of Statilius were opened and read, bringing a full confession from him (121-122).
  - Then those of Lentulus were opened and read (123-129).
    - After a denial Lentulus tried to break down the evidence of the Gauls and Volturcius (130-136);
    - then he broke down and confessed (137-141).
    - At Volturcius' request Lentulus' letter to Catiline was opened and read (142-149).
- Gabinius too confessed after some attempt at denial (150-152).
- Damaging as was the concrete evidence, the guilty reactions of the conspirators convicted them the more (152-159).

The Senate was then consulted about a course of action against the conspirators, and since the decree has not been published, I will give its details from memory (160-165):

- Thanks were decreed to me, to the praetors in charge of the arrest, and to my colleague in the consulship (166-172).
- Publius Lentulus was to resign the office of praetor and be put in jail (173-174).
- Cethegus, Statilius, and Gabinius were also to be jailed (174-176), together with five others who were implicated (176-188).
- A public thanksgiving in my honor was decreed, the first such honor for a civil magistrate (189-195).
- Lentulus has since publicly resigned (196-203).

The conspiracy is now crushed (204-207):

- Only incapable leaders are left behind at Rome (208-211).
- Hence Catiline was the only one to be feared (212-219).
  - He had to be forced to declare his hand (220-224),
  - since he would never have made the mistakes of Lentulus (225-231),
  - and his presence here would have made the suppression of the conspiracy extremely difficult (232-236).

The gods guided and protected us (237-247):
- Jupiter's statue was raised on the very day of the arrest of the conspirators (248-254).
- The plan of the conspirators to burn the city included the temples and shrines of the gods (255-257).
- Therefore the gods:
  - inspired my actions and helped me secure the proof of the conspiracy (258-262),
  - blinded Lentulus and his associates (263-266),
  - were responsible for the wholly unexpected cooperation of the Gauls (267-272).

Perōrātiō

Celebrate this deliverance which was accomplished so peacefully (273-279), for
- all previous civil disturbances ended in bloodshed (280-293),
- yet none of them aimed at the complete destruction of the state (294-301);
- hence our bloodless repression of this conspiracy is unique in our history (302-310).

I ask no other reward than this:
- that the memory of these deeds be kept alive in patriotic minds and hearts (311-316);
- in this living tradition of the Roman people shall I find immortality (317-325).

I look to you for my protection, since I must live with those I conquered (326-333),
- even though the memory of deeds nobly done is a real protection (334-338),
- and my purpose has always been to harass the wicked (339-341).
- This care you exercise in my regard will show your future protectors what to expect (342-345).

As for myself, since I have achieved the pinnacle of success (345-348), I can, only as a private citizen, live ever mindful of the deeds of my consulate (349-353);
- as for yourselves, pay homage to Jupiter and guard your homes this night while I see to it that you can now live in peace (354-359).

DIGEST OF THE IMPEACHMENT OF VERRES, FIRST HEARING

Exordium

Your own unpopularity and the discredit attached to these courts that has arisen from the common belief that a man of wealth, however guilty, cannot be convicted can now be dispelled (1-10),

because at this time Gaius Verres, already convicted in everyone's opinion, but according to his own boasting already acquitted by bribery, has been brought before the bar (11-15).

Therefore an honest verdict will restore your reputation.

Personally, I fear the underhanded methods and intrigues of Verres in this court (16-20), since he openly boasts about the power of his money (21-29).

His plans for corrupting this court are common knowledge; hence he fears nothing but the time set for the trial. For that reason he endeavored to block my appointment as prosecutor.

Prōpositiō

Now in the face of overwhelming evidence against him (30-37), he still boasts that he can 'buy' the time of his trial and so escape the present popular feeling and this honest jury (38-44).

He tried unsuccessfully to engineer a postponement of the trial (45-50).

Therefore it is clear that he puts all his hopes of escape in his money (51-57).

Nārrātiō

What talent or eloquence can even partially defend such a man as Verres (58-61)?

The stained and shameful record of his early career is splendid testimony to his character.

His criminal record in Sicily is unparalleled even in his own previous life (62-70):

laws were flouted,

extortion was common,

civil rights were disregarded,

national defense was neglected,

works of art were carried off and sanctuaries defiled,
decency forbids mentioning his personal crimes.

These crimes are common knowledge (71-77), but he makes an elaborate show of legal defense to cover up quite a different scheme (78-86).

Earlier he contracted to bribe the jury, but his efforts failed miserably (87-100).

Argūmentātiō

Now that Hortensius, Verres' advocate, is consul-elect, Verres has again resorted to bribery as I found out almost by chance (101-107).

Verres was congratulated upon Hortensius' election by Gaius Curio, a friend of mine, who assured Verres that this meant his acquittal.

This congratulation pointed to a bribery of the court and everyone so interpreted it (108-111) despite my witnesses and wealth of evidence (112-117).

I was alarmed at the possibility of Verres' acquittal but tried to conceal it (118-125).

Then his friend Metellus got the presidency of the Court of Extortion (126-129).

These were the plans against me:

Bribery agents and ward bosses were organized to prevent my election as aedile;

Sicilian gold now fought my election and this trial so that I could concentrate on neither issue (130-150); but

Hortensius' overtures to the Sicilians and Verres' vigorous campaign failed to stop my election.

After my election:

Verres and his friends attempted to escape this present jury and judge by dragging out the case into the new year when the friends of Verres would be in power as a result of the elections.

The consul-elect, Hortensius, reminded the Sicilians that his brother was now their governor, and that another brother would preside over the Court of Extortion (151-158)—a clear case of intimidation (159-165).

Plans and counterplans were made:

Verres boasted

that Hortensius is his creature, elected by his efforts;

that the court will be entirely new and suitable to him after January 1;

that the plans of the prosecutor would be brought to naught, since the various games, long speeches, and technical evasions will exhaust the prosecution;

that thus the case will come under the jurisdiction of Marcus Metellus.

Therefore haste is necessary lest I lose my prisoner:

I will not spend upon my speech of prosecution the full time allotted by law,

but I will prosecute by means of documents and witnesses (166-183),

and so reach an adjournment of the case before the first festival begins (184-187).

Hortensius is the one I have to reckon with:

His domination of the law courts undermines justice and is based in part on corrupt practices—a definite challenge for all my industry and determination (188-205).

Therefore as a public and patriotic service I warn evildoers to avoid bribery in this trial (206-218).

Even though Hortensius will be consul after January 1 and I only an aedile, yet the whole story of judicial crimes and villainies committed during the ten years since the transfer of the law courts from the Equestrian Order to the Senate will be exposed and proven in detail, and I shall deal sternly with offenders.

Possibly in this trial I shall find bribery if one can trust Verres' boasts (219-228) about amassing fortunes for advocates and judges.

Provincials will then ask for the abolition of the Court of Extortion, since it is cheaper to satisfy a governor's greed than to purchase his acquittal (229-239).

What a fine reputation for our courts to have (240-247)!

Hortātiō

This is a providential opportunity of delivering our order from unpopularity and hatred, from dishonor and disgrace that attaches to the fact that law courts in men's estimation have no existence worth the name. This is clearly established by the murmur of approval that greeted Pompey's desire to restore the power of the tribunes and their shout of approval for his plan to deal with corrupt law courts (248-271).

The eyes of the world are upon us. As you will pass verdict upon the prisoner, so the people of Rome will pass its verdict upon yourselves: Can a rich man be found guilty when senators make up the jury (272-281)?

This prisoner is so guilty that, if he is acquitted, it will be impossible to imagine any explanation but the most shameful (282-286), since

I will bring forth such well corroborated testimony that, no one will urge you to acquit this man as a personal favor (287-293).

You alone, gentlemen of the jury, can remove the stigma of injustice in these courts, since no others from our ranks can be found who are of equal eminence and distinction (293-300).

Therefore let this be an honest trial and let me lose my life rather than lose the resolve to bring any evildoers to task (301-306).

Let the judge be true to his duty in accord with his family's distinction and the precedents of law, so that the guilty will find that his fortune has heightened his guilt rather than secured an acquittal for him.

Perōrātiō

These are my plans:

I will not allow this case to drag on until a new administration is in power, since that would nullify all the efforts at redress for the Sicilians (307-323).

I will immediately call for witnesses to substantiate my charges. This will be no novelty in these courts (324-325); hence I'll state the charge, support it by questioning, argument, and comment, and then bring forward the witnesses to that charge (325-328).

The defense will have opportunity for cross-examination (328-336).

This is my indictment of Verres:

We submit that Verres is so guilty of crime (as we shall prove) that, even if we had time for a lengthy speech, there would be no need of it. I thank you, gentlemen.

(There followed the calling and interrogation of the witnesses for the prosecution.)

DIGEST OF THE IMPEACHMENT OF VERRES, SECOND HEARING[1]

I. The Flogging of Roman Citizens

Exordium

I have kept my pledge to the Sicilians and will now speak on behalf of Roman citizens (1-7).

Subtle reasoning and protracted proof are unnecessary, since all of Sicily is my witness to the truth of my charges (8-10).

Prōpositiō

Verres openly subjected Roman citizens to flogging just as if there were no distinction between citizen and slave (11-17). And his lictors flogged Roman citizens even without awaiting the orders of Verres (18-19).

Nārrātiō

The facts are these:

In the forum at Lilybaeum Gaius Servilius, a Roman citizen of Panhormus, was beaten with rods till he fell to the ground. All Lilybaeum saw it and all Sicily heard of it (20-26).

The charge? As if there could be any reason that would excuse the violation of Roman citizenship (27-31)! It was reported that Servilius talked rather freely about Verres' rascality and wickedness (32).

Upon summons Servilius came to Lilybaeum, but no one came forward to prosecute. Then one of Verres' lictors challenged Servilius to prove that Verres was making money by bribery. Servilius protested against being tried for a capital offense before a prejudiced court, since no one appeared to prosecute him.

[1] Toward the close of the first hearing Cicero outlined his plans for the prosecution of Verres. Since it was important that the trial be completed before the newly elected judges were to assume their duties, Cicero determined upon an expeditious procedure. He planned to state the charge, support it by questioning and argument, and then bring forward the witnesses to that charge. This Cicero does in the second hearing. Each charge may be considered as an oration in miniature, for a sufficient number of the elements of an oration are there to warrant our use of the standard terms in this outline.

Six lictors beat Servilius unmercifully until he fell to the ground. He was carried off half-dead and died soon after (33-39).

And this is only one of the punishments inflicted on Roman citizens. The Stone Quarries Prison at Syracuse was filled with Roman citizens who offended Verres (40-46).

Hortātiō

You, the jury, are rightfully indignant, because the rights of citizenship should be respected not only here at Rome but throughout the world (47-54).

And you, Verres, while treating Roman citizens as thieves and traitors, did you not think of your being brought to trial, of your being subjected to the authority of our laws and our courts (55-64)?

II. The Plundering and Execution of Roman Merchantmen

Prōpositiō prīma

Verres' monstrous appetite for cruelty led him on. Ships were seized in port, the voyagers put in the Stone Quarries, and the cargoes impounded (65-71).

Argūmentātiō

The charge? The same that he now alleges in his defense (72-74), that these wealthy merchants were fugitives from the dispersed armies of the rebel Sertorius (75-76).

By a display of their wares they tried to disprove Verres' charge (77-80), not foreseeing that such action would actually work their ruin (81-82).

Verres claimed that these goods were acquired from pirates, and therefore the merchants were put in the Stone Quarries and their goods impounded (82-85).

Prōpositiō secunda

When the prisons were full of honest merchants, guiltless Roman citizens were strangled, and the cry, "I am a Roman citizen" only increased their trials (86-92).

Argūmentātiō

This is proved by his own records of the prison, which were carefully kept (93-99). In them we often read the annotation: "The death penalty was inflicted upon them."

Hortātiō

Rome has waged many a war to avenge just such outrages against her citizens (100-106).

I do not complain about the arrest and robbery; my charge is that these men were put in prison and there were put to death (107-110).

My charges would arouse indignation even among foreigners (111-115) because the rights of Roman citizens are everywhere known and respected (115-117).

Refūtātiō

Verres charged that they were escaped Sertorians—rebels. Even if true there was no justification for the action, because the government had in effect pardoned the rebels after the defeat of Sertorius; moreover, Verres with his criminal record was not the one to hunt revolutionaries.

But the charge is false, as is proved by witnesses. These men were well-known merchants, innocent of crime and rebellion.

Verres saw to it that the heads of Roman citizens were covered when they were led to execution.

The outcry against him had made him not more merciful but more cautious (118-129), since people were making an inconveniently careful estimate of the number of missing pirates (130-133).

Perōrātiō

This, then, was the protection given our citizens in Sicily during the administration of Verres. Perils encountered in trade were not enough without having to risk further perils at the hand of the governor (134-138)!

Sicily our neighbor and dependency should have been a haven and home for Roman citizens (139-146).

III. The Crucifixion of a Roman Citizen

Exordium

How can I present the case of Publius Gavius, so incredible yet so well proved, so shocking that despite many entreaties I hesitated to bring it up in court (147-158)?

Verres' lesser crimes have exhausted my time and vocabulary. How, then, shall I describe this crowning deed of shame (159-163)?

Nārrātiō

I will let the bare facts speak for themselves (164-167):

Gavius of Consa, a Roman citizen, was thrown into prison by Verres. Gavius somehow escaped the Stone Quarries and fled to Messina. He talked openly at Messina that he was going to Rome and there would prefer charges against Verres (168-175).

But speaking thus at Messina was the same as saying it to the governor personally, since the town was Verres' stronghold (176-179).

Gavius was arrested. Verres came by chance to Messina and thanked the citizens for their solicitude for him (180-186).

In the forum the angry Verres orders preparations made to flog Gavius (187-191).

Gavius appealed to his right as a Roman citizen and offered proof that he was such (192-195).

But Verres claimed the man was a spy and ordered the flogging to proceed (196-199).

Gavius kept appealing to the fact of his citizenship—only to find that a cross was being prepared for him (200-208).

Thus our laws and the power of the tribunes, that should protect Roman citizens, were brought to naught by a man who owed his power to the favor of the Roman people (209-215).

The tears and groans of the bystanders—mostly Roman citizens—availed nothing (216-219).

Argūmentātiō

I did not press these charges in the earlier hearing for fear that the disturbed Romans would take justice into their own hands and punish Verres themselves, lest he escape the rigors of law (220-230).

Now I will prove my charge point by point (231-232):

You threw this Gavius into the Stone Quarries. I'll not prove it from the prison lists because then you may say that I picked just any person whose name happened to be Gavius, but I'll use witnesses. You may choose any of those whom I call and they will testify that it is this Gavius who was thrown into the Stone Quarries (233-239).

This Gavius was a citizen of Consa, and this is proved by the testimony of his fellow citizens (240-243).

You yourself, Verres, admitted that he cried out that he was a Roman citizen (244-249).

Therefore my witnesses are telling the truth; and note that these witnesses did not know Gavius personally, but testified only that they saw him flogged and crucified (250-255), and that despite his appeal to Roman citizenship, without hesitation and without investigation you sent him to the cross (256-260).

This one point: Your admission that he said he was a citizen is enough to convict you (261-265) since

that cry would have stopped the hand of a foreign executioner, yet it did not secure from you even a postponement of death (266-274);

this plea protects Romans, rich and poor alike, the world over (275-282), and if this protection is taken away, the world is closed to Romans (283-290).

Refūtātiō

You could easily have discovered the truth about Gavius' citizenship by summoning the Roman knight, Lucius Raecius, to whom Gavius appealed, and who was in Sicily at that time (291-299).

Hortātiō

But it was not merely against Gavius that Verres worked injustice but against us all (300-302),

for in putting Gavius on the cross and deliberately placing the cross where the dying man could look toward Italy and freedom, Verres made sport of the common liberties of us all (303-314), and with Gavius our rights and liberties were crucified (315-321).

Thus before all the world Verres flaunted his contempt for Roman citizenship (322-328).

Such a tale of cruelty would move even inanimate things, hence when addressing Roman senators I can rest assured that they will pronounce the cross a fitting punishment for Verres himself (329-338).

Perōrātiō

The fate of the ship captains, our allies, moved you to tears; how must we be affected by the fate of a kinsman, for all Roman citizens are kinsmen (339-342)?

All Romans scattered throughout the world look to you to protect their rights and their persons (343-348).

STYLISTIC DEVICES

All Latin authors use a great variety of stylistic devices. These form an integral part of Latin style both in oratory and in poetry. At times these devices appeal directly to the ear as in onomatopoeia, while on other occasions the imagination is stimulated by an unusual expression of an idea as in personification, or the mind is pleased by a new association of ideas as in oxymoron. These figures are not a mere ornament of style but are necessary for the complete expression of the author's concept and feeling.

Quite generally it is impossible to keep these figures when translating into English, since the genius of our tongue is quite different from that of the Romans. For this very reason a student must learn to see and appreciate them in the Latin if he is to begin to have some understanding of Latin style. And this perception of elements that are mostly untranslatable will highlight the necessity of studying the works of an author in the original rather than in mere translation.

No one, therefore, can fully understand and appreciate the writings of Cicero unless he is familiar with at least the more common figures of rhetoric and syntax which Cicero used to express fully his thought and emotions—an expression that was intended to heighten the effectiveness of language as a means of communicating the speaker's convictions and emotions.

Only the commoner and more easily understood figures are given here. If these are understood and their function observed, then at least a start will have been made in appreciating the beauty and effectiveness of the style of Cicero.

Word Order

Alliteration, repetition of the same letter at the beginning of successive words in order to appeal to the ear.

> *ut in perpetuā pāce esse possītis prōvidēbō—I shall see to it that you enjoy everlasting peace* (Cat. III, 358)

Anaphora, repetition of the same word at the beginning of successive phrases or clauses in order to secure emphasis.

Nihil agis, nihil mōlīris, nihil cōgitās—Nothing that you do, nothing that you plan, nothing that you think (Cat. I, 142-144)

nēmō tam improbus, tam perditus, tam tuī similis—no one so wicked, so depraved, so like yourself (Cat. I, 90-92)

Antithesis, strong contrast achieved through parallelism of words and ideas in order to bring the meaning into clear focus.

quōrum tibi auctōritās est vidēlicet cāra, vīta vīlissima—whose authority is indeed dear to you, but whose lives are worthless (Cat. I, 416-417)

Quid exspectās auctōritātem loquentium, quōrum voluntātem tacitōrum perspicis?—Why do you await the cogency of the spoken word when you see that silence indicates their will (Cat. I, 405-406)?

Assonance, repetition of the same vowel sounds in the first syllable of successive words in order to appeal to the ear.

clārissimō patre, avō, mājōribus—whose father, grandfather, and ancestors were renowned (Cat. I, 56)

Gājum Mānlium, audāciae satellitem atque administrum tuae—Gaius Manlius, your audacious attendant and accomplice (Cat. I, 118-119)

Asyndeton, omission of conjunctions that gives a staccatolike effect and impresses with its rapid accumulation of ideas.

templa deōrum immortālium, tēcta urbis, vītam omnium cīvium, Italiam tōtam ad exitium et vastitātem vocās—you destine to ruin and destruction the temples of the immortal gods, the homes in the city, the lives of all the citizens, the whole of Italy (Cat. I, 230-234)

appellāre, temptāre, sollicitāre poterat, audēbat—he was able (and) he dared to appeal to, to win over, (and) to stir up (Cat. III, 214)

perge quō coepistī: ēgredere aliquandō ex urbe; patent portae—proficīscere—continue on your way, leave the city now, the gates are open, depart (Cat. I, 193-196)

Chiasmus, inverted word order, e. g. noun adjective adjective noun, so called because the Greek letter 'chi' is formed if one phrase is written beneath the other and the similar parts of speech are connected with a straight line.

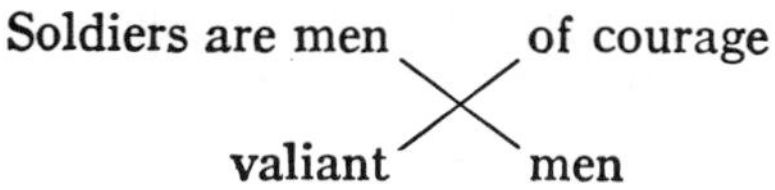

Such an arrangement throws stress on the 'courage' and helps to give variety of expression.

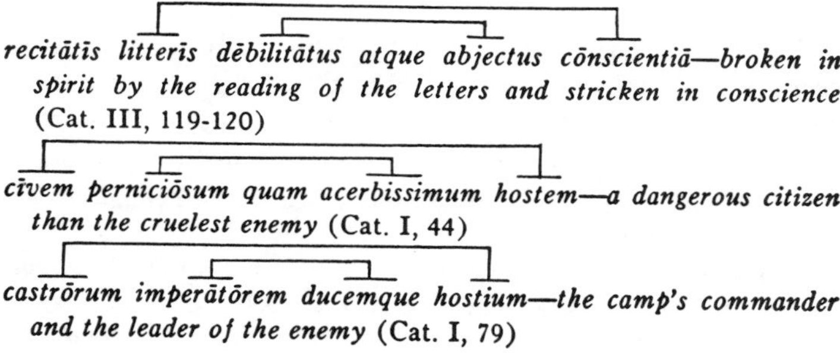

recitātīs litterīs dēbilitātus atque abjectus cōnscientiā—broken in spirit by the reading of the letters and stricken in conscience (Cat. III, 119-120)

cīvem perniciōsum quam acerbissimum hostem—a dangerous citizen than the cruelest enemy (Cat. I, 44)

castrōrum imperātōrem ducemque hostium—the camp's commander and the leader of the enemy (Cat. I, 79)

The following example contains a compound chiasmus:

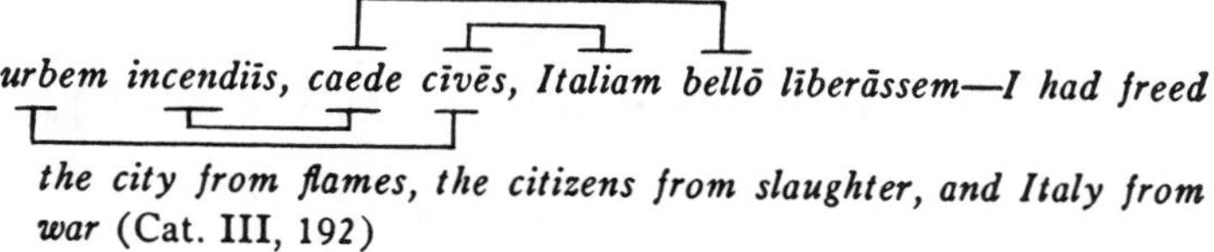

urbem incendiīs, caede cīvēs, Italiam bellō līberāssem—I had freed the city from flames, the citizens from slaughter, and Italy from war (Cat. III, 192)

Polysyndeton, the use of more conjunctions than is needed. Usually lends dignity and smoothness of rhythm.

ut, et quanta et quam manifesta et quā ratiōne invēstīgāta et comprehēnsa sint, vōs, quī et ignōrātis et exspectātis, scīre possītis—in order that you, who are both unaware of and await information about the affair, may know both its magnitude and its disclosure, and by what means it was investigated and discovered (Cat. III, 20-22)

Use of Words

Ellipsis, omission of some easily understood word or words in a sentence, in order to avoid monotony and to secure rapidity of narration.

domum meam relinquendam putārem: tū tibi urbem nōn (relinquendam) arbitrāris?—I would think that I would have to leave my home; do you not think that you would have to leave the city (Cat. I, 325-326)?

Quid tandem tē impedit? Mōsne mājōrum (tē impedit)?—What finally stops you? Is it the custom of our ancestors (that stops you) (Cat. I, 530-531)?

Hendiadys, two nouns are joined by a conjunction instead of using a noun in the genitive case or an adjective to modify one of the two nouns. This figure puts equal emphasis on the nouns instead of making one somewhat subordinate to the other.

ōra vultūsque—the expression on their faces (literally: *faces and expressions*) (Cat. I, 11)

dēclīnātiōne et . . . corpore—by a mere twist of the body (literally: *by a twist and by the body*) (Cat. I, 298)

vim et manūs—violent hands (literally: *force and hands*) (Cat. I, 410)

manūs ac tēla—armed hands (literally: *hands and weapons*) (Cat. I, 423)

Synecdoche, use of a part for the whole in order to secure variety.

ā tēctīs urbis ac moenibus—from the homes (roofs) and walls (Cat. I, 639)

ōra vultūsque—the expression on their faces (literally: *their mouths and countenances*) (Cat. I, 11)

Zeugma, use of one verb to govern two objects. If the fundamental meaning of the verb is considered, it can be applied to only one of the objects. Zeugma is the Greek word for 'yoke' as yoke of oxen.

omnis hic locus acervīs corporum et cīvium sanguine redundāvit—this entire place was filled with heaps of corpses and overflowed with the blood of citizens (Cat. III, 285-286)

The word *redundāvit* means 'overflowed with' and hence can properly be used only with *sanguine,* and yet by an extension of meaning it can also be applied to *acervīs corporum,* especially if we think of them as being piled in a restricted area and because of their number some of them roll out of the area. Note the chiasmus in this example.

Expression of Ideas

Anacoluthon, failure to complete the grammatical construction of a sentence due usually to the strong emotion of the speaker or writer.

> *Etenim sī mēcum patria . . . sī cūncta Italia, sī omnis rēs pūblica loquātur—For if the fatherland . . . if all Italy, if the republic should speak with me* (Cat. I, 513-516)

Then follow the supposed words of the fatherland, and the condition itself is never completed.

Apostrophe, address to a nonliving object as if it were alive in order to express the deep emotion of the speaker.

> *Ō nōmen dulce lībertātis! Ō jūs eximium nostrae cīvitātis!—O sweet name of liberty! O glorious right of citizenship* (Ver. II, 209)!

Climax, arrangement of ideas in ascending order for the purpose of securing forcefulness of expression.

> *Facinus est vincīre cīvem Rōmānum, scelus verberāre, prope parricīdium necāre—quid dīcam in crucem tollere?—It is a crime to bind a Roman citizen, it is an outrage to flog him, it is almost high treason to murder him, but what shall I say of crucifying him* (Ver. II, 315-316)?
>
> *nēmō tam improbus, tam perditus, tam tuī similis—no one so wicked, so depraved, so like to yourself* (Cat. I, 90-92)
>
> *ut Catilīnae profectiōne omnia patefacta, illūstrāta, oppressa, vindicāta esse videātis—in order that by Catiline's departure everything may be exposed, clearly brought to light, overwhelmed and punished* (Cat. I, 626-627)
>
> *quod nōn ego nōn modo audiam sed etiam videam plānēque sentiam—which I not only do not hear about, but also see, and clearly understand* (Cat. I, 145-147)

Hyperbole, obvious exaggeration, for the sake of producing a strong effect, by which something is represented as greater or more intense than it actually is.

alter fīnēs vestrī imperī nōn terrae sed caelī regiōnibus termināret—the one made your empire coextensive with the regions not of the earth but of the sky (Cat. III, 324-325)

ut ad ea probanda tōtam Siciliam testem adhibēre possem—in order that I may be able to use the whole of Sicily as my witness in proving these things (Ver. II, 9-10)

Irony, stating the opposite of what is meant. Irony is very frequently associated with sarcasm and ridicule, which are used by the speaker in order to secure a striking and highly effective statement of feelings.

Nōs autem, fortēs virī—And we brave men (implying that consuls and senators lack the real bravery needed to look to the good of the state rather than their own personal safety) (Cat. I, 28)

crēdō, erit verendum mihi—and I suppose I must fear (implying that there is no need to fear) (Cat. I, 84)

Litotes, an understatement. Much more is meant than is stated and for that reason the meaning stands out clearly.

neque enim sunt aut obscūra aut nōn multa—for they are not hidden, nor are they few in number (Cat. I, 291-292)

ex cīvitāte male pācātā—from a hardly civilized city (Cat. III, 267)

quae bellum populō Rōmānō facere et posse et nōn nōlle videātur—who seemed capable of waging war against the Roman people and not to be unwilling to do so (Cat. III, 268-269)

Metaphor, implied comparison. It usually results in a startling and emphatic expression.

exhauriētur ex urbe tuōrum comitum magna et perniciōsa sentīna reī pūblicae—the immensely dangerous bilge water of your companions will be drained from the city (Cat. I, 243-244)

stirps ac sēmen malōrum omnium—the root and seed of all evil (Cat. I, 592)

lūmina cīvitātis exstīncta sunt—the lights (leading men) of the city have been extinguished (killed) (Cat. III, 288)

perīculum . . . erit inclūsum penitus in vēnīs atque vīsceribus reī pūblicae—the danger will lie wholly hidden in the veins and vitals of the republic (Cat. I, 601-602)

Metonymy, substitution—use of a word or name that readily recalls another that is associated with it in meaning. Metonymy usually fastens upon some significant aspect of the object. Its use avoids monotonous repetition.

nōnnūllī sunt in hōc ōrdine—there are some in this group (the Senate) (Cat. I, 570)

quī . . . fascēs et secūrēs habēret—who has the rods and axes (who wields the powers of a Roman magistrate) (Ver. II, 213-214)

Monumentum sceleris audāciaeque suae—The monument to his bold crime (referring to the cross that was set up) (Ver. II, 326)

Oxymoron, a seeming contradiction. Its use startles the audience or reader and gives great emphasis.

cum tacent, clāmant—their silence shouts (Cat. I, 414)

Quae . . . tacita loquitur—Who though silent speaks (Cat. I, 345)

Paronomasia, a pun. A play on words which sharpens the meaning.

ut abs tē nōn ēmissus ex urbe sed immissus in urbem esse videātur—so that he may seem not to have been sent out of the city by you, but to have been sent against it (Cat. I, 525-526)

ut exsul potius temptāre quam cōnsul vexāre rem pūblicam possēs—so that as an exile he might be able to try the state rather than as consul to harass it (Cat. I, 504-505)

Personification, attributing personal qualities to an inanimate object in order to secure vividness.

Quae (patria) tēcum . . . loquitur—Who now speaks with you (Cat. I, 345)

sī tēcum . . . patria loquātur—if the fatherland should speak with you (Cat. I, 365)

Pleonasm, unnecessary fullness of expression. This is generally used when stateliness or dignity of expression is desired.

Quae cum ita sint, Catilīna, perge quō coepistī—Wherefore (since these things are so), Catiline, go your way (Cat. I, 192-193)

Ex quō mihi vēnit in mentem illud dīcere—Wherefore it occurs to me to mention this (Wherefore I mention this) (Ver. I, 229)

Preterition, a pretended omission. Its use emphasizes the things that are then mentioned and gives a cumulative effect.

Nam illa nimis antīqua praetereō—For I pass over those all too ancient instances (Cat. I, 38)

Praetermittō ruīnās fortūnārum tuārum—For I pass over in silence the ruin of your fortunes (Cat. I, 273)

Ac jam illa omittō—And now I omit those things (Cat. I, 290)

Repetition, saying a thing more than once for the sake of emphasis. It is frequently accompanied by anaphora.

Vīvis, et vīvis nōn ad dēpōnendam . . . audāciam—You live, and you live not to give up your boldness (Cat. I, 70-72)

Fuit, fuit ista quondam in hāc rē pūblicā virtūs—There was, there was at one time in this republic such valor (Cat. I, 42)

vīvēs, et vīvēs ita ut nunc vīvis—you will live, and you will live as you now are living (Cat. I, 95-96)

Rhetorical questions, queries that do not expect a reply. They are merely a forceful way of making a statement.

Meministīne mē . . . dīcere in senātū—Do you not remember my saying in the Senate (Cat. I, 113-115)

Quid tacēs?—Why do you keep quiet (Cat. I, 156)?

Num negāre audēs?—Do you dare deny it (Cat. I, 155)?

Quam rem pūblicam habēmus? In quā urbe vīvimus?—What kind of a state do we have? In what kind of a city do we live (Cat. I, 161-162)?

Simile, expressed comparison. It lends clarity and emphasis.

lūce sunt clāriōra nōbīs tua cōnsilia omnia—your plans, one and all, are clearer to us than the daylight (Cat. I, 111)

Ut saepe hominēs aegrī morbō gravī . . . prīmō relevārī videntur . . . sīc hic morbus quī est in rē pūblicā—just as men who are seriously ill often seem at first to be relieved . . . so this disease which is in the state (Cat. I, 603-608)

senātūs consultum vērum inclūsum in tabulīs tamquam in vāgīnā reconditum—a decree of the Senate on file in the archives just like a sword that is sheathed in a scabbard (Cat. I, 66-67)

INTRODUCTION

To the Student

You have heard it said that "all roads lead to Rome." Well, Rome is the subject of your study this year.

Last year you studied Caesar. The thought of that great general suggested an examination of the stuff of which leaders are made. The master idea of your study was leadership; and for the ideal leader you chose Christ. He became at once your master ideal and your ideal Master. In Him leadership took on flesh and blood, became incarnate before your eyes and it was

> . . . there then! the Master,
> *Ipse,* the only one, Christ, King, Head![1]

This year Cicero is your author. The master idea is conflict: conflict in the realm of government, of law, of religion; and the key word of the clash is Rome—Rome where these great struggles were fought out to the finish. You will hear Cicero summon all his eloquence before the Senate and the Roman people to defend Roman constitutional government against anarchy; you will hear him pleading before the Roman courts of law for justice against political corruption; you will see Rome purpled with the blood of martyrs who gave their lives for Christ in the conflict in which the kingdom of God triumphed over the empire of Caesar.

There at Rome you will find Cicero at the heart of the greatest political experiment in ancient times—the Roman Republic. As you listen to him speaking before the House, the Roman people, the court, your ear will grow attuned to certain phrases that recur, like the deep bass note of a bourdon stop: *senātus cōnsultum, in hōc sānctissimō gravissimōque cōnsiliō, contrā populum Rōmānum, imperium populī Rōmānī, fortūna populī Rōmānī.* It is the *senātus populusque Rōmānus,* the S. P. Q. R. that was em-

---

[1] Gerard Manley Hopkins, S. J., *The Wreck of the Deutschland.*

blazoned upon the Roman standards which Caesar led to war, that adorned the Roman rostra where Cicero spoke.

It took centuries for Rome to climb from kings to constitutional government. When it had reached its peak, this Roman Republic was built up of an aristocratic Senate and popular assemblies, with executive consuls and a whole series of magistrates mutually sharing power and limiting one another—the sort of system you have in the American Constitution, where Congress, the courts, the president, each acts as a check upon the other. This Roman Republic grew great and burst asunder, like Aesop's frog, in its efforts to expand itself into a constitutional world empire. The attempt at world domination failed because no institution can rise any higher than the men who compose it. The efficiency of governments, as of machinery, depends upon those who operate them. Fundamentally, the political problem is one of human character. What Goldsmith said of industrial England,

> Ill fares the land, to hastening ills a prey,
> Where wealth accumulates, and men decay,[1]

was true of imperial Rome. At Rome, as indeed everywhere, man is the old, the new problem. And since humanity changes its clothes but not its nature, succeeding generations have gone back to learn the lesson of man's decay and to draw fresh inspiration from the Roman Republic—its workings, its art of government, its genius for law, its mistakes. The comparison of the English Constitution to that of Rome is a commonplace. After all these centuries, American law still bears the stamp of the Roman mind. The democratic movements of the Middle Ages, as well as the leaders of the French Revolution, cited in their own defense the great names of the Roman Republic. And so you, too, can learn about these things from the few dramatic chapters in Roman government and law presented in this book.

One more thing: hand in hand with the decline and fall of the Roman Empire went the growth and rise of Christianity. And that

[1] Oliver Goldsmith, *The Deserted Village.*

puts you in contact with another and a greater clash. It dates from the day when two worlds stood face to face—Pilate, Roman governor of Palestine, and Christ, King of Kings. It grew into a struggle between the empire of Caesar and the kingdom of God—the rulers of this world and the kingdom of the next. And that conflict, too, went the road to Rome. It was towards Rome that Peter and Paul set their faces to the contest; at Rome died the Prince of the Apostles and the Apostle to the Gentiles, both giving their lives for Christ. It was at Rome, purpled with martyrs' blood, that Christianity took firm root and grew strong. From Rome the Church took what was best in the Roman genius for organization and embodied it in her ecclesiastical government. The Church's canon law is rooted in Roman legal theory and practice. Roman Cicero's mother tongue became the language of liturgy. Even today Christ's vicar still rules the Catholic Church from Rome, and when he writes a letter to the Catholic Church he still addresses it *urbī et orbī*. That is why each Catholic can say of himself: *cīvis Rōmānus sum.*

The fruit of last year's study was loyalty to Christ, King; this year it should be loyalty to Christ, head of that mystical body of which we are all members, the Church of Rome, and to His vicar, the Bishop of Rome.

Rome was not built in a day; still less can her whole story be told in a single third-year Latin text. Fortunately enough, however, as you just saw, it is also proverbial that all roads lead to Rome; and swift is the journey to it. Swift, too, is the trip from Rome to many another region in space—and, what is even more, in time. In God's Providence Rome is a city with an eternal destiny.

AVĒ RŌMA AETERNA!

PART I

ROMAN CONSTITUTIONAL GOVERNMENT VERSUS ANARCHY

PARTIES AND LEADERS IN ROMAN POLITICS

70-60 B.C.

The history of this decade leaves an impression somewhat like a confusion of a 'gangster' movie and a continual American political campaign. It is important to know something about the main actors.

THE SENATORIAL NOBLES

These were members of the optimate ('best') party, the aristocrats of Rome, men of high position and hereditary power. Among them were a few sincere men like Cato, who seems to have been the only man in Rome honestly determined to remove graft in government expenditures, or like Catulus, who was genuinely devoted to the vanishing republican ideals. On the whole, however, the party lacked leadership. Yet it was almost impossible to reach the consulate and the Senate unless one came from an aristocratic family. With justice, then, was Cicero, who had made his own way from obscure parentage (a *novus homō* in the Roman phrase), proud of attaining at last to the distinction of the consulate.

THE EQUESTRIAN ORDER

The knights, capitalists, bankers, and businessmen—the 'haves,' whose main interest was the maintenance of order and the protection of (their) property—made up this order.

THE POPULAR PARTY

The people's party was made up of men who professed the liberal principles of high-minded leaders of an older generation, but who were in reality mostly ambitious politicians making their way with political bargaining and promises. The clever Caesar (of later Gallic War fame) was their true leader. Crassus, Rome's wealthiest capitalist and a small-time military man, had been brought into unnatural association with Caesar and the *populārēs* by hopes of political advancement.

The Radicals

These were a mixed group of dispossessed farmers, ex-soldiers with no taste for work and memories of easy plunder, men about town, whom the 'night clubs' of Rome had impoverished and who were given to talking big over their wine, and a colorful and dissolute group of revolutionaries, the discontented of all classes. Among these latter Catiline was outstanding—a man of magnetic leadership and voracious vice whose characteristic quality was an unprincipled and haughty courage *(audācia)*.

Pompey

Pompey was the 'strong man' of Rome. His power rested on his generalship and his devoted armed forces, in face of which the civilian politicians were powerless and knew it. He was prevented only by indecision and a well-flattered vanity from making himself dictator of Rome.

Cicero

Cicero was an eminent lawyer and the greatest orator of his time. His prestige came of a brilliant legal career, during which he had attached to himself many influential clients. He was without military, financial, or political power in his own right, but destiny brought him forward as a consular candidate at a critical moment and catapulted him into a position of leadership.

Pompey and the People's Party

Just before the decade 70-60 B.C. we find the senatorial party strongly entrenched in a position of power. But Caesar and Crassus, by adroitly maneuvering Rome's 'Military Man No. 1'—Pompey—to their side and winning over the knights, soon began to get an edge over their senatorial rivals. At first the knights found this cultivation of the people's party quite profitable, but after they had secured the concessions they desired, they began to move toward the 'right.' This tendency to run into the arms of the senators became more pronounced as the people's party began to make overtures to the radicals (the knights, being capitalists, called these radicals 'ruffians' and 'debtors').

In 66 B. C. Pompey was given charge of the war then going on in the East and disappeared for a time from the Roman scene.

A 'Popular Front' against the Dictator-to-be

Everyone realized, of course, that when Pompey returned, he would return (if he only wished it) to rule Rome. All the efforts of the people's party, led by Caesar and Crassus, are directed during the years of Pompey's absence to setting up a counterpoise to his overmastering power, though all the while they ostensibly adhere to him. And so men of their own number are proposed for provincial campaigning in Spain and in Egypt in order to provide an opportunity for building an anti-Pompey military machine. But these and other schemes collapse, due largely to the opposition of the senatorial party which still controls most of the government agencies. At last it was evident to the people's party that to work their will they would have to destroy entirely the power of their senatorial rivals.

A Swing to the 'Left'

So they began to prepare the radical group, an explosive element well calculated to unseat the high-riding senators. The revolutionaries, Catiline and Manlius, were encouraged and abetted in various preliminary plots, but all these, too, for one reason or another failed.

Enter Cicero

In 64 B. C. Catiline and Antonius, also a radical, stood for the consulship with the strong support of the *populārēs*. Brilliantly campaigning against them was the orator and lawyer Cicero, a man of great personal gifts but indifferent political influence. Yet in this crisis the senators and the knights, both alarmed by the *populārēs'* policy of wooing the radicals, turned, reluctantly, to

Cicero as the only moderate leader strong enough to ward off a 'leftist' victory. Cicero and Antonius were elected.

Ballots versus Blood

The *populārēs* now saw no alternative except to engineer an open revolution. Constitutional attempts ('boring from within') had failed in the face of the united opposition of the vested interests. Pompey, too, would soon be returning. News of his continued victories was brought in by every fleet from the East. They had no time to waste. To allow the radicals to dissolve the government in blood, then to seize power themselves and build up a military machine of their own—this seems to have been their plan. Catiline and Manlius were the men to do it and would enjoy doing it. Manlius was sent off to enroll forces in Etruria; Catiline remained to intrigue at Rome.

The Crisis

All the parties now realized that the test of constitutional government was at hand. Cicero, when presiding as consul in an assembly, ostentatiously wore a breastplate and was surrounded by armed knights. The *populārēs* openly stood aloof, ready to profit from any embarrassment of the government and secretly, so it seems, continued to the last to encourage the anarchists. But Cicero's government was fully cognizant of the conspiracy, for his spies were everywhere. Not the least effective of these was the Roman lady Fulvia, mistress of one of Catiline's men and the betrayer of the secrets his tongue, loosened by wine and love, committed to her ear.

From then on events moved swiftly, and a news service of those days might have issued the following bulletins:

Bulletin

Rome, Oct. 18.—Today Cicero, in full Senate, communicated information of a general plot against the government. The Senate decreed a state of national emergency.

BULLETIN

Rome, Oct. 21.—The Senate today decreed martial law and gave the consuls wide dictatorial powers. Fresh information as to an imminent revolt is said to be in the hands of the government.

BULLETIN

Faesulae (Etruria), Oct. 27.—Gaius Manlius, leader of a camp of outlaws here, today issued a pronunciamento demanding cancellation of debts and similar legal 'reforms.' An armed march on Rome is hourly expected.

BULLETIN

Rome, Oct. 27.—News of insurrection in Etruria threw the city into alarm. Government officials ejected the gladiatorial slaves. The streets are closely patrolled. Government troops are said to be en route to Etruria under Quintus Marcius Rex. The city is rife with rumors of revolts in Apulia and at Capua. Notices of rewards for further information have appeared, and men are being enrolled in a national guard.

BULLETIN

Praeneste, Nov. 1.—A band of armed men last night attempted to seize the military fort here, but were beaten off by the garrison. This repulse is said to be due to secret counter preparations made several days ago on instruction from Rome.

MURDEROUS ATTEMPT ON CICERO

And so we come to the night between November 6 and 7. The quiet of Cicero's home is disturbed by a woman bringing urgent information for the consul. It is Fulvia. She has just come from a meeting with her lover, who has boasted to her that the morning will see Cicero out of the way. At a midnight meeting in the home of Marcus Laeca, two of Catiline's henchmen have promised him

—Courtesy of Produzione Consorzio Scipione S. A.

FULVIA AND CURIUS

Little does Curius think that the charming Fulvia, to whom he finds it so easy to confide the grandiose schemes of the revolution, is a government spy.

they will kill Cicero during the morning *salūtātiō*.[1] The guard around Cicero's house is at once strengthened; the leading men of the Senate are summoned and warned of the coming of the two conspirators. Cicero wants witnesses of the attempt, for thus only will the trustworthiness of his sources of information be proved beyond all doubt.

In the gray dawn the conspirators arrive to find their way barred; Cicero is yet to live for their undoing. This last attempt on his life again emphasizes the gravity of the government's position. Among other measures of state on this November 7 the consul calls an emergency meeting of the Senate for the following day.

For, though he and his friends are now certain of the conspiracy, his evidence is not cogent enough for legal action, and above all he must not move to his own destruction by striking too soon. He must force Catiline himself to make an open declaration of the fast-growing plot.

Rome's Domestic Enemy

The next day in a tense atmosphere—for rumor has got abroad of the attempt on the consul's life—the Senate assembles. There is an unusually good attendance; everyone senses the seriousness of the situation. Strong guards surround the Temple of Jupiter Stator, where the Senate meets only in time of national crisis. Beyond crowd the citizens of Rome, eager for news and anxious at the prospect of revolt and anarchy.

Onto such a scene walks Cicero, keyed at the excitement of danger and conscious that he, a man risen from the ranks of the common people, has become at last champion not of a party but of the Roman people and of its government. As he rises to speak, there in the midst of the Senate he sees the enemy of Rome, in a last audacious stroke, sitting in the governing body he plans

---

[1] It was the custom for prominent men at Rome to receive their friends and dependents early in the morning. During the visit the host would lie abed. This was the *salūtātiō*.

—Courtesy of Produzione Consorzio Scipione S. A.

ROMANS WELCOME CICERO TO THE SENATE

Some such scene may have met the eyes of Cicero as he made his way to the emergency meeting of the Senate on that critical eighth of November.

to murder. And Cicero, forgetting for once his prepared message, breaks into the impassioned words of a great orator and a great occasion. Facing the isolated figure of Catiline, "Quō usque tandem," he cries, "abūtēre,[1] Catilīna, patientiā nostrā?

First Oration against Catiline

Quam diū etiam furor iste tuus nōs ēlūdet?[2]
Quem ad fīnem sēsē effrēnāta[3] jactābit[4] audācia?

THE CITY IS IN TERROR

Nihilne[5] tē nocturnum praesidium Palātī,[6]
nihil urbis vigiliae,
nihil timor populī,

Words to Remember

tandem, adv., *at last, at length, finally.* Here it indicates impatience. Translate *pray; pray, tell me; I should like to know.*
patientia, ae, *patience, endurance* (cf. **patior, patienter**).
iste, ista, istud, *that, this.* **Iste** here implies contempt; Gr. 799.

---

[1] **abūtor, abūtī, abūsus sum,** 3, intr.; w. abl., *abuse, exhaust, try;* (**ab** + **ūtor**); **abūtēre** = **abūtēris.**

[2] **ēlūdō, ēlūdere, ēlūsī, ēlūsus,** 3, tr., *mock, make sport of, flout.*

[3] **effrēnātus, a, um,** *unbridled.* Suggests what comparison?

[4] **jactō,** 1, tr., *throw, hurl, cast, toss about;* **sē(sē) jactāre,** *to toss oneself about, to vaunt oneself.* **Sēsē jactābit** seems to picture Catiline's **audācia** as flinging itself about like an unbroken stallion, with no bridle to control it.

[5] **nihil;** adverbial accusative, taking the place of an emphatic **nōn.** Note the force gained by opening each item by the repetition of **nihil.** Recall the passage in St. Paul's Hymn to Charity (I Corinthians 13:3) where he uses this same sort of strong negative: "And if I distribute all my goods to feed the poor, and if I deliver my body to be burned, yet do not have charity, it profits me *nothing.*" Cicero gains an abrupt, machine-gunlike effect by dropping the **-ne tē** after the first of these **nihil** phrases.

[6] **Palātium, ī,** *the Palatine Hill,* a well-to-do residential district of Rome (cf. palace); **Palātī** = **Palātiī.**

nihil concursus bonōrum omnium,[7]
nihil hic mūnītissimus habendī senātūs locus,

[*In one sweeping gesture Cicero indicates the guards at the doorways and the solemn-visaged senators*]

nihil hōrum ōra vultūsque[8] mōvērunt?

YOUR PLANS ARE KNOWN

Patēre[9] tua cōnsilia nōn sentīs?
Cōnstrictam[10]
jam hōrum omnium scientiā tenērī
conjūrātiōnem tuam nōn vidēs?
Quid proximā, quid superiōre nocte ēgerīs,
ubi fuerīs,[11]
quōs convocāverīs,
quid cōnsilī[12] cēperīs
quem nostrum ignōrāre arbitrāris?

Words to Remember

concursus, ūs, *running together* (in more than one sense), *rally, assemblage, attack.*
ubi, interrog. adv., *where, in what place.*

---

7 On this excitement at Rome consult the *Flash* on page 7 under date of October 27.

8 **ōra vultūsque:** *the expression on the faces.* Often two nouns joined by **et** or **-que** are best rendered as if one modified the other. Literally the phrase means *the mouths and the faces.*

9 In excited denunciation Cicero wrenches the infinitive out of its usual position and places it in the more emphatic first place.

10 **cōnstrictus, a, um,** *checked, repressed* (cf. constriction). Used with **tenērī,** it means *held in check, held fast.* Again note the emphatic first place it is given.

11 Cicero refers to meetings such as the one at the house of Laeca.

12 **cōnsilī = cōnsiliī.**

YET WE DO NOT ACT!

Ō tempora, ō mōrēs![13] 2
senātus haec intellegit, cōnsul videt;
hic tamen vīvit.

[*He points emphatically at Catiline*]

Vīvit?
immō[14] vērō etiam in senātum venit,
fit pūblicī cōnsilī particeps,[15]
notat et dēsignat oculīs ad caedem ūnumquemque nostrum.[16]

Nōs autem, fortēs virī,[17] satisfacere[18] reī pūblicae vidēmur,
sī istīus furōrem ac tēla vītāmus.

Ad mortem tē, Catilīna, dūcī jussū cōnsulis jam prīdem oportēbat,
in tē cōnferrī pestem, quam tū in nōs omnēs jam diū māchināris.[19]

Words to Remember

notō, 1, tr., *mark down, note down* (cf. the phrase **Notā bene**, N. B.).
dēsignō, 1, tr., *point out, designate* (cf. **signum**).
ūnusquisque, ūnaquisque, ūnumquidque (**ūnus** + **quisque**), *each;* Gr. 836.
jussus, ūs, *bidding, command* (cf. **jubeō**).

---

13 **Ō tempora, ō mōrēs**, like the opening **Quō usque tandem**, is to Cicero what **Gallia est omnis dīvīsa in partēs trēs** is to Caesar. These words are familiar to students of Latin all over the world. Shakespeare puts in Cassius' mouth almost as empassioned a denunciation: "Age, thou art sham'd! Rome, thou hast lost the breed of noble bloods!" (*Julius Caesar*, Act I, Scene 2).

14 **immō**, adv., *more, more than that, on the contrary, nay rather;* alone, sometimes with **vērō**, it corrects the preceding sentence by implying that it was either an overstatement or an understatement.

15 **particeps, participis**, *taking part (in), sharing* (**pars** + **capiō**). Catiline was a senator and had a right to be present.

16 **nostrum**; why not **nostrī**? Gr. 123; 686.

17 There is irony in the words **fortēs virī**. The duty of consuls and senators was to look to the state's welfare, not their own necks.

18 **satisfaciō, satisfacere, satisfēcī, satisfactum**, 3, intr.; w. dat., *do enough, give satisfaction, satisfy* (**satis**, *enough* + **faciō**, *do*).

19 **māchinor**, 1, tr., *contrive, scheme, devise.*

OUR ANCESTORS WERE MORE 'DIRECT'

3 An vērō vir amplissimus, Pūblius Scīpiō,[20] pontifex maximus,[21]
Tiberium Gracchum,
mediocriter[22] labefactantem[23] statum[24] reī pūblicae,
prīvātus interfēcit:
Catilīnam, orbem terrae caede atque incendiīs vastāre cupientem,
nōs cōnsulēs perferēmus?[25]

Nam illa nimis[26] antīqua praetereō,[27]
quod[28] Gājus Servīlius Ahāla[29]
Spurium Maelium, novīs rēbus studentem,
manū suā occīdit.

Fuit, fuit[30] ista quondam in hāc rē pūblicā virtūs,

Words to Remember

amplus, a, um, *large, splendid, magnificent* (cf. ample).
quondam, adv., *formerly, once upon a time.*

---

[20] Publius Scipio was one of the prominent senators some eighty years earlier. He led a riot in which Tiberius Gracchus, a **populāris** and agitator for reform, was killed.

[21] **Pontifex maximus** was the official title of the high priest of the state religion.

[22] **mediocriter,** adv., *slightly* (cf. mediocre).

[23] **labefactō,** 1, tr., *disturb, shake, undermine.*

[24] **status, ūs,** *condition, position* (cf. status quo).

[25] **perferō, perferre, pertulī, perlātus,** irreg., tr., *endure, bear with.*

[26] **nimis,** adv., *too (much).*

[27] **praetereō, praeterīre, praeteriī(-īvī), praeteritum,** irreg., tr., *pass by, omit* (**praeter** + **eō**).

[28] **quod,** conj., *the fact that.*

[29] Gaius Servilius Ahala was a high official of the state in early Roman history. A certain Spurius Maelius was suspected of designing to make himself king. He refused to appear to answer the accusation, appealing to his supporters for protection. Thereupon Ahala killed him.

[30] **Fuit, fuit;** a solemn and melancholy repetition: *there was, there was once such (a high type of) manhood . . .*

ut virī fortēs ācriōribus[31] suppliciīs
cīvem perniciōsum quam acerbissimum[32] hostem coercērent.[33]

THE SENATE HAS AIMED A DECREE AT YOU

Habēmus senātūs cōnsultum in tē, Catilīna,
[*He whips his finger at Catiline*]
vehemēns et grave;
nōn deest reī pūblicae cōnsilium
neque auctōritās hūjus ōrdinis;
nōs, nōs, dīcō apertē, cōnsulēs dēsumus.

SUCH DECREES ONCE BROUGHT INSTANT EXECUTION

Dēcrēvit quondam senātus 4
ut Lūcius Opīmius,[34] cōnsul, vidēret 51
nē quid rēs pūblica dētrīmentī caperet.[35]
Nox nūlla intercessit.[36]

WORDS TO REMEMBER

vehemēns (*gen.* **vehementis**), *violent, impetuous, strong* (cf. **vehementer;** vehement).
dētrīmentum, ī, *loss, harm* (cf. detrimental); **dētrīmentum capere,** *to suffer loss.*

---

[31] **ācer, ācris, ācre,** *sharp, fierce.*

[32] **acerbus, a, um,** *bitter.*

[33] **coerceō,** 2, tr., *check, restrain* (cf. coercion).

[34] Lucius Opimius was a consul and leader of the senatorial party some years earlier. Acting under special powers from the Senate, he opposed the partisans of Gaius Gracchus, a popular agitator and younger brother of the Tiberius Gracchus mentioned in Note 20, page 14. In the struggle Gaius Gracchus and an associate, one Marcus Fulvius (lines 55 and 57), were killed.

[35] **Videant cōnsulēs nē quid rēs pūblica dētrīmentī capiat** was the stock senatorial formula for declaring a state of emergency. It was a proceeding not unlike the proclamation of martial law.

[36] **intercēdō, intercēdere, intercessī, intercessum,** 3, intr., *intervene.*

Interfectus est propter quāsdam sēditiōnum[37] suspīciōnēs
Gājus Gracchus,
  clārissimō patre, avō,[38] mājōribus;
occīsus est cum līberīs Mārcus Fulvius cōnsulāris.
Similī senātūs cōnsultō,
Gājō Mariō et Lūciō Valeriō,[39] cōnsulibus, est permissa rēs pūblica.
Num ūnum diem posteā
Lūcium Sāturnīnum,[39] tribūnum plēbis,[40]
et Gājum Servīlium,[39] praetōrem,
mors ac reī pūblicae poena remorāta[41] est?

YET WE FAIL TO EXECUTE THAT DECREE

At vērō nōs vīcēsimum[42] jam diem
patimur hebēscere[43] aciem[44] hōrum auctōritātis.
Habēmus enim ējus modī senātūs cōnsultum

Words to Remember

quīdam, quaedam, quoddam, *certain;* Gr. 820.
suspīciō, suspīciōnis, *suspicion, indication.*
līberī, līberōrum, *children.*

---

[37] **sēditiō, sēditiōnis,** *treason, revolt, rebellion.*

[38] **avus, ī,** *grandfather.*

[39] Gaius Marius and Lucius Valerius were consuls when the government was endangered by the agitation of the extreme leftists, Lucius Saturninus and Gaius Servilius. After an empowering decree of the Senate, the consuls incited the mob to kill Saturninus and Servilius, thereby removing the danger to the state in short order.

[40] **tribūnus (ī) plēbis,** *tribune of the people,* one of several magistrates elected by the people to watch over their interests.

[41] **remoror, 1,** tr., *keep waiting, fail to overtake* (cf. **moror, mora**).

[42] **vīcēsimus, a, um,** *twentieth.*

[43] **hebēscō, hebēscere,** 3, intr., *grow dull.*

[44] **aciēs, aciēī,** *edge* (literally), *line of battle* (more often in Caesar).

vērum inclūsum[45] in tabulīs[46] tamquam in vāgīnā[47] reconditum,[48]
quō ex senātūs cōnsultō
cōnfestim[49] tē interfectum esse, Catilīna, convēnit.
Vīvis, 5
et vīvis nōn ad dēpōnendam,
sed ad cōnfirmandam audāciam.

Cupiō, patrēs cōnscrīptī, mē[50] esse clēmentem,[51]
cupiō in tantīs reī pūblicae perīculīs nōn dissolūtum[52] vidērī
sed jam mē ipse inertiae nēquitiaeque condemnō.[53]

A TRAITOR SITS AMONG US

Castra sunt in Italiā contrā populum Rōmānum,

Words to Remember

vērum, adv., *but, yet.*
tamquam, adv., *as if, just as if, like.*
convenit, convenīre, convēnit, 4, intr.; acc. w. infin., *it is necessary, it is suitable.*
patrēs (patrum) cōnscrīptī (cōnscrīptōrum), *senators, gentlemen of the Senate. Conscript fathers* is meaningless. Individually senators were called **senātōrēs**; sitting as a body, the members of the House were addressed as **patrēs cōnscrīptī.**
inertia, ae, *inactivity* (cf. inert, inertia).

---

45 **inclūsus, a, um**, *thrust away, enclosed* (cf. **inclūdō**; inclose).

46 **tabula, ae**, *list, record, tablet.* Here, *in the archives* would be a good way of expressing the idea that the decree had been filed among the records of the Senate's proceedings.

47 **vāgīna, ae**, *scabbard.*

48 **reconditus, a, um**, *concealed, hidden* (cf. recondite).

49 **cōnfestim**, adv., *at once, immediately* (cf. **festināre**).

50 **mē**; this subject accusative is sometimes used after words like **volō**, which ordinarily take merely an infinitive to fill out their meaning, especially if the infinitive is **esse.**

51 **clēmēns** (*gen.* **clēmentis**), *mild, merciful.*

52 **dissolūtus, a, um**, *neglectful, remiss* (cf. dissolute).

53 **condemnō**, 1, tr.; gen. of the charge, *condemn.*

in Etrūriae[54] faucibus[55] collocāta,
crēscit in diēs singulōs hostium numerus;
eōrum autem castrōrum imperātōrem ducemque hostium
intrā moenia atque adeō in senātū vidētis,
intestīnam[56] aliquam cotīdiē perniciem reī pūblicae mōlientem.
Sī tē jam, Catilīna, comprehendī,
sī interficī jusserō,
crēdō,[57] erit verendum mihi
nē nōn potius hoc omnēs bonī sērius ā mē
quam quisquam crūdēlius factum esse dīcat.[58]

BUT THERE IS A JUST REASON WHY WE WAIT

Vērum ego hoc quod jam prīdem factum esse oportuit
certā dē causā nōndum addūcor ut faciam.
Tum dēnique interficiēre[59]

Words to Remember

singulī, ae, a, *each, one at a time, one each.*
intrā, prep. w. acc., *within.*
aliquis, aliqua, aliquod, indefinite adjective, *some, any;* Gr. 815.
cotīdiē, adv., *every day, daily.*
sērius, adv., *too late.*
quisquam, quidquam, *anyone, anything;* Gr. 843.
dēnique, adv., *at length, at last, thereupon, finally.*

---

[54] **Etrūria, ae,** *Etruria;* see map, page 57. Actually the camp was located at Faesulae (modern Fiesole) near Florence.

[55] **faucēs, faucium,** f., *jaws, throat, entrance, gateway, pass* (cf. fauces).

[56] **intestīnus, a, um,** *internal, civil* (cf. intestinal flu).

[57] **Crēdō** is ironical here; Cicero obviously supposes the opposite.

[58] **nē nōn . . . dīcat;** the whole clause is difficult because of what is omitted. Supply the words in parentheses: **nē nōn potius hoc omnēs bonī sērius ā mē (factum esse dīcant), quam (nē) quisquam (hoc) crūdēlius (ā mē) factum esse dīcat.** In English words are more apt to be omitted from the latter part of a sentence *(some played bridge; others, poker),* but in Latin it is often the other way *(some bridge; others poker played).*

[59] **interficiēre = interficiēris;** Gr. 1022.

—*Alinari*

CATILINE—DARK AND AUDACIOUS

cum jam nēmō tam improbus,
tam perditus,
tam tuī similis[60] invenīrī poterit
qui id nōn jūre factum esse fateātur.[61]

6 Quamdiū quisquam erit quī tē dēfendere audeat,
vīvēs,
et vīvēs ita ut nunc vīvis,
multīs meīs et firmīs praesidiīs obsessus,
nē commovēre tē contrā rem pūblicam possīs.

MEANWHILE, YOUR EVERY MOVE WILL BE KNOWN TO US

Multōrum tē etiam oculī et aurēs nōn sentientem,
sīcut[62] adhūc fēcērunt,
speculābuntur[63] atque custōdient.
Etenim quid est, Catilīna, quod jam amplius exspectēs,
sī neque nox tenebrīs obscūrāre[64] coetūs nefāriōs

WORDS TO REMEMBER

quamdiū, conj., *as long as* (**quam** + **diū**); Gr. 571.
obsideō, obsidēre, obsēdī, obsessus, 2, tr., *obstruct, blockade, besiege* (cf. obsession).
auris, auris, *ear* (cf. auricular confession).
adhūc, adv., *up to this time, hitherto* (**ad** + **hūc**).
etenim, *(and) really, (and) in fact, (for) truly* (**et** + **enim**). The word is used to link what went before with what is to come next.
tenebrae, tenebrārum, *darkness* (cf. the Office of Tenebrae).

---

60 This strong climax, **tam tuī similis**, is insulting, to say the least. The point Cicero is making is this: there were still numerous Catiline sympathizers (even in the Senate) who put no faith in reports of his proposed rebellion. Cicero must wait until the conspiracy is so plain that no political propaganda can make his action appear other than just and patriotic.

61 **fateor, fatērī, fassus sum**, 2, tr.; acc. w. infin., *own, admit*.

62 **sīcut**, conj., *just as, as;* Gr. 601.

63 **speculor**, 1, tr., *watch, spy upon* (cf. **speculātor**; speculation).

64 **obscūrō**, 1, tr., *hide, conceal* (cf. obscure).

nec prīvāta domus parietibus continēre
vōcēs conjūrātiōnis tuae potest,
sī illūstrantur,[65]
sī ērumpunt omnia?
Mūtā jam istam mentem, mihi crēde,[66]
oblīvīscere caedis atque incendiōrum.
Tenēris undique;
lūce sunt clāriōra nōbīs tua cōnsilia omnia,
quae jam mēcum licet recognōscās.

I KNEW THE DAY ON WHICH MANLIUS WOULD RAISE THE STANDARD OF REVOLT

Meministīne mē **7**
ante diem duodecimum Kalendās Novembrēs[67]
dīcere in senātū

WORDS TO REMEMBER

nec (neque), *and not, nor, neither.* **Neque** is used before vowels and consonants; **nec** rarely before vowels.
parietēs, parietum, m., *walls* (of a room), *partitions;* don't confuse with **mūrus** or **moenia.**
licet, licēre, licuit, 2, intr.; w. dat. of person; acc. w. infin., *it is allowed, it is permitted.* Here we have the less common usage of **licet** and the subjunctive without **ut;** Gr. 641.
recognōscō, recognōscere, recognōvi, recognitus, 3, tr., *review, recall* (cf. **cognōscō;** recognize).
duodecimus, a, um, *twelfth.*

---

[65] **illūstrō,** 1, tr., *light up, illuminate* (cf. illustration). **Illūstrantur** looks back at the phrase **nox tenebrīs obscūrāre,** just as **ērumpunt** has an eye on **prīvāta domus parietibus.**

[66] Don't translate **mihi crēde** too literally. The force is something like *take my advice,* or *take it from me.*

[67] **ante diem duodecimum Kalendās Novembrēs;** translate as if **diē duodecimō ante Kalendās Novembrēs** (cf. calender, November); **i. e.,** October 21 by Roman reckoning. See *Flash* under that date, page 7.

—*Courtesy of Produzione Consorzio Scipione S. A.*

CASTRA MANLIANA

Gaius Manlius and his supporters in their camp in Etruria discuss news from Rome and make plans for a march on the capital. Cicero's agents kept him fully informed of developments among the conspirators.

fore[68] in armīs certō diē,

qui diēs futūrus esset ante diem sextum Kalendās Novembrēs[69]
Gājum Mānlium,[70] audāciae satellitem[71] atque administrum[72]
tuae?

WORD TO REMEMBER

sextus, a, um, *sixth.*

---

68 **fore = futūrus** (**a, um**) **esse**; Gr. 360.

69 **ante diem sextum Kalendās Novembrēs**: October 27. See *Bulletin* under that date, page 7.

70 For Gaius Manlius see page 6.

71 **satelles, satellitis,** *attendant, henchman* (cf. satellite). The word implies a lower kind of service than **administer.**

72 **administer, administrī,** *helper, accomplice* (cf. **administrō**; administration).

Num mē fefellit, Catilīna,
nōn modo rēs[73] tanta, tam atrōx tamque incrēdibilis,
vērum, id quod multō magis est admīrandum, diēs?

I KNEW THE DATE YOU HAD SET FOR OUR SLAUGHTER

Dīxī ego īdem[74] in senātū
caedem tē optimātium[75] contulisse
in ante diem quīntum Kalendās Novembrēs[76]
tum cum multī prīncipēs cīvitātis
Rōmā nōn tam suī cōnservandī
quam tuōrum cōnsiliōrum reprimendōrum causā profūgērunt.
Num īnfitiārī[77] potes
tē illō ipsō diē,
meīs praesidiīs, meā dīligentiā circumclūsum,
commovēre tē contrā rem pūblicam nōn potuisse,
cum tū discessū cēterōrum,

Words to Remember

fallō, fallere, fefellī, falsus, 3, tr., *deceive, cheat, play* (someone) *false* (cf. infallibility).
quīntus, a, um, *fifth* (cf. quintuplets).
tum . . . cum, *at that time when.*
circumclūdō, circumclūdere, circumclūsī, circumclūsus, 3, tr., *enclose about, hedge in* (cf. **claudō, inclūdō**; enclosure).
discessus, ūs, *departure, withdrawal, absence.*
cēterī, ae, a, *the rest (of), the remainder* (cf. etc. = et cetera); Gr. 829.

---

[73] It is seldom that **rēs** is translated by *thing*. Find the word that fits the context. The **rēs** in question here is a *plot*, a *conspiracy*, an *enterprise*. The same holds for (**rēs**) **tanta**; not simply *so great* but rather *so ambitious*, or *so extensive*.

[74] **īdem**: *I also* (lit., *the same I*).

[75] **optimātēs, optimātium,** *the optimate party;* see page 3.

[76] **in ante diem quīntum Kalendās Novembrēs:** October 28.

[77] **īnfitior,** 1, tr.; acc. w. infin., *deny*.

nostrā tamen, quī remānsissēmus, caede
contentum tē esse dīcēbās?

I KNEW OF YOUR PLANS FOR PRAENESTE I BLOCKED THEM

8 Quid, cum tē Praeneste[78]
Kalendīs ipsīs Novembribus[79]
occupātūrum nocturnō impetū esse cōnfīderēs,
sēnsistīne illam colōniam[80]
meō jussū
meīs praesidiīs, custōdiīs, vigiliīs esse mūnītam?

SECRECY IS IMPOSSIBLE

Nihil agis,
nihil mōlīris,
nihil cōgitās[81]
quod nōn ego nōn modo audiam
sed etiam videam
plānēque sentiam.

Words to Remember

remaneō, remanēre, remānsī, remānsūrus, 2, intr., *remain behind* (cf. **maneō;** permanent).
contentus, a, um, *content(ed), satisfied.*
custōdia, ae, *sentinel, guard, protection.* **Custōdiīs** differs from **praesidiīs,** *garrison* (meaning the walls), and **vigiliīs,** *night watchmen.*

---

[78] **Praeneste, Praenestis,** n., *Praeneste,* a strong hill-city, twenty-five miles southeast of Rome, now Palestrina; see *Flash* under date of November 1, page 7.

[79] **Kalendīs ipsīs Novembribus:** *the very first day of November.*

[80] **colōnia, ae,** *colony.*

[81] **Nihil agis . . . cōgitās;** these short phrases must have been fired with machine-gunlike speed.

I KNOW WHAT YOU DID ON THE NIGHT BEFORE LAST

Recognōsce mēcum tandem noctem illam superiōrem;
jam intellegēs
  multō mē vigilāre ācrius ad salūtem
  quam tē ad perniciem reī pūblicae.
Dīcō tē priōre nocte vēnisse inter falcāriōs[82]—
  nōn agam obscūrē: in Mārcī Laecae domum—
convēnisse eōdem complūrēs ējusdem āmentiae scelerisque sociōs.[83]
Num negāre audēs?
[*He pauses—deathly, expectant silence*]
Quid[84] tacēs?
Convincam,[85] sī negās.

Words to Remember

vigilō, 1, intr., *am awake, am on guard* (cf. vigilant).
ācrius, comparative of **ācriter**, *sharply, keenly, piercingly.*
prior, prius, *former.* Here **priōre nocte** is the same night before last (**noctem illam superiōrem**).
obscūrē, adv., *darkly, obscurely.*
eōdem, adv., *to that same place, in the same place.*
āmentia, ae, *madness, folly* (cf. **mēns**).

---

[82] **inter falcāriōs:** *among the scythe makers, into the quarter of the sickle makers.* The various crafts and trades occupied exclusive sections at Rome, just as our produce markets and second-hand stores are usually grouped in one part of town. (Cf. **falx, falcis**, the pulling hooks in Caesar.)

[83] **complūrēs . . . sociōs**; the historian Sallust in his *Catilina* says: "intempestā nocte *(in the dead of night)* conjūrātiōnis prīncipēs convocat per M. Porcium Laecam" (27, 3-4).

[84] **quid:** *why?*

[85] **convincō, convincere, convīcī, convictus**, 3, tr., *prove, refute, convict.*

—*Alinari*

CICERO IN THE SENATE

The artist has well portrayed the varying reactions on the faces of the senators in the background.

HERE IN THE SENATE OF ROME . . . !

Videō enim esse hīc in senātū quōsdam quī tēcum ūnā fuērunt.[86]
Ō dī immortālēs![87] 9
Ubinam gentium sumus?[88]
Quam rem pūblicam habēmus?
In quā urbe vīvimus?
Hīc, hīc[89] sunt in nostrō numerō, patrēs cōnscrīptī,
[*With an emphatic gesture toward the members of the House*]
in hōc orbis terrae sānctissimō gravissimōque cōnsiliō,[90]
quī dē nostrō omnium interitū,
quī dē hūjus urbis atque adeō dē orbis terrārum exitiō cōgitent.
[*Indignant murmurs*]
Hōs ego videō cōnsul
et dē rē pūblicā sententiam rogō,

Words to Remember

ūnā, adv., *along (with), together.*
ubinam, adv., *where* (**ubi** + **nam**).
interitus, ūs, *death, destruction.*
sententia, ae, *opinion, vote.* **Sententiam rogāre** was the parliamentary phrase meaning *to ask an opinion, to call for a vote.*

---

[86] Some senators, like Catiline himself, were involved in the conspiracy—another reason for Cicero's caution.

[87] This entire dramatic outburst is brought on as Cicero realizes the full implication of the fact he has just disclosed: here before him in the very Senate house were men who but the night before had sat in on the revolutionary gathering at Laeca's. This was high treason.

[88] **Ubinam . . . sumus**: *Where in the world are we?* Gr. 691.

[89] **Hīc, hīc**; the repetition strengthens the seriousness of the situation: *here, right here in our midst . . .*

[90] **sānctissimō gravissimōque cōnsiliō**; notice the solemnity of these superlatives, weighted as they are with heavy *ō* sounds; **sānctus** often has the force of *revered, respected.*

et, quōs ferrō trucīdārī oportēbat,
eōs nōndum vōce vulnerō.

I KNOW EVERY DETAIL OF THAT MEETING

Fuistī igitur[91] apud Laecam illā nocte, Catilīna,
distribuistī partēs Italiae,
statuistī quō quemque proficīscī placēret,
dēlēgistī quōs Rōmae relinquerēs,
quōs tēcum ēdūcerēs,
discrīpsistī urbis partēs ad incendia,
cōnfirmāstī tē ipsum jam esse exitūrum,
dīxistī paulum tibi esse etiam nunc morae,
  quod ego vīverem.
Repertī sunt duo equitēs Rōmānī
  quī tē istā cūrā līberārent,
  et sē illā ipsā nocte paulō ante lūcem
  mē in meō lectō[92] interfectūrōs esse pollicērentur.

I KNEW OF MY PROJECTED 'REMOVAL'

10 Haec ego omnia,

Words to Remember

ferrum, ī, *iron, steel,* anything made of iron—*sword, spearpoint,* etc. (cf. ferric oxide; Fe, the chemical symbol for iron).
trucīdō, 1, tr., *slaughter, kill fiercely.*
apud, prep. w. acc., *among, in the presence of;* also *at the house of* (as here), *in the works of* (when referring to an author's writings).
discrībō, discrībere, discrīpsī, discrīptus, 3, tr., *apportion, divide* (cf. **scrībō**).
mora, ae, *delay* (cf. **moror**). **Morae** is genitive; Gr. 690.
cūra, ae, *care, concern.*

---

[91] **igitur,** adv., postp., *therefore.* It often resumes the thought after a digression—here the dramatic attack on the House.

[92] **lectus, ī,** *couch, bed.* Formal calls were made upon leading men in the early morning (**salūtātiō**). The host would be abed during the reception.

—*Courtesy J. Arthur Rank Organization, Inc.*

Apud Laecam

Neither the shadows of night could hide these criminal meetings, nor could the walls of private homes shut in the whispered conspiracy, since Cicero had made certain that numerous governmental agents were numbered among Catiline's followers, especially those at Rome.

vixdum[93] etiam coetū vestrō dīmissō,
comperī:
domum meam mājōribus praesidiīs mūnīvī atque firmāvī,
exclūsī eōs quōs tū ad mē salūtātum[94] māne mīserās,

Words to Remember

firmō, 1, tr., *strengthen, make secure*.(cf. **firmus**; firm).
exclūdō, exclūdere, exclūsī, exclūsus, 3, tr., *exclude, shut out* (cf. exclusive).
māne, adv., *in the morning, early*.

---

93 **vixdum**, adv., *scarcely yet, hardly even*.

94 **salūtō**, 1, tr., *greet, call on (formally), salute* (cf. **salūs**; salutary). **Salūtātum** is the supine; Gr. 213, 860.

cum illī ipsī vēnissent
quōs ego jam multīs ac summīs virīs
ad mē id temporis[95] ventūrōs esse praedīxeram.

LEAVE THE CITY!

Quae cum ita sint, Catilīna,
perge quō coepistī:
ēgredere aliquandō ex urbe;
patent portae—
proficīscere.

Nimium diū tē imperātōrem
tua illa Mānliāna[96] castra dēsīderant.

Ēdūc tēcum etiam omnēs tuōs;
sī minus, quam plūrimōs;[97]
pūrgā urbem.

Magnō mē metū līberāveris,
modo[98] inter mē atque tē mūrus intersit.

Words to Remember

pergō, pergere, perrēxī, perrēctum, 3, intr.; w. infin., ***keep straight, go straight, proceed.***
nimium, adv., *too, excessively.*
sī minus = sī nōn; Gr. 588.
pūrgō, 1, tr., *clean, purify* (cf. purge).
intersum, interesse, interfuī, interfutūrus, irreg., intr.; w. dat., ***am between, am among, take part in.***

---

[95] **id temporis:** *at that time;* Gr. 687.

[96] **Mānliānus, a, um;** adjective formed from **Mānlius;** meaning?

[97] **Ēdūc . . . plūrimōs;** the thought is highly compressed. Supplying a few words releases the pressure. **Ēdūc etiam omnēs tuōs tēcum (sī fierī potest); sī minus** (translate as if equal to **sī nōn omnēs**), **(at tamen ēdūc) quam plūrimōs.** Recall the imperatives, **dīc, dūc, fac,** and **fer** of **dīcō, dūcō, faciō,** and **ferō,** all of which drop the *e;* Gr. 1020.

[98] **modo,** conj., *if only, provided only, as long as;* Gr. 594.

YOU CANNOT REMAIN

Nōbīscum versārī jam diūtius nōn potes;
nōn feram,
nōn patiar,
nōn sinam.[99]
Magna[100] dīs immortālibus habenda est
atque huic ipsī Jovī[101] Statōrī[102] **11**
[With a gesture toward the statue of the god in whose temple they were]
antīquissimō custōdī hūjus urbis, grātia,
  quod hanc tam taetram,[103]
  tam horribilem
  tamque īnfestam reī pūblicae pestem
  totiēns jam effūgimus.
Nōn est saepius in ūnō homine[104]

Words to Remember

versor, 1, intr., *move about, dwell, engage in, remain.*
Juppiter, Jovis, *Jupiter* (cf. Jove, jovial).
Stator, Statōris, *the Stayer* (Protector), *Mainstay.*
horribilis, e, *dreadful, frightful, hideous.*
totiēns, adv., *so often, so many times.*

---

[99] **sinō, sinere, sīvī, situs, 3, tr.**; acc. w. infin.; **ut (nē),** *allow, permit.* **Nōn sinam** climaxes the triple negatives, **nōn feram, nōn patiar, nōn sinam.** The words are not mere synonyms. Try to imitate the rhythm and the build-up of these words in your translation.

[100] **Magna** goes with **grātia; grātiam habēre,** *to be thankful, to feel grateful.*

[101] Jupiter was the supreme god of the Romans.

[102] The temple to Jupiter the Stayer was vowed by Romulus when his troops were giving way to the Sabines, and built upon the spot where their flight was *stayed* by the god. At least so tradition had it.

[103] **taeter, taetra, taetrum,** *foul, hateful.*

[104] **in ūnō homine;** Catiline, that is, rather than Cicero. Cf. "Shall Rome stand under one man's awe?" (*Julius Caesar,* Act II, Scene 1).

summa salūs[105] perīclitanda reī pūblicae.
Quamdiū mihi cōnsulī dēsignātō,[106] Catilīna, īnsidiātus es,
nōn pūblicō mē praesidiō,
sed prīvātā dīligentiā[107] dēfendī.
Cum proximīs comitiīs cōnsulāribus
mē cōnsulem in campō[108]
et competītōrēs[109] tuōs interficere voluistī,
compressī cōnātūs tuōs nefāriōs amīcōrum praesidiō et cōpiīs,
nūllō tumultū pūblicē concitātō;[110]
dēnique, quotiēnscumque[111] mē petīstī,
per mē tibi obstitī,
quamquam vidēbam perniciem meam
cum magnā calamitāte reī pūblicae esse conjūnctam.

Words to Remember

perīclitor, 1, tr., *risk, endanger, try, test.*
comprimō, comprimere, compressī, compressus, 3, tr., *repress, suppress.*
cōnātus, ūs, *attempt* (cf. **cōnor**).
pūblicē, adv.; meaning?
obstō, obstāre, obstitī, 1, intr.; w. dat., *resist, stand in the way, prevent.*

---

105 **summa salūs**: *the highest interests*, or *the very existence.*

106 **cōnsulī dēsignātō**; the dative after **īnsidior**. The election of the consuls usually took place in July; a successful candidate would therefore be 'consul-elect' from that date until he took up his official duties on the first of the following January.

107 **prīvātā dīligentiā**: "(Cicerō) circum sē praesidia amīcōrum atque clientium *(clients)* occultē habēbat" (Sallust, *Catilina*, 26, 4).

108 **campus, ī**, *field*. Here the Campus Martius, the Field of Mars (cf. our Soldiers' Field), where election assemblies met.

109 **competītor, competītōris**; meaning? (Cf. **petō**; competition.) The men in question were D. Junius Silanus and L. Licinius, and one Servius Sulpicius who (like Catiline) also ran.

110 **concitō**, 1, tr., *arouse, agitate.* What Cicero means by **nūllō tumultū pūblicē concitātō** is that he didn't have to call out the militia.

111 **quotiēnscumque**, conj., *as often as.*

NOW UNIVERSAL ANARCHY IS YOUR AIM

Nunc jam apertē rem pūblicam ūniversam petis; **12**
templa deōrum immortālium,
tēcta urbis,
vītam omnium cīvium,
Italiam tōtam
ad exitium et vastitātem[112] vocās.

Quārē, quoniam id quod est prīmum
  et quod hūjus imperī disciplīnaeque mājōrum proprium[113] est,
  facere nōndum audeō,
faciam id quod est ad[114] sevēritātem lēnius,[115]
ad commūnem salūtem ūtilius.

  Nam sī tē interficī jusserō,
residēbit in rē pūblicā reliqua conjūrātōrum manus;
  sīn tū, quod tē jam dūdum hortor, exieris,

Words to Remember

ūniversus, a, um, *entire, all together* (lit., *turned to one;* **ūnus** + **vertō**; cf. universal).
quoniam, conj., *because, since, whereas.* Same as **quod** and **quia**; Gr. 572.
disciplīna, ae, *training, instruction, system* (cf. disciple).
resideō, residēre, resēdī, 2, intr., *settle down* (like dregs), *remain* (cf. **sedeō**; residue).
conjūrātor, conjūrātōris, *conspirator* (cf. **conjūrātiō**).
sīn, conj., *but if, if however;* Gr. 587.

---

[112] **vastitātem**; meaning? (What verb does it look like if you cut off the last part?)

[113] **proprius, a, um**; w. gen., *proper (to), peculiar (to), one's own;* Gr. 722, 723. Cicero has in mind such precedents as were set by men like Scipio and Ahala of whom he had made mention (cf. page 14).

[114] **ad**; here *in point of, with respect to, as regards.*

[115] **lēnis, e,** *soft, mild, gentle.*

exhauriētur[116] ex urbe
tuōrum comitum[117] magna et perniciōsa sentīna[118] reī pūblicae.

I EVEN DARE USE THE WORD 'EXILE'

13 Quid est,[119] Catilīna?
Num dubitās id, mē imperante, facere
quod jam tuā sponte faciēbās?
Exīre ex urbe jubet cōnsul hostem.[120]
Interrogās mē, num in exilium?
Nōn jubeō,
sed, sī mē cōnsulis, suādeō.
Quid est enim, Catilīna, quod tē jam in hāc urbe dēlectāre[121] possit?
in quā nēmō est
extrā istam conjūrātiōnem perditōrum hominum

Words to Remember

interrogō, 1, tr., *ask, question.*
cōnsulō, cōnsulere, cōnsuluī, cōnsultus, 3, tr. and intr.; w. acc. of person consulted; dat. of person whose interests are consulted, *consult, ask one's advice, plan, take thought for.*
suādeō, suādēre, suāsī, suāsus, 2, tr.; w. dat. of person, acc. of thing; acc. w. infin.; ut (nē), *advise, urge* (cf. **persuādeō**; suasive).

---

116 **exhauriō, exhaurīre, exhausī, exhaustus,** 4, tr., *draw off, drain* (cf. exhaust, exhausted).

117 **comes, comitis,** m., *companion, comrade, follower.*

118 **sentīna, ae,** *bilge (water).* The ship of state figure is common enough (cf. Longfellow's poem). Here Cicero makes bold to extend it a bit. If Catiline leaves, the rest of his 'gang' will go with him and there will be drained from the bottom of the ship large numbers of foul politicians.

119 **Quid est** anticipates the next question; *How now? What about this?*

120 **cōnsul hostem**; this had more force and dignity than the more personal **ego tē** would have had.

121 **dēlectō,** 1, tr., *delight, charm.*

qui tē nōn metuat,
nēmō quī nōn ōderit.

AND YOUR PRIVATE LIFE . . . !

Quae nota domesticae turpitūdinis nōn inūsta[122] vītae tuae est?
Quod prīvātārum rērum dēdecus[123] nōn haeret[124] in fāmā?
Quae libīdō ab oculīs,
quod facinus ā manibus umquam tuīs,
quod flāgitium ā tōtō corpore āfuit?
Cui tū adulēscentulō quem corruptēlārum[125] illecebrīs[126] irrētīssēs[127]
nōn aut ad audāciam ferrum
aut ad libīdinem facem praetulistī?[128]

Words to Remember

nota, ae, *mark, brand.*
libīdō, libīdinis, *desire, passion, lust.* An Anglicized form of the word (lĭ-bī'dō) has been popularized by modern psychology to express a motive force derived either from the sex instinct or from man's primal urge to live.
flāgitium, ī, *outrage, shameful deed.*
adulēscentulus, ī, *young lad.* (**-Ulus** is a diminutive suffix like the English *-let* in booklet, a small book.)
fax, facis, *torch, firebrand.*
praeferō, praeferre, praetulī, praelātus, irreg., tr., *carry in front of, bear before.*

---

122 **inūrō, inūrere, inussī, inūstus,** 3, tr., *burn in, brand.* The figure is borrowed from the branding of runaway slaves, criminals, and captives.

123 **dēdecus, dēdecoris,** n., *disgrace, dishonor.*

124 **haereō, haerēre, haesī, haesūrus,** 2, intr.; w. abl. or dat.; **in** w. abl., *stick* (cf. adhesive).

125 **corruptēla, ae,** *enticement (to vice).*

126 **illecebra, ae,** *allurement.*

127 **irrētiō,** 4, tr., *ensnare;* **irrētīssēs = irrētīvissēs.**

128 Torchbearers were necessary in the streets at night. Sallust tells of Catiline's fascinating but baneful influence over the young (*Catilina,* 14, 5-7).

—*Courtesy J. Arthur Rank Organization, Inc.*

YOUNG MEN WITH SWORDS

At Rome young men like those in Catiline's group carried a sword and used it—not always in play! The young men here shown would be no match for the soldier with his emblazoned shield, crested helmet, and heavier battle sword, but the present encounter is evidently a friendly one.

14 Quid vērō? nūper cum morte superiōris uxōris
novīs nūptiīs[129] domum vacuēfēcissēs,
nōnne etiam aliō incrēdibilī scelere hoc scelus cumulāstī?[130]

WORDS TO REMEMBER

uxor, uxōris, *wife.* (An uxorious husband is one who is dotingly fond of, or excessively submissive to, his wife. Some have suggested that Adam fell through uxoriousness.)
vacuēfaciō, vacuēfacere, vacuēfēcī, vacuēfactus, 3, tr., *empty* **(vacuus,** *empty* **+ faciō).**

---

129 **nūptiae, nūptiārum,** *wedding* (cf. nuptials).

130 **cumulō,** 1, tr., *crown, surmount.* Catiline's new bride-to-be, one Orestilla, "a woman praised for nothing but beauty," was as corrupt as Catiline himself. She objected to the son by his first wife. Catiline, it was said, removed the lady's objection by doing away with his son.

quod ego praetermittō et facile patior silērī,
  nē in hāc cīvitāte tantī facinoris immānitās[131]
  aut exstitisse aut nōn vindicāta esse videātur.
Praetermittō ruīnās[132] fortūnārum tuārum
  quās omnēs proximīs Īdibus[133] tibi impendēre sentiēs;
ad illa veniō quae nōn ad prīvātam ignōminiam vitiōrum tuōrum,
nōn ad domesticam tuam difficultātem ac turpitūdinem,
sed ad summam rem pūblicam
atque ad omnium nostrum vītam salūtemque pertinent.

CAN YOU LIVE AMONG MEN WHO KNOW YOU FOR A TRAITOR?

Potestne tibi haec lūx, Catilīna, **15**
aut hūjus caelī spīritus esse jūcundus,[134]
  cum sciās esse hōrum nēminem
    quī nesciat tē prīdiē Kalendās Jānuāriās,[135]
      Lepidō et Tullō[136] cōnsulibus,
    stetisse in comitiō cum tēlō?

Words to Remember

praetermittō, praetermittere, praetermīsī, praetermissus, 3, tr., *let pass by, overlook* (**praeter,** *by* + **mittō**). Cicero has a way of passing things over in silence and mentioning them just the same.
exsistō, exsistere, exstitī, 3, intr., *exist.*
ignōminia, ae, *disgrace, dishonor* (cf. ignominious defeat).
vitium, ī, *fault, crime.*
prīdiē, adv., *on the day before* (cf. **diēs**).

---

131 **immānitās, immānitātis,** *enormity, monstrosity.*

132 **ruīna, ae,** *downfall.* Cicero refers to the bankruptcy of Catiline's estate.

133 **Īdibus:** *the Ides of November* (the thirteenth). Creditors and bankers regularly called in loans on the Ides.

134 **jūcundus, a, um,** *pleasant, agreeable.*

135 **prīdiē Kalendās Jānuāriās:** December 31.

136 Lepidus and Tullus were consuls in 66 B. C.

manum
cōnsulum et prīncipum cīvitātis interficiendōrum causā parāvisse?
scelerī ac furōrī tuō nōn mentem aliquam aut timōrem tuum, sed fortūnam populī Rōmānī obstitisse?

YOUR MURDEROUS ATTEMPTS HAVE ALL BEEN FOILED

Ac jam illa omittō—
neque enim sunt aut obscūra
aut nōn multa commissa posteā—:
quotiēns tū mē dēsignātum
quotiēns vērō cōnsulem
interficere cōnātus es!
quot ego tuās petītiōnēs,[137]
ita conjectās ut vītārī posse nōn vidērentur,
parvā quādam dēclīnātiōne[138] et, ut ājunt, corpore effūgī!
Nihil agis,
nihil assequeris,
neque tamen cōnārī ac velle dēsistis.

Words to Remember

omittō, omittere, omīsī, omissus, 3, tr., *dismiss, omit* (cf. omission).
quotiēns, interrog. adv., *how often* (cf. quotient).
quot, indecl. adj., *how many.*
conjiciō, conjicere, conjēcī, conjectus, 3, tr., *hurl, throw, cast.*
ājunt: *they say.*
assequor, assequī, assecūtus sum, 3, tr., *attain, accomplish* (cf. **sequor**).
dēsistō, dēsistere, dēstitī, dēstitūrus, 3, intr., *cease, give up* (cf. desist).

---

137 **petītiō, petītiōnis,** *blow, thrust.* Cicero compares Catiline to a gladiator attempting to drive home thrust after thrust, only to find his adversary avoiding them by swift and well-timed movements. What similar comparison might we modern Americans make?

138 **dēclīnātiō, dēclīnātiōnis,** *swerve, twist.* **Dēclīnātiōne** and **corpore** go together; *by a mere twist of the body.*

Quotiēns jam tibi extorta[139] est ista sīca dē manibus! 16
Quotiēns excidit[140] cāsū aliquō et ēlāpsa est!
quae quidem quibus abs tē initiāta[141] sacrīs[142] ac dēvōta[143] sit nesciō,
quod eam necesse putās esse in cōnsulis corpore dēfīgere.[144]
Nunc vērō quae tua est ista vīta?
Sīc enim jam tēcum loquar,
nōn ut odiō permōtus esse videar, quō dēbeō,
sed ut misericordiā, quae tibi nūlla dēbētur.

NO FRIENDLY VOICE GREETED YOU

Vēnistī paulō ante in senātum.
Quis tē ex hāc tantā frequentiā,
tot ex tuīs amīcīs ac necessāriīs salūtāvit?[145]

Words to Remember

sīca, ae, *dagger.*
cāsus, ūs, *chance* (cf. casual acquaintance).
abs, *by;* form of preposition **ā** used before **tē.**
necesse, indecl. adj., *necessary.*
misericordia, ae, *mercy.*
necessārius, ī, *connection;* business associates and persons of that sort as well as friends.

---

[139] **extorqueō, extorquēre, extorsī, extortus,** 2, tr., *tear away, twist* (cf. extortion).

[140] **excidō, excidere, excidī,** 3, intr.; **ex (ē)** w. abl.; w. abl., *fall out, escape.*

[141] **initiō,** 1, tr., *dedicate* (cf. initiation).

[142] **sacra, sacrōrum,** *sacred rites.*

[143] **dēvoveō, dēvovēre, dēvōvī, dēvōtus,** 2, tr., *vow.* He speaks as if Catiline's dagger were set apart and consecrated to a special use like some sacred object.

[144] **dēfīgō, dēfīgere, dēfīxī, dēfīxus,** 3, tr.; **in** w. abl. or acc., *fix firmly, implant.*

[145] **salūtō, 1,** tr., *greet* (cf. salute, salutation).

Sī hoc post hominum memoriam[146] contigit nēminī,
vōcis exspectās contumēliam,
cum sīs gravissimō jūdiciō taciturnitātis oppressus?

YOU ARE DESERTED BY ALL

Quid quod[147] adventū tuō ista subsellia[148] vacuēfacta sunt
quod omnēs cōnsulārēs
qui tibi persaepe ad caedem cōnstitūtī fuērunt,
simul atque adsēdistī,[149]
partem istam subselliōrum[148] nūdam atque inānem relīquērunt,
quō tandem animō tibi ferendum putās?

YET, YOU REMAIN?

17 Servī mehercule[150] meī sī mē istō pactō metuerent
ut tē metuunt omnēs cīvēs tuī,
domum meam relinquendam putārem:
tū tibi urbem nōn arbitrāris?

Words to Remember

contingō, contingere, contigī, 3, intr.; w. dat., *happen to, fall to the lot of.*
contumēlia, ae, *reproach, indignity, affront* (cf. contumely).
taciturnitās, taciturnitātis, *silence* (cf. taciturn).
persaepe, adv., *very often.* What is the force of **per** in this compound?
simul atque (ac), *as soon as;* Gr. 556.
nūdus, a, um, *stripped, bare.*
inānis, e, *empty* (cf. an inane remark).
pactum, ī, *way, manner, agreement.* In the ablative, with words like **istō, quō,** it is tantamount to **istō modō, quōmodo.**

---

[146] **post hominum memoriam:** *within living memory, since the dawn of history.*
[147] **Quid quod:** *What (of this) that . . .*; a substantive clause; Gr. 657.
[148] **subsellium, ī,** *bench, seat.*
[149] **adsīdō, adsīdere, adsēdī,** 3, intr., *sit down, take one's seat.*
[150] **mehercule,** exclamation, *by Hercules, by heaven.*

—*Bettmann Archive*

CATILINE SITS ALONE

His fellow senators give a mute but effective show of disapproval by vacating the seats nearest him.

Et sī mē meīs cīvibus
injūriā suspectum tam graviter atque offēnsum vidērem,
carēre mē aspectū cīvium
quam īnfestīs omnium oculīs cōnspicī māllem:
tū, cum cōnscientiā scelerum tuōrum agnōscās[151] odium omnium,
jūstum et jam diū tibi dēbitum,
dubitās, quōrum mentēs sēnsūsque vulnerās,

WORDS TO REMEMBER

suspectus, a, um, *suspected.*
graviter, adv., *seriously* (cf. **gravis**).
offēnsus, a, um, *annoying* (cf. offensive).
cōnscientia, ae, *knowledge, consciousness* (cf. conscience).
sēnsus, ūs, *sense, emotion.*

---

[151] **agnōscō, agnōscere, agnōvī, agnitus,** 3, tr., *recognize* (cf. **cognōscō**).

eōrum aspectum praesentiamque vītāre?
Sī tē pārentēs[152] timērent atque ōdissent tuī
neque eōs ratiōne ūllā plācāre possēs,
ut opīnor,[153] ab eōrum oculīs aliquō concēderēs.
Nunc tē patria,[154]
quae commūnis est pārēns omnium nostrum,
ōdit ac metuit,
et jam diū nihil tē jūdicat nisi dē parricīdiō[155] suō cōgitāre;
hūjus tū neque auctōritātem verēbere[156]
nec jūdicium sequēre[156]
nec vim pertimēscēs?

OUR COMMON FATHERLAND PLEADS WITH YOU

18 Quae tēcum, Catilīna, sīc agit et quōdammodo[157] tacita loquitur:[158]
"Nūllum jam aliquot[159] annīs facinus exstitit nisi per tē,

Words to Remember

praesentia, ae, *presence.*
plācō, 1, tr., *calm, appease, pacify* (cf. placate).
aliquō, adv., *somewhere.*
pertimēscō, pertimēscere, pertimuī, 3, tr., *become thoroughly frightened, fear exceedingly.* The word is doubly intense; **per** + **timēscō** (strong form of **timeō**).

---

[152] **pārentēs;** there has been a steady gradation in Cicero's suppositions: slaves—citizens—parents.

[153] **opīnor,** 1, tr., *think* (cf. opinion).

[154] **Nunc tē patria;** here Cicero reaches a climax in the actual fear and hatred of the fatherland.

[155] **parricīdium, ī,** *impious murder;* the murder of a parent—*parricide.* The word is an extension of the personification of **patria** as **commūnis pārēns.**

[156] **verēbere;** short form for **verēberis. Sequēre** is also a short form.

[157] **quōdammodo,** adv., *after a fashion, in a way.*

[158] **tacita loquitur;** this is oxymoronic really, like the figure in *cruel kindness.* Cicero softens the bold word play by using the apologetic **quōdammodo.**

[159] **aliquot,** indecl. adj., *some, several.*

nūllum flāgitium sine tē:
tibi ūnī multōrum cīvium necēs,
tibi vexātiō dīreptiōque[160] sociōrum impūnīta fuit ac lībera;
tū nōn sōlum ad neglegendās lēgēs et quaestiōnēs,
vērum etiam ad ēvertendās perfringendāsque valuistī.

THE FATHERLAND HAS BEEN PATIENT

Superiōra illa, quamquam ferenda nōn fuērunt,
tamen, ut potuī, tulī:
nunc vērō mē tōtam esse in metū propter ūnum tē,
quidquid increpuerit,[161] Catilīnam timērī,
nūllum vidērī contrā mē cōnsilium inīrī posse
quod ā tuō scelere abhorreat,
nōn est ferendum.
Quam ob rem discēde
atque hunc mihi timōrem ēripe;
sī est vērus,
nē opprimar:

Words to Remember

nex, necis, *violent death, slaughter* (cf. **necō**).
vexātiō, vexātiōnis, *harassing, troubling* (cf. **vexō**; vexation).
neglegō, neglegere, neglēxī, neglēctus, 3, tr., *disregard, neglect* (cf. criminal negligence).
ēvertō, ēvertere, ēvertī, ēversus, 3, tr., *overthrow, upturn* (cf. **convertō, animadvertō**).
perfringō, perfringere, perfrēgī, perfrāctus, 3, tr., *break through, burst through* (cf. **frangō**; fractured).
abhorreō, abhorrēre, abhorruī, 2, intr.; **ab** (**ā**) w. abl., *shrink from, am averse to, am inconsistent with* (cf. abhorrent).
ob, prep. w. acc., *on account of, for;* **quam ob rem,** *wherefore.*
vērus, a, um, *true.*

---

[160] **dīreptiō, dīreptiōnis,** *plundering* (cf. **dīripiō**).

[161] **quidquid increpuerit:** *at every rumor, at every sound* (lit., *whatever makes a sound*).

sīn falsus,
ut tandem aliquandō timēre dēsinam."
19 Haec sī tēcum, ita ut dīxī, patria loquātur,
nōnne impetrāre dēbeat,
etiamsī[162] vim adhibēre nōn possit?

NO UPRIGHT CITIZEN WOULD RECEIVE YOU

Quid quod tū tē in custōdiam dedistī,
quod vītandae suspīciōnis causā
ad Mānium Lepidum[163] tē habitāre velle dīxistī?
Ā quō nōn receptus,
etiam ad mē venīre ausus es,
atque ut domī meae tē asservārem rogāstī.
Cum ā mē quoque id respōnsum tulissēs,
mē nūllō modō posse eīsdem parietibus[164] tūtō esse tēcum,
quī magnō in perīculō essem,

Words to Remember

dēsinō, dēsinere, dēsīvī, dēsitus, 3, intr., *stop, cease* (cf. **sinō**).
adhibeō, 2, tr., *employ, use, bring in.*
asservō, 1, tr., *keep, preserve, guard* (cf. **servō**).
quoque, adv., *also.*
respōnsum, ī, *answer* (cf. **respondeō**; response).

---

162 **etiamsī,** conj., *even if;* Gr. 598.

163 Manius Lepidus, a distinguished Roman. When accused of a serious crime a Roman citizen was not imprisoned pending trial, but simply put under the surveillance of some prominent citizen. Voluntarily to accept such surveillance (**custōdia**) was a sign of self-conscious innocence. Catiline had been accused of inciting a riot in connection with his earlier plots. In a bold attempt to gain support and sympathy he voluntarily sought some distinguished citizen (even Cicero!) to receive him into legal custody.

164 This sentence brings out clearly the difference between **parietēs** and **moenia. Murus** is much like **moenia**, except that the latter carries the notion of defensive fortification against enemies.

quod eīsdem moenibus continērēmur,
ad Quīntum Metellum,[165] praetōrem, vēnistī.
Ā quō repudiātus,[166]
ad sodālem[167] tuum, virum optimum, Mārcum Metellum,[168]
dēmigrāstī;[169]
quem tū vidēlicet et ad custōdiendum tē dīligentissimum
et ad suspicandum sagācissimum
et ad vindicandum fortissimum fore putāstī.
Sed quam longē vidētur ā carcere atque ā vinculīs abesse dēbēre
quī sē ipse jam dignum custōdiā jūdicārit?
Quae cum ita sint, Catilīna, **20**
dubitās, sī ēmorī aequō animō nōn potes,
abīre in aliquās terrās
et vītam istam, multīs suppliciīs jūstīs dēbitīsque ēreptam,
fugae sōlitūdinīque mandāre?
"Refer," inquis, "ad senātum";[170]

Words to Remember

vidēlicet, adv., *clearly, of course* (ironical).
sagāx (*gen.* **sagācis**), *shrewd* (cf. sagacious).
ēmorior, ēmorī, ēmortuus sum, 3, intr., *die*.
aequō animō: *with composure, resignedly* (**aequus, a, um**, *even, level, just*).
abeō, abīre, abiī, abitum, irreg., intr., *go away, depart*.
sōlitūdō, sōlitūdinis, *solitude* (cf. **sōlus**).
inquis: *you say;* used with direct quotations only, usually postpositive.

---

165 Quintus Metellus, a zealous member of the senatorial party.

166 **repudiō**, 1, tr., *reject* (cf. repudiate). **Repudiātus** is considerably stronger than the **nōn receptus** above.

167 **sodālis, sodālis**, m., *companion* (cf. sodality).

168 Catiline finally has to go to Marcus Metellus, one of his own men. Cicero's praise of Metellus is ironic.

169 **dēmigrō**, 1, intr., *go off* (cf. migration).

170 In parliamentary language **refer ad senātum** would be something like *put it before (up to) the House.*

id enim postulās,
et, sī hic ōrdō placēre sibi dēcrēverit tē īre in exilium,
obtemperātūrum[171] tē esse dīcis.

I WILL SHOW YOU WHAT THE SENATE THINKS OF YOU

Nōn referam,[172]
  id quod abhorret ā meīs mōribus,
et tamen faciam ut intellegās, quid hī dē tē sentiant.
Ēgredere ex urbe, Catilīna;
līberā rem pūblicam metū;
in exilium, sī hanc vōcem exspectās, proficīscere.
[*He pauses; the silence seems to deepen*]
Quid est? Ecquid[173] attendis,
ecquid animadvertis hōrum silentium?
Patiuntur, tacent.[174]
Quid[175] exspectās auctōritātem loquentium,
  quōrum voluntātem tacitōrum perspicis?
21 At sī hoc idem[176] huic adulēscentī optimō, Pūbliō Sēstiō,[177]

WORDS TO REMEMBER

attendō, attendere, attendī, attentus, 3, tr., *listen to, pay attention, heed* (cf. attend).
silentium, ī, *silence, stillness* (cf. **sileō**).

---

171 **obtemperō,** 1, intr., *conform, obey.*

172 To put the question of Catiline's exile before the Senate would have been unconstitutional. Hence, Cicero calls it repugnant to his own character.

173 **Ecquid:** *at all* (lit., *what at all, anything at all*); Gr. 842.

174 Exile was a supreme penalty and a disgrace for a Roman. Cicero deliberately and solemnly urges Catiline to go into exile. The Senate is silent; not a whisper of protest is heard. Cicero goes on to interpret this silence.

175 **Quid:** *Why?*

176 To what does **hoc idem** refer?

177 Publius Sestius, a prominent Roman.

sī fortissimō virō, Mārcō Mārcellō[178] dīxissem,
jam mihi cōnsulī hōc ipsō in templō
senātus jūre optimō vim et manūs[179] īntulisset.

HOW DID THE ROMAN CITIZENS OUTSIDE GREET YOU AS YOU ENTERED?

Dē tē autem, Catilīna,
cum quiēscunt,[180] probant;
cum patiuntur, dēcernunt;
cum tacent, clāmant;
neque hī sōlum
quōrum tibi auctōritās est vidēlicet cāra,
vīta vīlissima,[181]
sed etiam illī equitēs Rōmānī, honestissimī atque optimī virī,
cēterīque fortissimī cīvēs quī circumstant senātum,
quōrum tū et frequentiam vidēre
et studia percipere
et vōcēs paulō ante exaudīre potuistī.
Quōrum ego vix abs tē jam diū manūs ac tēla contineō,
eōsdem facile addūcam
ut tē, haec quae vastāre jam prīdem studēs relinquentem,
usque ad portās prōsequantur.

Words to Remember

probō, 1, tr.; acc. w. infin.; w. infin., *approve, prove* (cf. approbation).
sōlum, adv., *only*.
circumstō, circumstāre, circumstetī, 1, tr., *stand around* (**circum** + **stāre**).
prōsequor, prōsequī, prosecūtus sum, 3, tr., *escort, pursue* (cf. prosecute).

---

178 Marcus Marcellus, a renowned orator, thinker, and statesman.

179 **vim et manūs**: *violent hands;* like **dēclīnātiōne et corpore** in Note 138. The name of the figure is hendiadys.

180 **quiēscō, quiēscere, quiēvī**, 3, intr., *am quiet* (cf. **quiēs, requiēscat in pāce**; requiem, acquiesce).

181 **vīlissimus, a, um**, *most cheap, extremely worthless.*

BUT MY WORDS ARE WASTED!

22 Quamquam quid loquor?
  tē ut[182] ūlla rēs frangat?
  tū ut umquam tē corrigās?[183]
  tū ut ūllam fugam meditēre?[184]
  tū ut ūllum exilium cōgitēs?
Utinam tibi istam mentem dī immortālēs duint![185]

YOUR EXILE WILL RUIN ME

Tametsī videō,
  sī, meā vōce perterritus, īre in exilium animum indūxeris,[186]
quanta tempestās invidiae nōbīs,
  sī minus[187] in praesēns tempus, recentī memoriā scelerum tuōrum,
at in posteritātem impendeat.[188]

Words to Remember

quamquam quid: *and yet why.*
tametsī, conj., *and yet, although, though;* Gr. 598.
perterreō, 2, tr., *terrify greatly, frighten thoroughly.*
praesēns (*gen.* **praesentis**), *present, propitious.*
recēns (*gen.* **recentis**), *fresh, new* (cf. recent).
posteritās, posteritātis, *future generations* (cf. **posterī**; posterity).

---

182 These **ut** clauses may be taken as exclamatory questions with some such expression as **potestne fierī,** *is it possible that . . .,* understood; Gr. 637.

183 **corrigō, corrigere, corrēxī, correctus,** 3, tr., *improve* (cf. correct).

184 **meditor,** 1, tr., *consider* (cf. meditate).

185 **duint = dent.**

186 **animum indūxeris:** *you make up your mind.*

187 **sī minus:** *if not;* Gr. 588.

188 If Catiline merely went quietly into exile instead of to the camp of Manlius, the political enemies of Cicero would be able to laugh away all his elaborate predictions of Catiline's revolt and to raise the people against him for having hounded an innocent man into exile.

Sed est tantī,[189]
dummodo[190] ista sit prīvāta calamitās
et ā reī pūblicae perīculīs sējungātur.[191]

YOU ARE PAST REFORM

Sed tū ut vitiīs tuīs commoveāre,[192]
ut lēgum poenās pertimēscās,
ut temporibus reī pūblicae cēdās,
nōn est postulandum.
Neque enim is es, Catilīna,
ut tē aut pudor umquam ā turpitūdine
aut metus ā perīculō
aut ratiō ā furōre revocārit.[193]

AGAIN—GO!

Quam ob rem, ut saepe jam dīxī, proficīscere, **23**
ac, sī mihi inimīcō, ut praedicās, tuō cōnflāre[194] vīs invidiam,
rēctā perge in exilium:

WORDS TO REMEMBER

pudor, pudōris, *sense of shame, propriety, honor* (cf. **pudet**).
praedicō, 1, tr., *openly declare, proclaim.* Don't confuse **praedicō** with **praedīcō,** third conjugation, long ī.
rēctā (viā), *straightway.*

---

189 **tantī**; Gr. 700. For Cicero to say it was worth the price of his unpopularity was going pretty far. Like your modern statesman, he was quite sensitive to public opinion.

190 **dummodo**; Gr. 594.

191 **sējungō, sējungere, sējūnxī, sējūnctus,** 3, tr., *separate* (cf. **jungō**; junction).

192 **commoveāre = commoveāris.**

193 **revocārit = revocāverit.**

194 **cōnflō,** 1, tr., *blow, excite.*

vix feram sermōnēs hominum,
sī id fēceris;
vix mōlem istīus invidiae,
sī in exilium jussū cōnsulis īveris,
sustinēbō.

Sīn autem servīre meae laudī et glōriae māvīs,
ēgredere cum importūnā[195] scelerātōrum manū,
[*The phrases are hurled—fiercely—at Catiline*]
cōnfer tē ad Mānlium,
concitā perditōs cīvēs,
sēcerne tē ā bonīs,
īnfer patriae bellum,
exsultā impiō latrōciniō,
ut ā mē nōn ējectus ad aliēnōs,
sed invītātus ad tuōs īsse[196] videāris.

I KNOW YOUR PREPARATIONS

24 Quamquam quid ego tē invītem,
ā quō jam sciam esse praemissōs
quī tibi ad Forum Aurēlium[197] praestōlārentur[198] armātī?

Words to Remember

sermō, sermōnis, m., *talk, conversation;* **sermōnēs hominum,** *the talk of the town.*
mōlēs, mōlis, *burden, weight, mass* (cf. molecule).
scelerātus, a, um, *criminal* (cf. **scelus**).
sēcernō, sēcernere, sēcrēvī, sēcrētus, 3, tr., *separate* (cf. internal secretions).
exsultō, 1, intr., *revel, rejoice* (cf. exultation).

---

195 **importūnus, a, um,** *dangerous, savage.*
196 **īsse** = **iisse** (**īvisse**).
197 Forum Aurelium, a small town in Etruria.
198 **praestōlor,** 1, intr.; w. dat., *wait for.*

cui sciam pactam[199] et cōnstitūtam cum Mānliō diem?
ā quō etiam aquilam illam argenteam[200]
quam tibi ac tuīs omnibus
cōnfīdō perniciōsam ac fūnestam[201] futūram,
cui domī tuae sacrārium[202] scelerātum cōnstitūtum fuit,
sciam esse praemissam?
Tū ut[203] illā carēre diūtius possīs
quam venerārī ad caedem proficīscēns solēbās,
ā cūjus altāribus saepe istam impiam dexteram
ad necem cīvium trānstulistī?

Words to Remember

aquila, ae, *eagle, standard* (cf. aquiline nose). The chief standard of a legion was the image of an eagle with spread wings—as apt a symbol as the lion, king of beasts and a favorite with warriors.

argenteus, a, um, *silver* (cf. Argentina; Ag, the chemical symbol for silver).

altāria, altārium, *altar.* (Used only in the plural in classical Latin with singular meaning.)

---

[199] **pacīscor, pacīscī, pactus sum,** 3, tr. and intr., *agree, bargain* (cf. peace pact).

[200] In the time of Marius a silver eagle with outstretched wings was adopted as the ensign of the legion; only later were eagles sometimes of gold. The one mentioned here had been carried in the army of Marius in the campaign against the Cimbri (Sallust, *Catilina,* 59, 3). Recall the heroic standard-bearer of Caesar's invasion of Britain who stirred the famous tenth legion to the landing by plunging ahead and calling upon them not to allow the eagle to fall shamefully into the hands of the enemy (Henle, *Second Year Latin,* p. 110).

[201] **fūnestus, a, um,** *disastrous.*

[202] **sacrārium, ī,** *shrine* (cf. sacristy). The eagle of a legion was considered sacred and closely associated with the fortunes of its unit. At camp it was kept in a consecrated place near the commander's tent. Catiline is represented here as having a sort of sanctuary in his house for the special veneration of his silver idol.

[203] **ut;** used here with the subjunctive to express an incredulous question: *Is it possible that . . . ? Am I to suppose that . . . ?* See Note 182, page 48.

TO THAT CAMP YOU WILL AT LAST GO

25 Ībis tandem aliquandō
quō tē jam prīdem tua ista cupiditās effrēnāta ac furiōsa rapiēbat;
neque enim tibi haec rēs affert dolōrem,
sed quandam incrēdibilem voluptātem.
Ad hanc tē āmentiam nātūra peperit,
voluntās exercuit,
fortūna servāvit.
Numquam tū nōn modo[204] ōtium,[205]
sed nē bellum quidem nisi nefārium concupīstī.[206]
Nactus es,
ex perditīs atque ab omnī nōn modo fortūnā
vērum etiam spē dērelictīs[207] cōnflātam,[208]
improbōrum manum.

YOU WILL BE WITH YOUR OWN KIND

26 Hīc tū quā laetitiā perfruēre![209]
quibus gaudiīs exsultābis!

Words to Remember

cupiditās, cupiditātis, *desire, eagerness* (cf. **cupidus, a, um**).
effrēnātus, a, um, *unbridled.*
furiōsus, a, um, *mad, raging* (cf. furious).
nē . . . quidem, *not even.* (Always encloses the word or phrase emphasized.)
nancīscor, nancīscī, nactus sum, 3, tr., *obtain, fall in with.*

---

204 **nōn modo = nōn modo nōn.** The second **nōn** is omitted when the expression is balanced by **sed nē . . . quidem** with a single verb for both.

205 **ōtium, ī,** *peace.*

206 **concupīscō, concupīscere, concupīvī, concupītus,** 3, tr., *desire eagerly.*

207 **dērelictus, a, um,** *abandoned* (cf. **dērelinquō**; derelict).

208 **cōnflō,** 1, tr., *fuse together, weld together.*

209 **perfruēre = perfruēris.**

quantā in voluptāte bacchābere,[210]
cum in tantō numerō tuōrum
neque audiēs virum bonum quemquam
neque vidēbis!
Habēs ubi ostentēs[211] tuam illam praeclāram patientiam
famis, frīgoris, inopiae rērum omnium,
quibus tē brevī tempore cōnfectum esse sentiēs.
Tantum prōfēcī, cum tē ā cōnsulātū[212] reppulī, **27**
ut exsul potius temptāre
quam cōnsul vexāre rem pūblicam possēs,
atque ut id quod esset ā tē scelerātē susceptum,
latrōcinium potius quam bellum nōminārētur.

I WILL ANSWER AN APPARENT OBJECTION

Nunc, ut ā mē, patrēs cōnscrīptī,

Words to Remember

ostentō, 1, tr., *display* (cf. ostentation).
praeclārus, a, um, *famous, renowned.*
famēs, famis, *hunger, starvation* (cf. famine, famished).
frīgus, frīgoris, *cold* (cf. refrigerator).
cōnsulātus, ūs, *consulship, consulate.*
exsul, exsulis, *an exile.*
temptō, 1, tr., *make an attempt, try, test, try to win over* (cf. temptation).
vexō, 1, tr., *harass, ravage.*
scelerātē, adv., *criminally* (cf. **scelus, scelerātus**).
nōminō, 1, tr.; w. two accs., *call, name* (cf. nominations).

---

210 **bacchor, 1,** intr., *run wild, take wild delight;* **bacchābere = bacchāberis.** The word is strong and suggested to a Roman the frenzied orgies in honor of Bacchus, god of wine.

211 **Habēs ubi ostentēs:** *You have an opportunity to display;* **ubi** is used here in the sense of **(locum) in quō.**

212 **ā cōnsulātū;** Cicero used his influence to defeat Catiline in the consular election of 63 B.C.

—*Courtesy of Metro-Goldwyn-Mayer*

GALLEY SLAVES CHAINED TO THEIR OARS LIKE WORK ANIMALS

Love of liberty, charged with hatred and a desire for revenge that was enkindled by the harsh treatment meted out to slaves, drove into Catiline's ranks those who escaped or were released from the galleys.

quandam prope jūstam patriae querimōniam
dētester[213] ac dēprecer,
percipite, quaesō, dīligenter quae dīcam,
et ea penitus animīs vestrīs mentibusque mandāte.
Etenim sī mēcum patria,
quae mihi vītā meā multō est cārior,
sī cūncta Italia,
sī omnis rēs pūblica loquātur:

WORDS TO REMEMBER

querimōnia, ae, *complaint.*
dēprecor, 1, tr., *beg* (cf. **precēs**; deprecate).
quaesō, *I beg (you), I ask (you);* defective verb used only in first person.
penitus, adv., *deep down, deeply, utterly, thoroughly.*
cūnctus, a, um, *all, entire.*

---

213 **dētestor,** 1, tr., *ward off* (cf. detest).

YOU WILL LET THIS MAN GO?

"Mārce Tullī,[214] quid agis?

Tūne eum quem esse hostem comperistī,
quem ducem bellī futūrum vidēs,
quem exspectārī imperātōrem in castrīs hostium sentīs,
auctōrem sceleris,
prīncipem conjūrātiōnis,
ēvocātōrem[215] servōrum et cīvium perditōrum,
exīre patiēre,
ut abs tē nōn ēmissus ex urbe
sed immissus in urbem esse videātur?

Nōnne hunc in vincla[216] dūcī,
nōn ad mortem rapī,
nōn summō suppliciō mactārī[217] imperābis?

WHAT CAN BE PREVENTING YOU?

Quid tandem tē impedit? **28**

Mōsne mājōrum?

At persaepe etiam prīvātī in hāc rē pūblicā
perniciōsōs cīvēs morte multārunt.[218]

An lēgēs quae dē cīvium Rōmānōrum suppliciō rogātae sunt?[219]

---

[214] **Mārce Tullī**; vocative of **Mārcus Tullius** (Marcus Tullius Cicero). The fatherland, Italy, and the whole state is pictured as assuming a paternal attitude toward Cicero, fondly addressing him "Mark Tully."

[215] **ēvocātor**; compound of **ex** + **vocō** + **-tor**; meaning? This charge of drafting slaves into his service was serious and probably unfounded (cf. Sallust, *Catilina*, 56, 5). Rome always stood in dread of a slave uprising.

[216] **vincla** = **vincula.**

[217] **mactō,** 1, tr., *destroy, execute.*

[218] **multō,** 1, tr., *punish;* **multārunt** = **multāvērunt.**

[219] **rogātae sunt:** *have been passed.* A magistrate formally *asked* the people whether they approved a bill. Several laws had confirmed the ancient right of appeal to the people in capital cases: the first Valerian law, 503 B.C., and much later the *leges Porciae* and the *lex Sempronia* of the younger Gracchus.

At numquam in hāc urbe quī ā rē pūblicā dēfēcērunt
cīvium jūra tenuērunt.
An invidiam posteritātis timēs?

IS THIS YOUR GRATITUDE?

Praeclāram vērō populō Rōmānō refers grātiam,
qui tē, hominem per tē cognitum,[220]
nūllā commendātiōne mājōrum,
tam mātūrē ad summum imperium
per omnēs honōrum gradūs extulit,
sī propter invidiae aut alicūjus perīculī metum
salūtem cīvium tuōrum neglegis.

29 Sed sī quis est invidiae metus,
nōn est vehementius sevēritātis ac fortitūdinis invidia
quam inertiae ac nēquitiae pertimēscenda.
An, cum bellō vastābitur Italia,
vexābuntur urbēs,
tēcta ārdēbunt,
tum tē nōn exīstimās invidiae incendiō cōnflagrātūrum?"

Words to Remember

dēficiō, dēficere, dēfēcī, dēfectus, 3, tr. and intr.; **ab** (ā) w. abl., *fail, give out, revolt from.*
commendātiō, commendātiōnis, *excellence, worth.*
honor, honōris, *honor.*
gradus, ūs, *step* (cf. gradually). The rising steps of public office (**cursus honōrum**) were the quaestorship, aedileship, praetorship, consulship.
efferō, efferre, extulī, ēlātus, irreg., tr., *carry out, bear out;* passive, *am elated.*

---

220 **per tē cognitum:** *recognized (merely) for your own merit.* The phrase carries with it all we understand by the notion of a 'self-made man,' and stands in contrast to **commendātiō mājōrum,** those ancestral achievements which would give one a title to honor. Cicero was technically a **novus homō;** i. e., the first of his family to hold curule office.

Catiline's army assembled in Etruria to the north of Rome. An attack on the city would involve only a short march.

I WILL EXPLAIN MY HESITATION

Hīs ego sānctissimīs reī pūblicae vōcibus
et eōrum hominum quī hoc idem sentiunt mentibus
pauca respondēbō.

Ego, sī hoc optimum factū[221] jūdicārem, patrēs cōnscrīptī,
Catilīnam morte multārī,
ūnīus ūsūram[222] hōrae gladiātōrī[223] istī ad vīvendum nōn dedissem.
Etenim sī summī virī et clārissimī cīvēs
Sāturnīnī[224] et Gracchōrum[224]
et Flaccī[224] et superiōrum complūrium sanguine
nōn modo sē nōn contāminārunt
sed etiam honestārunt
certe verendum mihi nōn erat
nē quid, hōc parricīdā[225] cīvium interfectō,
invidiae mihi in posteritātem redundāret.[226]

I WOULD COUNT IT GLORY

Quodsī ea mihi maximē impendēret,
tamen hōc animō fuī semper,
ut invidiam virtūte partam
glōriam, nōn invidiam, putārem.

BUT ALL MUST BE CONVINCED

30 Quamquam nōnnūllī sunt in hōc ōrdine

Words to Remember

contāminō, 1, tr., *dishonor, pollute;* **contāminārunt = contāmināvērunt.**
honestō, 1, tr., *cover with honor, glory;* **honestārunt = honestāvērunt.**
partus, a, um, *born of, originating from* (cf. **pariō**).

---

[221] **factū**; Gr. 861-863.

[222] **ūsūra, ae,** *use, benefit* (cf. **ūtor**; usury).

[223] **gladiātor, gladiātōris,** *gladiator, ruffian.* The word is associated with **gladius** and has the notion of sword-bearing. The modern equivalent would be carrying a gun. Something like *gangster* would translate the idea.

[224] Saturninus, the Gracchi, and Flaccus (Marcus Fulvius Flaccus) were all met before. See Notes 34 and 39, pages 15 and 16.

[225] **parricīda, ae,** m., *murderer, parricide.*

[226] **redundō, 1,** intr., *flow back, contribute to* (cf. redound, redundancy).

quī aut ea quae imminent nōn videant
aut ea quae vident dissimulent;
quī spem Catilīnae mollibus[227] sententiīs aluērunt[228]
conjūrātiōnemque nāscentem nōn crēdendō corrōborāvērunt;[229]
quōrum auctōritāte multī nōn sōlum improbī,
vērum etiam imperītī,
sī in hunc animadvertissem,
crūdēliter et rēgiē[230] factum esse dīcerent.

ALL WILL SEE THE TRUTH IF ONLY CATILINE LEAVES!

Nunc intellegō,
sī iste, quō intendit, in Mānliāna castra pervēnerit,
nēminem tam stultum fore quī nōn videat
conjūrātiōnem esse factam,
nēminem tam improbum quī nōn fateātur.

WORDS TO REMEMBER

immineō, imminēre, 2, intr., *impend* (cf. imminent danger).
dissimulō, 1, tr., *disguise, dissemble* (cf. dissimulate). **Dissimulō** represents a thing which exists as not existing, whereas **simulō** represents a thing which does not exist as existing.
nāscor, nāscī, nātus sum, 3, intr., *am born* (cf. Nativity, native).
crūdēliter, adv., *cruelly, ruthlessly* (cf. **crūdēlitās**).
stultus, a, um, *stupid, dull* (cf. stultifying).
fateor, fatērī, fassus sum, 2, tr.; acc. w. infin., *admit, confess.*

---

227 **mollis, molle,** *soft, gentle.*

228 **alō, alere, aluī, altus (alitus),** 3, tr., *nourish, support* (cf. alimentary canal, alimony, coalition). By their half-hearted measures the members of the Senate have nourished Catiline's hopes and strengthened the newborn conspiracy by their incredulity. Notice the extended figure in the words **aluērunt, nāscentem,** and **corrōborāvērunt.**

229 **corrōborō,** 1, tr., *strengthen* (cf. corroborate).

230 **rēgiē,** adv., *despotically, like a king. Like a dictator* would give us the right flavor of **rēgiē.** Kings were considered tyrants, and monarchy of this sort was as unpopular with the Romans as totalitarianism is with us.

HIS DEATH IS NOT ENOUGH

Hōc autem ūnō interfectō,
intellegō hanc reī pūblicae pestem paulisper reprimī,
nōn in perpetuum comprimī posse.[231]
Quodsī sēsē ējēcerit,
sēcumque suōs ēdūxerit,
et eōdem cēterōs undique collēctōs naufragōs[232] aggregārit,
exstinguētur atque dēlēbitur
nōn modo haec tam adulta reī pūblicae pestis
vērum etiam stirps[233] ac sēmen malōrum omnium.

THE CONSPIRACY IS OF LONG GROWTH

31 Etenim jam diū, patrēs cōnscrīptī,
in hīs perīculīs conjūrātiōnis īnsidiīsque versāmur,
sed, nesciō quō pactō,[234]
omnium scelerum ac veteris furōris et audāciae mātūritās
in nostrī cōnsulātūs tempus ērūpit.

Words to Remember

aggregō, 1, tr., *gather together, add to* (cf. aggregation); **aggregārit = aggregāverit.**
exstinguō, exstinguere, exstīnxī, exstīnctus, 3, tr., *put out, quench, destroy* (cf. fire extinguisher, exstinct).
dēleō, dēlēre, dēlēvī, dēlētus, 2, tr., *destroy.*
adultus, a, um, *full grown, mature* (cf. adult).
sēmen, sēminis, *seed* (cf. seminary).
vetus (*gen.* **veteris**), *old.*
mātūritās, mātūritātis, *ripeness, full development* (cf. **mātūrus**; mature judgment).

---

231 **Hōc . . . posse**; notice how the first part of the sentence is loaded with long *ō's,* while the second part is fired with explosive labials, especially *p's.*

232 **naufragus, ī,** *castaway* (from a shipwreck; **nāvis** + **frangō**).

233 **stirps, stirpis,** *root.*

234 **nesciō quō pactō (modō)**: *somehow or other* (lit., *I know not in what way*).

IT WILL GROW WORSE IF WE ACT HASTILY

Hōc sī ex tantō latrōciniō iste ūnus tollētur,
vidēbimur fortasse ad breve quoddam tempus
cūrā et metū esse relevātī;[235]
perīculum autem residēbit,
et erit inclūsum penitus in vēnīs[236] atque vīsceribus[237] reī pūblicae.

Ut[238] saepe hominēs aegrī morbō[239] gravī,
cum aestū febrīque[240] jactantur,
sī aquam gelidam bibērunt,
prīmō relevārī videntur,
deinde multō gravius vehementiusque afflīctantur,[241]
sīc hic morbus[239] quī est in rē pūblicā,

WORDS TO REMEMBER

fortasse, adv., *perhaps* (cf. **forte**).
relevō, 1, tr., *lift up, raise, relieve.*
inclūdō, inclūdere, inclūsī, inclūsus, 3, tr., *shut in.*
aeger, aegra, aegrum, *sick, ill* (includes both mental and physical ills).
aestus, ūs, *heat, tide, swelling.*
jactō, 1, tr., *toss about, discuss.*
aqua, ae, *water* (cf. aqueduct).
gelidus, a, um, *icy-cold, frosty* (cf. congeal, gelatine).
bibō, bibere, bibī, bibitus, 3, tr., *drink* (cf. imbibe).

---

235 The terminology throughout the extended figure that follows is medical.

236 **vēna, ae**, *vein.*

237 **vīscera, vīscerum**, *vitals, vital organs.* **Vēnīs atque vīsceribus** is much like our *flesh and blood,* or *marrow and bones.*

238 **ut**: *just as.*

239 **morbus, ī**, *sickness, disease* (cf. **morior**; morbid fear).

240 **febris, febris**, *fever.*

241 **afflīctō**, 1, tr., *buffet, strike, distress.*

relevātus istīus poenā,
vehementius, reliquīs vīvīs, ingravēscet.[242]

LET LOYALTIES BECOME CLEAR!

32 Quārē sēcēdant[243] improbī,
sēcernant sē ā bonīs,
ūnum in locum congregentur,
mūrō dēnique, quod saepe jam dīxī, sēcernantur ā nōbīs;
dēsinant īnsidiārī domī suae cōnsulī,
circumstāre tribūnal praetōris urbānī,[244]
obsidēre cum gladiīs cūriam,[245]
malleolōs[246] et facēs ad īnflammandam urbem comparāre;
sit dēnique īnscrīptum in fronte ūnīuscūjusque
quid dē rē pūblicā sentiat.

A UNITED ROMAN FRONT

Polliceor hoc vōbīs, patrēs cōnscrīptī,
  tantam in nōbīs cōnsulibus fore dīligentiam,
  tantam in vōbīs auctōritātem,
  tantam in equitibus Rōmānīs virtūtem,

Words to Remember

vīvus, a, um, *alive, living* (cf. **vīvō**; vivacious).
tribūnal, tribūnālis, *tribunal.*
urbānus, a, um, *belonging to the city, of the city* (cf. **urbs**; urban).
frōns, frontis, *forehead, brow, front* (cf. frontal sinus).

---

242 **ingravēscō, ingravēscere, ingravēscī,** 3, intr., *grow worse, grow burdensome, am aggravated* (cf. **gravis**).

243 **sēcēdō, sēcēdere, sēcessī,** 3, intr., *go apart.*

244 The **praetor urbānus** was the judge in civil suits dealing with debts. It is obvious that Catiline's followers would attempt to intimidate him.

245 **cūria, ae,** *the Senate house, the House, the Curia.*

246 **malleolus, ī,** *firebrand.*

tantam in omnibus bonīs cōnsēnsiōnem,
ut Catilīnae profectiōne
omnia patefacta, illūstrāta, oppressa, vindicāta esse videātis.

[*He approaches Catiline, stands squarely in front of him; then, solemnly . . .*]

Hīsce[247] omnibus, Catilīna, 33
cum summā reī pūblicae salūte,
cum tuā peste ac perniciē,
cumque eōrum exitiō
qui sē tēcum omnī scelere parricīdiōque jūnxērunt,
proficīscere ad impium bellum ac nefārium.

WE CALL ON THE DIVINE PROTECTOR OF ROME

[*He addresses the statue of Jupiter Stator*]

Tū, Juppiter,[248]
quī eīsdem quibus haec urbs auspiciīs[249] ā Rōmulō[250] es cōnstitūtus,
quem Statōrem hūjus urbis atque imperī vērē nōmināmus,
hunc et hūjus sociōs ā tuīs cēterīsque templīs,
ā tēctīs urbis ac moenibus,

Words to Remember

cōnsēnsiō, cōnsēnsiōnis, *agreement* (cf. **sentiō**; consensus).
profectiō, profectiōnis, *a setting out, departure* (cf. **proficīscor**).
illūstrō, 1, tr., *reveal, bring to light.*
parricīdium, ī, *murder.*

---

247 **Hīsce = hīs + ce** (an emphatic suffix).

248 This invocation to the supreme god of the Romans gathered new solemnity from the fact that the speech was being delivered in the temple of Jupiter the Stayer.

249 **auspicium, ī,** *augury, omen;* pl., *auspices.*

250 Tradition had it that Romulus, the founder of Rome, had established the cult of Jupiter.

ā vītā fortūnīsque cīvium omnium arcēbis,
et hominēs bonōrum inimīcōs,
hostēs patriae,
latrōnēs Italiae,
scelerum foedere[251] inter sē ac nefāriā societāte conjūnctōs,
aeternīs suppliciīs vīvōs mortuōsque mactābis.

With that last threatening phrase still echoing in the temple, Catiline, we are told, rose to speak. He appealed against this upstart, this Cicero of no name or ancestry; he appealed to his own distinguished lineage. Was he not himself a senator, a patriot, a true-born Roman? But Cicero's facts as well as his rhetoric had taken effect, and the senators drowned the audacious voice of Catiline with cries of "Traitor! Traitor!" He, defiant still, glared about him, spoke some confused words of threat and strode from the temple.

CATILINE IN OPEN REBELLION

That same day he gave last-minute instructions to the conspirators at Rome and then set out to join the waiting band at Forum Aurelium. There he assumed the dress and manner of a consul and proceeded at once to the camp of Manlius. All this Cicero published the next day in a splendid speech to the people.

Words to Remember

arceō, arcēre, arcuī, 2, tr., *ward off* (cf. **coercēre**).
latrō, latrōnis, *bandit, robber* (cf. **latrōcinium**).
societās, societātis, *fellowship, companionship* (cf. **socius**; society).
aeternus, a, um, *eternal.*
mortuus, a, um, *dead* (cf. **mors, morior**; rigor [**rigēre,** *be stiff*] mortis, post-mortem, mortuary, mortify).

---

[251] **foedus, foederis,** *treaty, alliance* (cf. confederation).

A TRAP IS SPRUNG

But the conspirators within Rome were still active. Meanwhile the government watched and waited. And at last came opportunity. There were in Rome at this time ambassadors from the Allobroges, a Gallic tribe beyond the Alps but lately pacified. Lentulus—now Catiline's subordinate at Rome—conceived the plan of fomenting war in Gaul, thus at the same time embarrassing the government abroad and gaining swift Gallic cavalry for the army in Etruria. The Allobroges were approached, and . . . but let us rather hear Cicero's account of the facts, for he again published the official version in an address to the people of Rome.

Today a radio commentator or the president over a national television hookup would carry news of this kind to every citizen. In Rome the head of the government performed the same service for the assembled Roman citizens in the Forum. Let us turn back the dial of history and hear again the voice of Cicero ringing out over that eager and elated crowd. It is dusk in the Forum; Cicero, dignified, commanding, ascends the speaker's stand—the rostrum. There is a shout of acclaim, silence, and then:

Third Oration against Catiline

Rem pūblicam, Quirītēs, vītamque omnium vestrum, bona, fortūnās, conjugēs līberōsque vestrōs atque hoc domicilium clārissimī imperī,[1] fortūnātissimam pulcherrimamque urbem, hodiernō diē, deōrum immortālium summō ergā vōs amōre, labōribus,

WORDS TO REMEMBER

Quirītēs, Quirītium, *Roman citizens;* in their strictly civil capacity; generally used only in the vocative.
conjūnx, conjugis, c., *husband, wife.*
fortūnātus, a, um, *blessed, fortunate.*
hodiernō diē: *today, this day.*
ergā, prep. w. acc., *towards, for;* generally of friendly feelings.

[1] **imperī = imperiī.**

—*Black Star*

THE ROMAN FORUM

So might the Quirites have massed in the Forum that evening in ancient Rome when Cicero rose to tell the anxious citizens that at last their sacred temples, their homes, and their lives were safe from the firebrands and daggers of Catiline.

cōnsiliīs, perīculīs meīs, ē flammā atque ferrō ac paene ex faucibus[2] fātī ēreptam et vōbīs cōnservātam ac restitūtam vidētis.[3]

[*Shouts and applause*]

YOUR SAVIOR DESERVES EVERLASTING HONOR

Et sī nōn minus nōbīs jūcundī atque illūstrēs sunt eī diēs qui- 2
bus cōnservāmur quam illī quibus nāscimur, quod salūtis certa laetitia est, nāscendī incerta condiciō, et quod sine sēnsū nāscimur, cum voluptāte servāmur, profectō, quoniam illum[4] quī hanc urbem condidit, ad deōs immortālēs benevolentiā fāmāque sustulimus, esse apud vōs posterōsque vestrōs in honōre dēbēbit is[5] quī eandem hanc urbem conditam amplificātamque[6] servāvit.

Nam tōtī urbī, templīs, dēlūbrīs, tēctīs, ac moenibus subjectōs

---

Words to Remember

flamma, ae, *flame.*
paene, adv., *almost* (cf. peninsula, almost an island).
restituō, restituere, restitī, restitūtus, 3, tr., *restore* (cf. restitution).
jūcundus, a, um, *pleasant.*
illūstris, e, *bright, illustrious.*
incertus, a, um, *uncertain.*
benevolentia, ae, *affection.*
posterī, posterōrum, *descendants* (cf. posterity).
dēlūbrum, ī, *shrine.*
subjiciō, subjicere, subjēcī, subjectus, 3, tr.; w. acc. and dat., *throw under, expose to* (cf. subject).

---

[2] **faucēs, faucium,** f., *jaws, pass.*

[3] Discuss the contrast between the solemnity of this periodic sentence and the abrupt questions hurled at Catiline in the first oration. Has the situation anything to do with the changed style? What about the audience?

[4] Romulus, the mythical founder of Rome, who, according to legend, had been admitted to the company of the gods.

[5] Cicero, of course.

[6] **amplificō,** 1, tr., *extend, embellish.*

prope jam ignēs circumdatōsque restīnximus,[7] īdemque gladiōs in rem pūblicam dēstrictōs[8] rettudimus,[9] mucrōnēsque[10] eōrum ā jugulīs[11] vestrīs dējēcimus.

I WILL TELL YOU HOW THE CONSPIRATORS WERE BROUGHT TO JUSTICE

3 Quae quoniam in senātū illūstrāta, patefacta, comperta sunt per mē, vōbīs jam expōnam breviter, Quirītēs, ut, et quanta et quam manifesta et quā ratiōne invēstīgāta et comprehēnsa sint, vōs, quī et ignōrātis et exspectātis, scīre possītis.

EVEN AFTER CATILINE'S DEPARTURE, WE CONTINUED OUR PRECAUTIONS

Prīncipiō, ut Catilīna paucīs ante diēbus ērūpit ex urbe, cum sceleris suī sociōs, hūjusce[12] nefāriī bellī ācerrimōs ducēs, Rōmae relīquisset, semper vigilāvī et prōvīdī, Quirītēs, quemadmodum in tantīs et tam absconditīs īnsidiīs salvī esse possēmus.

Nam tum cum ex urbe Catilīnam ējiciēbam—nōn enim jam

Words to Remember

circumdō, circumdare, circumdedī, circumdatus, 1, tr., *put around, encompass, surround.*
invēstīgō, 1, tr., *detect, search out.*
prīncipium, ī, *beginning;* **prīncipiō:** *in the first place.*
quemadmodum, adv., *as, how.*
abscondō, abscondere, abscondī, absconditus, 3, tr., *put away, conceal, hide* (cf. abscond).

---

7 **restinguō, restinguere, restīnxī, restīnctus,** 3, tr., *put out, quench.*
8 **dēstrictus, a, um,** *unsheathed, drawn.*
9 **retundō, retundere, rettudī, retūsus,** 3, tr., *beat back, blunt.*
10 **mucrō, mucrōnis,** *point, sword point, dagger.*
11 **jugulum, ī,** *throat* (cf. jugular vein).
12 **hūjusce = hūjus + ce** (an emphatic suffix).

vereor hūjus verbī invidiam,[13] cum illa magis sit timenda quod vīvus exierit—sed tum cum illum exterminārī[14] volēbam, aut reliquam conjūrātōrum manum simul exitūram aut eōs quī restitissent īnfirmōs sine illō ac dēbilēs fore putābam.

THE MOST DANGEROUS CRIMINALS REMAINED AT HOME

Atque ego, ut vīdī, quōs maximō furōre et scelere esse īnflam- 4
mātōs sciēbam, eōs nōbīscum esse et Rōmae remānsisse, in eō omnēs diēs noctēsque cōnsūmpsī[15] ut quid agerent, quid mōlīrentur sentīrem ac vidērem, ut, quoniam auribus vestrīs propter incrēdibilem magnitūdinem sceleris minōrem fidem faceret ōrātiō mea, rem ita comprehenderem ut tum dēmum[16] animīs salūtī vestrae prōvidērētis, cum oculīs maleficium[17] ipsum vidērētis.

LENTULUS MADE THE FATAL BLUNDER

Itaque, ut comperī lēgātōs Allobrogum,[18] bellī trānsalpīnī[19] et

---

Words to Remember

simul, adv., *together, at the same time* (cf. simultaneous).
īnfirmus, a, um, *weak.*
dēbilis, e, *powerless.*
Allobrogēs, Allobrogum, *the Allobroges,* a tribe in southeastern Gaul.

---

[13] Now that Catiline is under arms in Etruria and has thus definitely shown himself a traitor, Cicero no longer fears the propaganda of the radical groups. His action in trying to drive Catiline out of Rome can now be called only patriotic. See Note 188, page 48.

[14] **exterminō**, 1, tr., *drive out, banish* (cf. exterminate).

[15] **cōnsūmō, cōnsūmere, cōnsūmpsī, cōnsūmptus**, 3, tr., *use up;* **diēs cōnsūmere;** in w. abl., *to spend days in.*

[16] **dēmum**, adv., *at length, finally.*

[17] **maleficium, ī,** *evil deed, crime.*

[18] These ambassadors had come to Rome to lay a complaint against the provincial governor. This circumstance led Lentulus to believe that the time was ripe for revolt.

[19] **trānsalpīnus, a, um,** *transalpine, across the Alps.*

tumultūs Gallicī[20] excitandī causā, ā Pūbliō Lentulō[21] esse sollicitātōs, eōsque in Galliam ad suōs cīvēs eōdemque itinere cum litterīs mandātīsque ad Catilīnam esse missōs, comitemque eīs adjūnctum esse Titum Volturcium,[22] atque huic ad Catilīnam esse datās litterās, facultātem[23] mihi oblātam putāvī ut, quod erat difficillimum, quodque ego semper optābam ab dīs immortālibus, tōta rēs nōn sōlum ā mē sed etiam ā senātū et ā vōbīs manifestō dēprehenderētur.

GOVERNMENT AGENTS LAID THE TRAP AT THE MULVIAN BRIDGE

5 Itaque hesternō diē[24] Lūcium Flaccum et Gājum Pomptīnum praetōrēs, fortissimōs atque amantissimōs reī pūblicae[25] virōs, ad mē vocāvī; rem exposuī; quid fierī placēret, ostendī. Illī autem, quī omnia dē rē pūblicā praeclāra atque ēgregia[26] sentīrent, sine

---

Words to Remember

excitō, 1, tr., *excite.*
comes, comitis, c., *companion.*
adjungō, adjungere, adjūnxī, adjūnctus, 3, tr.; w. dat.; **ad** w. acc., *join to.*
manifestō, adv., *clearly.*
Flaccus (ī), **Lūcius** (ī), *Lucius Flaccus,* a praetor.
Pomptīnus (ī), **Gājus** (ī), *Gaius Pomptinus,* a praetor.

---

[20] **Gallicus, a, um,** *Gallic, of Gaul* (cf. Gallicanism, a form of ecclesiastical nationalism originating in France).

[21] Publius Lentulus had been left behind to direct the plotting in Rome, but he proved a poor choice, as nature had not endowed him with the intelligence and energy necessary for the successful conspirator.

[22] Titus Volturcius was one of Catiline's agents. Little is known of him.

[23] **facultās, facultātis;** w. gen., *ability, opportunity (for).*

[24] **hesternō diē:** *yesterday.*

[25] **amantissimōs reī pūblicae:** *extremely patriotic* (lit., *most loving of the state*).

[26] **ēgregius, a, um,** *outstanding, remarkable* (cf. an egregious blunder).

—*Ewing Galloway*

THE MULVIAN BRIDGE TODAY

This modern bridge is built on the foundations of the ancient one where Cicero's agents arrested the revolutionaries and where, a little more than three and a half centuries later (October 28, 313), under the aegis of the cross that appeared to him in the sky, Constantine marched into battle.

recūsātiōne[27] ac sine ūllā morā negōtium suscēpērunt, et, cum advesperāsceret,[28] occultē ad pontem Mulvium pervēnērunt, atque ibi in proximīs vīllīs[29] ita bipertītō[30] fuērunt, ut Tiberis[31] inter eōs et pōns interesset.

WORDS TO REMEMBER

negōtium, ī, *business.*
occultē, adv., *secretly.*
Mulvius, a, um, *Mulvian,* a bridge across the Tiber, about two miles from Rome.

---

27 **recūsātiō, recūsātiōnis,** *refusal, objection* (cf. recusant).
28 **cum advesperāsceret:** *as dusk was coming on* (cf. vespers).
29 **vīlla, ae,** *country estate, farmhouse.*
30 **bipertītō,** adv., *in two sections* (cf. bipartite treaties).
31 **Tiberis, Tiberis,** m., *Tiber,* a river flowing past Rome to the sea.

Eōdem autem et ipsī sine cūjusquam suspīciōne multōs fortēs virōs ēdūxerant, et ego ex praefectūrā Reātīnā[32] complūrēs dēlēctōs adulēscentēs, quōrum operā ūtor assiduē in rē pūblicā, praesidiō cum gladiīs mīseram.

THE CAPTURE

6 Interim, tertiā ferē vigiliā exāctā,[33] cum jam pontem Mulvium magnō comitātū lēgātī Allobrogum ingredī inciperent, ūnāque Volturcius, fit in eōs impetus; ēdūcuntur et ab illīs gladiī et ā nostrīs. Rēs praetōribus erat nōta sōlis, ignōrābātur ā cēterīs.

THE DAMNING LETTERS ARE SEIZED

Tum interventū[34] Pomptīnī atque Flaccī pugna sēdātur. Litterae quaecumque erant in eō comitātū, integrīs signīs, praetōribus trāduntur; ipsī, comprehēnsī, ad mē, cum jam dīlūcēsceret,[35] dēdūcuntur.

Words to Remember

assiduē, adv., *constantly.*
comitātus, ūs, *retinue.*
ingredior, ingredī, ingressus sum, 3, tr., *advance, go.*
incipiō, incipere, incēpī, inceptus, 3, tr. and intr.; w. pres. infin., *begin* (cf. incipient cancer).
pugna, ae, *fight* (cf. **pugnō**).
sēdō, 1, tr., *stop, quiet, mitigate* (cf. sedative).
quīcumque, quaecumque, quodcumque, *whoever, whatever.*

---

[32] **praefectūra (ae) Reātīna (ae),** *the town of Reate,* about forty miles northeast of Rome. It was called a prefecture and governed by a praetor sent out from Rome. Cicero was its *patrōnus;* i. e., he acted as its attorney and legal adviser, and so could depend on its loyalty.

[33] **tertiā ferē vigiliā exāctā:** *about three o'clock in the morning;* **exigō, exigere, exēgī, exāctus,** 3, tr., *spend, end.*

[34] **interventus, ūs,** *intervention* (**inter** + **veniō,** *come between*).

[35] **cum jam dīlūcēsceret:** *at daybreak (when it was now growing light).*

THE SUSPECTS IN THE CITY ARE ROUNDED UP

Atque hōrum omnium scelerum improbissimum māchinātōrem Cimbrum Gabīnium, statim ad mē, nihil dum suspicantem, vocāvī; deinde item arcessītus est Lūcius Statilius, et post eum Gājus Cethēgus; tardissimē autem Lentulus[36] vēnit, crēdō[37] quod in litterīs dandīs praeter cōnsuētūdinem proximā nocte vigilārat.[38]

I PRESERVED THE EVIDENCE SCRUPULOUSLY

Cum summīs et clārissimīs hūjus cīvitātis virīs, quī, audītā rē, 7
frequentēs ad mē māne convēnerant, litterās ā mē prius[39] aperīrī quam ad senātum dēferrī placēret, nē, sī nihil esset inventum, temere ā mē tantus tumultus injectus[40] cīvitātī vidērētur, negāvī mē esse factūrum, ut dē perīculō pūblicō nōn ad cōnsilium pūblicum rem integram dēferrem.

Etenim, Quirītēs, sī[41] ea quae erant ad mē dēlāta reperta nōn

---

WORDS TO REMEMBER

māchinātor, māchinātōris, *contriver, schemer, plotter* (cf. **māchinor**).
Gabīnius (ī), **Cimber** (**Cimbrī**), *Cimber Gabinius,* one of Catiline's most dangerous gangsters.
arcessō, arcessere, arcessīvī, arcessītus, 3, tr., *summon.*
Statilius (ī), **Lūcius** (ī), *Lucius Statilius,* one of the confederates who was to have had part in the burning of Rome.
Cethēgus (ī), **Gājus** (ī), *Gaius Cethegus,* a conspirator noted for his rashness.
tardus, a, um, *slow* (cf. tardiness).
cōnsuētūdō, cōnsuētūdinis, *custom, habit.*
temere, adv., *recklessly, rashly* (cf. **temeritās**).

---

[36] Lentulus was notoriously a lover of ease.

[37] Spoken scornfully, alluding to the "sleepiness" of Lentulus. The letter over which he is represented as having "burned the midnight oil" contains, ironically enough, less than forty words (cf. page 79, lines 146-149).

[38] **vigilārat = vigilāverat.**

[39] **prius . . . quam = priusquam;** Gr. 564-568.

[40] **injiciō, injicere, injēcī, injectus,** 3, tr., *throw in, throw on* (cf. injection).

[41] Translate as if **etiam sī.**

—*Courtesy of Produzione Consorzio Scipione S. A.*

Disclosures in the Senate

Cicero, standing beside his colleague Antonius, informs the crowded and hastily convened Senate of the dramatic arrest of the Allobroges and Volturcius at the Mulvian Bridge earlier that day, as well as of the seizure of evidence that he tells the Senate will clearly brand Catiline and his associates as conspirators against the government.

essent, tamen ego nōn arbitrābar in tantīs reī pūblicae perīculīs esse mihi nimiam dīligentiam pertimēscendam.

I SUMMONED THE SENATE. THE HOME OF CETHEGUS WAS RAIDED

8 Senātum frequentem celeriter, ut vīdistis, coēgī. Atque intereā statim admonitū Allobrogum Gājum Sulpicium[42] praetōrem, fortem virum, mīsī quī ex aedibus Cethēgī, sī quid tēlōrum esset,

---

Words to Remember

nimius, a, um, *too much, excessive.*
intereā, adv., *meanwhile.*
admonitus, ūs, *advice, admonition* (cf. **moneō**).
aedēs, aedis, *temple;* pl., *house* (cf. edifice).

---

[42] Gaius Sulpicius was praetor in 63 B. C.

efferret; ex quibus ille maximum sīcārum numerum et gladiōrum extulit.

VOLTURCIUS WAS EXAMINED FIRST; HE TURNED STATE'S WITNESS

Intrōdūxī[43] Volturcium sine Gallīs. Fidem pūblicam[44] jussū senātūs dedī. Hortātus sum ut ea quae scīret sine timōre indicāret. Tum ille dīxit, cum vix sē ex magnō timōre recreāsset, ā Pūbliō Lentulō sē habēre ad Catilīnam mandāta et litterās ut servōrum praesidiō ūterētur, ut ad urbem quam prīmum cum exercitū accēderet; id autem eō cōnsiliō ut, cum urbem ex omnibus partibus, quemadmodum dēscrīptum distribūtumque erat, incendissent, caedemque īnfīnītam cīvium fēcissent, praestō esset ille quī et fugientēs exciperet et sē cum hīs urbānīs ducibus conjungeret.

THE TESTIMONY OF THE GALLIC AMBASSADORS

Intrōductī autem Gallī jūsjūrandum sibi et litterās ab Lentulō, 9
Cethēgō, Statiliō ad suam gentem datās esse dīxērunt, atque ita sibi ab hīs et ā Lūciō Cassiō esse praescrīptum ut equitātum in Italiam quam prīmum mitterent; pedestrēs sibi cōpiās nōn dē-

---

Words to Remember

recreō, 1, tr., *revive, restore, refresh* (cf. recreation). **recreāsset** = **recreāvisset.**
accēdō, accēdere, accessī, accessum, 3, intr.; **ad** w. acc., *approach, am added.*
dēscrībō, dēscrībere, dēscrīpsī, dēscrīptus, 3, tr., *map out, draw up.*
praestō, adv., *at hand.*
excipiō, excipere, excēpī, exceptus, 3, tr., *except, meet, receive.*
jūsjūrandum, jūrisjūrandī, *oath.*
Cassius (ī), **Lūcius** (ī), *Lucius Cassius,* another associate of Catiline.
praescrībō, praescrībere, praescrīpsī, praescrīptus, 3, tr., *prescribe, dictate.*

---

[43] That is, he was brought before the Senate.

[44] **fidem pūblicam:** *a pledge in the name of the state;* i. e., a pledge of clemency if he would turn state's evidence.

futūrās; Lentulum autem sibi cōnfirmāsse[45] ex fātīs Sibyllīnīs[46] haruspicumque[47] respōnsīs, sē esse tertium illum Cornēlium[48] ad quem rēgnum hūjus urbis atque imperium pervenīre esset necesse; Cinnam ante sē et Sullam fuisse; eundemque dīxisse fātālem hunc annum esse ad interitum hūjus urbis atque imperī, quī esset annus decimus post virginum absolūtiōnem,[49] post Capitōlī autem incēnsiōnem[50] vīcēsimus.

10 Hanc autem Cethēgō cum cēterīs contrōversiam fuisse dīxērunt quod Lentulō et aliīs Sāturnālibus[51] caedem fierī atque urbem incendī placēret, Cethēgō nimium id longum vidērētur.

Words to Remember

Sibyllīnus, a, um, *Sibylline.*
Cinna (ae), Cornēlius (ī), *Cornelius Cinna.*
Sulla (ae), Cornēlius (ī), *Cornelius Sulla.*
fātālis, e, *fated, destined* (cf. **fātum**).
contrōversia, ae, *dispute, quarrel.*

---

[45] **cōnfirmāsse = cōnfirmāvisse.**

[46] These Sibylline 'fates' were collections of prophecies that had as their authors certain ancient prophetesses known as Sibyls (cf. "Teste David cum Sibyllā" in the *Diēs Īrae*). They were highly esteemed at Rome and were consulted by the Senate in times of crisis.

[47] **haruspex, haruspicis,** m., *soothsayer, interpreter of the will of the gods.*

[48] There seems to have been a prophecy about three Cornelii who would rule Rome. Cornelius Cinna had ruled it in 86 B.C., Cornelius Sulla, 82-79 B.C., and Cornelius Lentulus fancied he was the last of the trio of Cornelii destined to hold this supreme power. He was the 'Man of Destiny' . . . so at least he told the Gauls.

[49] **virginum absolūtiōnem:** *the acquittal of the Vestal virgins.* There is no record of the case referred to here.

[50] **incēnsiō, incēnsiōnis,** *burning* (cf. **incendō**). The temple of Jupiter Capitoline was burned down in 83 B.C.

[51] **Sāturnālia, Sāturnālium,** *the Saturnalia,* festivities in honor of Saturn which began on December 17. These were days of license and unconventionality, like our Mardi Gras, a time therefore that would have been aptly chosen for the revolution. Thus today, for example, the Fourth of July might be a strategic time for a bank robbery.

THE LETTERS OF CETHEGUS

Ac nē longum sit,[52] Quirītēs, tabellās[53] prōferrī jussimus quae ā quōque dīcēbantur datae. Prīmum ostendimus Cethēgō signum. Cognōvit. Nōs līnum incīdimus. Lēgimus.

Erat scrīptum ipsīus manū Allobrogum senātuī et populō sēsē, quae eōrum lēgātīs cōnfirmāsset, factūrum esse; ōrāre ut item illī facerent quae sibi eōrum lēgātī recēpissent.

CETHEGUS' ARROGANCE BROKE DOWN

Tum Cethēgus, quī paulō ante aliquid tamen dē gladiīs ac sīcīs quae apud ipsum erant dēprehēnsa, respondisset, dīxissetque sē semper bonōrum ferrāmentōrum[54] studiōsum fuisse, recitātīs litterīs dēbilitātus atque abjectus cōnscientiā, repente conticuit.[55]

STATILIUS CONFESSES UNDER EXAMINATION

Intrōductus est Statilius. Cognōvit et signum et manum suam. **11**
Recitātae sunt tabellae in eandem ferē sententiam. Cōnfessus est.

Words to Remember

item, adv., *likewise*.
dēbilitātus, a, um, *stricken, broken* (cf. debilitated).
abjectus, a, um, *dejected, cast down* (cf. abject).
repente, adv., *suddenly*.

---

[52] **Ac nē longum sit:** *To make a long story short.*

[53] Short letters were written on tablets (**tabella, ae**) of wood fastened together by a sort of simple 'spiral' binding. The inside surfaces of the wood were hollowed out and filled with wax. To write one scratched the surface of the wax with a sharp-pointed instrument. The tablets were then closed and bound by a thread (**līnum, ī**) the knot of which was sealed with wax. Cicero had refused to break (**incīdō, incīdere, incīdī, incīsus**, 3, tr., *cut*) these seals (**signum, ī**) except in the presence of the Senate.

[54] **ferrāmentum, ī**, *weapon, iron piece.* He claimed to be a 'collector.'

[55] **conticēscō, conticēscere, conticuī**, 3, intr., *fall silent* (cf. **taceō**).

THE EXAMINATION OF LENTULUS

Tum ostendī tabellās Lentulō, et quaesīvī cognōsceretne signum. Adnuit![56] "Est vērō," inquam, "nōtum quidem signum, imāgō avī tuī,[57] clārissimī virī, quī amāvit ūnicē[58] patriam et cīvēs suōs; quae quidem tē ā tantō scelere, etiam mūta, revocāre dēbuit."

Leguntur eādem ratiōne ad senātum Allobrogum populumque litterae. Sī quid dē hīs rēbus dīcere vellet, fēcī potestātem.

LENTULUS ATTEMPTS A CROSS-EXAMINATION

Atque ille prīmō quidem negāvit; post autem aliquantō,[59] tōtō jam indiciō expositō atque ēditō, surrēxit. Quaesīvit ā Gallīs quid sibi esset cum eīs, quam ob rem domum suam vēnissent, itemque ā Volturciō.[60] Quī cum illī breviter constanterque respondissent per quem ad eum quotiēnsque vēnissent, quaesīssentque ab eō nihilne sēcum esset dē fātīs Sibyllīnīs locūtus, tum ille subitō, scelere dēmēns, quanta cōnscientiae vīs esset, ostendit.

Words to Remember

inquam: *I said;* always used with a direct quotation.
mūtus, a, um, *silent, mute.*
ēdō, ēdere, ēdidī, ēditus, 3, tr., *put forth, state, explain* (cf. editor).
surgō, surgere, surrēxī, surrēctum, 3, intr., *rise, stand up* (cf. Resurrection).
constanter, adv., *steadfastly* (cf. **stō**).
subitō, adv., *suddenly.*
dēmēns (*gen.* **dēmentis**), *mad, wild* (cf. **mēns**; dementia praecox).

---

[56] **adnuō, adnuere, adnuī**, 3, intr., *nod to, assent* (cf. **nūtus**).
[57] **imāgō avī tuī**: *the picture of your grandfather.* It was customary to place upon seals likenesses of distinguished ancestors.
[58] **ūnicē**, adv., *singularly* (cf. **ūnus**).
[59] **post autem aliquantō**: *after a short while.*
[60] Remember that Volturcius had turned state witness.

LENTULUS, TOO, BREAKS DOWN

Nam, cum id posset īnfitiārī, repente, praeter opīniōnem **12**
omnium, cōnfessus est. Ita eum nōn modo ingenium[61] illud et dīcendī exercitātiō,[62] quā semper valuit, sed etiam, propter vim sceleris manifestī atque dēprehēnsī, impudentia, quā superābat omnēs, improbitāsque dēfēcit.

THE MESSAGE TO CATILINE

Volturcius vērō subitō litterās prōferrī atque aperīrī jubet quās sibi ā Lentulō ad Catilīnam datās esse dīcēbat. Atque ibi vehementissimē perturbātus, Lentulus tamen et signum et manum suam cognōvit. Erant autem sine nōmine, sed ita:[63]

> "Quis sim, sciēs ex eō quem ad tē mīsī. Cūrā ut vir sīs, et cōgitā, quem in locum sīs prōgressus. Vidē quid tibi jam sit necesse, et cūrā ut omnium tibi auxilia adjungās, etiam īnfimōrum."[64]

EVEN THE CALLOUS GABINIUS COULD MAKE NO ANSWER

Gabīnius deinde intrōductus, cum prīmō impudenter respon-

WORDS TO REMEMBER

īnfitior, 1, tr.; acc. w. infin., *deny.*
impudentia, ae, *impudence, effrontery, shamelessness.*
improbitās, improbitātis, *depravity, recklessness* (cf. **improbus**).
impudenter, adv., *arrogantly* (cf. **impudentia**).

---

[61] **ingenium, ī,** *natural talent, ability, genius* (cf. ingenious contrivance).

[62] **exercitātiō, exercitātiōnis,** *training, exercise* (cf. **exerceō, exercitus**).

[63] The letter is also recorded by Sallust: "Quī sim, ex eō quem ad tē mīsī, cognōscēs. Fac cōgitēs, in quantā calamitāte sīs, et meminerīs tē virum esse. Cōnsīderēs, quid tuae ratiōnēs postulent. Auxilium petās ab omnibus, etiam ab īnfimīs" (*Catilina,* 44, 5). Though the same in substance, this version lacks the polish of Cicero's and perhaps shows Lentulus' haste more clearly.

[64] **īnfimus, a, um,** *lowest.*

dēre coepisset, ad extrēmum nihil ex eīs quae Gallī īnsimulābant negāvit.

THEIR VERY APPEARANCE CONVICTED THEM

13 Ac mihi quidem, Quirītēs, cum illa certissima vīsa sunt argūmenta atque indicia sceleris, tabellae, signa, manūs, dēnique ūnīuscūjusque cōnfessiō, tum multō certiōra illa, color, oculī, vultūs, taciturnitās.

Sīc enim obstupuerant,[65] sīc terram intuēbantur, sīc fūrtim[66] nōnnumquam[67] inter sēsē aspiciēbant, ut nōn jam ab aliīs indicārī, sed indicāre sē ipsī vidērentur.

I TOOK ADVICE OF THE SENATE

Indiciīs expositīs atque ēditīs, Quirītēs, senātum cōnsuluī dē summā rē pūblicā quid fierī placēret. Dictae sunt ā prīncipibus ācerrimae ac fortissimae sententiae, quās senātus sine ūllā varietāte est secūtus. Et quoniam nōndum est perscrīptum[68] senātūs cōnsultum, ex memoriā vōbīs, Quirītēs, quid senātus cēnsuerit expōnam.

Words to Remember

īnsimulō, 1, tr., *charge, allege* (cf. **simulō**).
argūmentum, ī, *argument, proof.*
cōnfessiō, cōnfessiōnis, *admission, confession* (cf. **cōnfiteor**).
color, colōris, *color.*
vultus, ūs, *look, expression, face, countenance.*
intueor, intuērī, intuitus sum, 2, tr., *fix my gaze on, fasten my eyes on* (cf. **tueor**; intuition).
aspiciō, aspicere, aspexī, aspectus, 3, tr., *glance at, look at* (cf. aspect).
varietās, varietātis, *diversity, variety.*

---

[65] **obstupēscō, obstupēscere, obstupuī**, 3, intr., *am stupified, am struck dumb.*
[66] **fūrtim**, adv., *stealthily* (cf. **fūrtum**; furtive).
[67] **nōnnumquam**, adv., *sometimes* (**nōn** + **numquam**, *not never*).
[68] **perscrīptus, a, um**, *written out.*

THE DECREE OF THE SENATE

Prīmum mihi grātiae verbīs amplissimīs aguntur, quod virtūte, cōnsiliō, prōvidentiā meā rēs pūblica maximīs perīculīs sit līberāta. Deinde Lūcius Flaccus et Gājus Pomptīnus, praetōrēs, quod eōrum operā fortī fidēlīque[69] ūsus essem, meritō ac jūre laudantur. Atque etiam virō fortī, collēgae meō,[70] laus impertītur,[71] quod eōs quī hūjus conjūrātiōnis participēs[72] fuissent ā suīs et ā reī pūblicae cōnsiliīs remōvisset.

THE CONVICTION OF THE CONSPIRATORS

Atque ita cēnsuērunt, ut Pūblius Lentulus, cum sē praetūrā **14**
abdicāsset,[73] in custōdiam trāderētur; itemque ut Gājus Cethēgus,
Lūcius Statilius, Pūblius Gabīnius, quī omnēs praesentēs erant,
in custōdiam trāderentur; atque idem hoc dēcrētum est in
Lūcium Cassium, quī sibi prōcūrātiōnem[74] incendendae urbis

WORDS TO REMEMBER

prōvidentia, ae, *preparation, foresight* (cf. providence; **prōvideō**).
ūtor, ūtī, ūsus sum, 3, intr.; w. abl., *use.*
removeō, removēre, remōvī, remōtus, 2, tr., *move back, remove.*
praetūra, ae, *the praetorship, the office of praetor.*
abdicō, 1, tr., *abdicate, renounce, resign.*

---

[69] **fidēlis, e,** *faithful, loyal, reliable* (cf. **fidēs**; fidelity).

[70] **collēgae meō:** *my colleague in the consulship.* This was Antonius, who had been a running mate of Catiline for the consulship (page 5). He is praised for breaking with the conspirators! Cicero won him over by promising him a lucrative provincial appointment after his term of office.

[71] **impertiō,** 4, tr., *give, bestow.*

[72] **particeps, participis,** c.; w. gen., *a sharer in.*

[73] Lentulus held office as a praetor; he had therefore first to be reduced to the status of a private citizen. The person of a Roman magistrate was regarded as inviolable.

[74] **prōcūrātiō, prōcūrātiōnis,** *office, charge, care.*

dēpoposcerat; in Mārcum Cēpārium,[75] cui ad sollicitandōs pastōrēs[76] Āpūliam[77] attribūtam esse[78] erat indicātum; in Pūblium Fūrium, quī est ex eīs colōnīs[79] quōs Faesulās[80] Lūcius Sulla dēdūxit; in Quīntum Annium Chīlōnem,[81] quī ūnā cum hōc Fūriō semper erat in hāc Allobrogum sollicitātiōne versātus; in Pūblium Umbrēnum,[82] lībertīnum[83] hominem, ā quō prīmum Gallōs ad Gabīnium perductōs esse cōnstābat.

A WISE AND GENEROUS MODERATION

Atque eā lēnitāte[84] senātus est ūsus, Quirītēs, ut, ex tantā conjūrātiōne tantāque hāc multitūdine domesticōrum hostium novem

---

Words to Remember

dēposcō, dēposcere, dēpoposcī, 3, tr., *demand, claim.*
Fūrius (ī), Pūblius (ī), *Publius Furius,* an associate of Catiline.
Sulla (ae), Lūcius (ī), *Lucius Sulla,* a former dictator.
sollicitātiō, sollicitātiōnis, *an inciting, an alluring, a tempting.*
perdūcō, perdūcere, perdūxī, perductus, 3, tr., *lead through, conduct, win over.*
multitūdō, multitūdinis, *crowd, multitude.*

---

75 Marcus Ceparius, a conspirator.

76 **pastor, pastōris,** *herdsman, shepherd* (cf. pastor of a parish and of a congregation; **grex, gregis,** *flock, herd*).

77 **Āpūlia, ae,** *Apulia,* a region of large estates in southern Italy, given to cattle raising. The herdsmen, mostly slaves, led a wild and lawless life—ready material for brigandage or revolution.

78 **attribuō, attribuere, attribuī, attribūtus,** 3, tr., *assign to, grant* (cf. divine attributes).

79 **colōnus, ī,** *settler* (cf. colonial policy).

80 Sulla, a former dictator at Rome (82-79 B.C.), had settled some of his ex-soldiers on land at Faesule (**Faesulae, Faesulārum**). Many of these, unused to the frugal and industrious life of the country, were eager for the spoils and excitement of revolution. Among these latter was the Publius Furius mentioned.

81 Quintus Annius Chilo, a conspirator.

82 Publius Umbrenus, another conspirator.

83 **lībertīnus, a, um,** *freed.*

84 **lēnitās, lēnitātis,** *leniency* (cf. **lēnis, e**).

—*Courtesy of Produzione Consorzio Scipione S. A.*

A Roman Senator Makes a Point

Freedom of discussion in the Roman Senate, just as in our own Senate, is a precious right enjoyed only by a free people.

hominum perditissimōrum poenā, rē pūblicā cōnservātā, reliquōrum mentēs sānārī[85] posse arbitrārētur.

A PUBLIC THANKSGIVING IN MY HONOR

Atque etiam supplicātiō dīs immortālibus prō singulārī eōrum 15
meritō meō nōmine dēcrēta est, quod mihi prīmum post hanc urbem conditam togātō[86] contigit, et hīs dēcrēta verbīs est: "quod

---

Words to Remember

supplicātiō, supplicātiōnis, *public thanksgiving, day of prayer.*
singulāris, e, *remarkable, distinguished, outstanding, alone.*
meritum, ī, *kindness, favor, merit, desert.*

---

[85] **sānō,** 1, tr., *heal, cure* (cf. board of sanitation).

[86] **togātō:** *as a civil magistrate;* opposed to **armātō** *(as a military man).*

urbem incendiīs, caede cīvēs, Italiam bellō līberāssem." Quae supplicātiō sī cum cēterīs supplicātiōnibus cōnferātur, hoc interest, quod[87] cēterae, bene gestā, haec ūna, cōnservātā rē pūblicā, cōnstitūta est.

THE RESIGNATION OF LENTULUS

Atque illud quod faciendum prīmum fuit factum atque trānsāctum est.[88] Nam Pūblius Lentulus, quamquam patefactīs indiciīs, cōnfessiōnibus suīs, jūdiciō senātūs nōn modo praetōris jūs vērum etiam cīvis āmīserat,[89] tamen magistrātū sē abdicāvit ut, quae religiō Gājō Mariō, clārissimō virō, nōn fuerat, quōminus[90] Gājum Glauciam,[91] dē quō nihil nōminātim erat dēcrētum, praetōrem occīderet, eā nōs religiōne in prīvātō Pūbliō Lentulō pūniendō līberārēmur.

THE CONSPIRACY IS CRUSHED!

16 Nunc quoniam, Quirītēs, cōnscelerātissimī perīculōsissimīque bellī nefāriōs ducēs captōs jam et comprehēnsōs tenētis, exīsti-

---

Words to Remember

magistrātus, ūs, *magistrate, magistracy.*
religiō, religiōnis, *scruple.*
Marius (ī), Gājus (ī), *Gaius Marius,* a consul.
nōminātim, adv., *by name.*
cōnscelerātus, a, um, *criminal* (cf. **scelus**).
perīculōsus, a, um, *dangerous* (cf. **perīculum**).

---

[87] **quod,** *that;* Gr. 658.

[88] **trānsigō, trānsigere, trānsēgī, trānsāctus,** 3, tr., *carry out, execute* (**trāns** + **agō**; cf. transaction).

[89] **āmittō, āmittere, āmīsī, āmissus,** 3, tr., *let go, lose.*

[90] **quōminus,** conj.; Gr. 646. The idea of preventing is in the word **religiō.**

[91] Gaius Glaucia, a corrupt demagogue. Acting on a general decree (naming no specific individual), Marius had not scrupled to execute this Gaius Glaucia, though at the time Glaucia was a praetor in office. Cicero is showing, by contrast, how carefully the legal formalities were observed in the case of Lentulus.

māre dēbētis omnēs Catilīnae cōpiās, omnēs spēs atque opēs, hīs dēpulsīs urbis perīculīs, concidisse.[92]

CATILINE'S DEPARTURE LEFT ONLY INCAPABLE LEADERS AT HOME

Quem quidem ego cum ex urbe pellēbam, hoc prōvidēbam animō, Quirītēs, remōtō Catilīnā, nōn mihi esse Pūblī Lentulī somnum[93] nec Lūcī Cassī adipēs[94] nec Gājī Cethēgī furiōsam temeritātem pertimēscendam.

CATILINE WAS THE ONE MAN TO BE FEARED

Ille erat ūnus timendus ex istīs omnibus, sed tam diū dum urbis moenibus continēbātur. Omnia nōrat,[95] omnium aditūs tenēbat; appellāre, temptāre, sollicitāre poterat, audēbat. Erat eī cōnsilium ad facinus aptum, cōnsiliō autem neque manus neque lingua deerat. Jam ad certās rēs cōnficiendās certōs hominēs dēlēctōs ac dēscrīptōs habēbat. Neque vērō, cum aliquid mandārat, cōnfectum putābat; nihil erat quod nōn ipse obīret, occurreret, vigilāret, labōrāret; frīgus, sitim,[96] famem ferre poterat.

Words to Remember

ops, opis, *power, help;* pl., *wealth, resources.*
temeritās, temeritātis, *rashness* (cf. **temere**).
dum, conj., *until, while.*
aditus, ūs, *approach, access, entrance.*
lingua, ae, *tongue, language.*
labōrō, 1, intr., *toil, am in difficulty.*

---

92 **concidō, concidere, concidī,** 3, intr., *fall down, collapse.*

93 **somnus, ī,** *sleep, drowsiness* (cf. somnolent).

94 **adeps, adipis,** m., *fat, corpulence.* Shakespeare represents Caesar as saying: "Let me have men about me that are fat: sleek-headed men and such as sleep o' nights: yond Cassius has a lean and hungry look; he thinks too much: such men are dangerous" (*Julius Caesar* 1:2).

95 **nōrat:** *he knew* (cf. **ignōrō**).

96 **sitim:** *thirst* (acc. sing.).

CATILINE HAD TO BE DRIVEN OUT

17 Hunc ego hominem tam ācrem, tam audācem, tam parātum, tam callidum,[97] tam in scelere vigilantem, tam in perditīs rēbus dīligentem, nisi ex domesticīs īnsidiīs in castrēnse[98] latrōcinium compulissem—dīcam id quod sentiō, Quirītēs—nōn facile hanc tantam mōlem malī ā cervīcibus vestrīs dēpulissem.

NEVER WOULD HE HAVE MADE THE MISTAKES OF LENTULUS

Nōn ille nōbīs Sāturnālia[99] cōnstituisset, neque tantō ante exitī ac fātī diem reī pūblicae dēnuntiāvisset, neque commīsisset, ut signum, ut litterae suae testēs manifestī sceleris dēprehenderentur.

Quae nunc, illō absente, sīc gesta sunt, ut nūllum in prīvātā domō fūrtum umquam sit tam palam inventum quam haec tanta in rē pūblicā conjūrātiō manifestō inventa atque dēprehēnsa est.

HOW DIFFERENT, HAD CATILINE REMAINED!

Quodsī Catilīna in urbe ad hanc diem remānsisset, quamquam, quoad[100] fuit, omnibus ējus cōnsiliīs occurrī atque obstitī, tamen,

---

Words to Remember

perdō, perdere, perdidī, perditus, 3, tr., *lose.*
compellō, compellere, compulī, compulsus, 3, tr., *drive together, collect.*
cervīcēs, cervīcium, *neck* (the nape of the neck).
dēnuntiō, 1, tr., *announce, threaten* (cf. denunciation).
absēns (*gen.* **absentis**), *absent.*
fūrtum, ī, *theft* (cf. **furtim**).
quam, adv., *as.*
obsistō, obsistere, obstitī, 3, intr.; w. dat., *block.*

---

[97] **callidus, a, um,** *clever, shrewd.*
[98] **castrēnsis, e,** *of the camp, pertaining to the camp* (cf. **castra**).
[99] See Note 51, page 76.
[100] **quoad,** *as long as;* Gr. 571.

—*Courtesy of Metro-Goldwyn-Mayer*

A Rising of Galley Slaves Caught in the Camera Eye of Hollywood

The Roman slave had no more rights than a cow or a mule. His master might mutilate, kill, or cast him out to die when old and feeble. Especially on the large plantations was the slave's life a combination of brutality and hard work. The large number of such slaves made them a constant danger. It is estimated that in 71 B.C. there were in Italy some thirteen or fourteen million slaves as against a free population of six or seven million. In the most desperate of slave revolts under Spartacus, the gladiator, two Roman armies were cut to pieces and many others defeated. All southern Italy was brought under the domination of the slaves. All captured Romans were tortured and killed. At last the soldier slaves were defeated, 12,300 dying on the field and 6,000 being crucified along the road from Capua to Rome. But the danger remained; and it is clear what a terrible charge in Roman eyes was Cicero's that Catiline was planning to arm and organize the slaves. The modern terms 'anarchist' and 'red' have a much milder emotional reaction than Cicero's *ēvocātor servōrum.*

ut levissimē dīcam, dīmicandum[101] nōbīs cum illō fuisset, neque nōs umquam, cum ille in urbe hostis esset, tantīs perīculīs rem pūblicam tantā pāce, tantō ōtiō,[102] tantō silentiō, līberāssēmus.

THE GODS DID GUIDE AND PROTECT US

Quamquam haec omnia, Quirītēs, ita sunt ā mē administrāta ut deōrum immortālium nūtū atque cōnsiliō et gesta et prōvīsa esse videantur.

21 Nam quis potest esse, Quirītēs, tam āversus ā vērō, tam praeceps,[103] tam mente captus[104] quī neget haec omnia quae vidēmus, praecipuēque hanc urbem, deōrum immortālium nūtū ac potestāte administrārī?

Etenim, cum esset ita respōnsum,[105] caedēs, incendia, interitum reī pūblicae comparārī, et ea per cīvēs, quae tum propter magnitūdinem scelerum nōnnūllīs incrēdibilia vidēbantur, ea nōn modo cōgitāta ā nefāriīs cīvibus, vērum etiam suscepta esse sēnsistis.

A REMARKABLE COINCIDENCE

Illud vērō nōnne ita praesēns est ut nūtū Jovis Optimī Maximī factum esse videātur ut, cum hodiernō diē māne per forum meō

Words to Remember

leve, adv., *lightly, mildly.*
nūtus, ūs, *nod, consent, will.*
āvertō, āvertere, āvertī, āversus, 3, tr.; **ab (ā)** w. abl., *turn from, turn away from, am hostile to.*
praecipuē, adv., *especially, particularly.*
forum, ī, *the forum.*

---

101 **dīmicō,** 1, intr.; **dē** w. abl., *contend (for), struggle (for).*

102 **ōtium, ī,** *tranquillity.*

103 **praeceps** (*gen.* **praecipitis**), *hasty, inconsiderate* (**prae** + **caput**; cf. precipitate).

104 **mente captus, a, um,** *beside oneself, out of one's mind, insane.*

105 Just previously there had been certain omens (lightning, earthquakes, etc.) which the soothsayers interpreted as foreboding ruin to Rome.

jussū et conjūrātī et eōrum indicēs[106] in aedem Concordiae[107] dūcerentur, eō ipsō tempore signum statuerētur?[108]

Quō collocātō atque ad vōs senātumque conversō, omnia quae erant cōgitāta contrā salūtem omnium illūstrāta et patefacta vīdistis.

THEY CONSPIRED AGAINST THE VERY GODS

Quō etiam mājōre sunt istī odiō suppliciōque dignī quī nōn 22
sōlum vestrīs domiciliīs atque tēctīs sed etiam deōrum templīs atque dēlūbrīs sunt fūnestōs[109] ac nefāriōs ignēs īnferre cōnātī.

I CANNOT TAKE THE CREDIT TO MYSELF

Quibus ego sī mē restitisse dīcam, nimium mihi sūmam, et nōn sim ferendus; ille, ille Juppiter restitit; ille Capitōlium, ille haec templa, ille cūnctam urbem, ille vōs omnēs salvōs esse voluit. Dīs immortālibus ducibus, hanc mentem, Quirītēs, voluntātemque suscēpī, atque ad haec tanta indicia pervēnī.

THE GODS BLINDED LENTULUS AND HIS ASSOCIATES

Jam vērō ā Lentulō cēterīsque domesticīs hostibus tam dēmenter tantae rēs crēditae et ignōtīs et barbarīs commissaeque litterae

---

WORDS TO REMEMBER

conjūrātī, conjūrātōrum, *conspirators.*
dēmenter, adv., *madly, foolishly* (cf. **mēns**; demented).
ignōtus, a, um, *unknown.*

---

106 **index, indicis,** *accuser, informer.*

107 **aedem Concordiae:** *the temple of Concord.*

108 To ward off the predicted destruction—according to the soothsayers—a statue of Jupiter had to be erected in the Forum and faced toward the east. Cicero regards it as more than a coincidence that it was only finally erected on the very day of the conspirators' arrest.

109 **fūnestus, a, um,** *deadly, fatal, destructive.*

—*Courtesy of Produzione Consorzio Scipione S. A.*

WE ARE SAVED!

A public thanksgiving was decreed in Cicero's honor amid great rejoicing.

numquam essent profectō, nisi ab dīs immortālibus huic tantae audāciae cōnsilium esset ēreptum.

WAS NOT THE ACTION OF THE GAULS ALTOGETHER BEYOND HUMAN EXPECTATIONS?

Quid vērō? Ut hominēs Gallī, ex cīvitāte male pācātā, quae gēns ūna restat quae bellum populō Rōmānō facere et posse et nōn nōlle videātur, spem imperī ac rērum maximārum ultrō sibi ā patriciīs[110] hominibus oblātam neglegerent vestramque salūtem suīs opibus antepōnerent,[111] id nōn dīvīnitus esse factum putātis, praesertim quī nōs nōn pugnandō sed tacendō superāre potuerint?

CELEBRATE YOUR PEACEFUL DELIVERANCE!

23 Quam ob rem, Quirītēs, quoniam ad omnia pulvīnāria[112] supplicātiō dēcrēta est, celebrātōte[113] illōs diēs cum conjugibus ac līberīs vestrīs. Nam multī saepe honōrēs dīs immortālibus jūstī habitī sunt ac dēbitī, sed profectō jūstiōrēs numquam. Ēreptī enim estis ex crūdēlissimō ac miserrimō interitū, ēreptī sine caede, sine sanguine, sine exercitū, sine dīmicātiōne;[114] togātī, mē ūnō togātō duce et imperātōre, vīcistis.

Words to Remember

profectō, adv., *actually, truly, indeed.*
dīvīnitus, adv., *providentially, from heaven.*
jūstus, a, um, *just, lawful.*
togātus, a, um, *clothed in the toga.*

---

[110] **patricius, a, um,** *aristocratic.* Lentulus and others of the conspirators were aristocrats by birth.

[111] **antepōnō, antepōnere, anteposuī, antepositus,** 3, tr.; w. acc. and dat., *put before, prefer to.*

[112] **ad omnia pulvīnāria:** *at all the shrines.* The **pulvīnar** was an elaborately decorated couch placed before the shrines of the gods.

[113] **celebrātōte:** *celebrate* (imperative, pl.).

[114] **dīmicātiō, dīmicātiōnis,** *struggle* (cf. **dīmicō**).

ALL PREVIOUS CIVIL DISTURBANCES ENDED IN BLOODSHED

24 Etenim recordāminī,[115] Quirītēs, omnēs cīvīlēs dissēnsiōnēs, nōn sōlum eās quās audīstis, sed eās quās vōsmet[116] ipsī meministis atque vīdistis. Lūcius Sulla Pūblium Sulpicium[117] oppressit; ējēcit ex urbe Gājum Marium, custōdem hūjus urbis, multōsque fortēs virōs partim ējēcit ex cīvitāte, partim interēmit.[118] Gnaeus Octāvius,[119] cōnsul, armīs expulit ex urbe collēgam; omnis hic locus acervīs corporum et cīvium sanguine redundāvit.[120]

Superāvit posteā Cinna cum Mariō;[121] tum vērō, clārissimīs virīs interfectīs, lūmina cīvitātis exstīncta sunt. Ultus est[122] hūjus

---

Words to Remember

cīvīlis, e, *civil.*
dissēnsiō, dissēnsiōnis, *strife, struggle, quarrel* (cf. dissension).
partim . . . partim, advs., *partly . . . partly.*
expellō, expellere, expulī, expulsus, 3, tr., *drive out.*
collēga, ae, m., *colleague, partner in office.*
acervus, ī, *heap, pile.*
lūmen, lūminis, *light.*

---

115 **recordāminī:** *recall to mind* (imperative, pl.); Gr. 708.

116 **vōsmet** = **vōs** + **met** (an emphatic suffix).

117 In 88 B.C. Publius Sulpicius proposed a law to substitute Gaius Marius for Lucius Sulla in command of the Roman army against Mithridates, a ruler in Asia Minor. Sulla marched on Rome and 'purged' the city of his enemies. Marius fled; Sulpicius was killed.

118 **interimō, interimere, interēmī, interemptus,** 3, tr., *do away with, kill.*

119 In 87 B.C. Gnaeus Octavius, an aristocrat and a partisan of Sulla, held the consulate with Lucius Cornelius Cinna, a democratic leader. They quarreled over certain proposals, and bloody rioting ensued. Before Octavius finally succeeded in driving out Cinna, some 10,000 persons are said to have perished.

120 **redundō,** 1, tr., *overflow (with), run (with)* (cf. redundant style).

121 Marius and his army brought Cinna back and took bitter vengeance on the aristocrats.

122 **ulcīscor, ulcīscī, ultus sum,** 3, tr., *take vengeance on, avenge.*

victōriae crūdēlitātem posteā Sulla;[123] nē dīcī quidem opus est[124] quantā dēminūtiōne[125] cīvium et quantā calamitāte reī pūblicae. Dissēnsit[126] Mārcus Lepidus ā clārissimō et fortissimō virō, Quīntō Catulō;[127] attulit nōn tam ipsīus interitus reī pūblicae lūctum[128] quam cēterōrum.

AND YET NONE OF THESE AIMED AT THE COMPLETE DESTRUCTION OF THE STATE

Atque illae tamen omnēs dissēnsiōnēs, erant ējus modī, Quirītēs, **25**
quae nōn ad dēlendam sed ad commūtandam rem pūblicam pertinērent. Nōn illī nūllam esse rem pūblicam, sed in eā quae esset sē esse prīncipēs, neque hanc urbem cōnflagrāre, sed sē in hāc urbe flōrēre[129] voluērunt.

Atque illae tamen omnēs dissēnsiōnēs, quārum nūlla exitium

Words to Remember

crūdēlitās, crūdēlitātis, *savagery, cruelty, severity.*
commūtō, 1, tr., *change* (cf. **mūtō**).

---

[123] Sulla, returning from the east with a victorious army, made himself dictator (83-79 B.C.). He posted proscription lists of those who were to be killed and whose property was to be forfeited to the state. His lists contained some 5,000 names. The ways of those who establish their power on might have not changed since Roman times.

[124] **opus est, esse, fuit,** intr.; w. dat. of person; w. abl. of thing, *it is necessary, there is need (of).*

[125] **dēminūtiō, dēminūtiōnis,** *loss, reduction.*

[126] **dissentiō, dissentīre, dissēnsī, dissēnsum,** 4, intr., *disagree, differ* (**dis,** *apart from* + **sentiō**).

[127] Sulla established an aristocratic constitution at Rome. Marcus Lepidus, a succeeding consul and a democrat, attempted to overthrow this Sullan constitution and was driven out by his colleague, Quintus Catulus.

[128] **lūctus, ūs,** *grief, mourning.*

[129] **flōreō, flōrēre, flōruī,** 2, intr., *flourish.*

reī pūblicae quaesīvit, ējus modī fuērunt ut nōn reconciliātiōne[130] concordiae[131] sed internecīōne[132] cīvium dījūdicātae sint.

YET HAVE WE ALL, WITHOUT BLOODSHED OR SORROW, SURVIVED THIS CONSPIRACY OF UNIVERSAL DESTRUCTION

In hōc autem ūnō post hominum memoriam maximō crūdēlissimōque bellō, quāle bellum nūlla umquam barbaria[133] cum suā gente gessit, quō in bellō lēx haec fuit ā Lentulō, Catilīnā, Cethēgō, Cassiō cōnstitūta ut omnēs quī, salvā urbe, salvī esse possent in hostium numerō dūcerentur, ita mē gessī, Quirītēs, ut salvī omnēs cōnservārēminī, et, cum hostēs vestrī tantum cīvium superfutūrum putāssent quantum īnfīnītae caedī restitisset, tantum autem urbis quantum flamma obīre nōn potuisset, et urbem et cīvēs integrōs incolumēsque servāvī.

I ASK NO OTHER REWARD THAN THAT THE MEMORY OF THESE DEEDS BE KEPT ALIVE IN PATRIOTIC MINDS AND HEARTS

26 Quibus prō tantīs rēbus, Quirītēs, nūllum ego ā vōbīs praemium virtūtis, nūllum īnsigne honōris, nūllum monumentum laudis postulābō praeterquam[134] hūjus diēī memoriam sempiter-

---

Words to Remember

dījūdicō, 1, tr., *decide* (cf. **jūdicō**).
quālis, e, *of such a sort, of such a kind, such as* (cf. quality).
supersum, superesse, superfuī, superfutūrus, irreg., intr.; w. dat., *survive, am left.*
incolumis, e, *safe.*
īnsigne, īnsignis, *mark, sign, insignia.*
sempiternus, a, um, *everlasting.*

---

130 **reconciliātiō, reconciliātiōnis,** *restoration, renewal.*
131 **concordia, ae,** *agreement, harmony.*
132 **internecīō, internecīōnis,** *massacre* (cf. **nex**).
133 **barbaria, ae,** *a foreign country* (cf. **barbarus**).
134 **praeterquam,** adv., *beyond, besides, except.*

nam. In animīs ego vestrīs omnēs triumphōs[135] meōs, omnia ōrnāmenta[136] honōris, monumenta glōriae, laudis īnsignia condī et collocārī volō.

I SHALL FIND IMMORTALITY IN THE LIVING TRADITION OF THE ROMAN PEOPLE

Nihil mē mūtum potest dēlectāre, nihil tacitum, nihil dēnique ējus modī quod etiam minus dignī assequī possint. Memoriā vestrā, Quirītēs, nostrae rēs alentur,[137] sermōnibus crēscent, litterārum monumentīs inveterāscent[138] et corrōborābuntur;[139] eandemque diem[140] intellegō, quam spērō aeternam fore, prōpāgātam[141] esse et ad salūtem urbis et ad memoriam cōnsulātūs meī, ūnōque tempore in hāc rē pūblicā duōs cīvēs exstitisse quōrum alter[142] fīnēs vestrī imperī nōn terrae sed caelī regiōnibus termināret, alter[143] hūjus imperī domicilium sēdēsque servāret.

Words to Remember

dēlectō, 1, tr., *delight, charm.*
spērō, 1, tr.; acc. w. infin., *hope.*
regiō, regiōnis, *boundary, limit.*
terminō, 1, tr., *bound, limit* (cf. railway terminal).
sēdēs, sēdis, *seat, abode, habitation.*

---

135 **triumphus, ī**, *triumph.* These triumphal processions were accorded victorious generals.

136 **ōrnāmentum, ī**, *decoration* (cf. **ōrnō**).

137 **alō, alere, aluī, altus (alitus)**, 3, tr., *nourish, maintain* (cf. alimentary canal).

138 **inveterāscō, inveterāscere, inveterāvī**, 3, intr., *grow old, am established, become fixed* (cf. **vetus**).

139 **corrōborō**, 1, tr., *strengthen.*

140 **diem**: *period of time* (not day).

141 **prōpāgō**, 1, tr., *grant, extend, prolong.*

142 Pompey, whose military exploits had made him the greatest living general.

143 Cicero himself.

I MUST LOOK TO YOU FOR FUTURE PROTECTION

27 Sed quoniam eārum rērum quās ego gessī nōn eadem est fortūna atque condiciō quae illōrum quī externa bella gessērunt, quod mihi cum eīs vīvendum est quōs vīcī ac subēgī,[144] illī hostēs aut interfectōs aut oppressōs relīquērunt, vestrum est, Quirītēs, sī cēterīs facta sua rēctē prōsunt, mihi mea nē quandō[145] obsint, prōvidēre.[146] Mentēs enim hominum audācissimōrum scelerātae ac nefāriae nē vōbīs nocēre possent ego prōvīdī; nē mihi noceant vestrum est prōvidēre.

BUT THE MEMORY OF DEEDS NOBLY DONE WILL BE MY SECURE PROTECTION

Quamquam, Quirītēs, mihi quidem ipsī nihil ab istīs jam nocērī potest. Magnum enim est in bonīs praesidium, quod mihi in perpetuum comparātum est, magna in rē pūblicā dignitās, quae mē semper tacita dēfendet, magna vīs cōnscientiae, quam quī neglegunt, cum mē violāre volent, sē ipsī indicābunt.

THE WICKED HAVE ALWAYS BEEN MY CHOSEN ENEMIES

28 Est enim in nōbīs is animus, Quirītēs, ut nōn modo nūllīus audāciae cēdāmus, sed etiam omnēs improbōs ultrō semper lacessāmus.[147]

Words to Remember

rēctē, adv., *rightly, correctly.*
prōsum, prōdesse, prōfuī, prōfutūrus, irreg., intr.; w. dat., *profit.*
obsum, obesse, obfuī, obfutūrus, irreg., intr.; w. dat., *am harmful.*
dignitās, dignitātis, *worth, esteem, honor.*
violō, 1, tr., *injure, outrage.*

---

144 **subigō, subigere, subēgī, subāctus**, 3, tr., *drive, conquer* (**sub** + **agō**).

145 **nē quandō**: *lest ever, that . . . never.*

146 Cicero rightly foresaw the danger, for he was later driven into exile precisely on charges of unconstitutional action in suppressing this conspiracy.

147 **lacessō, lacessere, lacessīvī, lacessītus**, 3, tr., *provoke, harass.*

YOU MUST SHOW IN MY CASE WHAT REWARD AWAITS YOUR DEFENDERS

Quodsī omnis impetus domesticōrum hostium, dēpulsus ā vōbīs, sē in mē ūnum converterit, vōbīs erit videndum, Quirītēs, quā condiciōne, posthāc eōs esse velītis quī sē prō salūte vestrā obtulerint invidiae perīculīsque omnibus; mihi quidem ipsī quid est quod jam ad vītae frūctum possit acquīrī,[148] cum praesertim neque in honōre vestrō neque in glōriā virtūtis quidquam videam altius quō mihi libeat[149] ascendere?

AS A PRIVATE CITIZEN I SHALL LIVE EVER MINDFUL OF THE DEEDS OF MY CONSULATE

Illud perficiam profectō, Quirītēs, ut ea quae gessī in cōnsulātū **29**
prīvātus tuear atque ōrnem,[150] ut, sī qua est invidia in cōnservandā rē pūblicā suscepta, laedat[151] invidōs, mihi valeat ad glōriam. Dēnique, ita mē in rē pūblicā trāctābō ut meminerim semper quae gesserim cūremque, ut ea virtūte, nōn cāsū, gesta esse videantur.

GUARD YOUR HOMES YET A WHILE LONGER

Vōs, Quirītēs, quoniam jam est nox, venerātī Jovem[152] illum,

---

WORDS TO REMEMBER

posthāc, adv., *after this.*
frūctus, ūs, *fruit, produce, profit.*
praesertim, adv., *especially, particularly.*
perficiō, perficere, perfēcī, perfectus, 3, tr., *perform, complete.*
tueor, tuērī, tuitus sum, 2, tr., *look at, protect.*
invidus, a, um, *envious, hostile.*
trāctō, 1, tr., *conduct, treat.*

---

148 **acquīrō, acquīrere, acquīsīvī, acquīsītus**, 3, tr., *add to* (cf. acquire).
149 **mihi libeat**: *I might desire.*
150 **ōrnō**, 1, tr., *fit out, adorn* (cf. **ōrnāmentum**).
151 **laedō, laedere, laesī, laesus**, 3, tr., *injure, harm* (cf. lesion).
152 Cicero here refers to the new statue of Jupiter standing in the Forum.

custōdem hūjus urbis ac vestrum, in vestra tēcta discēdite, et ea, quamquam jam est perīculum dēpulsum, tamen aequē ac[153] priōre nocte custōdiīs vigiliīsque dēfendite. Id nē vōbīs diūtius faciendum sit atque ut in perpetuā[154] pāce esse possītis prōvidēbō.[155]

THE END OF THE CONSPIRACY

After Cicero's speech to the people on the evening of December 3 neither the conspirators nor the government were idle. All day there had been rumors of secret preparations to liberate the prisoners by mob violence. The slaves and friends of Lentulus were known to be agitating among the lower classes. Some even said that Catiline was approaching the city to save the conspirators with his army. Because of these activities and rumors the government was afraid to keep the prisoners long in custody at Rome and yet, at the same time, afraid to execute them, for no Roman citizen could be put to death except by vote of the citizen assembly.

So on December 5 Cicero laid the case before the Senate. What course should they follow? A memorable debate ensued. Caesar argued for life imprisonment. Cicero swept away his arguments, pleading that no traitor could be considered a Roman citizen, that the conspirators had forfeited their rights. The extreme aristocrats backed Cicero and carried the Senate.

Across the Forum there stood an ancient prison, a subterranean vault twelve feet deep, later known as the Tullianum, in which condemned prisoners were kept for execution. Here then Cicero conducted Lentulus, Cethegus, Statilius, Gabinius, and Ceparius, surrounded by a strong guard of aristocrats. The Forum was crowded, but it was through an expectant silence that the small cortege passed. No delay was to permit a daring counterstroke. It was evening, and one by one the prisoners were let down into

---

153 **aequē ac**: *just as, much as* (lit., *equally*).

154 **perpetuus, a, um**, *unbroken, perpetual.*

155 There is an ominous hint at the fate of the conspirators in these closing words.

—*Courtesy of Produzione Consorzio Scipione S. A.*

LICTORS PRECEDING A ROMAN MAGISTRATE

Twelve lictors, marching in single file, always preceded the consul whenever he appeared in public. They bore the *fascēs,* which was a bundle of elm or birch rods tied together with a red strip and which enclosed an axe with the head outside. The *fascēs* were originally the symbol of power over life and limb, but came later to be merely the symbol of magisterial power. It was the duty of lictors to warn people to stand aside and pay homage to the magistrate.

the Tullianum and there, by torchlight, the deed was done. Cicero, standing at the door of the prison, cried out to the crowded Forum, "*Fuērunt, fuērunt.*" For thus did the Romans speak of the dead.

At the evil news from Rome, Catiline's army in Etruria dwindled to a small force of desperate men. Two Roman armies encompassed him, but he none the less maintained at first a strong position in the mountains, waiting with hope for developments elsewhere in Italy. At last his supplies were gone and he knew his fate. He threw his force on the nearest Roman army—that of Antonius—and on that day at least showed himself a Roman of the old stock. No quarter was asked, none given; when the battle was over the bodies of three thousand of Catiline's men covered the field rank by rank as they had stood in the fight, and among them was Catiline himself.

PART II

ROMAN LAW VERSUS POLITICAL CORRUPTION

THE IMPEACHMENT OF GAIUS VERRES BY THE PEOPLE OF SICILY ON A CHARGE OF EXTORTION DURING HIS THREE YEARS AS GOVERNOR

Attorney for the Prosecution

MARCUS TULLIUS CICERO

Attorney for the Defense

QUINTUS HORTENSIUS HORTALUS

THE IMPEACHMENT OF GAIUS VERRES

When we say, as we sometimes do, that the Rome of Cicero and Caesar was, despite its antiquity, very much of a modern city, we really mean that civilization, whether ancient or modern, is of a piece. After all, man, in trousers or toga, speaking Latin or Hindi or English, remains much the same. The vices and virtues of Chicago or Berlin or Bombay are the same as were the vices and virtues of ancient Rome, of Babylon, and of the cities on the Nile. Modern American cities have their racketeers and gangsters; their counterparts existed in old Rome.

And so, as we step into the Forum of ancient Rome, August 5, 70 B. C., the talk we hear on every side is not unfamiliar. The town is agog over the indictment of Verres. Everyone knows of him.

"He's been making politics a paying proposition for years," one dumpy middle-aged businessman tells us as we start off toward the law courts, "and he did well by himself these last three years as governor in Sicily. Why, he had to have a ship built to bring back the 'souvenirs' he picked up down there. The Sicilians came up hot after him with a list of accusations as long as your arm—pretty highhanded methods he used, they say. Mark Cicero took the case, and he's handling the charges against him. Cicero? A rising young lawyer, first-rate speaker, clever, too, and a deal more honest than most of those lawyers. Oh, but Verres will get off; he's got the brainiest lawyer money can buy, Hortensius—he could talk a jury into a coma. After all, Verres is a senator and with no one but senators allowed to sit on juries—well, thieves won't convict thieves, and every senator expects to make a little pocket money now and then. Laws? Well, as far as I can see, they're to keep the poor man in his place. Jugurtha was right, *omnia vēnālia Rōmae* (everything's for sale at Rome). The only thing to do is to get these senators off the jury, break their stranglehold on the courts, let some of the equites sit in judgment—and maybe we'll get a few convictions.

"That Hortensius is a clever fellow all right. Trying to get his friend Caecilius appointed prosecutor instead of Cicero was a sly trick. Cicero stopped them dead that time. Yes, sir, talked rings around Caecilius and got him laughed out of court. Well, if Cicero can outwit Hortensius and convict Verres, he's a made man. But you've got to remember, money talks nowadays. Another thing, they tried to crowd Cicero off this year's docket. Yes, they figured the incoming administration would be more friendly. Old Mark Metellus—good friend of Verres, you know, his campaign fund had a lot of Sicilian gold in it—well, old Mark will be presiding in the court and Hortensius himself, of course, is consul-elect. But Cicero fooled them. He went down to Sicily and got all his evidence in fifty days, had the case in court before Hortensius heard he'd left Sicily. But if Cicero takes a long time to present his case, they're still going to crowd him out, what with all these official vacations coming in between now and the new year. Well, here we are; that's Glabrio up there, presiding praetor—very decent fellow for a politician. The jury looks pretty good, too. They say Cicero didn't miss any tricks when they were selected—but after all they're still senators. Quite a crowd here—shhh, there's Cicero now; let's see what he can do with the odds on Hortensius."

The First Hearing

Quod erat optandum maximē, jūdicēs, et quod ūnum ad invidiam vestrī ōrdinis īnfāmiamque jūdiciōrum sēdandam maximē pertinēbat, id nōn hūmānō[1] cōnsiliō sed prope dīvīnitus datum atque oblātum vōbīs summō reī pūblicae tempore[2] vidētur. Inveterāvit enim jam opīniō perniciōsa reī pūblicae vōbīsque

---

WORDS TO REMEMBER

inveterāscō, inveterāscere, inveterāvī, 3, intr., *grow old, become established.*
opīniō, opīniōnis, *belief, reputation, opinion.*

---

[1] **hūmānus, a, um,** *human, refined.*
[2] **summō . . . tempore:** *at a great crisis . . .*

perīculōsa, quae nōn modo Rōmae sed etiam apud exterās nātiōnēs omnium sermōne percrēbuit,[3] hīs jūdiciīs quae nunc sunt pecūniōsum hominem, quamvīs sit nocēns, nēminem posse damnārī.

WE HAVE BEFORE THIS COURT A CLEAR-CUT TEST CASE: CAN A WEALTHY CRIMINAL BE CONVICTED?

Nunc in ipsō discrīmine ōrdinis jūdiciōrumque vestrōrum, cum 2
sint parātī quī cōntiōnibus et lēgibus hanc invidiam senātūs īnflammāre cōnentur, reus in jūdicium adductus est Gājus Verrēs, homō vītā atque factīs omnium jam opīniōne damnātus, pecūniae magnitūdine, suā spē et praedicātiōne[4] absolūtus.

AN HONEST VERDICT WILL RESTORE YOUR REPUTATION

"In this case, gentlemen, I appear as prosecutor, backed by the strong approval and keen interest of the nation; not to increase the unpopularity of your Order, but to help in allaying the discredit which is mine as well as yours. The character of the man I am prosecuting is such that you may use him to restore the lost good name of these Courts, to regain favour at home, and to give

---

Words to Remember

exterus, a, um, *foreign.*
pecūniōsus, a, um, *'monied,' wealthy* (cf. **pecūnia**).
quamvīs, adv. and conj., *as you will, ever so much, however much, although.*
nocēns (*gen.* **nocentis**), *guilty* (cf. innocent).
discrīmen, discrīminis, *crisis, difference, distinction* (cf. discriminating taste).
cōntiō, cōntiōnis, *a mass meeting, a public meeting.*
Verrēs (Verris), Gājus (ī), *Gaius Verres,* a Roman politician, governor of Sicily.
factum, ī, *thing done, a deed* (cf. **faciō**).
absolvō, absolvere, absoluī, absolūtus, 3, tr., *acquit.*

---

[3] **percrēbēscō, percrēbēscere, percrēbuī,** 3, intr., *become widely known.*
[4] **praedicātiō, praedicātiōnis,** *confident assertion, boasting.*

satisfaction abroad: he has robbed the Treasury, and plundered Asia and Pamphylia; he has behaved like a pirate in his city praetorship, and like a destroying pestilence in his province of
3 Sicily. You have only to pronounce against this man an upright and conscientious verdict, and you will continue to possess that public respect which ought always to belong to you. If, however, the vastness of his wealth shatters the conscience and the honesty of the judges in these Courts, I shall achieve one thing at least: it will be felt that the nation lacked the right judges in this case, and not that the judges lacked the right prisoner to convict, or the prisoner the right man to prosecute him."[5]

I FEAR THE UNDERHANDED METHODS AND THE INTRIGUES OF VERRES HERE IN THIS COURT

Equidem[6] ut dē mē cōnfitear, jūdicēs, cum multae mihi ā Gājō Verre īnsidiae terrā marīque factae sint, quās partim meā dīligentiā dēvītārim,[7] partim amīcōrum studiō officiōque reppulerim, numquam tamen neque tantum perīculum mihi adīre vīsus sum, neque tantō opere pertimuī, ut nunc in ipsō jūdiciō.

HE OPENLY BOASTS OF THE POWER OF HIS MONEY

4 Neque tantum mē exspectātiō accūsātiōnis meae[8] concursusque

---

WORDS TO REMEMBER

terrā marīque: *on land and sea.*
dēvītō, 1, tr., *avoid, escape* (cf. vītō).
officium, ī, *duty, loyalty, service, allegiance.*
tantō opere, *so much, so greatly.*

---

[5] Cicero, *The Verrine Orations*, edited by L. H. G. Greenwood. Loeb Classical Library, Harvard University Press. Vol. I, pp. 69-71.

[6] **equidem,** particle emphasizing the first person, *indeed, for my part.*

[7] **dēvītārim = dēvītāverim.**

[8] **exspectātiō accūsātiōnis meae:** *the public interest in my prosecution* (lit., *the waiting for my accusation*).

tantae multitūdinis—quibus ego rēbus vehementissimē perturbor—commovet, quantum istīus īnsidiae nefāriae, quās ūnō tempore mihi, vōbīs, Māniō Glabriōnī, praetōrī, populō Rōmānō, sociīs, exterīs nātiōnibus, ōrdinī, nōminī dēnique senātōriō facere cōnātur; quī ita dictitat eīs esse metuendum quī quod ipsīs sōlīs satis esset surripuissent,[9] sē tantum rapuisse ut id multīs satis esse possit; nihil esse tam sānctum quod nōn violārī, nihil tam mūnītum quod nōn expugnārī pecūniā possit.[10]

HIS PLANS FOR CORRUPTING THIS COURT ARE MATTER OF COMMON TALK

"If only the audacity of his designs were equalled by his secrecy in carrying them out, he might perhaps have contrived, at some time or in some detail, to hide them from me. But it has very fortunately come about, hitherto, that his incredible audacity has been accompanied by unparalleled folly. Just as he has been quite open in amassing his stolen wealth, so he has revealed quite clearly to everybody the plans and schemes by which he aims at corrupting his judges. He says he was really frightened once in his life—on the day when I first issued the summons against him; not only because he had newly arrived from his province to face a blaze of hatred and dislike, which, so far from being new, had

---

Words to Remember

Glabriō (Glabriōnis), Mānius (ī), *Manius Glabrio,* the praetor presiding in the Court of Extortion.
senātōrius, a, um, *senatorial.*
dictitō, 1, tr., *keep saying, boast, allege.*

---

[9] **surripiō, surripere, surripuī, surreptus,** 3, tr., *filch, steal secretly, purloin* (cf. surreptitiously).

[10] The cynic's principle, "Every man has his price." Compare with the remark of a Mexican president: "There is no Mexican general who can resist a gun-shot of $50,000."

burnt steadily for a long time past, but also because he had tumbled upon a time unsuitable for corrupting the Court.

HE TRIED TO BLOCK MY PROSECUTION

6 "That is why, when I had applied for a very short space of time in which to go and collect my evidence in Sicily, he found himself another man to apply for a period shorter by two days in which to do the like in Achaea; not with any idea that the latter should effect by his carefulness and energy what I have achieved by my own hard work and watchfulness—indeed, this collector of evidence in Achaea never got even so far as Brundisium; whereas I covered the whole of Sicily in fifty days, so effectively, that I took cognizance of the wrongs, and the documents recording the wrongs, of all the communities and individuals concerned: so that anyone could see quite clearly that Verres secured the man not to prosecute his own victim but to block the way for me."[11]

HE SEES THAT THE EVIDENCE AGAINST HIM IS OVERWHELMING

7 Nunc homō audācissimus atque āmentissimus hoc cōgitat. In-
31 tellegit mē ita parātum atque īnstrūctum[12] in jūdicium venīre ut nōn modo in auribus vestrīs, sed in oculīs omnium, sua fūrta atque flāgitia dēfīxūrus sim. Videt senātōrēs multōs esse testēs audāciae suae. Videt multōs equitēs Rōmānōs, frequentēs prae-

---

WORDS TO REMEMBER

āmēns (*gen.* **āmentis**), *mad, insane* (cf. **mēns**).
dēfīgō, dēfīgere, dēfīxī, dēfīxus, 3, tr.; **in** w. abl.; **in** w. acc., *fix firmly, plant.*

---

[11] Cicero, *The Verrine Orations,* edited by L. H. G. Greenwood. Loeb Classical Library. Vol. I, pp. 73-75.

[12] **īnstrūctus, a, um,** *equipped.*

—*Vitagraph Inc.*

LIBERTY UNDER LAW IN AMERICA

Today in a hundred courtrooms throughout our own country the traditions of Roman law and the very phrases of Cicero's language live on. Today, too, "I am an American citizen" carries with it all the rights and privileges that once attached to "I am a Roman citizen"—rights and privileges that can be only too easily lost if not guarded with constant vigilance.

tereā cīvēs atque sociōs, quibus ipse īnsignēs[13] injūriās fēcerit. Videt etiam tot tam gravēs ab amīcissimīs cīvitātibus lēgātiōnēs[14] cum pūblicīs auctōritātibus convēnisse.

BUT DOES THIS WORRY OUR FRIEND VERRES? FAR FROM IT. HE BOASTS THAT HE CAN 'BUY' THE TIME OF HIS TRIAL AND SO ESCAPE THE PRESENT POPULAR FEELING AND THIS HONEST JURY

Quae cum ita sint, usque eō dē omnibus bonīs male exīstimat, **8**
usque eō senātōria jūdicia perdita prōflīgātaque[15] esse arbitrātur, ut hoc palam dictitet, nōn sine causā sē cupidum pecūniae fuisse,

---

WORD TO REMEMBER

usque eō, *to such an extent.*

---

[13] **īnsignis, e,** *distinguished, prominent, conspicuous.*

[14] **lēgātiō, lēgātiōnis,** *embassy* (cf. **lēgātus**).

[15] **prōflīgātus, a, um,** *vile, corrupt.*

quoniam in pecūniā tantum praesidium experiātur[16] esse; sēsē—id quod difficillimum fuerit—tempus ipsum ēmisse jūdiciī suī, quō cētera facilius emere posteā posset, ut, quoniam crīminum vim subterfugere nūllō modō poterat, procellam[17] temporis dēvītāret.

HE DOES NOT HOPE TO GET OUT OF THIS BY ANY HONORABLE MEANS

9 Quodsī nōn modo in causā, vērum in aliquō honestō praesidiō, aut in alicūjus ēloquentiā aut grātiā,[18] spem aliquam collocāsset,[19] profectō nōn haec omnia colligeret[20] atque aucupārētur;[21] nōn usque eō dēspiceret contemneretque ōrdinem senātōrium, ut arbitrātū ējus[22] dēligerētur ex senātū quī reus fieret, quī, dum hic[23] quae opus essent comparāret, causam intereā ante eum dīceret.

THE ONLY ELOQUENCE ON WHICH HE RELIES IS THE ELOQUENCE OF HIS MONEY

10 Quibus ego rēbus quid iste spēret et quō animum intendat facile perspiciō. Quam ob rem vērō sē cōnfīdat aliquid perficere posse,

---

WORDS TO REMEMBER

subterfugiō, subterfugere, subterfūgī, 3, tr., *escape, avoid* (cf. subterfuge).
dēspiciō, dēspicere, dēspexī, dēspectus, 3, tr., *look down upon, despise.*
contemnō, contemnere, contempsī, contemptus, 3, tr., *scorn, contemn.*

---

16 **experiātur:** *he finds.*

17 **procella, ae,** *storm.*

18 The Romans were not unacquainted with the sort of legal influence and political 'pull' that comes from knowing the right persons.

19 **collocāsset = collocāvisset.**

20 **colligō, colligere, collēgī, collēctus,** 3, tr., *gather together, collect.*

21 **aucupor,** 1, tr., *look out for, watch for.*

22 **arbitrātū ējus:** *at his pleasure.*

23 Verres; Cicero refers to the attempt to crowd him out of the docket by bringing in another trumped-up case.

hōc praetōre et hōc cōnsiliō,[24] intellegere nōn possum. Ūnum illud intellegō—quod populus Rōmānus in rejectiōne jūdicum jūdicāvit —eā spē istum fuisse praeditum[25] ut omnem ratiōnem salūtis in pecūniā cōnstitueret; hōc ēreptō praesidiō ut nūllam sibi rem adjūmentō[26] fore arbitrārētur.

Etenim quod est ingenium[27] tantum, quae tanta facultās dīcendī aut cōpia,[28] quae istīus vītam, tot vitiīs flāgitiīsque convīctam,[29] jam prīdem omnium voluntāte jūdiciōque damnātam, aliquā ex parte possit dēfendere?

HIS EARLY CAREER IS SPLENDID TESTIMONY TO HIS CHARACTER!

"I pass over the stained and shameful record of his youthful **11**
days: what is the story of his quaestorship, the first stage in his official career? It is the story of how Gnaeus Carbo was robbed, by his own quaestor, of money belonging to the state: the story of a consular superior left helpless and deserted, of an army abandoned to its fate, of duty left undone, of the violation of the personal tie that the lot had imposed and hallowed. His term of service as adjutant was a disaster to the whole of the provinces of Asia and Pamphylia, where few private houses, very few cities, and not one single sanctuary escaped his depredations. It was

---

Words to Remember

rejectiō, rejectiōnis, *the challenging* (of jurors).
facultās, facultātis; w. gen., *ability, opportunity (for).*

---

[24] **cōnsiliō:** *panel of jurors.* By luck and clever challenging Cicero has secured an exceptionally honest set of **jūdicēs.**

[25] **praeditus, a, um;** w. abl., *gifted with, endowed with.*

[26] **adjūmentum, ī,** *help, aid, assistance* (cf. **adjuvō**). What kind of dative is **adjūmentō**?

[27] **ingenium, ī,** *natural talent, ability, genius.*

[28] **cōpia, ae,** *fullness* (of speech), *fluency.*

[29] **convīctus, a, um,** *convicted.*

now that he carried out, at Gnaeus Dolabella's expense, a fresh performance of the wickedness that had already distinguished his quaestorship, bringing discredit through his own misconduct on a man whom he had served not only as adjutant but as acting-quaestor also, and not merely failing to support him in the hour
12 of danger, but deliberately attacking and betraying him. His city praetorship was occupied in a plundering onslaught upon sanctuaries and public buildings, and in awarding, or failing to award, in the civil courts, personal and real property in violation of all legal precedents."[30]

HIS CRIMINAL RECORD IN SICILY IS UNPARALLELED EVEN IN HIS OWN PREVIOUS LIFE

Jam vērō omnium vitiōrum suōrum plūrima et maxima cōnstituit monumenta et indicia in prōvinciā Siciliā;[31] quam iste per triennium ita vexāvit ac perdidit ut ea restituī in antīquum statum[32] nūllō modō possit, vix autem per multōs annōs innocen-
13 tēsque praetōrēs aliquā ex parte recreārī posse videātur. Hōc praetōre, Siculī neque suās lēgēs neque nostra senātūs cōnsulta neque commūnia jūra tenuērunt. Tantum quisque[33] habet in

---

Words to Remember

Sicilia, ae, *Sicily.*
triennium, ī, *(a period of) three years.*
innocēns (*gen.* **innocentis**), *guiltless, innocent.*
Siculī, Siculōrum, *Sicilians.*

---

[30] Cicero, *The Verrine Orations,* edited by L. H. G. Greenwood. Loeb Classical Library. Vol. I, pp. 77-79.

[31] **in prōvinciā Siciliā**; Gr. 682.

[32] **status, ūs,** *position, condition, state.*

[33] **quisque, quidque,** indefinite pronoun, *each one, each thing, everyone;* Gr. 831.

Siciliā quantum hominis avārissimī et libīdinōsissimī[34] aut imprūdentiam[35] subterfūgit aut satietātī[36] superfuit.

EXTORTION WAS THE POLICY OF HIS ADMINISTRATION

"For the space of three years, the law awarded nothing to anybody unless Verres chose to agree; and nothing was so undoubtedly inherited from a man's father or grandfather that the courts would not cancel his right to it, if Verres bade them do so. Countless sums of money, under a new and unprincipled regulation, were wrung from the purses of the farmers; our most loyal allies were treated as if they were national enemies; Roman citizens were tortured and executed like slaves; the guiltiest criminals bought their legal acquittal, while the most honorable and honest men would be prosecuted in absence, and condemned and banished unheard; strongly fortified harbors, mighty and well-defended cities were left open to the assaults of pirates and buccaneers; Sicilian soldiers and sailors, our allies and our friends, were starved to death; fine fleets, splendidly equipped, were to
the great disgrace of our nation destroyed and lost to us. Famous 14
and ancient works of art, some of them the gifts of wealthy kings, who intended them to adorn the cities where they stood, others the gifts of Roman generals, who gave or restored them to the communities of Sicily in the hour of victory—this same governor stripped and despoiled every one of them. Nor was it only the civic statues and works of art that he treated thus; he also pillaged the holiest and most venerated sanctuaries; in fact, he has not left the people of Sicily a single god whose workmanship he

---

Word to Remember

avārus, a, um, *avaricious, greedy.*

---

[34] **libīdinōsus, a, um,** *intemperate, lustful* (cf. **libīdō**).

[35] **imprūdentia, ae,** *carelessness.*

[36] **satietās, satietātis,** *satiety* (cf. **satis**).

thought at all above the average of antiquity or artistic merit. As to his adulteries and the like vile offenses, a sense of decency makes me afraid to repeat the tale of his acts of wanton wickedness: and besides, I would not wish, by repeating it, to add to the calamities of those who have not been suffered to save their children and their wives from outrage at the hands of this lecherous scoundrel."[37]

HIS CRIMES ARE COMMON KNOWLEDGE

15 At enim haec ita commissa sunt ab istō ut nōn cognita sint ab omnibus? Hominem esse arbitror nēminem quī nōmen istīus audierit,[38] quīn[39] facta quoque ējus nefāria commemorāre possit; ut mihi magis timendum sit nē multa crīmina praetermittere[40] quam nē qua in istum fingere exīstimer. Neque enim mihi vidētur haec multitūdō, quae ad audiendum convēnit, cognōscere ex mē causam[41] voluisse, sed ea quae scit mēcum recognōscere.

HE MAKES AN ELABORATE SHOW OF LEGAL DEFENSE, BUT HIS REAL HOPE IS IN HIS INTRIGUES

Quae cum ita sint, iste homō āmēns ac perditus aliā mēcum ratiōne pugnat. Nōn id agit, ut alicūjus ēloquentiam mihi appōnat;[42] nōn grātiā, nōn auctōritāte cūjusquam, nōn potentiā

WORDS TO REMEMBER

commemorō, 1, tr., *repeat, relate, mention.*
fingō, fingere, fīnxī, fictus, 3, tr., *invent* (cf. fiction, fictitious).
potentia, ae, *might, force, power* (cf. potential energy).

---

[37] *The Verrine Orations,* edited by L. H. G. Greenwood. Vol. I, pp. 79-83.

[38] **audierit = audīverit.**

[39] **quīn = quī nōn**; Gr. 651.

[40] **praetermittō, praetermittere, praetermīsī, praetermissus,** 3, tr., *let go by, pass over.*

[41] **Causa** is used here in its legal sense of *case* or *facts of the case.*

[42] **appōnō, appōnere, apposuī, appositus,** 3, tr., *place at, place near, place by.*

nītitur.[43] Simulat hīs sē rēbus cōnfīdere; sed videō quid agat—neque enim agit occultissimē! Prōpōnit inānia[44] mihi nōbilitātis,[45] hoc est, hominum arrogantium,[46] nōmina, quī nōn tam mē impediunt quod nōbilēs sunt quam adjuvant quod nōtī sunt. Simulat sē eōrum praesidiō cōnfīdere, cum intereā aliud quiddam jam diū māchinētur.

I'LL TELL YOU WHAT HE IS REALLY DOING

Quam spem nunc habeat in manibus et quid mōliātur, breviter **16**
jam, jūdicēs, vōbīs expōnam, sed prius, ut[47] ab initiō rēs ab eō
cōnstitūta sit, quaesō, cognōscite.

Ut prīmum ē prōvinciā rediit, redemptiō[48] est hūjus jūdiciī facta grandī pecūniā.[49] Mānsit in condiciōne atque pactō[50] usque

---

Words to Remember

simulō, 1, tr., *pretend* (cf. simulated, simulation).
prōpōnō, prōpōnere, prōposuī, prōpositus, 3, tr., *put forward, propose.*
tam . . . quam, *as well . . . as, as much . . . as;* negatively, *not so much . . . as.*
māchinor, 1, tr., *plot, devise.*
initium, ī, *beginning* (cf. initial).
redeō, redīre, rediī, reditum, irreg., intr., *return.*

---

43 **nītor, nītī, nīxus sum**, 3, intr.; w. abl., *rely on.*

44 **Inānia** goes with **nōmina**. Verres makes an empty show of the great names of his supporters.

45 **nōbilitās, nōbilitātis**, *nobility.*

46 **arrogāns** (*gen.* **arrogantis**), *assuming, haughty, proud* (cf. arrogant).

47 **ut**, adv., *how.*

48 **redemptiō, redemptiōnis**, *a buying up, a bargain* (cf. **emō**; Redemption). Verres made a tentative agreement with a bribery agent to have the jury 'bought up.'

49 **grandī pecūniā**: *with a large sum of money, for 'big' money.*

50 **Mānsit . . . pactō**: *It remained in the form of a conditioned agreement . . .* The condition was the type of jury ultimately chosen. When the bribery agent saw that Cicero had obtained a set of jurors more honest than usual, he threw up the business.

ad eum fīnem dum jūdicēs rejectī sunt. Posteāquam[51] rejectiō jūdicum facta est—quod in sortītiōne[52] istīus spem[53] fortūna populī Rōmānī et in rejiciendīs jūdicibus mea dīligentia istōrum
17 impudentiam vīcerat—renuntiāta est[54] tōta condiciō. Praeclārē sē rēs habēbat.[55] Libellī[56] nōminum vestrōrum, cōnsiliīque hūjus in manibus erant omnium. Nūlla nota, nūllus color, nūllae sordēs[57] vidēbantur hīs sententiīs adlinī[58] posse; cum iste repente, ex alacrī[59] atque laetō,[60] sīc erat humilis[61] atque dēmissus[62] ut nōn modo populō Rōmānō, sed etiam sibi ipse condemnātus vidērētur.

WORD TO REMEMBER

rejiciō, rejicere, rejēcī, rejectus, 3, tr., *challenge;* used of the process of selecting jurors in which the attorneys had the right to challenge the selection of undesirable persons.

---

51 **posteāquam,** adv., *after that.*

52 **sortītiō, sortītiōnis,** *choice by lot.* A certain group of prospective jurors was picked by lot; from these the final jury was selected by the *'challenging'* (**rejectiō**).

53 **istīus spem:** *Verres' hope.* **Spem** is the object of **vīcerat.**

54 **renuntiāta est:** *was renounced.*

55 **Praeclārē sē rēs habēbat:** *Everything promised well* (lit., *The affair had itself splendidly*).

56 **libellus, ī,** *list.*

57 **sordēs, sordium,** f., *smudge* (cf. sordid story).

58 **adlinō, adlinere, adlēvī, adlitus,** 3, tr., *mark, smear, daub.* Cicero is making a reference to a notorious case in which Hortensius had figured as defense attorney. The jurors voted by ballot and in this particular case a sufficient number of them had been bribed. But the defense did not trust the men whom they had bought up. So to check on their votes the ballots of the bribed jurors were colored beforehand. It was not unusual to accept bribes from both sides.

59 **alacer, alacris, alacre,** *lively* (cf. alacrity).

60 **laetus, a, um,** *joyful.*

61 **humilis, e,** *low, humble.*

62 **dēmissus, a, um,** *cast down, depressed.*

BUT HE GOES BACK TO HIS OLD GAME

Ecce autem repente, hīs diēbus paucīs, comitiīs cōnsulāribus factīs, eadem illa vetera cōnsilia pecūniā mājōre repetuntur, eaedemque vestrae fāmae fortūnīsque omnium īnsidiae per eōsdem hominēs comparantur. Quae rēs prīmō, jūdicēs, pertenuī[63] nōbīs argūmentō indiciōque patefacta est; post, apertō suspiciōnis introitū,[64] ad omnia intima[65] istōrum cōnsilia sine ūllō errōre[66] pervēnimus.

THE ELECTION OF HORTENSIUS WAS THOUGHT BY ALL TO INSURE THE ACQUITTAL OF VERRES

"What happened was this. Hortensius had just been declared **18**
consul-elect, and was being escorted home from the Campus by a
large crowd of his supporters, when it chanced that they were met
by Gaius Curio. (I do not wish my reference to this gentleman
to be taken as disparaging him, but rather the reverse. If he had
wished that the remark I am going to quote should not be repeated, he would not have made it so openly in the hearing of
so large a gathering. None the less, what I am going to say shall
be said with cautious hesitation, showing that I am mindful of
his high rank, and of the personal friendship between us.) Just **19**
near the Arch of Fabius, he noticed Verres among the crowd,
called out to him, and congratulated him loudly. He said not a
word to the newly-elected consul Hortensius himself, nor to the
relatives and friends of Hortensius who were there at the time.

Words to Remember

ecce, interjection, *behold.*
repetō, repetere, repetīvī, repetītus, 3, tr., *seek back, demand, recollect.*

---

63 **pertenuis, e,** *very fine, slender.*
64 **introitus, ūs,** *entrance, door* (cf. Introit of the Mass).
65 **intimus, a, um,** *inmost* (cf. intimate).
66 **error, errōris,** *mistake, wandering* (cf. knights errant).

No, it was Verres with whom he stopped to talk, Verres whom he embraced and told to put aside all anxiety. 'I hereby inform you,' he said, 'that today's election means your acquittal.' This remark, being overheard by a number of honest gentlemen, was forthwith reported to me; or I should rather say, everyone told me of it as soon as he saw me. Some found it distressing, others absurd: it was absurd to those who regarded the issue of the case as depending on the credit of the witnesses, the methods of the prosecution, and the Court's power to decide, not on the consular election; distressing to those who could look further beneath the surface, and saw that this speech of congratulation pointed to the corruption of the members of the Court."[67]

THIS WAS THE COMMON TALK

20 Etenim sīc ratiōcinābantur,[68] sīc honestissimī hominēs inter sē et mēcum loquēbantur: apertē jam ac perspicuē[69] nūlla esse jūdicia. Quī reus prīdiē jam ipse sē condemnātum putābat, is, posteāquam dēfēnsor ējus cōnsul est factus, absolvitur!

HAS THE INFLUENCE OF A CONSUL-ELECT MORE WEIGHT THAN EVIDENCE AND WITNESSES?

Quid igitur?[70] quod tōta Sicilia, quod omnēs Siculī, omnēs negōtiātōrēs, omnēs pūblicae prīvātaeque litterae Rōmae sunt, nihilne id valēbit? nihil, invītō[71] cōnsule dēsignātō? Quid? jūdicēs

---

WORDS TO REMEMBER

dēfēnsor, dēfēnsōris, *advocate, defender, attorney.*
negōtiātor, negōtiātōris, *wholesale merchant, businessman* (cf. **negōtium**).

---

67 *The Verrine Orations,* edited by L. H. G. Greenwood. Vol. I, pp. 85-87.
68 **ratiōcinor,** 1, intr., *reason, think.*
69 **perspicuē,** adv., *clearly* (cf. perspicuous).
70 **igitur,** adv., postp., *therefore, then.*
71 **invītus, a, um,** *unwilling, unwillingly.*

—*Courtesy of Produzione Consorzio Scipione S. A.*

SCENE ON A ROMAN COUNTRY ESTATE

Many peaceful estates such as this one in Sicily's fertile fields made unwilling contribution to Verres' 'defense fund' through the legal fiction of new and unprincipled regulations governing suburban areas. Those that survived the ruinous levies were frequently confiscated by Verres upon the death of the owner.

nōn crīmina, nōn testēs, nōn exīstimātiōnem populī Rōmānī sequentur? Nōn. Omnia in ūnīus potestātē ac moderātiōne[72] vertentur.[73]

I WAS REALLY ALARMED

Vērē loquar, jūdicēs; vehementer mē haec rēs commovēbat. Optimus enim quisque[74] ita loquēbātur, "Iste quidem tibi ēripiē-

---

WORD TO REMEMBER

exīstimātiō, exīstimātiōnis, *opinion, reputation* (cf. **exīstimō**).

---

[72] **moderātiō, moderātiōnis,** *direction.*

[73] **vertentur:** *will depend upon;* **vertō, vertere, vertī, versus,** 3, tr., *turn, turn around, change.*

[74] **Optimus enim quisque;** Gr. 835.

tur; sed nōs[75] nōn tenēbimus jūdicia diūtius. Etenim quis poterit,
21 Verre absolūtō, dē trānsferendīs jūdiciīs recūsāre?"[76] Erat omnibus molestum;[77] neque eōs tam istīus hominis perditī subita[78] laetitia quam hominis amplissimī nova grātulātiō[79] commovēbat. Cupiēbam dissimulāre mē id molestē ferre;[80] cupiēbam animī dolōrem vultū tegere[81] et taciturnitāte[82] cēlāre.[83]

AND THEN HIS FRIEND METELLUS GOT THE PRESIDENCY OF THE EXTORTION COURT

Ecce autem, illīs ipsīs diēbus, cum praetōrēs dēsignātī sortīrentur[84] et Mārcō Metellō obtigisset[85] ut is dē pecūniīs repetundīs quaereret, nuntiātur mihi tantam istī grātulātiōnem[86] esse factam ut is domum quoque mitteret quī uxōrī suae nuntiārent.

WORD TO REMEMBER

grātulātiō, grātulātiōnis, *congratulation.*

---

[75] The senatorial party.

[76] **recūsō,** 1, tr., *refuse, raise objections, protest.*

[77] **molestus, a, um,** *distressing, unpleasant.*

[78] **subitus, a, um,** *sudden, unexpected.*

[79] Cicero refers to the words of Gaius Curio.

[80] **molestē ferre:** *to bear with difficulty, to be annoyed, to be uneasy, to take ill.*

[81] **tegō, tegere, tēxī, tēctus,** 3, tr., *cover, hide* (cf. **tēctum**).

[82] **taciturnitās, taciturnitātis,** *silence.*

[83] **cēlō,** 1, tr., *conceal.*

[84] **sortior,** 4, tr., *cast lots, draw lots.*

[85] **obtingō, obtingere, obtigī,** 3, intr.; w. dat. of person, *fall to the lot of.* Eight praetors were elected. Their specific offices were assigned by lot after their election. Marcus Metellus was a close friend of Verres and the presidency of the court **dē pecūniīs repetundīs** (the court *dealing with the recovery of money,* the Court of Extortion) fell to him.

[86] Verres' friends assumed that the choice of Metellus made Verres' acquittal certain.

I SOON LEARNED WHAT WAS GOING ON. THE BRIBERY AGENTS AND WARD BOSSES WERE ORGANIZED AGAINST ME

Sānē nē haec quidem rēs mihi placēbat: neque tamen tantō 22
opere quid in hāc sorte[87] metuendum mihi esset intellegēbam.
Ūnum illud ex hominibus certīs, ex quibus omnia comperī, re-
periēbam: fiscōs complūrēs cum pecūniā Siciliēnsī ā quōdam
senātōre ad equitem Rōmānum esse trānslātōs; ex hīs quasi
decem fiscōs ad senātōrem illum relīctōs esse comitiōrum meōrum
nōmine;[88] dīvīsōrēs omnium tribuum[89] noctū ad istum vocātōs.
Ex quibus quīdam, quī sē omnia meā causā facere dēbēre arbitrā- 23
bātur, eādem illā nocte ad mē vēnit; dēmōnstrat quā iste[90] ōrātiōne ūsus esset; commemorāsse[91] istum, quam līberāliter eōs
trāctāsset[92] et jam anteā, cum ipse praetūram petīsset,[93] et proxi-

---

WORDS TO REMEMBER

sānē, adv., *indeed, truly, of course.*
fiscus, ī, *a basket* (used for transporting coins).
Siciliēnsis, e, *Sicilian.*
dīvīsor, dīvīsōris, *bribery agent.*
līberāliter, adv., *generously.*

---

[87] **sors, sortis**, *lot.*

[88] Cicero was running for aedile; the elections for this office were held after those for consul and praetor. The 'certain senator' was going to handle Cicero's defeat himself with the money left at his house.

[89] **tribus, ūs**, f., *tribe.* The Roman citizens voted in divisions known as tribes. We would talk of wards or precincts.

[90] The 'certain senator.'

[91] **commemorāsse = commemorāvisse.**

[92] **trāctō**, 1, tr., *treat;* **trāctāsset = trāctāvisset.** This senator was a 'veteran' politician, having had several dealings with the bribery agents in previous elections.

[93] **petīsset = petīvisset.**

mīs cōnsulāribus praetōriīsque comitiīs; deinde continuō[94] esse pollicitum quantam vellent pecūniam sī mē aedīlitāte dējēcissent. Hīc aliōs negāsse[95] audēre; aliōs respondisse nōn putāre id perficī posse; inventum tamen esse fortem amīcum, ex eādem familiā,[96] Quīntum Verrem[97] Rōmiliā,[98] ex optimā dīvīsōrum disciplīnā,[99] patris istīus discipulum[100] atque amīcum, quī, HS quīngentīs mīlibus[101] dēpositīs, id sē perfectūrum pollicērētur; et fuisse tamen nōnnūllōs quī sē ūnā factūrōs esse dīcerent. Quae cum ita essent, sānē benevolō[102] animō mē ut magnōpere cavērem[103] praemonēbat.[104]

Words to Remember

praetōrius, a, um, *of or belonging to praetors, praetorian.*
aedīlitās, aedīlitātis, *the aedileship.*
magnōpere, adv., *greatly.*

---

[94] **continuō,** adv., *immediately, forthwith.*

[95] **negāsse = negāvisse.**

[96] **familia, ae,** *family* (in a wide sense).

[97] Quintus Verres, a relative of Gaius Verres.

[98] **Rōmiliā:** *of the Romilian tribe;* the ablative with **tribū** understood.

[99] **ex optimā dīvīsōrum disciplīnā:** *from the best school of bribery agents* (ironical). He had his training in bribery under Verres' father.

[100] **discipulus, ī,** *student, disciple.*

[101] **HS quīngentīs mīlibus:** *500,000 sesterces.* HS is a sign for the plural of **sestertius,** a coin about five cents in value (cf. $ for dollars). Hence the sum here is something like $25,000.

[102] **benevolus, a, um,** *kindly, friendly* (cf. **benevolentia**).

[103] **caveō, cavēre, cāvī, cautum,** 2, intr., *am on my guard, am careful* (cf. caution).

[104] **praemoneō,** 2, tr., *forewarn* (cf. premonition).

THROUGH HIS LAWYERS AND BRIBERY AGENTS VERRES WAS IMPEDING BOTH MY ELECTION AND THIS TRIAL

"Within the same short space of time I had now to face more 24
than one pressing anxiety. My election was upon me; and here, as in the trial, a great sum of money was fighting against me. The trial was approaching; and in this matter also those baskets of Sicilian gold were threatening me. I was deterred by concern for my election from giving my mind freely to the business of the trial; the trial prevented my devoting my whole attention to my candidature; and to crown it all, there was no sense in my trying to intimidate the bribery-agents, since I could see they were aware that the conduct of this present trial would tie my hands
completely. It was just at this moment that I heard for the first 25
time how Hortensius had sent the Sicilians word to call on him at his house—and how they had behaved like free and independent men, refusing to go when they understood why they were being sent for. And now began my election, which Verres supposed to be under his own control, like all the other elections of this year. He flew about, this great potentate, with his amiable and popular son, canvassing the tribes, and interviewing the family friends—to wit, the bribery-agents—and summoning them to the fray. As soon as this was noticed and understood, the people of Rome, with prompt enthusisam, ensured my not being thrust out of my office by the money of a man whose wealth had failed to lure me out of my honor.

AFTER MY ELECTION I FOUND VERRES AND HIS FRIENDS ATTEMPTING TO ESCAPE THIS PRESENT JURY AND JUDGE BY DRAGGING OUT THE CASE INTO THE NEW YEAR

"Once relieved of the heavy anxieties of my candidature, I be- 26
gan, with a mind much less occupied and distracted, to devote my thoughts and energies to the trial alone. I now discovered, gentlemen, that the plan of action formed and adopted by Verres and his friends was this: so to prolong proceedings, by whatever method might be necessary, that the trial should take place under the presidency of Marcus Metellus as praetor. This would have

several advantages. First, the strong friendly support of Marcus Metellus. Next, not only Hortensius would be consul, but Quintus Metellus too, the strength of whose friendship for Verres I will ask you to note: he has indeed given so clear a preliminary token of goodwill that Verres feels himself paid in full for those preliminary votes at the election."[105]

DID YOU EXPECT ME TO BE SILENT?

27 An mē tacitūrum tantīs dē rēbus exīstimāvistis? et mē, in tantō reī pūblicae exīstimātiōnisque meae perīculō, cuiquam cōnsultūrum potius quam officiō et dignitātī meae? Arcessit alter cōnsul dēsignātus[106] Siculōs. Veniunt nōnnūllī, propterea quod[107] Lūcius Metellus esset praetor in Siciliā. Cum eīs ita loquitur: sē cōnsulem esse; frātrem suum alterum Siciliam prōvinciam obtinēre, alterum esse quaesītūrum dē pecūniīs repetundīs;[108] Verrī nē nocērī possit[109] multīs ratiōnibus esse prōvīsum.

IF THIS ISN'T INTIMIDATION . . . !

28 Quid est, quaesō, Metelle, jūdicium corrumpere, sī hoc nōn est; testēs, praesertim Siculōs, timidōs hominēs et afflīctōs,[110] nōn

---

WORDS TO REMEMBER

corrumpō, corrumpere, corrūpī, corruptus, 3, tr., *corrupt, tamper with.*
timidus, a, um, *timorous, fearful.*

---

105 *The Verrine Orations,* edited by L. H. G. Greenwood. Vol. I, pp. 91-93.

106 This consul-elect was the colleague of Hortensius, Quintus Metellus Creticus. One of his brothers, Lucius Metellus, was governor of Sicily, and his other brother, Marcus Metellus, had been selected for the Court of Extortion—a powerful family 'team' and very likely to intimidate the Sicilians.

107 **propterea quod:** *because of the fact that.*

108 **alterum . . . repetundīs:** *the other one would preside over the Court of Extortion.*

109 **Possit** is used here impersonally.

110 **afflīctus, a, um,** *calamity-stricken, distressed.*

sōlum auctōritāte dēterrēre,[111] sed etiam cōnsulārī metū et duōrum praetōrum potestāte? Quid facerēs prō innocente homine et propinquō,[112] cum propter hominem perditissimum atque aliēnissimum dē officiō ac dignitāte dēcēdis,[113] et committis ut quod ille dictitat alicui quī tē ignōrat vērum esse videātur?

VERRES BOASTS THAT YOU, HORTENSIUS, ARE HIS CREATURE

"For Verres was reported to have been saying that you were 29
made consul, not, like the rest of your family, by fate, but by
his own exertions. Well then, he will have the two consuls, and
the president of the Court, to suit him. He says to himself: 'We
shall not only escape having Manius Glabrio as President of the
Court—a man who is far too conscientious and too subservient to
considerations of the national honour. We shall also gain in the
following ways. At present one of the judges is Marcus Caesonius,
who is the colleague of our prosecutor, and whose behaviour as a
judge has already been publicly tested and approved; a man
whom it must be most undesirable to have as member of any court
that we may try in any way to corrupt; for before this, when he
was a judge in the court over which Junius presided, he did not
simply take to heart the scandalous wickedness then committed,
but took steps to expose it quickly. We shall not have this man
as a judge after the 1st of January; nor shall we have Quintus 30
Manlius and Quintus Cornificius, two judges of entirely scrupulous
and upright character, because they will then be Tribunes of the
Plebs; that stern and upright judge Publius Sulpicius will have
to enter upon his magistracy on the 5th of December; Marcus
Crepereius, who belongs to an equestrian family of the strictest
traditions, Lucius Cassius, whose family has shown the highest
integrity in judicial as in all other matters, and Gnaeus Tremellius,
who is a particularly scrupulous and conscientious man—these

---

111 **dēterreō**, 2, tr., *frighten, intimidate.*

112 **propinquus, a, um**; w. dat., *near, close, relative.*

113 **dēcēdō, dēcēdere, dēcessī, dēcessum**, 3, intr., *depart from.*

three men of the fine old school have all been designated for military tribuneships, and after the 1st of January will not be judges. We shall also be having a supplementary ballot to fill the place of Marcus Metellus, since he is to preside over this actual Court. So that after the 1st of January, both the president and practically the whole of the Court will be changed; and thus we shall baffle the formidable threats of the prosecutor, and the widespread hopes that are centred upon this trial, just as we think best and
31 feel most inclined.' Today, the 5th of August, the Court did not assemble till three o'clock: they are already reckoning that today does not count at all. It is only ten days to the Votive Games that Gnaeus Pompeius is to hold; these games will occupy fifteen days, and will be followed immediately by the Roman Games. Thus it is not till after an interval of nearly forty days that they expect to begin their reply, at least, to the charges that we on this side shall have brought against them. They count on being able then, with the help of long speeches and technical evasions, to prolong the trial till the Games of Victory begin. These games are followed without a break by the Plebeian Games, after which there will be very few days, or none at all, on which the Court can sit. In this way they reckon that all the impetus of the prosecution will be spent and exhausted, and that the whole case will come up afresh before Marcus Metellus as president of the Court. Now so far as this gentleman is concerned, I should not have retained him as
32 a member of the Court, if I had had any doubts of his honesty; but even so, my feeling is that I would prefer this issue to be decided while he is only a member of the Court, and not when he is presiding over it; I would rather trust him under oath with his own voting-tablet, than not under oath with the voting-tablets of other persons."[114]

[114] *The Verrine Orations,* edited by L. H. G. Greenwood. Vol. I, pp. 95-99.

SHALL I WIN FAME BY ORATORY AND LOSE MY PRISONER?

Nunc ego, jūdicēs, jam vōs cōnsulō quid mihi faciendum pu-
tētis. Id enim cōnsiliī[115] mihi profectō tacitī dabitis quod egomet[116]
mihi necessāriō capiendum intellegō. Sī ūtar ad dīcendum meō
lēgitimō[117] tempore, meī labōris, industriae, dīligentiaeque capiam
frūctum, et ex accūsātiōne perficiam ut nēmō umquam post hominum memoriam parātior, vigilantior, compositior[118] ad jūdicium
vēnisse videātur. Sed in hāc laude industriae meae, reus nē ēlābā-
tur, summum perīculum est. Quid est igitur quod fierī possit?
Nōn obscūrum, opīnor, neque absconditum.[119] Frūctum istum **33**
laudis quī ex perpetuā ōrātiōne percipī potuit in alia tempora re-
servēmus; nunc hominem tabulīs, testibus, prīvātīs pūblicīsque
litterīs auctōritātibusque accūsēmus. Rēs omnis mihi tēcum erit,
Hortensī.[120] Dīcam apertē: sī tē mēcum dīcendō ac dīluendīs[121]
crīminibus in hāc causā contendere putārem, ego quoque in accū-
sandō atque in explicandīs crīminibus operam cōnsūmerem. Nunc,

---

Words to Remember

necessāriō, adv., *unavoidably, necessarily.*
accūsātiō, accūsātiōnis, *charge, prosecution, method of conducting the prosecution, complaint.*
opīnor, 1, tr., *think.*
reservō, 1, tr., *reserve.*
tabula, ae, *tablet, list, record.*
explicō, 1, tr., *unfold, develop, state, explain.*
cōnsūmō, cōnsūmere, cōnsūmpsī, cōnsūmptus, 3, tr., *use up* (cf. consumption).

---

[115] What case is **cōnsiliī**? Why? Gr. 687.

[116] **egomet** = **ego** + **met** (an emphatic suffix).

[117] **lēgitimus, a, um**, *legal, allotted by law.*

[118] **compositus, a, um**, *well-prepared, with everything in order.*

[119] **abscondō, abscondere, abscondī, absconditus**, 3, tr., *put away, conceal, hide* (cf. **reconditum**; abscond).

[120] **Hortensius, ī**, *Hortensius*, one of the great lawyers and orators of Cicero's time. **Hortensī** is the vocative.

[121] **dīluō, dīluere, dīluī, dīlūtus**, 3, tr., *palliate, weaken, remove* (cf. dilute).

—*Alinari*

The Games Are On!

The Roman games contained spectacle and entertainment of every kind. Lasting for days, they occupied the whole attention of the populace. All official business was suspended. A series of such celebrations gave Hortensius—as he thought—the opportunity of protracting Verres' case so that it would come under the new and more favorable administration.

quoniam pugnāre contrā mē īnstituistī nōn tam ex tuā nātūrā quam ex istīus tempore et causā, necesse est istīus modī ratiōnī aliquō cōnsiliō obsistere.

YOUR PLAN AND MY COUNTERPLAN

Tua ratiō est, ut secundum bīnōs lūdōs[122] mihi respondēre in- 34
cipiās; mea, ut ante prīmōs lūdōs comperendinem.[123] Ita fīet ut tua ista ratiō exīstimētur astūta,[124] meum hoc cōnsilium necessārium.[125]

WHAT DO I MEAN WHEN I SAY I HAVE YOU, HORTENSIUS, TO RECKON WITH?

Vērum illud quod īnstitueram dīcere, mihi rem tēcum esse, hūjusmodī est. Ego cum hanc causam Siculōrum rogātū[126] recēpis-

---

WORDS TO REMEMBER

īnstituō, īnstituere, īnstituī, īnstitūtus, 3, tr.; w. infin., *begin, undertake.*
lūdus, ī, *game* (cf. interlude).

---

[122] **secundum bīnōs lūdōs:** *after both the festivals.* The trial had begun on August 5. The celebration in honor of the end of the war in Spain was to run from August 15 to September 1. On September 4 the **Lūdī Rōmānī** would begin and last until September 15. If Cicero used the ordinary method of giving a long introduction he would occupy all the time up to the adjournment for the Games. Hortensius felt he could fill out the time after the **bīnī lūdī** until October 27, after which other festivals would pretty well eliminate business until the new year. Thus the case would escape the present court and administration.

[123] **comperendinō,** 1, tr., *reach an agreement, adjourn.* After each side had presented its case, a date was set for the final argumentation and verdict. This setting of a date was called the **comperendinātiō.** Cicero intends to have both sides finish before the first games begin. The **comperendinātiō** would thus be forced on Hortensius and a verdict rendered before the new year.

[124] **astūtus, a, um,** *clever, ingenious* (cf. astute).

[125] **necessārius, a, um,** *necessary, urgent.*

[126] **rogātū:** *at the request of.*

sem, idque mihi amplum et praeclārum exīstimāssem,[127] eōs velle meae fideī dīligentiaeque perīculum facere[128] quī innocentiae[129] abstinentiaeque[130] fēcissent; tum susceptō negōtiō, mājus mihi quiddam prōposuī, in quō meam in rem pūblicam voluntātem

35 populus Rōmānus perspicere posset. Nam illud mihi nēquāquam[131] dignum industriā cōnātūque meō vidēbātur, istum ā mē in jūdicium, jam omnium jūdiciō condemnātum vocārī, nisi ista tua intolerābilis[132] potentia[133] et ea cupiditās quā per hōsce[134] annōs in quibusdam jūdiciīs ūsus es, etiam in istīus hominis dēspērātī[135] causā interpōnerētur. Nunc vērō, quoniam haec tē omnis dominātiō[136] rēgnumque jūdiciōrum tantō opere dēlectat, et sunt hominēs quōs libīdinis īnfāmiaeque suae neque pudeat[137] neque taedeat[138] —quī, quasi dē industriā,[139] in odium offēnsiōnemque populī Rō-

---

Words to Remember

interpōnō, interpōnere, interposuī, interpositus, 3, tr., *put between, interpose.*
offēnsiō, offēnsiōnis, *disfavor, dislike, disapproval.*

---

127 **exīstimāssem = exīstimāvissem.**

128 **perīculum facere:** *to make trial of, to test.*

129 **innocentia, ae,** *integrity, honesty.*

130 **abstinentia, ae,** *self-control.*

131 **nēquāquam,** adv., *not at all.*

132 **intolerābilis, e,** *unsupportable, intolerable.*

133 Hortensius, a much older and more powerful man than Cicero, was the leading lawyer of the day and dominated the courts. Cicero insinuates that this domination is undermining justice and is based in part on corrupt practices (**cupiditās**). By breaking Hortensius' power in this case he will free the courts and do a public and patriotic service.

134 **hōsce = hōs + ce** (an emphatic suffix).

135 **dēspērātus, a, um,** *desperate* (cf. **spēs**).

136 **dominātiō, dominātiōnis,** *domination.*

137 **pudet, pudēre, puduit,** 2, tr., *it shames, is ashamed, feel shame;* Gr. 714-716.

138 **taedet, taedēre, taeduit (taesum est),** 2, tr., *it wearies;* Gr. 714-716.

139 **dē industriā:** *of set purpose.*

mānī inruere[140] videantur—hoc mē profiteor suscēpisse magnum fortasse onus et mihi perīculōsissimum vērum tamen dignum[141] in quō omnēs nervōs[142] aetātis[143] industriaeque meae contenderem.

HERE, THEN, IS MY CHALLENGE TO BRIBERY AND CORRUPTION!

Quoniam tōtus ōrdō[144] paucōrum improbitāte et audāciā pre- 36
mitur et urgētur[145] īnfāmiā jūdiciōrum, profiteor huic generī hominum mē inimīcum accūsātōrem,[146] odiōsum,[147] assiduum,[148] acerbum adversārium.[149] Hoc mihi sūmō, hoc mihi dēposcō, quod agam in magistrātū,[150] quod agam ex eō locō[151] ex quō mē populus Rōmānus ex Kalendīs Jānuāriīs[152] sēcum agere dē rē pūblicā ac dē hominibus improbīs voluit. Hoc mūnus[153] aedīlitātis meae

---

Words to Remember

profiteor, profitērī, professus sum, 2, tr.; acc. w. infin., *avow openly, profess.*
onus, oneris, n., *burden, cargo* (cf. onerous).
acerbus, a, um, *bitter.*

---

140 **inruō, inruere, inruī,** 3, intr., *rush into.*

141 For this special usage of **dignus** with a characteristic clause see Gr. 635.

142 **nervus, ī,** *muscle.*

143 **aetās, aetātis,** *age, time of life.*

144 The senators, all of whom bore the infamy of legal corruption because of the criminal intrigues of a few. By blaming the situation on a few Cicero avoids antagonizing the whole senatorial order.

145 **urgeō, urgēre, ursī,** 2, tr., *press upon, burden.*

146 **accūsātor, accūsātōris,** *prosecutor.*

147 **odiōsus, a, um,** *hateful, troublesome* (cf. odious).

148 **assiduus, a, um,** *unrelenting, pertinacious.*

149 **adversārius, ī,** *opponent* (cf. **ad, vertō**).

150 Despite the 'well-oiled' machinery of his opponents, Cicero had been elected aedile prior to the opening of this trial.

151 As a public official in the popular assemblies.

152 **ex Kalendīs Jānuāriīs:** *from the first of January;* when he would go into office.

153 **mūnus, mūneris,** n., *function, duty, gift.*

populō Rōmānō amplissimum pulcherrimumque polliceor. Moneō, praedīcō, ante dēnuntiō;[154] quī aut dēpōnere aut accipere[155] aut recipere aut pollicērī[156] aut sequestrēs[157] aut interpretēs[158] corrumpendī jūdiciī solent esse, quīque ad hanc rem aut potentiam aut impudentiam suam professī sunt, abstineant[159] in hōc jūdiciō manūs animōsque ab hōc scelere nefāriō.

I WILL FIGHT THE WHOLE COMPANY OF CORRUPT POLITICIANS AND LAWYERS

37 "Hortensius will then be consul, endowed with supreme command and authority, while I shall be an aedile, nothing much greater than an ordinary citizen: yet the thing that I now promise to do is of such a kind, so welcome and acceptable to the people of Rome, that the consul himself must seem even less than an ordinary citizen, if that were possible, when matched against me on this issue.

"The whole story shall not only be recalled, but set forth and corroborated in detail, the story of all the judicial crimes and villainies that have been committed during the ten years since the
38 transfer of the law-courts to the Senate. The people of Rome shall learn from me how it is that, so long as the law-courts were in the hands of the Equestrian Order, for nearly fifty years together, not even the faintest suspicion rested upon one single Roman knight, gentlemen, when sitting as a judge, of accepting a bribe to give a particular verdict; how it is that, when the courts had been transferred to the Senatorial Order, and the power of the people over you as individuals had been taken away, Quintus Calidius observed, upon being convicted, that a man of praetorian

---

154 **ante dēnuntiō:** *I make this preliminary proclamation.*

155 **aut dēpōnere aut accipere:** *to receive or give deposits for bribery.*

156 **aut recipere aut pollicērī:** *to undertake to offer or to offer bribes.*

157 **sequester, sequestris,** *an agent.*

158 **interpres, interpretis,** m., *a go-between* (cf. interpreter).

159 **abstineō, abstinēre, abstinuī, abstentus,** 2, tr., *keep off, keep clear, hold off* (cf. **abstinentia**).

rank could not decently be convicted for less than thirty thousand pounds; how it is that, when Quintus Hortensius was president of the Extortion Court, the penalty inflicted on the condemned senator Publius Septimius was assessed with express reference to the fact of his having received a bribe as judge; that in the cases of
the senators Gaius Herennius and Gaius Popilius, who were both **39**
found guilty of embezzlement, and of Marcus Atilius, who was found guilty of treason, the fact was established that they had taken bribes as judges; that when Gaius Verres was presiding at a trial as City Praetor, senators were found to vote against a man whom they were condemning without having attended his trial; that a senator was once found who, when sitting as a judge, in one and the same case received money from the accused man with which to bribe the other judges, and from the prosecutor to vote
for the accused man's condemnation. And now, what words can **40**
I find to deplore that foul and disastrous blot upon the honor of our whole Order, the fact that in this land of ours, with the law-courts in the Senatorial Order's hands, such a thing happened as that the voting-tablets, given to judges who were under oath, were marked with wax of different colours? With all these facts I promise you I will deal sternly and faithfully."[160]

WHAT IF IN THIS VERY TRIAL I FIND CORRUPTION AND INTRIGUE?

Quō mē tandem animō fore putātis, sī quid in hōc ipsō jūdiciō intellēxerō similī aliquā ratiōne esse violātum atque commissum? Praesertim cum plānum facere multīs testibus possim, Gājum Verrem in Siciliā, multīs audientibus, saepe dīxisse, sē habēre

Word to Remember

plānus, a, um, *clear, plain.*

[160] *The Verrine Orations*, edited by L. H. G. Greenwood. Vol. I, pp. 105-107.

hominem potentem,[161] cūjus fīdūciā prōvinciam spoliāret: neque sibi sōlī pecūniam quaerere, sed ita triennium illud praetūrae Siciliēnsis distribūtum habēre ut sēcum praeclārē agī dīceret sī ūnīus annī quaestum[162] in rem suam converteret; alterum patrōnīs et dēfēnsōribus trāderet; tertium illum ūberrimum[163] quaestuōsissimumque[164] annum tōtum jūdicibus reservāret.

I THINK THE VERY PERSONS FOR WHOSE BENEFIT THIS LAW OF EXTORTION WAS PASSED WILL DEMAND ITS REPEAL

41 Ex quō mihi vēnit in mentem illud dīcere (quod apud Mānium Glabriōnem nūper cum in rejiciendīs jūdicibus[165] commemorāssem,[166] intellēxī vehementer populum Rōmānum commovērī), mē arbitrārī fore ut nātiōnēs exterae lēgātōs ad populum Rōmānum mitterent ut lēx dē pecūniīs repetundīs jūdiciumque tollerētur.[167] Sī enim jūdicia nūlla sint, tantum ūnumquemque ablātūrum putant, quantum sibi ac līberīs suīs satis esse arbitrētur; nunc, quod, ējusmodī jūdicia sint, tantum ūnumquemque auferre, quantum sibi, patrōnīs, advocātīs,[168] praetōrī, jūdicibus, satis futūrum

---

Words to Remember

fīdūcia, ae, *trust, confidence.*
spoliō, 1, tr., *plunder, despoil.*
patrōnus, ī, *patron.*
auferō, auferre, abstulī, ablātus, irreg., tr., *carry off, take away.*

---

161 **potēns** (*gen.* **potentis**), *powerful* (cf. **possum**).

162 **quaestus, ūs,** *gain, profit.*

163 **ūber** (*gen.* **ūberis**), *rich, fertile.*

164 **quaestuōsus, a, um,** *full of gain, profitable.*

165 **in rejiciendīs jūdicibus:** *when the challenging of the jurors was taking place.*

166 **commemorāssem = commemorāvissem.**

167 The point of the remark is more evident if we remember that this law of extortion was passed precisely to bring relief to the provincials.

168 **advocātus, ī,** *lawyer* (cf. advocate).

sit; hoc profectō īnfīnītum esse; sē avārissimī hominis cupiditātī satisfacere[169] posse, nocentissimī victōriae nōn posse.

A FINE REPUTATION, INDEED!

Ō commemoranda jūdicia praeclāramque exīstimātiōnem[170] nos- 42
trī ōrdinis! cum sociī populī Rōmānī jūdicia dē pecūniīs repetundīs fierī nōlunt, quae ā mājōribus nostrīs sociōrum causā com-
parāta sunt. An iste umquam dē sē bonam spem habuisset, nisi
dē vōbīs malam opīniōnem animō imbibisset?[171] Quō mājōre
etiam—sī fierī potest—apud vōs odiō esse dēbet quam est apud
populum Rōmānum, cum in avāritiā,[172] scelere, perjūriō,[173] vōs
suī similēs esse arbitrētur.

THIS IS A PROVIDENTIAL OPPORTUNITY!

Cui locō,[174] per deōs immortālēs, jūdicēs, cōnsulite ac prōvidēte. 43
Moneō praedīcōque—id quod intellegō—tempus hoc vōbīs dīvīnitus datum esse ut odiō, invidiā, īnfāmiā, turpitūdine tōtum ōrdinem līberētis. Nūlla in jūdiciīs sevēritās, nūlla religiō, nūlla
dēnique jam exīstimantur esse jūdicia. Itaque ā populō Rōmānō
contemnimur, dēspicimur: gravī diūturnāque[175] jam flagrāmus[176]
īnfāmiā. Neque enim ūllam aliam ob causam populus Rōmānus 44

---

[169] **satisfaciō, satisfacere, satisfēcī, satisfactum,** 3, intr.; w. dat., *make restitution to, appease.*

[170] **Ō commemoranda . . . exīstimātiōnem**; accusative of exclamation; Gr. 759.

[171] **imbibō, imbibere, imbibī,** 3, tr., *conceive, become saturated with* (lit., *drink in*).

[172] **avāritia, ae,** *avarice.*

[173] **perjūrium, ī,** *perjury.*

[174] **Cui locō:** *Against this state of affairs.*

[175] **diūturnus, a, um,** *long-standing.*

[176] **flagrō,** 1, intr., *am aflame.*

tribūnīciam[177] potestātem tantō studiō requīsīvit; quam cum poscēbat, verbō illam poscere vidēbātur, rē vērā jūdicia poscēbat. Neque hoc Quīntum Catulum,[178] hominem sapientissimum atque amplissimum, fūgit, quī Gnaeō Pompējō,[179] virō fortissimō et clārissimō, dē tribūnīciā potestāte referente,[180] cum esset sententiam rogātus, hōc initiō est summā cum auctōritāte ūsus, patrēs cōnscrīptōs jūdicia male et flagitiōsē[181] tuērī; quodsī in rēbus jūdicandīs populī Rōmānī exīstimātiōnī satisfacere voluissent, nōn tantō opere hominēs fuisse tribūnīciam potestātem dēsīderātūrōs.[182]

45 Ipse dēnique Gnaeus Pompējus, cum prīmum cōntiōnem ad urbem cōnsul dēsignātus habuit, ubi—id quod maximē exspectārī vidēbātur—ostendit sē tribūnīciam potestātem restitūtūrum, factus est in eō strepitus et grāta[183] cōntiōnis admurmurātiō.[184] Idem in

---

Words to Remember

tribūnīcius, a, um, *of tribunes.*

requīrō, requīrere, requīsīvī, requīsītus, 3, tr., *seek again, search for, demand, miss, need.*

poscō, poscere, poposcī, 3, tr.; w. acc. of person; **ab (ā)** w. abl. of person; w. acc. of thing; **ut (nē)**, *demand.*

sapiēns (*gen.* **sapientis**), *wise* (cf. a sapient remark).

strepitus, ūs, *noise* (cf. obstreperous children).

---

177 Cicero says that the recent agitation for the restoration of the tribunes with wide powers to protect the people is the result of the corrupt judiciary; a telling argument against the senators who violently opposed the tribune. Give them just courts, says Cicero—and the people will let you abolish the office of tribune.

178 Quintus Catulus, an eminent leader of the senatorial party.

179 Gnaeus Pompeius, the distinguished general and political leader.

180 **Referente** was the technical word for introducing a bill in an assembly. See Note 170, page 45.

181 **flagitiōsē,** adv., *criminally, shamefully.*

182 **voluissent . . . fuisse . . . dēsīderātūrōs;** conditional sentence in indirect discourse; Gr. 669-671.

183 **grātus, a, um;** w. dat., *acceptable, pleasing.*

184 **admurmurātiō, admurmurātiōnis,** *a murmur of approval.*

eādem cōntiōne cum dīxisset populātās[185] vexātāsque esse prōvinciās; jūdicia autem turpia ac flagitiōsa[186] fierī; et reī sē prōvidēre ac cōnsulere velle; tum vērō nōn strepitū sed maximō clāmōre suam populus Rōmānus significāvit[187] voluntātem.

THE EYES OF ROME ARE ON THIS COURT

Nunc autem hominēs in speculīs[188] sunt: observant[189] quemad- 46
modum sēsē ūnusquisque vestrum gerat in retinendā religiōne
cōnservandīsque lēgibus. Vident adhūc post lēgem tribūnīciam,
ūnum senātōrem hominem vel[190] tenuissimum esse damnātum:
quod tametsī nōn reprehendunt[191] tamen magnōpere quod laudent
nōn habent. Nūlla est enim laus, ibi esse integrum,[192] ubi nēmō
est quī aut possit aut cōnētur corrumpere. Hoc est jūdicium in 47
quō vōs dē reō, populus Rōmānus dē vōbīs jūdicābit. In hōc
homine statuētur, possitne, senātōribus jūdicantibus, homō nocen-
tissimus pecūniōsissimusque damnārī.

ACQUIT THIS MAN—YOU CONVICT YOURSELVES!

Deinde est ējusmodī reus in quō homine nihil sit praeter summa peccāta maximamque pecūniam; ut, sī līberātus sit, nūlla alia

---

WORDS TO REMEMBER

turpis, e, *shameful, base* (cf. **turpitūdō**).
tenuis, e, *fine, thin, slender, poor.*

---

[185] **populor,** 1, tr., *plunder, lay waste.*

[186] **flagitiōsus, a, um,** *criminal, shameful.*

[187] **significō,** 1, tr., *signify, express* (cf. **signum**).

[188] **specula, ae,** *a watch tower* (cf. **speculor**).

[189] **observō,** 1, tr., *watch, observe.*

[190] **vel,** adv. w. superlative, *the very, even.*

[191] **reprehendō, reprehendere, reprehendī, reprehēnsus,** 3, tr., *blame, admonish.*

[192] **integer, integra, integrum,** *honest.* The unique instance cited was no test case; the senator condemned was not a 'monied' man.

—*Courtesy of Metro-Goldwyn-Mayer*

VERRES IN SICILY

While governor in Sicily, Verres became quite a collector of art, and extortion by the illegal invasion of private homes was his favorite device for securing items for his collection. In so acting he not only flouted the Roman laws, which in common with all civilized law attempted to protect the privacy of a man's home, but he also showed his contempt for the special courts of justice known as the *quaestiōnēs perpetuae dē pecuniīs repetundīs* which had been established to deal with such violations of human rights.

suspīciō, nisi ea quae turpissima est, residēre possit. Nōn grātiā, nōn cognātiōne,[193] nōn aliīs rēctē factīs, nōn dēnique aliquō mediocrī[194] vitiō, tot tantaque ējus vitia sublevāta[195] esse vidēbuntur.

48 Postrēmō[196] ego causam sīc agam, jūdicēs, ējusmodī rēs, ita nōtās, ita testātās,[197] ita magnās, ita manifestās prōferam, ut nēmō ā vōbīs ut istum absolvātis per grātiam cōnētur contendere. Habeō

WORD TO REMEMBER

prōferō, prōferre, prōtulī, prōlātus, irreg., tr., *bring forward, extend.*

---

193 **cognātiō, cognātiōnis,** *relationship.*

194 **mediocris, e,** *moderate, small.*

195 **sublevō,** 1, tr., *lift up, palliate.*

196 **postrēmō,** adv., *at last, finally.*

197 **testātus, a, um,** *corroborated, proved by evidence.*

autem certam viam atque ratiōnem quā omnēs illōrum cōnātūs
invēstīgāre et cōnsequī possim. Ita rēs ā mē agētur ut in eōrum
cōnsiliīs omnibus nōn modo aurēs hominum, sed etiam oculī
populī Rōmānī interesse videantur. Vōs aliquot[198] jam per annōs 49
conceptam[199] huic ōrdinī turpitūdinem atque īnfāmiam dēlēre ac
tollere potestis. Cōnstat inter omnēs, post haec cōnstitūta jūdicia
quibus nunc ūtimur, nūllam hōc splendōre[200] atque hāc dignitāte
cōnsilium fuisse. Hīc sī quid erit offēnsum, omnēs hominēs nōn
jam ex eōdem ōrdine aliōs magis idōneōs—quod fierī nōn potest—
sed alium omnīnō ōrdinem ad rēs jūdicandās quaerendum arbitrā-
buntur.

LET THIS BE AN HONEST TRIAL OR ELSE . . .

Quāpropter,[201] prīmum ab dīs immortālibus, quod spērāre mihi 50
videor, hoc idem, jūdicēs, optō, ut in hōc jūdiciō nēmō improbus praeter eum quī jam prīdem inventus est reperiātur; deinde, sī plūrēs improbī fuerint, hoc vōbīs, hoc populō Rōmānō, jūdicēs, cōnfirmō, vītam mehercule[202] mihi prius quam[203] vim persevērantiamque[204] ad illōrum improbitātem persequendam dēfutūram.

Word to Remember

persequor, persequī, persecūtus sum, 3, tr., *follow through, pursue, press hard.*

---

[198] **aliquot,** indecl. adj., *some, several, a few, not many.*

[199] **conceptus, a, um,** *brought forth, conceived, incurred.*

[200] **splendor, splendōris,** *eminence, distinction.*

[201] **quāpropter,** adv., *wherefore.*

[202] **mehercule,** exclamation, *by Hercules!* Here as Cicero brings the first hearing to a solemn close, it assumes the dignity of a public oath. It could be rendered as *so may God help me.* Recall, in President Roosevelt's solemn declaration of war on Japan, the phrase, "so help us God."

[203] **prius quam = priusquam.**

[204] **persevērantia, ae,** *perseverance.*

LET THE JUDGE BE TRUE TO HIS DUTY

51 "But indeed this same scandal, for which, when once committed, I thus undertake to secure drastic punishment at the cost of toil and danger and hostility to myself, you, Manius Glabrio, with the help of your strength and wisdom and watchfulness, can prevent from coming to pass at all. Be the champion of our courts of law: be the champion of justice and integrity, of honour and conscience: be the champion of the Senate, that it may pass the test of this trial, and recover the esteem and favour of the Roman people. Think of the great place you hold, of the duty that you owe to Rome, and the tribute that you owe to your own ancestors. Remember the Acilian Law, your father's work—the law whereby the nation gained efficient courts and strictly honourable judges
52 to deal with extortion claims. You are hedged about with an army of great precedents, forbidding you to forget the high honour your family has won, reminding you night and day of your gallant father, of your wise grandfather, of your noble father-in-law. Show therefore the keen vigour of your father Glabrio, by repelling the assaults of unscrupulous knaves; show the foresight of your grandfather Scaevola, by anticipating the plots now being hatched against your honour and the honour of these gentlemen; show the steadfastness of your father-in-law Scaurus, by letting no man succeed in shaking you out of the truth and certainty of your judgment: and the people of Rome shall see, that when a man of high honour and integrity is presiding over a court of chosen judges, the accused, if he be guilty, will find that his vast fortune has tended rather to heighten belief in his guilt than to furnish him with the means of escaping his doom."[205]

I WILL NOT ALLOW THIS CASE TO DRAG ON UNTIL A NEW ADMINISTRATION IS IN

53 Mihi certum est nōn committere ut in hāc causā praetor nōbīs cōnsiliumque mūtētur. Nōn patiar rem in id tempus addūcī ut

---

[205] *The Verrine Orations,* edited by L. H. G. Greenwood. Vol. I, pp. 115-117.

Siculī quōs adhūc servī dēsignātōrum cōnsulum nōn mōvērunt,
cum eōs novō exemplō[206] ūniversōs arcesserent, eōs tum līctōrēs
cōnsulum vocent; ut hominēs miserī, anteā sociī atque amīcī
populī Rōmānī, nunc servī ac supplicēs,[207] nōn modo jūs suum
fortūnāsque omnēs eōrum imperiō āmittant,[208] vērum etiam dē-
plōrandī[209] jūris suī potestātem nōn habeant. Nōn sinam[210] pro- **54**
fectō causā ā mē perōrātā,[211] quadrāgintā[212] diēbus interpositīs,
tum nōbīs dēnique responderī cum accūsātiō nostra in oblīviō-
nem[213] diūturnitātis[214] adducta sit: nōn committam ut tum rēs jū-
dicētur cum haec frequentia tōtīus Italiae Rōmā discesserit, quae
convēnit ūnō tempore undique comitiōrum, lūdōrum, cēnsendī-
que[215] causā. Hūjus jūdiciī et laudis frūctum et offēnsiōnis perīculum vestrum, labōrem sollicitūdinemque[216] nostram, scientiam
quid agātur, memoriamque quid ā quōque dictum sit, omnium
putō esse oportēre.

I WILL ADOPT AN EXPEDITIOUS METHOD

Faciam hoc nōn novum, sed ab eīs quī nunc prīncipēs nostrae **55**
cīvitātis sunt ante factum, ut testibus ūtar statim: illud ā mē

WORD TO REMEMBER

līctor, līctōris, *lictor.*

---

206 **exemplum, ī,** *precedent.* Cicero refers to the attempt on the part of Hortensius, the consul-elect, to intimidate the Sicilian delegation.

207 **supplex, supplicis,** m., *suppliant.*

208 **āmittō, āmittere, āmīsī, āmissus,** 3, tr., *let go, lose.*

209 **dēplōrō,** 1, tr., *remonstrate (about).*

210 **sinō, sinere, sīvī, situs,** 3, tr.; acc. w. infin.; **ut (nē),** *allow, permit.*

211 **perōrō,** 1, tr., *end, conclude, close* (cf. peroration).

212 **quadrāgintā,** *forty.*

213 **oblīviō, oblīviōnis,** *oblivion.*

214 **diūturnitās, diūturnitātis,** *length of time, passage of time.*

215 **cēnsendī:** *of being enrolled in the census.*

216 **sollicitūdō, sollicitūdinis,** *anxiety.*

novum, jūdicēs, cognōscētis, quod ita testēs cōnstituam ut crīmen tōtum explicem; ut, ubi id interrogandō, argūmentīs, atque ōrātiōne firmāverō tum testēs ad crīmen accommodem:[217] ut nihil inter illam ūsitātam[218] accūsātiōnem atque hanc novam intersit,[219] nisi quod in illā tum cum omnia dicta sunt testēs dantur; hīc in singulās rēs dabuntur; ut illīs quoque eadem interrogandī facultās, argūmentandī[220] dīcendīque sit. Sī quis erit quī perpetuam ōrātiōnem accūsātiōnemque dēsīderet, alterā āctiōne audiet; nunc id quod facimus, eā ratiōne facimus ut malitiae[221] illōrum cōnsiliō
56 nostrō occurrāmus—necessāriō fierī intellegat. Haec prīmae āctiōnis erit accūsātiō.

THE CHARGE

"We submit that Gaius Verres has been guilty of many acts of lust and cruelty towards Roman citizens and Roman allies, of many outrageous offences against God and man; and that he has, moreover, illegally robbed Sicily of four hundred thousand pounds. This fact we will use witnesses, and private records, and official written statements, to make so plain to you that you will conclude that, even had we had days to spare and time to speak at leisure, there would still have been no need to speak at any great length.—I thank you, gentlemen."[222]

Word to Remember

āctiō, āctiōnis, *suit, process* (of trial), *indictment, accusation, hearing.*

---

[217] **accommodō, 1,** tr.; **ad** w. acc.; w. dat., *fit to, adapt* (cf. accommodations).

[218] **ūsitātus, a, um,** *usual.*

[219] **nihil . . . intersit; nihil interest inter . . . atque** is the idiomatic way of saying *there is no difference between . . . and . . .*

[220] **argūmentor, 1,** intr., *argue.*

[221] **malitia, ae,** *wickedness, trickery* (cf. malice).

[222] *The Verrine Orations,* edited by L. H. G. Greenwood. Vol. I, p. 121.

VERRES IS CONDEMNED

Cicero's strategy achieved its purpose. Checkmated at every point, with the weight of evidence overwhelmingly against him, Verres went into voluntary exile. In his absence, he was condemned to perpetual banishment and assessed full compensation for the Sicilians. Yet, even so, it is probable that the Sicilians never recovered a fraction of their due—perhaps too much of it had already vanished into the pockets of powerful men at Rome.

The rest of the Verrine orations Cicero published as a pamphlet to insure his reputation by showing to the world the extent of his evidence and the power of his pleading. Yet, so skillfully are they written, so dramatically and forcefully, that it is hard to believe they were never delivered in the praetor's court.

The extract which follows is one of the most striking in the whole case and brilliantly portrays the respect for the personal rights of a Roman citizen which Roman custom and law inculcated.

I HAVE KEPT MY PLEDGE TO THE SICILIANS. I COME NOW TO SPEAK ON BEHALF OF ROMAN CITIZENS—OF YOU AND ME

The Second Hearing (Book 5)

Satis est factum Siculīs, satis officiō ac necessitū- **139**
dinī,[1] jūdicēs, satis prōmissō[2] nostrō ac receptō.[3] Reliqua est ea causa, jūdicēs, quae jam nōn recepta sed innāta,[4] neque dēlāta ad mē sed in animō sēnsūque meō penitus affīxa[5] atque īnsita[6] est; quae nōn ad

[1] **necessitūdō, necessitūdinis,** *connection.* Cicero refers to the personal relations he had established with the Sicilians during his term as quaestor in the island. They remembered him as an exceptionally honest administrator.

[2] **prōmissum, ī,** *promise.*

[3] **receptum, ī,** *an engagement, an undertaking* (lit., *a thing received* or *agreed to*). Cicero had accepted the case and had therefore an obligation in justice to defend the Sicilians.

[4] **innātus, a, um,** *inborn.* Defense of Roman rights is instinctive in a Roman, a corollary of the law of self-preservation.

[5] **affīxus, a, um,** *fastened, fixed, entwined.*

[6] **īnsitus, a, um,** *placed in, residing in.*

sociōrum salūtem sed ad cīvium Rōmānōrum, hoc est ad ūnīuscūjusque nostrum, vītam et sanguinem pertinet.

DO NOT EXPECT SUBTLE REASONING OR PROTRACTED ARGUMENTS, BUT PLAIN FACTS OF WHICH ALL SICILY IS WITNESS

In quā nōlīte ā mē, quasi dubium sit aliquid, argūmenta, jūdicēs, exspectāre. Omnia quae dīcam sīc erunt illūstria ut ad ea probanda tōtam Siciliam testem adhibēre possem.

HE PUT ROMAN CITIZENS TO DEATH WITHOUT SHAME. WHAT DID THEIR CITIZENSHIP MEAN TO HIM?

Furor enim quīdam, sceleris et audāciae comes, istīus effrēnā-
tum animum importūnamque[7] nātūram tantā oppressit āmentiā
ut numquam dubitāret in conventū palam supplicia quae in con-
victōs maleficiī[8] servōs cōnstitūta sunt ea in cīvēs Rōmānōs ex-
140 prōmere.[9] Virgīs quam multōs cecīderit, quid ego commemorem?
Tantum brevissimē, jūdicēs, dīcō: nūllum fuit omnīnō cīvitātis,
istō praetōre, in hōc genere discrīmen.

EVEN HIS SUBORDINATES VIOLATED THE PERSONS OF ROMAN CITIZENS

Itaque jam cōnsuētūdine ad corpora cīvium Rōmānōrum, etiam sine istīus nūtū, ferēbātur manus ipsa līctōris.

WORDS TO REMEMBER

conventus, ūs, *meeting, assembly, assizes, community.*
virga, ae, *twig, bough, rod* (for flogging), *wand.*
caedō, caedere, cecīdī, caesus, 3, tr., *cut down, fell, strike, beat, kill.*

---

[7] **importūnus, a, um,** *savage.*
[8] **maleficium, ī,** *evil deed, crime* (cf. **male, faciō**).
[9] **exprōmō, exprōmere, exprōmpsī, exprōmptus,** 3, tr., *bring forth.*

DO YOU REMEMBER THE FORUM AT LILYBAEUM? DO YOU RECALL ONE GAIUS SERVILIUS—A ROMAN CITIZEN?

Num potes hoc negāre, Verrēs, in forō Lilybaeī,[10] maximō conventū, Gājum Servīlium, cīvem Rōmānum ē conventū Panhormitānō,[11] veterem negōtiātōrem, ad tribūnal,[12] ante pedēs tuōs, ad terram virgīs et verberibus abjectum? Audē hoc prīmum negāre, sī potes! Nēmō Lilybaeī[10] fuit quīn[13] vīderit; nēmō in Siciliā quīn[13] audierit. Plagīs cōnfectum dīcō ā līctōribus tuīs cīvem Rōmānum ante oculōs tuōs concidisse.

AND WHAT REASON DID YOU GIVE?—AS IF ANY REASON COULD EXCUSE THE VIOLATION OF ROMAN CITIZENSHIP!

At quam ob causam, dī immortālēs! Tametsī injūriam faciō **141**
commūnī causae[14] et jūrī cīvitātis; quasi enim ūlla possit esse causa cūr hoc cuiquam cīvī Rōmānō jūre accidat,[15] ita quaerō

Words to Remember

Servīlius (ī), **Gājus** (ī), *Gaius Servilius,* a Roman businessman.
verbera, verberum, n., *stripes, whipping, flogging, blows* (cf. reverberation).
plaga, ae, *blow.*
concidō, concidere, concidī, 3, intr., *fall down, collapse.*

---

[10] **Lilybaeum, ī,** *Lilybaeum,* a city in Sicily. See the map on page 159.

[11] **Panhormitānus, a, um,** *of the city of Panhormus.*

[12] **ad tribūnal:** *before the tribunal,* where judgments were given. Notice the force and dramatic value of the accumulation of details given by Cicero.

[13] **quīn;** Gr. 650-651.

[14] **commūnī causae:** *the common interest of all citizens.* "When I ask for Verres' excuse for his treatment of Servilius," Cicero says equivalently, "I do not mean to imply that there could ever be an excuse for so mistreating a Roman citizen." Verres' excuse in this instance was so outrageous that Cicero wished to make a point of it.

[15] **accidit, accidere, accidit,** 3, intr.; w. dat. of person; **ut (ut nōn),** *it happens* (cf. accident).

quae in Servīliō[16] causa fuerit. Ignōscite[17] in hōc ūnō, jūdicēs; in cēterīs enim nōn magnōpere causās requīram.

Locūtus erat līberius dē istīus improbitāte atque nēquitiā. [*Here Cicero relates how the reports of such talk were carried to Verres, how Gaius was brought to Lilybaeum for trial on a trumped-up charge, and how he violently objected in court before Verres to the illegality of the case.*]

AND HOW DID VERRES ANSWER THE JUST DEMANDS OF THIS ROMAN CITIZEN?

142 Haec[18] cum maximē loquerētur, sex līctōrēs circumsistunt, valentissimī[19] et ad pulsandōs[20] verberandōsque hominēs exercitātissimī;[21] caedunt ācerrimē virgīs; dēnique proximus līctor[22]—dē quō jam saepe dīxī—Sēxtius,[23] conversō bacillō,[24] oculōs miserō[25] tundere[26] vehementissimē coepit. Itaque ille, cum sanguis ōs

---

WORDS TO REMEMBER

verberō, 1, tr., *beat, flog* (cf. **verbera**).
ōs, ōris, n., *mouth, face, expression.*

---

[16] **in Servīliō:** *in the case of Servilius.*
[17] **ignōscō, ignōscere, ignōvī, ignōtum,** 3, intr.; w. dat., *forgive.*
[18] **Haec** refers to Servilius' objections to the illegal prosecution.
[19] **valentissimus, a, um,** *very powerful, strong-armed* (cf. **valeō**).
[20] **pulsō,** 1, tr., *strike, knock, assault* (cf. pulse).
[21] **exercitātissimus, a, um,** *very practiced, past master* (cf. **exerceō**).
[22] **proximus līctor:** *the governor's right-hand man* (lit., *the lictor next to him*).
[23] Sextius, whom Cicero mentions frequently in similar assaults.
[24] **bacillum, ī,** *stick, cane;* the lictor's official *rod* (cf. bacillus).
[25] **miserō;** dative referring to Servilius; Gr. 727.
[26] **tundō, tundere, tutudī, tūnsus,** 3, tr., *pound, strike.*

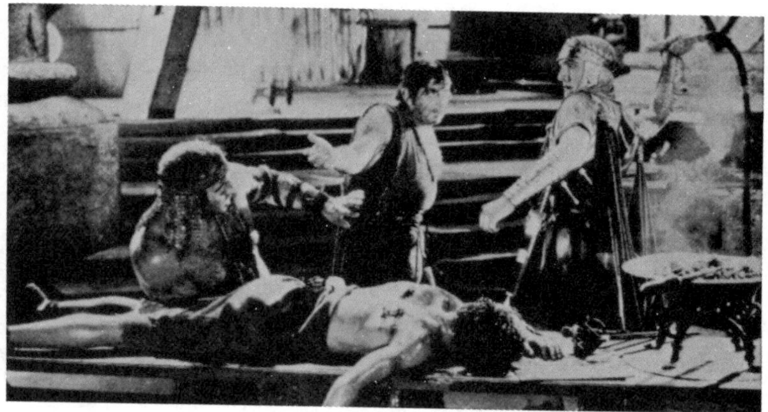

—*Courtesy of Paramount Pictures*

A Roman Torture Chamber

According to Roman law the hot iron and the scourge were reserved for slaves and noncitizens. Yet Verres applied both liberally to citizens and provincials alike to persuade them to contribute to his 'expense fund.' Protestations raised against such illegal actions such as these brought no alleviation, but rather caused Verres to proceed to even sterner measures.

oculōsque complēsset,[27] concidit. Sīc ille affectus, illinc[28] tum prō mortuō sublātus, perbrevī[29] posteā est mortuus.

BUT THIS IS ONLY ONE OF MANY SIMILAR INSTANCES

Nam quid ego dē cēterīs cīvium Rōmānōrum suppliciīs singil- 143
lātim[30] potius quam generātim[31] atque ūniversē[32] loquar? Carcer 41

Word to Remember

afficiō, afficere, affēcī, affectus, 3, tr.; w. abl., *affect, treat with.*

---

[27] **complēsset = complēvisset.**

[28] **illinc,** adv., *thence.*

[29] **perbrevī,** adv., *very shortly, soon* (cf. **brevis**).

[30] **singillātim,** adv., *individually.*

[31] **generātim,** adv., *generally.*

[32] **ūniversē,** adv., *on the whole.*

ille quī est ā crūdēlissimō tyrannō[33] Dionysiō[34] factus Syrācūsīs, quae "Lautumiae"[35] vocantur, in istīus[36] imperiō domicilium cīvium Rōmānōrum fuit.

Ut[37] quisque istīus animum aut oculōs offenderat,[38] in Lautumiās statim conjiciēbātur.

YOU ARE INDIGNANT AT THIS OF COURSE—FOR YOU EXPECT THE RIGHTS OF CITIZENSHIP TO BE RESPECTED NOT ONLY HERE BUT THROUGHOUT THE WORLD

Indignum hoc videō vidērī omnibus, jūdicēs; et id jam priōre āctiōne, cum haec testēs dīcerent, intellēxī. Retinērī enim putātis oportēre jūra lībertātis nōn modo hīc, ubi tribūnī plēbis,[39] ubi cēterī magistrātūs, ubi forum plēnum jūdiciōrum, ubi senātūs auctōritās, ubi aestimātiō[40] populī Rōmānī et frequentia, sed,

---

Words to Remember

Syrācūsae, Syrācūsārum, *Syracuse,* one of the principal cities of Sicily.
lautumiae, lautumiārum, *a stone quarry.*
indignus, a, um; w. abl., *unworthy, not deserving (of).*
plēbs, plēbis, *the people, the masses.*

---

33 **tyrannus, ī,** *tyrant.*

34 The elder Dionysius, who ruled the city of Syracuse despotically 406-367 B.C. The **Lautumiae** dated from an early period but this Dionysius enlarged it. Tyrants have their own uses for prisons and concentration camps.

35 The prison was called the Stone Quarry because it was cut out of the living rock. Places of this sort usually merit names like the Black Hole of Calcutta, the Rock (Alcatraz), and the Big House.

36 **istīus**; Verres'.

37 **ut,** *whenever;* Gr. 556.

38 **offendō, offendere, offendī, offēnsus,** 3, tr., *offend.* For the tense see Gr. 544.

39 The peculiar duty of the **tribūnī plēbis** was to protect personal rights. Their houses were open day and night to permit any citizen to make instant appeal for protection.

40 **aestimātiō, aestimātiōnis,** *judgment, appraisal.*

ubicumque[41] terrārum et gentium violātum jūs cīvium Rōmānōrum sit, statuitis id pertinēre ad commūnem causam lībertātis et dignitātis.

DID YOU DARE TO TREAT ROMAN CITIZENS LIKE THIEVES AND TRAITORS?

In externōrum hominum maleficōrum[42] scelerātōrumque, in **144**
praedōnum hostiumque custōdiās[43] tū tantum numerum cīvium Rōmānōrum inclūdere ausus es? Numquamne tibi jūdiciī, numquam cōntiōnis, numquam hūjus tantae frequentiae, quae nunc animō tē inīquissimō[44] īnfestissimōque intuētur, vēnit in mentem?[45] Numquam tibi populī Rōmānī absentis dignitās, numquam speciēs[46] ipsa hūjusce[47] multitūdinis in oculīs animōque versāta est? Numquam tē in hōrum cōnspectum reditūrum, numquam in forum populī Rōmānī ventūrum, numquam sub lēgum et jūdiciōrum potestātem cāsūrum esse dūxistī?

WHAT NOURISHED HIS MONSTROUS APPETITE FOR CRUELTY?

At quae erat ista libīdō crūdēlitātis exercendae? Quae tot sce- **145**
lerum suscipiendōrum causa? Nūlla, jūdicēs—praeter praedandī[48]

Words to Remember

praedō, praedōnis, m., *pirate, robber.*
cōnspectus, ūs, *sight, vision.*
cadō, cadere, cecidī, cāsūrus, 3, intr., *fall, am slain.*

---

41 **ubicumque,** adv., *wherever.* For **terrārum** and **gentium** see Gr. 691.

42 **maleficus, a, um,** *wicked* (cf. **maleficium**).

43 **custōdiās:** *prisons intended for . . .*

44 **inīquus, a, um,** *uneven, unjust, unfavorable.*

45 **Numquam . . . vēnit in mentem:** *Did there never come into your mind (the thought) of . . .*

46 **speciēs, speciēī,** *appearance.*

47 **hūjusce = hūjus + ce** (an emphatic suffix).

48 **praedor, 1,** intr., *get booty, plunder.*

novam singulāremque ratiōnem. Quaecumque enim nāvis ex Asiā,[49] quae ex Syriā, quae Tyrō,[50] quae Alexandrīā[51] vēnerat, statim certīs indicibus et custōdibus[52] tenēbātur; vectōrēs[53] omnēs in Lautumiās conjiciēbantur; onera atque mercēs in praetōriam domum[54] dēferēbantur.

146 At quae causa tum subjiciēbātur ab ipsō, jūdicēs, hūjus tam nefāriae crūdēlitātis? Eadem quae nunc in dēfēnsiōne commemorābitur.

LET ANYONE COME TO SICILY WITH RICH MERCHANDISE, "AHA!" CRIES OUR VIGILANT GOVERNOR, "A TRAITOR! TO THE STONE QUARRY: THE WEALTH TO MY HOME FOR SAFEKEEPING!"

Quīcumque accesserant ad Siciliam paulō plēniōrēs, eōs Sertōriānōs[55] mīlitēs esse atque ā Diāniō[56] fugere dīcēbat.

Words to Remember

nāvis, nāvis, *ship.*
Syria, ae, *Syria.*
index, indicis, m., *accuser, informer.*
merx, mercis, *merchandise.*
dēfēnsiō, dēfēnsiōnis, *the defense* (in a trial).

---

[49] **Asia, ae,** *Asia (Minor).*

[50] **Tyrus, ī,** f., *Tyre.*

[51] **Alexandrīa, ae,** *Alexandria.* Cicero mentions the more important ports and countries of the Mediterranean with which Sicily carried on extensive commerce.

[52] Verres had stationed groups of professional informers and squads of special police at all the ports to handle these cases.

[53] **vector, vectōris,** *voyager.*

[54] Cicero refers to the official residence of the governor. Verres did not leave the confiscated goods in the hands of the police.

[55] **Sertōriānus, a, um,** *Sertorian.* Sertorius was leader of a revolt in Spain. Verres would accuse these wealthy merchants of being fugitives from the dispersed armies of Sertorius, attempting by their disguise to escape the penalty of their treason.

[56] **Diānium, ī,** *Dianium;* a promontory in Spain used as a base by Sertorius.

—*Courtesy of Paramount Pictures*

A ROYAL PLEASURE YACHT ON A ROMAN LAKE

It was for luxuries such as these that the Romans reaped the wealth of the provinces of the Roman Empire. Especially during the imperial period these sumptuous yachts of the emperors, their extensive palaces furnished without thought of expense, and the protracted and costly banquets which they held were but applications on a grander scale of the principle of the right to plunder at will by which Verres lived.

Illī ad dēprecandum perīculum prōferēbant aliī purpuram Tyriam,[57] tūs[58] aliī atque odōrēs[59] vestemque linteam,[60] gemmās[61] aliī et margarītās,[62] vīna nōnnūllī Graeca[63] vēnālēsque Asiāticōs[64] ut intellegerētur ex mercibus quibus ex locīs nāvigārent.

Nōn prōvīderant eās ipsās sibi causās esse perīculī quibus argūmentīs[65] sē ad salūtem ūtī arbitrābantur. Iste enim haec eōs

---

[57] **purpura (ae) Tyria (ae),** *Tyrian purple;* a cloth famous in the ancient world.

[58] **tūs, tūris,** *incense.*

[59] **odor, odōris,** *odor.* Translate *perfumes.*

[60] **vestis (is) lintea (ae),** *linen fabric.*

[61] **gemma, ae,** *precious stone.*

[62] **margarīta, ae,** *pearl* (cf. Margaret).

[63] **vīnum (ī) Graecum (ī),** *Greek wine.*

[64] **vēnālēs Asiāticōs:** *Asiatic slaves* (lit., *Asiatics for sale*).

[65] **Argūmentīs** is in apposition with **quibus;** *as arguments, as proofs.*

ex pīrātārum societāte adeptōs esse[66] dīcēbat. Ipsōs in Lautumiās abdūcī[67] imperābat. Nāvēs atque onera diligenter asservanda[68] cūrābat.

AND ONCE IN PRISON THESE ROMAN CITIZENS WERE SLAUGHTERED WHOLESALE

147 Hīs īnstitūtīs cum complētus jam mercātōrum carcer esset, tum illa fīēbant quae Lūcium Suettium,[69] equitem Rōmānum, lēctissimum virum, dīcere audīstis, et quae cēterōs audiētis. Cervīcēs in carcere frangēbantur indignissimē cīvium Rōmānōrum, ut illa vōx et implōrātiō, "Cīvis Rōmānus sum," quae saepe multīs in ultimīs terrīs opem inter barbarōs et salūtem tulit, ea mortem illīs acerbiōrem et supplicium mātūrius[70] ferret.

DO YOU DARE DENY THESE STATEMENTS OR EVEN ACCUSE ME OF EXAGGERATION?

Quid est, Verrēs? quid ad haec cōgitās respondēre? Num mentīrī[71] mē? num fingere aliquid? num augēre[72] crīmen? Num

---

Words to Remember

pīrāta, ae, m., *pirate.*
asservō, 1, tr., *keep in custody.*
īnstitūtum, ī, *design, practice, device, institution.*
lēctissimus, a, um, *excellent.*
implōrātiō, implōrātiōnis, *entreaty, pleading.*

---

[66] **adipiscor, adipiscī, adeptus sum,** 3, tr., *reach, obtain, get possession of.*

[67] **abdūcō, abdūcere, abdūxī, abductus,** 3, tr., *lead away.*

[68] For the use of the gerundive with **cūrō** see Gr. 883.

[69] Lucius Suettius, one of Cicero's witnesses.

[70] **mātūrius,** adv., *sooner, more quickly.*

[71] **mentior,** 4, intr., *lie.*

[72] **augeō, augēre, auxī, auctus,** 2, tr., *increase, exaggerate.*

quid[73] hōrum dīcere istīs tuīs dēfēnsōribus audēs? Cedō[74] mihi, quaesō, ex ipsīus sinū[75] litterās Syrācūsānōrum quās iste ad arbitrium suum cōnfectās esse arbitrātur; cedō[74] ratiōnem carceris, quae dīligentissimē cōnficitur, quō quisque diē datus in custōdiam, quō mortuus, quō necātus sit.

[*The records from Syracuse are here read by the clerk. Cicero* **148**
goes on to prove from them that all the imprisoned Roman citi-
zens were murdered.]

ROME HAS WAGED MANY A WAR TO AVENGE JUST SUCH OUTRAGES AGAINST HER CITIZENS

Sī quī[76] rēx, sī qua[76] cīvitās exterārum gentium, sī qua[76] nātiō **149**
fēcisset aliquid in cīvēs Rōmānōs ējusmodī, nōnne pūblicē vindicārēmus? nōnne bellō persequerēmur? Possēmus hanc injūriam ignōminiamque nōminis Rōmānī inultam[77] impūnītamque dīmittere? Quot bella mājōrēs nostrōs et quanta suscēpisse arbitrāminī, quod cīvēs Rōmānī injūriā affectī, quod nāviculāriī[78] retentī, quod mercātōrēs spoliātī dīcerentur?

Words to Remember

Syrācūsānī, Syrācūsānōrum, *the Syracusans, the inhabitants of Syracuse.*
arbitrium, ī, *will, desire, judgment, wish* (cf. arbitrary; **arbitror**).
necō, 1, tr., *kill, murder* (cf. **nex**).

---

[73] **quid = aliquid.**

[74] **cedō:** *give;* irregular imperative.

[75] **sinus, ūs,** *fold;* here referring to the fold of the toga over the breast, a place where papers might be carried—i. e., out of Verres' own documents. We might say "out of his own brief case."

[76] **quī, qua (quae), quod,** *some, any;* Gr. 841.

[77] **inultus, a, um,** *unavenged, unrevenged* (cf. **ulcīscor**).

[78] **nāviculārius, ī,** *seaman* (cf. **nāvis**).

I AM NOT COMPLAINING MERELY ABOUT THE ARREST AND ROBBERY OF ROMAN CITIZENS

At ego jam retentōs nōn queror. Spoliātōs ferendum putō. Nāvibus, mancipiīs,[79] mercibus ademptīs,[80] in vincula mercātōrēs esse conjectōs et IN VINCULĪS CĪVĒS RŌMĀNŌS NECĀTŌS ESSE arguō.[81]

MY CHARGES WOULD AROUSE INDIGNATION EVEN AMONG FOREIGNERS; FOR THE RIGHTS OF ROMAN CITIZENS ARE EVERYWHERE KNOWN AND RESPECTED

150 Sī haec apud Scythās[82] dīcerem, nōn hīc in tantā multitūdine cīvium Rōmānōrum, nōn apud senātōrēs, lēctissimōs cīvitātis, nōn in forō populī Rōmānī dē tot et tam acerbīs suppliciīs cīvium Rōmānōrum, tamen animōs etiam barbarōrum hominum permovērem. Tanta enim hūjus imperiī amplitūdō,[83] tanta nōminis Rōmānī dignitās est apud omnēs nātiōnēs, ut ista in nostrōs hominēs crūdēlitās nēminī concessa esse videātur.

[*At this point Cicero takes up Verres' alleged charge that the men he put to death were escaped Sertorians, rebels against the Roman government. Cicero shows that, even if true, there was no justification for the action of the governor. The government had, in practical policy at least, pardoned the rebels after the defeat of Sertorius; moreover, Verres, with his criminal record, was*

Word to Remember

queror, querī, questus sum, 3, tr., *complain of, lament* (cf. **querimōnia**).

---

[79] **mancipium, ī,** *a taking by the hand* (**manus** + **capiō**), an old Roman form for the purchase of any property in the presence of five witnesses; translate *slave.*

[80] **adimō, adimere, adīmī, ademptus,** 3, tr.; w. dat. of person, *take away.*

[81] **arguō, arguere, arguī,** 3, tr., *maintain, charge.*

[82] **Scytha, ae,** m., *a Scythian.* The Scythians were barbarians in Asia. They are used as a symbol for remote and unknown peoples. We might say "in Tibet" or "in central Africa."

[83] **amplitūdō, amplitūdinis,** *renown, honor.*

not the man to become a zealot in hunting down the revolutionaries. But the charge was false as well. By the testimony of direct witnesses Cicero proves that these citizens in question were well-known merchants, men innocent of crime and rebellion alike.]

WHY DID YOU BEGIN TO EXECUTE ROMAN CITIZENS WITH THEIR HEADS COVERED? THE OUTCRY AGAINST YOU HAD MADE YOU NOT MORE MERCIFUL BUT MORE CAUTIOUS

Quid dē illā multitūdine dīcēmus quī, capitibus involūtīs, in **156**
pīrātārum captīvōrumque[84] numerō prōdūcēbantur ut secūrī ferīrentur? Quae ista nova dīligentia? Quam ob causam abs tē ex-
cōgitāta?[85] An tē Lūciī Flāviī[86] cēterōrumque dē Lūciō Hērenniō[87]
vōciferātiō commovēbat? An Mārcī Anniī,[88] gravissimī atque
honestissimī virī, summa auctōritās paulō dīligentiōrem timidiō-
remque fēcerat? quī nūper prō testimōniō, nōn advenam[89] nesciōquem nec aliēnum, sed eum cīvem Rōmānum quī omnibus in illō
conventū nōtus, quī Syrācūsīs nātus esset, abs tē secūrī percus-
sum esse[90] dīxit. Post hanc illōrum vōciferātiōnem, post hanc **157**

Words to Remember

involūtus, a, um, *covered.*
prōdūcō, prōdūcere, prōdūxī, prōductus, 3, tr., *lead forth, protect, bring forth.*
secūris, secūris (abl. -ī), *axe.*
feriō, ferīre, 4, tr., *strike.*
vōciferātiō, vōciferātiōnis, *outcry* (cf. **vōx**; vociferous).
testimōnium, ī, *proof, testimony, witness.*
nesciōquī, nesciōqua, nesciōquod, *some;* Gr. 819.

---

84 **captīvus, ī,** *prisoner, captive.*
85 **excōgitō,** 1, tr., *think out.*
86 Lucius Flavius, a Roman citizen and merchant.
87 Lucius Herennius, another Roman citizen, also a merchant.
88 Marcus Annius, a distinguished Roman citizen.
89 **advena, ae,** *stranger, guest.*
90 **percutiō, percutīre, percussī, percussus,** 4, tr., *strike, beat.*

commūnem fāmam atque querimōniam,[91] nōn mītior[92] in suppliciō sed dīligentior esse coepit.

Capitibus involūtīs cīvēs Rōmānōs ad necem prōdūcere īnstituit —quōs tamen idcircō necābat palam, quod hominēs in conventū (id quod anteā dīxī) nimium dīligenter praedōnum numerum requīrēbant.

THIS THEN WAS THE PROTECTION GIVEN OUR CITIZENS DURING YOUR ADMINISTRATION IN SICILY

Haecine[93] plēbī Rōmānae, tē praetōre, est cōnstitūta condiciō, haec negōtiī gerendī spēs, hoc capitis vītaeque discrīmen?[94] Parumne multa[95] mercātōribus sunt necessāriō perīcula subeunda[96] fortūnae, nisi etiam hae formīdinēs[97] ab nostrīs magistrātibus atque in nostrīs prōvinciīs impendēbunt?

BY EVERY RIGHT THIS SICILY SHOULD HAVE BEEN A HAVEN AND A HOME TO ROMAN CITIZENS

Ad eamne rem fuit haec suburbāna[98] ac fidēlis[99] Sicilia, plēna optimōrum sociōrum honestissimōrumque cīvium, quae cīvēs Rōmānōs omnēs suīs ipsa sēdibus libentissimē[100] semper accēpit, ut, quī usque ex ultimā Syriā atque Aegyptō[101] nāvigārent, quī

WORD TO REMEMBER

idcircō, adv., *therefore, for this reason.*

---

91 **querimōnia, ae,** *complaint* (cf. querulous).

92 **mītis, e,** *gentle, merciful.*

93 **haecine = haec + ci** (emphatic suffix) **+ ne** (interrogative enclitic).

94 **capitis vītaeque discrīmen:** *danger to life and limb.*

95 **parum multa:** *too few.*

96 **subeō, subīre, subiī, subitum,** irreg., intr., *undergo.*

97 **formīdō, formīdinis,** *fear, dread.*

98 **suburbānus, a, um,** *suburban, near Rome.*

99 **fidēlis, e,** *loyal* (cf. fidelity).

100 **libentissimē,** adv., *most willingly.*

101 **Aegyptus, ī,** f., *Egypt.*

apud barbarōs propter togae[102] nōmen in honōre aliquō fuissent, quī ex praedōnum īnsidiīs, quī ex tempestātum perīculīs profūgissent, in Siciliā secūrī ferīrentur, cum sē jam domum vēnisse arbitrārentur?

HOW CAN I ADEQUATELY PRESENT THE INCREDIBLE CASE OF PUBLIUS GAVIUS?

Nam quid ego dē Pūbliō Gāviō, Cōnsānō mūnicipe, dīcam, **158**
jūdicēs? aut quā vī vōcis, quā gravitāte verbōrum, quō dolōre animī dīcam? tametsī dolor nōn dēficit; ut[103] cētera[104] mihi in dīcendō digna rē, digna dolōre meō suppetant,[105] magis labōrandum est. Quod crīmen ējusmodī est ut, cum prīmum ad mē dēlātum est, ūsūrum mē illō nōn putārem; tametsī enim vērissimum esse intellegēbam, tamen crēdibile[106] fore nōn arbitrābar. Coāctus lacrimīs omnium cīvium Rōmānōrum quī in Siciliā negōtiantur, adductus Valentīnōrum,[107] hominum honestissimōrum, omniumque

---

WORDS TO REMEMBER

Gāvius (ī), **Pūblius** (ī), *Publius Gavius,* a Roman citizen carrying on business in Sicily.
Cōnsānus, a, um, *of Consa,* a town in Italy.
mūniceps, mūnicipis, m., *burgess, citizen, fellow-citizen.*
gravitās, gravitātis, *weight, solemnity, seriousness* (cf. gravity).
lacrima, ae, *tear* (cf. lacrimal glands).
negōtior, 1, intr., *carry on business, engage in trade.*

---

102 **toga, ae,** *the toga;* used here as symbolic of Roman citizenship since the toga was the distinctive dress of Romans, just as kilts are of Scotchmen or the fez of Mohammedans.

103 **Ut** depends on **labōrandum est.**

104 **cētera**; eloquence, force, etc. Sorrow, says Cicero, is indeed present; it is only necessary to make the other things (**cētera**) worthy of the subject.

105 **suppetō, suppetere, suppetīvī,** 3, intr., *am at hand, hold out.*

106 **crēdibilis, e,** *credible.*

107 **Valentīnī, Valentīnōrum,** *the inhabitants of Vibo* (also known as Valentia), a town in southern Italy.

Rhēgīnōrum testimōniīs multōrumque equitum Rōmānōrum, quī cāsū tum Messānae fuērunt, dedī tantum priōre āctiōne testium, rēs ut nēminī dubia esse posset.

HIS LESSER CRIMES HAVE EXHAUSTED MY TIME AND MY VOCABULARY. HOW SHALL I DESCRIBE THIS CROWNING DEED OF SHAME?

159 Quid nunc agam?[108] Cum jam tot hōrās dē ūnō genere ac dē istīus nefāriā crūdēlitāte dīcam, cum prope omnem vim verbōrum ējusmodī quae scelere istīus digna sint aliīs in rēbus cōnsūmpserim, neque hoc prōvīderim ut varietāte crīminum vōs attentōs[109] tenērem,[110] quemadmodum dē tantā rē dīcam?

I WILL LET THE BARE FACT SPEAK FOR ITSELF

Opīnor, ūnus modus atque ūna ratiō est. Rem in mediō pōnam, quae tantum habet ipsa gravitātis ut neque mea—quae nūlla est—neque cūjusquam ad īnflammandōs vestrōs animōs ēloquentia requīrātur.

HERE ARE THE FACTS

160 Gāvius hic, quem dīcō, Cōnsānus, cum in illō numerō cīvium Rōmānōrum ab istō in vincula conjectus esset et, nesciō quā ratiōne,[111] clam ē Lautumiīs profūgisset Messānamque vēnisset—quī

Words to Remember

Rhēgīnī, Rhēgīnōrum, *the inhabitants of Rhegium,* a city in southern Italy just across the strait from Sicily.
cāsū, adv., *by chance.*
Messāna, ae, *Messina.*

---

[108] **agam**; Gr. 510.
[109] **attentus, a, um,** *attentive.*
[110] For the tense of **tenērem** see Gr. 539.
[111] **nesciō quā ratiōne:** *I know not by what means, somehow or other.*

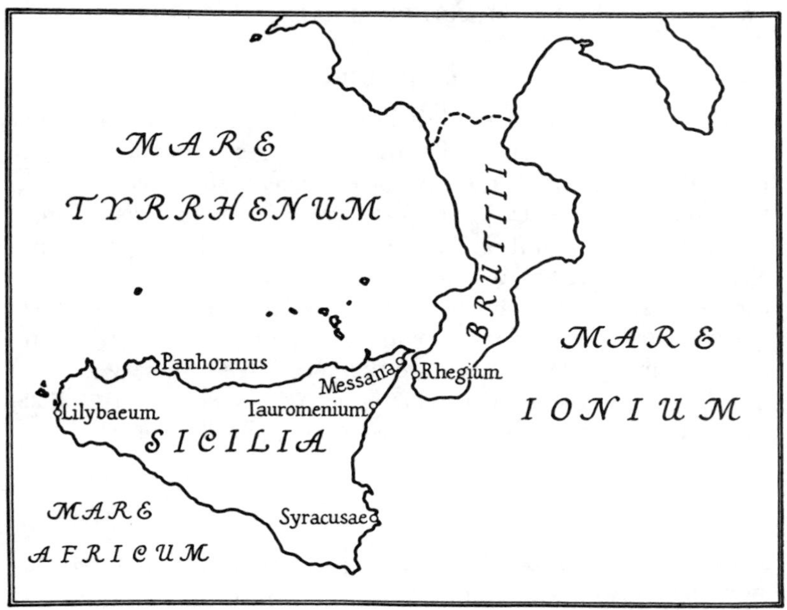

At the narrowest point of the Strait of Messina Italian soil is but two and a half miles from the Sicilian seacoast, but this might as well have been a hundred miles for Publius Gavius of Consa as he hung on his cross and paid with his life for threatening to bring Verres to court on a charge of illegal arrest.

tam prope jam Italiam et moenia Rhēgīnōrum[112] vidēret et ex illō metū mortis ac tenebrīs quasi lūce lībertātis et odōre[113] aliquō lēgum recreātus revīxisset[114]—loquī Messānae et querī coepit sē cīvem Rōmānum in vincula conjectum, sibi rēctā[115] iter esse Rōmam, Verrī sē praestō[116] advenientī futūrum.

---

112 Gavius could look across the strait from Messina and see this free Roman town.

113 **odor, odōris,** *odor.* Translate *fresh air, atmosphere.*

114 **revīvīscō, revīvīscere, revīxī,** 3, intr., *am revived, breathe freely.*

115 **rēctā,** adv., *directly, straightway.* Gavius' big mistake was to start threatening Verres before he had cleared the shores of Sicily.

116 **praestō,** adv., *at hand.* Gavius would wait at Rome to prosecute Verres on his return from Sicily.

GAVIUS IS ARRESTED

Nōn intellegēbat miser nihil interesse[117] utrum haec Messānae an apud ipsum in praetōriō[118] loquerētur. Nam, ut anteā vōs docuī, hanc sibi iste urbem dēlēgerat[119] quam habēret adjūtrīcem[120] scelerum, fūrtōrum receptrīcem,[121] flāgitiōrum[122] omnium cōnsciam.[123] Itaque ad magistrātum Māmertīnum statim dēdūcitur Gāvius, eōque ipsō diē cāsū Messānam Verrēs venit. Rēs ad eum dēfertur: esse cīvem Rōmānum quī Syrācūsīs in Lautumiīs sē fuisse quererētur, quem, jam ingredientem nāvem et Verrī nimis[124] atrōciter[125] minitantem,[126] ā sē[127] retrāctum[128] esse et asservātum, ut ipse in eum statueret quod vidērētur. Agit hominibus grātiās, et eōrum benevolentiam ergā sē dīligentiamque collaudat.[129]

Word to Remember

Māmertīnus, a, um, *Mamertine, of Messina*. The inhabitants of Messina were called Mamertines.

---

[117] **nihil interesse:** *it made no difference, it mattered little.*

[118] **praetōrium, ī,** *the governor's house.*

[119] Verres had involved the officials of Messina in his crimes and his profits in order to bind the city to him as an ally. Gavius was as dangerous to the magistrates of Messina as to Verres himself.

[120] **adjūtrīx, adjūtrīcis,** m., *accomplice, helper, assistant* (cf. **adjuvō**).

[121] **receptrīx, receptrīcis,** m., *receiver* (cf. **recipiō**).

[122] **flāgitium, ī,** *outrage, shameful deed.*

[123] **cōnscius, a, um,** *sharing in the knowledge, privy to;* used of those who have guilty knowledge of crimes.

[124] **nimis,** adv., *too much, too.*

[125] **atrōciter,** adv., *angrily.*

[126] **minitor,** 1, intr.; w. dat., *threaten.*

[127] The officials of Messina are speaking. They seized Gavius.

[128] **retrahō, retrahere, retrāxī, retrāctus,** 3, tr., *drag back.* They dragged Gavius off the boat.

[129] **collaudō,** 1, tr., *praise* (cf. **laudō**).

FURIOUS ANGER OF VERRES

Ipse īnflammātus scelere et furōre in forum vēnit. Ārdēbant 161
oculī. Tōtō ex ōre crūdēlitās ēminēbat.[130] Exspectābant omnēs, quō tandem prōgressūrus aut quidnam[131] āctūrus esset—cum repente hominem[132] prōripī[133] atque in forō mediō nūdārī[134] ac dēligārī et virgās expedīrī[135] jubet.

CIVIS ROMANUS SUM!

Clāmābat ille miser SĒ CĪVEM ESSE RŌMĀNUM, mūnicipem Cōnsānum; meruisse[136] cum Lūciō Raeciō, splendidissimō[137] equite Rōmānō, quī Panhormī negōtiārētur, ex quō haec Verrēs scīre posset.

"A SPY!"—VERRES

Tum iste sē[138] comperisse eum speculandī[139] causā in Siciliam ab ducibus fugitīvōrum[140] esse missum; cūjus reī neque index,

---

WORDS TO REMEMBER

dēligō, 1, tr., *fasten (down), tie.*
Raecius (ī), **Lūcius** (ī), *Lucius Raecius,* a prominent Roman.
Panhormus, ī, f., *Panhormus,* a city in Sicily.

---

130 **ēmineō, ēminēre, ēminuī,** 2, intr., *shine forth, gleam out* (cf. eminent).

131 **quisnam, quaenam, quidnam,** interrog. pron., *who, what.*

132 **hominem**; Gavius.

133 **prōripiō, prōripere, prōripuī, prōreptus,** 3, tr., *drag out, drag forth.*

134 **nūdō, 1,** tr.; w. abl., *make bare, strip* (cf. **nūdus**).

135 **expediō,** 4, tr., *bring forth, provide.*

136 **mereō,** 2, tr., *merit, deserve.* Here it is a short form of the technical term for serving in the army, **stīpendia merēre.** Gavius was a veteran and had seen service with Lucius Raecius, a prominent Roman.

137 **splendidus, a, um,** *distinguished.*

138 A verb of saying (e. g., **dīxit**) is understood.

139 **speculor, 1,** intr., *spy.*

140 **fugitīvus, ī,** *fugitive, deserter;* the slaves under Spartacus who were at this time fighting off Roman armies in southern Italy.

neque vēstīgium[141] aliquod, neque suspīciō cuiquam esset ūlla; deinde jubet undique hominem vehementissimē verberārī.

FROM THE LASH GAVIUS HAD ONE APPEAL

162 Caedēbātur virgīs in mediō forō Messānae cīvis Rōmānus, jūdicēs; cum intereā nūllus gemitus, nūlla vōx alia illīus miserī inter dolōrem crepitumque[142] plāgārum audiēbātur nisi haec, "CĪVIS RŌMĀNUS SUM!" Hāc sē commemorātiōne cīvitātis omnia verbera dēpulsūrum cruciātumque ā corpore dējectūrum arbitrābātur.[143] Is nōn modo hoc nōn perfēcit ut virgārum vim dēprecārētur, sed, cum implōrāret saepius ūsūrpāretque[144] nōmen cīvitātis, crux, crux, inquam, īnfēlīcī[145] et aerumnōsō,[146] quī numquam istam pestem vīderat comparābātur.

LIBERTY! JUSTICE!

163 Ō nōmen dulce[147] lībertātis! Ō jūs eximium[148] nostrae cīvitātis!

Words to Remember

gemitus, ūs, *groan.*
commemorātiō, commemorātiōnis, *mention, proclaiming* (cf. **commemorō**).
cruciātus, ūs, *torture.*
implōrō, 1, tr.; w. acc. of person and **ut** (**nē**); **ab** (**ā**) w. abl. of person and acc. of thing, *entreat.*

---

141 **vēstīgium, ī,** *clue, trace* (cf. vestige).

142 **crepitus, ūs,** *sound* (cf. **increpō**).

143 It was unconstitutional to scourge Roman citizens even when guilty of crimes.

144 **ūsūrpō,** 1, tr., *use, make use of.*

145 **īnfēlīx** (*gen.* **īnfēlīcis**), *hapless, unhappy.*

146 **aerumnōsus, a, um,** *wretched, full of hardship.*

147 **dulcis, e,** *sweet.*

148 **eximius, a, um,** *glorious, proud.*

Ō Lēx Porcia[149] Lēgēsque Semprōniae![150] Ō graviter dēsīderāta et aliquandō reddita[151] plēbī Rōmānae tribūnīcia potestās! Hūcine[152] tandem omnia reccidērunt[153] ut cīvis Rōmānus in prōvinciā populī Rōmānī, in oppidō foederātōrum,[154] ab eō quī beneficiō[155] populī Rōmānī fascēs[156] et secūrēs habēret dēligātus in forō virgīs caederētur?

TORTURE!

Quid? cum ignēs candentēsque[157] lāminae[158] cēterīque cruciātūs admovēbantur,[159] sī tē illīus acerba implōrātiō et vōx miserābilis[160] nōn inhibēbat,[161] nē cīvium quidem Rōmānōrum quī tum aderant flētū[162] et gemitū maximō commovēbāre?[163]

I DID NOT WISH TO PRESS THIS CHARGE IN THE EARLIER HEARING

In crucem tū agere ausus es quemquam quī sē cīvem Rōmānum esse dīceret? Nōluī tam vehementer agere hoc prīmā āctiōne, jū-

---

149 **Lēx Porcia**: *the Law of Porcius.* This law forbade the scourging of Roman citizens.

150 **Lēgēs Semprōniae**: *the Laws of Sempronius.* By this legislation a Roman citizen could appeal to the popular assembly at Rome against any death sentence, a right equivalent to our trial by jury. Cicero appeals to these basic laws as we would to the Constitution or the Bill of Rights.

151 **reddō, reddere, reddidī, redditus,** 3, tr., *give back.*

152 **hūcine** = **hūc** *(hither)* + **ci** (emphatic suffix) + **ne.**

153 **recidō, recidere, reccidī,** 3, intr., *fall back* (cf. recede).

154 **foederātus, a, um,** *federated;* towns guaranteed special privileges by Rome.

155 **beneficium, ī,** *benefit, good deed* (cf. **bene, faciō, maleficium**).

156 **fascēs, fascium,** f., *the lictor's rods* (cf. fascism). The rods and axes were the symbols of the power of a Roman magistrate.

157 **candēns** (*gen.* **candentis**), *white-hot.*

158 **lāmina, ae,** *metal plate.*

159 **admoveō, admovēre, admōvī, admōtus,** 2, tr., *apply.*

160 **miserābilis, e,** *wretched, pitiful.*

161 **inhibeō,** 2, tr., *restrain* (cf. inhibition).

162 **flētus, ūs,** *weeping, tears.*

163 **commovēbāre** = **commovēbāris.**

dicēs—nōluī. Vīdistis enim ut[164] animī multitūdinis in istum dolōre et odiō et commūnis perīculī metū concitārentur.

Statuī egomet[165] mihi tum modum et ōrātiōnī meae et Gājō Numitōriō, equitī Rōmānō, prīmō hominī, testī meō. Et Glabriōnem, id quod sapientissimē fēcit, facere laetātus sum,[166] ut repente cōnsilium in mediō testimōniō dīmitteret.[167]

Etenim verēbātur nē populus Rōmānus ab istō eās poenās vī repetīsse[168] vidērētur quās veritus esset nē iste lēgibus et vestrō jūdiciō nōn esset persolūtūrus.[169]

164 Nunc, quoniam explōrātum est omnibus quō locō causa tua sit et quid dē tē futūrum sit, sīc tēcum agam.

I WILL PROVE MY CHARGE POINT BY POINT

Gāvium istum quem repentīnum[170] speculātōrem fuisse dīcis ostendam in Lautumiās Syrācūsīs ā tē esse conjectum, neque id sōlum ex litterīs ostendam Syrācūsānōrum nē possīs dīcere mē, quia sit aliquis in litterīs Gāvius, hoc fingere et ēligere nōmen ut hunc illum esse possim dīcere; sed ad arbitrium tuum testēs dabō quī istum ipsum Syrācūsīs abs tē in Lautumiās conjectum esse dīcant.

Words to Remember

Numitōrius (ī), **Gājus** (ī), *Gaius Numitorius,* a Roman knight.
speculātor, speculātōris, *spy.*
ēligō, ēligere, ēlēgī, ēlēctus, 3, tr., *pick out, choose* (cf. elective courses).

---

164 **ut,** *how;* introducing an indirect question.

165 **egomet** = **ego** + **met** (an emphatic suffix).

166 **laetor,** 1, intr., *am glad* (cf. **laetitia**).

167 **ut . . . dīmitteret;** noun clause of result in apposition with **id.** Glabrio adjourned the sitting for fear of mob violence; Gr. 637.

168 **repetīsse** = **repetīvisse.**

169 **persolvō, persolvere, persolvī, persolūtus,** 3, tr., *pay.*

170 **repentīnus, a, um,** *sudden.*

HE WAS A CITIZEN OF CONSA

Prōdūcam etiam Cōnsānōs, mūnicipēs illīus ac necessāriōs, quī tē nunc sērō[171] doceant,[172] jūdicēs nōn sērō,[171] illum Pūblium Gāvium quem tū in crucem ēgistī cīvem Rōmānum et mūnicipem Cōnsānum, nōn speculātōrem fugitīvōrum fuisse.

YOU ADMITTED YOURSELF THAT HE CRIED OUT HE WAS A ROMAN CITIZEN

Cum haec omnia, quae polliceor, cumulātē[173] tuīs proximīs[174] **165**
plāna fēcerō, tum istuc[175] ipsum tenēbō quod abs tē mihi datur, eō contentum mē esse dīcam. Quid enim nūper tū ipse, cum populī Rōmānī clāmōre atque impetū perturbātus exsiluistī,[176] quid, inquam, locūtus es? Illum[177] quod moram suppliciō quaereret, ideō[178] clāmitāsse[179] sē esse cīvem Rōmānum, sed speculātōrem fuisse.

THIS IS THE TESTIMONY OF EYEWITNESSES

Jam[180] meī testēs vērī sunt. Quid enim dīcit aliud Gājus Numitōrius? quid Mārcus et Pūblius Cottiī,[181] nōbilissimī homines,

---

Word to Remember

clāmitō, 1, tr., *keep shouting.*

---

[171] **sērō**, adv., *too late.*

[172] **doceō, docēre, docuī, doctus,** 2, tr.; w. acc. of person; **dē** w. abl. of thing; acc. w. infin., *inform, teach.*

[173] **cumulātē**, adv., *amply, fully, abundantly.*

[174] **proximīs**: *supporters.*

[175] **istuc = istud.**

[176] **exsiliō, exsilīre, exsiluī,** 4, intr., *jump up.*

[177] Gavius.

[178] **ideō**, adv., *therefore.*

[179] **clāmitāsse = clāmitāvisse.**

[180] **Jam** indicates that this is a conclusion from the words of Verres. *Very well then . . .*

[181] Marcus and Publius Cottius, Roman citizens resident in eastern Sicily.

ex agrō Tauromenītānō?[182] quid Quīntus Luccēius,[183] quī argentāriam[184] Rhēgiī[185] maximam fēcit? Adhūc enim testēs ex eō genere ā mē sunt datī, nōn quī nōvisse[186] Gāvium, sed sē vīdisse dīcerent, cum is, quī sē cīvem Rōmānum esse clāmāret, in crucem agerētur.

YOU ADMIT HE CRIED OUT HIS CITIZENSHIP—YET, WITHOUT HESITATION, WITHOUT INVESTIGATION, YOU SENT HIM TO THE CROSS!

Hoc tū, Verrēs, idem dīcis. Hoc tū cōnfitēris illum clāmitāsse[187] sē cīvem esse Rōmānum; apud tē nōmen cīvitātis nē tantum quidem valuisse ut dubitātiōnem[188] aliquam, ut crūdēlissimī taeterrimīque[189] suppliciī aliquam parvam moram saltem[190] posset afferre.

THIS ONE POINT IS ENOUGH

166 Hoc teneō, hīc haereō,[191] jūdicēs, hōc sum contentus ūnō. Omittō ac neglegō cētera. Suā cōnfessiōne induātur[192] ac jugulētur[193] necesse est.[194] Quī esset ignōrābās. Speculātōrem esse suspicābāre.[195] Nōn quaerō quā suspīciōne. Tuā tē accūsō ōrātiōne; cīvem Rōmānum sē esse dīcēbat.

---

[182] **ager (agrī) Tauromenītānus (ī),** *the Tauromenium district,* in eastern Sicily.

[183] Quintus Lucceius, a prominent banker of Rhegium.

[184] **argentāria, ae,** *a bank, banking house.*

[185] **Rhēgium, ī,** *Rhegium,* a town in southern Italy just across from Sicily.

[186] **nōscō, nōscere, nōvī, nōtus,** 3, tr., *know.*

[187] **clāmitāsse = clāmitāvisse.**

[188] **dubitātiō, dubitātiōnis,** *hesitation* (cf. **dubitō**).

[189] **taeter, taetra, taetrum,** *hateful, horrible.*

[190] **saltem,** adv., *at least.*

[191] **haereō, haerēre, haesī, haesūrus,** 2, intr., *stick.*

[192] **induō, induere, induī, indūtus,** 3, tr., *put on* (here used as of a noose or snare); *entangle, catch.*

[193] **jugulō,** 1, tr., *cut the throat, murder.* Here it carries through the metaphor of **induō** and means *strangle*—much like our idea of giving a person "enough rope to hang himself."

[194] The subjunctive is frequently used after **necesse est** without **ut**; Gr. 641.

[195] **suspicābāre = suspicābāris.**

THAT CRY WOULD HAVE STOPPED THE HAND OF A FOREIGN EXECUTIONER!

Sī tū apud Persās[196] aut in extrēmā Indiā[197] dēprehēnsus, Verrēs, ad supplicium dūcerēre,[198] quid aliud clāmitārēs nisi tē cīvem esse Rōmānum? et sī tibi ignōtō apud ignōtōs, apud barbarōs, apud hominēs in extrēmīs atque ultimīs gentibus positōs, nōbile et illūstre apud omnēs nōmen tuae cīvitātis prōfuisset—ille, quisquis erat, quem tū in crucem rapiēbās, quī tibi esset ignōtus, cum cīvem sē Rōmānum esse dīceret apud tē praetōrem, sī nōn effugium,[199] nē moram quidem mortis mentiōne[200] atque ūsūrpātiōne[201] cīvitātis assequī potuit?

THIS PLEA PROTECTS ROMANS—RICH AND POOR ALIKE—THE WORLD OVER

Hominēs tenuēs, obscūrō locō nātī, nāvigant. Adeunt ad ea **167**
loca quae numquam anteā vīdērunt, ubi neque nōtī esse eīs quō vēnērunt neque semper cum cognitōribus esse possunt. Hāc ūnā tamen fīdūciā cīvitātis nōn modo apud nostrōs magistrātūs, quī et lēgum et exīstimātiōnis perīculō continentur, neque apud cīvēs sōlum Rōmānōs, quī et sermōnis et jūris et multārum rērum societāte jūnctī sunt, fore sē tūtōs arbitrantur; sed, quōcumque vēnerint, hanc sibi rem praesidiō spērant esse futūram.

WORD TO REMEMBER

cognitor, cognitōris, *voucher, witness of one's identity* (cf. **cognōscō**).

---

[196] **Persae, Persārum,** m., *Persians.*

[197] **India, ae,** *India.*

[198] **dūcerēre = dūcerēris.**

[199] **effugium, ī,** *escape.*

[200] **mentiō, mentiōnis,** *mention.*

[201] **ūsūrpātiō, ūsūrpātiōnis,** *use* (of the word), *claim.*

—*Alinari*

THE MAD EMPEROR CALIGULA

Under the emperors the traditions of law and liberty for which Cicero stood were often almost entirely forgotten. Emperors like Nero and Caligula thought nothing of condemning to death not only Roman citizens but even senators of the Roman people.

TAKE AWAY THIS PROTECTION AND YOU CLOSE THE WORLD TO ROMANS

Tolle hanc spem, tolle hoc praesidium cīvibus Rōmānīs; cōn- **168**
stitue nihil esse opis in hāc vōce "CĪVIS RŌMĀNUS SUM," posse impūnē[202] praetōrem aut alium quemlibet[203] supplicium quod velit in eum cōnstituere quī sē cīvem Rōmānum esse dīcat, quod[204] eum quis[205] ignōret—jam omnēs prōvinciās, jam omnia rēgna, jam omnēs līberās cīvitātēs, jam omnem orbem terrārum, quī semper nostrīs hominibus maximē patuit, cīvibus Rōmānīs istā dēfēnsiōne[206] praeclūseris.[207]

YOU COULD EASILY HAVE DISCOVERED THE TRUTH

Quid, sī Lūcium Raecium, equitem Rōmānum, quī tum in Siciliā erat, nōminābat, etiamne id magnum fuit Panhormum litterās mittere? Asservāssēs[208] hominem custōdiīs Māmertīnōrum tuōrum, vīnctum, clausum[209] habuissēs dum Panhormō Raecius venīret:[210] cognōsceret[211] hominem, aliquid dē summō suppliciō remitterēs; sī ignōrāret, tum, sī ita tibi vidērētur, hoc jūris in omnēs cōnstituerēs ut quī neque tibi nōtus esset neque cognitō-

---

Word to Remember

vinciō, vincīre, vīnxī, vīnctus, 4, tr., *bind, bind in prison* (cf. **vinculum**).

---

202 **impūnē,** adv., *with impunity.*

203 **alium quemlibet:** *any other person at all;* Gr. 844.

204 **Quod** is a conjunction, not a pronoun.

205 **quis = aliquis.**

206 **istā dēfēnsiōne:** *by that line of defense* (by admitting the plea of Verres).

207 **praeclūdō, praeclūdere, praeclūsī, praeclūsus,** 3, tr., *shut off* (cf. preclude).

208 **asservāssēs = asservāvissēs.**

209 **claudō, claudere, clausī, clausus,** 3, tr., *shut, imprison* (cf. claustrophobia).

210 **venīret;** Gr. 568.

211 Understand **sī** before **cognōsceret.**

rem locuplētem[212] daret, quamvīs cīvis Rōmānus esset, in crucem tollerētur.

BUT AFTER ALL IT WAS NOT MERELY AGAINST THIS GAVIUS THAT VERRES WORKED INJUSTICE BUT AGAINST US ALL!

169 Sed quid ego plūra dē Gāviō? quasi tū Gāviō tum fuerīs īnfestus ac nōn nōminī, generī, jūrī cīvium hostis. Nōn illī, inquam, hominī sed causae commūnī lībertātis inimīcus fuistī.

YOU MADE SPORT OF HIS ROMAN RIGHTS

Quid enim attinuit,[213] cum Māmertīnī mōre atque īnstitūtō suō[214] crucem fīxissent post urbem in Viā Pompēiā,[215] tē jubēre in eā parte fīgere quae ad fretum[216] spectāret, et hoc addere,[217] quod negāre nūllō modō potes, quod omnibus audientibus dīxistī palam, tē idcircō illum locum dēligere ut ille, quoniam sē cīvem Rōmānum esse dīceret, ex cruce Italiam cernere[218] ac domum suam prōspicere[219] posset? Itaque illa crux, sōla, jūdicēs, post

---

Words to Remember

fīgō, fīgere, fīxī, fīxus, 3, tr., *fasten, drive in, fix.*
fretum, ī, *strait* (of water).
spectō, 1, tr., *look at, look towards.*

---

212 **locuplēs** (*gen.* **locuplētis**), *rich, wealthy.*

213 **attineō, attinēre, attinuī, attentum,** 2, intr., *pertain to, mean.*

214 It was usual to execute criminals outside the city at some customary spot. In this case Verres, for reasons of his own, ordered a deviation from custom.

215 **Via (ae) Pompēia (ae),** *the Via Pompeia,* a highway running out of Messina.

216 The strait between Sicily and Italy. Remember that from Messina one could see Italy across the strait.

217 **addō, addere, addidī, additus,** 3, tr., *add.*

218 **cernō, cernere,** 3, tr.; acc. w. infin., *discern.*

219 **prōspiciō, prōspicere, prōspexī, prōspectus,** 3, tr., *see afar, view from a distance.*

conditam Messānam illō in locō fīxa est. Italiae cōnspectus ad eam rem ab istō dēlēctus est ut ille in dolōre cruciātūque moriēns perangustō[220] fretō dīvīsa servitūtis[221] ac lībertātis jūra cognōsceret; Italia autem alumnum[222] suum servitūtis extrēmō summōque suppliciō affīxum[223] vidēret.

WITH GAVIUS OUR RIGHTS AND LIBERTY WERE CRUCIFIED!

Facinus est vincīre cīvem Rōmānum, scelus verberāre, prope **170**
parricīdium necāre—quid dīcam in crucem tollere? Verbō satis dignō tam nefāria rēs appellārī nūllō modō potest. Nōn fuit hīs omnibus iste contentus—spectet, inquit, patriam! in cōnspectū lēgum lībertātisque moriātur! Nōn tū hōc locō Gāvium, nōn ūnum hominem nesciōquem,[224] cīvem Rōmānum, sed commūnem lībertātis et cīvitātis causam in illum cruciātum et crucem ēgistī.

HE FLAUNTED BEFORE THE WORLD HIS CONTEMPT FOR ROMAN CITIZENSHIP

Jam vērō vidēte hominis[225] audāciam. Nōnne eum graviter tulisse[226] arbitrāminī quod illam cīvibus Rōmānīs crucem nōn posset

---

WORD TO REMEMBER

servitūs, servitūtis, f., *slavery* (cf. **servus**).

---

[220] **perangustus, a, um,** *very narrow.*

[221] The Romans thought of crucifixion as a punishment intended primarily for slaves.

[222] **alumnus, ī,** *son* (cf. alumni association).

[223] **affīgō, affīgere, affīxī, affīxus,** 3, tr., *fix to, suspend.*

[224] **ūnum hominem nesciōquem:** *one man, I don't know who; some fellow or other;* Gr. 819.

[225] **hominis;** Verres.

[226] So much did Verres hate Roman citizens that he would gladly have planted that cross in the most prominent parts of Rome itself.

in forō,[227] nōn in comitiō, nōn in rōstrīs[228] dēfīgere? Quod enim hīs locīs in prōvinciā suā celebritāte[229] simillimum, regiōne proximum potuit, ēlēgit. Monumentum sceleris audāciaeque suae voluit esse in cōnspectū Italiae, vestibulō[230] Siciliae, praetervectiōne[231] omnium quī ultrō citrōque[232] nāvigārent.

AND I AM SPEAKING TO ROMAN CITIZENS AND TO SENATORS WHO ARE THE HEAD AND FOUNTAIN OF ROMAN RIGHTS

171 Sī haec nōn ad cīvēs Rōmānōs, nōn ad aliquōs amīcōs nostrae cīvitātis, nōn ad eōs quī populī Rōmānī nōmen audīssent, dēnique, sī nōn ad hominēs vērum ad bēstiās,[233] aut etiam—ut longius prōgrediar—sī in aliquā dēsertissimā[234] sōlitūdine ad saxa[235] et ad scopulōs[236] haec conquerī[237] ac dēplōrāre[238] vellem, tamen omnia mūta atque inanimāta[239] tantā et tam indignā rērum acerbitāte[240] commovērentur. Nunc vērō cum loquar apud senātōrēs populī Rōmānī, lēgum et jūdiciōrum et jūris auctōrēs, timēre nōn dēbeō nē nōn ūnus iste[241] cīvis Rōmānus illā cruce dignus, cēterī omnēs similī perīculō indignissimī jūdicentur.

---

[227] **forō**; the forum at Rome.

[228] **rōstra, rōstrōrum,** *platform, rostra;* the speaker's stand in the Roman forum. There is tragic irony in the word, for it was upon the rostra at Rome that Cicero's dismembered head and hands were transfixed in disgrace at the order of Mark Antony.

[229] **celebritās, celebritātis,** *populousness.*

[230] **vestibulum, ī,** *entrance, entrance gate* (cf. vestibule). Here at Messina people regularly passed over from Italy to Sicily.

[231] **praetervectiō, praetervectiōnis,** *a passing by, a passageway.* The spot overlooked the strait through which a steady stream of commerce flowed.

[232] **ultrō citrōque:** *back and forth.*

[233] **bēstia, ae,** *wild animal.*

[234] **dēsertus, a, um,** *deserted.*

[235] **saxum, ī,** *rock.*

[236] **scopulus, ī,** *crag.*

[237] **conqueror, conquerī, conquestus sum,** 3, tr., *complain of.*

[238] **dēplōrō,** 1, tr., *weep over.*

[239] **inanimātus, a, um,** *lifeless, inanimate.*

[240] **acerbitās, acerbitātis,** *harshness, bitterness* (cf. **acerbus**).

[241] **ūnus iste**; Verres.

ALL ROMANS SCATTERED THROUGHOUT THE WORLD LOOK TO YOU TO PROTECT THEIR RIGHTS AND THEIR PERSONS

172 Paulō ante, jūdicēs, lacrimās in morte miserā atque indignā nauarchōrum[242] tenēbāmus, et rēctē ac meritō sociōrum innocentium miseriā[243] commovēbāmur—quid nunc in nostrō sanguine tandem facere dēbēmus?

Nam cīvium Rōmānōrum omnium sanguis conjūnctus exīstimandus est, quoniam et salūtis omnium ratiō et vēritās postulat. Omnēs hōc locō cīvēs Rōmānī, et quī adsunt et quī ubīque[244] sunt, vestram severitātem dēsīderant, vestram fidem implōrant, vestrum auxilium requīrunt; omnia sua jūra, commoda,[245] auxilia, tōtam dēnique lībertātem in vestrīs sententiīs versārī arbitrantur.

---

242 **nauarchus, ī,** *ship captain.* Cicero refers to an earlier charge.

243 **miseria, ae,** *misery, sad fate.*

244 **ubīque,** adv., *everywhere.*

245 **commodum, ī,** *advantage, interest, convenience* (cf. **accommodō**).

PART III

ROME VERSUS CHRISTIANITY

CHRIST CONQUERS THE EMPIRE

—*Ewing Galloway*

THE COLOSSEUM TODAY

A mute reminder of pagan Rome still standing, an ancient relic in the Rome of the popes.

PROLOGUE

Pagan Rome developed an admirable system of law which recognized and protected many of the natural rights of the human person. But the benefit of law extended in its fullness to a relatively small favored class—Roman citizens. In the vast army of slaves at the base of Roman society the law saw little more than a species of property. Their torture and execution never drew indignant reproaches from the mouth of a Cicero. Besides, Roman legal theory, especially under the Empire, terminated in the omnipotent state; beyond it there were no spiritual rights, above all, no spiritual society of independent and supernatural power.

When Christianity entered into the society of Rome, it saved and protected all that was good in it and yet went grandly beyond it. It brought a new dignity to man—to all men, slave and free, foreigner and Roman alike, and gathered them into a new and higher society, the Church of Christ. Old Rome turned all its machinery of law and government against this new power, but in the end, the Rome of the emperors gave place to the new Rome, the Rome of the popes.

The story of that clash between Christ and the Empire begins with Pilate's condemnation of our Lord to the cross.

PILATE THE ROMAN GOVERNOR CONDEMNS CHRIST THE SON OF GOD TO THE CROSS

DATE: The eve of the Pasch, probably A. D. 29-30.

SCENE: Before the governor's palace at Jerusalem. A frenzied mob supports the chief priests of the Jews as they accuse Christ of blasphemy and of sedition against Tiberius, the reigning emperor. Pilate, intimidated by the violence of the mob, has just had Christ cruelly flogged, hoping thereby to satisfy the blood lust of the Jews and to arouse, perhaps, their pity.

Exīvit ergō[1] iterum[2] Pīlātus forās[3] et dīcit eīs. "Ecce addūcō vōbīs eum forās ut cognōscātis quia[4] nūllam inveniō in eō causam." (Exīvit ergō Jēsūs portāns corōnam[5] spīneam[6] et purpureum[7] vestīmentum.[8]) Et dīcit eīs: "Ecce homō." Cum ergō vīdissent eum pontificēs[9] et ministrī,[10] clāmābant, dīcentēs: "Crucifīge, crucifīge eum." Dīcit eīs Pīlātus: "Accipite eum vōs et crucifīgite. Ego enim nōn inveniō in eō causam." Respondērunt eī Jūdaeī: "Nōs lēgem habēmus, et secundum lēgem dēbet morī, quia fīlium Deī sē fēcit."

Cum ergō audīsset Pīlātus hunc sermōnem, magis timuit. Et ingressus est praetōrium[11] iterum[2] et dīxit ad Jēsum: "Unde es tū?" Jēsūs autem respōnsum nōn dedit eī. Dīcit ergō eī Pīlātus: "Mihi nōn loqueris? Nescīs quia[4] potestātem habeō crucifīgere

---

[1] **ergō**, adv., *accordingly, therefore, then.*

[2] **iterum**, adv., *again.*

[3] **forās**, adv., *forth, out of doors.*

[4] **quia**, conj., *that;* introducing a noun clause. In classical Latin the accusative with the infinitive would be used.

[5] **corōna, ae,** *crown.*

[6] **spīneus, a, um,** *of thorns.*

[7] **purpureus, a, um,** *purple.*

[8] **vestīmentum, ī,** *garment.*

[9] **pontifex, pontificis,** m., *chief priest, pope.*

[10] **minister, ministrī,** *servant.*

[11] **praetōrium, ī,** *the governor's hall.*

—*Bettmann Archive*

CHRIST BEFORE PILATE

Pilate had the power to free Christ, but he failed to do so because his ambitions outweighed the Roman's traditional sense of what was right.

tē et potestātem habeō dīmittere tē?" Respondit Jēsūs: "Nōn habērēs potestātem adversum[12] mē ūllam nisi tibi datum esset dēsuper.[13] Propterea[14] quī mē trādidit tibi mājus peccātum habet."

Et exinde[15] quaerēbat Pīlātus dīmittere eum; Jūdaeī autem clāmābant dīcentēs: "Sī hunc dīmittis, nōn es amīcus Caesaris;[16] omnis enim quī sē rēgem facit contrādīcit[17] Caesarī."

Pīlātus autem cum audīsset hōs sermōnēs, addūxit forās Jēsum et sēdit prō tribūnālī, in locō quī dīcitur Lithostrōtos,[18] Hebraicē[19] autem Gabbatha.[29] Erat autem parascēvē[21] Paschae,[22] hōra quasi

---

12 **adversum**, prep. w. acc., *against.*

13 **dēsuper**, adv., *from above.*

14 **propterea**, adv., *therefore.*

15 **exinde**, adv., *from henceforth.*

16 Caesar was the title of the Roman emperors. At this time Tiberius was the reigning Caesar.

17 **contrādīcō, contrādīcere, contrādīxī, contrādictum**, 3, intr.; w. dat., *speak against.*

18 Lithostrotos, the Greek name for the place, means *paved with stone.*

19 **Hebraicē**, adv., *in Hebrew.*

20 The meaning of the Hebrew name, Gabbatha, is uncertain.

21 **parascēvē**: *the day of preparation, the eve.*

22 **Pascha, ae**, *the Pasch.*

sexta, et dīcit Jūdaeīs: "Ecce rēx vester." Illī autem clāmābant: "Tolle, tolle, crucifīge eum!" Dīcit eīs Pīlātus: "Rēgem vestrum crucifīgam?" Respondērunt pontificēs: "Nōn habēmus rēgem nisi Caesarem." Tunc ergō trādidit eīs illum ut crucifīgerētur.

POPE PETER DEFIES THE AUTHORITY OF THE JEWS

After the coming of the Holy Spirit, the apostles, strengthened by grace and conscious of a God-given mission, began to preach the 'good news' of Christ to all the Jews. The priests soon had them arrested and imprisoned, but the apostles knew that they were endowed with a higher power, Christ's very own.

Adveniēns autem prīnceps sacerdōtum[1] et quī cum eō erant, convocāvērunt concilium et omnēs seniōrēs fīliōrum Israēl; et mīsērunt ad carcerem ut addūcerentur. [*But the apostles had been let out during the night by an angel and were preaching in the Temple. The officers went there and brought them to the council of the priests.*] Et cum addūxissent illōs, statuērunt in conciliō. Et interrogāvit eōs prīnceps sacerdōtum,[1] dīcēns: "Praecipiendō[2] praecēpimus vōbīs nē docērētis in nōmine istō.[3] Et ecce replēstis[4] Jērūsālem doctrīnā[5] vestrā, et vultis indūcere super[6] nōs sanguinem hominis istīus."

Respondēns autem Petrus et apostolī[7] dīxērunt: "OBĒDĪRE[8] OPORTET DEŌ MAGIS QUAM HOMINIBUS!"

---

[1] **sacerdōs, sacerdōtis,** c., *priest.*

[2] **praecipiō, praecipere, praecēpī, praeceptum,** 3, intr.; w. dat., *order.* This repetition of the same word (**praecipiendō praecēpimus**) is a typical Hebrewism.

[3] Jesus.

[4] **repleō, replēre, replēvī, replētus,** 2, tr., *fill;* **replēstis = replēvistis.**

[5] **doctrīna, ae,** *teaching, doctrine.*

[6] **super,** prep. w. acc., *over, upon.*

[7] **apostolus, ī,** *apostle.*

[8] **obēdiō,** 4, intr.; w. dat., *obey.*

PAUL APPEALS TO HIS RIGHTS AS A ROMAN CITIZEN

After his conversion Paul later returned to Jerusalem and went into the Temple. When the Jews recognized him—knowing him as they did for a convert to Christ—a riot broke out in the Temple and spread throughout the city. Paul was rescued and arrested by the Roman soldiers. He was just on the point of being flogged and put to the torture when—

Dīcit astantī[1] sibi centuriōnī Paulus: "Sī[2] hominem Rōmānum et indemnātum[3] licet vōbīs flagellāre?"[4] Quō audītō, centuriō accessit ad tribūnum et nuntiāvit eī, dīcēns: "Quid āctūrus es? Hic enim homō cīvis Rōmānus est."

Accēdēns autem tribūnus, dīxit illī: "Dīc mihi sī[5] tū Rōmānus cīvis es?" At ille dīxit: "Etiam."[6] Et respondit tribūnus: "Ego multā summā[7] cīvīlitātem[8] hanc cōnsecūtus sum." Et Paulus ait:[9] "Ego autem et nātus sum." Prōtinus[10] ergō discessērunt ab illō quī eum tortūrī erant.[11] Tribūnus quoque timuit postquam rescīvit[12] quia cīvis Rōmānus esset et quia alligāsset[13] eum.

---

1 **astō, astāre, astitī,** 1, intr., *stand beside.*

2 **Sī** is here used to introduce a question, like **an.**

3 **indemnātus, a, um,** *uncondemned.*

4 **flagellō,** 1, tr., *flog.*

5 **sī,** *whether.*

6 **Etiam** is often used in giving affirmative answers; *yes.*

7 **multā summā:** *for a large sum of money.*

8 **cīvīlitās, cīvīlitātis (cīvitās, cīvitātis),** *citizenship.*

9 **ait:** *he said.*

10 **prōtinus,** adv., *straightway.*

11 **tortūrī erant:** *were going to torture.*

12 **rescīscō, rescīscere, rescīvī, rescītus,** 3, tr., *ascertain.*

13 **alligō,** 1, tr., *bind;* **alligāsset = alligāvisset.**

PAUL APPEALS TO CAESAR

The Roman governor Felix kept Paul in prison two years without deciding his case. When Festus, who succeeded Felix, came into office, at the instigation of the Jews he again examined Paul.

Fēstus alterā diē sēdit prō tribūnālī et jussit Paulum addūcī. Quī cum perductus esset, circumstetērunt eum quī ab Jerosolymā[1] dēscenderant Jūdaeī multās et gravēs causās objicientēs[2] quās nōn poterant probāre, Paulō ratiōnem reddente:[3] "Quoniam[4] neque in lēgem Jūdaeōrum neque in templum neque in Caesarem quidquam[5] peccāvī."[6]

Fēstus autem volēns grātiam praestāre[7] Jūdaeīs, respondēns Paulō, dīxit: "Vīs Jerosolymam[1] ascendere, et ibi dē hīs jūdicārī apud mē?" Dīxit autem Paulus: "Ad tribūnal Caesaris stō, ibi mē oportet jūdicārī. Jūdaeīs nōn nocuī sīcut tū melius nōstī.[8] Sī enim nocuī aut dignum morte aliquid fēcī, nōn recūsō[9] morī; sī vērō nihil est eōrum quae hī accūsant mē, nēmō potest mē illīs dōnāre.[10] CAESAREM APPELLŌ!" Tunc Fēstus, cum conciliō locūtus, rēspondit: "Caesarem appellāstī?[11] Ad Caesarem ībis!"

---

[1] **Jerosolyma, ae,** *Jerusalem;* **Jerosolyma, Jerosolymōrum** also used.

[2] **objiciō, objicere, objēcī, objectus,** 3, tr., *throw in the way of, put in the way of, expose.*

[3] **ratiōnem reddō, reddere, reddidī, redditus,** 3, tr., *give an account.*

[4] Do not translate **quoniam**; the word is here equivalent to quotation marks.

[5] **quidquam**: *in anything;* it is used here as the object of the intransitive verb **peccō**; Gr. 756.

[6] **peccō,** 1, intr., *offend.*

[7] **praestō, praestāre, praestitī, praestitus,** 1, tr., *exhibit, furnish.*

[8] **nōscō, nōscere, nōvī, nōtus,** 3, tr., *know;* **nōstī = nōvistī.**

[9] **recūsō,** 1, tr.; w. infin.; **quōminus, nē (quīn),** *refuse.*

[10] **dōnō,** 1, tr.; w. acc. of person and abl. of thing, *give a gift, present, make a gift of.*

[11] **appellāstī = appellāvistī.**

—*Courtesy of Paramount Pictures*

In the Dungeons of the Colosseum

Here Christians from every walk of life awaited death from beast or gladiator to make festival for the blood-hungry eyes of the Roman rabble.

PETER AND PAUL MARTYRED AT ROME

Paul appealed to Rome, and to Rome he was sent. There persecution was raging. The fire that had laid waste ten of Rome's fourteen districts had inflamed also a mass of prejudices. In terror the mad Emperor Nero, a matricide and incendiary, blamed the Christians. Small wonder that the Roman police, who had been hounding Christians for three years, should now lay hands upon their leaders—Peter and Paul. Tradition has it that they were martyred on the same day. But death could not be inflicted in the same way, for Paul was a Roman citizen and Peter was not. Paul was beheaded; Peter was crucified—head down as he had requested, unworthy to die the same death as his Master.

United in life, united in death at Rome, Peter and Paul remained united in the hearts of the early Christians. The catacombs of St. Sebastian have this simple invocation inscribed upon their walls:

PETRE ET PAULE, PETITE

Heresy has tried to divide them, to set one against the other, but the Church still keeps them united. On June 29 she celebrates the martyrdom of Peter and Paul and at vespers on that feast sings this thrilling song to Rome:

Ō Rōma fēlīx, quae duōrum prīncipum
Es consecrāta[1] glōriōsō[2] sanguine!
Hōrum cruōre[3] purpurāta[4] cēterās
Excellis[5] orbis ūna pulchritūdinēs.[6]

---

[1] **consecrō,** 1, tr., *consecrate, make sacred.*

[2] **glōriōsus, a, um,** *glorious.*

[3] **cruor, cruōris,** *blood.*

[4] **purpurātus, a, um,** *purpled, incarnadined.*

[5] **excellō, excellere, exceluī, excelsus,** 3, tr., *excel.*

[6] **pulchritūdō, pulchritūdinis,** *beauty.*

MARTYRDOM UNDER THE EMPERORS

A human document of great interest has come down to us from a martyrdom under Septimius Severus and Caracalla. The account was composed partly by an unknown eyewitness, partly by Perpetua, one of the martyrs, in prison. We can see in the simple story the excitement of people aroused by blood lust or pity, the sorrow of relatives, the little human touches of friendship and common prayer, and the fellowship of suffering. All were steadfast to the death and are honored as saints in the Church.

As our story opens, the slave Revocatus and the slave girl Felicity, together with Saturninus, Secundulus, and Perpetua, a matron of distinguished family, have been arrested on a charge of being Christians. They are joined in their imprisonment, voluntarily, by Saturus, who, it seems, had converted them. Perpetua tells of their condemnation:

Aliō diē cum prandērēmus,[1] subitō raptī sumus ut audīrēmur, et pervēnimus ad forum.[2] Rūmor[3] statim per vīcīnās[4] forī partēs cucurrit,[5] et factus est populus immēnsus.[6] Ascendimus in catastam.[7] Interrogātī cēterī cōnfessī sunt. Ventum est ad mē. Et appāruit[8] pater īlicō[9] cum fīliō meō;[10] et extrāxit[11] mē dē gradū,

---

[1] **prandeō, prandēre, prandī, prānsum**, 2, intr., *eat breakfast.*

[2] The forum at Carthage in northern Africa, where the scene of the martyrdom is laid.

[3] **rūmor, rūmōris,** *rumor, report.*

[4] **vīcīnus, a, um,** *neighboring.*

[5] **currō, currere, cucurrī, cursum**, 3, intr., *run.*

[6] **immēnsus, a, um,** *large.*

[7] **catasta, ae,** *a platform.*

[8] **appāreō, appārēre, appāruī, appāritum**, 2, intr., *appear.*

[9] **īlicō**, adv., *there, on the spot.*

[10] Perpetua was a young mother.

[11] **extrahō, extrahere, extrāxī, extractus**, 3, tr., *draw from.*

—*Courtesy of RKO Pictures, Inc.*

THE OFFICIAL BOX

Amid the splendor of pagan display the Roman officials sit in state to watch the death agony of their Christian subjects, who preferred, for Christ's sake, to exchange life in this world for a life in heaven with God—an attitude which is as incomprehensible to the materialist of today as it was to the pagan living in the time of the Caesars.

dīcēns: "Supplicā,[12] miserēre īnfantī."[13] Et Hilariānus[14] prōcūrātor[15] quī tunc locō prōcōnsulis[16] Minuciī Timiniānī[17] dēfūnctī[18] jūs gladiī[19] accēperat: "Parce,"[20] inquit, "cānīs[21] patris tuī; parce[20] īnfantiae[22] puerī. Fac sacrum[23] prō salūte Imperātōrum." Et ego respondī: "Nōn faciō." Et Hilariānus[14] dīxit: "Chrīstiāna

---

[12] **supplicō,** 1, tr., *sacrifice.* The Christians had only to offer sacrifice to the pagan gods to be released.

[13] **īnfāns, īnfantis,** c., *infant.*

[14] **Hilariānus, ī,** *Hilarianus,* the imperial collector of revenues. He was presiding in place of the proconsul who had recently died.

[15] **prōcūrātor, prōcūrātōris,** *collector.*

[16] **prōcōnsul, prōcōnsulis,** *proconsul.*

[17] **Timiniānus** (ī), **Minucius** (ī), *Minucius Timinianus,* a proconsul.

[18] **dēfūnctus, a, um,** *dead.*

[19] **jūs gladiī:** *the power of pronouncing capital sentence.*

[20] **parcō, parcere, pepercī, parsūrus,** 3, intr.; w. dat., *spare.*

[21] **cānī, cānōrum,** *grey hairs.*

[22] **īnfantia, ae,** *infancy.*

[23] **sacrum, ī,** *sacrifice.*

es?" Et ego respondī: "Chrīstiāna sum." . . . Tunc nōs ūniversōs prōnuntiat,[24] et damnat ad bēstiās; et hilarēs[25] dēscendimus ad carcerem.

On the birthday of the Emperor, March 7, A. D. 203, they were led into the arena. "Illūxit,"[26] says the ancient writer, "diēs victōriae illōrum, et prōcessērunt dē carcere in amphitheātrum[27] quasi in caelum itūrī." They were all exposed to the wild beasts, and last of all Felicity, the maiden slave, and Perpetua, the noble matron, were thrown by an enraged cow—in cruel mockery of their sex. Perpetua, on regaining her breath and her wits, called her brother and others to her and said: "In fide stāte et invicem[28] omnēs dīligite et passiōnibus[29] nostrīs nē scandalīzēminī."[30] Then all of them—mangled and half-dead from the beasts—were given the *coup de grâce* by the gladiators to the huge delight of the blood-hungry mob.

HERE ARE THE MARTYRS
SATURUS SATURNINUS
REVOCATUS SECUNDULUS
FELICITY AND PERPETUA
WHO SUFFERED ON THE NONES OF MARCH
[*From the ancient memorial stone discovered at Carthage, 1907.*]

---

24 **prōnuntiō**, 1, tr., *sentence.*

25 **hilaris, e,** *joyful, cheerful* (cf. hilarious, Hilary).

26 **illūcēscō, illūcēscere, illūxī**, 3, intr., *dawn.*

27 **amphitheātrum, ī,** *amphitheater.* These ancient 'bowls' were as common in Roman cities and towns as ball parks are throughout the United States.

28 **invicem**, adv., *mutually, one another.*

29 **passiō, passiōnis,** *suffering.*

30 **scandalīzō**, 1, tr., *scandalize.*

CYPRIAN THE BISHOP BEARS WITNESS UNTO BLOOD

About fifty years after the martyrdom of Perpetua another persecution was raging in Roman territory. There was a certain Cyprian, bishop of Carthage in North Africa, a convert, formerly a distinguished lawyer and a man of position and influence. In the first stage of the persecution he had been arrested and sent into exile, from which, however, he later returned. But a new edict decreed death to all Christian bishops and priests. Cyprian was brought before the proconsul, Galerius Maximus. He is being examined:

Galērius Maximus prōcōnsul Cypriānō epīscopō[1] dīxit: "Tū es Thascius Cypriānus?" Cypriānus epīscopus[1] respondit: "Ego sum." Galērius Maximus prōcōnsul dīxit: "Tū pāpam[2] tē sacrilegae[3] mentis hominibus praebuistī?"[4] Cypriānus epīscopus[1] respondit: "Ego." Galērius Maximus prōcōnsul dīxit: "Jussērunt tē sacrātissimī[5] imperātōrēs caeremōniārī."[6] Cypriānus epīscopus dīxit: "Nōn faciō." Galērius Maximus ait: "Cōnsule tibi." Cypriānus epīscopus respondit: "Fac quod tibi praeceptum est;[7] in rē tam jūstā nūlla est cōnsultātiō."[8]

Galērius Maximus collocūtus[9] cum conciliō sententiam vix et

---

[1] **epīscopus, ī,** *bishop.*

[2] **pāpa, ae,** *bishop, pope.*

[3] **sacrilegus, a, um,** *impious.* A Christian was 'impious' as regards the pagan deities.

[4] **praebeō,** 2, tr., *offer, show.*

[5] **sacrātus, a, um,** *sacred, holy.*

[6] **caeremōnior,** 1, intr., *offer sacrifice.*

[7] **praecipiō, praecipere, praecēpī, praeceptum,** 3, intr.; w. dat., *order.*

[8] **cōnsultātiō, cōnsultātiōnis,** *consideration.* Cyprian means that his duty is so plain there is no room for reconsideration.

[9] **colloquor, colloquī, collocūtus sum,** 3, intr., *talk, confer with.*

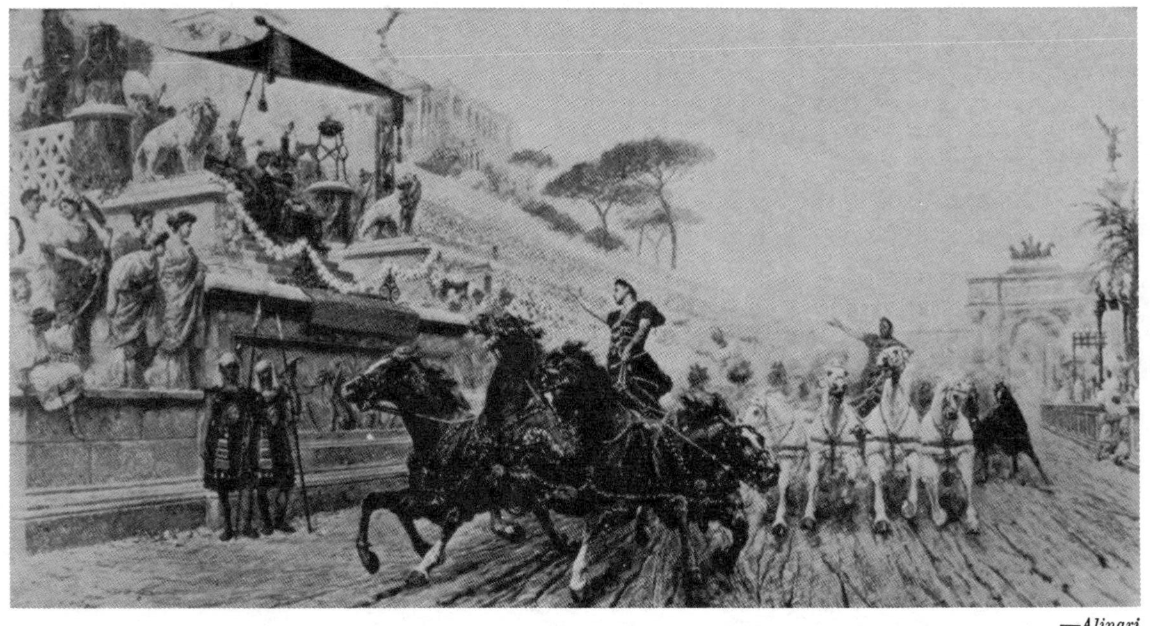

—*Alinari*

HAIL, CAESAR!

No Christian ever could or can now submit to the deification of the emperor or his identification with an omnipotent state. Loyal subjects of emperor and state they always have been, just as they are today of any lawfully constituted government. But between the worship of emperor or state and the worship of Christ they could make but one choice.

aegrē[10] dīxit verbīs hūjusmodī: "Diū sacrilegā mente vīxistī et plūrimōs nefāriae tibi cōnspīrātiōnis[11] hominēs aggregāstī[12] et inimīcum tē diīs Rōmānīs et religiōnibus sacrīs[13] cōnstituistī nec tē piī[14] et sacrātissimī prīncipēs Valerius et Galliēnus[15] Augustī et Valeriānus nōbilissimus Caesar ad sectam[16] caeremōniārum[17] suārum revocāre potuērunt, et ideō[18] cum sīs nēquissimōrum[19] crīminum auctor et signifer[20] dēprehēnsus, eris ipse documentō[21] hīs quōs scelere tuō tēcum aggregāstī; sanguine tuō sānciētur[22] disciplīna." Et hīs dictīs dēcrētum[23] ex tabellā recitāvit: "Thascium Cypriānum gladiō animadvertī placet." Cypriānus epīscopus dīxit: "DEŌ GRĀTIĀS."

And so he, too, like multitudes of others, was led out to give the supreme witness to Christ. Calm, as befitted a successor of the apostles, he received the stroke of the executioner, and became, for all time, a hero of the faith.

---

[10] **aegrē**, adv., *with difficulty*. Cyprian was a prominent and respected personage.

[11] **cōnspīrātiō, cōnspīrātiōnis**, *conspiracy*.

[12] **aggregō**, 1, tr., *join to* (cf. aggregation).

[13] **sacer, sacra, sacrum**, *holy*.

[14] **pius, a, um**, *pious*.

[15] Gallienus was the son of Emperor Valerian (253-260) and had been named coruler by his father. Recall that Caesar and Augustus were titles given to Roman emperors.

[16] **secta, ae**, *following of, observance*.

[17] **caeremōnia, ae**, *sacred rite*.

[18] **ideō**, adv., *therefore*.

[19] **nēquissimus, a, um**, *most wicked* (cf. **nēquitia**).

[20] **signifer, signiferī**, *standard bearer, leader* (**signum** + **ferō**).

[21] **documentum, ī**, *lesson, example*. What case is **documentō**? Why?

[22] **sānciō, sāncīre, sānxī, sānctus**, 4, tr., *establish, confirm* (cf. sanctions).

[23] **dēcrētum, ī**, *judgment* (cf. **dēcernō**).

"LICET CHRISTIANOS ESSE"—CONSTANTINE

[*As the Edict of Milan* (A. D. 313) *might have been headlined.*]

On October 28, A. D. 312, Constantine marched into battle at the Mulvian Bridge. He was completely victorious, and this victory he attributed to the God of the Christians and a vision of the cross which he is said to have seen at midday in the sky emblazoned with the words: *In hōc signō vincēs.*

At any rate, in the following year he and his coemperor, Licinius, issued from Milan the famous edict by which Christians were given full liberty under the law to practice their religion. The following is an excerpt from the official text of the decree.

Cum fēlīciter,[1] tam ego Constantīnus Augustus quam ego Licinius Augustus apud Mediōlānum[2] convēnissēmus atque ūniversa quae ad commoda[3] et sēcūritātem[4] pūblicam pertinērent in tractū[5] habērēmus, haec—inter cētera quae vidēbāmus plūribus hominibus prōfutūra—vel in prīmīs ōrdinanda[6] esse crēdidimus quibus dīvīnitātis[7] reverentia[8] continēbātur ut darēmus ET CHRĪSTIĀNĪS ET OMNIBUS LĪBERAM POTESTĀTEM SEQUENDĪ RELIGIŌNEM QUAM QUISQUE VOLUISSET quō[9] quidem dīvīnitās in sēde caelestī nōbīs atque omnibus quī sub potestāte nostrā sunt cōnstitūtī plācāta ac propitia[10] possit

---

1 **fēlīciter,** adv., *fortunately, happily.*

2 **Mediōlānum, ī,** *Milan.*

3 **commodum, ī,** *advantage, interest, convenience.*

4 **sēcūritās, sēcūritātis,** *security.*

5 **in tractū:** *under consideration.*

6 **ōrdinō,** 1, tr., *regulate.*

7 **dīvīnitās, dīvīnitātis,** *the divinity.*

8 **reverentia, ae,** *reverence, worship.*

9 **quō,** *so that;* introducing a purpose clause.

10 **propitius, a, um,** *well-disposed.*

exsistere. Itaque hōc cōnsiliō salūbrī[11] ac rēctissimā[12] ratiōne ineundum esse crēdidimus ut nūllī omnīnō facultātem abnegandam[13] putārēmus quī vel observātiōnī[14] Chrīstiānōrum vel eī religiōnī mentem suam dederat quam sibi aptissimam esse sentīret ut possit nōbīs summa dīvīnitās, cūjus religiōnī līberīs mentibus obsequimur,[15] in omnibus solitum[16] favōrem[17] suum benevolentiamque praestāre.

---

[11] **salūbris, e,** *beneficial* (cf. **salūs**).

[12] **rēctus, a, um,** *right.*

[13] **abnegō,** 1, tr., *refuse, deny* (cf. **negō**).

[14] **observātiō, observātiōnis,** *observance.*

[15] **obsequor, obsequī, obsecūtus sum,** 3, intr.; w. dat., *submit to.*

[16] **solitus, a, um,** *accustomed, usual.*

[17] **favor, favōris,** *favor.*

—*Ewing Galloway*

Ave Roma Nobilis!

The goal of the pilgrim eyes of all the Christian world.

ROME—THE CAPITAL OF CHRISTENDOM

And so Rome—where so often had echoed that cry, *Chrīstiānī ad leōnēs,*[1] where Paul and Pope Peter had died—became the Rome of the popes, the capital of Christendom, the spiritual center of the world. To its great white Father the Indians of North America would look for guidance, as well as the cultured of China, the wise men of India, the king on his throne, and the worker in the slums.

So did it appear to the pilgrims of the Middle Ages who, as they marched up to Rome's gates, chanted the ancient song of St. Peter Damian:

Ō Rōma nōbilis, orbis et domina,[2]
Cūnctārum urbium excellentissima,[3]
Roseō[4] martyrum sanguine rubea,[5]
Albīs[6] et virginum līliīs[7] candida;[8]
Salūtem dīcimus tibi per omnia;
Tē benedīcimus:[9] salvē[10] per saecula!

---

1 **leō, leōnis,** m., *lion.*

2 **domina, ae,** *mistress.*

3 **excellēns** (*gen.* **excellentis**), *superior, remarkable, surpassing.*

4 **roseus, a, um,** *rosy.*

5 **rubeus, a, um,** *red.*

6 **albus, a, um,** *(dead) white* (cf. the alb, a long white vestment).

7 **līlium, ī,** *lily.*

8 **candidus, a, um,** *(shining) white.* (Candidates for office were so called among the Romans because they were always clothed in white.)

9 **benedīcō, benedīcere, benedīxī, benedictus,** 3, tr., *bless, praise.*

10 **salvē:** *hail;* imperative.

ST. AMBROSE DEFIES THE EMPEROR

But the rights of the Christian Church, won by long ages of suffering, were retained only by constant effort. Eternal vigilance is the price of liberty. Thus again, toward the close of the fourth century, we find St. Ambrose, bishop of Milan, defending the rights of the Church against the powerful Auxentius. The following paragraph is from a sermon delivered A. D. 386 against Auxentius.

Tribūtum[1] Caesaris est, nōn negātur; ecclēsia Deī est. Caesarī utique[2] nōn dēbet adjicī,[3] quia jūs Caesaris esse nōn potest Deī templum. Quod cum honōrificentiā[4] imperātōris dictum nēmō potest negāre. Quid enim honōrificentius[5] quam ut imperātor ecclēsiae fīlius dīcātur? Quod cum dīcātur, sine peccātō dīcitur; cum grātiā dīcitur. Imperātor enim intrā ecclēsiam, nōn suprā[6] ecclēsiam est; bonus enim imperātor quaerit auxilium ecclēsiae, nōn refūtat.[7]

---

1 **tribūtum, ī,** *tribute.*

2 **utique,** adv., *certainly, surely, without fail.*

3 **adjiciō, adjicere, adjēcī, adjectus,** 3, tr., *add to, hurl to.*

4 **honōrificentia, ae,** *honor, acknowledgment of honor.*

5 **honōrificentior, ius,** *more honorable.*

6 **suprā,** prep. w. acc., *above.*

7 **refūtō,** 1, tr., *repress, oppose.*

THE POPES TODAY—WORLD LEADERS

Through the ages the Church in its popes and sainted leaders has continued to guide and govern the great mass of Christians who acknowledge Christ's vicar at Rome. In our own days scholars like Leo XIII, Pius X, Pius XI, and Pius XII have assumed a spiritual leadership extending far beyond the limits of the Church, a leadership acknowledged by all those who love peace, justice, and liberty under law. Pius XI it was who, in Ciceronic language, condemned Communism as an *inventum*[1] *quod dēnique hūmānae*[2] *persōnae*[3] *jūra, dignitātem, lībertātem dētrectat*[4] *ac dēnegat.*[5]

At the solemn funeral services for the same Holy Father, Angelo Perrugini spoke thus of his dedication to peace:

Nōn est hic locus, ēminentissimī[6] Prīncipēs, nōn est tempus singula persequendī quae complōrātus[7] Pontifex praeclārē gessit. Sed, quoniam mihi contigit, jussū mandātōque vestrō[8] dē diūturnō[9] glōriōsōque pontificātū[10] verba facere, ēnītar,[11] ut praecipuam[12] ējus apostolicī mūneris[13] partem per summa capita re-

---

1 **inventum, ī,** *thing discovered, invention.*

2 **hūmānus, a, um,** *human, refined.*

3 **persōna, ae,** *person.*

4 **dētrectō,** 1, tr., *reject.*

5 **dēnegō,** 1, tr., *deny.*

6 **ēminēns** (*gen.* **ēminentis**), *illustrious, eminent.*

7 **complōrātus, a, um,** *lamented.*

8 **jussū mandātōque vestrō:** *by your order and command.*

9 **diūturnus, a, um,** *long.*

10 **pontificātus, ūs,** *pontificate.*

11 **ēnītor, ēnītī, ēnīxus sum,** 3, intr., *try.*

12 **praecipuus, a, um,** *principal, main.*

13 **mūnus, mūneris,** *function, duty, gift.*

feram, eam scīlicet[14] pecūliāriter[15] attinentem[16] ad doctrīnam ex Litterīs Encyclicīs[17] dēsūmptam,[18] quae quidem ideō datae sunt,[19] ut suāděrent ac fovērent[20] pācem mentium et animōrum, pācem domesticam et cīvīlem, pācem inter populōs gentēsque ūniversās, jūxtā[21] illud signum: *Pāx Chrīstī in Rēgnō Chrīstī.*

On March 2, 1939 His Eminence Camillo Caccia Dominioni proclaimed from the balcony of the Vatican Basilica to the crowds below and to the radio audience of the world the election of Pius XII to succeed Pius XI: "Annuntiō[22] vōbīs gaudium magnum. Habēmus pāpam, Ēminentissimum ac Reverendissimum[23] Cardinālem[24] Eugenium Pacelli,[25] quī sibi nōmen imposuit Pium XII."

The next day, March 3, Pius XII spoke to the world by radio and left no doubt that he would champion the causes dear to the heart of his great predecessor Pius XI. Said Pius XII:

Ac Nostrō huic paternō nuntiō ōmen[26] pācis adjicere invītātiōnemque[27] cupimus. Pācem, dīcimus, quam Noster piae recordātiōnis Dēcessor[28] tam impensē[29] hominibus suāsit tamque

---

[14] **scīlicet**, adv., *namely.*

[15] **pecūliāriter**, adv., *especially, particularly.*

[16] **attineō, attinēre, attinuī, attentus,** 2, intr., *pertain to.*

[17] **Litterae (Litterārum) Encyclicae (Encyclicārum),** *Encyclicals.*

[18] **dēsumō, dēsūmere, dēsūmpsī, dēsūmptus,** 3, tr., *take from.*

[19] **ideō datae sunt:** *were written with a view to.*

[20] **foveō, fovēre, fōvī, fōtus,** 2, tr., *nourish, favor.*

[21] **jūxtā,** prep. w. acc., *according to.*

[22] **annuntiō,** 1, tr., *make known, announce, proclaim.*

[23] **reverendus, a, um,** *reverend.*

[24] **cardināl, cardinālis,** m., *cardinal.*

[25] **Eugenius (ī) Pacelli,** *Eugenio Pacelli.*

[26] **ōmen, ōminis,** *omen, sign.*

[27] **invītātiō, invītātiōnis,** *invitation.*

[28] **Noster piae recordātiōnis Dēcessor:** *our predecessor of pious memory.*

[29] **impensē,** adv., *earnestly.*

ēnīxīs[30] precibus[31] implōrāvit, ut suam Deō vītam prō conciliandā[32] hominum concordiā ultrō dēvovēret.[33] Pācem, Deī mūnus pulcherrimum, quae exsuperat[34] omnem sēnsum; pācem dēnique, quae ex jūstitiā cāritāteque oritur. Ad pācem illam adhortāmur[35] omnēs, quae animōs amīcitiā Deī conjūnctōs refovet,[36] quaeque domesticum convīctum[37] sacrō Jēsū Chrīstī amōre temperat[38] atque compōnit;[39] ad pācem quae nātiōnēs ac gentēs per mūtuum[40] frāternumque auxilium conjungit; ad pācem dēnique atque concordiam ita inter nātiōnēs īnstaurandam,[41] ut singulae gentēs mūtuā cōnsēnsiōne, amīcō foedere[42] atque adjūtrīce[43] operā, ad ūniversae hominum familiae prōfectum[44] fēlīcitātemque,[45] aspīrante[46] juvanteque[47] Deō, contendant.

The year 1958 witnessed the death of the beloved Pius XII on October 8. Twenty days after his death the conclave of cardinals chose as his successor Angelo Giuseppe Roncalli, patriarch of Venice, who upon being told of his election said (as quoted in *Acta Apostolicae Sēdis*):

Audiēns verba tua "tremēns"[48] factus sum ego, et timeō. Quae

---

[30] **ēnīxus, a, um,** *strong, eager.*
[31] **precēs, precum,** f., *prayers, entreaties.*
[32] **conciliō,** 1, tr., *win over, conciliate.*
[33] **dēvoveō, dēvovēre, dēvōvī, dēvōtus,** 2, tr., *offer, dedicate, sacrifice.*
[34] **exsuperō,** 1, tr., *surpass.*
[35] **adhortor,** 1, tr., *exhort.*
[36] **refoveō, refovēre, refōvī, refōtus,** 2, tr., *cherish again, revive.*
[37] **convīctus, ūs,** *life.*
[38] **temperō,** 1, tr., *regulate.*
[39] **compōnō, compōnere, composuī, compositus,** 3, tr., *compose.*
[40] **mūtuus, a, um,** *mutual.*
[41] **īnstaurō,** 1, tr., *reestablish.*
[42] **foedus, foederis,** *treaty, agreement.*
[43] **adjūtrīx, adjūtrīcis,** *an assistant, a helper.*
[44] **prōfectus, ūs,** *progress.*
[45] **fēlīcitās, fēlīcitātis,** *happiness.*
[46] **aspīrō,** 1, tr., *favor.*
[47] **juvō, juvāre, jūvī, jūtus,** 1, tr., *help, please.*
[48] **tremō, tremere, tremuī,** 3, intr., *tremble, quake.*

sciō dē meā paupertāte[49] et vilitāte[50] sufficiunt[51] ad meam confūsiōnem.[52] Sed cum videam in vōtīs[53] Frātrum meōrum Ēminentissimōrum Sānctae Rōmānae Ecclēsiae Cardinālium signum voluntātis Deī, acceptō[54] ēlectiōnem[55] ab ipsīs factam: et caput meum et dorsum[56] meum inclīnō[57] ad calicem[58] amāritūdinis[59] et ad patientiam Crucis. In sollemnitāte[60] Chrīstī Rēgis cantāvimus[61] omnēs: "Dominus jūdex noster: Dominus lēgifer[62] noster: Dominus rēx noster, ipse salvābit[63] nōs."

The newly elected Pope then said to the conclave:

Vocābor[64] Jōannēs. Nōmen Nōbīs dulce,[65] quia nōmen patris Nostrī; nōmen Nōbīs suāve,[66] quia titulāre[67] est humilis[68] paroeciae[69] in quā baptismum[70] accēpimus: nōmen sollemne[71] innumerābilium[72] Cathedrālium,[73] quae in tōtō orbe terrārum

---

49 **paupertās, paupertātis,** *poverty, moderate means.*

50 **vilitās, vilitātis,** *worthlessness.*

51 **sufficiō, sufficere, suffēcī, suffectum,** 3, intr., *am sufficient.*

52 **confūsiō, confūsiōnis,** *confusion, blushing.*

53 **vōtum, ī,** *vote, wish.*

54 **acceptō,** 1, tr., *accept, take.*

55 **ēlectiō, ēlectiōnis,** *choice, election.*

56 **dorsum, ī,** *back (of a man).*

57 **inclīnō,** 1, tr., *bend, bow down.*

58 **calix, calicis,** m., *chalice.*

59 **amāritūdō, amāritūdinis,** *bitterness.*

60 **sollemnitās, sollemnitātis,** *festival, celebration.*

61 **cantō,** 1, tr. and intr., *sing, chant.*

62 **lēgifer, lēgifera, lēgiferum,** *lawgiving* (**lēx** + **ferō**).

63 **salvō,** 1, tr., *save.*

64 **vocō,** 1, tr., *name, call.*

65 **dulcis, e,** *sweet (of taste or smell), pleasant, loved.*

66 **suāvis, e,** *agreeable, delightful.*

67 **titulāris, e,** *titular.* Before **titulāre** understand **nōmen.**

68 **humilis, e,** *humble, lowly.*

69 **paroecia, ae,** *parish.*

70 **baptismum, ī,** *baptism.*

71 **sollemnis, e,** *solemn, religious.*

72 **innumerābilis, e,** *countless.*

73 **cathedrālis, cathedrālis,** *cathedral.*

habentur . . . nōmen quod in seriē[74] pervetustā[75] Rōmānōrum Pontificum gaudet dē maximō prīmātū[76] plūrālitātis.[77] Sunt enim ēnumerātī[78] Summī Pontificēs, quibus nōmen Jōannēs, vīgintī duo. . . .

Sed nōmen Jōannēs Nōbīs et tōtī Ecclēsiae cārissimum pecūliārī[79] modō dīligimus: et quidem ob duplicem[80] ējus appellātiōnem:[81] scīlicet[82] ob appellātiōnem[81] duōrum virōrum quī propinquiōrēs fuērunt, et sunt, Chrīstō Dominō, ūniversī mundī Redemptōrī[83] Dīvīnō et Ecclēsiae Fundātōrī.[84]

Jōannēs Baptista[85] precursor[86] Dominī: quī nōn erat certē ille lūx, sed testimōnium erat dē lūmine: et vērē fuit testimōnium invictum[87] vēritātis, jūstitiae, lībertātis, in praedicātiōne,[88] in baptismō[89] paenitentiae,[90] in profūsō[91] sanguine.

Et alter Jōannēs discipulus et ēvangelista,[92] Chrīstō et Mātrī suae dulcissimae[93] summopere[94] dīlēctus,[95] quī suprā[96]

---

74 **seriēs, seriēī,** *series, chain, unbroken line of descent.*
75 **pervetustus, a, um,** *very old, ancient.*
76 **prīmātus, ūs,** *primacy, first place, pre-eminence.*
77 **plūrālitās, plūrālitātis,** *plurality, greater number.*
78 **ēnumerō,** 1, tr., *count up, number.*
79 **pecūliāris, e,** *proper, special.*
80 **duplex** (*gen.* **duplicis**), *twofold, double.*
81 **appellātiō, appellātiōnis,** *naming, calling by name.*
82 **scīlicet,** adv., *namely.*
83 **redemptor, redemptōris,** *redeemer.*
84 **fundātor, fundātōris,** *founder.*
85 **baptista, ae,** m., *baptist, one who baptizes.*
86 **precursor, precursōris,** *forerunner, precursor.*
87 **invictus, a, um,** *unconquerable, invincible.*
88 **praedicātio, praedicatiōnis,** *preaching.*
89 **baptismus, ī,** *baptism.*
90 **paenitentia, ae,** *penance.*
91 **profundō, profundere, profūdī, profūsus,** 3, tr., *pour forth, shed copiously.*
92 **ēvangelista, ae,** m., *evangelist.*
93 **dulcis, e,** *sweet (of taste or smell), pleasant, loved.*
94 **summopere,** adv., *most especially.*
95 **dīlēctus, a, um,** *loved, beloved.*
96 **suprā,** prep. w. acc., *on, above.*

pectus[97] Dominī in cena[98] recubuit,[99] et inde hausit[100] cāritātem[101] illam cūjus fuit usque ad prōvectam[102] senectūtem[103] flamma vīvāx[104] et apostolica.

Faxit Deus[105] ut uterque Jōannēs clāmitet[106] in ecclēsiā ūniversā per humillimum[107] ministerium[108] pastōrāle[109] Nostrum, . . . clāmitet[106] Clērō[110] et populō ūniversō hoc opus Nostrum, quō cupimus parāre Dominō plēbem perfectam,[111] rectās[112] facere sēmitās[113] ējus, ut sint prāva[114] in directa[115] et aspera[116] in viās plānās:[117] ut videat omnis carō[118] salūtāre[119] Deī. . . .

Concēdat benignissimus[120] Deus, Venerābilēs Frātrēs, ut Nōs, quī eōdem nōmine insignīmur[121] ac prīmus in hāc Summōrum Pontificum seriē,[122] eādem etiam sanctitāte[123] vītae, eādemque

---

97 **pectus, pectoris,** n., *breast.*

98 **cena, ae,** *supper.*

99 **recumbō, recumbere, recubuī,** 3, intr., *to lie, lie down.*

100 **hauriō, haurīre, hausī, haustus,** 4, tr., *draw, drain.*

101 **cāritās, cāritātis,** *love.*

102 **prōvectus, a, um,** *advanced.*

103 **senectus, senectūtis,** *old age.*

104 **vīvāx** (*gen.* **vīvācis**), *tenacious of life, long-lived.*

105 **Faxit Deus:** *may God grant.*

106 **clāmitō,** 1, tr., *cry out aloud, announce.*

107 **humilis, e,** *humble, lowly.*

108 **ministerium, ī,** *ministry, service.*

109 **pastōrālis, e,** *pastoral.*

110 **clērus, ī,** *the clergy.*

111 **perfectus, a, um,** *perfect.*

112 **rectus, a, um,** *straight.*

113 **sēmita, ae,** *path, way.*

114 **prāvus, a, um,** *crooked.*

115 **directus, a, um,** *straight, direct.*

116 **asper, aspera, asperum,** *rough, uneven.*

117 **plānus, a, um,** *level, smooth.*

118 **carō, carnis,** *flesh.*

119 **salūtāris, e,** *saving, salutary* (used here as a neuter noun: *salvation*).

120 **benignus, a, um,** *good, benignant, kind.*

121 **insigniō, insignīre, insignīvī, insignītus,** 4, tr., *to call (by name), to name.*

122 **sēries, seriēī,** *chain, unbroken line of descent.*

123 **sanctitās, sanctitātis,** *sanctity.*

animī fortitūdine, usque ad profūsiōnem[124] sanguinis, sī Dominō placuerit, dīvīnā adjuvante grātiā, ēnitēre[125] possīmus.

Despite the world's joy and the ovations that hailed his election to the Chair of St. Peter, the Pontiff's heart was heavy, for he was keenly aware of the struggle going on in the world. He had said to the Cardinals at his coronation: "Ōs Nostrum est sine vōce, sed cor[126] Nostrum patet ad vōs," and open it did in the following telegram to a prominent victim of persecution, which with only a few changes was also sent to another victim, Cardinal Stepinac:

Dīlēctō[127] Fīliō Nostrō Cardinālī[128] Jōsēphō Mindszenty, Strigoniēnsī[129] Archiepiscopō.[130] Vehementer dolentēs,[131] quod in Nostrā ad Petrī Solium[132] assumptiōne[133] tē hīc paternā[134] cāritāte amplectī[135] nequīmus,[136] tibi, dīlēcte[127] Fīlī Noster, singulārem Apostolicam Benedictiōnem[137] caelestium mūnerum auspicem,[138] impertīmus.[139]

---

124 **profūsiō, profūsiōnis,** *shedding, effusion.*
125 **ēniteō, ēnitēre, ēnituī,** 2, intr., *shine forth, shine out.*
126 **cor, cordis,** n., *heart.*
127 **dīlēctus, a, um,** *beloved.*
128 **cardināl, cardinālis,** m., *cardinal.*
129 **Strigoniēnsis, e,** *of Esztergom.*
130 **archiepiscopus, ī,** *archbishop.*
131 **doleō, dolēre, doluī, dolitum,** 2, intr., *grieve.*
132 **solium, iī,** *chair, seat.*
133 **assumptiō, assumptiōnis,** *receiving, taking.*
134 **paternus, a, um,** *fatherly.*
135 **amplector, amplectī, amplexus sum,** 3, tr., *embrace.*
136 **nequeō, nequīre, nequīvī, nequitum,** 4, intr., *am unable.*
137 **benedictiō, benedictiōnis,** *blessing, benediction.*
138 **auspex, auspicis,** *the beginning, harbinger.*
139 **impertiō, impertīre, impertīvī, impertītus,** 4, tr., *impart, bestow.*

THE TWO STANDARDS

Victory in the clash between Christ and His foes depends upon the generosity with which each individual Christian fights under the standard of the Cross. Long since has the Roman eagle been replaced by the *Vexilla*[1] *Regis*—the *signum crucis.*

In hōc signō vincēs—so it seemed to Ignatius of Loyola. Himself a soldier, he had been wounded in the siege of Pampeluna. But the cannon ball that fractured his leg did not shatter his dreams of conquest; it only changed his allegiance. Why should Don Iñigo risk life and limb under the flag of an earthly ruler when his could be certain victory under the banner of the eternal King of Kings?

In his recruiting manual, *The Spiritual Exercises,* St. Ignatius with one bold stroke cut the globe into two worlds in conflict:

Quartā diē fiet meditātiō[2] dē duōbus vexillīs,[1] ūnō quidem Jēsū Chrīstī optimī nostrī imperātōris; alterō vērō Lūciferī,[3] hostis hominum capitāllissimī.[4] . . . Erit consīderātiō[5] Chrīstī ex ūnā parte, et ex alterā Lūciferī,[3] quōrum uterque omnēs hominēs ad sē vocat, sub vexillō[1] suō congregandōs.

St. Ignatius then sketches the diametrically opposed campaign plans of the rival leaders for the souls of men:

Trēs consurgunt[6] perfectiōnis[7] gradūs,[8] vidēlicet paupertās,[9]

---

[1] **vexillum, ī,** *standard, flag, banner.*

[2] **meditātiō, meditātiōnis,** *meditation, mental prayer.*

[3] **Lūcifer, Lūciferī,** *Lucifer,* prince of the fallen angels (**lūx** + **ferō**).

[4] **capitālis, e,** *relating to the head, first, chief* (cf. **caput**).

[5] **consīderātiō, consīderātiōnis,** *reflection, consideration.*

[6] **consurgō, consurgere, consurrēxī, consurrēctum,** 3, intr., *arise, spring up.*

[7] **perfectiō, perfectiōnis,** *perfection.*

[8] **gradus, ūs,** *step, interval.*

[9] **paupertās, paupertātis,** *poverty.*

abjectiō suī,[10] atque humilitās,[11] quae ex diametrō[12] dīvitiīs,[13] honōrī, et superbiae[14] opponuntur,[15] ac virtūtēs omnēs statim intrōdūcunt.

He concludes the consideration by instructing us to make three *colloquia* or prayers:

Colloquium[16] [prīmum] ad Virginem beātam, implōranda est per eam ā Fīliō grātia, ut recipī possim et manēre sub Vexillō[1] Ējus; . . . secundum [colloquium[16]] ad Chrīstum hominem dīrigitur,[17] ut mihi ā Patre impetret illud idem; tertium [colloquium[16]] ad Patrem, ut annuat[18] petītiōnī.[19]

It is the timeless choice which Pilate gave the Jews: Christ or Barabbas. *Quī nōn est mēcum, contrā mē est.* For the founder of the Company of Jesus the forces in conflict were as clearly distinguishable as black and white. Ever after Pampeluna his steady vision saw life

. . . wind
Off her once skeined stained veined variety upon, all on two spools; part, pen, pack
Now her all in two flocks, two folds—black, white; right, wrong.[20]

In fact, when Ignatius was still unsure what shape his new service would take, Christ appeared to him on the way to the Eternal City and said, "*Tibi propitius erō Rōmae.*" And it was at Rome that things disposed themselves in his favor.

---

[10] **abjectiō suī:** *contempt of self.*
[11] **humilitās, humilitātis,** *humility.*
[12] **ex diametrō:** *diametrically.*
[13] **dīvitiae, dīvitiārum,** *riches.*
[14] **superbia, ae,** *pride.*
[15] **oppōnō, oppōnere, opposuī, oppositum,** 3, intr.; w. dat., *oppose.*
[16] **colloquium, iī,** *prayer (conversation).*
[17] **dīrigō, dīrigere, dīrēxī, dīrēctus,** 3, tr., *direct.*
[18] **annuō, annuere, annuī, annūtum,** 3, intr.; w. dat., *pay heed to, listen to.*
[19] **petītiō, petītiōnis,** *petition, prayer.*
[20] Gerard Manley Hopkins, S. J., *Spelt from Sibyl's Leaves.*

EPILOGUE

"No servant is greater than his master. If they have persecuted me, they will persecute you." Christianity's struggle ended in Rome only to begin anew in other lands and other times. The spirit of Nero and Diocletian has never died, nor has the spirit of Peter and Paul, of Felicity and Perpetua. In every age and in every land Christians have given their blood in love and loyalty to Christ, to His church, to His vicar on earth—a proof of devotion greater than which no man can give. From Stephen that spirit of loyalty had spread to Rome. England saw it in Campion and More. And when the fire Christ had come to cast upon the world had kindled all Europe and leaped the ocean, America saw it in Jogues, Brebeuf, and their companions. The procession of palms goes on—on to the Eternal City of which St. John spoke:

> After this I saw a great multitude which no man could number, out of all nations and tribes and peoples and tongues, standing before the throne and before the Lamb, clothed in white robes, and with palms in their hands. And they cried with a loud voice, saying, "Salvation belongs to our God who sits upon the throne, and to the Lamb." . . . And one of the elders spoke and said . . . "These are they who have come out of the great tribulation, and have washed their robes and made them white in the blood of the Lamb. Therefore they are before the throne of God, and serve him day and night in his temple, and he who sits upon the throne will dwell with them. They shall neither hunger nor thirst any more, neither shall the sun strike them nor any heat. For the Lamb who is in the midst of the throne will shepherd them, and will guide them to the fountains of the waters of life, and God will wipe away every tear from their eyes."[1]

Here is a promise of the end of blood and sweat and tears—the end of conflict in eternal life. But as long as men on earth follow the Lamb of God, this saying is true:

SANGUIS MARTYRUM: SEMEN CHRISTIANORUM

---

[1] Apocalypse 7:9-17.

PART IV

EXERCISES BASED ON CICERO

LESSON 1: DIRECT QUESTIONS; *QUIS, QUID*

VOCABULARY

audācia, ae	*boldness* *daring* *recklessness*
Catilīna, ae, *m.*	*Catiline*
scientia, ae	*knowledge*
vigilia, ae	*night watch* *guard*
oculus, ī	*eye*
incendium, ī	*fire* *conflagration*
conjūrātiō, conjūrātiōnis	*conspiracy* *plot*
Cicerō, Cicerōnis	*Cicero*
fīnis, fīnis, *m.*	*end* (pl.) *territory*
furor, furōris	*rage* *frenzy* *madness*
mōs, mōris, *m.*	*manner* *custom* (pl.) *character*
pestis, pestis	*plague* *ruin*
pūblicus, a, um	*public*
nocturnus, a, um	*nocturnal* *nightly*
quam, *adv.*	*how*
ignōrō, *1, tr.; acc. w. infin.*	*not know* *am unaware* *overlook*

convocō, ***1, tr.***	*call together* *summon together*
pateō, patēre, patuī, ***2, intr.***	*lie open* *am open* *extend*
vītō, ***1, tr.***	*avoid* *shun*
jam, ***adv.***	*already* *now*
vērō, ***adv. and conj.; postp.***	*in truth* *but* *of course*
jam prīdem **jam diū** **jam dūdum**	*long (since)* *long (ago)*

RELATED ENGLISH WORDS

Ours is often referred to as the age of *science*. The ***vigil*** of Christmas is a day of fast and abstinence. The *oculist* told the old gentleman to wear a pair of bifocals instead of his ridiculous mon*ocle*. *Final* examinations. He attended one of the *public* schools. The neighborhood was terrified by the *furious* attacks of *nocturnal* prowlers. *Ignorance* of a law does not always excuse one from responsibility. He told a *patent* lie before the *convocation*. *Incendiary* bombs work havoc on thickly populated areas.

RELATED LATIN WORDS

Sciō; vigilō; nox; noctū; vocō; audāx; incendō.

IDIOM

Jam diū, jam dūdum, and **jam prīdem** are used as follows:

I have long (since) been . . . **Jam diū** or **jam dūdum** with the present.

You have long (since) been desiring our death.
Jam diū mortem nostram cupis.

I had long (since) been . . . **Jam prīdem** or **jam dūdum** with the imperfect.

You had long (since) been desiring our death.
Jam prīdem mortem nostram cupiēbās.

ASSIGNMENT: *First Oration against Catiline,* lines 1-31; GRAMMAR 140, 141; 502-508; Review GRAMMAR 14-71.

MEMORY: Precēs Cotīdiānae, page 214.

EXERCISE 1

Translate:

1. Quis erat Catilīna et ubi erat? 2. Nōnne Cicerō in senātum venit? 3. Num populus Rōmānus omnia intellēxit? 4. Quis dēsignāverat ūnumquemque nostrum ad caedem? 5. Intellēxitne cōnsul conjūrātiōnem cōnstrictam[1] jam omnium scientiā tenērī? 6. Quam diū vīderat cōnsul conjūrātiōnem esse factam? 7. Cōnsulēs vīdērunt, senātus intellēxit, iste tamen vīvēbat; vērō in senātum vēnit; notābat et dēsignābat ad caedem ūnumquemque eōrum. 8. Quid proximā nocte ēgistī? 9. Quō tandem tempore venient tempora bona? 10. Urbis vigiliae mē nōn movent. 11. Cōnsul Catilīnae furōrem vīdit. 12. Utrum vīvis in urbe annōn? 13. Hominēs bonī loca pūblica et concursum populī saepe vītant. 14. Urbem mūnītam nocturnō impetū cēpērunt. 15. Quō ībis? 16. Quam diū in hāc urbe vīxistī? 17. Nunc vērō quae tua est ista vīta? 18. Quōs amīcōs convocāstī?[2] 19. Quid agis? 20. Nōs omnēs multa ignōrāmus et ignōrābimus. 21. Urbis portae patēbant. 22. An omnia mala vītāre possumus? 23. In tē cōnferrī jam prīdem oportēbat pestem quam tū in nōs omnēs jam diū parās. 24. Cōnsulēs, virī fortēs, jam prīdem Catilīnae furōrem ac tēla vītābant. 25. Jam dūdum oportēbat Catilīnam ad mortem jussū cōnsulis dūcī. 26. Jam diū timōrem populī vītāmus. 27. Locum habendī

---

[1] **cōnstrictus, a, um,** *held in check, checked, repressed.*
[2] See Gr. 1023.

senātūs jam prīdem mūniēbant. 28. Superiōre nocte cōnsulēs in senātū vīdī. 29. Quid vīdistī in urbe? Vīdimus incendium senātūs. 30. Imperātor sēnsit sua consīlia patēre. 31. Utrum putās urbem nostram esse pulchram[1] annōn? 32. Num sēnsit populus Rōmānus urbem praesidiīs vigiliīsque esse mūnītam? 33. Quibuscum vēnērunt in senātum? 34. Quōcum vīvis in urbe? 35. Chrīstus usque ad fīnem patientiam habuit. 36. Hostium audācia atque furor nostrōs usque ad fugam mōvērunt. 37. Hostēs incendium urbis jam dūdum cupiēbant.

"BUT LET YOUR SPEECH BE, 'YES, YES'; 'NO, NO'"[2]

Now you may be wondering how to answer a question in Latin; at least how to say Yes and No.

For *yes:* (1) use **ita, ita est, sīc, sānē, etiam, utique, certē, vērō, omnīnō,** or **profectō;** or (2) simply repeat the emphatic word.

1. **Vidēsne locum? Ita.**
2. **Intelligisne hoc? Intelligō.**

For *no:* **(1)** use **nōn, minimē, nēquāquam, haudquāquam, nūllō modo;** (2) repeat the emphatic word with a negation; or (3) use **immō** with the addition of the contrary.

1. **Fuistīne in urbe illā nocte? Nūllō modo.**
2. **Habēmusne senātum hāc in urbe? Nōn habēmus.**
3. **Eratne bonus Catilīna? Immō malus.**

EXERCISE 2

Respondē Latīnē:

1. Quis es? 2. Ubi vīvis? 3. Quid proximā nocte ēgistī? 4. Quō tempore hunc in locum vēnistī? 5. Quōcum vēnistī? 6. Vīvisne in urbe? 7. Quis erat Cicerō? 8. Nōnne factus est Cicerō cōnsul? 9. Num omnia vīderat? 10. Quō tempore sēnsit conjūrātiōnem

---

[1] **pulcher, pulchra, pulchrum,** *beautiful, noble, glorious.*

[2] Matthew 5:37.

esse factam? 11. Quam diū vīxit in urbe? 12. Ubi convocāvit senātum? 13. Mūnītusne erat locus habendī senātūs? 14. Num Catilīna haec omnia intellēxit? 15. Sēnsitne Catilīna cōnsilia sua patēre? 16. Erantne mōrēs Catilīnae bonī? 17. Num senātus populusque Rōmānus ignōrāvit omnia? 18. Quem ad fīnem facta erat conjūrātiō? 19. Nōnne mōvit Catilīnam timor bonōrum omnium? 20. Eratne Cicerō bonus? 21. Intelligisne haec omnia? 22. Sumusne omnēs in urbe?

EXERCISE 3

Translate:

1. Where are you living? 2. You live in the city, don't you? 3. How long will you live in the city? 4. The people did not know about Catiline's daring, did they? 5. Did Cicero already know everything? 6. At what time did Cicero come into the Senate? 7. With whom did he come? 8. Whom had Catiline called together on that night? 9. But where were the consuls? 10. Of course you understand all this,[1] don't you? 11. The Roman people overlooked Catiline's recklessness. 12. They came last night. 13. Good times are now coming. 14. At what time will they come? 15. About that I, in truth, know nothing. 16. The night before last I saw the night watches of the Senate. 17. The city gates were open and they saw the fire. 18. Cicero had long since fortified a place for holding the Senate. 19. Where will the enemy flee? 20. He won't now hold the Senate in the city, will he? 21. Don't you think the conspiracy is exposed?[2] 22. Did the Roman people know all this[1] or were they unaware (of it)? 23. The saints pursue the knowledge of God even to the end of life. 24. You ought long ago to have been led to (your) death. 25. We have long been shunning the plague. 26. Don't you know that the consul sees your plot? 27. You summoned those men together last night. 28. We will avoid your mad weapons.[3] 29. Our territory extends all the way to the river.

---

[1] Use the plural.

[2] Use **pateō**.

[3] mad weapons = madness and weapons.

30. You have long been trying to avoid the attacks of the enemy. 31. The nocturnal guards of the city move me not at all. 32. "Catiline," says Cicero, "has long been making a plan against the lives of all of us." 33. He even comes into the Senate. 34. Or do you think we do not know about the nightly conflagrations? 35. There was rage in the consul's eyes because of the public ruin.

PRECĒS CHRĪSTIĀNAE COTĪDIĒ FACIENDAE[1]

Signum Crucis

In nōmine Patris et Fīliī et Spīritūs Sānctī. Āmēn.

Pater Noster

They had seen Him praying. One of the disciples said to Him: "Lord, teach us to pray . . ." And He said to them, "When you pray, say: Our Father . . ."

Christ's answer was not a learned lecture on the need, nature, and manner of prayer. His was the direct, concrete answer. He gave them a master prayer upon which to model.

There is a unity, a simple charm about the sixfold petitions of the Pater. For God three things are asked: that He be given glory as Father, dominion as King, service as Master; three things for man: that God give him provision as Father, pardon as King; protection as Master.

When you are wondering how to pray, take a lesson from the masterpiece which came from the Master who said, "When you pray, say:

" 'Pater noster, quī es in caelīs, sānctificētur[2] nōmen tuum. Adveniat rēgnum tuum. Fīat voluntās tua, sīcut in caelō et in

[1] Christian Prayers to Be Recited Daily. These prayers, all of which were given in First Year Latin, are repeated here so that they may be memorized and used for the daily class prayer. Let the students take turns leading prayers.

[2] **sānctificō**, 1, tr., *sanctify, hallow* (cf. All Hallows, the old word for All Saints).

terrā. Pānem nostrum cotīdiānum[1] dā nōbīs hodiē.[2] Et dīmitte[3] nōbīs dēbita[4] nostra, sīcut et nōs dīmittimus[3] dēbitōribus[5] nostrīs. Et nē nōs indūcās in tentātiōnem:[6] sed līberā nōs ā malō. Āmēn.' "

Ave Maria

She was at prayer—"breathless with adoration"—when on a sudden Gabriel comes from God, speaks to the maid at Nazareth, "Hail, Mary, full of grace." Here was forever the companion to the Lord's Prayer, the Angelic Salutation to Our Lady.

Avē, Marīa, grātiā plēna; Dominus tēcum; benedicta[7] tū in mulieribus,[8] et benedictus[7] frūctus[9] ventris[10] tuī Jēsūs. Sāncta Marīa, Mater Deī, ōrā prō nōbīs peccātōribus,[11] nunc et in hōrā mortis nostrae. Āmēn.

Doxologia

Glōria Patrī, et Fīliō, et Spīrituī Sānctō. Sīcut erat in prīncipiō, et nunc, et semper, et in saecula saeculōrum. Āmēn.

---

[1] **cotīdiānus, a, um,** *daily, everyday;* sometimes spelled **quotīdiānum.**
[2] **hodiē,** adv., *today, on this day* (**hōc** + **diē**).
[3] **dīmittō, dīmittere, dīmīsī, dīmissus,** 3, tr., *send away, dismiss, forgive.*
[4] **dēbitum, ī,** *debt, offense.*
[5] **dēbitor, dēbitōris,** *debtor.*
[6] **tentātiō, tentātiōnis,** *temptation, trial, test.*
[7] **benedictus, a, um,** *blessed.*
[8] **mulier, mulieris,** *woman.*
[9] **frūctus, ūs,** *fruit.*
[10] **venter, ventris,** *womb.*
[11] **peccātor, peccātōris,** *sinner.*

LESSON 2: INDIRECT QUESTIONS

VOCABULARY

poena, ae **supplicium, ī**	*punishment* *penalty*
cōnsultum, ī	*decree* *resolution* (of the Senate)
cīvis, cīvis, *m.*	*citizen* *fellow citizen*
orbis (orbis) terrārum (*sometimes* terrae)	*world*
praetor, praetōris	*praetor*
manus, ūs, *f.*	*hand* *band*
rēs (reī) pūblica (ae)	*state*
rēs (rērum) novae (novārum)	*revolution* (lit., *new things*)
antīquus, a, um	*ancient* *former*
clārus, a, um	*famous* *loud* *clear*
perniciōsus, a, um	*dangerous* *destructive*
prīvātus, a, um	*private* *personal (personally)*
cōnsulāris, e	*of consular rank* *ex-consul* (as a noun)
apertē, *adv.*	*openly* *plainly*
omnīnō, *adv.*	*altogether*
dēcernō, dēcernere, dēcrēvī, dēcrētus, *3, tr.; w. infin. if subject is the same;* ut (nē) *if subject is different*	*determine* *decide* *decree*

permittō, permittere, permīsī, permissus, *3, tr.; w. dat. of person; acc. of thing;* **ut (nē)**	*give over* / *entrust*
at, *conj.*	*but*
quōmodo, *adv.*	*how*

RELATED ENGLISH WORDS

Penal laws. The Romans had great *civic* pride. *Manu*script. The Hammond organ has two *manuals*. We study Latin not for its *antiquarian* but for its literary value. His was a *pernicious* influence on the government. *Republic.*

ASSIGNMENT: *First Oration against Catiline,* lines 32-63; GRAMMAR 660-662; Review GRAMMAR 186-207, 315-316, 352-356.

MEMORY: *First Oration against Catiline,* lines 1-11.

EXERCISE 4

Translate; explain the italicized words:

1. Cicerō senātōrēs rogat quid dē rē pūblicā *sentiant.* 2. "Quid," inquit, "dē rē pūblica sentītis?" 3. Senātōrēs quid dē rē pūblicā sentīre *dēbērent* nōn intellēxērunt. 4. Cicerō rogāvit quid Catilīna ante lūcem *ēgisset.* 5. Rogābō quis mē *exspectet.* 6. Nōn omnēs ignōrāmus ubi *fuerīs.* 7. Scīsne hoc? 8. Sciō quid *factūrus sīs.* 9. Multōrum nōs etiam oculī nōn sentientēs saepe vident. 10. At oculī omnium senātōrum in Catilīnam versī sunt.[1] 11. Utrum cōnsulāris es *annōn*? 12. Rogāvī num cōnsulāris essēs *necne.* 13. *Mēne* exspectābis annōn? 14. Quid antīquī illī *dēcrēverint* omnīnō ignōrō. 15. Cicerō scīvit ubi Catilīna *fuisset,* quid *ēgisset,* quōs *convocāsset,* quid cōnsilī *cēpisset.* 16. Nōn ignōrō quot *sint* cōnsulārēs in senātū. 17. Quid *dīceret* Chrīstus multī nōn intellēxērunt. 18. Nōn videō quōmodo vōx populī *possit* esse vōx Deī. 19. *Utrum* vīs apertē loquī *an* tacēbis?[2] 20. Num cōnsul *vellet* apertē loquī an

[1] **vertō, vertere, vertī, versus,** 3, tr., *turn.*

[2] **taceō,** 2, tr. and intr., *pass over in silence, am silent.*

tacēret omnēs ignōrāvimus. 21. Rogāvit mē num vōx cōnsulis ab omnibus senātōribus *audīrētur*. 22. Sciō cūr vōx cōnsulis nōn *audiātur* ab omnibus quī in senātū sunt. 23. Chrīstus rogāvit Petrum num *posset* sēcum ūnam hōram vigilāre.[1] 24. Omnēs hominēs poenās lēgum antīquārum timent. 25. Nōnne est summa reī pūblicae poena mors? 26. Cicerō habuit senātūs cōnsultum in Catilīnam vehemēns et grave, quō ex senātūs cōnsultō ad mortem dūcī jam prīdem oportēbat. 27. Chrīstus ad summum supplicium est ductus. 28. Cicerō in senātū Catilīnam fore[2] in armīs certō diē apertē dīxit. 29. Tempore Catilīnae cīvēs Rōmānī armīs terrēbantur. 30. Catilīna orbem terrae caede atque incendiīs vastāre cupiēbat. 31. Multa urbis loca ad incendia dēsignābantur. 32. Catilīna undique tenēbātur; lūce erant clāriōra sua cōnsilia omnia. 33. Praetōrēs manū cōnsulis occīsī sunt. 34. At tandem ad locum parvā cum mīlitum manū vēnit praetor. 35. Cōnsul manū suā praetōrem novīs rēbus studentem occīdit. 36. Bellum est rēs omnīnō perniciōsa.

EXERCISE 5

Translate:

1. He did not know how many famous men were in the Senate. 2. Cicero knew where Catiline had been, what he had done, how many men he had called together. 3. Did you hear me, or didn't you? 4. The praetor asked the people whether they heard him or not. 5. The consul wished to know what every man felt about this serious punishment. 6. Cicero was not unaware of Catiline's whereabouts.[3] 7. According to the senatorial decree he ought long ago to have been given a severe penalty. 8. Can you hear my voice, or isn't it loud enough? 9. Not all the citizens were able to hear the praetor's voice; it was not clear. 10. Many did not understand what Christ was saying. They had eyes, but could not see; minds[4]

---

[1] **vigilō**, 1, intr., *am watchful, am awake, am alert.*

[2] **fore = futūrus (a, um) esse**; Gr. 360.

[3] Translate *where Catiline was.*

[4] *mind,* **mēns, mentis.**

but could not understand. 11. Pilate, the Roman leader, asked Christ whether He was a king or not. 12. Christ plainly said that He was a king, but that His kingdom was not of this world. 13. But on that very night a private citizen killed the consul. 14. He had not decided to what part of the world he would go. 15. They asked openly where he would go. 16. You said you had determined to go out of the city. 17. The consul asked the citizens how they had summoned bands of soldiers. 18. They had long desired to kill the dangerous enemies of the state. 19. Whom did the Roman people fear? 20. Cicero asked his men whether Catiline was arousing many dangerous men against the state. 21. No one knew where Catiline was. 22. The people were altogether unaware of the extent of the danger.[1] 23. He asked how the plans had been made. 24. Did not Judas give Christ over to the hands of His enemies? 25. In former times the state was often entrusted to one man because of fear of revolution. 26. Even ancient wars were very destructive. 27. The praetor killed the ex-consul personally. 28. The leading men determined to avoid personal danger altogether.

EXERCISE 6

Imitate the word order and structure of the model in translating:

MODEL: **Fuit, fuit ista quondam in hāc rē pūblicā virtūs**
ut virī fortēs acriōribus suppliciīs
cīvem perniciōsum quam acerbissimum hostem coercērent.

1. There was in Abraham[2] such great virtue that he was eager to lead his son to death rather than[3] fail to do the will[4] of God.
2. There was once in this nation such manly courage that good

---

[1] Use an indirect question.
[2] Use the same word.
[3] *rather than:* **potius quam.**
[4] *will,* **voluntās, voluntātis.**

men would lead a citizen to a more severe death than a great enemy.

3. There was in this man such recklessness that he desired to destroy the whole world with fire and slaughter rather than defend the state.

SIGHT TRANSLATION[1]

DĒ POPULĪ RŌMĀNĪ PRĪNCIPIBUS

In prīncipiō populus Rōmānus rēgēs habuit. Prīmus Rōmānōrum rēx erat Rōmulus. Rōmulus erat rēx bonus et urbem Rōmam mūnīvit. Omnēs quī in urbe vīvēbant nihil timōris habuērunt. Populus Rōmānus Rōmulum laudāvit. Rōmānī septem omnīnō habuērunt rēgēs.

At posteā populus Rōmānus cōnsulēs habuit. Duo erant cōnsulēs quī ā populō dēligēbantur.[2] Imperium cōnsulis erat maximum. Tempore conjūrātiōnis Catilīnae ūnus ex cōnsulibus erat Cicerō. Cicerō vīderat conjūrātiōnem esse factam. Locum habendī senātūs mūnīvit. Omnēs senātōrēs convocāvit. In senātum vēnit. Dē conjūrātiōne ignōrāvit nihil. Omnia Catilīnae cōnsilia patefēcit.[3]

Posteā imperātōrēs populum Rōmānum regēbant.[4] Omnium imperatōrum maximus erat Augustus Caesar. Cum autem nōn omnēs imperātōrēs essent bonī, cīvitās Rōmāna ā barbarīs superāta est.

Respondē Latīnē:

1. In prīncipiō ā quibus regēbantur[4] Rōmānī?
2. Quis erat prīmus populī Rōmānī rēx?

---

[1] These short bits of Sight Translation are for reading. They need not be translated into English; in fact, it is better if they are not. They should be read aloud, with meaningful phrasing, rather slowly, more than once if necessary, with a view to grasping the thought directly. The Latin questions should help one to test whether the passage was understood or not. They should be answered in Latin.

[2] **dēligō, dēligere, dēlēgī, dēlēctus,** 3, tr., *choose, select.*

[3] **patefaciō, patefacere, patefēcī, patefactus,** 3, tr., *open, disclose.*

[4] **regō, regere, rēxī, rēctus,** 3, tr., *rule, guide.*

3. Nōnne erat Rōmulus bonus?
4. Quid ēgit Rōmulus?
5. Cūr laudāvērunt eum Rōmānī?
6. Quot rēgēs habuērunt Rōmānī?
7. Quot erant cōnsulēs Rōmānī?
8. Ā quō dēligēbantur?[1]
9. Eratne eōrum imperium maximum?
10. Quis erat cōnsul tempore conjūrātiōnis Catilīnae?
11. Quid fēcit Cicerō?
12. Quī posteā regēbant[2] populum Rōmānum?
13. Quis erat imperātor omnium maximus?
14. Num omnēs imperātōrēs Rōmānī erant bonī?

[1] **dēligō, dēligere, dēlēgī, dēlēctus.** 3, tr., *choose, select.*
[2] **regō, regere, rēxī, rēctus,** 3, tr., *rule, guide.*

LESSON 3: WISHES

VOCABULARY

nēquitia, ae	*criminal negligence* *wickedness*
moenia, moenium	*walls* *fortifications*
jūs, jūris, *n.*	*right* *justice*
voluntās, voluntātis	*will*
perniciēs, perniciēī	*disaster* *destruction*
improbus, a, um	*wicked* *depraved*
perditus, a, um	*desperate* *abandoned*
crūdēlis, e	*cruel*
modus, ī	*manner* *kind*
ējus modī **hūjus modī**	*of this kind* *of this sort*
nōndum, *adv.*	*not yet*
potius, *adv.*	*rather*
comprehendō, comprehendere, comprehendī, comprehēnsus, *3, tr.*	*grasp* (in a physical or intellectual sense) *arrest*
crēscō, crēscere, crēvī, crētum, *3, intr.*	*grow* *increase* (in size, power, age, etc.)
dēpōnō, dēpōnere, dēposuī, dēpositus, *3, tr.*	*lay down* *give up*
mōlior, mōlīrī, mōlītus sum, *4, tr.*	*undertake*

inveniō, invenīre, invēnī, inventus, ***4, tr.; acc. w. infin.*** — *come upon* / *find (out)* / *discover*

RELATED ENGLISH WORDS

The *jury* returned a verdict of guilty. Lucifer brought *perdition* upon himself and his host. We *comprehend* a thing when we grasp it with our minds. South America is rich in *deposits* of ore. Edison had a remarkable *inventive* genius.

RELATED LATIN WORDS

Pōnō; veniō.

IDIOM

We have allowed . . . for twenty days . . .
This is the twentieth day that we have permitted . . .
For twenty days now we have permitted . . .

Nōs vīcēsimum jam diem[1] patimur.[2]

ASSIGNMENT: *First Oration against Catiline,* lines 64-98; GRAMMAR 511-513.

MEMORY: *First Oration against Catiline,* lines 12-20.

EXERCISE 7

Translate and explain the italicized words:

1. Tempora bona *veniant*. 2. Utinam rēgnum Chrīstī *veniat*. 3. Utinam bonī *sīmus* usque ad fīnem vītae. 4. Nē ad mortem *dūcant* virum fortem. 5. *Adveniat* rēgnum tuum. 6. Chrīstus *vincat,* Chrīstus *rēgnet,* Chrīstus *imperet*. 7. Utinam Caesar mortem *vītāsset*. 8. Utinam Cicerō *vīveret*. 9. Utinam Jūdas Chrīstum nē *trādidisset*. 10. *Inveniāmus* viam. 11. *Fīat* voluntās Deī ab omnibus, in omnī locō, omnī tempore. 12. Utinam nē orbis

---

[1] Accusative case; Gr. 761.

[2] Present tense.

terrārum hominum nēquitiā *vastētur*. 13. Tempora bona in rē pūblicā nostrā *veniant*. 14. Utinam mīlitēs moenia *tenuissent*. 15. *Vīvat* cōnsul! *Vīvat* urbs nostra! *Vīvat* rēs pūblica nostra! *Vīvat* populus noster! *Vīvant* jūra nostra! 16. Utinam omnēs hominēs bonīs mōribus *studērent*. 17. Utinam Jūdaeī Chrīstum ad mortem nē *dūxissent*. 18. Utinam omnēs post mortem ad Deum *veniāmus*. 19. Ad multōs annōs *vīvās*. 20. Utinam omnēs improbī perditīque hominēs nēquitiam *dēpōnerent* et reī pūblicae jūra *servārent*. 21. Cicerō vīdit manum improbōrum perniciem reī pūblicae cotīdie mōlientem. 22. Nē *crēscat* bellōrum crūdēlium numerus. 23. Certā dē causā praetor nōndum hominem perditum comprehenderat. 24. Tempora bona nōndum vēnērunt. 25. Cīvēs improbī novās rēs in cīvitāte potius quam bella externa[1] mōliuntur. 26. Ējus modī senātūs cōnsultum nōndum habēmus. 27. Utinam omnēs hominēs *comprehendissent* quae essent cīvis prīvātī jūra. 28. Utinam nōs omnēs virtūte in diēs singulōs *crēscāmus*. 29. Audāciam potius *dēpōnat* quam *cōnfirmet*. 30. Praetōrēs quī omnia jūre faciunt nōndum invenīrī possunt. 31. Antīquī jam prīdem arbitrābantur sē posse hominem novīs rēbus studentem occīdere. 32. Pūblius Scīpiō Tiberium Gracchum prīvātus interfēcit. 33. Mors vītārī nōn potest.

EXERCISE 8

Translate:

1. May Christ's kingdom come. 2. Would that all depraved and desperate citizens would not lay down their lives for[2] the destruction of the state. 3. Would that the disaster had not come at that time. 4. May he not come. 5. (Long) live Christ, King! 6. Would that men were not cruel. 7. May good times come. 8. The enemy have not yet come up to the city walls. 9. Would that the rights of citizens were grasped by the Senate. 10. Would that the alarm[3]

[1] **externus, a, um,** *foreign, external.*

[2] Use **ad.**

[3] alarm = fear.

of the people had moved Catiline. 11. Would that all men desired the reign of Christ. 12. Would that we may have patience.[1] 13. May you live many years. 14. May we avoid destruction of this kind in our state. 15. Praised be Jesus Christ! 16. May he not discover the ancient fortifications. 17. Would that the cities of Europe[2] had not been ravaged by war. 18. Would that all Christians were devoted to the will of God. 19. The leader of the plot was depraved rather than cruel. 20. May citizens of this sort not be found within[3] the walls of our city. 21. May his virtue increase. 22. Would that the band of desperate men had been arrested because of their wickedness. 23. The depraved soldiers did not give up the slaughter of the citizens. 24. We have awaited you for twenty days now. 25. The Roman people had long been eager for a revolution. 26. Brutus killed Caesar with his own hand. 27. He had long undertaken the destruction of the city. 28. This is the twentieth day that we have not come upon the consul in the Senate. 29. The conspiracy was growing because of the consul's criminal negligence.

EXERCISE 9

Imitate the word order and structure of the model in translating:

MODEL: Tum dēnique interficiēre,
cum jam nēmō tam improbus,
tam perditus,
tam tuī similis invenīrī poterit
quī id nōn jūre factum esse fateātur.

1. Then at length will all men be happy[4] when no one will be found so wicked, so abandoned, as not to love God.

---

[1] *patience,* **patientia, ae.**
[2] *Europe,* **Eurōpa, ae.**
[3] *within,* **intrā,** prep. w. acc.
[4] *happy,* **beātus, a, um.**

2. Then at last shall we conquer the enemy when no one will be found so cowardly,[1] so desperate, as not to fight for the state.

3. Then at length will the whole world have peace when no one will be found so foolish,[2] so depraved, as not to preserve the rights of all nations.

NOTE ON TRANSLATION

Although the vocabularies give only a few English equivalents for the Latin words, the English meanings of any Latin word are not, so to speak, frozen. Actually the words and expressions can be and often must be changed to other synonyms and constructions to make good English sentences. Translate ideas rather than words.

When you meet an unfamiliar word in translating from English to Latin, do not immediately rush to the English-Latin vocabulary in the back of the book, only to surrender with some such excuse as, "We haven't had that word." Instead, analyze the meaning of the unfamiliar expression; see whether you haven't had Latin words which MEAN the same thing in English. In Exercise 10, for example, don't let the phrase *popular alarm* baffle you. Think of the meaning and the use of the word *alarm*—don't be alarmed; have no fear. The idea behind *alarm* is the same as the idea behind the word *fear*. As for *popular*, is it not merely *of the people* in disguise? The phrase *popular alarm* is simply **timor populī.**

EXERCISE 10

A Patriot Speaks to a Tyrant

Translate:

You have long since been desiring to ravage our city. You have long since been eager for a revolution. Are you indifferent to[3] the popular alarm? Don't you see that all brave men in this city

---

[1] *cowardly,* **ignāvus, a, um.**

[2] *foolish,* **stultus, a, um.**

[3] Translate *nothing moved by.*

know everything? Don't you see that your plans are known by all the people? Which one of us in this state do you think is unaware of what you did last night, or the night before last? The whole world knows that you have a fortified place where your band betakes itself.

Oh that all good men may adopt some plan.[1] Would that we had acted. We see and understand everything; we do nothing. May the time come when those who are eager for revolution may be led to (their) death.

[1] *may adopt some plan:* **quid cōnsilī capiant.**

LESSON 4: TENSE USAGE

VOCABULARY

dīligentia, ae	*care* *carefulness*
mēns, mentis	*mind*
coetus, ūs	*meeting* *gathering*
domus, ūs, *f. (Gr. 67-68; 915-917)*	*home* *house*
nefārius, a, um	*wicked* *impious*
atrōx (*gen.* **atrōcis**)	*savage* *fierce*
incrēdibilis, e	*unbelievable* *extraordinary*
admīror, *1, tr.*	*wonder at* *am surprised at*
mūtō, *1, tr.*	*change*
audeō, audēre, ausus sum, *2, intr.; w. infin. (Gr. 345)*	*dare*
ērumpō, ērumpere, ērūpī, ēruptum, *3, intr.;* **ex (ē)** *w. abl.*	*burst forth* *rush forth*
profugiō, profugere, profūgī, profugitum, *3, intr.*	*flee from* *run away*
custōdiō, *4, tr.*	*guard*
oblīvīscor, oblīvīscī, oblītus sum, *3, tr.; w. gen. of persons, gen. or acc. of things, acc. of neuter prons. or adjs.; acc. w. infin.*	*forget*
meminī, meminisse, *tr.; w. gen. of persons, gen. or acc. of things, acc. of neuter prons. or adjs.; acc. w. infin. (Gr. 436-442)*	*remember* *bear in mind*

magis, ***comparative adv.***	*more*
multō, ***abl. of degree of difference (Gr. 771)***	*much* *by much*
nōn modo . . . sed (etiam) **nōn modo . . . vērum (etiam)**	*not only . . . but (also)*

RELATED ENGLISH WORDS

A *multi*millionaire has, or is reputed to have, two million dollars or more. To be *oblivious* of a favor is unpardonable. A student should always be *diligent*. People with little emotional control often become *mental* cases. The *dome* of St. Peter's in Rome is one of the largest in the world. Catiline's was a *nefarious* scheme against his own country. World War II was not without its *atrocities*. Light travels at an almost *incredible* speed. *Admiration.* God is *immutable*. Volcanic *eruptions*. *Custody.*

RELATED LATIN WORDS

Dīligenter; crēdō; audācia; ēruptiō; fugiō; custōs.

IDIOM

I also said . . .
I said likewise . . .
(I, the same one, said . . .)
Dīxī ego īdem . . .

ASSIGNMENT: *First Oration against Catiline,* lines 99-135; GRAMMAR 436-442; 480-497; Review GRAMMAR 72-88.

MEMORY: *First Oration against Catiline,* lines 21-31.

EXERCISE 11

Translate and explain the tense of the italicized words:

1. "*Vēnī,*" inquit, "et hīc sum in senātū." 2. Cicerō locum habendī senātūs magnā cum dīligentiā *mūnīverat*. 3. Omnēs cīvēs bonī virtūtī *student*. 4. Auctōritās hūjus reī pūblicae *est* omnī locō

bona. 5. Cicerō omnia quae Catilīna *fēcerat* nōn modo audīvit sed etiam vīdit. 6. Ūnus cōnsul in cīvitāte *vīvēbat*, alter diū in prōvinciā *fuerat*. 7. Omnēs hominēs mortem *patiuntur*. 8. Cicerō in senātum *venit*, omnēs *convocat*, omnia *patefacit*.[1] 9. *Fuit* magna quondam in rē pūblicā Rōmānā virtūs. 10. Cōnsul hostem ad mortem dūcere *audēbat*. 11. Ex urbe mūnītā *ērumpēmus*. 12. Omnēs quī *audīverant* Chrīstum admīrātī sunt. 13. Chrīstus omnia fēcit quae Pater *dīxerat*. 14. Tum hominēs mortem propter virtūtem *patiēbantur*. 15. Omnēs cīvēs domūs suās incrēdibilī dīligentiā *custōdiēbant*. 16. Oculus *est* lūx mentis. 17. Neque nox tenebrīs obscūrāre[2] neque prīvāta domus parietibus continēre nefāriōs coetūs tuōs *potest*. 18. Catilīna cum suīs improbīs novīs rēbus *studēbat*. 19 *Venit* tandem bellum atrōx. 20. Cōnsulis dīligentiam multō magis *admīrābantur* quam praetōris audāciam. 21. Hominēs saepe mentem *mūtant*. 22. Cicerō nōndum facere *audēbat* id quod facere *dēbēbat*. 23. Cīvēs ex senātū *ērumpunt*. 24. Etiam ex oppidīs *profugiunt*. 25. Concursum reprimere *potuit* nēmō. 26. Multa *oblīvīscimur* omnēs, etiam quae nōs meminisse *oportet*. 27. Cīvēs improbī multō ācrius ad perniciem reī pūblicae *vigilant* quam bonī ad ējus salūtem. 28. Nunc, nunc, patrēs cōnscrīptī, *oportet* nōs agere. 29. Vērum nōs hoc quod jam prīdem factum esse *oportuit* certā dē causā nōndum *addūcimur* ut faciāmus. 30. Cōnsul in castra ante lūcem *vēnit*. 31. Cicerō multō ante in senātum *vēnerat*. 32. Rogāvit mē quid *exspectāvissem*. 33. Dux tenebrās noctis *exspectābat*. 34. Cicerō jam dūdum auctōritātem senātūs *exspectābat*. 35. Catilīna, dux hostium et conjūrātiōnis imperātor, ā suīs cotīdiē[3] *exspectābātur*. 36. Nēmō nunc Catilīnam dēfendere *audet*. 37. Nōs autem facere quod majōrēs fēcērunt nōn *audēmus*. 38. Reī pūblicae hostis intrā moenia, atque adeō in senātum nunc *venit*. 39. Cīvēs bonī et reī pūblicae hostēs eīsdem[4] moenibus nunc

---

[1] **patefaciō, patefacere, patefēcī, patefactus,** 3, tr., *open, disclose.*

[2] **obscūrō,** 1, tr., *hide.*

[3] **cotīdiē,** adv., *daily.*

[4] **īdem, eadem, idem,** *same;* Gr. 137.

continentur. 40. Cōnsul jam diū ab hostium manū ac tēlīs *continētur*. 41. Petrus *meminerat* Chrīstī verba et illā nocte ūsque ad lacrimās[1] est commōtus. 42. Chrīstus peccātōris numquam[2] *est oblītus*. 43. Meministīne omnia quae dīxit Cicerō in senātū, an multa *es oblītus*?

EXERCISE 12

Translate:

1. In former times the consuls led men to death much more easily. 2. For a long time Cicero kept avoiding Catiline's mad weapons.[3] 3. Christ did nothing which the Father had not told Him. 4. No Christian is unaware that there is one God. 5. The number of wicked gatherings in this city is unbelievable. 6. We have long since been defending not only our city, but our homes and our lives against the savage attacks of impious men. 7. The Roman people had in ancient times had great authority; but the Senate took this out of their hands. 8. But Cicero checked the plot with extraordinary carefulness. (As) consul he not only saw everything, but also heard about the wicked gatherings. 9. We shall all suffer death. 10. The influence of one good man can move many to virtue. 11. The bill[4] of the Senate had been severe. 12. By a like decree of the House[5] all men who had dared to come into the city with weapons had been killed. 13. Cicero was not moved to the point of[6] fear, for he was not that sort of man. 14. They all wondered at the things which Christ said. They guarded His words[7] with great care in their minds. 15. The soldiers had run away from the camp and no one dared to guard the baggage. 16. Christians know that all authority comes from God. 17. All

---

[1] **lacrima, ae,** *a tear.*

[2] **numquam,** adv., *never.*

[3] mad weapons = madness and weapons.

[4] bill = decree.

[5] Use **senātus.**

[6] *to the point of:* **usque ad.**

[7] *word,* **verbum, ī.**

the citizens will live; but their leader will be led to death. 18. God is the Father of all men. 19. Night and day he lived in fear because of the fierce conspiracy. 20. He has come with his father. 21. The band of citizens fled from the house. 22. All authority is in Christ's hand, for He is God. 23. All good Christians strive to become like Christ. 24. Catiline said nothing; he had forgotten all the things he desired to say to the meeting. 25. Is patience[1] a Christian virtue? 26. We all forget many things which we ought to bear in mind. 27. The Romans not only guarded their cities, but also fortified them with walls. 28. God saw all things that He had made and they were good. 29. Peter remembered what Christ had said. 30. The savage enemy burst forth from the camp with extraordinary frenzy. 31. He did not change his mind, but rushed from the city to the camp. 32. They were much more surprised at the unbelievable care with which he guarded his home. 33. For many days now there has been a camp of enemies in Italy. 34. Christians have long understood that it behooved Christ to be led to death.

EXERCISE 13

Translate:

All your plans are perfectly plain[2] to us. Where you were on the night before last, whom you sent out of the city, what impious men you summoned together—we all know and understand. You are held in on all sides by the agents[3] of the government. You cannot lift a finger[4] against the city, the consuls, the state. Don't you perceive this? Don't you see that we know everything? You ought long ago to have changed your plans and to have forgotten the slaughter of your fellow citizens and the destruction of the state.

---

1 *patience,* **patientia, ae.**

2 *perfectly plain,* **clārissimus, a, um.**

3 agent = guard.

4 *to lift a finger:* **commōvēre tē.**

EX MISSALĪ RŌMĀNŌ[1]

Ex Ordinario Missae

The Mass has been called a drama in two acts. The first part is an exchange of words, the second an exchange of gifts. In the first part of the Mass we speak to God, God speaks to us.

At the foot of the altar all confess their sins and ask pardon—priest, altar boy, people. In this spirit the priest ascends, reads the Introit that sets the tone for the feast, and returns to the center with the ninefold plea, the *Kyrie Eleison.* Here with sorrow and repentance, quickly yielding to joy and gratitude, he breaks into a hymn of praise. The words re-echo upon the sanctuary with all the splendor of the angel choir that sang the first Christmas carol. For a moment we are shepherds keeping the night watch over sheep in the hills of Bethlehem. For a moment the glory of God shines around us and we hear "a multitude of the heavenly host praising God and saying":

Glōria in excelsīs[2] Deō. Et in terrā pāx hominibus bonae voluntātis. Laudāmus tē. Benedīcimus[3] tē. Adōrāmus[4] tē. Glōrificāmus[5] tē. Grātiās agimus tibi propter magnam glōriam tuam. Domine Deus, Rēx caelestis,[6] Deus Pater omnipotēns.[7] Domine Fīlī ūnigenite, Jēsū Chrīste, Domine Deus, Agnus[8] Deī, Fīlius Patris. Quī tollis peccāta mundī, miserēre nōbīs. Quī tollis peccāta mundī, suscipe dēprecātiōnem[9] nostram. Quī sedēs ad dextram[10] Patris, miserēre nōbīs. Quoniam tū sōlus sānctus. Tū sōlus Dominus.

---

1 These selections are taken from the Roman Missal. Some are from the Ordinary of the Mass, the part which never changes; others are from the Proper for the seasons and feasts of the year, which change from day to day.

2 **in excelsīs:** *in the highest.*

3 **benedīcō, benedīcere, benedīxī, benedictus,** 3, tr., *bless.*

4 **adōrō,** 1, tr., *adore.*

5 **glōrificō,** 1, tr., *glorify.*

6 **caelestis, e,** *heavenly.*

7 **omnipotēns** (*gen.* **omnipotentis**), *almighty.*

8 **agnus, ī,** *lamb.*

9 **dēprecātiō, dēprecātiōnis,** *prayer.*

10 **dexter, dextra, dextrum,** *right.*

Tū sōlus altissimus, Jēsū Chrīste. Cum Sānctō Spīritū in glōriā Deī Patris. Āmēn.

Ex Proprio de Sanctis

Turning toward the people the celebrant says, "Dominus vōbīscum"; to which the altar boy answers, "Et cum spīritū tuō."

And now the speaking to God continues. The priest, uniting himself with the server, the congregation, and the whole *ecclēsia*[1] *ōrāns,* says—in the plural, notice:

Ōrēmus: Deus, cūjus ūnigenitus per vītam, mortem et resurrēctiōnem suam nōbīs salūtis aeterna praemia comparāvit: concēde,[2] quaesumus:[3] ut, haec mystēria[4] sācrātissimō[5] beātae Marīae rosāriō[6] recolentēs,[7] et imitēmur,[8] quod continent, et quod prōmittunt,[9] assequāmur.[10] Per eundem Dominum nostrum Jēsum Chrīstum, Fīlium tuum. Quī tēcum vīvit et rēgnat in ūnitāte Spīritūs Sānctī Deus, per omnia saecula saeculōrum. Āmēn.

This prayer, taken from the Mass of the Feast of the Holy Rosary, October 7, is characteristic of the structure of most prayers: first, an address to God under some aspect pertinent to the feast; then a petition revolving about the feast; this is asked "through Christ our Lord," and sealed with the universal Amen.

---

[1] **ecclēsia, ae,** *church.*

[2] **concēdō, concēdere, concessī, concessus,** 3, tr., *grant.*

[3] **quaesumus:** *we beseech.*

[4] **mystērium, ī,** *mystery.*

[5] **sācrātus, a, um,** *sacred.*

[6] **rosārium, ī,** *rosary.*

[7] **recolō, recolere, recoluī, recultus,** 3, tr., *celebrate, commemorate.*

[8] **imitor,** 1, tr., *imitate, copy.*

[9] **prōmittō, prōmittere, prōmīsī, prōmissus,** 3, tr., *promise.*

[10] **assequor, assequī, assecūtus sum,** 3, tr., *attain, reach.*

LESSON 5: USE OF DEMONSTRATIVE, REFLEXIVE, AND INTENSIVE PRONOUNS

VOCABULARY

exitium, ī	*ruin* *destruction*
scelus, sceleris, *n.*	*crime*
complūrēs, complūra	*several* *many*
immortālis, e	*immortal* *deathless*
hīc, *adv.*	*here*
plānē, *adv.*	*clearly* *plainly*
cotīdiē, *adv.*	*daily*
īdem, eadem, idem *(Gr. 137; 813-814)*	*same*
cōgitō, *1, tr. and intr.; acc. w. infin.*	*ponder* *think* *contemplate*
vulnerō, *1, tr.*	*wound*
taceō, *2, tr. and intr.*	*pass over in silence* *am silent*
cōnfīdō, cōnfīdere, cōnfīsus sum, *3, intr.; w. dat. of person; abl. of thing; acc. w. infin.*	*trust* *rely on*

RELATED ENGLISH WORDS

We believe in the *immortality* of the soul. For a long time during World War II it was thought that the European fortress was *invulnerable*. *Tacit* permission. The right kind of self-*confidence* is not to be frowned upon.

RELATED LATIN WORDS

Plūrēs; mors; vulnus.

IDIOM

There are those who . . . *There are some who . . .* *Some . . .*	**Sunt quī** with the subjunctive; Gr. 633-636

There are those who contemplate the destruction of us all.

Sunt quī dē nostrō omnium interitū cōgitent.

ASSIGNMENT: *First Oration against Catiline,* lines 136-170; GRAMMAR 790-814; Review GRAMMAR 123-141.

MEMORY: *First Oration against Catiline,* lines 1-31.

EXERCISE 14

Translate and explain the italicized pronouns and adjectives:

1. Omnēs sumus *hōc* in locō. 2. Patrēs nostrī sunt *eō* in locō. 3. Cicerō erat in *illō* locō. 4. *Iste* furor tuus nōn movet nōs. 5. Cicerō et Catilīna erant Rōmānī; *hic* conjūrātiōnem faciēbat, *ille* conjūrātiōnem patefēcit.[1] 6. *Hanc* urbem mūniēmus; *illam* nōn cōnfirmābimus. 7. Omnia *illa* in senātū dīxit. 8. *Iī* quī perditī improbīque sunt, cīvēs bonī esse nōn possunt. 9. Cicerō *ille* erat dux populī Rōmānī. 10. Brūtus Caesarem *illum* manū suā interfēcit. 11. *Iste* Catilīna dē suae urbis atque adeō dē orbis terrārum exitiō cōgitābat. 12. An tacēbimus dē *hōc* incrēdibilī scelere? 13. *Tē* movēre contrā rem pūblicam nūllō modō potes. 14. Tempore Cicerōnis hominēs perditī *sē* movēre in urbem mūnītam nōn potuērunt. 15. Utinam possīmus omnēs vidēre *nōs* sīcut aliī hominēs nōs vident. 16. Complūrēs cīvēs ad eandem urbem *sē* contulērunt. 17. Plānē nēmō potest aliīs dare quod *ipse* nōn habet. 18. Cicerō *sē* laudāvit usque ad mortem. 19. Utinam nē sīmus

---

[1] **patefaciō, patefacere, patefēcī, patefactus, 3, tr.,** ***open, disclose.***

laudātōrēs[1] temporis *nostrī*. 20. Utinam tibi *istam* mentem dī immortālēs darent! 21. Caesar dīxit *suōs* venīre. 22. Catilīna jam prīdem *sē* nocturnō impetū urbem occupātūrum cōnfīdēbat. 23. Catilīna omnēs suōs *sēcum* venīre jussit. 24. *Ipse* Chrīstus ad mortem duōbus cum hominibus improbīs ductus est. Sed ūnus ex *illīs* Chrīstī patientiā est mōtus. Chrīstus *ējus* virtūtem cōnfirmāvit. "Hodiē,"[2] inquit, "*mēcum* eris in caelīs." At *ille* quī quondam improbus perditusque erat hōrā mortis in sānctōrum numerō habētur. 25. Chrīstus ad *suōs* vēnit, et *suī* eum interfēcērunt. 26. *Ipsa* virtūs est bona in sē. 27. Cōnsul hostēs reī pūblicae nōndum vōce vulnerābat. 28. Cicerō sē *ipse* laudāvit usque ad fīnem. 29. Dē nostrā *ipsōrum* perniciē cotīdiē cōgitābant. 30. Nōnne tuum *ipsīus* patrem vidēbis? 31. *Ipse* dīxit. 32. Catilīna manum convocāvit. *Ipse, eōrum* dux, illā nocte ad eōs vēnit. 33. Cicerō nocturnum praesidium mūnīvit, *ipse* cum tēlō in senātum vēnit. 34. Omnēs scientiā *ipsōrum* sānctōrum cōnfirmārī possumus. 35. Ego vērō urbis exitium *ipse* eō tempore plānē vīdī. 36. Eundem locum incendiō vastāvērunt. *Ipsī* manū *suā* cīvēs bonōs occīderant. 37. Quid[3] tacētis? 38. Nostrīs temporibus cīvis prīvātus nōn potest hostem pūblicum *suā* auctōritāte occīdere. 39. *Illī* antīquī Rōmānī dē quibus Cicerō dīxit, hoc *ipsum* fēcērunt. 40. Imperātor *suōs* in castra dūxit. *Ipse* contrā hostem *sē* contulit. 41. Cum vēnerō, *ipse* tē vidēbō. 42. *Vōbīscum* cotīdiē sit Deus. 43. Nēmō vīderat hominem quī tantam audāciam habuit. *Iste* enim nihil cupīvit nisi[4] reī pūblicae exitium. 44. Certā dē causā pater *ējus* jussit *eum* ad *sē* venīre. 45. Neque vīdī ūllō locō hominem tam improbum, tam perditum, tam Catilīnae similem. 46. Castra sunt in *ipsā* Italiā posita. *Ipse* dux in senātum vēnerat. 47. Utinam Deus nōs contrā omnia hostis perīcula cotīdiē cōnfirmet. 48. *Eōrum* autem ducem in senātū vidētis. 49. Cōnfirmāstī tē *ipsum* jam esse exitūrum.

---

[1] **laudātor, laudātōris**; from what verb is this noun formed? Meaning?
[2] **hodiē**, adv., *today*.
[3] **quid**, *why*.
[4] **nisi**, conj., *except*.

EXERCISE 15

Translate:

1. There are some who do not love their leaders. 2. Here, here in our midst[1] are those who plainly desire the very destruction of the city. 3. This man's boldness does not move me one bit.[2] 4. What was the reason for[3] this crime? 5. I myself am clearly unaware. 6. The leader said that his camp had been pitched in Italy. 7. Cicero himself said the same thing. 8. Several were wounded in that (famous) battle. 9. This citizen is good; that one is wicked. 10. There were some who were eager to lead Christ to death. 11. The famous leader Caesar led his men to Rome against the Senate's authority. 12. Clearly no human being[4] is immortal. 13. Would that we had been silent about the crime. 14. We cannot trust so great a number of the enemy. 15. The commander himself had no definite plan. 16. In that same place several soldiers are being wounded daily. 17. There are some who do not fear God. 18. Would that we might all avoid eternal[5] death. 19. For a definite reason Cicero had fortified the very place for holding the Senate. 20. Would that Italy had not had a desperate leader; but she was led to her ruin by one man. 21. When you come I myself shall see you. 22. Virtue is good in itself. 23. He daily pondered many crimes, but he did nothing about them. 24. Several Romans thought that they could rely on the deathless gods.

EXERCISE 16

A Patriot Addresses His Countrymen

Translate:

"Here, right here in our number, fellow citizens, there are those who are making a conspiracy against our city, our state, our

---

[1] *in our midst:* **in nostrō numerō.**

[2] Translate *moves me nothing.*

[3] Translate *of;* Gr. 685.

[4] Use **homō, hominis.**

[5] *eternal,* **aeternus, a, um.**

people. Day by day the number of those eager for revolution increases. Here, right here in our state, there is a camp fortified against us all. The leader of that band of wicked and desperate men you see in the city and even in the Senate. But we, the leaders of the people, what are we doing? We fortify here one place, here another. We avoid the mad weapons[1] of this desperate commander and think we are doing everything.

"Ought he not long ago to have been led to death? Our fathers were not men of this sort. When they saw with their own eyes that a conspiracy had been made, they slew[2] the wicked men with their own hands. They fortified the city. They strengthened all good citizens against the danger.

"Would that we had in these our times men of this sort. Would that we, leaders of the people, had the virtue of our fathers. But we have long allowed this man and all his wicked band to strengthen themselves in boldness, nay[3] in madness. The whole situation[4] is serious, fellow citizens. This is the time when we ought to act. We can no longer avoid the mad thrusts[5] of the enemy. God is for us, and when God is for us who can be against us!"

---

[1] mad weapons = madness and weapons.

[2] slay = kill.

[3] *nay,* **immō vērō**, adv.

[4] situation = thing.

[5] mad thrusts = madness and weapons.

LESSON 6: CONDITIONAL SENTENCES

VOCABULARY

līberō, *1, tr.*	*free* *liberate*
placet, placēre, placuit, placitum, *2, intr.; w. dat.; w. infin.; acc. w. infin.;* **ut (nē)**	*it pleases* *it seems good*
dēsīderō, *1, tr.*	*miss* *long for*
comperiō, comperīre, comperī, compertus, *4, tr.; acc. w. infin.*	*find out* *discover (as certain)*
ēdūcō, ēdūcere, ēdūxī, ēductus, *3, tr.*	*lead out*
praedīcō, praedīcere, praedīxī, praedictus, *3, tr.; acc. w. infin.*	*say* *foretell*
statuō, statuere, statuī, statūtus, *3, tr.; w. infin.*	*set up* *place* *determine*
dēligō, dēligere, dēlēgī, dēlēctus, *3, tr.*	*choose* *pick out*
quodsī, *conj.*	*but if*
aliquandō, *adv.*	*at some time* *at length*
paulō, *abl. of degree of difference (modifying* **ante, post,** *or a comparative)*	*(by) a little*
paulum, *adv. or noun w. gen.*	*a little*

RELATED ENGLISH WORDS

"Give me *liberty* or give me death." The Parliament was waiting on the royal *placet*. The chairman of the meeting was unable to achieve the one *desideratum*. It is not always safe to *predict* which of two well-matched teams will win a game. *Statute*.

RELATED LATIN WORDS

Līber; reperiō; dūcō; dīcō.

ASSIGNMENT: *First Oration against Catiline,* lines 171-207; GRAMMAR 581-588; Review GRAMMAR 240-282.

MEMORY: *First Oration against Catiline,* lines 148-157.

EXERCISE 17

Translate; explain the construction of the italicized words:

1. Nōs autem, fortēs cīvēs, cōnsulem *laudāmus* sī istīus furōrem ac tēla *vītat.* 2. Sī tē interficī *jusserō,* an placēbit populō Rōmānō? 3. *Sīn autem* tē comprehendī jusserō, nēmō erit tam improbus tamque perditus quī tē dēsīderet. 4. Praetōrēs sēcum ēdūcere voluērunt omnēs Catilīnae amīcōs, *sī minus,* quam plūrimōs. 5. Sī cīvēs meī *timerent* mē, ex urbe aliquandō ēgrederer. 6. Convincam,[1] sī *negās*! 7. Haec sī in senātū *dīxissem,* cōnsulibus nōn *placuisset.* 8. Haec sī tēcum *loquar,* quid *cōgitēs*? 9. Nisi Cicerō Catilīnam ad mortem dūcere *statuisset,* Rōma metū nōn *esset līberāta.* 10. Sī rēx *essem,* magnā cum dīligentiā amīcōs dēligerem. 11. Sī in castrīs *essem,* domum meam *dēsīderārem.* 12. *Sī* scelus est pūblicum *nōn* prīvātum, acriōribus suppliciīs reprimī dēbet. 13. Sīn autem haec *praedīxerō,* plānē *negābis.* 14. Sī praetōrēs paulō ante lūcem *vēnissent,* omnia *comperissent.* 15. Quodsī Catilīna eō tempore in castra Mānliāna *ēgressus esset,* hoc omnibus cīvibus nunc *placēret.* 16. Sī aliquandō tibi placuerit hāc in urbe paulum manēre, apud mē vīvere *poteris.*

EXERCISE 18

Translate:

1. If it should please Catiline to go out of the city, he would free the state from fear. 2. If Cicero had not foretold this, the people would not have found it out. 3. If Catiline had not come

---

[1] **convincō, convincere, convīcī, convictus,** 3, tr., *prove, refute, convict.*

into the Senate a little before, Cicero would not have said these things. 4. If Catiline should at some time go out of the city, would Cicero remain? 5. If Cicero had not feared the people, he would have determined to lead Catiline to death. 6. If you at length leave[1] the city, you will free me from fear. 7. But if it seems good to you, pick out several brave men. 8. I foretold to the Senate that you had determined to kill me. 9. If you were not living in the city, you would long for your home. 10. If the praetors had been led to his house a little before night, they would have discovered the wicked gathering. 11. But if we were away from home, we would miss our friends a little. 12. If I place guards at the gates, no one will be able to enter the city. 13. If the soldiers whom he set up at the bridge had been brave, they would have driven the enemy back.

EXERCISE 19

Translate:

1. If we have long been fearing Catiline, why do we not order him to be killed? 2. If that desperate man should dare to come into the Senate, we would lead him out. 3. If he had had a definite reason, he would clearly have told us. 4. If we have not been able to defend the state by our carefulness, we will not be able to defend it by the sword. 5. If Cicero had not fortified the place for holding the Senate, Catiline and his men would have seized it. 6. If God is good, why do not all men love Him? 7. If Christ were not God, we would not give Him the highest praise. 8. If Catiline had killed Cicero, Rome would have been laid waste. 9. A state cannot be strong unless the citizens choose good leaders. 10. If you shun recklessness, you will grow in knowledge. 11. We did not fortify our very own city. 12. No man can understand God as God understands Himself. 13. But if you should come a little before midnight you would find me at home. 14. If my brother were living, I would not miss him.

[1] leave = go out.

EXERCISE 20

Imitate the word order and structure of the model in translating:

MODEL: Dīxistī paulum tibi esse etiam nunc morae quod ego vīverem.

1. You said that you were in serious danger because I had come.
2. You said that even then you remained a little longer because the consul was more careful than you yourself.
3. He said he even now had some fear because the consul knew his plans.

EXERCISE 21

A Patriot Addresses a Colonial Convention in the American Revolution

Translate:

"Here in our own number, in this serious assembly of the colonies,[1] there are men who ponder about the destruction of our colonies[1] and of all of us. There are men who have determined to hand us over to our enemies, to make peace against our wills with the English, finally,[2] to surrender the liberty which we have received from our ancestors and which we are now fighting to preserve."

EXERCISE 22

Translate orally:

1. Where are you going? 2. I shall fight up to the end. 3. You have long been making attacks against us all. 4. Shall we not lead this plague of the state to death? 5. It seemed good to the Senate that Catiline be led to death. 6. Or do you think Catiline

---

[1] *colony,* **colōnia, ae.**

[2] *finally,* **dēnique, adv.**

a good man? 7. Do you know how long Christ was on earth? 8. What are you now undertaking? 9. The consul himself ought to kill him. 10. Washington defended the state against its enemies. 11. No one could be found so wicked as not to praise Washington. 12. There is no one who does not know that Washington was a brave man. 13. Washington has been called the "Father of His Country."[1] 14. The British were laying waste the towns and cities of the colonies.[2] 15. Washington drove them back by his own diligence and by the help of all good men. 16. Our state was not only preserved but also liberated by him. 17. Great thanks do we owe to God that He gave us this man. 18. All Americans should keep Washington ever[3] before their eyes.[4]

EXERCISE 23

Imitate the word order and structure of the model in translating:

**MODEL: Nōbīscum versārī jam diūtius nōn potes,
nōn feram,
nōn patiar,
nōn sinam.**

1. He can no longer remain in the city, the consul will not permit[5] it, the Senate will not allow it, the immortal gods will not suffer it.

2. We are not unaware of your plot. We hear all, we learn all, we understand all.

3. You can no longer fight against your fellow citizens; I will not endure[6] it nor suffer it.

---

[1] *country,* **patria, ae.**

[2] *colony,* **colōnia, ae.**

[3] Translate *always.*

[4] *to keep before the eyes:* **ob oculōs habēre.**

[5] *permit,* **sinō, sinere, sīvī, situs,** 3, tr.; acc. w. infin.

[6] endure = bear.

4. You are now able to enter upon your plan. The consul will do nothing. He will neither hear nor see the plot.

5. You cannot make war on the state any longer. Neither your friends nor your enemies will permit[1] it. The immortal gods themselves will not allow it.

[1] *permit,* **sinō, sinere, sīvī, situs,** 3, tr.; acc. w. infin.

LESSON 7: THE VOCATIVE; COMMANDS

VOCABULARY

comitia, comitiōrum	*assembly* *elections*
exilium, ī	*exile*
tēctum, ī	*roof* *house*
templum, ī	*temple* *shrine*
sevēritās, sevēritātis	*strictness* *sternness*
calamitās, calamitātis	*disaster* *misfortune*
tumultus, ūs	*uproar* *disorder*
īnfestus, a, um	*hostile* *threatening*
extrā, *prep. w. acc.*	*outside (of)* *beyond*
quamquam, *conj. (Gr. 595)*	*although* *and yet*
quārē, *adv.* (quā + rē)	*wherefore*
dubitō, *1, tr. and intr.; w. infin.;* dē *w. abl.*	*doubt* *hesitate*
effugiō, effugere, effūgī, *3, tr. and intr.*	*flee from* *escape*
metuō, metuere, metuī, *3, tr.;* nē (nē nōn, ut); *w. infin.*	*fear*
īnsidior, *1, intr.; w. dat.*	*waylay* *plot*
ōdī, ōdisse, *tr.* *(Gr. 443-448, 451)*	*hate*

meā (tuā, suā) sponte	*of my (your, his, their) own accord*
quīdam, quiddam, *defin. pronoun (Gr. 820)*	*a certain one* *a certain thing*
quīdam, quaedam, quoddam *(Gr. 820)*	*certain*

RELATED ENGLISH WORDS

When you ask your father for an *extra* allowance you want something beyond what he usually gives you. *Extramural* athletics are games in competition with outside teams. *Indubitably.* Some guests have the *odious* habit of staying too long. Fires that start of their own accord are said to be caused by *spontaneous* combustion.

RELATED LATIN WORDS

Fugiō; īnsidiae; ōdium.

ASSIGNMENT: *First Oration against Catiline,* lines 208-257; GRAMMAR 462-463; 514-518; 678; Review GRAMMAR 28; 208, 216-218, 283, 289-291, 317, 327, 354, 357, 377, 383, 388, 394, 421, 441, 1020.

MEMORY: *First Oration against Catiline,* lines 158-170.

EXERCISE 24

Translate; explain the italicized constructions:

1. *Nē cōgitent* dē hāc calamitāte. 2. *Tacēte* omnēs! 3. *Nōlīte occupāre* templum. 4. *Nē negāverīs* tē esse socium meum. 5. *Audiāmus* quid dīcat ōrātor.[1] 6. *Nē cōgitēmus* mala dē sociīs nostrīs. 7. Sociī Rōmam *cōnservent*. 8. *Reprimite,* mīlitēs, hostium impetum. 9. "*Mementō* meī, Domine, cum vēnerīs in rēgnum tuum." 10. *Estōte* fortēs in exiliō vestrō. 11. *Ostende* nōbīs, Domine, viam salūtis. 12. *Mūtā* jam istam mentem. 13. *Oblīvīscere* caedis

[1] **ōrātor, ōrātōris,** *orator, speaker.*

atque incendiōrum. 14. *Exeant* ex urbe cum omnibus sociīs suīs. 15. *Recognōsce* tandem mēcum noctem illam superiōrem. 16. *Mementō,* homō, fīnem tuum. 17. *Nōlī* diūtius *dubitāre*. 18. *Nē dīxerīs* istud. 19. Per tuās viās, Domine, *dūc* nōs quō tendimus[1] ad salūtem aeternam. 20. Bella premunt nōs, Domine, *dā* virtūtem, *fer* auxilium. 21. *Venī,* fīlī mī, et *adjuvā* mē. 22. Tēcta urbis *petāmus*. 23. *Venī,* Sāncte Spīritus, *dā* nōbīs lūcem. 24. *Audī,* Domine, ōrātiōnem meam et clāmor meus ad tē *veniat*. 25. Ab omnī malō *līberā* nōs, Domine. 26. Sāncte Petre, *ōrā* prō nōbīs. 27. *Ōrēmus* et prō amīcīs et prō inimīcīs[2] nostrīs. 28. *Venīte,* laudēmus Dominum. 29. *Videāmus,* amīcī, quid sit in hāc urbe. 30. Quōs amīcōs habētis eōsque bonōs, firmiter *tenēte*. 31. Dux suā sponte mortem potius quam exilium petīvit. 32. Ōdī tumultum comitiōrum. 33. Mīles quīdam proximīs comitiīs cōnsulāribus Cicerōnem interficere voluit. 34. Quamquam exilium est malum, sunt quī nōn dubitent hanc poenam prō rē pūblicā accipere. 35. Catilīna nōn dē exiliō sed dē bellō īnfestō cōgitābat. 36. Tōtum templum mūnīvērunt. 37. Quārē omnēs hominēs sevēritātem exiliī metuunt et hanc calamitātem effugere cupiunt. 38. Exspectāte mē extrā urbis moenia. 39. Quamquam cōnsul hostem et ōdit et metuit nōlēbat eum in exilium mittere. 40. Hostēs quīdam cotīdiē cīvibus īnsidiābantur. 41. "Quam diū," inquit Cicerō, "mihi cōnsulī dēsignātō īnsidiātus es!" 42. Sī mē amīcī timērent atque ōdissent meī, ab eōrum oculīs concēderem.[3]

EXERCISE 25

Translate orally:

1. Illā nocte complūrēs ējusdem āmentiae scelerisque sociī in Marcī Laecae domum convēnērunt. 2. Nōn modo dē ējus sevēritāte audīvī sed etiam ipsam vīdī. 3. Audī, serve bone, vōcem dominī tuī. 4. Cicerō cōnsilia Catilīnae nōn sōlum intellēxit sed etiam

---

[1] **tendō, tendere, tetendī, tentus,** 3, tr., *stretch out, hold out, direct one's course.*

[2] **inimīcus, ī,** *enemy* (personal).

[3] **concēdō, concēdere, concessī, concessus,** 3, tr. and intr., *withdraw, yield.*

repressit. 5. Taceāmus omnēs intrā hōs parietēs. 6. Cūr oportet nōs tacēre? 7. Mīlitēs nocturnō impetū urbem occupāvērunt. Nōn enim mūnīta erat. 8. Num haec negāre audēs? 9. Prīncipēs quīdam cīvitātis Rōmā profugērunt tum cum Catilīna eōs ad caedem notāvit. 10. Utinam animae[1] nostrae ā peccātō cōnserventur. 11. Fīlius nihil ēgit, nihil cōgitāvit quod nōn pater ējus nōn modo audīvit sed etiam vīdit plānēque sēnsit. 12. Sociī Catilīnae inter sē quaedam loquēbantur. 13. Chrīstus inter duōs hominēs perditōs est crucifīxus.[2] 14. Ego īdem haec dīxī. 15. Cicerō enim vīderat in senātū quōsdam quī ūnā cum Catilīnā fuērunt. 16. Rēs pūblica propter cōnsulis dīligentiam ad breve quondam tempus ā timōre līberāta est. 17. Cicerō īdem dīxit sē mūnīvisse eundem locum. 18. Mīlitēs ad templum tandem vēnērunt. 19. In tēcta impetum fēcērunt. 20. Sociī Catilīnae inter sē dē omnī scelere loquēbantur. 21. Cor[3] Jēsū, dīc nōbīs "Salūs vestra ego sum." 22. Chrīstus est prīnceps pācis. 23. In hāc cīvitāte urbem mūnītam habēmus nūllam. 24. Quārē cōnsul suā sponte nōn dubitāvit exilium petere. 25. Ēdūc tēcum omnēs tuōs; pūrgā urbem.

EXERCISE 26

Translate:

1. Ponder over[4] these matters well, my boy. 2. Let us not only be silent, but also avoid disorder. 3. Don't deny that you were at Laeca's house. 4. Seize the town, soldiers, but spare the houses of the citizens. 5. Lord, lead us to Thy kingdom. 6. Do good; avoid evil. 7. Let the consuls free the state from disaster. 8. Change your mind, my son. 9. Let's always be prepared. 10. Gentlemen of the Senate, do not hesitate to change your minds about this misfortune. 11. Wherefore do not fear his sternness. 12. I also said that I would plot against him at the consular elections. 13. Forget fire and sword. 14. Let him not deny that he was in the assembly.

---

[1] **anima, ae,** *soul.*

[2] **crucifīgō, crucifīgere, crucifīxī, crucifīxus,** 3, tr., *crucify.*

[3] **cor, cordis,** n., *heart.*

[4] Translate *about.*

15. Let them not waylay the praetor at his house. 16. Let us avoid this threatening war. 17. Cicero likewise said that the companions of his crime had met under the same roof. 18. Let the leading men flee from Rome. 19. Don't deny that you said this. 20. Let the soldiers fortify not only the Senate but also the houses of the leading men. 21. I also said he would go to the camp outside the city walls of his own accord. 22. There was a certain disorder in the city because of one man. 23. Let us pray not only for our friends but also for our enemies. 24. Let us ask why they are being sent into exile. 25. At length the leader was silent. He had spoken a long time; nay,[1] too long. 26. Do not trust this man. 27. Let him not plot against the state. 28. Let him go together[2] with all his men. 29. Let there be no disorder in this most holy temple. 30. Although the disaster was most threatening, certain men did not hesitate to resist it. 31. Do not entrust the state to dangerous citizens. 32. Let us find a way. 33. Let us guard our liberty with the greatest care.

EXERCISE 27

Translate:

Change your minds, citizens; you can no longer preserve your safety. Go, fortify your homes, prepare yourselves against the enemy. There is a camp pitched in Italy against you. The enemy will make an attack at a time when you are not expecting it. Strengthen your courage, defend your homes, guard your people. We are held in on all sides. We must all fight to preserve our liberty.

And you, soldiers, be brave. Fight the enemy to the end—to death. Bring safety to your citizens, freedom[3] to your city, glory to your country.[4]

---

[1] *nay,* **immō,** adv.

[2] *together,* **ūnā,** adv.

[3] *freedom,* **lībertās, lībertātis.**

[4] *country,* **patria, ae.**

SIGHT TRANSLATION

DĒ RŌMĀ, URBE AETERNĀ

Rōma est urbs clāra. Rōmulus, rēx prīmus, urbī nōmen dedit. Flūmen Tiberis urbem dīvidit. Aliae sunt urbēs in Italiā, sed omnium clārissima est Rōma. Rōma est caput Italiae. Hāc in urbe senātus habēbātur. Cōnsulēs senātum convocābant. In senātū alter cōnsul cōnsilium cēpit, alter nihil dīxit. Cicerō senātum propter conjūrātiōnis timōrem in locō mūnītō habuit. Omnēs in hunc locum vēnērunt. Cicerō in senātum venit, omnia dīcit, omnia patefacit; nihil ignōrat, nihil vītat. Catilīna erat etiam in senātū. Nōn sē movet. Multa sentit, nihil dīcit.

Tempore Cicerōnis cīvēs Rōmānī erant superbī.[1] Omnēs aliī hominēs barbarī vocābantur. Cīvēs Rōmānī in tōtō orbe terrae vīvēbant. Nōn omnēs barbarī auctōritātī Rōmānae fāvērunt.[2] Nūllus cīvis Rōmānus ad mortem dūcēbātur. Barbarī autem jussū praetōris ad mortem jam prīdem dūcēbantur. Ad mortem vītandam hominēs saepe dīxērunt sē esse cīvēs Rōmānōs.

Posteā urbs Rōma facta est Chrīstiāna. Omnēs Chrīstiānī intellēxērunt Rōmam esse caput ecclēsiae[3] Catholicae. Sānctus Petrus et Sānctus Paulus in urbe Rōmā mortem propter Chrīstum passī sunt. Rōma est usque ad nostrum tempus caput ecclēsiae[3] Catholicae, semperque erit. Pius duodecimus[4] est pater omnium Chrīstiānōrum in orbe terrārum. Saepe litterās dat "urbī et orbī." Suprēmam auctōritātem in ecclēsiā[3] Catholicā habet. Locum tenet Petrī, immō vērō ipsīus Chrīstī.

Hōc modō nōs omnēs sumus cīvēs Rōmānī. Sānctus Paulus quondam clāmāvit:[5] "Cīvis Rōmānus sum!" Omnēs Catholicī dīcimus: "Ave Rōma aeterna! Cīvēs Rōmānī sumus!" Utinam sīmus bonī Rōmae aeternae cīvēs!

---

[1] **superbus, a, um,** *proud.*

[2] **faveō, favēre, fāvī, fautum,** 2, intr.; w. dat., *am well disposed, favor, befriend.*

[3] **ecclēsia, ae,** *church.*

[4] **duodecimus, a, um,** *twelfth.*

[5] **clāmō,** 1, tr.; acc. w. infin., *cry aloud, shout.*

Respondē Latīnē:

1. Quālis[1] urbs est Rōma?
2. Quis dedit Rōmae nōmen suum?
3. Suntne aliae urbēs in Italiā?
4. Num sunt clāriōrēs quam Rōma?
5. Quae urbs est caput Italiae?
6. Quā in urbe habēbātur senātus?
7. Quī convocābant senātum?
8. Quot erant cōnsulēs?
9. Quid agēbat alter cōnsul in senātū?
10. Cūr mūnīvit Cicerō locum habendī senātūs?
11. Quid fēcit Cicerō in senātū?
12. Quid dīxit Catilīna?
13. Quō nōmine Rōmānī aliōs hominēs vocābant?
14. Ubi vīvēbant cīvēs Rōmānī?
15. Quid sēnsērunt barbarī dē Rōmānōrum auctōritāte?
16. Num cīvēs Rōmānī ad mortem dūcēbantur?
17. Quōmodo dūcēbantur barbarī ad mortem?
18. Quōmodo saepe vītābant mortem?
19. Nōnne Rōma facta est Chrīstiāna?
20. Quae urbs est ecclēsiae[2] Catholicae caput?
21. Quā in urbe sunt Petrus Paulusque passī?
22. Quam ob rem passī sunt?
23. Estne Rōma caput ecclēsiae[2] Catholicae?
24. Quis est pater omnium Chrīstiānōrum?
25. Cūr litterae ējus dantur "urbī et orbī"?
26. Quis habet suprēmam auctōritātem in ecclēsiā Rōmānā?
27. Cūjus locum tenet Pius duodecimus?
28. Nōnne sumus omnēs hōc modō cīvēs Rōmānī?
29. Quid quondam clāmāvit Paulus?
30. Estne Rōma hōc modō aeterna?
31. Quid apertē dīcimus omnēs Catholicī?

---

[1] **quālis, e,** interrog. adj., *what kind.*

[2] **ecclēsia, ae,** *church.*

LESSON 8: TIME; NUMERALS

VOCABULARY

fāma, ae	*reputation, fame, rumor*
difficultās, difficultātis	*trouble, difficulty*
turpitūdō, turpitūdinis	*shame, disgrace*
facinus, facinoris, *n.*	*deed, misdeed, outrage*
domesticus, a, um	*of the home, domestic*
nūper, *adv.*	*recently*
umquam, *adv.*	*ever, at any time*
vindicō, *1, tr.*	*punish, deliver, set free*
stō, stāre, stetī, statum, *1, intr.*	*stand*
sileō, silēre, siluī, *2, intr.*	*am silent, keep silent*
impendeō, impendēre, *2, intr.; w. dat.*	*overhang, threaten*
nesciō, *4, tr.; acc. w. infin.*	*not know, am ignorant*

RELATED ENGLISH WORDS

Some people have a *vindictive* disposition. *Silence* is golden. The murals of Michelangelo are *famous*. Dogs and cats are *domestic* animals. A *constant* friend is one who stands by you when you are in trouble. *Obstacles* stand in the way. *Impending* dangers.

RELATED LATIN WORDS

Facilis; turpiter; domus; obstō; sciō.

ASSIGNMENT: *First Oration against Catiline,* lines 258-289; GRAMMAR 112-118; 919-924.

MEMORY: *First Oration against Catiline,* lines 148-179.

EXERCISE 28

Translate; explain the italicized expressions:

1. Quamquam cōnsul *duās hōrās* in senātū locūtus est, nōn omnēs eum audīvērunt. 2. Tertiā autem diē *ūnam tantum hōram* dīxit. 3. *Quīnque diēbus* cōram[1] populō Rōmānō loquētur. 4. *Abhinc multōs annōs* patrēs nostrī hunc locum mūnīvērunt. 5. Catilīna cupiēbat *certīs post diēbus* ad castra proficīscī. 6. Equitēs Rōmānī domum Cicerōnis paulō *ante lūcem* vēnērunt. 7. *Paucīs post diēbus* domum suam mūnīvit atque firmāvit. 8. *Post mortem* Caesaris bella domestica reī pūblicae Rōmānae *multōs annōs* impendēbant. 9. Dux populum *trēs hōrās* hortābātur. Tum dēnique siluit. Vōx enim ējus jam diūtius audīrī nōn potuit. 10. *Multōs jam annōs* cōpiae Rōmānae in difficultātibus versābantur. 11. Quid proximā, quid *superiōre nocte* ēgerīs nesciō. 12. Omnēs Catilīnae amīcī stābant *illō diē* in armīs. 13. *Superiōre nocte* facinus incrēdibile compertum est. 14. Quamquam fuistī apud Laecam *illā nocte,* nihil agere potuistī. 15. *Eōdem tempore* reliquōs sociōs hortābātur. 16. Quamquam eum saepe vindicāvērunt semper siluit. 17. Hominēs prīvātī saepe propter calamitātēs pūblicās patiuntur. 18. Per tōtam vītam cōnsul voluit imperium Rōmānum et ā peste pūblicā et ā calamitāte prīvātā cōnservāre. 19. *Prīmā lūce* amīcum vocāvit, grātiās eī ēgit, eum dīmīsit. 20. Calamitātēs commūnēs saepe ūtilēs sunt ad hominēs inter

---

[1] **cōram,** prep. w. abl., *before.*

sē conjungendōs. 21. Quamquam *tempore bellī* hominēs saepe bonō commūnī student, *tempore pācis* bonum prīvātum volunt. 22. Chrīstus *trēs annōs* vītam pūblicam vīxit. 23. *Post trēs annōs* hostēs eum ad mortem dūxērunt. 24. *Quot hōrās* erat Chrīstus in cruce? 25. *Tertiā autem hōrā* Chrīstus vōce magnā exclāmāvit:[1] "Pater mī, in manūs tuās commendō[2] spīritum meum." 26. Et inclīnātō capite[3] ēmīsit[4] spīritum. 27. Tenebrae factae sunt *eō tempore* quō Chrīstus mortuus est. 28. *Tertiā autem diē,* Chrīstus, dux vītae, resurrēxit.[5] 29. Magna Deō habenda est atque Fīliō ējus grātia. 30. Populus grātiās Cicerōnī ēgit propter ējus dīligentiam. 31. Dēbēmus semper amīcōrum fāmam servāre. 32. Cōnsul pauca dīxit hominibus quī hoc idem sentīrent. 33. Jam diū haec horribilis reī pūblicae pestis cīvibus impendet. 34. Dux cōnsulem gladiō interfēcit. 35. Cīvēs saepe prīvātā dīligentiā potius quam pūblicō praesidiō sē dēfendunt. 36. Sociī inter sē scelere nūper conjunctī domestica sunt pestis. 37. Chrīstus autem ē manibus eōrum effūgit; nōn enim vēnerat tempus ējus. 38. Duō equitēs Rōmānī sēsē *illā ipsā nocte paulō ante lūcem* mē interfectūrōs esse pollicitī sunt. 39. *Decem hōrās* in comitiīs stetit. 40. An umquam *trēs hōrās* in senātū es locūtus?

EXERCISE 29

Translate:

1. You wished to set me free five days ago. 2. We shall disclose[6] your misdeed within three days. 3. Two days before the battle Catiline left Rome. 4. They waited five days because of the domestic trouble. 5. After Caesar's death domestic wars threatened Rome. 6. For three hours the people stood outside the Senate.

---

[1] exclāmō, 1, tr., *cry out, exclaim.*

[2] commendō, 1, tr., *commit to, entrust to.*

[3] inclīnātō capite: *bowing his head.*

[4] ēmittō, ēmittere, ēmīsī, ēmissus, 3, tr., *send forth.*

[5] resurgō, resurgere, resurrēxī, resurrēctum, 3, intr., *rise, rise again.*

[6] *disclose,* patefaciō, patefacere, patefēcī, patefactus, 3, tr.

Finally[1] the leader came out. 7. He had not recently spoken to them. 8. A certain man reported Catiline's plans to us. 9. In war people are eager to punish the enemy. 10. On the sixth day they discovered the outrage. 11. On the eighth day the crime was punished. 12. For ten days the soldiers defended themselves against the domestic disaster. 13. At dawn my friend called me. 14. Or do you think that the leaders of the state can at any time keep silent about these disgraces of the home? 15. The consul had been in public life for ten years; for the remaining years of his life he fled the public eye.[2] 16. In war domestic difficulties threaten many citizens. 17. They had long been ignorant of the consul's reputation. 18. What shame has ever been absent from your meetings? 19. If the deed had been done, a rumor of it would have been heard throughout the whole town; no one would have been able to deliver the citizens from the threatening trouble.

NOTE ON TRANSLATION

In translating continuous passages like the exercise which follows, do not lean too heavily upon the English-Latin vocabulary; rely rather upon a thoroughgoing familiarity with the idiom of Cicero.[3] Thus, whereas you will get little help from the vocabulary in translating such phrases as *I shall not deal in the dark,* a bit of paging through Cicero—or better still, your own memory—will yield **nōn agam obscūrē.** In fact, the slavish pursuit of words in the vocabulary may even lead you onto the wrong track. Thus, *take my word for it* might give you **capiō** and **verbum;** but if you look rather for the IDEA and ask yourself how Cicero puts it, you will be on the right road with the phrase **mihi crēde.**

Again, *to put up with* has nothing to do with **pōnere.** Translating ideas rather than words, you realize that the idea behind *putting up with* is *tolerating, bearing,* or *enduring,* which will be

---

[1] *finally,* **tandem,** adv.

[2] public eye = eyes of the people.

[3] See pages 345-349 for a list of word-groups and idioms.

expressed by some such word as **patior, sinō,** or **ferō.** Very often these continuous passages will remind you of definite sections in Cicero. Your best help in translating will therefore be a careful study of the corresponding passages.

EXERCISE 30

AN ANGRY FATHER TO HIS WAYWARD SON

Translate:

I have long wanted to talk plainly to you. Now I can no longer be silent. In truth, I shall not deal in the dark, but I shall tell you all I know.

Do you think I don't know where you were last night? What friends you had with you? What places you visited? The eyes and ears[1] of many people spy[2] on you without your realizing[3] it. Neither night with its darkness[4] nor private homes with their walls[5] can hold in your wicked gatherings. It all comes to light.[6] It all bursts forth.

Change your mind, my son. Take my word for it; forget this sort of life. How long do you think my patience will put up with this disgrace of the home?

There was once upon a time[7] such manliness in you that you would do what you were told. Recently things have changed (themselves) and domestic difficulties are threatening. I give you a command sharp and severe: This sort of thing ought never again[8] happen. I shall no longer warn you. A word to the wise is sufficient.[9] I've spoken.

---

[1] *ear,* **auris, auris,** m.

[2] *spy,* **speculor, 1,** tr.

[3] *realize,* **sentiō, sentīre, sēnsī, sēnsus, 4,** tr.; acc. w. infin.

[4] *darkness,* **tenebrae, tenebrārum.**

[5] Use **parietēs, parietum,** m.

[6] Use the passive of **illustrō, 1,** tr., *reveal, bring to light.*

[7] *once upon a time,* **quondam,** adv.

[8] *again,* **iterum,** adv.

[9] *A word to the wise is sufficient:* **Verbum sapientī sat est.**

GENERAL REVIEW EXERCISES

EXERCISE 31

Translate orally:

1. Cicerō senātūs cōnsultum habuit vehemēns et grave. 2. Similī senātūs cōnsultō, aliī cōnsulēs hostēs reī pūblicae ad mortem dūxerant. 3. Ex hōc senātūs cōnsultō Catilīnam ad mortem dūcī jam prīdem oportēbat. 4. Nōs ējus modī senātūs cōnsultum nōn habēmus. 5. Cicerō magnam tenēbat auctōritātem; alter cōnsul auctōritātem habuit nūllam. 6. Auctōritās senātūs movēbat Catilīnam nihil. 7. Hominēs reī pūblicae auctōritāte ad mortem dūcuntur. 8. Omnis auctōritās ex Deō venit. 9. Ūnus ex cīvibus bonīs haec mihi dīxit. 10. Cōnsul bona omnium cīvium movēbat ex urbe. 11. Propter timōrem omnēs cīvēs in locum mūnītum vēnērunt. 12. Cīvibus haec omnia dīxit; neque ūllam rem ignōrāverat. 13. Cīvēs fortēs mortem propter reī pūblicae auctōritātem saepe patiuntur. 14. Cīvis Rōmānus sum. 15. Interrogāvērunt eum num cīvis Rōmānus esset. 16. Hostium manus omnēs cīvēs bonōs interficere cupiēbat. 17. Num interfēcērunt hostem pūblicum? 18. Ūnus est Deus, Pater omnium. 19. "Cupiō," inquit Cicerō, "cupiō, patrēs cōnscrīptī, auctōritātem senātūs esse magnam." 20. Pater meus vir gravis est et fortis. 21. Nōnne patientia virtūs est magna? 22. Catilīna virtūtem habuit nūllam. 23. Illō ipsō diē patrēs eōrum vēnērunt. 24. Diē atque nocte omnēs cīvēs propter ūnum hominem patiēbantur. 25. Omnēs Chrīstiānī bonī cum Chrīstō patiuntur. 26. Aliquandō tēcum veniam. 27. Omnēs enim urbēs mihi similēs videntur. 28. Omnēs quī in senātum vēnerant gravēs fortēsque erant. 29. Tēlum longum cēpit. 30. Magnā cum manū in alteram urbem sē contulit. 31. Nox nūlla erat ējus modī. 32. Ignōrāvēruntne omnēs cīvēs conjūrātiōnem esse factam? Nūllō modō. 33. Convocāvitne Cicerō senātum ūnum in locum? 34. Auctōritātem in ūnō homine posuērunt. 35. Propter mortem ūnīus Chrīstī omnēs hominēs locum in caelīs habent. 36. Erat similis

patrī. 37. Nūllus homō neque habuit neque habet neque habēbit virtūtem Chrīstī. 38. Chrīstus enim est Deus. 39. Catilīna cum tēlō in comitiīs stetit. 40. Cicerō in senātum magnā cum manū sē contulit. 41. In quā urbe vīvimus? 42. In hōc gravī cōnsiliō sunt reī pūblicae hostēs. 43. At manus hostium in rē pūblicā jam diū vīvit. 44. Tōta auctōritās erat in alterō cōnsule. 45. Chrīstus omnia apertē dīxit. 46. In conciliō Hērōdis[1] Chrīstus dīxit nihil. 47. Dēcrēverat enim senātus ut cōnsulēs vidērent nē quid dētrīmentī rēs pūblica caperet. 48. Ējus modī furōrem pater ējus nōn patiētur. 49. At prīvātī in hāc rē pūblicā cīvēs ad mortem dūxērunt. 50. Videō enim nūllam esse aliam viam. 51. Quid est enim virtūs? 52. Neque enim erat Catilīna ējus modī vir. 53. In prīncipiō Deus fēcit caelum et orbem terrae. 54. Quid fēcit Deus alterō diē? 55. Nōnne factus est homō ex terrā? 56. Nōnne vīdit Deus omnia esse bona? 57. Num omnēs hominēs sentiunt omnia esse bona? 58. Dum[2] Chrīstus in terrā vīvēbat, bona et faciēbat et dīcēbat. 59. Chrīstus auctōritātem reī pūblicae nōn ignōrāvit, immō vērō apertē notāvit. 60. Habetne Chrīstus superiōrem in nōs auctōritātem quam rēs pūblica?

EXERCISE 32

Translate orally:

1. Catilīna vīvēbat, et vīvēbat nōn ad dēpōnendam, sed ad cōnfirmandam audāciam. 2. Vērum Cicerō id quod jam prīdem factum esse oportēbat certā dē causā nōndum addūcēbātur ut faceret. 3. Castra erant in Italiā contrā populum Rōmānum collocāta; crēscēbat in diēs singulōs hostium numerus; eōrum autem imperātor et dux hostium erat ipse Catilīna. 4. Iste intrā moenia atque adeō in senātum vēnerat. 5. Intestīnae[3] cīvitātis perniciēī cotīdiē studēbat. 6. Italiam tōtam cupiēbat vastāre. 7. Cōnsul, senātus, cīvēs, populus Rōmānus, urbs Rōma, tōta Italia erat in

[1] **Hērōdes, Hērōdis,** *Herod.*

[2] **dum,** conj., *while.*

[3] **intestīnus, a, um,** *internal, civil.*

perīculō propter istum ūnum. 8. At Cicerō cupiēbat esse clēmēns;[1] nōn cupiēbat in tantīs reī pūblicae perīculīs Catilīnam ad mortem dūcere. 9. Cicerō sēnsit nēminem dē conjūrātiōne istīus ignōrāre. 10. Nēminī tamen dīxit. 11. Catilīna cum improbōrum manū ad castra sē contulit. 12. Cīvēs perditī ad causam Catilīnae in diēs movēbantur. 13. In tantō Rōmānōrum numerō aliquī improbī perditīque cīvēs Catilīnam esse ducem bonum sēnsērunt. 14. Ego vērō nūllō tempore tantam auctōritātem, tantam patientiam, tantam virtūtem vīderam. 15. Haec ego omnia intellēxī. 16. Chrīstus Judaeōs contrā sē cōnsilium cēpisse intellēxit. 17. Illō ipsō diē Chrīstus passus est. 18. Proximā nocte, "Pater," inquit, "fīat voluntās tua." 19. "Quid," inquit Cicerō, "dē rē pūblicā sentis?" 20. Spīritus Sānctus omnēs Chrīstiānōs cōnfirmat. 21. Nēmō erat tam perditus tamque improbus quī nōn vidēret conjūrātiōnem esse factam. 22. Utinam rēs pūblica Rōmāna perniciem vītāsset! 23. Ego tēcum vīvere jam diūtius nōn possum. 24. Cicerō nōn pūblicō sē praesidiō, sed prīvātā dīligentiā dēfendit. 25. Intrā moenia atque adeō in senātū erat hostium dux.

EXERCISE 33

Translate:

1. How long will you continue[2] to hate Rome? 2. How long he will continue[2] to hate Rome, we do not know. 3. You have now long been hating Rome. 4. He had long been plotting against the citizens. 5. For five days have we now allowed this man to live. 6. I also said that he was plotting against the lives of us all. 7. There are some who are plotting against the lives of all the citizens. 8. Cicero himself said this. 9. He said he would leave Rome. 10. Cicero said they could not remain in Rome any longer. 11. The conspirators[3] fled to save[4] themselves. 12. He ordered the guards to defend his house. 13. Did Catiline leave Rome? 14. Sure-

---

[1] **clēmēns** (*gen.* **clēmentis**), *merciful.*

[2] Do not translate; Gr. 489.

[3] *conspirator,* **conjūrātor, conjūrātōris.**

[4] *save,* **cōnservō, 1,** tr.

ly you don't fear this man? 15. Didn't he say this? 16. Or are you waiting to kill me? 17. Who of us does not know his plans? 18. He asked whether Catiline would leave the city or not. 19. Will you leave the city or not? 20. He asked whether the Senate feared Catiline. 21. We know with whom you were at the last elections. 22. Has he set out for the camp? 23. Was Catiline recently at Rome? 24. When[1] will he set out from Rome? 25. Did they march five days? 26. He left Rome at the third hour. 27. The soldiers hastened to Rome. 28. There was a great disaster in Gaul. 29. He marched through the province. 30. He will leave within ten days. 31. After several days they were killed. 32. Shortly before dawn a messenger arrived. 33. Many years later several people praised him. 34. Five days ago Catiline left Rome. 35. For many days now we have been hearing Cicero.

EXERCISE 34

Translate:

1. How long then will you remain at Rome? 2. Does not the garrison of the city move you? 3. Don't you fear the eyes of all good men? 4. Didn't Catiline see that Cicero knew his plans? 5. Nevertheless he dares to come into the Senate. 6. Do you ask whether he was present at the meeting? 7. Didn't the Senate and the consuls understand this? 8. Are there some who would defend Catiline? 9. Was not Catiline long plotting against the city? 10. He asked Catiline whether he would leave the city. 11. "Depart," he said, "the gates are open." 12. You said you feared me. You said you hated me. You also said that I would be killed. 13. I know what you and your men did last night. 14. Do you think I am ignorant of what plans you made? 15. Five days before the battle Catiline was at Rome. 16. One day afterwards he was killed. 17. He said he was defending himself. 18. Was there anyone[2] at Rome who did not fear you? 19. There was no one so

[1] *when*, **quandō**, interrog. adv.

[2] Gr. 843.

wicked as to defend the enemies of the state. 20. All this I discovered within two hours. 21. Do you hesitate to go into exile? 22. Did he fortify his home with stronger guards? 23. Shortly before dawn he came to Rome. 24. He asked whether he hesitated to go into exile. 25. I advise this.

EXERCISE 35

Translate orally:

1. Set out for Rome. 2. Leave the city. 3. March through the province. 4. I will come within three days. 5. Four years ago he was killed. 6. We will find him within three days. 7. He asked whether they had come to Rome. 8. Four days ago they came to Rome. 9. Was he at home? 10. Did he see anyone?[1] 11. Whom did he see? 12. There are some who do not fear you. 13. He had long been desiring this. 14. At the third hour he discovered the plot. 15. He waited three days. 16. He asked whether they would come or not. 17. Where was the camp? 18. Do you dare deny it? 19. Was anyone there? 20. Let them depart, each[2] to his own home. 21. Is there anyone (at all)[1] who believes this? 22. Do not fear. 23. Free us from this danger. 24. I did not know the size of the camp.[3] 25. They do not know where the camp is. 26. They did not know the location of the camp.[4] 27. He came into the Senate on the fifth day. 28. He knew the identity of the conspirators.[3] 29. He did not know the time of their arrival.[5] 30. He did not know the place of assembly.[6]

---

[1] Gr. 843.

[2] Gr. 832.

[3] Use an indirect question.

[4] What construction?

[5] Use an indirect question introduced by **quandō,** *when,* or **quō tempore.**

[6] Translate *where they would assemble.*

LESSON 9: ACCUSATIVE WITH THE INFINITIVE

VOCABULARY

frequentia, ae	*crowd* *throng*
jūdicium, ī	*judgment* *trial*
odium, ī	*hatred*
aspectus, ūs	*sight* *look* *appearance*
pārēns, pārentis, *c.*	*parent*
jūstus, a, um	*just* *lawful*
obscūrus, a, um	*obscure* *dark*
quidem, *adv.*	*indeed* *at least*
ut, *conj.* sīc . . . ut, *conj.*	*as* *just as*
careō, carēre, caruī, caritūrus, *2, intr.; w. abl.*	*am without* *want* *lack*
concēdō, concēdere, concessī, concessus, *3, tr. and intr.*	*withdraw* *yield*
opprimō, opprimere, oppressī, oppressus, *3, tr.*	*overwhelm* *surprise*
ēlābor, ēlābī, ēlāpsus sum, *3, intr.*	*slip away* *escape*
cōnspicor, *1, tr.; acc. w. infin.*	*observe* *perceive*
suspicor, *1, tr.; acc. w. infin.*	*suspect*
mālō, mālle, māluī, *tr.; acc. w. infin.*	*prefer*

RELATED ENGLISH WORDS

The debater disregarded one important *aspect* of the question. The school cannot assume all *parental* responsibilities. Both sides were willing to make generous *concessions*. *Oppressive* weather. A *lapse* of memory.

RELATED LATIN WORDS

Frequēns; ōdī; premō.

ASSIGNMENT: *First Oration against Catiline,* lines 290-337; GRAMMAR 408-410, 425-429; 897-903; Review GRAMMAR 209-211, 219-227, 284-286, 292-300, 318, 328, 336-338, 889.

EXERCISE 36

Translate; explain the italicized verbs:

1. Dīcō tē *venīre* paulō ante lūcem. 2. Dīcō tē *vēnisse* paulō ante lūcem. 3. Dīcō tē *ventūrum esse* paulō ante lūcem. 4. Pārentēs meī dīxērunt sē urbem *relinquere*. 5. Pārentēs meī dīxērunt sē urbem *relīquisse*. 6. Pārentēs meī dīxērunt sē urbem *relictūrōs esse*. 7. Cicerō putāvit Catilīnam ex urbe *profectūrum esse*. 8. Eques quīdam pollicitus est sē Cicerōnem in lectō[1] *interfectūrum esse*. 9. Cicerō autem negāvit sē *vulnerātum esse*. 10. Cōnsulēs putant rem pūblicam ā metū *esse līberātam*. 11. Dux scīvit magnam equitum partem intrā mūrōs *relictam esse*. 12. Trāditum est Rōmānōrum rēgēs bonōs *fuisse*. 13. Cōnsul dīcitur ex urbe *exīre*. 14. Cicerō vidētur metū *movērī*. 15. Vīsum est senātuī et cōnsulibus hostēs *dīmittī*. 16. Quis est quī haec *ferat*? 17. Erant in senātū quī dē reī pūblicae interitū *cōgitārent*. 18. Mīlitēs dīxērunt sē mālle *morī* potius quam in exilium *īre*. 19. Nōn possumus diū aspectū pārentum *carēre*. 20. Suspicātus sum pārentēs eum interfēcisse. 21. Vīdimus ex cīvium frequentiā virum jūstum *ēlābī*. 22. Nōn ignōrāmus, cīvēs, nōs ab hoste *opprimī*. 23. Mālō cum amīcīs ā frequentiā *concēdere*. 24. Puerī pārentēs ā

[1] **lectus, ī,** *couch, bed.*

longē[1] cōnspicātī sunt. 25. Chrīstus autem sē Sānctum Spīritum missūrum pollicitus est.

EXERCISE 37

Translate:

1. The consul says that he can no longer bear this sort of boldness. 2. Christ said that He would lead men out of darkness[2] into the light. 3. There are some who do not wish to dismiss the Roman knights. 4. He said that he himself did not suspect his parents' hatred. 5. He went right up to[3] the gates, but he did not escape. 6. Are there those in this Senate who desire to destroy Rome, its walls, its homes? 7. You say that these men are even now[4] in arms. 8. He said he would not[5] leave a large part of the cavalry within[6] the walls. 9. They promised to free the city from fear. 10. I say that these companions in[7] crime came on that very night. 11. There are some (people) who praise God on account of fear. 12. The sight of a throng always overwhelms me. 13. I say that I cannot be without my parents. 14. I say that the enemy was in arms. 15. I say that the enemy will be in arms. 16. They thought that the people had been freed from the boldness of one man. 17. They thought that Catiline had been wounded in battle. 18. I say that my parents will always be just. 19. The consul indeed is said to have slipped away from the crowd. 20. It is thought that he was suspected of hatred. 21. I hear that after the trial the crowd withdrew. 22. The appearances of things often hinder our judgment. 23. We could not see anything; it was a dark day and the house lacked light. 24. The general thought he could surprise the enemy, but they did not yield. 25. Good parents at least

---

[1] **ā longē**: *from afar, from a distance.*

[2] *darkness,* **tenebrae, tenebrārum.**

[3] right up to = all the way to.

[4] Use **etiam nunc** or **etiam jam.**

[5] Translate *he denied that he would.*

[6] *within,* **intrā**, prep. w. acc.

[7] Translate *of.*

should discover what their children want. 26. We should speak of our friends just as we prefer them to speak of us. 27. It is not lawful to hold (one's) parents in hatred.

EXERCISE 38

Imitate the word order and structure of the model in translating:

MODEL: Sīc enim jam tēcum loquar,
nōn ut odiō permōtus esse videar, quō dēbeō,
sed ut misericordiā, quae tibi nūlla dēbētur.

1. For I shall now act not as one seeming to be moved by fear, but by patriotism.[1]
2. For I shall now order you to be led to death, not that you may suffer, as you deserve,[2] but that the state may be without fear.
3. For I shall now praise God, not as a sinner[3] moved by fear, as I ought, but as a son moved by love, which is most certainly due[4] God.
4. For I shall now speak to you, my son, not that I may appear to be moved by anger,[5] as I ought, but by carefulness about your reputation which ought to be most dear to you and to me.

EXERCISE 39

Translate orally:

1. Quōmodo timōrem populī tibi ferendum putās? 2. Haec omnia cōnsul bene tulit. 3. Dīxī ego īdem mē paulō ante ex urbe exitūrum. 4. Cōnsul hostem ex urbe exīre jussit. 5. "Quae cum ita sint," inquit Cicerō, "perge quō coepistī; ēgredere aliquandō ex urbe, patent portae—proficīscere." 6. Ēgredere ex urbe; līberā

---

[1] *patriotism,* **amor (amōris) patriae.**

[2] as you deserve = as you ought.

[3] *sinner,* **peccātor, peccātōris.**

[4] due = owing to.

[5] *anger,* **īra, ae.**

rem pūblicam metū; proficīscere! 7. Sociī quī apud Laecam convēnerant ējus domum relīquērunt. 8. Audīvī equitem Rōmānum ad mē missum esse. 9. Ēdūc tēcum omnēs sociōs tuōs nefāriōs. 10. Cum intellēxit coetum esse dīmissum, Cicerō domum suam mājōribus praesidiīs mūnīvit atque firmāvit. 11. Petrus ter[1] negāvit sē Chrīstum scīre. 12. Pollicitus erat sē Dominum secūtūrum esse usque ad fīnem. 13. Jūstus quidem Deī voluntātem māvult. 14. Vōx potest mentēs hominum tamquam gladius corpora vulnerāre. 15. Utinam omnī cūrā līberārēmur! 16. Duō sociī noctem fore obscūram suspicātī sunt. 17. Catilīna paulō ante in senātum vēnerat. 18. Semper in mente habēre dēbēmus summam reī pūblicae salūtem. 19. Summī clārissimīque cīvēs ex urbe exierant propter metum. 20. Nōs omnēs scīmus Catilīnam partēs urbis inter sociōs distribuisse. 21. Equitēs Rōmānī erant virī summī atque clārissimī. 22. Odium, ut scīmus omnēs, hominis jūdicium impedit.

EX MISSĀLĪ RŌMĀNŌ

Ex Proprio de Sanctis

In the first part of the Mass we speak to God; we confess our sins, praise and thank Him, ask for favors suggested by the feast of the day. Then God speaks to us; sometimes through the voice of a prophet of the Old Law, sometimes through a letter of St. Paul in the New Testament. The lesson for the Feast of the Holy Guardian Angels (October 2) is typical.

Lectiō librī Exodī:[2]

Haec dīcit Dominus Deus: Ecce, ego mittam angelum meum, quī praecēdat[3] tē, et custōdiat in viā, et intrōdūcat[4] in locum

---

[1] **ter**, adv., *thrice, three times.*

[2] *A reading from the Book of Exodus.*

[3] **praecēdō, praecēdere, praecessī, praecessus**, 3, tr. and intr., *go before, precede.*

[4] **intrōdūcō, intrōdūcere, intrōdūxī, intrōductus**, 3, tr., *bring in, introduce.*

quem parāvī. Observā[1] eum, et audī vōcem ējus, nec contemnendum[2] putēs: quia nōn dīmittet, cum peccāveris,[3] et est nōmen meum in illō. Quod sī audīeris vōcem ējus et fēceris omnia quae loquor, inimīcus[4] erō inimīcīs tuīs et afflīgam[5] afflīgentēs tē; praecēdetque[6] tē angelus meus.[7]

God continues to speak to us in the Gospel, this time chiefly through His Son. We rise to full height, sign our foreheads, lips, and breast with the Sign of the Cross. The priest changes from the Epistle to the Gospel side of the altar and, as he does on the Feast of the Holy Guardian Angels, reads:

Sequentia sānctī evangeliī secundum Matthēum:[8]

In illō tempore accessērunt[9] discipulī ad Jēsum, dīcentēs: Quis, putās, mājor est in rēgnō caelōrum? Et advocāns[10] Jēsūs parvulum,[11] statuit eum in mediō eōrum et dīxit: Āmēn, dīcō vōbīs, nisi conversī[12] fuerītis et efficiāminī sīcut parvulī,[11] nōn intrābitis[13] in rēgnō caelōrum . . . Vidēte, nē contemnātis[2] ūnum ex hīs pusillīs;[14] dīcō enim vōbīs, quia angelī eōrum in caelīs semper vident faciem[15] Patris meī quī in caelīs est.[16]

---

1 **observō, 1,** tr., *heed, observe.*

2 **contemnō, contemnere, contempsī, contemptus,** 3, tr., *despise, scorn* (cf. contempt).

3 **peccō, 1,** intr., *sin.*

4 **inimīcus, ī,** *enemy* (personal).

5 **afflīgō, afflīgere, afflīxī, afflīctus,** 3, tr., *strike, dash down* (cf. afflict).

6 **praecēdō, praecēdere, praecessī, praecessus,** 3, tr. and intr., *go before, precede.*

7 Exodus 23:20-23.

8 *The continuation of the holy Gospel according to St. Matthew.*

9 **accēdō, accēdere, accessī, accessum,** 3, intr.; **ad** w. acc., *move to, approach.*

10 **advocāns; ad + vocō;** meaning?

11 **parvulus, ī,** *child, little boy.*

12 **convertō, convertere, convertī, conversus; con + vertō;** meaning?

13 **intrō,** 1, intr., *enter.*

14 **pusillus, a, um,** *small, tiny.*

15 **faciēs, faciēī,** *face.*

16 Matthew 18:1-10.

LESSON 10: PLACE; ABLATIVE ABSOLUTE

VOCABULARY

custōdia, ae	*guard* *custody*
patria, ae[1]	*fatherland* *native land* *country*
vinculum, ī	*bond* (pl.) *chains* (pl.) *prison*
carcer, carceris	*prison*
quaestiō, quaestiōnis	*inquiry* *investigation* *law court*
impūnītus, a, um	*unpunished*
dignus, a, um; *w. abl. (Gr. 775)*	*worthy (of)*
falsus, a, um	*false*
tacitus, a, um	*silent* *silently* *quiet* *quietly*
habitō, ***1, tr.***	*live* *dwell*
impetrō, ***1, tr.;*** **ab (ā)** ***w. abl. of person; acc. of thing;*** **ut (nē)**	*obtain* (by asking)
jūdicō, ***1, tr.; acc. w. infin.***	*judge*
adhibeō, ***2, tr.;*** **ad** ***w. acc.***	*employ* *use*
valeō, valēre, valuī, ***2, intr.; w. infin.***	*am strong* *am influential* *am well*

[1] Really **patria terra,** from the adjective **patrius, a, um.**

discēdō, discēdere, discessī, discessum, ***3, intr.;*** **ab (ā), ex (ē),** ***or*** **dē** ***w. abl.*** — *depart*, *withdraw*

RELATED ENGLISH WORDS

It was not hard to see the *fallacy* of his argument. *Convalescents* are people who are in the process of recovering their strength. The prisoner was taken into *custody*. Christ was subjected to many *indignities* during His Passion. *Patriotism. Incarceration.* He disobeyed his superior officer with *impunity*. The *inhabitants* of an island are those who dwell there. *Impetratory* prayer. If you are *prejudiced* against a person, your opinion is based upon a judgment previously made. *Avail. Valid. Valence.*

RELATED LATIN WORDS

Custōs; vinciō; quaerō; fallō; taceō; valē.

ASSIGNMENT: *First Oration against Catiline,* lines 338-386; GRAMMAR 912-914; 915-917.

EXERCISE 40

Translate; explain the italicized phrases:

1. *Quaestiōne factā,* hostēs patriae ad carcerem ductī sunt. 2. Quamquam nōn jūdicāvērunt eōs dignōs esse morte, tamen eōrum amīcī nōn valuērunt eōs impūnītōs *ē custōdiā* ēripere. 3. *Ad patriam* tandem aliquandō reversus est; decem jam annōs in exiliō habitāverat. 4. Vinculum omnium virtūtum est cāritās. 5. *Conjūrātiōne compertā,* Cicerō erat omnī laude dignus. 6. *Duce mortuō,* omnēs amīcī tacitī ējus *domō* discessērunt. 7. Ēripe mē, Domine, *dē* falsōrum amīcōrum *manū*. 8. Castra sunt *in Italiā* contrā populum Rōmānum collocāta. 9. *In quā urbe* vīvis? 10. *In hōc sānctissimō gravissimōque cōnsiliō* sunt quī vim adhibēre nōn valeant. 11. Quot carcerēs sunt *in hāc cīvitāte*? 12. *Lepidō et Tullō cōnsulibus,* Catilīna *in comitiō* cum tēlō stābat. 13. Nōn autem potuit tēla *ex castrīs* ēripere. 14. *Ipsō in templō* cīvēs complūrēs tacitī prō patriā pācem cotīdiē impetrābant. 15. Exīre

ex urbe jussit cōnsul hostem. 16. Quis *ex hāc tantā frequentiā,* tot ex tuīs amīcīs tēcum locūtus est? 17. Ēgredere *ex urbe,* Catilīna, līberā rem pūblicam *metū;* in exilium, sī hanc vōcem exspectās, discēde. 18. At saepe etiam prīvātī *in hāc rē pūblicā* cīvēs falsōs vinculīs dignōs jūdicāvērunt. 19. Ā cīvium oculīs discēdant falsī neque cum bonīs diūtius habitent. 20. Homō quī sē ipse jam dignum custōdiā jūdicat nōn potest longē ā carcere atque ā vinculīs abesse. 21. *Ēruptiōne*[1] *factā,* omnēs quī in carcere erant ad proximam urbem effūgērunt. 22. Judaeī Petrum *in carcerem* conjēcērunt; illā autem ipsā nocte Petrus, *angelō duce,* ē vinculīs ēreptus est. 23. Discēdant omnēs improbī perditīque hominēs ā templīs, ā tēctīs urbis ac moenibus, ā cīvitāte, immō vērō, ā patriā—*in exilium* proficīscantur. 24. Quotiēns jam ēlāpsa est ista sīca *dē manibus tuīs*! 25. Mediā autem nocte hostēs tacitī *dē mūrīs* discessērunt. 26. *Quaestiōne* paulō ante *habitā,* cōnsul in senātum vēnit. 27. Nōnne hunc *in vincula* dūcī dēbēre jūdicās? 28. *Omnibus impūnītīs* ūnum in locum *convocātīs,* cōnsul dīligēns voluit quaestiōnem habēre. 29. Hīc, hīc in nostrō numerō sunt quī impūnītī bellum in patriam īnferant. 30. Hoc sī vērum jūdicās, apertē loquere; sīn falsum, tacē.

EXERCISE 41

Translate:

1. When the gathering had been dismissed, the consul went into the Senate. 2. Cicero led the enemies of the country to death without any public disorder.[2] 3. During my consulship[2] Rome was preserved from a great disaster. 4. When the Senate had been summoned, the consul collected the swords from the private houses. 5. There is no one at Rome who will judge that you are worthy of custody. 6. Did he escape unpunished from the hands of the soldiers? 7. Lead the men into Italy. 8. They withdrew from Rome and dwelt in a neighboring town. 9. They were not able to

---

[1] **ēruptiō, ēruptiōnis,** *a breaking out, a bursting forth.*

[2] Use an ablative absolute.

lead the army through the province. 10. They did not know the whereabouts of the prison.[1] 11. After his death they said many false things about him. 12. The army marched into its native land. 13. After an investigation had been obtained, the careful consul saved several men from prison. 14. Enemies of the state are worthy of chains. 15. They all silently departed from their fatherland. 16. The general was not influential (enough) to use violence in the private inquiry about the soldiers. 17. At Rome the citizens knew how strong the law courts were. 18. The bond of friendship is strong. 19. Those who live in small towns are often quiet. 20. How are you? I am well.

SIGHT TRANSLATION

DĒ GRACCHŌRUM MĀTRE

[Pars Prīma]

Cornēlia erat fīlia Pūbliī Scīpiōnis Āfricānī,[2] quī Hannibalem vīcit. Uxor facta est Tiberiō Semprōniō Gracchō.[3] Fīliōs duōs habuērunt, quōrum senior Tiberius, minor Gājus.

Ōlim[4] mulier[5] nōbilis ornāmenta[6] sua Cornēliae ostendēbat. Quae Cornēlia propter pulchritūdinem[7] laudāvit, sed deinde[8] fīliōs suōs ad sē vocāvit: "Haec," inquit, "sunt ornāmenta[6] mea."

Tiberius Gracchus erat ōrātor[9] clārus et mīles fortis. Ā populō Rōmānō et laudābātur et dīligēbātur.

Ējus tempore per tōtam Italiam erat magnus numerus servōrum. Cīvēs multī, quī agrōs habitāre nōn potuērunt, jam in urbem vēnerant et Rōmae vīvēbant. Rēs pūblica Rōmāna magnō in

---

1 Use an indirect question.

2 Publius Scipio Africanus, a famous Roman general.

3 Tiberius Sempronius Gracchus, member of a famous Roman family.

4 **ōlim**, adv., *once*.

5 **mulier, mulieris**, *woman*.

6 **ornāmentum, ī**, *jewel* (cf. ornament).

7 **pulchritūdō, pulchritūdinis**, *beauty, charm*.

8 **deinde**, adv., *next, thereupon*.

9 **ōrātor, ōrātōris**, *speaker, orator*.

perīculō jam diū versābātur. Tiberius Gracchus et frāter Gājus studēbant rem pūblicam servāre. Voluērunt multōs cīvēs ex urbe in agrōs redūcere et agrōs pūblicōs, quī jam diū in manibus paucōrum erant, distribuere.[1] Inimīcī[2] autem Tiberiī eum novīs rēbus studēre putāvērunt. Hanc ob causam eum occīdērunt.

Respondē Latīnē:

1. Cūjus fīlia erat Cornēlia?
2. Quem vīcerat Pūblius Scīpiō?
3. Cūjus uxor facta est Cornēlia?
4. Quot fīliōs habuērunt?
5. Quis erat senior? Quis minor?
6. Nōnne erant ornāmenta[3] mulieris[4] nōbilis pulchra?[5]
7. Habuitne ornāmenta[3] Cornēlia?
8. Quālis[6] ōrātor[7] erat Tiberius? Quālis[6] mīles?
9. Num tempore Tiberiī cīvēs in agrīs vīvere potuērunt?
10. Cūr nōn?
11. Quem in locum sē contulērunt?
12. Nōnne rēs pūblica Rōmāna in perīculō versābātur?
13. Quid facere voluērunt frātrēs Gracchī?
14. In quōrum manibus erant agrī?
15. Num facile erat redūcere cīvēs ex urbe in agrōs?
16. Putāsne Gracchōs vērē novīs rēbus studuisse?
17. Num Tiberius jūre[8] occīsus est?

---

[1] **distribuō, distribuere, distribuī, distribūtus,** 3, tr., *assign, distribute.*
[2] **inimīcus, ī,** *enemy* (personal).
[3] **ornāmentum, ī,** *jewel.*
[4] **mulier, mulieris,** *woman.*
[5] **pulcher, pulchra, pulchrum,** *beautiful.*
[6] **quālis, e,** interrog. adj., *of what sort, what kind of.*
[7] **ōrātor, ōrātōris,** *speaker, orator.*
[8] **jūre,** adv., *justly, rightly.*

LESSON 11: THE GERUND AND THE GERUNDIVE

VOCABULARY

invidia, ae	*envy* *hatred* *unpopularity*
studium, ī	*zeal* *eagerness* *devotion*
adulēscēns, adulēscentis	*young man*
tempestās, tempestātis	*storm* *weather*
cārus, a, um	*dear*
cēterī, ae, a ***(Gr. 829)***	*the rest (of)* *the remainder*
honestus, a, um	*upright* *honorable*
vix, ***adv.***	*hardly* *scarcely* *barely* *with difficulty*
dummodo, ***conj. (Gr. 594)***	*if only* *provided only* *as long as*
clāmō, ***1, tr.; acc. w. infin.***	*cry aloud* *shout*
frangō, frangere, frēgī, frāctus, ***3, tr.***	*break* *destroy*
postulō, ***1, tr.;*** **ab (ā)** ***w. abl. of person; acc. of thing;*** **ut (nē);** ***acc w. infin.***	*demand*
revocō, ***1, tr.***	*call back* *recall*

percipiō, percipere, percēpī, perceptus, *3, tr.; acc. w. infin.* — *learn of*; *perceive*

exaudiō, *4, tr.; acc. w. infin.* — *catch sound of*; *hear*

serviō, *4, intr.; w. dat.* — *serve*

RELATED ENGLISH WORDS

One should avoid *invidious* remarks. A *student* is one who presumably has some devotion to knowledge. An *adolescent* is one who is on the way to becoming an adult. Who wrote *The Tempest*? *Etc.* is the abbreviation for **et cetera** *(and the rest)*. *Exclamation* point. A *fractured* skull is not necessarily fatal. *Postulates* of reason. The president *revoked* his decision. Have you ever had an *audition* in a radio studio?

RELATED LATIN WORDS

Studeō; adulēscentulus; perfrangō; vocō; audiō; servitūs; servus.

ASSIGNMENT: *First Oration against Catiline,* lines 387-449; GRAMMAR 864-883; Review GRAMMAR 212, 228-230, 288, 304-306, 319, 329, 342, 344, 380, 385, 391, 396, 397, 418, 424, 429.

EXERCISE 42

Translate; explain the italicized constructions:

1. In senātū paene *clāmandum* est, sī exaudīrī vīs. 2. Cicerō loquēbātur dē invidiā cīvium honestōrum *vītandā*. 3. Rōmae complūrēs adulēscentēs *pugnandī* cupidī erant. 4. Cēterī cīvēs urbis *mūniendae* causā sē dedērunt. 5. Omnēs adulēscentēs vix intellegere videntur tempus esse *loquendī,* tempus *tacendī*. 6. Hominēs *cōgitandō* invidiam superāre possunt. 7. Putāvī tē fore dīligentissimum ad *custōdiendum*. 8. Ējus studium vix est *dēpōnendum*. 9. Tempestās invidiae nōbīs est *metuenda*. 10. Pārentēs sunt multō cāriōrēs omnibus cēterīs amīcīs. 11. Sed tū ut lēgum

poenās timeās, ut temporibus reī pūblicae cēdās, nōn est *postulandum.* 12. Saepe in mentem *revocanda* est mors. 13. Rōmae *vīvendī* causā vēnit. 14. Percipite, omnēs, invidiam esse *dēpōnendam.* 15. Chrīste, audī nōs; Chrīste, exaudī nōs. 16. Complūra tēcta tempestāte fracta sunt. 17. Voluntās mala *frangenda* est. 18. Vix umquam ā nōbīs *cēdendum* est temporibus. 19. Ad urbem *mūniendam* missī sunt. 20. Nōbīs *eundum* est. 21. Patriae *serviendum* est. 22. Interrogās mē num *Deō serviendum* sit. 23. Dē hīs difficultātibus mihi *tacendum* est. 24. Dīxit *populō ā cōnsule serviendum* esse. 25. Vix erat imperītus[1] *loquendī.*

EXERCISE 43

Translate:

1. We ought always to avoid envy. 2. There is a time for[2] speaking and a time for[2] keeping silent. 3. This young man's zeal in conquering difficulties should be praised. 4. Our dear parents were crying aloud, but they could not be heard because of the storm. 5. The weather was suitable for setting out. 6. The young man had to leave his dear native land. 7. The rest of the upright citizens should be recalled from exile. 8. We were scarcely able to catch the sound of his voice. 9. If you want to be heard in this place, you have to shout. 10. Carefulness must always be demanded. 11. Nothing could break Catiline's boldness as long as he was at Rome. 12. A good soldier must never yield to the enemy. 13. We must carefully perceive what is being done by the consul.

EXERCISE 44

Translate:

1. Nihilne hic mūnītissimus habendī senātūs locus tē movet? 2. Vīvis tamen ad cōnfirmandam audāciam. 3. Eritne hoc mihi metuendum? 4. Virtūs ējus multō magis est admīranda. 5. Suī

---

[1] **imperītus, a, um**; w. gen., *unskilled (in), inexperienced (in).*

[2] Translate *of.*

cōnservandī causā profūgērunt. 6. Magna grātia dīs immortālibus est habenda. 7. Manum prīncipum interficiendōrum causā parāvistī. 8. Num putās domum tuam relinquendam esse? 9. Audācia ējus, cīvēs Rōmānī, nōn est ferenda. 10. Vītandae suspīciōnis causā mēcum īvistī. 11. Ad vindicandum fortis est. 12. Tū ut aliquandō mentem istam mūtēs, nōn est postulandum. 13. Nōn ūnam dabō tibi hōram ad vīvendum. 14. Complūrēs adulēscentēs perditōs urbis mūniendae causā convocāvit. 15. Bellī vītandī causā lēgātum mīsit. 16. Studiō dīcendī semper valuit. 17. Cum illō est nōbīs pugnandum. 18. Efficiam nē diūtius vōbīs sit timendum. 19. Hoc optimum tempus est pugnandī. 20. Catilīna urbis capiendae cupidus est. 21. Ad custōdiendum est dīligentissimus. 22. Tempus est nōn dīcendī, sed agendī. 23. Haec calamitās magnā cum patientiā ferenda est. 24. In montibus erat pugnandum. 25. Cicerōnis nōn est oblīvīscendum. 26. Līberīs ā mīlitibus parcendum[1] est. 27. Nōbīs eundum est. 28. Senātuī ā cōnsule persuādendum est.

EXERCISE 45

Imitate the word order and the structure of the model in translating:

MODEL: **Quōrum ego vix abs tē jam diū manūs ac tēla continēō,**
eōsdem facile addūcam
ut tē, haec quae vastāre jam prīdem studēs relinquentem,
usque ad portās prōsequantur.

1. I shall easily persuade the very men who have long been desiring to lead you to death to praise you once you have spoken to the Roman people.

2. These men had long been fearing the Germans. Yet Caesar easily persuaded them to follow him courageously as he led the legions against the enemy.

---

[1] **parcō, parcere, pepercī, parcitūrus,** 3, intr.; w. dat., *spare.*

EXERCISE 46

Translate:

1. Our minds must be strengthened by thinking on these noble men. 2. We must serve God. 3. This is a splendid time to free the state from this danger. 4. We must listen to what he said. 5. Cicero had to drive the wicked Catiline out of Rome. 6. The courageous king did not fear the Romans. 7. This is not to be wondered at. 8. He sent men to capture the city. 9. We must conquer or die. 10. He is prepared for speaking. 11. His madness is not to be borne. 12. We must spare the children. 13. He was sent to arouse the Gauls. 14. This is not to be feared. 15. He should be put to death. 16. Dangerous citizens should be restrained. 17. His plots must be avoided. 18. The state must be freed from dangers. 19. Cicero should be praised by all men. 20. We must avoid war.

EXERCISE 47

Translate:

1. We must trust this man. 2. That young man is to be praised. 3. Cicero said virtue was to be praised. 4. Cicero was always prepared for speaking. 5. We must demand the captured slaves. 6. This is a good time for summoning the people. 7. They should never destroy this city. 8. We must destroy him as if he were a plague. 9. This must not be reported to the Senate. 10. You must go into exile, Catiline. 11. This indeed is not to be asked for. 12. You must fear the penalties of the laws. 13. He must forget the slaughter of citizens. 14. They came for the sake of seeing their dear fatherland. 15. Young men are not always to be persuaded by their parents; they must often be commanded. 16. God ought to be served by all men, in all places, at all times. 17. The eagerness of youth[1] is not to be broken, provided only it can be restrained.

---

[1] youth = young men.

EX MISSĀLĪ RŌMĀNŌ

Ex Ordinario

With God's good news (the Gospel) finished, the first part of the Mass comes to a close, but not without a public profession of faith. Standing we say, "I believe . . ." Although we said "*ōrēmus*" in the prayers, "*laudāmus*" in the Gloria, faith is a personal matter. That is why we shift to the singular when we say:

Crēdō in ūnum Deum, Patrem omnipotentem, factōrem caelī et terrae, vīsibilium[1] omnium et invīsibilium.[2] Et in ūnum Dominum Jēsum Chrīstum, Fīlium Deī ūnigenitum. Et ex Patre natum ante omnia saecula. Deum dē Deō, lūmen dē lūmine, Deum vērum dē Deō vērō. Genitum, nōn factum, consubstantiālem Patrī; per quem omnia facta sunt. Quī propter nōs hominēs et propter nostram salūtem dēscendit dē caelīs. Et incarnātus est dē Spīritū Sānctō ex Marīā virgine, et homō factus est. Crucifīxus etiam prō nōbīs, sub Pontiō Pīlātō passus et sepultus est.[3] Et resurrēxit tertiā diē, secundum Scrīptūrās. Et ascendit in caelum; sedet ad dexteram Patris. Et iterum ventūrus est cum glōriā jūdicāre vīvōs et mortuōs; cūjus rēgnī nōn erit fīnis. Et in Spīritum Sānctum, Dominum et vīvificantem,[4] quī ex Patre Fīliōque prōcēdit. Quī cum Patre et Fīliō simul adōrātur, et conglōrificātur;[5] quī locūtus est per prophētās. Et ūnam sānctam, catholicam et apostolicam ecclēsiam. Cōnfiteor ūnum baptisma in remissiōnem peccātōrum. Et exspectō resurrēctiōnem mortuōrum. Et vītam ventūrī saeculī. Āmēn.

---

[1] **vīsibilis, e,** *visible.*

[2] **invīsibilis, e; in + vīsibilis;** meaning?

[3] **sepeliō, sepelīre, sepelīvī, sepultus,** 4, tr., *bury.*

[4] **vīvificō,** 1, tr., *give life to* (i. e., the spiritual life of grace).

[5] **conglōrificō,** 1, tr., *glorify.*

LESSON 12: REVIEW

VOCABULARY

laetitia, ae	*joy* *gladness*
inimīcus, ī	*enemy* (personal)
gaudium, ī	*delight* *pleasure*
latrōcinium, ī	*robbery* *brigandage*
laus, laudis	*praise*
voluptās, voluptātis	*pleasure*
dexter, dextra, dextrum **dexter, dextera, dexterum**	*on the right* *right*
impius, a, um	*impious* *undutiful*
numquam, *adv.*	*never*
armō, *1, tr.*	*arm* *equip*
concitō, *1, tr.*	*stir up* *instigate*
invītō, *1, tr.*	*invite*
exerceō, *2, tr.*	*train* *carry on*
soleō, solēre, solitus sum, *2, intr.; w. infin.*	*am accustomed*
ējiciō, ējicere, ējēcī, ējectus, *3, tr.*	*throw out*
pariō, parere, peperī, partus, *3, tr.*	*bring forth* *bear*
praemittō, praemittere, praemīsī, praemissus, *3, tr.*	*send ahead*
rapiō, rapere, rapuī, raptus, *3, tr.*	*snatch* *seize*

afferō, afferre, attulī, allātus, ***irreg., tr.***	*bring to* / *report*
prōficiō, prōficere, prōfēcī, prōfectus, ***3, tr.;*** **ut (nē)**	*effect* / *accomplish*
trānsferō, trānsferre, trānstulī, trānslātus, ***irreg., tr.***	*carry over* / *transfer*
veneror, ***1, tr.***	*reverence*
perfruor, perfruī, perfrūctus sum, ***3, intr.; w. abl.***	*enjoy*

RELATED ENGLISH WORDS

Is *Laetare* Sunday in Advent or in Lent? Nero lived a *voluptuous* life. Some ball players are *ambidextrous*. At one time Germany regarded France's every move as *inimical*. *Alarmists* are scaremongers. The unruly member was *ejected* from the Senate. The notion of bearing young is contained in *parent, parturition, parturient*. *Rapacious*. *Rapture*. Ask for a *transfer* to the other car. We give Mary a special kind of *veneration*.

RELATED LATIN WORDS

Latrō; laudō; amīcus; arma; exercitus; jaciō; pārēns; mittō; ferō.

IDIOM

In Latin, adjectives of praise or blame are not made to agree directly with a proper noun. A general noun like **vir, mīles, urbs,** and so forth is put in apposition to the proper noun and the adjective is made to agree with this general noun.

The excellent Metellus . . .	**Metellus, vir optimus . . .**
The courageous Marcellus . . .	**Mārcellus, vir fortissimus . . .**
The illustrious Gracchi . . .	**Clārissimī cīvēs, Gracchī . . .**
The upright and excellent Roman knights . . .	**Equitēs Rōmānī, honestissimī atque optimī virī . . .**

ASSIGNMENT. *First Oration against Catiline,* lines 450-507.

EXERCISE 48

Translate:

1. Paulum laudis semper hominibus affert laetitiam atque gaudium. 2. Brevis voluptās saepe parit dolōrem magnum. 3. Chrīstus sedet ad dexteram Patris. 4. Omnia arma atque tēla impiō latrōciniō ab inimīcīs sunt rapta. 5. Quodsī mīlitēs Rōmānōs, honestissimōs atque fortissimōs virōs, praemīsisset, cīvēs ab inimīcīs numquam concitātī essent. 6. Num ab amīcīs tuīs, virīs optimīs, invītātus es? 7. Utinam nē urbs nostra bellō potius quam latrōciniō vexārētur. 8. Rōmānī, virī fortissimī, ad hostēs repellendōs sē brevī tempore armāvērunt. 9. Omnēs adulēscentēs cotīdiē exercēre sē solēbant. 10. Sīn autem sēsē ējēcerit, sēcumque suōs ēdūxerit, prōficiet ut haec reī pūblicae pestis tandem aliquandō removeātur.[1] 11. Sī inimīcus patriae in exilium rapiātur, amīcōrum laetitiā atque domūs gaudiīs perfruī diūtius nōn possit. 12. Cicerō, vir optimus, inimīcōs suōs ad dexteram senātūs partem trānstulit. 13. Deus est semper et ubīque[2] omnibus hominibus venerandus.

EXERCISE 49

Translate:

1. Quam rem pūblicam habēmus? 2. Quod facinus ā manibus umquam tuīs āfuit? 3. Quō tandem animō[3] hoc tibi ferendum putās? 4. Dēcrēvit senātus ut cōnsul vidēret nē quid rēs pūblica dētrīmentī caperet. 5. Vērum ego hoc quod jam prīdem factum esse oportuit certā dē causā nōndum faciō. 6. Quamdiū quisquam erit quī tē dēfendere audeat, vīvēs. 7. Cōnsul dīxit sē vidēre posse in senātū quōsdam quī ūnā cum Catilīnā fuērunt. 8. Cicerō interrogāvit num Catilīna dubitāret id, cōnsule imperante, facere quod jam suā sponte faceret. 9. Nēmō est quī hominem perditum nōn metuat, nēmō quī nōn ōderit. 10. An invidiam timēs? 11. Propter invidiae et perīculī timōrem praetōrēs ad locum mūnītum sē contu-

---

[1] **removeō, removēre, remōvī, remōtus,** 2, tr., *remove.*

[2] **ubīque,** adv., *everywhere.*

[3] **animus, ī,** *soul, mind, spirit.*

lērunt. 12. "Quī," inquit Chrīstus, "nōn est mēcum est contrā mē." 13. Spēs etiam pācis brevis erat nūlla. 14. Quodsī fieret, tamen invidiam virtūte partam glōriam, nōn invidiam, putārem. 15. Dē eōrum mentibus quī hoc idem sentiunt pauca dīcam. 16. Aliēna rapere latrōcinium est. 17. Fidem nostram crēdendō exercēmus. 18. Hostēs gladiōs, tēla, arma contrā patriam comparābant. 19. Concitā perditōs cīvēs! Īnfer patriae bellum! 20. In tantō numerō cīvium neque audīvī amīcum quemquam neque vīdī. 21. Dīligentiā pārentum adulēscēns ab omnī malō servātur. 22. Catilīna improbōrum manum nactus erat. 23. Fortēs dē fugā vix cōgitant. 24. Audīte, quaesō, dīligenter quae dīcam et ea animīs[1] vestrīs mentibusque mandāte. 25. Sī hoc idem huic adulēscentī optimō dīxissem, jam mihi cōnsulī hōc ipsō in templō senātus ultrō vim et manūs īntulisset. 26. Sī in exilium tuā sponte īveris, omnēs tuī ex urbe tēcum exibunt. 27. Sī in hunc hominem animadvertissem, omnēs hoc crūdēliter factum esse dīcerent. 28. Dē tē autem cum tacent, clāmant. 29. Sīn autem servīre meae laudī et glōriae māvīs, ēgredere ex urbe, cōnfer tē ad castra tua. 30. Vīs, in exercendīs adulēscentibus, est vītanda. 31. Utinam Rōmam, urbem clārissimam, aliquandō vidēre possim!

EXERCISE 50

Translate:

1. We all try to enjoy some gladness and delight in this brief life of ours. 2. Praise is good if it comes from others and not from ourselves. 3. My parents have been invited to the city. 4. They reported the impious robbery to the praetors. 5. The life of man on earth has its joys and its sorrows. 6. Many brief pleasures bring to those who enjoy them a certain grief. 7. They carried the swords over from his house to mine in their right hands. 8. If the wicked robbery had been reported within a short time, the consul would never have transferred the soldiers. 9. If my enemies were armed, they would snatch my sword from my own right hand.

---

[1] **anīmus, ī,** *soul, mind, spirit.*

10. They were accustomed to reverence the gods in their temples daily. 11. The will of a young man should be trained. 12. Cicero was accustomed to train himself daily by speaking. 13. The soldiers were sent ahead to stir up the citizens. 14. Mary is the mother of God; she bore Christ who is God. 15. The undutiful servant was thrown out of the home.

SIGHT TRANSLATION

DĒ GRACCHŌRUM MĀTRE

[Pars Secunda]

Exspectābat Cornēlia domī fīlium Tiberium, quī tribūnus plēbis[1] erat et ā populō Rōmānō dīligēbātur quod agrōs pauperibus[2] distribuere jam prīdem cupiēbat. "Utinam," inquit Cornēlia amīcīs servīsque, "domum veniat fīlius meus."

Tum concursus cīvium in viā audītur. Servus quīdam, "Jam," inquit, "fīlius abest, domina."[3]

"Nōnne," inquit Cornēlia, "clāmōrem populī et vōcēs amīcōrum audīs?"

Nunc veniunt ante oculōs mātris Gracchōrum. Tacent omnēs. Corpus enim Tiberiī domum portant. Tribūnus plēbis[1] ab inimīcīs occīsus erat.

Omnēs circumstābant. Nēmō loquī potuit. Māter Gracchōrum, mulier[4] optima, prīmō dīxit nihil. Tandem haec locūta est. "Multās jam hōrās fīlium meum exspectō. Hodiē[5] eum mortuum maximē[6] et dīligō et laudō, nam fortem sē ostendit. Nunc enim ego sum omnium mulierum[4] beātissima. Pater meus Hannibalem superāvit. Vir meus glōriam sibi ex Hispaniā[7] reportāvit. Fīliōs duōs reī pūblicae dedī. Tiberius hīc est—prō patriā mortuus;

---

1 **plēbs, plēbis,** *the people.*

2 **pauper, pauperis,** *a poor man, the poor.*

3 **domina, ae,** *mistress, lady.*

4 **mulier, mulieris,** *woman.*

5 **hodiē,** adv., *today.*

6 **maximē,** adv., *especially.*

7 **Hispania, ae,** *Spain.*

Gājus adhūc vīvit—prō patriā et ille omnēs vīrēs dabit. Vōbīs, amīcī, grātiās agō quod corpus Tiberiī meī ad mē portāvistis. Nunc dīs immortālibus grātiās agere volō. Mulierem[1] ad deōrum templum dūcite—Scīpiōnis fīliam, Gracchī uxōrem, mātrem Gracchōrum!"

Populus Rōmānus semper laudāvit hanc mulierem[1] fortem. Cīvēs monumentum[2] Cornēliae, mulierī[1] optimae atque fortissimae, dēdicāvērunt[3] brevī cum inscriptiōne,[4] "Māter Gracchōrum."

Respondē Latīnē:

1. Quem exspectābat Cornēlia domī?
2. Nōnne erat Tiberius tribūnus plēbis?[5]
3. Cūr ā populō Rōmānō dīligēbātur Tiberius?
4. Quid dīxit Cornēlia amīcīs et servīs?
5. Ubi audiēbātur clāmor cīvium?
6. Cūr tacēbant omnēs quī in domum Cornēliae vēnerant?
7. Ā quibus est occīsus Tiberius Gracchus?
8. Quid dīxit māter Tiberiī in prīncipiō?
9. Posteā quid dīxit?
10. Cūr laudāvit fīlium Cornēlia?
11. Quid dīxit Cornēlia dē patre? Quid dē virō suō?
12. Quid dīxit dē Gājō?
13. Quibus grātiās ēgit Cornēlia?
14. Quōmodo laudāvērunt Cornēliam Rōmānī?
15. Quae inscriptiō[4] erat in monumentō?[2]
16. Quid putās dē mātre Gracchōrum?

---

[1] **mulier, mulieris,** *woman.*
[2] **monumentum, ī,** *memorial.*
[3] **dēdicō, 1,** tr., *dedicate, consecrate.*
[4] **inscriptiō, inscriptiōnis,** *inscription.*
[5] **plēbs, plēbis,** *the people.*

LESSON 13: THE GENITIVE AS AN ADJECTIVE EQUIVALENT; THE DATIVE OF POSSESSION

VOCABULARY

animus, ī	*soul* *mind* *spirit*
auctor, auctōris	*originator* *author* *instigator*
fortitūdō, fortitūdinis	*courage* *bravery*
amor, amōris	*love*
sanguis, sanguinis, *m.*	*blood*
vērus, a, um	*true* *real*
maximē, *adv.*	*especially* *mostly* *mainly*
prope, *adv.*	*almost* *nearly*
cōnflagrō, *1, intr.*	*burn* *am on fire*
ārdeō, ārdēre, ārsī, ārsum, *2, intr.; w. infin.*	*am aflame* *blaze*
ēmittō, ēmittere, ēmīsī, ēmissus, *3, tr.*	*send forth* *send out*
immittō, immittere, immīsī, immissus, *3, tr.*	*send into* *send against*

RELATED ENGLISH WORDS

At the end of the play the crowd shouted, "*Author!*" St. Stephen, the protomartyr, was a man of *fortitude*. *Consanguinity* is blood relationship. The strikers were charged with *arson*. *Conflagration.* He was an *ardent* admirer of Beethoven. The cat *emitted* a howl when Tommy trod on its tail.

RELATED LATIN WORDS

Fortis; mittō.

ASSIGNMENT: *First Oration against Catiline*, lines 508-569; Grammar 680-699; 725.

EXERCISE 51

Translate; explain the italicized words:

1. Cicerō certē dīxit Catilīnam nōn sōlum esse auctōrem *sceleris*, prīncipem *conjūrātiōnis*, sed etiam *castrōrum* imperātōrem et maximē *hostium* ducem. 2. Propter *ūnīus ducis* fortitūdinem omnēs mīlitēs sē sanguinem prō patriā datūrōs respondērunt. 3. Catilīna sē *urbem Rōmam* incēnsūrum esse pollicitus erat. 4. *Ūnus ex mīlitibus, omnium* fortissimus, respondit nēminem *hostium* sē impedīre posse. 5. Ējusmodī hominēs semper amōre *patriae* ārdent. 6. Sī quid *novī* audiās, dīligenter attende. 7. Prope tōta *urbs Rōma* ārdēbat. 8. Adventū *Catilīnae* omnēs cōnsulārēs ex senātū prope discessērunt. 9. Servīs ex urbe ēmissīs, pārentēs *adulēscentium* Rōmae mānsērunt. 10. Sīn autem hostēs in oppidum immīsissem, prope omnia tēcta cōnflagrāvissent. 11. Nihilne tē *hōrum* ōra vultūsque mōvērunt? 12. Nōn ignōrāmus quid *cōnsiliī* cēperīs. 13. Quem *nostrum* haec ignōrāre arbitrāris? 14. Nōn deest reī pūblicae cōnsilium. 15. Paulum mihi etiam nunc est *perīculī* quod inimīcus vīvit. 16. Ubi *gentium* sumus? 17. Sunt *mihi* duo gladiī. 18. *Cicerōnis* dīligentiā est urbs Rōma servāta. 19. Quid *novī*? Nihil *novī*. 20. Laus *suī* odium parit. 21. Cāritās *Chrīstī* urget[1] nōs. 22. Dēbēmus omnēs amōre *Deī* potius quam timōre movērī. 23. Catilīna interitum omnium cīvitātis *prīncipum* dēcrēverat. 24. Magna *cīvium* pars intrā moenia continēbātur.

---

[1] **urgeō, urgēre, ursī,** 2, tr., *push, impel.*

25. *Nōs omnēs* vidēmur hāc in vītā satis *dolōris* habēre. 26. Martyrēs[1] erant hominēs *magnae fortitūdinis*. 27. Sīs *bonō animō*. 28. *Hī omnēs* ūnā vōce respondērunt sē nihil *novī* scīre. 29. Erat *cōnsulī* domus in proximō oppidō. 30. Utinam *mihi* esset plūs *temporis* ad studendum![2]

EXERCISE 52

Translate:

1. Many men are unaware of the force of the word[3] liberty. 2. He was sent forth from the city of Rome at the instigation of the consul.[4] 3. The fear of danger never hinders a brave soldier. 4. The general sent his men against the right part of the army. 5. But if he should make no answer,[5] give him enough time to think about the matter. 6. Good citizens are inflamed with patriotism.[6] 7. If the consul had not been careful, almost the whole city of Rome would have been burned. 8. Almost all the ancient Christians gave their blood for the love of Christ. 9. The young man carefully replied that there was no news. 10. Fortitude is a great virtue, especially in[7] soldiers. 11. The fear of God is certainly the beginning[8] of real knowledge. 12. There is yet[9] a little danger. 13. Cicero's house was fortified by stronger guards. 14. The consul did not have enough authority[10] in the Senate. 15. Where in the world can true liberty be found? 16. He sought more news. 17. What news (is there)? (There is) no news. 18. With the arrival of Cicero all of those who had been speaking were silent. 19. The

---

[1] **martyr, martyris,** *martyr.*

[2] **ad studendum:** *for studying.*

[3] *word,* **vōx, vōcis.**

[4] Use an ablative absolute.

[5] Translate *answer nothing.*

[6] Translate *love of country.*

[7] Translate *of.*

[8] *beginning,* **initium, ī.**

[9] *yet,* **adhūc,** adv.

[10] Use the dative of possession.

fear of death hindered the slaves. 20. This is a good time for[1] speaking about the laws of the state. 21. One of the consuls said that there was no danger. 22. God should be reverenced by all of us. 23. All of the citizens tried to hinder his approach.[2] 24. The saints were men of extraordinary patience. 25. My parents have a home in the city and a house in the neighboring town. 26. The blood of Christ is the dear price[3] of all our souls.

EXERCISE 53

Translate:

[*An excerpt from an imaginary address of a Catholic before the French Chamber of Deputies in 1901 when, under Masonic influence, the deputies were considering legislation which would exile the teaching orders.*]

"Even if[4] you said you wished to preserve and defend the welfare of us all, yet[5] in secret you had long been plotting against the welfare of all Catholics. All your wicked attacks we resisted by our own diligence, by the help of our friends, by the grace of God. But now you are openly attacking all religion,[6] the churches[7] and homes of France, the faith of all Frenchmen, and their very souls you are bringing to ruin and disaster. Christ did not say that we would be victorious[8] in every danger, but this He did say, that against His church[7] the gates of hell[9] would not prevail.[10] In God then is all our hope placed."

---

1 Translate *of.*

2 Translate *him approaching.*

3 *price,* **pretium, ī.**

4 See Gr. 598.

5 *yet,* **tamen,** adv.

6 *religion,* **religiō, religiōnis.**

7 *church,* **ecclēsia, ae.**

8 to be victorious = to conquer.

9 *hell,* **īnferus, ī.**

10 *prevail,* **praevaleō, praevalēre, praevaluī, praevalitūrus,** 2, intr.

EX MISSĀLĪ RŌMĀNŌ

Ex Ordinario

So far the Mass has been a matter of words; now those words go into action. And the action is one of giving gifts to God. All the italicized words in the prayers which follow express an offering, a giving. With the priest we offer God bread, wine, ourselves —all we have, all we are.

We Offer Bread

Suscipe, sāncte Pater, omnipotēns aeterne Deus, hanc immaculātam[1] hostiam,[2] quam ego indignus[3] famulus[4] tuus *offerō*[5] tibi, Deō meō vīvō[6] et vērō, prō innumerābilibus[7] peccātīs, et offēnsiōnibus,[8] et negligentiīs[9] meīs, et prō omnibus circumstantibus, sed et prō omnibus fidēlibus[10] Chrīstiānīs vīvīs[6] atque dēfūnctīs;[11] ut mihi et illīs prōficiat[12] ad salūtem in vītam aeternam. Āmēn.

We Offer Wine

Offerimus[5] tibi, Domine, calicem[13] salūtāris,[14] tuam dēprecantēs clēmentiam;[15] ut in cōnspectū[16] dīvīnae mājestātis[17] tuae prō

---

[1] **immaculātus, a, um,** *spotless* (cf. Immaculate Conception).

[2] **hostia, ae,** *host, wafer.*

[3] **indignus, a, um,** *unworthy.*

[4] **famulus, ī,** *servant.*

[5] **offerō, offerre, obtulī, oblātus,** irreg., tr., *offer, present.*

[6] **vīvus, a, um,** *living, alive.*

[7] **innumerābilis, e,** *countless, numberless.*

[8] **offēnsiō, offēnsiōnis,** *offense, wrong.*

[9] **negligentia, ae,** *failing, defect.*

[10] **fidēlis, e,** *faithful.*

[11] **dēfūnctus, a, um,** *dead.*

[12] **prōficiō, prōficere, prōfēcī, prōfectum,** 3, intr.; w. dat., *avail, am profitable.*

[13] **calix, calicis,** *chalice, cup.*

[14] **salūtāre, salūtāris,** *salvation.*

[15] **clēmentia, ae,** *mercy, clemency.*

[16] **cōnspectus, ūs,** *sight, presence.*

[17] **mājestās, mājestātis,** *majesty.*

nostrā et totīus mundī salūte cum odōre[1] suāvitātis[2] ascendat. Āmēn.

We Offer Ourselves

In spīritū humilitātis,[3] et in animō contrītō[4] *suscipiāmur* ā tē, Domine; et sīc fīat sacrificium[5] nostrum in cōnspectū[6] tuō hodiē[7] ut placeat tibi, Domine Deus.

---

[1] **odor, odōris,** *fragrance, odor.*
[2] **suāvitās, suāvitātis,** *sweetness, pleasantness.*
[3] **humilitās, humilitātis,** *humility, lowliness.*
[4] **contrītus, a, um,** *crushed, contrite.*
[5] **sacrificium, ī,** *sacrifice.*
[6] **cōnspectus, ūs,** *sight.*
[7] **hodiē,** adv., *today.*

LESSON 14: GENERAL GRAMMAR REVIEW

VOCABULARY

īnsidiae, īnsidiārum	*ambush* *plot* *snare*
imperītus, a, um; *w. gen.*	*unskilled (in)* *inexperienced (in)*
nōnnūllī, ae, a	*some*
paulisper, *adv.*	*for a short time*
vērē, *adv.*	*indeed* *truly*
īnflammō, *1, tr.*	*set on fire*
congregō, *1, tr.*	*gather into a flock* *gather together*
colligō, colligere, collēgī, collēctus, *3, tr.*	*bring together*
īnscrībō, īnscrībere, īnscrīpsī, īnscrīptus, *3, tr.*	*write on* *inscribe*
intendō, intendere, intendī, intentus, *3, tr.; w. dat.;* ad *or* in *w. acc.*	*stretch to* *am bound for*
comprimō, comprimere, compressī, compressus, *3, tr.*	*check*
patefaciō, patefacere, patefēcī, patefactus, *3, tr.* (*passive,* patefīō)	*open* *disclose*

RELATED ENGLISH WORDS

Avoid *insidious* remarks in your conversation. There is an interesting relationship between the word pastor (**pastor, pastōris,** *shepherd*) and *congregation* (cf. **grex, gregis,** *flock*). Non-*inflammable* material. A stamp *collection.* The *inscription* above Christ's cross was written in Hebrew, in Greek, and in Latin. Cicero's first oration against Catiline is an *inflammatory* speech.

RELATED LATIN WORDS

Nūllus; paulum; vēritās; scrībō; intentus; premō.

ASSIGNMENT: *First Oration against Catiline,* lines 570-645.

EXERCISE 54

Translate:

1. Īnsidiīs patefactīs, nōnnūllī tamen dubitābant. 2. Sī omnēs improbī ūnum in locum congregārentur, haec reī pūblicae pestis paulisper reprimerētur, nōn in perpetuum comprimerētur. 3. Dux suōs colligere nōn potuit; erat enim imperītus bellī. 4. Nōn possumus conjungere nōs cum amīcīs in perpetuum. 5. Hoc in Chrīstī cruce īnscrīptum erat: Jēsūs Nazarēnus,[1] Rēx Jūdaeōrum (INRI). 6. Sī Catilīna in castra Mānliāna vērē intendisset, sine ūllā morā pervēnisset. 7. Sī ex hōc tantō latrōciniō iste ūnus tollētur, vidēbimur paulisper esse līberātī; perīculum autem remanēbit. 8. Dux ūnum ex mīlitibus ad tēcta īnflammanda praemīsit. 9. Pārentēs sīc tēcum agere, sīc tēcum loquī dēbent. 10. Nōn omnēs memoriam mortis aequō animō patimur. 11. Servī sī mē istō modō metuerent ut tē metuunt omnēs cīvēs tuī, domum meam relinquendam putārem. 12. Catilīna putāvit amīcum suum, virum optimum, Mārcum Metellum fore dīligentissimum ad custōdiendum, ad vindicandum fortissimum. 13. Eōrum ego vix abs tē jam diū manūs ac tēla contineō. 14. Cīvēs īsdem moenibus tūtō cum hūjusmodī hominibus esse nōn possunt. 15. Ējusmodī adulēscentēs nōn longē ā carcere absunt. 16. Mōrēs mājōrum impedīre mē nōn possunt. 17. "Tolle crucem tuam," inquit, "et sequere mē." 18. "Sine mē nihil potestis facere." 19. Eō ipsō annō cōnsul factus est. 20. Haec sī ā Deō petam, nōnne impetrāre dēbeam? 21. Clāmor loquentium exaudītus est. 22. Quodsī hostēs timērent, ā moenibus paulisper sē cōnferrent. 23. An amīcōrum invidiam timēs? 24. Pārentēs in adulēscentibus corrigendīs[2] odiō permovērī numquam

---

[1] **Nazarēnus, a, um,** *of Nazareth, Nazarene.*

[2] **corrigō, corrigere, corrēxī, corrēctus,** 3, tr., *correct, improve, alter.*

dēbent. 25. Cīvitātis auctōritās hominibus bonīs cārissima est. 26. Adulēscentem domum mīsērunt ad gaudium pārentibus afferendum. 27. Hominēs armātōs ad bellum impium patriae īnferendum invītat. 28. Nōn sōlum urbs Rōma sed etiam cūncta Italia jam diū in hīs perīculīs īnsidiīsque versābātur. 29. Inimīcōrum injūriae nōn sunt semper vindicandae. 30. Cicerō intellēxit, sī iste, quō intendēbat, in Mānliāna castra pervēnisset, nēminem tam stultum fore quī nōn vidēret conjūrātiōnem esse factam, nēminem tam falsum quī nōn apertē dīceret.

EXERCISE 55

Translate:

1. There are some in the Senate who do not seem to understand the snares of our enemies. 2. Cicero wanted everything to be opened to the eyes of the people. 3. If we cannot check this plot forever, then let us repress it for a short while. 4. All the soldiers were gathered together in one place. 5. If the consul had been unskilled in speaking, he would never have been able to set the minds of the citizens on fire. 6. He brought all the citizens of the towns together and joined them as a leader. 7. If these words[1] had not been written on the cross, many of those who were present[2] would not have known why Christ had been led to death. 8. The soldier was bound for home. 9. We cannot truly understand why our laws have been taken away.

EX MISSĀLĪ RŌMĀNŌ

From the Canon

We offered to God bread, wine, and with the bread and cup ourselves. Now God gives us in return the body and blood of His Son to be the food of our souls. As the priest bows in awe before receiving God's good gift, he prays:

---

[1] *word,* **verbum, ī.**

[2] *am present,* **adsum, adesse, adfuī, adfutūrus,** irreg., intr.; w. dat.

Domine Jēsū Chrīste, quī dīxistī apostolīs tuīs: pācem relinquō vōbīs, pācem meam dō vōbīs, nē respiciās[1] peccāta mea, sed fidem ecclēsiae tuae; eamque secundum voluntātem tuam pācificāre et coadūnāre dignēris.[2] Quī vīvis et rēgnās Deus per omnia saecula saeculōrum. Āmēn.

Domine Jēsū Chrīste, Fīlī Deī vīvī, quī ex voluntāte Patris, cooperante[3] Spīritū Sānctō, per mortem tuam mundum vīvificāstī,[4] līberā mē per hoc sacrōsānctum[5] corpus et sanguinem tuum ab omnibus inīquitātibus[6] meīs, et ūniversīs malīs. Et fac mē tuīs semper inhaerēre[7] mandātīs, et ā tē numquam sēparārī[8] permittās. Quī cum eōdem Deō Patre, et Spīritū Sānctō vīvis et rēgnās Deus in saecula saeculōrum. Āmēn.

Perceptiō[9] corporis tuī, Domine Jēsū Chrīste, quod ego indignus sūmere praesūmō,[10] nōn mihi prōveniat[11] in jūdicium et condemnātiōnem,[12] sed prō tuā pietāte[13] prōsit[14] mihi ad tūtāmentum[15] mentis et corporis, et ad medēlam percipiendam.[16] Quī vīvis et rēgnās cum Deō Patre in ūnitāte Spīritūs Sānctī Deus, per omnia saecula saeculōrum. Āmēn.

---

1 **respiciō, respicere, respexī, respectus,** 3, tr. and intr., *regard, look at.*

2 **eamque . . . dignēris:** *and deign to give her peace and unity agreeably to Thy will.*

3 **cooperor,** 1, tr., *cooperate.*

4 **vīvificō,** 1, tr., *give life to* (i. e., the spiritual life of grace); **vīvificāstī = vīvificāvistī.**

5 **sacrōsānctus, a, um,** *most sacred.*

6 **inīquitās, inīquitātis,** *sinfulness.*

7 **inhaereō, inhaerēre, inhaesī, inhaesum,** 2, intr.; w. abl. or dat., *cling to* (cf. adhesive).

8 **sēparō,** 1, tr., *separate.*

9 **perceptiō, perceptiōnis,** *partaking.*

10 **praesūmō, praesūmere, praesūmpsī, praesūmptus,** 3, tr., *presume, venture.*

11 **prōveniō, prōvenīre, prōvēnī, prōventum,** 4, intr., *turn to, conduce to.*

12 **condemnātiō, condemnātiōnis,** *condemnation, damnation.*

13 **prō tuā pietāte:** *by reason of Thy loving kindness.*

14 **prōsum, prōdesse, prōfuī, prōfutūrus,** irreg., intr.; w. dat., *benefit, profit.*

15 **tūtāmentum, ī,** *protection, safeguard* (cf. **tūtus**).

16 **et ad medēlam percipiendam:** *and an effective remedy.*

LESSON 15: COMMON EXPRESSIONS OF PURPOSE

VOCABULARY

fātum, ī	*prophetic utterance* *fate* *doom*
domicilium, ī	*abode* *domicile*
verbum, ī	*word*
ignis, ignis, *m.*	*fire*
magnitūdō, magnitūdinis	*size* *greatness*
condiciō, condiciōnis	*condition* *state* (pl.) *terms*
pulcher, pulchra, pulchrum	*beautiful*
manifestus, a, um	*clear* *evident*
salvus, a, um	*safe*
breviter, *adv.*	*briefly*
restō, restāre, restitī, *1, intr.*	*remain*
prōvideō, prōvidēre, prōvīdī, prōvīsus, *2, tr.;* ut (nē)	*see ahead* *provide* *take care*
expōnō, expōnere, exposuī, expositus, *3, tr.; acc. w. infin.*	*explain* *disembark* *line up*
condō, condere, condidī, conditus, *3, tr.*	*found* *build*

RELATED ENGLISH WORDS

Macaulay had such a fine memory that with a few minutes' study he could repeat a long poem *verbatim*. The tiresome *verbiage* of after-dinner speakers is *proverbial*. The *ignition* system of a combustion engine. The sailors were unable to *salvage* the cargo from the wrecked ship. "*Brevity* is the soul of wit." The Christian views the world as being governed by the fatherly *providence* of God, not by the inexorable *fate* of the pagans. An *expository* paragraph.

RELATED LATIN WORDS

Brevis; magnus; stō; videō; pōnō; salvō.

ASSIGNMENT: *Third Oration against Catiline,* lines 1-38; GRAMMAR 546-549; 729-731; Review GRAMMAR 864, 870-877.

EXERCISE 56

Translate; explain the italicized constructions:

1. Ipse in senātum vēnit *quō facilius* rērum condiciōnem manifestīs verbīs *expōneret*. 2. Praetōrēs domicilia custōdiēbant ut omnēs in hīs tantīs perīculīs atque fātī īnsidiīs salvī esse *possent*. 3. Cōnsul rem populō breviter exposuit *ad cōnfirmandum* eōrum *timōrem* quī in urbe restābant. 4. Haec mihi dīxit ut manifestum mihi *esset* urbem Rōmam ā Rōmulō conditam esse. 5. Post urbem Rōmam conditam Rōmānī jūra semper custōdiēbant ut omnēs cīvēs salvī esse *possent*. 6. Mīlitēs omnia facere dēbent nē umquam domicilia pulchra igne *incendantur*. 7. Sunt quī nihil *prōvideant*. 8. Sānctus Paulus multa pulchra dīxit ut hominum animōs ad Chrīstum *dūceret*. 9. *Auxiliō praetōribus* complūrēs adulēscentēs mīsit. 10. Haec pulchra verba *nōnnūllīs salūtī* fuērunt. 11. Catilīna Rōmā *bellī excitandī causā* profectus est. 12. Duōs praetōrēs ad domicilium praemīsī ut quid mōlīrētur reī pūblicae hostis *invenīrem*. 13. Amīcum rogat ut sē paulum *exspectet*. 14. Haec dīxit nē improbōrum fātum ā populō *intelligerētur*. 15. Praetor ad domicilium profectus est ut, sī quid tēlōrum in-

venīret, *efferret*. 16. *Ad hanc* reī pūblicae *condiciōnem vītandam,* cōnsul pauca verba nōbīscum locūtus est. 17. Senātōrēs breviter in senātū restitērunt *suī cōnservandī causā*. 18. Rōmulus fātō Rōmam *urbis condendae causā* ductus est. 19. Cōnsul custōdēs extrā mūrum *praesidiō* relīquit. 20. Pārentis mors semper est *nōbīs magnō dolōrī*. 21. Spēs vītae aeternae cōnsequendae est *omnibus Chrīstiānīs gaudiō*. 22. Mors nōn est omnīnō *dolōrī*. 23. Utinam omnēs amīcī essent nōbīs *praesidiō*. 24. Nōnne sunt quī *vīvant* ut voluptāte *perfruantur*? 25. Deus sit nōbīs in vītā *gaudiō* in morte *praesidiō* in aeternum *salūtī*. 26. Propter magnitūdinem sceleris compertī, nōnnūllī etiam in senātū dē cōnsulis verbīs dubitāvērunt.

EXERCISE 57

Translate:

1. In a few words he briefly explained that he had come to their abode so that they might be free from the fear of fire. 2. When the peace terms of the enemy had been explained,[1] the consul remained in the camp for three hours to make a decision about an affair of such greatness. 3. If this youth should now hear about the fate of his parents, it would be a great grief to him. 4. The praetor left a guard at the gates of the beautiful abode as a protection against fire. 5. The ancients who founded our country left laws to guard our rights. 6. He did all he could in order that the desperate band of criminals might be snatched from the clutches[2] of doom. 7. Those who left their fatherland to found our city were men of great soul. 8. It is clear that God sent His Son for our salvation.[3] 9. The beautiful city of Rome was founded many years before the time of Christ. 10. This victory is a great joy to us, but a grief to the enemy. 11. He will come to see his dear parents. 12. They have a beautiful domicile[4] at Rome. 13. God will provide if we trust

[1] Use an ablative absolute.

[2] Say *hands*.

[3] Use a double dative.

[4] Use the dative of possession.

Him. 14. If the government[1] sends these upright citizens into exile, they will found a new city in which to dwell. 15. The Lord be to me a protection in this life and salvation in the life which will come after death. 16. He explained the whole thing to the people so that no one might be unaware of what was being done. 17. Christ spoke openly in order to be safe from the envy of those who hated Him. 18. I say this so that no one may think that I fear unpopularity.

EXERCISE 58

Imitate the word order and the structure of the model in translating:

MODEL: **Itaque hesternō diē**
Lūcium Flaccum et Gājum Pomptīnum, praetōrēs,
fortissimōs et amantissimōs reī pūblicae virōs,
ad mē vocāvī,
rem exposuī,
quid fierī placēret, ostendī.

1. And so two hours later he captured Lentulus and Cethegus, utterly[2] abandoned and wicked men; he sent them to Rome; he threw them into prison.
2. And so he attacked Corinth,[3] a beautiful and renowned city, by land and by sea;[4] after five days he took it, and for ten days burned its houses, its domiciles, its temples.
3. And so on that very night he took the child[5] Jesus and Mary, His most holy mother, and fled into Egypt,[6] and lived there for many years.
4. And so he heard both Cicero and Hortensius, the renowned

---

[1] Use **rēs (reī) pūblica (ae).**
[2] Use superlatives.
[3] *Corinth,* **Corinthus, ī.**
[4] *by land and by sea:* **terrā marīque.**
[5] *child,* **īnfāns, īnfantis.**
[6] *Egypt,* **Aegyptus, ī.**

orators,[1] speaking in the Forum.[2] This was five years ago. He praised them and asked them to train him to speak in the Senate.

EXERCISE 59

Translate:[3]

[*From an Imaginary Report of a Regional Director of the G-Men.*]

"When I learned that Public Enemy No. 1 was in the city, I sent for Wellington and Reynolds, two trustworthy officers.[4] I explained the matter to them and showed them what I wanted done. I sent them to see whether he was really the man we wanted and what he was doing or planning to do. I ordered them to find out everything so that the crimes of this fellow would be perfectly clear, not only to them but to the jurors.[5]

"These two courageous men not only undertook the job without delay or objection,[6] but they captured the man himself on that same day and led him to jail."

---

[1] *orator,* **ōrātor, ōrātōris.**

[2] *forum,* **forum, ī.**

[3] It will be necessary to study Cicero carefully to discover ways of translating this exercise. Sentences will have to be changed and expressions altered. Ask yourself how Cicero might have said "Public Enemy No. 1," "What he was planning to do," etc.

[4] *officer,* **praetor, praetōris.**

[5] *juror,* **jūdex, jūdicis.**

[6] *objection,* **recūsātiō, recūsātiōnis.**

LESSON 16: DELIBERATIVE QUESTIONS; CONCESSIVE SUBJUNCTIVE

VOCABULARY

opera, ae	*services* *pains* *efforts*
mandātum, ī	*instruction* *order*
frequēns (*gen.* frequentis)	*in large numbers* *crowded*
nōtus, a, um	*known* *well-known*
deinde, *adv.*	*next* *thereupon*
optō, *1, tr.; w. infin.;* ut (nē)	*desire* *hope for* *pray for*
sollicitō, *1, tr.*	*stir up* *tempt*
dēprehendō, dēprehendere, dēprehendī, dēprehēnsus, *3, tr.*	*catch* *catch in the act* *surprise*
offerō, offerre, obtulī, oblātus, *irreg., tr.*	*present* *offer*
dēferō, dēferre, dētulī, dēlātus, *irreg., tr.;* ad *w. acc.*	*carry away* *report (to)*

RELATED ENGLISH WORDS

A *mandate* is a commission, an order. *Notorious,* originally meaning 'well-known,' now has a derogatory sense; a notorious criminal, for example. *Optional. Solicit.* An *oblation* is an offering.

RELATED LATIN WORDS

Mandō; ignōrō; comprehendō; ferō.

ASSIGNMENT: *Third Oration against Catiline,* lines 39-86; GRAMMAR 509, 510; 519.

EXERCISE 60

Translate; explain the italicized words:

1. Quid *faceret* rēx? 2. In hīs tantīs reī pūblicae perīculīs quid *dīcam*? 3. Hunc ego ad mortem nōn *dūcam*? 4. Nē *fuerit* magnō corpore; tamen erat mihi timendum. 5. Operā ējus nōn *ūterer*? 6. *Sit* nōtus; *sit* clārus; honestus nōn est. 7. Quid *optāret* cōnsul nisi mortem? 8. Frequentēs *veniant,* timor populī movet mē nihil. 9. Deinde vēnit ad sollicitandōs cīvēs perditōs. 10. In ipsīs autem cīvibus sollicitandīs est dēprehēnsus. 11. Quid *offerāmus* Deō quī tot nōbīs bona dedit? 12. Mandātum ad cōnsulēs *dēferat;* hoc mihi placēbit. 13. Quis hoc *neget*? 14. Nē *fuerit* vērum! Quid ergō?[1] 15. *Sint* fortēs! Eōs nōn timeō. 16. Quō sē *cōnferent*? 17. Quam diū *manēret* in urbe? 18. Gladium huic r estī *trāderem*? 19. *Sint* ējus mandāta difficilia; tamen violanda[2] nōn sunt. 20. Deinde frequentēs optāvērunt praetōris operam ad hostem nōtum dēprehendendum. 21. Sī haec omnia ad prīncipēs cīvitātis dēlātā essent, hostium īnsidiae dēprehēnsae essent. 22. Omnēs cīvēs nōtī operam suam cōnsulibus obtulērunt. 23. Sī jūdicāvissēs Catilīnam dignum morte, an eī ūnam ad vīvendum hōram dedissēs? 24. *Haec locūtus,* Cicerō tandem aliquandō siluit. 25. *Hīs dictīs,* conjūrātiō comperta vidēbātur. 26. Nōn *Rōmae* sed in Italiā erant castra Mānliana. 27. Omnēs quī in exilium discesserant Rōmam ad patriam sunt reversī. 28. Nesciō cūr cōnsul ausus sit dē turpitūdine domesticā loquī; fāmae enim cīvis prīvātī nocēbat.

---

[1] **ergō,** adv., *therefore, then.*

[2] **violō,** 1, tr., *violate, injure, outrage.*

EXERCISE 61

Translate:

1. Granted that they didn't come in large numbers, our services were not altogether[1] offered in vain.[2] 2. Suppose it is true; no one will believe he gave this order. 3. To whom was I to report this serious matter? 4. What was he to say next? 5. Thanks to[3] his pains I was able to get the thing I had long hoped for. 6. Where were the fleeing soldiers to betake themselves? 7. What was the praetor to say about this instruction? 8. Because of the consul's care and the efforts of the praetor the well-known commander was unable to tempt the citizens. 9. What was the consul to say to the crowded Senate? 10. The enemy of the state was thereupon caught in the very crime of stirring up the slaves. 11. I had long desired to present myself and my services to the government.[4] 12. A well-known senator was surprised in his own home. He had long been privately reporting the state's instructions to the enemy. 13. An opportunity[5] next offered itself to Cicero for which he had long prayed. 14. How was the slave to carry all the swords away from my house? 15. Granted that he is a man of virtue, still he did violate[6] the rights of the citizens.

EXERCISE 62

Translate:

We were in the midst of[7] many grave dangers. In Italy there was a camp of wicked and abandoned men who wished to burn the city and slaughter the citizens. There were enemies even at Rome; yes, the commander in chief and leader of the enemy was

---

[1] *altogether,* **omnīnō**, adv.
[2] *in vain,* **frūstrā**, adv.
[3] Translate *because of.*
[4] Translate *state.*
[5] *opportunity,* **facultās, facultātis**; w. gen.
[6] *violate,* **violō**, 1, tr.
[7] Use **versor** w. **in.**

in the city against which he so desired to make impious war. In the Senate itself I saw conspirators,[1] and I was forced to ask them their opinion[2] on public affairs. And, what was most to be feared, these men did not hesitate to solicit the Gauls to make war on our legions.

What were we to do? Where were we to turn?[3] What orders were to be given? Whose services used? Thereupon an opportunity[4] offered itself for which I had always prayed. The enemies of the state were caught. I saved the city; I freed the citizens from fear; I snatched the homes of the citizens and the temples of the gods from ruin and destruction.

Granted that Catiline was a citizen; granted that the conspirators[1] were Romans. Who would not praise me for my care in guarding the state?

EXERCISE 63

[General Review]

Translate:

1. He besieged[5] Corinth,[6] a beautiful and renowned city, by land and by sea.[7] 2. I have saved this well-known city. 3. I sent men ahead to capture the Gauls. 4. I explained what I wanted done. 5. He led them to jail. 6. They ordered the leader of the enemy to be killed. 7. I sent scouts[8] to find what the enemy was doing. 8. I sent this fellow to get the weapons. 9. He said he had always been a friend of mine. 10. Leave the city. 11. You have long been trying to kill me. 12. What would anyone[9] say? 13. I said likewise

---

[1] *conspirators,* **conjūrātī, conjūrātōrum.**

[2] Use an indirect question.

[3] *turn,* **vertō, vertere, vertī, versus,** 3, tr. (Always takes an object in Latin.)

[4] *opportunity,* **facultās, facultātis;** w. gen.

[5] *besiege,* **obsideō, obsidēre, obsēdī, obsessus,** 2, tr.

[6] *Corinth,* **Corinthus, ī.**

[7] *by land and sea:* **terrā marīque.**

[8] *scout,* **explōrātor, explōrātōris.**

[9] *anyone,* **quisquam, quidquam.**

that you would try to kill us all. 14. Would that the courageous Cicero were alive. 15. Let him come. 16. Don't say that. 17. Change your mind. 18. If he should leave, the city would be freed from danger. 19. Free me from fear. 20. Let it be granted that he is brave. 21. Surely you don't dare say this? 22. Why did he come into the Senate? 23. If your parents hated you, what would you do? 24. If Rome had been destroyed, we should not be reading[1] Cicero. 25. If you know what Catiline is doing, why don't you throw him into chains? 26. If he comes to your house, do not hesitate to kill him. 27. Who would blame[2] the soldiers? 28. What was Cicero to do? 29. I shall now act not as one moved by fear but as one moved by patriotism. 30. If all criminals were in jail, we should be free from fear. 31. He said he would leave Rome. 32. There was a revolt[3] in Gaul. 33. They marched through the province. 34. There were many abandoned men at Rome.

---

[1] *read,* **legō, legere, lēgī, lēctus,** 3, tr. What tense? Note the meaning; Gr. 593.

[2] *blame,* **reprehendō, reprehendere, reprehendī, reprehēnsus,** 3, tr.

[3] *revolt,* **dēfectiō, dēfectiōnis.**

LESSON 17: REVIEW OF THE ABLATIVE

VOCABULARY

indicium, ī	*information* *proof*
potestās, potestātis	*power*
īnfīnītus, a, um	*endless* *extensive*
studiōsus, a, um; *w. gen.*	*fond of* *eager for*
aliquis, aliquid *(Gr. 815)*	*someone* *something*
aliquis, aliqua, aliquod *(Gr. 815)*	*some*
amō, *1, tr.*	*love*
indicō, *1, tr.; acc. w. infin.*	*point out* *accuse*
recitō, *1, tr.*	*read aloud*
cūrō, *1, tr.;* ut (nē)	*care for* *take care*
cēnseō, cēnsēre, cēnsuī, cēnsus, *2, tr.;* ut (nē); *acc. w. infin.*	*am of the opinion* *think*
cōnfiteor, cōnfitērī, cōnfessus sum, *2, tr.; acc. w. infin.*	*admit* *confess*
intrōdūcō, intrōdūcere, intrōdūxī, intrōductus, *3, tr.*	*bring in*
legō, legere, lēgī, lēctus, *3, tr.*	*read*

RELATED ENGLISH WORDS

An *amateur* musician plays for love of music, not as a means of making a living. A *sinecure* is a job without much to take care of. *Introduce. Lectures* are etymologically, and unfortunately actually, discourses that are read.

RELATED LATIN WORDS

Possum; studeō; cūra; dūcō.

ASSIGNMENT: *Third Oration against Catiline,* lines 87-165; GRAMMAR 762-780.

EXERCISE 64

Translate; explain the italicized words:

1. Rōmae cōnsulēs tempore bellī erant hominēs *īnfīnītā potestāte.* 2. Indicia clārissima *ā praetōre* intrōducta sunt. 3. Aliquis in rē pūblicā semper est studiōsus *potestātis.* 4. Cēnseō indicium senātuī *ā cōnsule* recitandum. 5. Cūrāvit urbem *moenibus* mūniendam. 6. Multī cīvēs *obscūrō locō* nātī sunt. 7. Cōnsul litterās *magnā* cum *dīligentiā* recitāvit. 8. Cōnfiteor hominēs *mōribus* inter sē differre. 9. Alter cōnsul *paulō* diūtius locūtus est. 10. Amīcus meus studiōsissimus est *legendī.* 11. Saepe indicāvit pārentēs *ā suīs līberīs* amārī. 12. Etsī[1] hic cōnsul potestātis studiōsus nōn est, tamen est *aliquā potestāte* dignus. 13. Sunt quī cēnseant potestātem esse cāriōrem *vītā.* 14. Deus ipse omnia quae vīdēmus *īnfīnītā potestāte* fēcit; tamen sunt quī eum nōn ament.

EXERCISE 65

Translate:

1. The information had been brought into the Senate by the consul. 2. He thought that he should use his extensive power. 3. I am always fond of reading. 4. If the letters had not been read aloud by the consuls, no one would have admitted the proof. 5. Let the consul take care that no one in the Senate be eager for endless power. 6. If some information is brought in, we can accuse the men who read the letters. 7. If you love your parents, they will love you. 8. There are many who are fond of receiving letters, few who are eager to write letters. 9. Something was being pointed

---

[1] **etsī**, conj., *although, even if.*

out by the praetor. 10. A little while before Cethegus had said something about the swords which had been taken from his house. 11. But when the letters had been read aloud, he admitted the plot. 12. They were of the opinion that the city ought to be destroyed by fire. 13. Caesar became a man of extensive power and the highest authority, but he was killed at the violent hands of friends. 14. We differ among ourselves in character. 15. Free the state from fear. 16. Catiline was born of famous parents. 17. The leader admitted that he was not contented[1] with the power the Senate had given him. 18. I am of the opinion that much more can be brought about by virtue than by power. 19. With exceptional[2] care did I guard the lives and liberty of all the citizens. 20. Catiline was a man of extreme[2] recklessness. 21. The state has been freed from terrible[2] dangers.

EXERCISE 66

Translate; explain the italicized constructions:

1. Rēs pūblica *cōnsiliō* et *dīligentiā* Cicerōnis est servāta. 2. Optimus quisque laudēs aliōrum *cum gaudiō* audit. 3. Gladiōs *ā vōbīs* dējēcimus. 4. Cōnsilia eōrum *per mē* comperta sunt. 5. Expōnam vōbīs *quā ratiōne* comperta sint. 6. Adhūc sunt *nōbīscum*. 7. *Oculīs* jam scelus vidēmus. 8. Gallī *ā Lentulō* sollicitātī sunt. 9. *Magnō comitātū* advēnērunt lēgātī. 10. Gladiī *ā nostrīs* ēdūcuntur. 11. Litterae *ā mē* nōn sunt apertae. 12. Cicerō et Catilīna inter sē *virtūte* maximē differunt. 13. *Audāciā* omnēs superās. 14. Jussit eum quam prīmum advenīre *cum exercitū*. 15. Sē *cum hīs* conjungere statuit. 16. Erat eī *cum cēterīs* contrōversia. 17. Ipsīus *manū* scrīptae erant. 18. Haec autem potestās tē nōn revocāvit *ā maximō scelere*. 19. *Timōre* permōtus haec fēcit. 20. *Scientiā dīcendī* omnēs aliōs superābat. 21. Rōmānī

[1] *contented*, **contentus, a, um.**

[2] Where English writers prefer adjectives of quality (terrible, excellent, splendid, etc.), the Romans showed a preference for adjectives of quantity (*magnus, maximus, tantus,* etc.). Notice how frequently such adjectives are used by Cicero. Learn to translate them by appropriate English adjectives.

erant hominēs *magnī animī*. 22. Rēs pūblica *maximīs perīculīs* līberāta est. 23. Haec *animō* prōvidēbam. 24. Haec omnia deōrum immortālium voluntāte certissimē gesta sunt. 25. Vir *magnī nōminis* est. 26. Eratne Cicerō homō *magnō corpore*? 27. Mihi *cum eīs* quōs vīcī vīvendum est. 28. *Custōdiīs vigiliīsque* urbem dēfendī. 29. *Omnibus vīribus* cōnābor. 30. Nēmō *Cicerōne* erat loquendī studiōsior.

EXERCISE 67

Translate:[1]

1. It is indeed a well-known seal. 2. Be brave. 3. The letter was to this effect. 4. (He), most profoundly moved . . . 5. And not to make a long story . . . 6. It is the portrait of your grandfather. 7. He got to his feet. 8. And, to be brief . . . 9. Letters in his own handwriting . . . 10. The content of these letters was about the same. 11. And to make a long story short . . . 12. The letters were anonymous. 13. Play the man. 14. Crazed by his crime . . . 15. Keep your head up. 16. It ought to have made you shrink from such a crime. 17. (He), violently agitated . . . 18. A connoisseur of fine ironware . . . 19. And to cut the story short . . . 20. (He spoke) to about the same effect . . . 21. He was singularly patriotic and civic-minded. 22. At first he said yes. 23. He asked them what business he had with them. 24. His experience in public speaking failed him. 25. His answer was brief and firm. 26. The letter was unsigned. 27. In the long run he denied none of the allegations of the Gauls. 28. Every now and then they exchanged stealthy glances. 29. The Senate adopted these extremely harsh and uncompromising proposals without any amendments. 30. I shall explain the bill of the House from memory. 31. And not to bore you . . . 32. You shall learn my identity from the man whom I've sent you. 33. Collecting iron tools was his favorite hobby.

---

[1] Idiomatic and correct Latin equivalents for the phrases and sentences in this exercise will be found by examining the Latin text assigned for the lesson. As far as possible avoid using vocabularies or dictionaries.

EXERCISE 68

The Traitor Is Condemned

Translate:

I brought in the other man. He seemed to be very agitated.[1] We showed him the letters which the officers[2] had taken from his house a little while before. They were unsigned.[1] At first he said they were not written in his hand, but at last, overcome by the proof, he admitted that they were his. But he cried out that he had written them through fear,[3] that he was a most patriotic man,[1] that he had not wished to destroy the government and his fellow citizens. But his crime was so terrible[1] that the judges were not moved by pity.[4] They forthwith ordered him to be shot.[1]

CICERO'S SENSE OF HUMOR

We hardly think of the serious-minded Cicero, thundering against Catiline in *illō sānctissimō gravissimōque cōnsiliō,* as a man possessed of rare wit. Yet there were those who referred to him as the 'consular buffoon,' and there were several books of Cicero's jokes in circulation at Rome. We find traces of this wit in the irony with which he deals with the embarrassed conspirators in the Third Oration, especially his references to the sleepy Lentulus and the hot-headed Cethegus.[5] In some of the hearings of the Verrines Cicero descended even to puns, and—what is even more unpardonable—the wordplay often involved the defendant's name.[6]

The fifth-century writer Macrobius is responsible for the fol-

[1] Use a Roman equivalent from Cicero.

[2] *officer,* **praetor, praetōris.**

[3] Translate *led on by fear* or *moved by fear.*

[4] *pity,* **mīsericordia, ae.**

[5] See especially the *Third Oration against Catiline,* lines 71-72 and 117-120.

[6] One involved a play on Verres' name and the word **verrō,** *sweep.* Cicero speaks of Verres having gone to Sicily **ad verrendam prōvinciam** *(to make a clean sweep of the province).* **But it is hazardous to try to translate a pun.**

lowing samples of Cicero's wit. These he culled principally from a collection of jokes made by Cicero's secretary, Tiro.

Sed mīror[1] omnēs vōs joca[2] tacuisse Cicerōnis, in quibus fācundissimus,[3] ut in omnibus, fuit. Cicerō, cum apud Damasippum[4] cēnāret[5] et ille, mediocrī[6] vīnō[7] positō, dīceret: "Bibite Falernum[8] hoc; annōrum quadrāgintā[9] est." "Bene," inquit, "aetātem fert."[10]

Īdem cum Lentulum, generum[11] suum, exiguae statūrae[12] hominem, longō gladiō accīnctum[13] vīdisset, "Quis," inquit, "generum[11] meum ad gladium alligāvit?"[14]

Nec Quīntō Cicerōnī frātrī pepercit.[15] Nam cum in eā prōvinciā quam ille rēxerat[16] vīdisset imāginem ējus ingentibus līneāmentīs[17] usque ad pectus[18] ex mōre pictam[19] (erat autem Quīntus ipse statūrae[20] parvae), ait. "Frāter meus dīmidius[21] mājor est quam tōtus."

---

1 **mīror,** 1, tr., *marvel, am amazed.*

2 **jocus, ī** (pl., **jocī** and **joca**), *joke, jest.* Here **joca** is the object of **tacuisse.**

3 **fācundus, a, um,** *fluent, ready.*

4 **Damasippus, ī,** *Damasippus.*

5 **cēnō,** 1, intr., *dine* (cf. cenacle).

6 **mediocris, e,** *indifferent, middling, second-rate.* The word is important for the joke.

7 **vīnum, ī,** *wine.*

8 **Falernum, ī,** *Falernian wine,* a fine wine made of grapes grown in the Falernian country in the district of Campania.

9 **quadrāgintā,** *forty.* The older the wine, the better.

10 **Bene aetātem fert:** *It doesn't show its age at all* (lit., *It carries its age well*).

11 **gener, generī,** *son-in-law.*

12 **exiguae statūrae:** *of small build.* What kind of genitive?

13 **accingō, accingere, accīnxī, accīnctus,** 3, tr., *gird* (cf. cincture).

14 **alligō,** 1, tr., *tie to, bind to.*

15 **parcō, parcere, pepercī, parcitūrus,** 3, intr.; w. dat., *spare.*

16 **regō, regere, rēxī, rēctus,** 3, tr., *guide, rule.*

17 **ingentibus līneāmentīs:** *in huge strokes.*

18 **pectus, pectoris,** n., *breast.*

19 **pictus, a, um,** *painted, colored.*

20 **statūra, ae,** *build, stature.*

21 **dīmidius, a, um,** *halved, divided in half.* This refers to the picture of Quintus, showing head and shoulders; **tōtus** refers to Quintus himself.

Cicerō Cūriō[1] multum dē annīs aetātis[2] suae mentientī[3] dīxit: "Tum ergō cum ūnā dēclāmābāmus[4] nōn erās nātus." Īdem, Fabiā[5] dīcente trīgintā[6] sē annōs habēre,[7] "Vērum est," inquit; "nam hoc illam[8] vīgintī[9] annīs audiō."

---

1 **Cūrius, ī,** *Curius.*

2 **aetās, aetātis,** *age.*

3 **mentior,** 4, tr. and intr., *lie.*

4 **dēclāmō,** 1, tr. and intr., *practice speaking in public.* Curius and Cicero were fellow students, but Curius was trying to make out that he was much younger than he was.

5 **Fabia, ae,** *Fabia.*

6 **trīgintā,** *thirty.*

7 What is the corresponding English idiom?

8 **Illam** is the subject of **dīcere,** to be supplied.

9 **vīgintī,** *twenty.*

LESSON 18: RESULT CLAUSES; NOUN CLAUSES INTRODUCED BY *QUOMINUS* AND *QUOD*

VOCABULARY

testis, testis, *m.*	*witness*
aptus, a, um; *w. dat.;* ad *w. acc.*	*fitted for* *fitted to*
prīmum, *adv.*	*first*
meritō, *adv.* **jūre, *adv.***	*rightly* *justly*
modo, *adv.*	*only* *just now*
palam, *adv.*	*openly*
quōminus, *conj. (Gr. 646)*	*from* *that . . . not*
dēpellō, dēpellere, dēpulī, dēpulsus, *3, tr.*	*drive away* *expel*
occurrō, occurrere, occurrī, occursum, *3, intr.; w. dat.*	*go to meet*
obeō, obīre, obiī, obitus, *irreg., tr.*	*undergo*
pūniō, *4, tr.*	*punish*
cōnstat, cōnstāre, cōnstitit, *1, intr.; acc. w. infin.*	*it is certain*
accidit, accidere, accidit, *3, intr.; w. dat. of person;* ut (ut nōn)	*it happens*

RELATED ENGLISH WORDS

Aptitude tests indicate for what sort of work one's talent and background best suit him. The New *Testament* bears witness to the life and teaching of Jesus Christ. *Occurrence. Punitive.*

RELATED LATIN WORDS

Prīmus; jūs; minus; pellō; eō; stō.

ASSIGNMENT: *Third Oration against Catiline,* lines 166-236; GRAMMAR 550-555; 646-649; 657-659.

EXERCISE 69

Translate; explain the italicized constructions:

1. Sīc omnibus perīculīs occurrere dēbēmus, *ut* ea *vincāmus*. 2. Hostēs nōn eī erant *quī* facile *dēpellerentur*. 3. Testēs adeō metuērunt *ut* palam loquī *nōn possent*. 4. Cōnstat hoc scelus esse tantum *ut* meritō ac jūre *pūniātur*. 5. Nūllum perīculum est tam grave *quīn* bene obīrī *possit*. 6. Tam aptus erat ad loquendum *ut* nunc cōnsul factus *sit*. 7. Bene accidit *quod* praetōrēs eīs *occurrerunt*. 8. *Quod* testēs sē in custōdiam *dedērunt* bene factum est. 9. Nihil obstat *quōminus* hae litterae in lūcem *ēdantur*.[1] 10. Prīmum hostēs impediāmus *quōminus* nostrōs *dēpellant*. 11. Prohibēbimus eum *nē* testēs modo *pūniat*. 12. Illud magis est timendum *quod* vīvus *exiit*. 13. Bene accidit *quod* tē *vīdī*. 14. Cōnstat eōs nōbīscum fore. 15. Illum hortātus sum ut sine timōre omnia expōneret. 16. Testis palam dīxit sē litterās ad Catilīnam scrīptās habēre. 17. Ōrāvit ut omnia quae pollicitī essent facerent. 18. Respondit sē semper bonārum imāginum[2] studiōsum fuisse. 19. Servī nōn erant aptī ad perīculum obeundum. 20. Omnia comperit esse vēra. 21. Tēla ita conjecta sunt ut vītārī nōn posse *vidērentur*. 22. Tam audācter prōgressī sunt mīlitēs nostrī ut hostēs *fugerent*. 23. Adeō bene vīxit *ut* amīcōrum meminisse eī gaudiō magnō *sit*. 24. Eōs laudāvit quod Deum amārent. 25. Chrīstus tertiā diē resurrēxit sīcut dīxit.

EXERCISE 70

Translate:

1. It was fortunate that the witness did not die. 2. That I am fitted to undergo these hardships[3] I owe to you. 3. So great was

---

[1] **in lūcem ēdo, ēdere, ēdidī, ēditus,** 3, tr., *publish.*

[2] **imāgō, imāginis,** *picture, image.*

[3] hardship = difficulty.

their fear that the witnesses were prevented from speaking openly. 4. So severely were the citizens punished that they were expelled from their country. 5. The crime was so terrible that the witnesses were unable to read about it. 6. First he went to meet the praetor. Then he tried to prevent him from speaking openly. 7. It is certain that the friends of Catiline will prevent the consul from driving him away. 8. His was a mind fitted for understanding the customs of the people. 9. If Catiline plotted against his country, he ought rightly and justly to be punished. 10. It is certain that these young men are not just now fitted for the army.

EXERCISE 71

Translate:

1. They fought so bravely that they conquered the enemy. 2. Cicero defended the state so bravely that now we all praise him. 3. They were the sort of men who would conspire against the state. 4. His unpopularity was so great that he left Rome. 5. His crimes were so numerous and so terrible that the Senate forthwith condemned[1] him. 6. The witnesses were so numerous that he finally confessed everything. 7. Would that he had so lived that we could praise him. 8. Would that you had spoken in such a way that we could trust you. 9. The crimes were so clear that no one defended him. 10. Cicero was so careful that the state was freed from dangers. 11. They fought so bravely that Cicero praised them. 12. Catiline was so daring that even[2] Cicero feared him. 13. So great was his speed[3] that the enemy was unable to waylay him. 14. He so bore himself in public affairs that it was clear that his deeds were not those of chance[4] but of virtue.

---

[1] *condemn,* **condemnō, 1, tr.**

[2] Use **ipse.**

[3] *speed,* **celeritās, celeritātis.**

[4] *chance,* **cāsus, ūs.**

EXERCISE 72

Imitate the word order and the structure of the model in translating:

MODEL: Ille erat ūnus timendus ex istīs omnibus,
sed
tam diū dum urbis moenibus continēbātur.

1. Sin alone should be feared by all[1] of you, but only as long as you are in[2] this world.
2. God must be loved more than all else, but in such a way that you love men with that same love.
3. Liberty must be protected[3] with all diligence, but in such a way that law and peace also are preserved.

EXERCISE 73

Translate orally:

1. The state was saved from dangers. 2. We were rescued from dangers. 3. We were saved by Cicero. 4. The Gaul was captured by the Romans. 5. He surpassed all in the science of speaking. 6. The leaders went with the Gauls. 7. He saved the state by his care and counsel. 8. Our lives were saved by the diligence and courage of Cicero. 9. Caesar surpassed all in the science of fighting. 10. He was a man of great courage. 11. The letters were unsigned. 12. His was a mind fitted for crime. 13. We were saved by the will of the gods. 14. We sent the letters through a Gaul. 15. They wanted to come before dawn. 16. We must guard our liberty with great care. 17. These things were carried out in his absence. 18. He did not wish to talk about the matter with others present. 19. He alone was to be feared among them all. 20. If he had remained in the city, we should still be[2] in danger. 21. Would that I had escaped. 22. Would that you had not written those

---

[1] Remember that **omnis** never takes the genitive.

[2] Use **versor,** 1, intr.

[3] *protect,* **dēfendō, dēfendere, dēfendī, dēfēnsus,** 3, tr.

letters. 23 May the state be saved. 24. He learned of the plots through the Gauls. 25. They send letters by the Gauls.

EXERCISE 74

Translate:[1]

1. His was a mind fitted for the planning of crime. 2. To put it mildly . . . 3. He and only he was the man to be afraid of. 4. So peacefully, so tranquilly, so silently . . . 5. To say the least . . . 6. Neither tongue nor hand failed his thoughts. 7. He was a man diligent in iniquity. 8. So long in advance . . . 9. The day of destruction and fate . . . 10. He saw to every detail himself. 11. All doors opened to his grasp. 12. He had the ability and the audacity. 13. He hand-picked definite men to see definite jobs through. 14. I shall speak out my mind. 15. Caught, ever so red-handed . . . 16. We would have been forced to fight it out with him.

EX MISSĀLĪ RŌMĀNŌ

Ex Ordinario Missae

"In the beginning God created heaven, and earth." So starts the Book of Genesis in which Moses first tells of the beginning of the march of time. St. John opens his Gospel with the same words—*In prīncipiō*. But John refers rather to the eternal procession of the Word who became man in time. Though the expressions used in John's prelude are simple, they carry with them the whole doctrine of the Church on the Incarnation. Notice two inescapable truths enumerated: the Word is God; and the Word was made flesh.

In prīncipiō erat Verbum, et Verbum erat apud Deum, et Deus erat Verbum. Hoc erat in prīncipiō apud Deum. Omnia per ipsum

[1] Idiomatic and correct Latin equivalents for the phrases in this exercise will be found by examining the Latin text assigned for the lesson. As far as possible avoid using vocabularies or dictionaries.

facta sunt; et sine ipsō factum est nihil, quod factum est. In ipsō vīta erat, et vīta erat lūx hominum. Et lūx in tenebrīs lūcet,[1] et tenebrae eam nōn comprehendērunt. Fuit homō missus ā Deō, cuī nōmen erat Jōannēs. Hic vēnit in testimōnium, ut testimōnium perhibēret[2] dē lūmine, ut omnēs crēderent per illum. Nōn erat ille lūx, sed ut testimōnium perhibēret[2] dē lūmine. Erat lūx vēra, quae illūminat[3] omnem hominem venientem in hunc mundum. In mundō erat, et mundus per ipsum factus est, et mundus eum nōn cognōvit. In propria[4] vēnit, et suī eum nōn recēpērunt. Quotquot[5] autem recēpērunt eum, dedit eīs potestātem fīliōs Deī fierī, hīs, quī crēdunt in nōmine ējus: quī nōn ex sanguinibus, neque ex voluntāte carnis,[6] neque ex voluntāte virī, sed ex Deō nātī sunt. ET VERBUM CARŌ[6] FACTUM EST, et habitāvit in nōbīs: et vīdimus glōriam ējus, glōriam quasi Ūnigenitī ā Patre, plēnum grātiae et vēritātis.

And the Mass ends with two grateful words often repeated during the Sacrifice: *Deō grātiās.*

---

[1] **lūceō, lūcēre, lūxī**, 2, intr., *shine, give light.*

[2] **perhibeō**, 2, tr., *give, grant, afford.*

[3] **illūminō**, 1, tr., *light up, enlighten.*

[4] **proprius, a, um**, *one's own.*

[5] **quotquot**, indecl. adj., *as many as.*

[6] **carō, carnis**, *flesh.*

LESSON 19: COMPARATIVE CLAUSES; ABLATIVE OF COMPARISON

VOCABULARY

vērum, ī	*truth* *reality*
monumentum, ī	*monument* *memorial*
externus, a, um	*foreign*
male, ***adv.***	*badly* *poorly*
ultrō, ***adv.***	*unasked* *unprovoked*
convertō, convertere, convertī, conversus, ***3, tr.***	*turn about*
nōlō, nōlle, nōluī, ***tr.; w. infin.; acc. w. infin.;*** **ut (nē)** *(Gr. 405-407, 419-424)*	*am unwilling* *do not wish*

RELATED ENGLISH WORDS

We *verify* facts when we make sure they are true. To speak badly of a person is to *malign* him. A *monumental* work. *External.* A *malapropos* remark is badly to the purpose, inappropriate. *Convertible.*

RELATED LATIN WORDS

Vēritās; malus; vertō.

IDIOM

It is the duty of, part of, character of, sign of, quality of, and so forth is translated by the genitive of nouns, but by the neuter nominative singular of possessive pronouns.

> **Mīlitis bonī est fortiter pugnāre.**
> *It is the mark of a good soldier to fight bravely.*

Vestrum est nē mihi mea facta obsint prōvidēre.
It is your duty to see to it that my deeds do not injure me.

ASSIGNMENT: *Third Oration against Catiline,* lines 237-358; GRAMMAR 599-610; Review GRAMMAR 89-111.

EXERCISE 75

Translate:

1. Monumentum in hāc urbe nōn tantum est quantum audīveram. 2. Ducis est mandāre; oboedīre[1] mīlitis. 3. Haec omnia quae tibi dīxī tam vēra sunt quam incrēdibilia. 4. Patrum est puerōs in virtūte exercēre. 5. Nōn tot adsunt[2] in senātū quot cōnsul vocāverat. 6. Testis est vēra loquī. 7. Cīvēs nōluērunt eadem audīre ac semper. 8. Nostrum est Deō servīre. 9. Quō altius loquēris, eō melius audīrī poteris. 10. Post haec autem rogāvit Pīlātum Jōsēphus ab Arimathaeā[3] ut tolleret corpus Jēsū; et permīsit Pīlātus. Vēnit ergō Jōsēphus et tulit corpus. 11. Erat ibi monumentum novum, in quō nōndum quisquam positus erat. Ibi ergō posuērunt Jēsum. 12. Testēs autem vērum dīcere nōluērunt. 13. Ipse cōnsul bellum ultrō cum externīs male pācātīs gerēbat. 14. Ad populum tum conversus, eōs ut vēra audīrent hortātus est. 15. Nōluī male respondēre; nōluī ultrō loquī. 16. Cōnsulis est prōvidēre nē rēs pūblica quid dētrīmentī capiat. 17. Quotiēs Catilīna vītam cōnsulis petīvit, totiēs ē manibus ējus effūgit. 18. Neque tālis erat Catilīna quālis Cicerō. 19. Sīc respondit testis ut ipse respondissem.

EXERCISE 76

Translate:

1. All your plans are clearer to us than the light of day. 2. Glory is dearer to me than life itself. 3. This is the same man we saw at

[1] **oboediō, oboedīre,** 4, intr., *obey.*

[2] **adsum, adesse, adfuī, adfutūrus,** irreg., intr.; w. dat., *am present, support.*

[3] **ab Arimathaeā:** *of Arimathea,* a city in Judea. Its site is unknown, but it was probably between Jerusalem and Joppa.

Rome. 4. "Theirs not to reason why;[1] theirs not to make reply; theirs but to do and die." 5. It is our duty to provide for the welfare of both body and soul. 6. He did not wish to act as I had ordered him. 7. The more he spoke the less they listened.[2] 8. It is the part of a good witness to tell the truth. 9. The memorial was not so beautiful as I thought. 10. The army was not so great as he had thought. 11. You are just the same as you always were. 12. In the Senate there were as many opinions as there were men. 13. He is as careful as he is brave. 14. He acted in the same way as you would. 15. It is the duty of a consul to look to[3] the welfare of the state. 16. The monument which they had set up was larger than you would have thought. 17. Just as Caesar was the greatest Roman general, so Cicero was the greatest Roman orator.[4] 18. The foreign soldiers were as barbarous as they were brave. 19. The general turned about to his soldiers and said the same thing he had said a little before. 20. These foreigners speak poorly. 21. The more quickly you leave this place, the better. 22. Some foreign people wage war unprovoked. 23. It happened exactly as Cicero had foreseen.

EXERCISE 77

Translate:

1. It is, to be sure, a well-known seal. 2. Be brave. 3. The letters were anonymous. 4. To put it mildly . . . 5. He was a man diligent in iniquity. 6. We have been saved by Cicero. 7. Free me from these dangers. 8. The man was very agitated. 9. The letters were unsigned. 10. They were written in his own hand. 11. He recognized the seal. 12. Would that I had escaped. 13. He praised them for defending the Senate. 14. We ought to thank God. 15. He surpassed all his friends in the science of speaking. 16. Gaul was pacified by Caesar. 17. Your duty is to defend

---

[1] *to reason why:* **causam quaerere.**

[2] *listen,* **attendō, attendere, attendī, attentus,** 3, tr.

[3] *look to,* **prōvideō, prōvidēre, prōvīdī, prōvīsus,** 2, tr.; **w.** dat.; **dē w.** abl.

[4] *orator,* **ōrātor, ōrātōris.**

me. 18. It is the duty of a good soldier to defend the state. 19. I shall take care that you may all dwell in peace. 20. Would that Caesar had not pacified the Gauls. 21. He said the enemy were coming. 22. Five years ago we saw this man in Rome. 23. He said he would never come to Rome. 24. It happened that they met the enemy in a forest. 25. It happened that there was a full moon[1] that night. 26. Who would rightly blame[2] me? 27. He asked me to help them. 28. It is fortunate that you were not killed. 29. He came here for the sake of seeing the town. 30. If you were at Rome, you would see the Pope.[3] 31. If Caesar were alive, he would be a world leader. 32. Within three days we shall arrive at the mountains. 33. Let him leave the city. 34. If we fear God, why should we fear men? 35. They acted as if[4] they were moved by hatred. 36. Do not kill that man. 37. Two hours later Lentulus was captured. 38. Public Enemy No. 1 has been captured. 39. They undertook the business without delay. 40. I sent men there to capture the enemy. 41. Suddenly he confessed all. 42. He spoke to the same effect. 43. He rose to his feet. 44. It was the portrait of his grandfather. 45. We showed him the same letters that had been taken from his house. 46. When you came into the Senate a little while ago, who of all these men saw you?

EXERCISE 78

Translate:[5]

1. All the world about us is ruled by the will and power of God. 2. If I should say that I had thwarted them, I should take too much credit to myself. 3. I am of this mind. 4. The defense of loyal men counts for much. 5. I see no higher pinnacle of glory.

---

[1] *moon,* **lūna, ae.**

[2] *blame,* **reprehendō, reprehendere, reprehendī, reprehēnsus,** 3, tr.

[3] *pope,* **pāpa, ae.**

[4] *as if,* **quasi,** conj.; Gr. 611.

[5] Idiomatic and correct Latin equivalents for the phrases in this exercise will be found by examining the assigned Latin text. As far as possible avoid using vocabularies and dictionaries.

6. I would be intolerable. 7. A state imperfectly pacified . . . 8. They are able and not unwilling to make war. 9. I ask no other reward than the everlasting remembrance of this day. 10. He kept both the city and the citizens safe and sound. 11. Without bloodshed . . . 12. The bright lights of statesmanship were snuffed out. 13. Within living memory . . .

EXERCISE 79

Translate orally:

1. The letters were unsigned. 2. To put it mildly, we have been saved from great dangers. 3. He surpassed all the Romans in the science of speaking. 4. He denied that he had written the letters. 5. Would that you had not taken those letters. 6. He recognized the portrait of his father. 7. He went to Rome with all speed. 8. His was a mind fitted for crime. 9. He praised them for fighting bravely. 10. Since this is so, let us praise them. 11. They are worthy of dire punishment. 12. Finally, to make a long story short, we led them all to death. 13. They recognized their seals. 14. The letters were written in his own handwriting. 15. All this world which we see is governed by the power of God. 16. You have long been plotting against the lives of all of us. 17. The gates are open, go! 18. He sent men ahead to capture the camp. 19. May it come out well. 20. It is the sign of a real saint to love God above all things.

EXERCISE 80

Translate:

We have been living,[1] fellow Americans,[2] in difficult times; our government has been saved at last from pressing[3] dangers. Our country has been in danger not only because of plots and dissensions of the citizens but also because of foreign wars and the

---

[1] Use **versor.**

[2] *fellow Americans,* **cīvēs (cīvium) Americānī (Americānōrum).**

[3] Use a common adjective of quantity.

attacks of hostile nations. Can anyone[1] deny that we have been saved from all these dangers not merely by the efforts and energy[2] of the government[3] but also by the will and power of God, who defends the liberty and safety of the good? We ought, then, certainly to give thanks to God; we have been saved by Him from the sword, from fire, from destruction itself.

---

1 *anyone,* **quisquam, quidquam**; Gr. 843.

2 *energy,* **studium, ī.**

3 Use **cōnsul** in the plural to indicate the executive department of the government.

LESSON 20: ADVERSATIVE CLAUSES; GENITIVE OF THE CHARGE

VOCABULARY

īnfāmia, ae	*dishonor* *disgrace*
ēloquentia, ae	*eloquence*
reus, ī	*defendant* *the accused (person)*
jūdex, jūdicis	*judge* *juror* (voc. pl.) *gentlemen of the jury*
nātiō, nātiōnis	*tribe* *nation*
caput, capitis	*head*
crīmen, crīminis	*accusation* *crime*
accūsō, ***1, tr.; w. gen. of the charge***	*accuse*
condemnō, ***1, tr.; w. gen. of the charge***	*condemn*
damnō, ***1, tr.; w. acc. of person; gen. or abl. of thing***	*harm* *condemn* *sentence*
capite damnāre	*to sentence to death*
adsum, adesse, adfuī, adfutūrus, ***irreg., intr.; w. dat.***	*am present* *support*

RELATED ENGLISH WORDS

A *judicious* person judges carefully before giving an opinion or taking action. *International.* Not all nations inflict *capital* punishment for murder. *Criminal* negligence. *Infamy. Indemnity* is compensation for harm sustained.

RELATED LATIN WORDS

Fāma; jūdicō; loquor; sum.

ASSIGNMENT: Selections from *The Impeachment of Gaius Verres,* pages 104-126; GRAMMAR 595-598, 628; 717-718.

EXERCISE 81

Translate; explain the italicized constructions:

1. *Quamquam* reus crīmen *negāvit,* jūdicēs eum fūrtī condemnārunt. 2. *Quamquam* nihil dignum morte *fēcerat,* adulēscēns damnātus est capite. 3. *Quamvīs* honestī *essent* testēs, jūdex eōrum verbīs nōn crēdidit. 4. *Etiamsī* testēs nōn *adessent,* tamen reus propter īnfāmiam condemnātus esset. 5. *Licet* jūdex ēloquentiae studiōsissimus *sit,* male loquitur. 6. *Ut* vīrēs nōn *adsint,* tamen est laudanda voluntās. 7. Quō plūs eum *nēquitiae* accūsāvērunt, eō plūs negāvit. 8. *Quamvīs* facile *sit* nātiōnēs externās *bellī* accūsāre, tamen nōn omnēs celeriter condemnandae sunt. 9. Tantum erat crīmen ut reus nūllā ēloquentiā salvus esse posset. 10. *Cum* crīmen negāre *posset,* repente cōnfessus est. 11. *Quamquam* Cicerō *vidēbat* perniciem suam cum magnā calamitāte reī pūblicae esse conjūnctam, tamen perīculum prīvātum nōn vītāvit. 12. Quam īnfāmiam, *quamquam* ferenda nōn *fuit,* tamen, ut potuit, tulit.

EXERCISE 82

Translate:

1. Although I am being accused of an unbelievable crime, gentlemen of the jury, still you cannot rightly and justly sentence me to death. 2. Although he could have denied it, he suddenly confessed everything. 3. Granted that the accusation was true, the defendant ought not to have been condemned without witnesses. 4. However careful the consul was, he was not always present in the Senate. 5. Although he supported the cause of the foreign nation by his eloquence, the people did not want to go to war.

6. The judge injured the reputation of the accused man, even if he did it unwillingly.[1] 7. Even if his dishonor was great, he should not have been condemned by those jurors. 8. Even if he had not received a serious head wound, the brave soldier would have died. 9. Although the state has been saved, we are not yet free from danger. 10. Although he answered thus, I will not yet throw him into prison. 11. Although the letters were unsigned, we knew who wrote them. 12. Although it was night, he did not return to Rome. 13. Although they were worthy of severe punishment, he did nothing. 14. Although they had no cavalry, they conquered. 15. Even if he had had cavalry, he would not have conquered. 16. Even if the letters were unsigned, I should nevertheless know who wrote them. 17. Although you may be rich,[2] you are not happy.[3] 18. However good you are, there will be some who hate you. 19. They were captured although they exercised[4] care.

EXERCISE 83

Translate:

1. Although you have long been plotting against us, still I do not fear you. 2. Even though you may not believe it, I know what you did last night. 3. Even though he should dare to come into the Senate, I would not order him to be arrested. 4. Although you have long been trying to kill us all, you cannot lift a finger[5] against the state. 5. Even though I should order you to be led to death, the rest of your band would yet live. 6. Even though you are the most wicked of men, still you can't deny that you said this. 7. Even though he is worthy of death, let us not condemn him. 8. Do not kill him even though he is an enemy of the state. 9. Although there are some here who defend Catiline, I say that

---

[1] *unwilling,* **invītus, a, um.**

[2] *rich,* **dīvēs (*gen.* dīvitis).**

[3] *happy,* **beātus, a, um.**

[4] *exercise,* **ūtor, ūtī, ūsus sum,** 3, intr.; w. abl.

[5] *lift a finger,* **mē (tē, sē) commoveō, commovēre, commōvī, commōtus,** 2, tr.

he is the worst enemy of the state, the most wicked of men. 10. Although he ought to be led to death, I will not yet order this. 11. Even if he changed his mind, he would still be an object of hate[1] to me. 12. Even though you came together at night, I know who were with you. 13. Even though he had denied it, we would have put him in prison. 14. Even though he did not arrest Catiline, he knew what he was going to do. 15. Even if some were praising him, I should not. 16. Though he set out for Rome in the morning,[2] he did not arrive before night. 17. If you have done this, you will be put in prison. 18. If it is your duty to defend the state, why don't you do so? 19. Granted that Caesar had considerable genius,[3] none the less I cannot admire[4] his character. 20. You have not defended me, although it is your duty to do so. 21. Although we are free from danger at last, it is still your duty to defend me. 22. Although he should come into the Senate, I would not arrest him. 23. Even if he should not go out of Rome, we should not fear him. 24. Although they were very careful, none the less the praetors sent by Cicero captured them. 25. Supposing it to be true, still we should not be afraid. 26. Although we had taken the letters from his house, still he denied he had written them.

CICERO'S LETTERS

In Cicero's speeches we have a picture of the orator; in his letters a cross section of Cicero the man. Written to family and friends, the eight hundred or so letters that survive vary in length from a few lines to several pages. They are naturally less formal in style than the orations—now chatty, now frank, now moody, now weighted down with worry even to the point of despair. Here we see Cicero's character stripped of its official public dress, clothed in all its personal weakness. Some have thought it indis-

---

[1] *an object of hate:* **odiō**; dative of purpose.

[2] *in the morning,* **māne**, adv.

[3] *genius,* **ingenium, ī.**

[4] Use **admīror.**

creet of Cicero so to have laid bare the most intimate workings of his own self. Even so, with all their indecision, their inconsistency, their self-centeredness these intensely human documents reveal a man of high ideals.

When reading a letter of Cicero one often feels like a person overhearing a telephone conversation. Correspondence, like telephone calls, involves two parties. Let us listen to at least one side of an anxious chat which Cicero and his son Marcus have with his wife Terentia and his daughter Tullia. Dated January 22, 49 B. C., when Caesar and Pompey were in open conflict, the letter was written from Cicero's villa at Formiae. Cicero was still trying to make up his mind which side to take. Meanwhile he is worried about his wife and daughter at Rome; he asks them to decide whether they will stay in Rome or join him at Formiae, tells them to secure their house by barricades, and instructs them to keep him posted:

TULLIUS TERENTIAE SUAE ET PATER SUĀVISSIMAE FĪLIAE, CICERŌ MATRĪ ET SORŌRĪ S. D. PLŪR.[1]

Cōnsīderandum[2] vōbīs etiam atque etiam,[3] animae meae,[4] dīligenter putō, quid faciātis, Rōmaene sītis an mēcum in aliquō tūtō locō; id nōn sōlum meum cōnsilium est, sed etiam vestrum. Mihi veniunt in mentem haec: Rōmae vōs esse tūtō posse per

[1] **Tullius . . . S. D. Plūr.:** *Tully to his Terentia and Daddy to his very sweet daughter, Cicero to his mother and sister—(both) send heartiest greetings.* This is one variation of the Roman letter heading, the equivalent of our salutation. The name of the sender is in the nominative, the person to whom it was sent in the dative, followed by some such greeting as the one used here. **S. D. Plūr.** is the standard abbreviation for **Salūtem dīcit plūrīmam** (lit., *Says very many greetings*). Sometimes only S. D. (**Salūtem dīcit:** *Sends regards*) was used. In more formal correspondence great attention was paid to forenames and titles, and the formula was S. V. B. E. V. (**Sī valēs, bene est; valeō:** *If you are well, 'tis well; I am well*). Roman letters usually ended abruptly with some brief phrase like **valē** *(good-by)*, followed by the date and address.

[2] **cōnsīderō,** 1, tr., *consider, reflect upon.*

[3] **etiam atque etiam:** *again and again.*

[4] **animae meae:** *my dears.*

Dolābellam,[1] eamque rem posse nōbīs adjūmentō[2] esse, sī quae vīs aut sī quae rapīnae[3] fierī coeperint; sed rūrsus[4] illud[5] mē movet, quod videō omnēs bonōs abesse Rōmā et eōs mulierēs[6] suās sēcum habēre. Haec autem regiō, in quā ego sum, nostrōrum est cum oppidōrum, tum etiam praediōrum,[7] ut et multum esse mēcum et, cum abieritis, commodē[8] in nostrīs praediīs[9] esse possītis.

Mihi plānē nōn satis cōnstat adhūc, utrum[10] sit melius. Vōs vidēte, quid aliae faciant istō locō fēminae,[11] et nē, cum velītis, exīre nōn liceat. Id velim dīligenter etiam atque etiam[12] vōbīscum et cum amīcīs cōnsīderētis.[13]

Domus ut prōpugnācula[14] et praesidium habeat, Philotīmō[15] dīcētis.[16] Et velim tabellāriōs īnstituātis[17] certōs, ut cotīdiē ali-

---

[1] **per Dolābellam:** *under Dolabella's protection;* Gr. 975. Dolabella, Cicero's son-in-law, had joined Caesar's party. Cicero was leaning somewhat to Pompey's side. If Terentia and Tullia stayed at Rome they could enjoy Dolabella's protection.

[2] **adjūmentum, ī,** *help, aid, protection* (cf. **adjuvō**).

[3] **rapīna, ae,** *plundering, pillage* (cf. **rapiō**).

[4] **rūrsus,** adv., *again, on the other hand.*

[5] **Illud** anticipates the substantive clause **quod . . . habēre.**

[6] **mulier, mulieris,** *woman.*

[7] **nostrōrum . . . praediōrum:** *consists both of towns under our patronage and of estates which I own.*

[8] **commodē,** adv., *readily, easily.*

[9] **praedium, ī,** *estate, farm.*

[10] **utrum:** *which of the two.*

[11] **fēmina, ae,** *woman.*

[12] **etiam atque etiam:** *again and again.*

[13] **cōnsīderō,** 1, tr., *consider, reflect upon.*

[14] **prōpugnāculum, ī,** *rampart, place of defense* (against the looting common in times of political disturbance).

[15] **Philotīmus, ī,** *Philotimus,* Terentia's steward, whose dishonesty Cicero refers to in other letters.

[16] The future indicative is here used in a command; Gr. 491.

[17] **velim tabellāriōs īnstituātis:** *please organize letter-carriers* (lit., *I should like you to arrange;* Gr. 500). The Romans had no postal system like ours. Letters were carried by messengers.

quās ā vōbīs litterās accipiam; maximē autem date operam, ut valeātis, sī nōs vultis valēre.

VIIII Kal. Formiīs[1]

---

[1] **VIIII Kal. Formiīs**: *Formiae, January 22.* **VIIII Kal.** probably **IX Kalendās Februāriās,** *the ninth day before the Calends of February.*

LESSON 21: CAUSAL CLAUSES; ABLATIVE OF CAUSE, PRICE; GENITIVE OF INDEFINITE VALUE

VOCABULARY

industria, ae	*exertion* *hard work* *energy*
pecūnia, ae	*money*
nihilum, ī	*nothing*
mercātor, mercātōris	*merchant*
genus, generis, *n.*	*race* *kind*
anteā, *adv.*	*before*
quasi, *adv. and conj. (Gr. 611)*	*as if* *just as* *nearly*
emō, emere, ēmī, emptus, *3, tr.*	*buy*
vēndō, vēndere, vēndidī, vēnditus, *3, tr.*	*sell*
cōnstō, cōnstāre, cōnstitī, cōnstātum, *1, intr.; w. abl. or gen.*	*cost*
gaudeō, gaudēre, gāvīsus sum, *2, intr.*	*rejoice* *am glad*
necesse est, esse, fuit, *intr.; w. infin. (Gr. 641, 892)*	*it is necessary*

RELATED ENGLISH WORDS

An *industrious* person exerts himself. Mr. Micawber in Dickens' *David Copperfield* was always being embarrassed by *pecuniary* circumstances. *Mercantile* is an adjective referring to merchants. The *Gentiles* are the races of other than Jewish blood. To *preempt* land is to settle upon it with the privilege of buying it if one wishes. *Vendor*.

RELATED LATIN WORDS

Merx; ante; gaudium; necessārius.

ASSIGNMENT: Selections from *The Impeachment of Gaius Verres,* pages 127-154; Grammar 572-576, 578-580; 700-705; 781-784; 788-789.

EXERCISE 84

Translate; explain the italicized constructions:

1. Aliquī mercātōrēs pecūniam nōn habent *quia* labōrem atque industriam *vītant*. 2. Domum emere nōluī *quod* nōn *esset* mihi satis pecūniae. 3. Adulēscēns Chrīstum secūtus nōn est *quia* multa bona *habēret* quae vēndere nōlēbat. 4. Eam amō *nōn quod* ējusdem generis *sit* sed quod pulchra est. 5. Et ingressus in templum, Chrīstus ējēcit eōs *quoniam* in domō ōrātiōnis *vēnderent* et *emerent*. 6. Quae *cum* ita *sint,* necesse est diūtius exspectāre. 7. Gāvīsus est *quod* pecūniam mercātōribus nōn *dedī*. 8. Omnēs Chrīstiānī *spē* gaudent. 9. *Prae dolōre* loquī nōn potuit. 10. Chrīstus ab amīcō *pretiō*[1] servī vēnditus est. 11. Nōs autem Chrīstus ēmit *sanguine suō*. 12. Mīlitēs gaudēbant *quasi* domum *vīdissent*. 13. Mēcum loqueris *quasi* reus *essem*. 14. Dēbēmus amīcōs vērōs *permagnī* facere. 15. Multa quae anteā *maximī* aestimāvī,[2] nunc minōris habeō. 16. Hominēs hūjus generis *nihilī* putō. 17. *Quoniam* haec in senātū *comperta sunt,* vōbīs omnia expōnam. 18. *Tantī* est, sī ex urbe eās. 19. Sānctī honōrem *parvī* faciunt. 20. Praetōrēs *laudāvit* quod sine morā negōtium *suscēpissent*. 21. Quae *cum* ita *sint,* eum in vincula conjicere dēbēmus. 22. *Cum* haec omnia magna atque pulchra *videāmus,* nōnne Deum esse cōnfirmāre dēbēmus? 23. *Hāc victōriā* gāvīsus, Rōmam īvit. 24. Victōria multō *sanguine* cōnstābat. 25. Vōs, *quoniam* jam *est* nox, domōs vestrās discēdite. 26. Gaudeō *quod* hostēs *subēgistī*.[3] 27. Amīcus meus *īdem* est *quī* semper fuit.

---

[1] **pretium, ī,** *price.*

[2] **aestimō,** 1, tr.; w. gen. or abl. of price, *value, estimate, regard.*

[3] **subigō, subigere, subēgī, subāctus,** 3, tr., *drive, conquer.*

EXERCISE 85

Translate:

1. The merchants were glad because of the victory. 2. It cost much bloodshed,[1] but it was worth it. 3. As it is now night, depart from your toil to your homes. 4. Christ bought us all for the dear price of His blood. 5. These Roman merchants have much money because they buy things for nearly nothing and sell them at a great price. 6. The three kings rejoiced because they saw Jesus and Mary. 7. There are those who love God not because He is good in Himself, but because they do not wish to be condemned forever. 8. Several things which I valued highly before, I now hold for nothing. 9. It is necessary to defend oneself and one's country with energy and toil. 10. Hard work overcomes every difficulty. 11. There are those who hate foreign races as if they were enemies. 12. Thanks to the exertion and work of the consul we have been preserved just as if we had not undergone any danger. 13. Since the state has been saved, we ought to give thanks to God. 14. This victory cost considerable slaughter. 15. Since he answered thus, we shall throw him into prison. 16. Because the letters were unsigned, we did not know who wrote them. 17. As it is now night, we ought to return to Rome. 18. He thinks little of honor. 19. The people rejoiced on account of this victory. 20. He praised the soldiers because they had defended the city. 21. They are worthy of more severe punishment because they have plotted against their own fellow citizens. 22. I am glad that you came. 23. It is of less value. 24. They were conquered because they had no cavalry. 25. For the sake of money and because of his patriotism, he wished to live at Rome. 26. There was grief throughout the whole city because Cicero had been killed. 27. The Romans prospered[2] because they were brave. 28. Throughout the whole city there were bodies of those who had been slain.

---

[1] bloodshed = blood.

[2] *prosper*, **flōreō, flōrēre, flōruī**, 2, intr.

29. We have long been fearing you since we know that you desired to burn the city and kill the citizens.

EXERCISE 86

Translate orally:

1. The letters were unsigned. 2. Gaul was imperfectly pacified. 3. He said there had been a controversy about this matter. 4. He begged them to defend him. 5. He said he had always been a connoisseur of portraits. 6. His was a mind fitted by nature for crime. 7. To put it mildly, they did not wish to help us. 8. He urged them to speak without fear. 9. He surpasses all in the art of speaking. 10. They recognized the letters. 11. It is worth while. 12. I consider him of small worth. 13. The gates are open. 14. Would that Cicero had not died. 15. They will see to it that they dwell in everlasting peace. 16. He discovered that everything was true. 17. They could have conquered us. 18. The plots were discovered by the will of God. 19. The state has been saved from terrible dangers. 20. It is now night. 21. Depart to your homes. 22. He waged many foreign wars. 23. All the attacks of wicked citizens have been turned against me alone. 24. Would that you had come. 25. May I see you again. 26. I have incurred unpopularity in the administration of the state. 27. May it avail for my glory. 28. May you ever defend the state. 29. He blamed them for not defending the state. 30. May they come. 31. These men have not heeded the voice of conscience. 32. Their deeds have benefited them. 33. You must see to it that I am not killed. 34. Yours it is to defend me and my children. 35. The letters were to about the same effect. 36. They can no longer injure me. 37. May I see Rome some day. 38. He said they would come. 39. I thought the others would leave. 40. They asked us to help them. 41. Cicero asked the Romans to defend him. 42. The state, though silent, asks you to defend it. 43. Would that you had not been captured. 44. Would that you were at Rome. 45. He said these things had been done by virtue and not by chance. 46. He urged them to confess. 47. I shall see to it that you will not long have to do this.

48. They were in perpetual peace. 49. Since it is now night, return to your homes. 50. We ought to thank God.

EXERCISE 87

Translate:

I have spent my days and nights in this toil that you may live forever in peace. I have ever thought it the part of a good consul to see to it that the citizens be free from danger and from fear. Since the lot of those who engage in politics[1] is not the same as the lot of those who engage in literature,[2] for whilst against the former[3] the attacks of all wicked and impious men are turned, the writings of the latter[3] are read only by the good and are neglected[4] by the wicked, your part it is—if I justly and rightly have a certain hope of glory[5] and fame—to defend my name and my deed against the enemies of this city and of all of you. In you, fellow citizens, I place my hope of safety and of everlasting praise.

CICERO'S TRAINING IN ORATORY

It is not surprising that one as successful in the art of oratory as Cicero should have written something about the theory of that art. In *Dē Ōrātōre* he discusses the basic training of the ideal public speaker; in the historical dialogue *Brūtus, dē Clārīs Ōrātōribus* he gives a history and evaluation of Rome's greatest speakers—a Who's Who of Roman orators. When Cicero came to his own day he was unable to resist the *ego* that had so often betrayed his tongue into the words *nunc pauca dē mē dīcam.* Toward the close of the dialogue Rome's first orator tells of his own study, training, and experience in these words:

---

[1] Use **versor in rē pūblicā.** Compare this sentence with the sentence that begins on page 96, *Third Oration against Catiline,* line 326.

[2] Use **versor in litterīs.**

[3] See Gr. 795.

[4] *neglect,* **neglegō, neglegere, neglēxī, neglēctus, 3, tr.**

[5] Use an objective genitive.

Eram cum Stōicō Diodotō,[1] quī, cum habitāvisset apud mē mēcumque vīxisset, nūper est domī meae mortuus. Huic ego doctōrī[2] et ējus artibus[3] variīs[4] atque multīs ita eram tamen dēditus ut ab exercitātiōnibus[5] ōrātōriīs[6] nūllus diēs vacuus[7] esset. Commentābar dēclāmitāns,[8] sīc enim nunc loquuntur, saepe cum M. Pīsōne et cum Q. Pompējō[9] aut cum aliquō cotīdiē; idque faciēbam multum etiam Latīnē, sed Graecē[10] saepius, vel quod Graeca[10] ōrātiō plūra ornāmenta suppeditāns[11] cōnsuētūdinem similiter[12] Latīnē dīcendī afferēbat, vel quod ā Graecīs[10] summīs doctōribus,[2] nisi Graecē[10] dīcerem, neque corrigī[13] possem neque docērī.[14]

Tum prīmum nōs ad causās et prīvātās et pūblicās adīre coepimus, nōn ut in forō discerēmus,[15] quod plērīque[16] fēcērunt, sed ut, quantum nōs efficere potuissēmus, doctī[14] in forum venīrēmus. Eōdem tempore Molōnī dedimus operam;[17] dictātōre[18] enim Sullā lēgātus ad senātum dē Rhodiōrum praemiīs[19] vēnerat. Itaque

---

[1] **Stōicus** (ī) **Diodotus** (ī), *Diodotus the Stoic.* This philosopher had lived at Rome and given instructions to Cicero, especially in logic.

[2] **doctor, doctōris,** *teacher.*

[3] **ars, artis,** *art.*

[4] **varius, a, um,** *different, various.*

[5] **exercitātiō, exercitātiōnis,** *training, exercise.*

[6] **ōrātōrius, a, um**; adjective from **ōrātor**; meaning?

[7] **vacuus, a, um,** *free, empty.*

[8] **Commentābar dēclāmitāns:** *I used to practice declamation.*

[9] Marcus Piso and Quintus Pompey were friends of Cicero.

[10] **Graecus, a, um,** *Greek;* **Graecē:** *in Greek.*

[11] **plūra ornāmenta suppeditāns:** *supplying more rhetorical ornaments.*

[12] **similiter,** adv., *in like manner, similarly.*

[13] **corrigō, corrigere, corrēxī, corrēctus,** 3, tr., *correct, improve.*

[14] **doceō, docēre, docuī, doctus,** 2, tr., *teach, train.*

[15] **discō, discere, didicī,** 3, tr. and intr., *learn.*

[16] **plērīque, plērōrumque,** *the majority, almost all.*

[17] **Molōnī dedimus operam:** *I studied under Molo.* Molo of Rhodes was a famous teacher under whom Cicero later studied at Rhodes itself.

[18] **dictātor, dictātōris,** *dictator.*

[19] **dē Rhodiōrum praemiīs:** *about claims of the people of Rhodes* (i. e., reimbursement for their losses in the war with Mithridates).

prīma causa pūblica, prō Sex. Rōsciō[1] dicta, tantum commendātiōnis[2] habuit ut nōn ūlla esset quae nōn digna nostrō patrōciniō[3] vidērētur.

Erat eō tempore in nōbīs summa gracilitās[4] et īnfirmitās[5] corporis, prōcērum et tenue collum;[6] quī habitus[7] et quae figūra[8] nōn procul[9] abesse putātur ā vītae perīculō,[10] sī accēdit labor et laterum magna contentiō;[11] eōque magis hoc eōs quibus eram cārus commovēbat quod omnia sine remissiōne,[12] sine varietāte, vī summā vōcis et tōtīus corporis contentiōne[13] dīcēbam. Itaque cum mē et amīcī et medicī[14] hortārentur ut causās agere dēsisterem, quodvīs[15] potius perīculum mihi adeundum quam ā spērātā dīcendī glōriā discedendum putāvī. Sed cum cēnsērem remissiōne[12] et moderātiōne[16] vōcis et commūtātō genere dīcendī mē et perīculum vītāre posse et temperātius[17] dīcere, ut cōnsuētūdinem dīcendī mūtārem, ea causa mihi in Asiam[18] proficīscendī fuit.

Itaque cum essem biennium[19] versātus in causīs, et jam in forō celebrātum[20] meum nōmen esset, Rōmā sum profectus. Cum vēnis-

---

1 Sextus Roscius.

2 What case is **commendātiōnis**? Why?

3 **patrōcinium, ī,** *patronage, defense.*

4 **gracilitās, gracilitātis,** *slimness, thinness, slenderness.*

5 **īnfirmitās, īnfirmitātis,** *weakness, illness.*

6 **prōcērum et tenue collum:** *a long thin neck.*

7 **habitus, ūs,** *appearance, condition.*

8 **figūra, ae,** *shape, form, figure.*

9 **procul,** adv., *far off, at a distance.*

10 A slender build of this sort would indicate physical weakness.

11 **laterum magna contentiō:** *the severe strain on the lungs.* There would be danger of pleurisy or tuberculosis.

12 **remissiō, remissiōnis,** *relaxation, easing up.*

13 **contentiō, contentiōnis,** *strain, exertion.*

14 **medicus, ī,** *doctor.*

15 **quīvīs, quaevīs, quodvīs,** *any at all, what you please*; Gr. 844.

16 **moderātiō, moderātiōnis,** *control, restraint.*

17 **temperātius,** adv., *more restrainedly, with more moderation.*

18 **Asia, ae,** *Asia (Minor).*

19 **biennium, ī,** *(a period of) two years* (**bis + annus**).

20 **celebrātus, a, um,** *well-known.*

sem Athēnās,[1] studium philosophiae,[2] numquam intermissum,[3] ā prīmāque adulēscentiā[4] cultum[5] et semper auctum[6] renovāvī.[7] Post ā mē Asia[8] tōta peragrāta est,[9] fuīque cum summīs quidem ōrātōribus, quibuscum exercēbar ipsīs libentibus.[10]

Quibus nōn contentus, Rhodum[11] vēnī, mēque ad eundem quem Rōmae audīveram Molōnem[12] applicāvī,[13] cum āctōrem in vērīs causīs scrīptōremque praestantem[14] tum in notandīs animadvertendīsque vitiīs et īnstituendō docendōque prūdentissimum.[15] Is dedit operam,[16] sī modo id cōnsequī potuit, ut nimis[17] redundantēs[18] nōs et superfluentēs[19] juvenīlī[20] quādam dīcendī impūnitāte[21] et

---

1 **Athēnae, Athēnārum,** *Athens.*

2 **studium** (ī) **philosophiae,** *the study of philosophy.*

3 **intermittō, intermittere, intermīsī, intermissus,** 3, tr., *interrupt.*

4 **adulēscentia, ae,** *youth.*

5 **colō, colere, coluī, cultus,** 3, tr., *cultivate, cherish* (cf. culture).

6 **augeō, augēre, auxī, auctus,** 2, tr. and intr., *increase, enrich.*

7 **renovō,** 1, tr., *renew, refresh.*

8 **Asia, ae,** *Asia (Minor).*

9 **peragrō,** 1, tr., *wander through, pass over, traverse.*

10 **ipsīs libentibus:** *with their good will.*

11 **Rhodus, ī,** *Rhodes,* an island off Asia Minor famous for its school of rhetoric.

12 **Molō, Molōnis,** *Molo.*

13 **applicō,** 1, tr., *attach to, apply to, connect with.*

14 **āctōrem in vērīs causīs scrīptōremque praestantem:** *plaintiff for real cases and an outstanding writer.* These 'real cases' were distinguished from the stock cases of mock trials used in oratorical training.

15 **īnstituendō docendōque prūdentissimum:** *most prudent in instructing and teaching.*

16 **operam dō, dare, dedī, datus,** 1, tr., *pay attention to, take care that.*

17 **nimis,** adv., *too much, too.*

18 **redundō,** 1, tr., *run over, overflow* (cf. redundant).

19 **superfluō, superfluere, superflūxī, superflūxum,** 3, intr., *flow over* (cf. superfluous).

20 **juvenīlis, e,** *youthful.*

21 **impūnitās, impūnitātis,** *freedom* (cf. impunity).

licentiā[1] reprimeret et quasi extrā rīpās[2] diffluentēs[3] coercēret.[4] Ita recēpī mē bienniō[5] post nōn modo exercitātior,[6] sed prope mūtātus; nam et contentiō[7] nimia vōcis resēderat, et quasi dēferverat[8] ōrātiō, lateribusque[9] vīrēs et corporī mediocris habitus[10] accesserat.

---

1 **licentia, ae,** *license, liberty* (to do what one pleases).

2 **rīpa, ae,** *bank* (of a river).

3 **diffluō, diffluere, difflūxī, difflūxum,** 3, intr., *flow in different directions.*

4 **coerceō,** 2, tr., *check.* This whole figure pictures the stream of oratory overflowing its banks. The more mature Cicero had learned how to restrain his youthful flood of words.

5 **biennium, ī,** *(a period of) two years.*

6 **exercitātus, a, um,** *well-trained.*

7 **contentiō, contentiōnis,** *strain, exertion.*

8 **dēfervescō, dēfervescere, dēfervī,** 3, intr., *cease boiling, cool off.*

9 **latus, lateris,** n., *side;* **latera, laterum,** *lungs.*

10 **mediocris habitus:** *medium build.* Cicero's frail body had taken on some weight.

GENERAL REVIEW EXERCISES

EXERCISE 88

Translate:

1. Although we have saved your lives and fortunes, there is still a little danger. 2. You have all been saved from destruction by the extraordinary help of the immortal gods. 3. You have been snatched from death itself by my efforts and plans. 4. If life is dearer to us than all other things, ought we not to praise Cicero for saving us from ruin and destruction? 5. He asked whether the plans of the conspirators were not clear to all good men. 6. Who would not praise Cicero for putting the dangerous Catiline to death? 7. Granted that he was a citizen, he was an enemy of the state. 8. I shall explain to you how this enemy of the state was captured. 9. Ought not Cicero to be held in honor among all men? 10. Did not Catiline leave the city a few days ago?

EXERCISE 89

Translate:

1. Although the letters were handed over to the praetors, they did not read them. 2. If I had not summoned them then, they would have fled from the city. 3. Although he recognized his seal, he would not[1] confess. 4. Cicero himself did not read the letters. 5. They praised Cicero for not reading them. 6. It happened that many illustrious men came to Cicero's house within a few hours. 7. Would that they had never written those letters! 8. I sent Sulpicius to see what weapons were at the house of Cethegus. 9. Although many weapons were found at his house, he denied that he was an enemy of the state. 10. "I have always been," he said, "a collector[2] of fine weapons."

---

[1] Use **nōlō.**

[2] Use **studiōsus, a, um.**

EXERCISE 90

Translate:

1. Catiline must be cast out of the city. 2. Although these men were at Rome, I did not yet dare to order them to be thrown into prison. 3. There were some in Rome who did not know what plans these men were making. 4. I wanted to explain the affair in such a way that you would see the plots of the enemies with your own eyes. 5. I spent my days and nights in providing for your safety. 6. I wanted the whole matter to be understood not only by myself, not only by the Senate, but also by you. 7. He said that they had undertaken the business[1] without any delay. 8. He sent the excellent Flaccus to capture the Gauls. 9. Who would blame[2] Cicero for acting as he did? 10. Praise and renown were dearer to Cicero than money or even life itself.

EXERCISE 91

Translate:

1. I encouraged them to speak freely. 2. I asked them what they knew about the matter. 3. Catiline had ordered him to come to the city with slaves within a few days. 4. All the friends of Catiline were very much afraid of Cicero. 5. Catiline had said that the city had to be burned. 6. He had ordered them to kill all the citizens who resisted them. 7. "Lentulus," said the Gauls, "gave us letters and money for your nation. He said he would make us all citizens. He also said that he was the man who by fate was to gain power over the whole city and all Italy." 8. They praised Cicero for freeing them from fear and for saving their lives and their fortunes. 9. The cavalry of the Gauls was better than that[3] of the Romans. 10. Although some did not wish to destroy the city, Catiline said it had to be burned.

---

[1] *business,* **negōtium, ī.**

[2] *blame,* **reprehendō, reprehendere, reprehendī, reprehēnsus, 3, tr.**

[3] Do not translate *that.*

EXERCISE 92

Translate:

1. He promised to do everything they wanted.[1] 2. Granted that he was brave! Granted that he was learned![2] What of it? 3. Cicero asked him whether he recognized the seal. 4. "Certainly," he said, "it is the image of my grandfather. Am I to be condemned on these charges because someone[3] used my seal?" 5. Although at first he denied everything, he finally confessed and was led off to prison. 6. Be a man! Take care to gain for yourself the help of even the slaves. 7. Although he had taken the letters from his house, still he denied he had written them.

EXERCISE 93

Translate:

Gentlemen of the Senate, have we not most certain proofs of their guilt?[4] Recall to your minds the letters, the seals, the handwriting. Recall their own words and those[5] of the Gauls. I have spent my days and nights so that this might all be clear to you. Who would not condemn these dangerous citizens? Who would not free the state from danger and from fear by their death? Can there be those in this assembly who do not hate and fear the dangerous Catiline, the wicked Lentulus, and that pest of the state, Cethegus? Granted that they are citizens. Who would not consider them the enemies of the state rather than patriots? The fatherland, so to speak,[6] has long been defending and cherishing[7] them, but they have hated it, and have long been desiring one thing only, to destroy that fatherland, to burn the homes of us all and even the temples of the immortal gods.

---

[1] What tense?

[2] *learned,* **doctus, a, um.**

[3] *someone,* **nesciōquis, nesciōquid;** Gr. 819.

[4] guilt = crime.

[5] Do not translate *those.*

[6] *so to speak:* **ut ita dīcam.**

[7] *cherish,* **colō, colere, coluī, cultus,** 3, tr.

WORD-GROUPS AND IDIOMS[1]

FIRST ORATION AGAINST CATILINE

quem ad fīnem: *to what limit? how far?*
proximā nocte: *last night.*
superiōre nocte: *the night before last.*
jussū cōnsulis: *at the consul's bidding, by order of the consul.*
ex senātūs cōnsultō: *in accordance with the senatorial decree, according to the bill of the House.*
in diēs: *day by day, each day.*
in diēs singulōs: *each successive day, day after day.*
mihi crēde: *take my advice, take it from me, take my word for it, upon my word.*
in armīs esse: *to be under arms, to be in arms.*
priōre nocte: *night before last.*
obscūrē agere: *to deal in the dark, to be vague.*
sententiam rogāre: *to ask an opinion, call upon to vote.*
apud Laecam: *at Laeca's house, at Laeca's.*
paulum morae: *a little delay, some delay.*
paulō ante lūcem: *a little before dawn, just before sunrise.*
id temporis: *at that particular time, just at that moment.*
quae cum ita sunt: *under these circumstances, and since this is so.*
grātiam habēre: *to be thankful, to feel grateful.*
summa salūs reī pūblicae: *the highest interests of the state, the state's very existence.*
mē imperante: *at my bidding, by my order.*
Lepidō et Tullō cōnsulibus: *during the consulship of Lepidus and Tullus.*
post hominum memoriam: *within living memory, since the dawn of history.*

---

[1] Some words go together naturally, others assume new colors when combined. These word-groups and idioms, listed in the order in which they occur in the text, are to be mastered by the pupil.

ūllā ratiōne: *by any means, in any way.*
ad Lepidum habitāre: *to live at the house of Lepidus, to stop at Lepidus's.*
ad senātum referre: *to put up to the House, to lay before the Senate.*
vīs et manūs: *violent hands.*
manūs ac tēla: *weaponed hands.*
animum indūcere: *to make up one's mind.*
in praesēns tempus: *for the present.*
in posteritātem / **in posterum**: *for the future.*
est tantī: *it is worth it, it is worth while.*
quam ob rem: *wherefore, on that account.*
vix feram: *I shall hardly be able to endure, I shall find it hard to take.*
quaesō: *please, I beg you, kindly tell me.*
lēgēs quae rogātae sunt: *laws that have been passed.*
grātiam referre: *to return a favor, to requite.*
hoc idem sentīre: *to feel the same way, to share the same opinion.*

THIRD ORATION AGAINST CATILINE

ex faucibus fātī: *from the jaws of doom.*
minōrem fidem facere: *to command less confidence, to fail to convince.*
facultātem offere: *to present an opportunity.*
manifestō dēprehendere: *to catch red-handed.*
amantissimus reī pūblicae: *extremely patriotic.*
cum advesperāsceret: *as dusk was coming on.*
tertiā ferē vigiliā exāctā: *about three o'clock in the morning, when the third watch was all but spent.*
integrīs signīs: *with unbroken seals, unopened.*
cum jam dīlūcēsceret: *at daybreak, at dawn, when day was now dawning.*
praeter cōnsuētūdinem: *contrary to one's custom.*
audītā rē: *on hearing the news.*

frequentēs convēnērunt: *they gathered in crowds, they came together in large numbers.*
ex aedibus Cethēgī: *from Cethegus's home.*
eō cōnsiliō ut: *with a view to.*
ac nē longum sit: *to make a long story short, not to bore you.*
ipsīus manū scrīptum: *in his own handwriting.*
paulō ante: *a moment before.*
aliquid respondēre: *to make some answer or other.*
in eandem ferē sententiam: *to much the same effect, of about the same import.*
facere potestātem dīcendī: *to offer an opportunity to speak.*
post autem aliquantō: *but after a while.*
quid mihi cum vōbīs est: *what business have I with you, what have I got to do with you.*
praeter opīniōnem omnium: *contrary to everyone's expectation.*
ex memoriā: *by heart, from memory.*
in custōdiam trādere: *to put under surveillance.*
meō nōmine: *in my name, on my account, in my honor.*
post hanc urbem conditam: *since the founding of this city.*
factum atque trānsāctum est: *it is done and over with.*
ut levissimē dīcam: *to say the least, to put the case very mildly.*
āversus ā vērō: *hostile to truth.*
mente captus: *beside oneself, out of one's mind.*
cīvēs integrōs incolumēsque servāre: *to keep the citizens safe and sound.*
rēs quās ego gessī: *my exploits, my achievements.*

IMPEACHMENT OF VERRES

terrā marīque: *on land and sea.*
ūnō tempore: *at one and the same time.*
arbitrātū ējus: *at his pleasure.*
animum intendere: *to direct one's thoughts, to turn one's attention.*
aliquā ex parte: *to some degree, in some measure.*
per triennium: *for three years.*

nūllō modō: *in no way, by no means.*
ab initiō: *from the first, at the beginning.*
praeclārē sē rēs habēbat: *everything promised well, things looked bright.*
hīs diēbus paucīs: *during these past few days.*
invītō cōnsule dēsignātō: *because of the consul-elect's reluctance.*
Verre absolūtō: *if Verres be acquitted, with Verres's release.*
esse omnibus molestum: *to be a source of annoyance to everybody.*
molestē ferre: *to be annoyed, to take hard, to bear ill.*
illīs ipsīs diēbus: *during those very days.*
dē pecūniīs repetundīs: *dealing with recovery of money, concerning extortion.*
eādem illā nocte: *on that very same night.*
benevolō animō: *kindheartedly, generously.*
rēs omnis mihi tēcum est: *the whole business is between you and me.*
perīculum facere: *to test, to make trial of.*
dē industriā: *of set purpose, deliberately, willfully.*
sēcum praeclāre agere: *to fare admirably, to do well by oneself.*
mihi vēnit in mentem: *it occurs to me.*
sī fierī potest: *if possible.*
rē vērā: *in reality, as a matter of fact.*
neque hoc Quīntum Catulum fūgit: *and this fact did not escape the attention of Quintus Catulus.*
cōnstat inter omnēs: *it is generally agreed, all agree.*
fierī nōn pōtest: *it is impossible.*
novō exemplō: *by an unprecedented circumstance, by an innovation.*
hīs īnstitūtīs: *by these devices, in accordance with this practice.*
in vincula conjicere: *to throw into prison, to put in chains.*
capitibus involūtīs: *with covered heads, blindfolded.*
tē praetōre: *during your praetorship.*
propter togae nōmen: *out of respect for the toga, out of regard for Roman citizenship.*
nāvem ingredī: *to board a ship, to go aboard ship.*

stīpendia merēre: *to serve in the army, to see service.*
in crucem agere: *to condemn to the cross, to crucify.*
ad arbitrium tuum: *at your wish, as you please.*
hoc tū idem dīcis: *you also say, you also admit this fact.*
obscūrō locō nātus: *born of humble station.*
in crucem tollere: *to lift up on the cross, to crucify.*
mōre atque īnstitūtō: *according to well-established custom.*
ūnus homō nesciōquis: *some individual or other.*
ultrō citrōque: *back and forth.*
ut longius prōgrediar: *to go one step further.*

A LIFE OF CICERO

Marcus Tullius Cicero was born in Arpinum, a town in the Volscian Mountains, some sixty miles southeast of Rome, on January 3, 106 B. C. He was therefore six years older than Caesar. His parents were plebeians, but his father, a good businessman with ambitions for his sons, moved the family to Rome, where Marcus and his younger brother Quintus began their education.

At seventeen Cicero saw service in the army during the Social War (90-88 B. C.), but he came back to Rome with more taste for civil than for military service. He had long since developed a keen interest in the Forum, which was to the ancient Roman all that Wall Street, the White House, and the Supreme Court are to us. Here were the rostra from which orators addressed the people, and in those days the rostra took the place of our newspapers and radio.

But Cicero would not mount the speaker's platform unprepared. He must train for it. For six years he gave himself over to the study of logic, rhetoric, philosophy, and speech, under the best instructors at Rome. Not a day went by without some practice in public speaking—sometimes in Latin, often in Greek.

Meanwhile Rome had twice been bathed in blood. Marius had seized the government and purged it of aristocrats. Sulla had come back from Asia Minor and restored the aristocracy in yet another blood bath.

Marcus Tullius was twenty-five years old when he pleaded his first case in the law courts in 81 B. C. Success was instant, but ill-health threatened him. Of frail build and with an intense disposition, the young lawyer could not stand the strain of speaking. At the advice of doctors and friends he gave up the practice of law in 79 B. C. and took a trip abroad. At Athens he audited lectures in philosophy, at Rhodes he sat for a time under his old speech professor, Molo. He returned to Rome a changed man. He had developed a more effortless manner of speaking; he had regained his strength and with it his reputation as a pleader. So much so, that he felt the time had now come for him to enter public life. It was about this time that he married Terentia, a woman of wealth and position. They had two children. Tullia, the daughter, was their pride and joy; Marcus, the son, was something of a disappointment.

As praetor of Sicily in 75 B. C., Cicero's justice so won the confidence of all Sicilians that, five years later, they called upon him to champion their rights against the political machinery whereby Verres, their governor, had robbed and maltreated them. Not the weight of Verres' gold, nor even the strategy of Hortensius, Rome's top-ranking lawyer of that period, could win the case. Cicero had hardly opened it when Hortensius abandoned Verres and the Sicilian boss fled into exile.

In giant strides the popular young lawyer took the ***cursūs honōrum***, the rising steps to political office. As aedile in 69 B. C. he did not display the wealth of a Caesar, but his good taste in staging the public games won him no less acclaim. As praetor in 66 B. C. he handled both civil and criminal suits with justice. That year he mounted the rostra for the first time. There was only one more step to climb before reaching the top. On January 1, 63 B. C., two days before his forty-third birthday Cicero took over the first office of the land. He was consul. But a more detailed story of the events of this period is told elsewhere in this book (pages 11-99).

At the end of his term, in December of that eventful year, Cicero was not allowed to make a farewell speech to the people from the rostra. He had put the Catilinarian conspirators to death without trial. Such injustice deprived him of the right to speak. It was the beginning of the end. Cicero retired to the private practice of law.

During the First Triumvirate (Pompey, Caesar, and Crassus) Cicero's enemies were contriving to have him exiled from Rome. In fact he had no sooner voluntarily retired to Thessalonica than a formal decree banishing him from a radius within four hundred miles of Rome was passed.

With Caesar absent in Gaul, Pompey favored Cicero's recall and by August of the year 57 B. C. his return was voted by the popular assembly. He came back to Rome amid demonstrations of joy.

But things were different now. The all-but-totalitarian government of the triumvirs had no room for freedom of speech. The voice of Cicero was silenced. He left in 51 B. C. to administer the province of Cilicia, but was happy to return to Rome where civil storms were threatening.

On January 11, 49 B. C., in open defiance of Pompey and the Senate, Caesar crossed the Rubicon. "The die was cast." The indecisive Cicero sided with Pompey and went to Greece. After Caesar had gained control in the Battle of Pharsalus, the embarrassed Cicero returned to Italy upon the assurance by the generous Caesar that all had been forgiven.

On the Ides of March, 44 B. C., Caesar fell beneath the daggers of conspiracy. With the downfall of the conspirators, Mark Antony tried to usurp the functions of dictator. Cicero now came forward in one last attempt to champion the Roman Republic. Before the Senate and from the rostra he attacked Antony in a series of orations known as the Phillippics. In vain, Antony, Lepidus, and Octavian had formed a second triumvirate. Again there was a blood purge like that of Marius and Sulla. Late in November of 43 the triumvirs published a list of seventeen obnoxious men who were to be put out of the way at once. The name of Marcus Tullius Cicero headed the list.

News of his proscription reached Cicero at his Tusculan villa, some fifteen miles southeast of Rome. From Antium he tried to take ship, but contrary winds drove the boat back to shore somewhat farther south at Formiae. Here Antony's assassins, hot on the trail, overtook Rome's greatest orator as he was being carried in flight on a litter by a band of faithful slaves. In the woods just short of the seacoast they prepared to make one last stand with their master. But Cicero surrendered. His head and hands were struck off and brought back to Rome. There in the Forum, at

Antony's command, they were nailed mute and motionless to the rostra.

Statesman, Orator, and Prose Master

Himself something of a political idealist, Cicero undoubtedly misread his time. In this he was not unlike the American idealist, Woodrow Wilson. He was unable to sympathize with the realism of those dictators who had little patience with the crumbling constitutional government of the Roman Republic. He wavered, he halted, he went now one way now another, always hoping to rescue the old form of government. Meanwhile the reins of government fell into the hands of men of action like Caesar. But that same strongly emotional temperament which made Cicero a poor statesman, made him a great orator. And though many have been harsh in their judgment of him as a statesman, no one denies him supremacy in oratory. His name has been associated with that of the Greek Demosthenes as one of the foremost orators of antiquity.

Cicero's was a talent suited for oratory. He had a mind of wide range, a heart of deep feeling, a keen memory, a fine personal appearance—and with it all a persistent industry in striving to cultivate these natural powers, a sure sense of form, and an easy command of language.

To many of us today, nourished on the more informal me-to-you technique of modern radio, the formal oratorical style of Cicero may seem a bit strange. Our ears are more in tune with the fireside chat of a President Roosevelt than the classical form of a Ciceronic speech. And yet—radio or rostra—at the heart of oratory is that fine art of persuasion which never changes. And it is that spirit, that soul of a speech we must get at. Nor is the more formal style out of date. The speeches of England's prime minister of World War II are rather in the classical tradition. And even the balcony technique of dictatorship reminds us not a little of the Roman rostra—and say what we may about the cause of Hitler or Mussolini, no one can doubt the persuasiveness of their oratory.

We have some fifty complete orations of Cicero today, fragments of twenty others, and the titles of thirty speeches which have been lost. Elsewhere mention is made of his works on oratorical theory and practice (pages 336-341) and his correspondence (pages 328-331). Later in life, during his enforced political inactivity, Cicero turned to philosophy, partly to distract his own mind, partly to make the best of Greek thought available for his countrymen. A dozen or so of these philosophical essays have survived and seven others were known to antiquity. His essays on Old Age *(Dē Senectūte)* and on Friendship *(Dē Amīcitiā)* are still favorites. Though not particularly original in his thought, Cicero did give to Latin a philosophical vocabulary that prepared the way not only for pagan writers, but also for the Latin literature of Christian theology.

This is Cicero—Rome's first orator, master of prose and model of literary style to our day. "He created a language," says the distinguished classical scholar J. W. Mackail, "which remained for sixteen centuries that of the civilized world, and used that language to create a style which nineteen centuries have not replaced, and in some respects have scarcely altered. He stands in prose, like Virgil in poetry, as the bridge between the ancient and modern world."

CICERO TODAY

One never reads a great author of antiquity, such as Cicero, without sometimes being forced to exclaim: How modern the ancients are! Really great literature never grows old; in fact it helps us to understand and interpret what often seems so new to us today. The classics are not merely a sort of Olde Curiosity Shoppe—they are as modern as a department store.

But the student must keep his eyes open for his own needs. For your guidance we list here a large number of topics for discussion. These will guide your thinking as you study the speeches; they will also furnish topics for class discussions, subjects for themes, and problems for Latin clubs. They may even suggest ideas for dramatizations or radio skits.

Topics for Discussion

1. Citizenship and Patriotism in Cicero's Speeches
2. Cicero's High-Mindedness and Sense of Responsibility in Government
3. President Wilson and Cicero: Political Idealists in Conflict with Realistic Men of Action
4. Public Opinion and Politics, Then and Now
5. Cicero's Hankering after the Good Old Days and the Good Old Roman Virtues
6. Success or Failure—an Evaluation of Cicero's Life
7. Democracy and Dictatorship, Old and New
8. Roman Blood Baths and Communist Purges
9. Roman Racketeering and Modern Gangsters
10. Politics or Government—Graft, Bribery, and the Like
11. Provincial Maladministration and Colonial Oppression
12. Criminal Prosecution; Subterfuge Past and Present
13. Cicero and Roman Religion
14. Does the Appeal to Jupiter in the Catilinarians Show a Tendency to Monotheism?

15. Cicero and Divine Providence
16. Cicero's Egotism and the Vanity of Dictators
17. Invective in the First Catilinarian and in Modern Political Campaigns
18. Compromise in Cicero; the Political Idealist and the Real Situation
19. From Rostra to Radio and Television
20. Consul and Senate, President and Congress, Prime Minister and Parliament
21. The Merits of a Television Report by the President at a Time of National Emergency
22. Traces of Wit in the Third Catilinarian
23. Private Life and Public Office; Would Modern Newspapers Countenance the 'Smearing' Cicero Gave Catiline in the First Oration?
24. Ancient Custody and Modern Parole
25. Parliamentary Procedure and Formulae: A Comparative Study of American Congressional and Roman Senatorial Practice
26. The Roman Eagle and the Stars and Stripes on Iwo Jima
27. Roman Praetors in the Third Catilinarian and the American F. B. I.
28. Comparison of Cicero's Story of the Encounter at the Mulvian Bridge, Caesar's Report of a Battle, and a Communique in World War II
29. The Cross-Examination of Volturcius, Cethegus, Lentulus, and the Gauls
30. From Tabellarii to Air Mail: A Study of Ancient Letter Carrier Service and Modern Mail
31. The Character of Catiline as Shown in the Third Oration and in Sallust
32. The Celebration of the Saturnalia and the Feast of Christmas
33 The Looting of Sicily and the Spoils of Present-day Political Machines
34. Boss Verres

35. Court Pleading, Ancient and Modern

36. The *Tribunus Plebis* and Democracy

37. Money Talks; in Latin, English, or Any Language.

38. Hortensius' Stalling for Time and the Technique of Appealing to Higher Courts

39. Roman Reputation for Justice in the Provinces

40. The *Lautumniae* and the Black Hole of Calcutta

41. *Civis Romanus Sum!*

42. Crucifixion in Cicero

43. The Cross-Examination of Verres by Cicero, on the Charge that Gavius Was a Spy

44. Phrases in Cicero Which Literally Have the Flavor of Modern Slang

45. Cicero's Ambition and Industry

46. The Self-Made Statesman: A Sympathetic Study of Marcus Tullius Cicero and Abraham Lincoln.

REVIEW WORD LIST

FOR THIRD YEAR

audācia, ae	*boldness* *daring* *recklessness*
Catilīna, ae, *m.*	*Catiline*
scientia, ae	*knowledge*
vigilia, ae	*night watch* *guard*
oculus, ī	*eye*
incendium, ī	*fire* *conflagration*
conjūrātiō, conjūrātiōnis	*conspiracy* *plot*
Cicerō, Cicerōnis	*Cicero*
fīnis, fīnis, *m.*	*end* (pl.) *territory*
furor, furōris	*rage* *frenzy* *madness*
mōs, mōris, *m.*	*manner* *custom* (pl.) *character*
pestis, pestis	*plague* *ruin*
pūblicus, a, um	*public*
nocturnus, a, um	*nocturnal* *nightly*
quam, *adv.*	*how*
ignōrō, *1, tr.; acc. w. infin.*	*not know* *am unaware* *overlook*

convocō, *1, tr.*	*call together* *summon together*
pateō, patēre, patuī, *2, intr.*	*lie open* *am open* *extend*
vītō, *1, tr.*	*avoid* *shun*
jam, *adv.*	*already* *now*
vērō, *adv. and conj.; postp.*	*in truth* *but* *of course*
jam prīdem **jam diū** **jam dūdum**	*long (since)* *long (ago)*
poena, ae **supplicium, ī**	*punishment* *penalty*
cōnsultum, ī	*decree* *resolution* (of the Senate)
cīvis, cīvis, *m.*	*citizen* *fellow citizen*
orbis (orbis) terrārum (*sometimes* terrae)	*the world*
praetor, praetōris	*praetor*
manus, ūs, *f.*	*hand* *band*
rēs (reī) pūblica (ae)	*state*
rēs (rērum) novae (novārum)	*revolution*
antīquus, a, um	*ancient* *former*
clārus, a, um	*famous* *loud* *clear*
perniciōsus, a, um	*dangerous* *destructive*

prīvātus, a, um	*private* *personal* *personally*
cōnsulāris, e	*of consular rank* *ex-consul* (as a noun)
apertē, ***adv.***	*openly* *plainly*
omnīnō, ***adv.***	*altogether*
dēcernō, dēcernere, dēcrēvī, dēcrētus, ***3, tr.; w. infin. if subject is the same;*** **ut (nē)** ***if subject is different***	*determine* *decide* *decree*
permittō, permittere, permīsī, permissus, ***3, tr.; w. dat. of person; acc. of thing;*** **ut (nē)**	*give over* *entrust*
at, ***conj.***	*but*
quōmodo, ***adv.***	*how*
nēquitia, ae	*criminal negligence* *wickedness*
moenia, moenium	*walls* *fortifications*
jūs, jūris, ***n.***	*right* *justice*
voluntās, voluntātis	*will*
perniciēs, perniciēī	*disaster* *destruction*
improbus, a, um	*wicked* *depraved*
perditus, a, um	*desperate* *abandoned*
crūdēlis, e	*cruel*
modus, ī	*manner* *kind*
ējus modī **hūjus modī**	*of this kind* *of this sort*
nōndum, ***adv.***	*not yet*

potius, ***adv.***	*rather*
comprehendō, comprehendere, comprehendī, comprehēnsus, ***3, tr.***	*grasp* (in a physical or intellectual sense) *arrest*
crēscō, crēscere, crēvī, crētum, ***3, intr.***	*grow* *increase* (in size, power, age, etc.)
dēpōnō, dēpōnere, dēposuī, dēpositus, ***3, tr.***	*lay down* *give up*
mōlior, mōlīrī, mōlītus sum, ***4, tr.***	*undertake*
inveniō, invenīre, invēnī, inventus, ***4, tr.; acc. w. infin.***	*come upon* *find (out)* *discover*
dīligentia, ae	*care* *carefulness*
mēns, mentis	*mind*
coetus, ūs	*meeting* *gathering*
domus, ūs, ***f.***	*home* *house*
nefārius, a, um	*wicked* *impious*
atrōx (*gen.* atrōcis)	*savage* *fierce*
incrēdibilis, e	*unbelievable* *extraordinary*
admīror, ***1, tr.***	*wonder at* *am surprised at*
mūtō, ***1, tr.***	*change*
audeō, audēre, ausus sum, ***2, intr.; w. infin.***	*dare*
ērumpō, ērumpere, ērūpī, ēruptum, ***3, intr.;*** **ex (ē)** ***w. abl.***	*burst forth* *rush forth*
profugiō, profugere, profūgī, profugitum, ***3, intr.***	*flee from* *run away*
custōdiō, ***4, tr.***	*guard*

oblīvīscor, oblīvīscī, oblītus sum, ***3, tr.; w. gen. of persons, gen. or acc. of things, acc. of neuter prons. or adjs.; acc. w. infin.***	*forget*
meminī, meminisse, ***tr.; w. gen. of persons, gen. or acc. of things, acc. of neuter prons. or adjs.; acc. w. infin.***	*remember* *bear in mind*
magis, ***comparative adv.***	*more*
multō, ***abl. of degree of difference***	*much* *by much*
nōn modo . . . sed (etiam) **nōn modo . . . vērum (etiam)**	*not only . . . but (also)*
exitium, ī	*ruin* *destruction*
scelus, sceleris, ***n.***	*crime*
complūrēs, complūra	*several* *many*
immortālis, e	*immortal* *deathless*
hīc, ***adv.***	*here*
plānē, ***adv.***	*clearly* *plainly*
cotīdiē, ***adv.***	*daily*
īdem, eadem, idem	*same*
cōgitō, ***1, tr. and intr.; acc. w. infin.***	*ponder* *think* *contemplate*
vulnerō, ***1, tr.***	*wound*
taceō, ***2, tr. and intr.***	*pass over in silence* *am silent*
cōnfīdō, cōnfīdere, cōnfīsus sum, ***3, intr.; w. dat. of person; abl. of thing; acc. w. infin.***	*trust* *rely on*
līberō, ***1, tr.***	*free* *liberate*
placet, placēre, placuit, placitum, ***2, intr.; w. dat.; w. infin.; acc. w. infin.;*** **ut (nē)**	*it pleases* *it seems good*

dēsīderō, ***1, tr.***	*miss* *long for*
comperiō, comperīre, comperī, compertus, ***4, tr.; acc. w. infin.***	*find out* *discover (as certain)*
ēdūcō, ēdūcere, ēdūxī, ēductus, ***3, tr.***	*lead out*
praedīcō, praedīcere, praedīxī, praedictus, ***3, tr.; acc. w. infin.***	*say* *foretell*
statuō, statuere, statuī, statūtus, ***3, tr.; w. infin.***	*set up* *place* *determine*
dēligō, dēligere, dēlēgī, dēlēctus, ***3, tr.***	*choose* *pick out*
quodsī, ***conj.***	*but if*
aliquandō, ***adv.***	*at some time* *at length*
paulō, ***abl. of degree of difference (modifying*** **ante, post,** ***or a comparative)***	*(by) a little*
paulum, ***adv. or noun w. gen.***	*a little*
comitia, comitiōrum	*assembly* *elections*
exilium, ī	*exile*
tēctum, ī	*roof* *house*
templum, ī	*temple* *shrine*
sevēritās, sevēritātis	*strictness* *sternness*
calamitās, calamitātis	*disaster* *misfortune*
tumultus, ūs	*uproar* *disorder*
īnfestus, a, um	*hostile* *threatening*
extrā, ***prep. w. acc.***	*outside (of)* *beyond*

quamquam, *conj.*	*although* *and yet*
quārē, *adv.* (quā + rē)	*wherefore*
dubitō, *1, tr. and intr.; w. infin.;* dē *w. abl.*	*doubt* *hesitate*
effugiō, effugere, effūgī, *3, tr. and intr.*	*flee from* *escape*
metuō, metuere, metuī, *3, tr.;* nē (nē nōn, ut); *w. infin.*	*fear*
īnsidior, *1, intr.; w. dat.*	*waylay* *plot*
ōdī, ōdisse, *tr.*	*hate*
meā (tuā, suā) sponte	*of my (your, his, their) own accord*
quīdam, quiddam, *defin. pron.*	*a certain one* *a certain thing*
quīdam, quaedam, quoddam	*certain*
fāma, ae	*reputation* *fame* *rumor*
difficultās, difficultātis	*trouble* *difficulty*
turpitūdō, turpitūdinis	*shame* *disgrace*
facinus, facinoris, *n.*	*deed* *misdeed* *outrage*
domesticus, a, um	*of the home* *domestic*
nūper, *adv.*	*recently*
umquam, *adv.*	*ever* *at any time*
vindicō, *1, tr.*	*punish* *deliver* *set free*

stō, stāre, stetī, statum, *1, intr.*	*stand*
sileō, silēre, siluī, *2, intr.*	*am silent* *keep silent*
impendeō, impendēre, *2, intr.; w. dat.*	*overhang* *threaten*
nesciō, *4, tr.; acc. w. infin.*	*not know* *am ignorant*
frequentia, ae	*crowd* *throng*
jūdicium, ī	*judgment* *trial*
odium, ī	*hatred*
aspectus, ūs	*sight* *look* *appearance*
pārēns, pārentis, *c.*	*parent*
jūstus, a, um	*just* *lawful*
obscūrus, a, um	*obscure* *dark*
quidem, *adv.*	*indeed* *at least*
ut, *conj.* **sīc . . . ut, *conj.***	*as* *just as*
careō, carēre, caruī, caritūrus, *2, intr.; w. abl.*	*am without* *want* *lack*
concēdō, concēdere, concessī, concessus, *3, tr. and intr.*	*withdraw* *yield*
opprimō, opprimere, oppressī, oppressus, *3, tr.*	*overwhelm* *surprise*
ēlābor, ēlābī, ēlāpsus sum, *3, intr.*	*slip away* *escape*
cōnspicor, *1, tr.; acc. w. infin.*	*observe* *perceive*

suspicor, *1, tr.; acc. w. infin.*	*suspect*
mālō, mālle, māluī, *tr.; acc. w. infin.*	*prefer*
custōdia, ae	*guard* *custody*
patria, ae	*fatherland* *native land*
vinculum, ī	*bond* (pl.) *chains* (pl.) *prison*
carcer, carceris	*prison*
quaestiō, quaestiōnis	*inquiry* *investigation* *law court*
impūnītus, a, um	*unpunished*
dignus, a, um; *w. abl.*	*worthy (of)*
falsus, a, um	*false*
tacitus, a, um	*silent* *silently* *quiet* *quietly*
habitō, *1, tr.*	*live* *dwell*
impetrō, *1, tr.;* ab (ā) *w. abl. of person; acc. of thing;* ut (nē)	*obtain* (by asking)
jūdicō, *1, tr.; acc. w. infin.*	*judge*
adhibeō, *2, tr.;* ad *w. acc.*	*employ* *use*
valeō, valēre, valuī, *2, intr.; w. infin.*	*am strong* *am influential* *am well*
discēdō, discēdere, discessī, discessum, *3, intr.;* ab (ā), ex (ē), *or* dē *w. abl.*	*depart* *withdraw*
invidia, ae	*envy* *hatred* *unpopularity*

studium, ī	*zeal* *eagerness* *devotion*
adulēscēns, adulēscentis	*young man*
tempestās, tempestātis	*storm* *weather*
cārus, a, um	*dear*
cēterī, ae, a	*the rest (of)* *the remainder*
honestus, a, um	*upright* *honorable*
vix, ***adv.***	*hardly* *scarcely* *barely* *with difficulty*
dummodo, ***conj.***	*if only* *provided only* *as long as*
clāmō, ***1, tr.; acc. w. infin.***	*cry aloud* *shout*
frangō, frangere, frēgī, frāctus, ***3, tr.***	*break* *destroy*
postulō, ***1, tr.;*** **ab (ā)** ***w. abl. of person; acc. of thing;*** **ut (nē);** ***acc. w. infin.***	*demand*
revocō, ***1, tr.***	*call back* *recall*
percipiō, percipere, percēpī, perceptus, ***3, tr.; acc. w. infin.***	*learn of* *perceive*
exaudiō, ***4, tr.; acc. w. infin.***	*catch sound of* *hear*
serviō, ***4, intr.; w. dat.***	*serve*
laetitia, ae	*joy* *gladness*
inimīcus, ī	*enemy* (personal)

gaudium, ī	*delight* *pleasure*
latrōcinium, ī	*robbery* *brigandage*
laus, laudis	*praise*
voluptās, voluptātis	*pleasure*
dexter, dextra, dextrum **dexter, dextera, dexterum**	*on the right* *right*
impius, a, um	*impious* *undutiful*
numquam, *adv.*	*never*
armō, *1, tr.*	*arm* *equip*
concitō, *1, tr.*	*stir up* *instigate*
invītō, *1, tr.*	*invite*
exerceō, *2, tr.*	*train* *carry on*
soleō, solēre, solitus sum, *2, intr.; w. infin.*	*am accustomed*
ējiciō, ējicere, ējēcī, ējectus, *3, tr.*	*throw out*
pariō, parere, peperī, partus, *3, tr.*	*bring forth* *bear*
praemittō, praemittere, praemīsī, praemissus, *3, tr.*	*send ahead*
rapiō, rapere, rapuī, raptus, *3, tr.*	*snatch* *seize*
afferō, afferre, attulī, allātus, *irreg., tr.*	*bring to* *report*
prōficiō, prōficere, prōfēcī, prōfectus, *3, tr.;* ut (nē)	*effect* *accomplish*
trānsferō, trānsferre, trānstulī, trānslātus, *irreg., tr.*	*carry over* *transfer*
veneror, *1, tr.*	*reverence*
perfruor, perfruī, perfrūctus sum, *3, intr.; w. abl.*	*enjoy*

animus, ī	*soul* *mind* *spirit*
auctor, auctōris	*originator* *author* *instigator*
fortitūdō, fortitūdinis	*courage* *bravery*
amor, amōris	*love*
sanguis, sanguinis, *m.*	*blood*
vērus, a, um	*true* *real*
maximē, *adv.*	*especially* *mostly* *mainly*
prope, *adv.*	*almost* *nearly*
cōnflagrō, *1, intr.*	*burn* *am on fire*
ārdeō, ārdēre, ārsī, ārsum, *2, intr.; w. infin.*	*am aflame* *blaze*
ēmittō, ēmittere, ēmīsī, ēmissus, *3, tr.*	*send forth* *send out*
immittō, immittere, immīsī, immissus, *3, tr.*	*send into* *send against*
īnsidiae, īnsidiārum	*ambush* *plot* *snare*
imperītus, a, um; *w. gen.*	*unskilled (in)* *inexperienced (in)*
nōnnūllī, ae, a	*some*
paulisper, *adv.*	*for a short time*
vērē, *adv.*	*indeed* *truly*
īnflammō, *1, tr.*	*set on fire*

congregō, *1, tr.*	*gather into a flock* *gather together*
colligō, colligere, collēgī, collēctus, *3, tr.*	*bring together*
īnscrībō, īnscrībere, īnscrīpsī, īnscrīptus, *3, tr.*	*write on* *inscribe*
intendō, intendere, intendī, intentus, *3, tr.;* ad *or* in *w. acc.*	*stretch to* *am bound for*
comprimō, comprimere, compressī, compressus, *3, tr.*	*check*
patefaciō, patefacere, patefēcī, patefactus, *3, tr.* (*passive,* patefīō)	*open* *disclose*
fātum, ī	*prophetic utterance* *fate* *doom*
domicilium, ī	*abode* *domicile*
verbum, ī	*word*
ignis, ignis, *m.*	*fire*
magnitūdō, magnitūdinis	*size* *greatness*
condiciō, condiciōnis	*condition* *state* (pl.) *terms*
pulcher, pulchra, pulchrum	*beautiful*
manifestus, a, um	*clear* *evident*
salvus, a, um	*safe*
breviter, *adv.*	*briefly*
restō, restāre, restitī, *1, intr.*	*remain*
prōvideō, prōvidēre, prōvīdī, prōvīsus, *2, tr.;* ut (nē)	*see ahead* *provide* *take care*
expōnō, expōnere, exposuī, expositus, *3, tr.; acc. w. infin.*	*explain* *disembark* *line up*

condō, condere, condidī, conditus, *3, tr.*	*found* *build*
opera, ae	*services* *pains* *efforts*
mandātum, ī	*instruction* *order*
frequēns (*gen.* frequentis)	*in large numbers* *crowded*
nōtus, a, um	*known* *well-known*
deinde, *adv.*	*next* *thereupon*
optō, *1, tr.; w. infin.;* ut (nē)	*desire* *hope for* *pray for*
sollicitō, *1, tr.*	*stir up* *tempt*
dēprehendō, dēprehendere, dēprehendī, dēprehēnsus, *3, tr.*	*catch* *catch in the act* *surprise*
offerō, offerre, obtulī, oblātus, *irreg., tr.*	*present* *offer*
dēferō, dēferre, dētulī, dēlātus, *irreg., tr.;* ad *w. acc.*	*carry away* *report (to)*
indicium, ī	*information* *proof*
potestās, potestātis	*power*
īnfīnītus, a, um	*endless* *extensive*
studiōsus, a, um; *w. gen.*	*fond of* *eager for*
aliquis, aliquid	*someone* *something*
aliquis, aliqua, aliquod	*some*

amō, *1, tr.*	*love*
indicō, *1, tr.; acc. w. infin.*	*point out* *accuse*
recitō, *1, tr.*	*read aloud*
cūrō, *1, tr.;* ut (nē)	*care for* *take care*
cēnseō, cēnsēre, cēnsuī, cēnsus, *2, tr.;* ut (nē) ; *acc. w. infin.*	*am of the opinion* *think*
cōnfiteor, cōnfitērī, cōnfessus sum, *2, tr.; acc. w. infin.*	*admit* *confess*
intrōdūcō, intrōdūcere, intrōdūxī, intrōductus, *3, tr.*	*bring in*
legō, legere, lēgī, lēctus, *3, tr.*	*read*
testis, testis, *m.*	*witness*
aptus, a, um; *w. dat.;* ad *w. acc.*	*fitted for* *fitted to*
prīmum, *adv.*	*first*
meritō, *adv.* jūre, *adv.*	*rightly* *justly*
modo, *adv.*	*only* *just now*
palam, *adv.*	*openly*
quōminus, *conj.*	*from* *that . . . not*
dēpellō, dēpellere, dēpulī, dēpulsus, *3, tr.*	*drive away* *expel*
occurrō, occurrere, occurrī, occursum, *3, intr.; w. dat.*	*go to meet*
obeō, obīre, obiī, obitus, *irreg., tr.*	*undergo*
pūniō, *4, tr.*	*punish*
cōnstat, cōnstāre, cōnstitit, *1, intr.; acc. w. infin.*	*it is certain*
accidit, accidere, accidit, *3, intr.; w. dat. of person;* ut (ut nōn)	*it happens*

vērum, ī	*truth* *reality*
monumentum, ī	*monument* *memorial*
externus, a, um	*foreign*
male, *adv.*	*badly* *poorly*
ultrō, *adv.*	*unasked* *unprovoked*
convertō, convertere, convertī, conversus, *3, tr.*	*turn about*
nōlō, nōlle, nōluī, *tr.; w. infin.; acc. w. infin.;* ut (nē)	*am unwilling* *do not wish*
īnfāmia, ae	*dishonor* *disgrace*
ēloquentia, ae	*eloquence*
reus, ī	*defendant* *the accused (person)*
jūdex, jūdicis	*judge* *juror* (voc. pl.) *gentlemen of the jury*
nātiō, nātiōnis	*tribe* *nation*
caput, capitis	*head*
crīmen, crīminis	*accusation* *crime*
accūsō, *1, tr.; w. gen. of the charge*	*accuse*
condemnō, *1, tr.; w. gen. of the charge*	*condemn*
damnō, *1, tr.; w. acc. of person; gen. or abl. of thing*	*harm* *condemn* *sentence*
capite damnāre	*to sentence to death*
adsum, adesse, adfuī, adfutūrus, *irreg., intr.; w. dat.*	*am present* *support*

industria, ae	*exertion* *hard work* *energy*
pecūnia, ae	*money*
nihilum, ī	*nothing*
mercātor, mercātōris	*merchant*
genus, generis, *n.*	*race* *kind*
anteā, *adv.*	*before*
quasi, *adv. and conj.*	*as if* *just as* *nearly*
emō, emere, ēmī, emptus, *3, tr.*	*buy*
vēndō, vēndere, vēndidī, vēnditus, *3, tr.*	*sell*
cōnstō, cōnstāre, cōnstitī, cōnstātum, *1, intr.; w. abl. or gen.*	*cost*
gaudeō, gaudēre, gāvīsus sum, *2, intr.*	*rejoice* *am glad*
necesse est, esse, fuit, *intr.; w. infin.*	*it is necessary*

CLASSIFIED WORD LIST[1]

NOUNS OF THE FIRST DECLENSION

(LIKE *TERRA, AE*)

amīcitia, ae	*friendship*
***causa, ae**	*cause* *reason*
cōpia, ae	*supply* *abundance*
fortūna, ae	*fortune*
fossa, ae	*ditch*
***fuga, ae**	*flight*
Gallia, ae	*Gaul*
glōria, ae	*fame* *glory*
grātia, ae	*favor* *influence* *grace* (in Christian Latin)
***hōra, ae**	*hour*
injūria, ae	*injustice* *wrong*
inopia, ae	*scarcity* *want*
Italia, ae	*Italy*
Marīa, ae	*Mary*
memoria, ae	*memory*
nātūra, ae	*nature*
nauta, ae	*sailor*
porta, ae	*gate*

---

[1] Words marked with an asterisk are second-year words; all others belong to the required vocabulary of the first six units of FIRST YEAR LATIN.

prōvincia, ae	*province*
Rōma, ae	*Rome*
silva, ae	*forest*
terra, ae	*earth* *land*
via, ae	*road* *way*
victōria, ae	*victory*
vīta, ae	*life*

PLURAL NOUNS OF THE FIRST DECLENSION

(LIKE *TERRAE, TERRĀRUM*)

***angustiae, angustiārum**	*defile* *narrow place* *difficulties*
cōpiae, cōpiārum, *f.*	*troops* *forces* (a military term)
grātiae, grātiārum	*thanks*
litterae, lĭtterārum	*letter* (i. e., *an epistle*) *dispatch*

MASCULINE NOUNS OF THE SECOND DECLENSION

(LIKE *SERVUS, Ī*)

ager, agrī	*field*
amīcus, ī	*friend*
***annus, ī**	*year*
Chrīstiānus, ī	*Christian*
Chrīstus, ī	*Christ*
Deus, ī	*God*

dominus, ī	*master* *Lord*
fīlius, ī	*son*
Gallus, ī	*a Gaul*
gladius, ī	*sword*
lēgātus, ī	*envoy* *lieutenant*
locus, ī (*pl.*, loca, locōrum)	*place*
mundus, ī	*world*
mūrus, ī	*wall*
numerus, ī	*number*
nuntius, ī	*messenger* *message*
populus, ī	*people* *nation*
puer, puerī	*boy*
Rōmānus, ī	*a Roman*
servus, ī	*slave* *servant*
***socius, ī**	*companion* *ally*
tribūnus, ī	*tribune*
***ventus, ī**	*wind*
vir, virī	*man*

NEUTER NOUNS OF THE SECOND DECLENSION

(LIKE *BELLUM, Ī*)

auxilium, ī	*help* *aid*
bellum, ī	*war*
caelum, ī	*sky* *heaven*

concilium, ī	*council*
cōnsilium, ī	*plan* *counsel*
frūmentum, ī	*grain* (pl., *crops*)
imperium, ī	*command* *power* *empire*
oppidum, ī	*town*
***peccātum, ī**	*mistake* *sin* (in Christian Latin)
perīculum, ī	*danger*
***pīlum, ī**	*javelin*
praemium, ī	*reward*
***praesidium, ī**	*garrison* *protection*
proelium, ī	*battle*
rēgnum, ī	*kingdom* *royal power*
signum, ī	*standard* *signal* *sign*
tēlum, ī	*dart*
vallum, ī	*wall* *rampart*

PLURAL NEUTER NOUNS OF THE SECOND DECLENSION

(LIKE *BELLA, BELLŌRUM*)

arma, armōrum	*arms*
auxilia, auxiliōrum	*reinforcements*
castra, castrōrum	*camp*
hīberna, hībernōrum	*winter quarters*

impedīmenta, impedīmentōrum	*baggage* *baggage train*

MASCULINE AND FEMININE NOUNS OF THE THIRD DECLENSION

(LIKE *LĒX, LĒGIS*)

***auctōritās, auctōritātis**	*authority* *influence*
Caesar, Caesaris	*Caesar*
***cāritās, cāritātis**	*charity* *love*
centuriō, centuriōnis	*centurion*
cīvitās, cīvitātis	*state*
clāmor, clāmōris	*shouting* *shout*
cōnsul, cōnsulis, *m.	*consul*
***crux, crucis**	*cross*
custōs, custōdis	*guard*
***dolor, dolōris**	*pain* *sorrow*
dux, ducis	*leader*
eques, equitis	*horseman* (pl., *cavalry*)
frāter, frātris (frātrum)	*brother*
homō, hominis	*man*
imperātor, imperātōris	*commander in chief* *general*
labor, labōris	*effort* *toil*
legiō, legiōnis, *f.*	*legion*
lēx, lēgis	*law*
***lībertās, lībertātis**	*liberty*
lūx, lūcis	*light*

māter, mātris (mātrum)	*mother*
mīles, mīlitis	*soldier*
nox, noctis	*night*
obses, obsidis, *c*.	*hostage*
ōrātiō, ōrātiōnis	*speech* *prayer*
ōrdō, ōrdinis, *m*.	*rank* (of soldiers)
pater, patris (patrum)	*father*
pāx, pācis	*peace*
***pes, pedis, *m*.**	*foot* (of an animal, mountain, etc.; or a unit of measure)
prīnceps, prīncipis	*chief* *leading man*
***ratiō, rationis**	*method* *reason* *plan* *way*
rēx, rēgis	*king*
salūs, salūtis	*safety* *welfare* *salvation*
***timor, timōris**	*fear*
vēritās, vēritātis	*truth*
virtūs, virtūtis	*courage* *virtue*
vōx, vōcis	*voice* *cry*

PLURAL NOUNS OF THE THIRD DECLENSION

(LIKE *LĒGĒS, LĒGUM*)

***mājōrēs, mājōrum, *m*.**	*ancestors* *forefathers*

MASCULINE AND FEMININE NOUNS OF THE THIRD DECLENSION

(LIKE *PARS, PARTIS*)

caedēs, caedis	*slaughter*
***classis, classis**	*fleet*
***cohors, cohortis**	*cohort* (a division of a legion containing 600 men)
collis, collis, *m.*	*hill*
gēns, gentis	*tribe*
hostis, hostis	*enemy* (in war)
mōns, montis, *m.*	*mountain*
mors, mortis	*death*
pars, partis	*part*
pōns, pontis, *m.*	*bridge*
urbs, urbis	*city*

PLURAL NOUNS OF THE THIRD DECLENSION

(LIKE *FĪNĒS, FĪNIUM*)

fīnēs, fīnium, *m.*	*territory*
vīrēs, vīrium, *f.	*strength* *force*

NEUTER NOUNS OF THE THIRD DECLENSION

(LIKE *FLŪMEN, FLŪMINIS*)

agmen, agminis	*column* (of soldiers) *army* (on the march)
corpus, corporis, *n.*	*body*
flūmen, flūminis	*river*

iter, itineris, *n*.	*journey* *march* *route*
nōmen, nōminis	*name*
***tempus, temporis, *n*.**	*time*
vulnus, vulneris, *n*.	*wound*

NOUNS OF THE FOURTH DECLENSION

(LIKE *PORTUS, ŪS*)

adventus, ūs	*arrival* *coming*
equitātus, ūs	*cavalry*
exercitus, ūs	*army*
impetus, ūs	*attack*
metus, ūs	*fear*
***passus, ūs**	*a pace* (a measure = 5 Roman feet)
portus, ūs	*harbor*
senātus, ūs	*senate*
spīritus, ūs	*breath* *spirit*

NOUNS OF THE FIFTH DECLENSION

(LIKE *RĒS, REĪ*)

aciēs, aciēī	*battle line*
diēs, diēī, *m*. *(f.)	*day*
fidēs, fideī	*faith* *reliability* *faithfulness*

rēs, reī	*thing* *affair*
spēs, speī	*hope*

ADJECTIVES OF THE FIRST AND SECOND DECLENSIONS

(LIKE *MAGNUS, A, UM*)

aliēnus, a, um	*unfavorable* *another's* *foreign*
altus, a, um	*high* *deep*
angustus, a, um	*narrow*
***barbarus, a, um**	*barbarian* *foreign*
bonus, a, um	*good*
***certus, a, um**	*certain* *fixed*
Chrīstiānus, a, um	*Christian*
cupidus, a, um; *w. gen.*	*eager* *desirous*
***dubius, a, um**	*doubtful* *uncertain*
***extrēmus, a, um**	*outermost* *farthest* *last*
fīnitimus, a, um; *w. dat.*	*neighboring* *next*
***firmus, a, um**	*strong* *vigorous*
idōneus, a, um; *w. dat. or* ad *w. acc.	*suitable* *proper* *convenient*

lātus, a, um	*wide*
longus, a, um	*long*
magnus, a, um	*great* *large*
malus, a, um	*bad*
***maximus, a, um**	*greatest*
***medius, a, um**	*middle*
***meus, a, um**	*my* *mine*
***minimus, a, um**	*smallest*
multus, a, um	*much* (pl., *many*)
novus, a, um	*new*
***optimus, a, um**	*best*
parātus, a, um; *w. pres. infin. or* ad *w. acc.	*prepared (for)*
***parvus, a, um**	*small*
***paucī, ae, a**	*few*
***pessimus, a, um**	*worst*
plēnus, a, um; *w. gen. or abl.*	*full*
***plūrimus, a, um**	*very many* *the greatest number* (pl., *the most*)
***prīmus, a, um**	*first*
proximus, a, um; *w. dat.	*nearest* *next*
***quantus, a, um**	*how much* *how large*
reliquus, a, um	*remaining* *the rest of*
Rōmānus, a, um	*Roman*
sānctus, a, um	*holy* *saint*
***secundus, a, um**	*second*
***summus, a, um**	*highest*

***suus, a, um**	*his (own)* *her (own)* *its (own)* *their (own)*
***tantus, a, um**	*so great*
***tertius, a, um**	*third*
tūtus, a, um	*safe*
***tuus, a, um**	*your* (of one person) *yours* *your own*
***ultimus, a, um**	*farthest* *last*

ADJECTIVES OF THE FIRST AND SECOND DECLENSIONS

(LIKE *MISER, MISERA, MISERUM*)

līber, lībera, līberum	*free*
miser, misera, miserum	*wretched*

ADJECTIVES OF THE FIRST AND SECOND DECLENSIONS

(LIKE *INTEGER, INTEGRA, INTEGRUM*)

integer, integra, integrum	*fresh* *uninjured* *whole*
***noster, nostra, nostrum**	*our* *ours* *our own*
***vester, vestra, vestrum**	*your* (of more than one person) *yours* *your own*

ADJECTIVES OF THE FIRST AND SECOND DECLENSIONS

(LIKE *ŪNUS, A, UM* IN THE GENITIVE AND DATIVE SINGULAR)

***alius, alia, aliud**	*other* *another*
***alter, altera, alterum**	*second* *the other* (of two) *the one* (of two)
***nūllus, a, um**	*no* *none*
***sōlus, a, um**	*alone* *only* (as an adjective)
***tōtus, a, um**	*whole* *all of* *the whole of*
***ūllus, a, um**	*any*
***ūnus, a, um**	*one*
***uterque, utraque, utrumque**	*each* (of two) *both* (of two)

ADJECTIVES OF THE THIRD DECLENSION

(LIKE *GRAVIS, E*)

brevis, e	*short*
commūnis, e	*common*
difficilis, e	*difficult*
facilis, e	*easy*
fortis, e	*brave* *strong*
gravis, e	*heavy* *severe* *serious*

nōbilis, e	*noble* *renowned*
omnis, e	*all* *every*
similis, e; *w. gen. or dat.*	*like* *similar*
***tālis, e**	*such* *of such a kind*
ūtilis, e; ad *w. acc.*	*useful (for)*

ADJECTIVES OF THE THIRD DECLENSION

(LIKE *ĀCER, ĀCRIS, ĀCRE*)

***ācer, ācris, ācre**	*sharp* *fierce* *eager*
***celer, celeris, celere**	*swift*

ADJECTIVES OF THE THIRD DECLENSION

(LIKE *AUDĀX; gen. AUDĀCIS*)

***audāx (*gen.* audācis)**	*daring* *bold* *courageous*

ADJECTIVES OF THE THIRD DECLENSION

(LIKE *DĪLIGĒNS; gen. DĪLIGENTIS*)

***dīligēns (*gen.* dīligentis)**	*careful* *exact*

COMPARATIVE ADJECTIVES

(LIKE *GRAVIOR, GRAVIUS*)

***mājor, mājus**	*greater*
***melior, melius**	*better*
***minor, minus**	*smaller*
***pējor, pējus**	*worse*
***superior, superius**	*higher* *former*
***ulterior, ulterius**	*farther*

IRREGULAR AND MIXED NOUNS AND ADJECTIVES

dī, deōrum (***abl. and dat.*** **dīs**)	*gods*
Jēsūs, ū (***declined:*** **Jēsūs, Jēsū, Jēsū, Jēsum, Jēsū**)	*Jesus*
mīlle passūs** (pl.,*** **mīlia passuum**)	*a mile*
nēmō, nēminis** (**nūllīus, nūllō,** ***and **nūllā** ***usually used in place of*** **nēminis** ***and*** **nēmine**)	*no one*
nihil** (short form:*** **nīl**), ***n., indecl. noun***	*nothing*
parum,** ***indecl. noun; w. gen.	*too little* *not enough*
***plūrēs, plūra**	*more*
plūs, plūris,** ***n.; w. gen.	*more*
quot,** ***indecl. adj.	*how many*
satis,** ***indecl. noun; w. gen.	*enough*
tot,** ***indecl. adj.	*so many*
vīs** (gen.*** **vis** [***rare***]; ***acc.*** **vim**; ***abl.*** **vī**)	*force* *power* *violence*

ADVERBS

ācriter	*bitterly* *eagerly*
***adeō**	*so* *to such a degree*
***bene**	*well*
celeriter	*swiftly*
***cūr**	*why*
***diū**	*a long time* *long* (of time)
diūtius	*longer*
etiam	*also*
***facile**	*easily*
***facilius**	*more easily*
ferē	*almost*
fortiter	*bravely* *strongly*
ibi	*there*
interim	*meanwhile*
***ita**	*so* *in such a manner* *thus*
longē	*far* *by far*
***magis**	*more*
***magnōpere**	*greatly*
***male**	*badly*
***melius**	*better*
***minus**	*less*
***multum**	*much* *greatly*
***nihil**	*not* *not at all*
nōn	*not*

nunc	*now*
***nūper**	*lately*
***parum**	*little* *too little*
***pējus**	*worse*
***plūs**	*more*
posteā	*afterwards*
***prope**	*near*
***propius**	*nearer*
***quam**	*than*
***quō**	*whither* *where* (of motion)
saepe	*often*
***satis**	*sufficiently*
semper	*always*
***sīc**	*so* *in such a manner*
statim	*at once* *immediately*
***tam**	*so* *to such a degree*
tamen	*nevertheless*
tum	*then* *at that time*
***tūtō**	*safely*
***ubi**	*where*
undique	*from all sides* *on all sides*
usque	*all the way (to)* *even (to)* *up (to)*
vehementer	*greatly* *violently*

PRONOUNS

***ego, meī**	*I*
***hic, haec, hoc**	*this*
***ille, illa, illud**	*that* *he, she, it, they,* etc.
***ipse, ipsa, ipsum**	*self*
***is, ea, id**	*that* *he, she, it, they,* etc.
nōs, nostrī	*we*
***quī, quae, quod**	*who* *what* *which* *that*
***quis, quid**	*who* *what*
***suī**	*himself (him)* *herself (her)* *itself (it)* *themselves (them)*
***tū, tuī**	*you* (sing.)
vōs, vestrī	*you* (pl.)

NUMERALS

***centum**	*one hundred*
***decem**	*ten*
***duo, duae, duo**	*two*
mīlle** ***(indecl. adj. in sing.; **mīlia, mīlium,** ***neuter noun in pl.)***	*thousand*
***quattuor**	*four*
***trēs, tria**	*three*

PREPOSITIONS

ab (ā), *w. abl.	*by* (agent) *away from* *from*
ad, *w. acc.*	*to* *until* *at* *for* (with adjectives)
ante, *w. acc.	*before* (of time or place) *in front of*
apud, *w. acc.	*among* *in the presence of*
contrā, *w. acc.	*against* *opposite*
cum, *w. abl.*	*with*
dē, *w. abl.	*down from* *out of* *from* *concerning* *about*
ex (ē), *w. abl.	*out of* *from*
in, *w. abl.*	*in* *on*
in, *w. acc.*	*in* *into* *against* *upon* *onto* *on*
inter, *w. acc.*	*between* *among*
per, *w. acc.*	*through*
post, *w. acc.*	*after* *behind*

praeter, *w. acc.	*except* *past* *contrary to*
prō, *w. abl.*	*in front of (before)* *on behalf of (for)*
propter, *w. acc.*	*on account of*
sine, *w. abl.*	*without*
sub, *w. abl.	*under* *at the foot of*
sub, *w. acc.	*under* *beneath* *up to* *about* } of time *toward* } of time
trāns, *w. acc.*	*across*

OTHER WORDS, IDIOMS, AND PARTICLES

avē, *interjection	*hail!*
causā, *preceded by gen.	*for the sake of*
in perpetuum	*forever*
in prīmīs	*especially* (lit., *among the first things*)
in prīncipiō	*in the beginning*
in saecula saeculōrum	*world without end* *forever*
***nē**[1]	*not* (with commands, wishes, and hortatory subjunctives)
-ne *(added to emphatic word—generally to the verb—and put first in the sentence)	particle used in asking questions

---

[1] **Nē** is also a conjunction; see page 410.

nōnne** ***(generally first in its clause)	word used in asking questions when the answer 'yes' is expected
num** ***(generally first in its clause)	word used in asking questions when the answer 'no' is expected
prīmā lūce	*at dawn*
***utinam**	particle used in wishes
vī** (abl. of*** **vīs**)	*violently* *by force*

VERBS OF THE FIRST CONJUGATION

(LIKE *LAUDŌ*)

adjuvō, adjuvāre, adjūvī, adjūtus, *1, tr.*	*help* *aid*
administrō, *1, tr.*	*manage* *attend to*
appellō, *1, tr.*	*address* *call (upon)*
with two accs.	*call*
appropinquō, *1, intr.; w. dat. or* ad *w. acc.*	*draw near to* *approach*
collocō, *1, tr.*	*place* *station*
comparō, *1, tr.*	*get ready* *prepare*
cōnfirmō, *1, tr.	*encourage* *strengthen*
with acc. w. infin.	*affirm*
conjūrō, *1, intr.	*conspire* *form a conspiracy*

cōnservō, *1, tr.*	*preserve* *spare*
dēmōnstrō, *1, tr.; acc. w. infin.	*show* *point out*
dō, dare, dedī, datus, *1, tr.*	*give*
exīstimō, *1, tr.; acc. w. infin.	*think*
explōrō, *1, tr.*	*reconnoiter* *find out*
expugnō, *1, tr.*	*storm* *take by storm*
exspectō, *1, tr.*	*wait for* *wait*
imperō, *1, tr.; w. dat. of person	*levy (on)*
***with* ut (nē)**	*order* *command*
incitō, *1, tr.*	*incite* *arouse*
laudō, *1, tr.*	*praise*
mandō, *1, tr.; w. dat. of person	*commit* *entrust*
***with* ut (nē)**	*command*
negō, *1, tr.; acc. w. infin.	*deny* *say . . . not*
nuntiō, *1, tr.; acc. w. infin.	*announce* *report*
occupō, *1, tr.*	*seize*
oppugnō, *1, tr.*	*attack* *assault* *storm*
ōrō, *1, tr.;* ut (nē)	*beg* *pray*
pācō, *1, tr.	*pacify*
parō, *1, tr.; w. pres. infin.	*prepare* *get ready*

perturbō, *1, tr.*	*confuse* *disturb*
portō, *1, tr.*	*carry*
pugnō, *1, intr.*	*fight*
*putō, *1, tr.; acc. w. infin.*	*think*
*rogō, *1, tr.;* ut (nē)	*ask* *request*
servō, *1, tr.*	*guard* *keep*
superō, *1, tr.*	*overcome* *conquer* *surpass*
vastō, *1, tr.*	*lay waste* *ravage*
*vetō, vetāre, vetuī, vetitus, *1, tr.; acc. w. pres. infin.*	*forbid*
vocō, *1, tr.*	*call*

VERBS OF THE SECOND CONJUGATION

(LIKE *MONEŌ*)

*commoveō, commovēre, commōvī, commōtus, *2, tr.*	*alarm* *arouse*
compleō, complēre, complēvī, complētus, *2, tr.; w. abl.*	*fill (with)*
contineō, continēre, continuī, contentus, *2, tr.*	*restrain* *hold in*
*dēbeō, *2, tr.; w. pres. infin.*	*ought* *owe*
habeō, *2, tr.*	*have*
*jubeō, jubēre, jussī, jussus, *2, tr.; acc. w. pres. infin.;* ut (nē)	*order* *command*
maneō, manēre, mānsī, mānsūrus, *2, intr.*	*remain*

moneō, ***2, tr.;*** **ut (nē)**	*warn* *advise*
moveō, movēre, mōvī, mōtus, ***2, tr.***	*move*
noceō, nocēre, nocuī, nocitūrus,** ***2, intr.; w. dat.	*harm* *injure*
obtineō, obtinēre, obtinuī, obtentus, ***2, tr.***	*hold* *occupy*
oportet, oportēre, oportuit,** ***2, intr.; acc. w. pres. infin.	*it behooves* *it is necessary*
permoveō, permovēre, permōvī, permōtus,** ***2, tr.	*arouse* *influence*
persuādeō, persuādēre, persuāsī, persuāsum,** ***2, intr.; w. dat.; **ut (nē)**	*persuade*
pertineō, pertinēre, pertinuī, ***2, intr.;*** **ad** ***w. acc.***	*pertain to* *stretch to*
prohibeō,** ***2, tr.; w. abl. of separation	*ward off (from)* *prevent*
respondeō, respondēre, respondī, respōnsus,** ***2, tr.; acc. w. infin.	*answer*
retineō, retinēre, retinuī, retentus, ***2, tr.***	*hold back* *keep*
studeō, studēre, studuī,** ***2, intr.; w. dat. or pres. infin.; acc. w. infin.; **ut (nē)**	*am eager (for)* *strive (after)* *am devoted (to)*
sustineō, sustinēre, sustinuī, sustentus, ***2, tr.***	*sustain* *withstand*
teneō, tenēre, tenuī, tentus, ***2, tr.***	*hold*
terreō, ***2, tr.***	*terrify*
timeō, timēre, timuī, ***2, tr.; w. pres. infin.***	*fear (to)*
videō, vidēre, vīdī, vīsus, ***2, tr.; acc. w. infin.***	*see*

VERBS OF THE THIRD CONJUGATION

(LIKE *MITTŌ*)

***abdō, abdere, abdidī, abditus,** *3, tr. (always with an object in Latin)*	*hide* *conceal*
***addūcō, addūcere, addūxī, adductus,** *3, tr.;* **ut (nē)**	*lead to* *induce* *influence*
agō, agere, ēgī, āctus, *3, tr.*	*drive* *do* *act* *treat* *give* (*w.* **grātiās**)
***animadvertō, animadvertere, animadvertī, animadversus,** *3, tr.; acc. w. infin.*	*attend to* *notice*
cēdō, cēdere, cessī, cessūrus, *3, intr.*	*give way* *yield*
cognōscō, cognōscere, cognōvī, cognitus, *3, tr.; acc. w. infin.*	*learn* *find out*
***cōgō, cōgere, coēgī, coāctus,** *3, tr.; acc. w. infin.*	*bring together* *collect* *force*
***committō, committere, commīsī, commissus,** *3, tr.*	*commit* *allow*
***conjungō, conjungere, conjūnxī, conjūnctus,** *3, tr.*	*join together* *unite*
***cōnscrībō, cōnscrībere, cōnscrīpsī, cōnscrīptus,** *3, tr.; acc. w. infin.*	*enroll* *write*
***cōnstituō, cōnstituere, cōnstituī, cōnstitūtus,** *3, tr.; w. pres. infin.*	*place* *set up* *decide* *determine*
contendō, contendere, contendī, *3, intr.; w. pres. infin.*	*strive* *contend* *hasten*

crēdō, crēdere, crēdidī, crēditus, *3, tr. and intr.; w. dat. of person to whom or in whom; acc. w. infin.	*believe* *trust* *entrust*
dēdō, dēdere, dēdidī, dēditus, *3, tr. (always with an object in Latin)	*give up* *devote* *surrender*
dēdūcō, dēdūcere, dēdūxī, dēductus, *3, tr.*	*lead* *lead away*
dēfendō, dēfendere, dēfendī, dēfēnsus, *3, tr.*	*defend*
dīcō, dīcere, dīxī, dictus, *3, tr.; acc. w. infin.	*say* *tell*
dīligō, dīligere, dīlēxī, dīlēctus, *3, tr.	*love*
dīmittō, dīmittere, dīmīsī, dīmissus, *3, tr.*	*send away* *dismiss*
dispōnō, dispōnere, disposuī, dispositus, *3, tr.	*distribute* *station*
dīvidō, dīvidere, dīvīsī, dīvīsus, *3, tr.	*divide* *separate*
dūcō, dūcere, dūxī, ductus, *3, tr.*	*lead* *guide*
gerō, gerere, gessī, gestus, *3, tr.*	*carry* *carry on* *wage* (*w.* **bellum**)
incendō, incendere, incendī, incēnsus, *3, tr.*	*set fire to* *burn*
incolō, incolere, incoluī, *3, tr.	*inhabit* *dwell in*
***indūcō, indūcere, indūxī, inductus, *3, tr.;* ut (nē)**	*lead in* *lead on* *influence*
īnstruō, īnstruere, īnstrūxī, īnstrūctus, *3, tr.*	*draw up* *equip*
intellegō, intellegere, intellēxī, intellēctus, *3, tr.; acc. w. infin.	*understand* *perceive*

jungō, jungere, jūnxī, jūnctus, *3, tr.	*join* *unite*
mittō, mittere, mīsī, missus, *3, tr.*	*send*
occīdō, occīdere, occīdī, occīsus, *3, tr.*	*kill*
ostendō, ostendere, ostendī, ostentus, *3, tr.; acc. w. infin.	*show* *tell*
pellō, pellere, pepulī, pulsus, *3, tr.*	*drive* *repulse* *rout*
petō, petere, petīvī, petītus, *3, tr.;* ut (nē)	*seek* *beg* *request*
pōnō, pōnere, posuī, positus, *3, tr.*	*put* *place* *set* *pitch* (*w.* **castra**)
premō, premere, pressī, pressus, *3, tr.*	*press* *press hard*
***quaerō, quaerere, quaesīvī, quaesītus, *3, tr.;* ut (nē)**	*seek* *ask*
redūcō, redūcere, redūxī, reductus, *3, tr.	*lead back* *draw back*
relinquō, relinquere, relīquī, relictus, *3, tr.	*leave* *leave behind*
remittō, remittere, remīsī, remissus, *3, tr.	*send back* *return* *release*
repellō, repellere, reppulī, repulsus, *3, tr.	*beat back* *drive back*
reprimō, reprimere, repressī, repressus, *3, tr.	*press back* *check* *restrain*
resistō, resistere, restitī, *3, intr.; w. dat.	*remain behind* *resist* *withstand*

sūmō, sūmere, sūmpsī, sūmptus, *3, tr.	*take* *assume*
tollō, tollere, sustulī, sublātus, *3, tr.	*lift up* (passive, *am elated*) *take away*
trādō, trādere, trādidī, trāditus, *3, tr.*	*hand over*
trādūcō, trādūcere, trādūxī, trāductus, *3, tr.; two accs. or acc. and* trāns *w. acc.	*lead across* *lead over*
vincō, vincere, vīcī, victus, *3, tr.*	*conquer*
vīvō, vīvere, vīxī, vīctūrus, *3, intr.	*live*

VERBS OF THE FOURTH CONJUGATION

(LIKE *AUDIŌ*)

aperiō, aperīre, aperuī, apertus, *4, tr.	*open* *uncover* *expose*
audiō, *4, tr.; acc. w. infin.*	*hear*
conveniō, convenīre, convēnī, conventum, *4, intr.*	*come together* *assemble*
impediō, *4, tr.	*hinder* *impede*
mūniō, *4, tr.*	*fortify* *construct* (*w.* **viam** *or* **viās**)
perveniō, pervenīre, pervēnī, perventum, *4, intr.;* in *or* ad *w. acc.*	*arrive*
reperiō, reperīre, repperī, repertus, *4, tr.; acc. w. infin.	*find (out)*
sciō, *4, tr.; acc. w. infin.	*know*
sentiō, sentīre, sēnsī, sēnsus, *4, tr.; acc. w. infin.	*feel* *perceive* *think*
veniō, venīre, vēnī, ventum, *4, intr.*	*come*

-IŌ VERBS OF THE THIRD CONJUGATION

(LIKE *CAPIŌ*)

accipiō, accipere, accēpī, acceptus, *3, tr.	*receive* *take*
capiō, capere, cēpī, captus, *3, tr.	*take* *capture*
cōnficiō, cōnficere, cōnfēcī, cōnfectus, *3, tr.	*accomplish* *finish* *exhaust*
cōnspiciō, cōnspicere, cōnspexī, cōnspectus, *3, tr.	*observe* *perceive*
***cupiō, cupere, cupīvī, cupītus, *3, tr.; w. pres. infin.; acc. w. infin.;* ut (nē)**	*desire*
dējiciō, dējicere, dējēcī, dējectus, *3, tr.	*hurl down* *cast down*
***efficiō, efficere, effēcī, effectus, *3, tr.;* ut (ut nōn *or* nē)**	*bring about* *cause*
ēripiō, ēripere, ēripuī, ēreptus, *3, tr.; w. dat. of person or thing from which;* ab (ā) *or* ex (ē) *w. abl.	*take away* *save from*
faciō, facere, fēcī, factus, *3, tr.	*do* *make*
fugiō, fugere, fūgī, fugitūrus, *3, intr.	*flee*
interficiō, interficere, interfēcī, interfectus, *3, tr.	*kill*
jaciō, jacere, jēcī, jactus, *3, tr.	*throw* *hurl*
perspiciō, perspicere, perspexī, perspectus, *3, tr.; acc. w. infin.	*view* *inspect* *perceive*
praeficiō, praeficere, praefēcī, praefectus, *3, tr.; w. dat. of thing of which	*put in command of*
recipiō, recipere, recēpī, receptus, *3, tr.	*take back*
with a reflexive pronoun	*withdraw* *recover*

rejiciō, rejicere, rejēcī, rejectus, *3, tr.	*hurl back* *drive back* *repel*
suscipiō, suscipere, suscēpī, susceptus, *3, tr.	*undertake* *take (upon oneself)*

DEPONENT VERBS OF THE FIRST CONJUGATION

(LIKE *LAUDOR*)

arbitror, *1, tr.; acc. w. infin.	*think* *consider*
***cohortor, *1, tr.;* ut (nē)**	*encourage*
cōnor, *1, tr.; w. pres. infin.	*try* *attempt*
***hortor, *1, tr.;* ut (nē)**	*urge* *encourage*

DEPONENT VERBS OF THE SECOND CONJUGATION

(LIKE *MONEOR*)

polliceor, *2, tr.; acc. w. infin. (usually future)	*promise*
***vereor, *2, tr.; w. pres. infin. or* nē (ut)**	*fear (to)*

DEPONENT VERBS OF THE THIRD CONJUGATION

(LIKE *MITTOR*)

cōnsequor, cōnsequī, cōnsecūtus sum, *3, tr.	*follow up* *overtake* *gain*
loquor, loquī, locūtus sum, *3, tr. and intr.	*talk* *speak*

proficīscor, proficīscī, profectus sum, *3, intr.	*set out* *depart*
revertor, revertī, {revertī, / reversus sum,} *3, intr.	*return*
sequor, sequī, secūtus sum, *3, tr.	*follow* *pursue*
ūtor, ūtī, ūsus sum, *3, intr.; w. abl.	*use* *employ* *exercise*

DEPONENT VERBS OF THE FOURTH CONJUGATION

(LIKE *AUDIOR*)

orior, orīrī, ortus sum, *4, intr.	*rise* *arise*
potior, *4, intr.; w. abl. or gen.	*get possession of* *become master of*

DEPONENT *-IŌ* VERBS OF THE THIRD CONJUGATION

(LIKE *CAPIOR*)

aggredior, aggredī, aggressus sum, *3, tr.	*advance to* *attack*
ēgredior, ēgredī, ēgressus sum, *3, intr.	*go out*
morior, morī, mortuus sum, *3, intr.	*die*
patior, patī, passus sum, *3, tr.; acc. w. infin.	*suffer* *allow*
prōgredior, prōgredī, prōgressus sum, *3, intr.	*go forward* *advance* *proceed*

IRREGULAR VERBS

(*EŌ* AND ITS COMPOUNDS)

adeō, adīre, adiī(-īvī), aditus, *irreg., tr.	*go to* *approach* *visit*
eō, īre, īvī (iī), itum, *irreg., intr.	*go*
exeō, exīre, exiī(-īvī), exitum, *irreg., intr.	*go out*
ineō, inīre, iniī(-īvī), initus, *irreg., tr.	*go into* *enter upon*
trānseō, trānsīre, trānsiī(-īvī), trānsitus, *irreg., tr.	*go across* *cross* *pass*

IRREGULAR VERBS

(*FERŌ* AND ITS COMPOUNDS)

cōnferō, cōnferre, contulī, collātus, *irreg., tr.	*bring together* *compare*
with a reflexive pronoun	*betake oneself*
differō, differre, distulī, dīlātus, *irreg., tr.	*scatter* *put off* *differ*
ferō, ferre, tulī, lātus, *irreg., tr.	*bear* *bring* *carry*
īnferō, īnferre, intulī, illātus, *irreg., tr.; w. dat. of person	*bring (upon)* *inflict (upon)* *inspire (in)*
referō, referre, rettulī, relātus, *irreg., tr.	*bring back* *report* *refer*

IRREGULAR VERBS

(*SUM* AND ITS COMPOUNDS)

absum, abesse, āfuī, āfutūrus, *irreg., intr.;* ab (ā) *w. abl.*	*am away* *am distant*
dēsum, deesse, dēfuī, dēfutūrus, *irreg., intr.; w. dat.	*am lacking* *am absent* *fail*
possum, posse, potuī, *irreg., intr.; w. pres. infin.	*am able* *can*
praesum, praeesse, praefuī, praefutūrus, *irreg., intr.; w. dat.	*am over* *am in command of*
sum, esse, fuī, futūrus, *irreg., intr.*	*am*

OTHER IRREGULAR VERBS

***coepī, coepisse, coeptus sum, *tr.; w. pres. infin.*[1]**	*began* *have begun*
***fīō, fierī, factus sum, *intr.;* ut (ut nōn)**	*am made* *am done* *become* *happen*
***volō, velle, voluī, *tr.; w. pres. infin.; acc. w. infin.;* ut (nē)**	*am willing* *wish*

VERBAL IDIOMS

certiōrem (-ēs) faciō, facere, fēcī, factus, *3, tr.; acc. w. infin.;* dē *w. abl.	*inform* (lit., *make more certain)*
cōnsilium capiō, capere, cēpī, captus, *3, tr.	*make a plan*

---

[1] When **coepī** governs a passive infinitive it is changed to the passive form, **coeptus sum**. It is, however, translated as ACTIVE.

in fugam dō, dare, dedī, datus, *1, tr.	*put to flight*
inquit *(with direct quotations only; usually placed after the first word or phrase of the quotation)	*he says* *he said*
inter sē dō, dare, dedī, datus, *1, tr.*	*exchange*
iter faciō, facere, fēcī, factus, *3, tr.	*march* *make a journey*
memoriā teneō, tenēre, tenuī, tentus, *2, tr.; acc. w. infin.*	*keep in memory* *remember*
miserēre; *w. dat. or gen.	*have mercy (on)*
nactus, a, um (*perfect participle of* nancīscor)	*having obtained possession of* *having met with* *having found*
nōlī, *w. pres. infin.* **nōlīte, *w. pres. infin.***	*be unwilling*
pedem referō, referre, rettulī, relātus, *irreg., tr.	*retreat* *fall back*
proelium committō, committere, commīsī, commissus, *3, tr.	*join battle* *begin battle*

CONJUNCTIONS

atque (ac)	*and*
aut	*or*
aut . . . aut	*either . . . or*
autem, *postp.*	*however*
***cum**	*when* *since*
***cum prīmum**	*as soon as*
enim, *postp.*	*for*
et	*and*
et . . . et	*both . . . and*

itaque	*therefore* *and so*
nam	*for*
***nē**	*that . . . not* (in negative purpose clauses and noun clauses after verbs of 'willing') *in order that not* (in negative purpose clauses)
neque	*nor* *and . . . not*
neque . . . neque	*neither . . . nor*
***postquam**	*after*
-que	*and*
***quia**	*because*
***quō**	*that* *in order that* (in purpose clauses containing a comparative adverb or adjective)
***quod**	*because*
***quoniam**	*because*
sed	*but*
sīcut	*as*
***ubi**	*when*
***ut**	*that* (in noun, purpose, and result clauses) *in order that* (in purpose clauses)
***ut prīmum**	*as soon as*

LATIN-ENGLISH VOCABULARY

ab (**ā**), *prep. w. abl.*, by *(agent)*, away from, from.

abdicō, *1, tr.*, abdicate, renounce, resign.

abdō, abdere, abdidī, abditus, *3, tr.*, hide, conceal. *(Always takes an object.)*

abeō, abīre, abiī(-īvī), abitum, *irreg., intr.*, go away, depart.

abhinc, *adv.*, ago.

abhorreō, abhorrēre, abhorruī, *2, intr.; ab (ā) w. abl.*, shrink from, am averse to, am inconsistent with.

abjectus, a, um, dejected, cast down.

abs, *form of preposition **ab**, used before **tē**.*

abscondō, abscondere, abscondī, absconditus, *3, tr.*, put away, conceal, hide.

absēns (*gen.* **absentis**), absent.

absolvō, absolvere, absolvī, absolūtus, *3, tr.*, acquit.

absum, abesse, āfuī, āfutūrus, *irreg., intr.; ab (ā) w. abl.*, am away, am distant.

ac, *conj.*, and; *in comparative clauses*, as, than; **īdem, eadem, idem . . . ac**, the same . . . as.

accēdō, accēdere, accessī, accessum, *3, intr.; ad w. acc.*, come to, approach, am added.

accidit, accidere, accidit, *3, intr.; w. dat. of person; ut (ut nōn)*, it happens; **bene accidit**, it is fortunate (Gr. 659).

accipiō, accipere, accēpī, acceptus, *3, tr.*, receive, take.

accūsātiō, accūsātiōnis, charge, prosecution, method of conducting the prosecution, complaint.

accūsō, *1, tr.; w. gen. of the charge*, accuse.

ācer, ācris, ācre, sharp, fierce, eager.

acerbus, a, um, bitter.

acervus, ī, heap, pile.

aciēs, aciēī, battle line.

ācriter, *adv.*, bitterly, eagerly.

āctiō, āctiōnis, suit, process *(of trial)*, indictment, accusation, hearing.

ad, *prep. w. acc.*, to, until, at, for, before; **ad īnfimum**, to the bottom, at the bottom; **ad multam noctem**, far into the night; **ad ūnum**, to a man, without exception *(generally with **omnēs**)*.

addūcō, addūcere, addūxī, adductus, *3, tr.; ut (nē)*, lead to, induce, influence.

adeō, *adv.*, so, to such a degree; **atque adeō**, and even.

adeō, adīre, adiī(-īvī), aditus, *irreg., tr.*, go to, approach, visit, undergo, encounter.

adhibeō, *2, tr.; ad w. acc.*, employ, use, apply.

adhūc, *adv.*, up to this time, hitherto.

aditus, ūs, approach, access, entrance.

adjiciō, adjicere, adjēcī, adjectus, *3, tr.*, hurl to, add.

adjungō, adjungere, adjūnxī, adjūnctus, *3, tr.; w. dat.; ad w. acc.*, join to.

adjuvō, adjuvāre, adjūvī, adjūtus, *1, tr.*, help, aid.

administrō, *1, tr.*, manage, attend to.

admīror, *1, tr.*, wonder at, am surprised at.

admonitus, ūs, advice, admonition.

adōrō, *1, tr.*, adore.

adsum, adesse, adfuī, adfutūrus, *irreg., intr.; w. dat.*, am present, support.

adulēscēns, adulēscentis, young man.

adulēscentulus, ī, young lad.

adultus, a, um, full grown.

adveniō, advenīre, advēnī, adventum, *4, intr.*, come to, reach, arrive, come.

adventus, ūs, arrival, coming.
advocō, *1, tr.,* call, summon.
aedēs, aedis, temple; *pl.* house.
aedīlitās, aedīlitātis, the aedileship.
aeger, aegra, aegrum, sick, ill.
aequus, a, um, even, level, just; **aequō animō,** with composure, resignedly.
aestus, ūs, heat, tide, swelling.
aeternus, a, um, eternal, everlasting.
afferō, afferre, attulī, allātus, *irreg., tr.,* bring to, report.
afficiō, afficere, affēcī, affectus, *3, tr.; w. abl.,* affect, treat with.
Āfricānus, ī. *See* **Scīpiō Āfricānus.**
ager, agrī, field.
aggredior, aggredī, aggressus sum, *3, tr.,* advance to, attack.
aggregō, *1, tr.,* gather together, add to, join to.
agmen, agminis, column *(of soldiers),* army *(on the march).*
agō, agere, ēgī, āctus, *3, tr.,* drive, do, act, treat, lead; **grātiās agere,** to give thanks, to thank.
ait, he said.
ājunt, they say.
aliēnus, a, um, unfavorable, another's, foreign.
aliquandō, *adv.,* at some time, at length.
aliquantus, a, um, some.
aliquis, aliqua, aliquod, *indefinite adj.,* some, any (Gr. 815).
aliquis, aliquid, someone, something (Gr. 815).
aliquō, *adv.,* somewhere.
aliter, *adv.,* otherwise; **sīn aliter,** but if not.
alius, alia, aliud, other, another.
Allobrogēs, Allobrogum, the Allobroges, *a tribe in southeastern Gaul.*
altāria, altārium, altar *(plural with singular meaning).*
alter, altera, alterum, second, the other *(of two),* the one *(of two).*
altus, a, um, high, deep.
āmēn, amen.
āmēns (*gen.* **āmentis**), mad, insane.
āmentia, ae, madness, folly.
amīcitia, ae, friendship.
amīcus, a, um; *w. dat.,* friendly.
amīcus, ī, friend.
amō, *1, tr.,* love.
amor, amōris, love.
amplus, a, um, large, splendid, magnificent.
an, *conj.,* or, or rather; **utrum . . . an,** whether . . . or.
angelus, ī, angel.
angustiae, angustiārum, defile, narrow place, difficulties.
angustus, a, um, narrow.
animadvertō, animadvertere, animadvertī, animadversus, *3, tr.; acc. w. infin.,* attend to, notice, punish.
animus, ī, soul, mind, spirit; **aequō animō,** with composure, resignedly; **bonō animō sum, esse, fuī, futūrus,** *irreg., intr.,* am of good cheer.
annōn, or not.
annus, ī, year.
ante, *adv.,* before *(time).*
ante, *prep. w. acc.,* before, in front of.
anteā, *adv.,* before; **paulō anteā,** shortly before.
antīquus, a, um, ancient, former.
aperiō, aperīre, aperuī, apertus, *4, tr.,* open, uncover, expose.
apertē, *adv.,* openly, plainly.
apostolicus, a, um, apostolic.
apostolus, ī, apostle.
appellō, *1, tr.,* address, call (upon), appeal to; *w. two accs.,* call.
appropinquō, *1, intr.; w. dat. or ad w. acc.,* draw near to, approach.
aptus, a, um; *w. dat.; ad w. acc.,* fitted to, fitted for.
apud, *prep. w. acc.,* among, in the presence of, near, at the house of, in the works of.
aqua, ae, water.
aquila, ae, eagle, standard.
arbitrium, ī, will, desire, judgment, wish.

arbitror, *1, tr.; acc. w. infin.,* think, consider.
arceō, arcēre, arcuī, *2, tr.,* ward off.
arcessō, arcessere, arcessīvī, arcessītus, *3, tr.,* summon.
ārdeō, ārdēre, ārsī, ārsum, *2, intr.; w. infin.,* am aflame, blaze.
argenteus, a, um, silver.
argūmentum, ī, argument, proof.
arma, armōrum, arms, weapons.
armō, *1, tr.,* arm, equip.
ascendō, ascendere, ascendī, ascēnsus, *3, tr. and intr.; **ad** or **in** w. acc.,* go up, ascend.
aspectus, ūs, sight, look, appearance.
aspiciō, aspicere, aspexī, aspectus, *3, tr.,* glance at, look at.
assequor, assequī, assecūtus sum, *3, tr.,* attain, accomplish, pursue, overtake.
asservō, *1, tr.,* keep, preserve, guard.
assiduē, *adv.,* constantly.
at, *conj.,* but.
atque (ac), *conj.,* and; *in comparative clauses,* as, than; **atque adeō,** and even; **simul atque,** as soon as; **īdem, eadem, idem . . . atque,** the same . . . as.
atrōx (*gen.* **atrōcis**), savage, fierce.
attendō, attendere, attendī, attentus, *3, tr.,* listen to, pay attention, heed.
auctor, auctōris, originator, author, instigator.
auctōritās, auctōritātis, authority, influence.
audācia, ae, boldness, daring, recklessness.
audācter, *adv.,* boldly, bravely.
audāx (*gen.* **audācis**), daring, bold, courageous.
audeō, audēre, ausus sum, *2, intr.; w. infin.,* dare.
audiō, *4, tr.; acc. w. infin.,* hear, listen.
auferō, auferre, abstulī, ablātus, *irreg., tr.,* carry off, take away.
Augustus, ī, Augustus.
auris, auris, ear.
aut, *conj.,* or, **aut . . . aut,** *conjs.,* either . . or
autem, *conj., postp.,* however; **sīn autem,** but if.
auxilium, ī, help, aid; *pl.,* reinforcements.
avārus, a, um, avaricious, greedy.
avē, *interjection,* hail.
āvertō, āvertere, āvertī, āversus, *3, tr.; **ab (ā)** w. abl.,* turn (away) from, am hostile to

baptisma, baptismatis, *n.,* baptism.
barbarus, a, um, barbarian, foreign.
barbarus, ī, a barbarian.
beātus, a, um, blessed, happy.
bellum, ī, war; **bellum gerō, gerere, gessī, gestus,** *3, tr.,* wage war.
bene, *adv.,* well; **bene accidit, accidere, accidit,** *3, intr., or* **bene fit, fierī, factus est,** *irreg., intr.,* it is fortunate (GR. 659).
benevolentia, ae, affection, good will.
bēstia, ae, wild beast.
bibō, bibere, bibī, bibitus, *3, tr.,* drink.
bonus, a, um, good; **bonō animō sum, esse, fuī, futūrus,** *irreg., intr.,* am of good cheer.
brevis, e, short, brief.
breviter, *adv.,* briefly.

cadō, cadere, cecidī, cāsūrus, *3, intr.,* fall, am slain.
caedēs, caedis, slaughter.
caedō, caedere, cecīdī, caesus, *3, tr.,* cut down, fell, strike, beat, kill.
caelestis, e, heavenly.
caelum, ī, sky, heaven.
Caesar, Caesaris, Caesar.
calamitās, calamitātis, disaster, misfortune.
capiō, capere, cēpī, captus, *3, tr.,* take, capture; **cōnsilium capere,** to adopt a plan, to make a plan; **dētrīmentum capere,** to suffer loss; **mente captus (a, um),** beside oneself, out of one's mind, insane.

Capitōlium, ī, the temple of Jupiter Capitoline, the Capitoline Hill.

caput, capitis, head; **capite damnō,** *1, tr.*, sentence to death.

carcer, carceris, prison.

careō, carēre, caruī, caritūrus, *2, intr.; w. abl.*, am without, want, lack.

cāritās, cāritātis, charity, love.

cārus, a, um, dear.

Cassius (ī), **Lūcius** (ī), Lucius Cassius.

castra, castrōrum, camp; **castra pōnō, pōnere, posuī, positus,** *3, tr.*, pitch camp.

cāsus, ūs, chance; **cāsū,** by chance.

Catholicus, a, um, Catholic.

Catilīna, ae, *m.*, Catiline.

Catulus (ī), **Quīntus** (ī), Quintus Catulus.

causa, ae, cause, reason, case, facts of the case; **causā;** *w. gen.*, for the sake of; **quā dē causā,** and for this reason, wherefore, therefore.

cēdō, cēdere, cessī, cessūrus, *3, intr.*, give way, yield.

celer, celeris, celere, swift.

celeriter, *adv.*, swiftly, quickly.

cēnseō, cēnsēre, cēnsuī, cēnsus, *2, tr.; ut (nē); acc. w. infin.*, think, am of the opinion, assess.

centum, *indecl. numeral,* one hundred.

centuriō, centuriōnis, centurion.

certē, *adv.*, certainly.

certus, a, um, certain, fixed, definite; **certiōrem (-ēs) faciō, facere, fēcī, factus,** *3, tr.; acc. w. infin.; dē w. abl.*, inform.

cervīx, cervīcis *(generally plural even when singular in English),* neck.

cēterī, ae, a, the rest (of), the remainder.

Cethēgus (ī), **Gājus** (ī), Gaius Cethegus.

Chrīstiānus, a, um, Christian.

Chrīstiānus, ī, a Christian.

Chrīstus, ī, Christ.

Cicerō, Cicerōnis, Cicero.

Cinna (ae), **Cornēlius** (ī), Cornelius Cinna.

circiter, *adv.*, about.

circum, *prep. w. acc.*, around, about.

circumclūdō, circumclūdere, circumclūsī, circumclūsus, *3, tr.*, enclose about, hedge in.

circumdō, circumdare, circumdedī, circumdatus, *1, tr.*, put around, surround, encompass.

circumstō, circumstāre, circumstetī, *1, tr.*, stand around, surround.

cīvīlis, e, civil.

cīvis, cīvis, *m.*, citizen, fellow citizen.

cīvitās, cīvitātis, state, citizenship.

clam, *adv.*, secretly.

clāmitō, *1, tr.; acc. w. infin.*, keep shouting.

clāmō, *1, tr.; acc. w. infin.*, cry aloud, shout.

clāmor, clāmōris, shouting, shout.

clārus, a, um, famous, loud, clear.

classis, classis (*abl.* **e** *or* **ī**), fleet.

coepī, coepisse, coeptus sum, *tr.; w. pres. infin.*, began, have begun (Gr. page 82, footnote 1).

coetus, ūs, meeting, gathering, company.

cōgitō, *1, tr. and intr.; acc. w. infin.; dē w. abl.*, ponder, think, contemplate.

cognitor, cognitōris, voucher, witness of one's identity.

cognōscō, cognōscere, cognōvī, cognitus, *3, tr.; acc. w. infin.*, learn, find out, recognize.

cōgō, cōgere, coēgī, coāctus, *3, tr.; acc. w. pres. infin.*, drive together, collect, force, compel.

cohors, cohortis, cohort.

cohortor, *1, tr.; ut (nē),* encourage.

collēga, ae, *m.*, colleague, partner in office.

colligō, colligere, collēgī, collēctus, *3, tr.*, bring together, collect, gather together.

collis, collis, *m.*, hill.

collocō, *1, tr.,* place, station.
color, colōris, color.
comes, comitis, *c.,* companion.
comitātus, ūs, retinue.
comitia, comitiōrum, assembly, elections.
comitium, ī, place of assembly; *pl.,* assembly, elections.
commemorātiō, commemorātiōnis, mention, proclaiming.
commemorō, *1, tr.,* repeat, relate, mention.
commendātiō, commendātiōnis, excellence, worth.
committō, committere, commīsī, commissus, *3, tr.,* commit, allow; **proelium committere,** to join battle, to begin battle.
commoveō, commovēre, commōvī, commōtus, *2, tr.,* alarm, arouse.
commūnis, e, common.
commūtō, *1, tr.,* change.
comparō, *1, tr.,* get ready, prepare.
compellō, compellere, compulī, compulsus, *3, tr.,* drive together, collect.
comperiō, comperīre, comperī, compertus, *4, tr.; acc. w. infin.,* find out, discover (as certain).
competītor, competītōris, rival, competitor.
compleō, complēre, complēvī, complētus, *2, tr.; w. abl.,* fill (with).
complūrēs, complūra, several, many.
comprehendō, comprehendere, comprehendī, comprehēnsus, *3, tr.,* grasp, arrest, take, seize.
comprimō, comprimere, compressī, compressus, *3, tr.,* check, repress, suppress.
cōnātus, ūs, attempt.
concēdō, concēdere, concessī, concessus, *3, tr.,* withdraw, yield, allow.
concidō, concidere, concidī, *3, intr.,* fall down, collapse.
concilium, ī, council, assembly.
concitō, *1, tr.,* stir up, instigate, arouse, agitate.
concordia, ae, concord, union, agreement.
concursus, ūs, running together, rally, assemblage, attack.
condemnō, *1, tr.; w. gen. of the charge,* condemn.
condiciō, condiciōnis, condition, state, terms.
condō, condere, condidī, conditus, *3, tr.,* build, found, conceal.
cōnferō, cōnferre, contulī, collātus, *irreg., tr.,* bring together, compare, set, appoint; *w. reflexive pronoun,* betake oneself.
cōnfessiō, cōnfessiōnis, admission, confession.
cōnficiō, cōnficere, cōnfēcī, cōnfectus, *3, tr.,* accomplish, finish, exhaust.
cōnfīdō, cōnfīdere, cōnfīsus sum, *3, intr.; w. dat. of person; abl. of thing; acc. w. infin.,* trust, rely on.
cōnfirmō, *1, tr.,* encourage, strengthen; *w. acc. w. infin.,* affirm.
cōnfiteor, cōnfitērī, cōnfessus sum, *2, tr.; acc. w. infin.,* confess, admit.
cōnflagrō, *1, intr.,* burn, am on fire.
congregō, *1, tr.,* gather into a flock, gather together.
conjiciō, conjicere, conjēcī, conjectus, *3, tr.,* hurl, throw, cast; **in vincula conjicere,** to throw into prison.
conjungō, conjungere, conjūnxī, conjūnctus, *3, tr.,* join together, unite.
conjūnx, conjugis, *c.,* husband, wife.
conjūrātī, conjūrātōrum, conspirators.
conjūrātiō, conjūrātiōnis, conspiracy, plot.
conjūrātor, conjūrātōris, conspirator.
conjūrō, *1, intr.,* conspire, form a conspiracy.
cōnor, *1, tr.; w. pres. infin.,* try, attempt.
Cōnsānus, a, um, of Consa, *a town in Italy.*
cōnscelerātus, a, um, criminal.
cōnscientia, ae, knowledge, consciousness.

cōnscrībō, cōnscrībere, cōnscrīpsī, cōnscrīptus, *3, tr.; acc. w. infin.*, enroll, write; **patrēs (patrum) cōnscrīptī (cōnscrīptōrum),** senators, gentlemen of the Senate.

cōnsēnsiō, cōnsēnsiōnis, agreement.

cōnsequor, cōnsequī, cōnsecūtus sum, *3, tr.*, follow up, overtake, gain.

cōnservō, *1, tr.*, preserve, spare, save.

cōnsilium, ī, plan, counsel, council, deliberative body; **cōnsilium capiō, capere, cēpī, captus,** *3, tr.*, adopt a plan, make a plan.

cōnspectus, ūs, sight, vision.

cōnspiciō, cōnspicere, cōnspexī, cōnspectus, *3, tr.*, observe, perceive.

cōnspicor, *1, tr.; acc. w. infin.*, observe, perceive.

cōnstanter, *adv.*, steadfastly.

Constantīnus, ī, Constantine, *a Roman emperor.*

cōnstat, cōnstāre, cōnstitit, *1, intr.; acc. w. infin.*, it is certain, it is established.

cōnstituō, cōnstituere, cōnstituī, cōnstitūtus, *3, tr.; w. pres. infin.*, place, set up, decide, determine.

cōnstō, cōnstāre, cōnstitī, cōnstātum, *1, intr.; w. abl. or gen.*, cost.

consubstantiālis, e, of the same nature, consubstantial.

cōnsuētūdō, cōnsuētūdinis, custom, habit, usage, practice.

cōnsul, cōnsulis, *m.*, consul.

cōnsulāris, e, of consular rank; *as a noun,* ex-consul.

cōnsulātus, ūs, consulship, consulate.

cōnsulō, cōnsulere, cōnsuluī, cōnsultus, *3, tr. and intr.; w. acc. of person consulted; dat. of person whose interests are consulted,* consult, ask one's advice, plan, take thought for.

consultum, ī, decree, resolution *(of the Senate).*

cōnsūmō, cōnsūmere, cōnsūmpsī, cōnsūmptus, *3, tr.*, use up.

contāminō, *1, tr.*, dishonor, pollute.

contemnō, contemnere, contempsī, contemptus, *3, tr.*, despise, contemn, scorn.

contendō, contendere, contendī, *3, intr.; w. pres. infin.*, strive, contend, hasten.

contentus, a, um, contented, satisfied.

contineō, continēre, continuī, contentus, *2, tr.*, restrain, hold in.

contingō, contingere, contigī, *3, intr.; w. dat.; **ut (ut nōn),*** happen to, fall to the lot of.

cōntiō, cōntiōnis, public meeting, mass meeting.

contrā, *prep. w. acc.*, against, opposite.

contrōversia, ae, dispute, quarrel.

contumēlia, ae, reproach, indignity, affront.

conveniō, convenīre, convēnī, conventum, *4, intr.*, come together, assemble.

convenit, convenīre, convēnit, *4, intr.; w. infin.*, it is necessary, it is suitable.

conventus, ūs, meeting, assembly, assizes, community.

convertō, convertere, convertī, conversus, *3, tr.*, turn about, change, wheel about.

convocō, *1, tr.*, call together, summon together.

cōpia, ae, supply, abundance; *pl.*, troops, forces.

Cornēlia, ae, Cornelia, *a Roman name.*

corpus, corporis, *n.*, body.

corrumpō, corrumpere, corrūpī, corruptus, *3, tr.*, corrupt, tamper with.

cotīdiē, *adv.*, every day, daily.

crēdō, crēdere, crēdidī, crēditus, *3, tr. and intr.; w. dat. of person to whom or in whom; acc. w. infin.*, believe, trust, entrust.

crēscō, crēscere, crēvī, crētum, *3, intr.*, grow, increase *(in size, power, age, etc.).*

crīmen, crīminis, accusation, crime, charge.

cruciātus, ūs, torture.

crucifīgō, crucifīgere, crucifīxī, crucifīxus, *3, tr.*, crucify.
crūdēlis, e, cruel.
crūdēlitas, crūdēlitātis, savagery, cruelty, severity.
crūdēliter, *adv.*, cruelly, ruthlessly.
crux, crucis, cross.
cum, *prep. w. abl.*, with.
cum, *conj.*, when, since, although; **cum prīmum,** *conj.*, as soon as; **tum . . . cum,** at the time when.
cūnctus, a, um, all, entire.
cupiditās, cupiditātis, desire, eagerness.
cupidus, a, um; *w. gen.*, eager, desirous.
cupiō, cupere, cupīvī, cupītus, *3, tr.; w. pres. infin.; acc. w. infin.;* ***ut (nē)***, desire.
cūr, *interrog. adv.*, why.
cūra, ae, care, concern.
cūrō, *1, tr.;* ***ut (nē)***, care for, take care (GR. 883).
custōdia, ae, guard, custody, protection, sentinel.
custōdiō, *4, tr.*, guard.
custōs, custōdis, *m.*, watchman, guard.
Cypriānus (ī), Thascius (ī), Thascius Cyprian, *bishop of Carthage.*

damnō, *1, tr.; w. acc. of person; gen. or abl. of thing*, harm, condemn, sentence *(to punishment)*; **capite damnāre,** to sentence to death.
dē, *prep. w. abl.*, down from, out of, from, concerning, about, for, according to; **dē pecūniīs repetundīs,** concerning extortion.
dēbeō, *2, tr.; w. pres. infin.; w. dat.*, ought, owe.
dēbilis, e, powerless.
dēbilitātus, a, um, stricken, broken.
decem, *indecl. numeral*, ten.
dēcernō, dēcernere, dēcrēvī, dēcrētus, *3, tr.; w. infin. if subject is same;* ***ut (nē)*** *if subject is different*, determine, decide, decree.
decimus, a, um, tenth.
dēdō, dēdere, dēdidī, dēditus, *3, tr.*, give up, devote, surrender. *(Always takes an object.)*
dēdūcō, dēdūcere, dēdūxī, dēductus, *3, tr.*, lead, lead away.
dēfendō, dēfendere, dēfendī, dēfēnsus, *3, tr.*, defend.
dēfēnsiō, dēfēnsiōnis, the defense.
dēfēnsor, dēfēnsōris, advocate, defender, attorney.
dēferō, dēferre, dētulī, dēlātus, *irreg., tr.;* ***ad*** *w. acc.*, carry away, report (to).
dēficiō, dēficere, dēfēcī, dēfectus, *3, tr. and intr.;* ***ab (ā)*** *w. abl.*, fail, give out, revolt from.
dēfīgō, dēfīgere, dēfīxī, dēfīxus, *3, tr.;* ***in*** *w. abl.;* ***in*** *w. acc.*, fix firmly, plant.
deinde, *adv.*, next, thereupon.
dējiciō, dējicere, dējēcī, dējectus, *3, tr.*, hurl down, cast down.
dēlectō, *1, tr.*, delight, charm.
dēleō, dēlēre, dēlēvī, dēlētus, *2, tr.*, destroy.
dēligō, *1, tr.*, fasten (down), tie.
dēligō, dēligere, dēlēgī, dēlēctus, *3, tr.*, choose, pick out.
dēlūbrum, ī, shrine.
dēmēns (*gen.* **dēmentis**), mad, wild.
dēmenter, *adv.*, madly, foolishly.
dēmōnstrō, *1, tr.; acc. w. infin.*, show, point out.
dēnique, *adv.*, at length, at last, thereupon, finally.
dēnuntiō, *1, tr.*, announce, threaten.
dēpellō, dēpellere, dēpulī, dēpulsus, *3, tr.*, drive away, expel.
dēpōnō, dēpōnere, dēposuī, dēpositus, *3, tr.*, lay down, give up.
dēposcō, dēposcere, dēpoposcī, *3, tr.*, demand, claim.
dēprecor, *1, tr.*, beg (off), implore.
dēprehendō, dēprehendere, dēprehendī, dēprehēnsus, *3, tr.*, catch, catch in the act, surprise.

dēscendō, dēscendere, dēscendī, dēscēnsum, *3, intr.*, climb down, descend.

dēscrībō, dēscrībere, dēscrīpsī, dēscrīptus, *3, tr.*, map out, draw up.

dēsīderō, *1, tr.*, miss, long for.

dēsignātus, a, um, elected, elect.

dēsignō, *1, tr.*, point out, designate.

dēsinō, dēsinere, dēsīvī, dēsitus, *3, intr.*, stop, cease.

dēsistō, dēsistere, dēstitī, dēstitūrus, *3, intr.; w. infin.*, cease, give up.

dēspiciō, dēspicere, dēspexī, dēspectus, *3, tr.*, despise.

dēsum, deesse, dēfuī, dēfutūrus, *irreg., intr.; w. dat.*, am lacking, am absent, fail, am wanting.

dētrīmentum, ī, loss, harm; **dētrīmentum capiō, capere, cēpī, captus,** *3, tr.*, suffer loss.

Deus, ī (*voc.* **Deus;** *pl., nom.* **dī** *or* **diī;** *abl. and dat.* **dīs** *or* **diīs**), God.

dēvītō, *1, tr.*, avoid.

dexter, dextera (dextra), dexterum (dextrum), on the right, right.

dīcō, dīcere, dīxī, dictus, *3, tr.; acc. w. infin.*, say, tell.

dictitō, *1, tr.*, keep saying, boast, allege.

diēs, diēī, *m. (f.)*, day; **hodiernō diē,** today, this day; **perendinō diē,** on the day after tomorrow.

differō, differre, distulī, dīlātus, *irreg., tr.*, scatter, put off, differ.

difficilis, e, difficult.

difficultās, difficultātis, difficulty, trouble.

dignitās, dignitātis, worth, esteem, honor.

dignus, a, um; *w. abl.*, worthy (of).

dījūdicō, *1, tr.*, decide.

dīligēns (*gen.* **dīligentis**), careful, exact.

dīligenter, *adv.*, carefully.

dīligentia, ae, care, carefulness, diligence.

dīligō, dīligere, dīlēxī, dīlēctus, *3, tr.*, love.

dīmittō, dīmittere, dīmīsī, dīmissus *3, tr.*, send away, dismiss.

discēdō, discēdere, discessī, discessum, *3, intr.; ab (ā), ex (ē), or dē w. abl.*, depart, withdraw, go away.

discessus, ūs, departure, withdrawal, absence.

disciplīna, ae, training, instruction, system, obedience.

discipulus, ī, disciple, pupil.

discrībō, discrībere, discrīpsī, discrīptus, *3, tr.*, apportion, divide.

discrīmen, discrīminis, crisis, difference, distinction.

dispōnō, dispōnere, disposuī, dispositus, *3, tr.*, distribute, station.

dissēnsiō, dissēnsiōnis, strife, struggle, quarrel.

dissimulō, *1, tr.*, disguise, dissemble, pretend not to.

distribuō, distribuere, distribuī, distribūtus, *3, tr.; w. dat.; in w. acc.*, distribute among, allot.

diū, *adv.*, a long time, long *(of time)*; **jam diū,** long ago, long since, now for a long time *(w. pres. indicative)*.

diūtissimē, *adv.*, longest.

diūtius, *comparative adv.*, longer.

dīvidō, dīvidere, dīvīsī, dīvīsus, *3, tr.*, divide, separate.

dīvīnitās, dīvīnitātis, the divinity.

dīvīnitus, *adv.*, providentially, from heaven.

dīvīnus, a, um, divine.

dīvīsor, dīvīsōris, bribery agent.

dō, dare, dedī, datus, *1, tr.*, give; **in fugam dare,** to put to flight; **inter sē dare,** to exchange; **operam dare,** to take pains, to give attention.

doceō, docēre, docuī, doctus, *2, tr.; acc. w. infin.*, teach, inform.

doctrīna, ae, teaching, doctrine.

dolor, dolōris, pain, sorrow, grief.

domesticus, a, um, of the home, domestic.

domicilium, ī, abode, domicile.

dominus, ī, master, Lord.

domus, ūs, *f.*, house, home (Gr. 915-917).
dubitō, *1, tr. and intr.; w. infin.; dē w. abl.*, doubt, hesitate.
dubius, a, um, doubtful, uncertain.
dūcō, dūcere, dūxī, ductus, *3, tr.*, lead, guide.
dūdum, *w.* **jam,** already, now for a long time *(w. pres. indicative)*, then for a long time *(w. imperfect indicative)*.
dum, *conj.*, until, while (Gr. 564-570).
dummodo, *conj.*, if only, provided only, as long as (Gr. 594).
duo, duae, duo, two (Gr. 115).
duodecimus, a, um, twelfth.
dux, ducis, leader.

ē (ex), *prep. w. abl.*, from, out of, away from.
ecce, *interjection*, behold.
ecclēsia, ae, church.
ēditus, a, um, elevated, high.
ēdō, ēdere, ēdidī, ēditus, *3, tr.*, put forth, state, explain.
ēdūcō, ēdūcere, ēdūxī, ēductus, *3, tr.*, lead out, draw out.
efferō, efferre, extulī, elātus, *irreg., tr.*, carry out, bear out; *passive*, am elated.
efficiō, efficere, effēcī, effectus, *3, tr.; ut (ut nōn or nē)*, bring about, cause.
effrēnātus, a, um, unbridled.
effugiō, effugere, effūgī, *3, tr. and intr.*, flee from, escape.
ego, meī, I.
ēgredior, ēgredī, ēgressus sum, *3, intr.*, go out, march out.
ējiciō, ējicere, ējēcī, ējectus, *3, tr.*, throw out.
ējus modī (ējusmodī), of this kind, of this sort.
ēlābor, ēlābī, ēlāpsus sum, *3, intr.*, slip away, escape.
ēligō, ēligere, ēlēgī, ēlēctus, *3, tr.*, pick out, choose.
ēloquentia, ae, eloquence.
ēminēns (*gen.* **ēminentis**), illustrious, eminent.
ēmittō, ēmittere, ēmīsī, ēmissus, *3, tr.*, send forth, send out.
emō, emere, ēmī, emptus, *3, tr.*, buy.
ēmorior, ēmorī, ēmortuus sum, *3, intr.*, die.
enim, *conj., postp.*, for.
eō, *adv.*, thither, to that place, there; **quō . . . eō,** *used in comparing comparatives* (Gr. 607); **usque eō,** to such an extent.
eō, īre, īvī (iī), **itum,** *irreg., intr.*, go.
eōdem, *adv.*, to that same place, in the same place.
eques, equitis, horseman; *pl.*, cavalry.
equitātus, ūs, cavalry.
ergā, *prep. w. acc.*, towards *(generally of friendly feelings)*, for.
ergō, *adv.*, accordingly, therefore, then.
ēripiō, ēripere, ēripuī, ēreptus, *3, tr.; w. dat. of person or thing from which; ab (ā) or ex (ē) w. abl.*, take away, save from, snatch.
ērumpō, ērumpere, ērūpī, ēruptum, *3, intr.; ex (ē) w. abl.*, burst forth, rush forth.
et, *conj.*, and; **et . . . et,** *conjs.*, both . . . and.
etenim, *conj.*, (and) really, (and) in fact, (for) truly.
etiam, *adv.*, also, even.
etiamsī, *conj.*, although, even if.
etsī, *conj.*, although, even if.
ēvertō, ēvertere, ēvertī, ēversus, *3, tr.*, overthrow, upturn.
ēvocātor, ēvocātōris, one who calls to arms, recruiter, enlister, drafter.
ex (ē), *prep. w. abl.*, out of, from, away from.
exaudiō, *4, tr.; acc. w. infin.*, catch sound of, hear.
excelsīs, in, in the highest.
excipiō, excipere, excēpī, exceptus, *3, tr.*, except, meet, receive.
excitō, *1, tr.*, excite, arouse.

exclūdō, exclūdere, exclūsī, exclūsus, *3, tr.,* exclude, shut out.
exeō, exīre, exiī(-īvī), exitum, *irreg., intr.,* go out.
exerceō, *2, tr.,* train, carry on.
exercitus, ūs, army.
exilium, ī, exile.
exīstimātiō, exīstimātiōnis, opinion, reputation.
exīstimō, *1, tr.; acc. w. infin.,* think.
exitium, ī, ruin, destruction.
expellō, expellere, expulī, expulsus, *3, tr.,* drive out.
explicō, *1, tr.,* unfold, develop, state, explain.
explōrō, *1, tr.,* reconnoiter, find out.
expōnō, expōnere, exposuī, expositus, *3, tr.; acc. w. infin.,* explain, disembark, line up.
expugnō, *1, tr.,* storm, take by storm.
exsistō, exsistere, exstitī, *3, intr.,* exist.
exspectō, *1, tr.,* wait for, wait.
exstinguō, exstinguere, exstīnxī, exstīnctus, *3, tr.,* put out, quench, destroy.
exsul, exsulis, an exile.
externus, a, um, foreign.
exterus, a, um, foreign.
extrā, *prep. w. acc.,* outside (of), beyond.
extrēmus, a, um, outermost, farthest, last.

facile, *adv.,* easily.
facilis, e, easy.
facinus, facinoris, *n.,* deed, misdeed, outrage, crime.
faciō, facere, fēcī, factus, *3, tr.,* do, make; *w. gen. of indefinite value,* regard; **certiōrem (-ēs) facere;** *acc. w. infin.; dē w. abl.,* to inform; **fīnem facere;** *w. gen.,* to finish; **iter facere,** to march, to make a journey; **vim facere,** to use force.
factor, factōris, creator.
factum, ī, thing done, deed.
facultās, facultātis; *w. gen.,* ability, opportunity (for).
falcāriōs, inter, in the section of the scythe makers.
fallō, fallere, fefellī, falsus, *3, tr.,* deceive, cheat, play (someone) false.
falsus, a, um, false.
fāma, ae, fame, reputation, rumor.
famēs, famis, hunger, starvation.
familia, ae, family, household.
fātālis, e, fated, destined.
fateor, fatērī, fassus sum, *2, tr.; acc. w. infin.,* admit, confess.
fātum, ī, prophetic utterance, fate, doom.
fax, facis, torch, firebrand.
fēlix (*gen.* **fēlīcis**), happy, fortunate.
ferē, *adv.,* almost.
feriō, ferīre, *4, tr.,* strike.
ferō, ferre, tulī, lātus, *irreg., tr.,* bear, bring, carry, endure; **graviter ferre,** to take hard (ill).
ferrum, ī, iron, steel, spearpoint.
Festus, ī, Festus, *a Roman governor.*
fidēs, fideī, faith, reliability, faithfulness.
fīdūcia, ae, trust, confidence.
fīgō, fīgere, fīxī, fīxus, *3, tr.,* fasten, drive, fix.
fīlius, ī, son.
fīnēs, fīnium, *m.,* territory, boundary.
fingō, fingere, fīnxī, fictus, *3, tr.,* invent.
fīnis, fīnis, *m.,* end, termination; *pl.,* boundary, territory; **fīnem faciō, facere, fēcī, factus,** *3, tr.; w. gen.,* finish.
fīnitimus, a, um; *w. dat.,* neighboring, next.
fīō, fierī, factus sum, *intr.; ut (ut nōn),* am made, am done, become, happen; **bene fit,** it is fortunate (GR. 659); **certior fierī,** to be informed.
firmiter, *adv.,* firmly, steadfastly.
firmō, *1, tr.,* strengthen, make secure, establish.

firmus, a, um, strong, vigorous.
fiscus, ī, a basket *(used for transporting coins).*
Flaccus (ī), **Lūcius** (ī), Lucius Flaccus, *a praetor.*
flāgitium, ī, outrage, shameful deed.
flamma, ae, flame.
flūmen, flūminis, river.
forās, *adv.,* forth, out of doors.
fortasse, *adv.,* perhaps, probably, possibly.
fortis, e, brave, strong.
fortiter, *adv.,* bravely, strongly.
fortitūdō, fortitūdinis, courage, bravery.
fortūna, ae, fortune.
fortūnātus, a, um, blessed, fortunate.
forum, ī, forum.
fossa, ae, ditch.
frangō, frangere, frēgī, frāctus, *3, tr.,* break, destroy.
frāter, frātris (frātrum), brother.
frāternus, a, um, fraternal.
frequēns (*gen.* **frequentis**), in large numbers, crowded.
frequentia, ae, throng, crowd, assembly.
fretum, ī, strait *(of water).*
frīgus, frīgoris, *n.,* cold.
frōns, frontis, forehead, brow, front.
frūctus, ūs, fruit, produce, profit.
frūmentum, ī, grain; *pl.,* crops.
fuga, ae, flight; **in fugam dō, dare, dedī, datus,** *1, tr.,* put to flight.
fugiō, fugere, fūgī, fugitūrus, *3, tr. and intr.,* flee.
fugitīvus, ī, fugitive, deserter.
fūnestus, a, um, deadly, fatal, destructive.
furiōsus, a, um, mad, raging.
Fūrius (ī), **Pūblius** (ī), Publius Furius.
furor, furōris, rage, frenzy, madness.
fūrtum, ī, theft, robbery.

Gabīnus (ī), **Cimber** (**Cimbrī**), Cimber Gabinus, *a conspirator.*
Gallia, ae, Gaul.
Gallus, ī, a Gaul.
gaudeō, gaudēre, gāvīsus sum, *2, intr.,* rejoice, am glad.
gaudium, ī, delight, pleasure, joy.
Gāvius (ī), **Pūblius** (ī), Publius Gavius, *a Roman citizen carrying on business in Sicily.*
gelidus, a, um, icy-cold, frosty.
gemitus, ūs, groan.
genitus, a, um, begotten, born.
gēns, gentis, tribe; **ubinam gentium,** where in the world.
genus, generis, *n.,* race, kind.
Germānus, ī, a German.
gerō, gerere, gessī, gestus, *3, tr.,* carry, carry on; **bellum gerere,** to wage war; **rēs (rērum) gestae (gestārum),** exploits, achievements.
Glabriō (Glabriōnis), Mānius (ī), Manius Glabrio, *the praetor presiding in the Court of Extortion.*
gladius, ī, sword.
glōria, ae, fame, glory.
glōriōsus, a, um, glorious.
Gracchus (ī), **Gājus** (ī), Gaius Gracchus, *a famous Roman statesman and reformer.*
Gracchus (ī), **Tiberius** (ī), Tiberius Gracchus, *a famous Roman statesman, brother of Gaius.*
gradus, ūs, step.
grātia, ae, influence, grace *(in Christian Latin),* good graces; *pl.,* thanks; **grātiās agō, agere, ēgī, āctus,** *3, tr.,* give thanks, thank; **grātiam habeō,** *2, tr.,* am grateful; **grātiam referō, referre, rettulī, relātus,** *irreg., tr.,* show gratitude.
grātulātiō, grātulātiōnis, congratulation.
gravis, e, heavy, severe, serious.
gravitās, gravitātis, weight, solemnity, seriousness.
graviter, *adv.,* seriously; **graviter ferō, ferre, tulī, lātus,** *irreg., tr.,* take hard (ill).

habeō, *2, tr.*, have; **grātiam habēre**, to be grateful; **ōrātiōnem habēre**, to deliver a speech.
habitō, *1, tr.*, live, dwell.
haereō, haerēre, haesī, haesūrus, *2, intr.; w. abl. or dat.;* ***in*** *w. abl.*, stick.
Hannibal, Hannibalis, *m.*, Hannibal, *a great Carthaginian general.*
hīc, *adv.*, here.
hic, haec, hoc, this; **hūjus modī**, of this kind, of this sort.
hodiē, *adv.*, today, on this day.
hodiernō diē, today, this day.
homō, hominis, man *(a human being).*
honestō, *1, tr.*, cover with honor, glory.
honestus, a, um, upright, honorable.
honor, honōris, honor.
hōra, ae, hour.
horribilis, e, dreadful, frightful, hideous.
Hortēnsius, ī, Hortensius, *a famous lawyer of Cicero's day.*
hortor, *1, tr.;* ***ut (ut nē)***, urge, encourage, exhort.
hostis, hostis, enemy *(in war).*
hūc, *adv.*, hither.
hūjus modī, of this kind, of this sort.

ibi, *adv.*, there.
idcircō, *adv.*, therefore, for this reason.
īdem, eadem, idem, same (Gr. 137; 813-814); **īdem, eadem, idem . . . quī, quae, quod (ac, atque)**, the same . . . as.
idōneus, a, um; *w. dat. or* ***ad*** *w. acc.*, suitable, proper, convenient.
igitur, *adv., postp.*, therefore, then.
ignis, ignis, *m.*, fire.
ignōminia, ae, disgrace, dishonor.
ignōrō, *1, tr.; acc. w. infin.*, not know, am unaware, overlook.
ignōtus, a, um, unknown.
ille, illa, illud, that, he, she, it, the former, the famous (Gr. 134; 795, 798).
illūstris, e, bright, illustrious.
illūstrō, *1, tr.*, reveal, bring to light.
imāgō, imāginis, image, picture, portrait, statue.
immineō, imminēre, *2, intr.*, impend.
immittō, immittere, immīsī, immissus, *3, tr.*, send into, send against.
immō, *adv.*, on the contrary, by no means, by all means; **immō verō**, *adv.*, nay, on the contrary.
immortālis, e, deathless, immortal.
impedīmenta, impedīmentōrum, baggage, baggage train.
impediō, *4, tr.*, hinder, impede.
impendeō, impendēre, *2, intr.; w. dat.*, overhang, threaten.
imperātor, imperātōris, commander in chief, general, emperor.
imperītus, a, um; *w. gen.*, unskilled (in), inexperienced (in).
imperium, ī, command, power, empire.
imperō, *1, tr.; w. dat. of person;* ***ut (nē)***, levy (on), order, command.
impetrō, *1, tr.;* ***ab (ā)*** *w. abl. of person; acc. of thing;* ***ut (nē)***, obtain *(by asking).*
impetus, ūs, attack.
impius, a, um, impious, undutiful.
implōrātiō, implōrātiōnis, entreaty, pleading.
implōrō, *1, tr.; w. acc. of person;* ***ut (nē); ab (ā)*** *w. abl. of person and acc. of thing*, entreat.
impōnō, impōnere, imposuī, impositus, *3, tr.*, place upon, put on, give to.
improbitās, improbitātis, wickedness, depravity, recklessness, dishonesty.
improbus, a, um, wicked, depraved.
impudenter, *adv.*, arrogantly.
impudentia, ae, impudence, effrontery, shamelessness.
impūnītus, a, um, unpunished.
in, *prep. w. abl.*, in, on; *prep. w. acc.*, into, against, upon, onto, on, towards.
in excelsīs, in the highest.

in fugam dō, dare, dedī, datus, *1, tr.,* put to flight.
in perpetuum, forever.
in prīmīs, *lit.,* among the first things, especially.
in prīncipiō, in the beginning, in the first place.
in saecula saeculōrum, world without end, forever.
inānis, e, empty.
incarnātus, a, um, made flesh.
incendium, ī, fire, conflagration.
incendō, incendere, incendī, incēnsus, *3, tr.,* set fire to, burn.
incēnsiō, incēnsiōnis, burning.
incertus, a, um, uncertain, indefinite, vague.
incipiō, incipere, incēpī, inceptus, *3, tr. and intr.; w. pres. infin.,* begin, undertake.
incitō, *1, tr.,* incite, arouse.
inclūdō, inclūdere, inclūsī, inclūsus, *3, tr.,* shut in, include, confine.
incolō, incolere, incoluī, *3, tr.,* inhabit, dwell in.
incolumis, e, safe, unhurt.
incrēdibilis, e, unbelievable, extraordinary.
inde, *adv.,* thence, from that place, from there.
index, indicis, *m.,* accuser, informer.
indicium, ī, information, proof; **per indicium,** through informers.
indicō, *1, tr.; acc. w. infin.,* point out, accuse.
indignus, a, um; *w. abl.,* unworthy, not deserving (of), disgraceful.
indūcō, indūcere, indūxī, inductus, *3, tr.; ut (nē),* lead in, lead on, influence.
industria, ae, exertion, hard work, energy.
ineō, inīre, iniī(-īvī), initus, *irreg., tr.,* go into, enter upon.
inertia, ae, inactivity.
īnfāmia, ae, dishonor, disgrace, infamy.
īnferō, īnferre, intulī, illātus, *irreg., tr.; w. dat. of person,* bring (upon), inflict (upon), inspire (in); **bellum īnferre,** to make war on.
īnfestus, a, um, hostile, threatening.
īnfimus, a, um, lowest; **ad īnfimum,** to the bottom, at the bottom.
īnfīnītus, a, um, endless, extensive.
īnfirmus, a, um, weak.
īnfitior, *1, tr.; acc. w. infin.,* deny.
īnflammātus, a, um, inflamed.
īnflammō, *1, tr.,* set on fire.
ingenium, ī, natural talent, ability, genius.
ingredior, ingredī, ingressus sum, *3, tr.,* advance, go.
inimīcus, ī, enemy *(personal).*
initium, ī, beginning.
injūria, ae, injustice, wrong.
innocēns (*gen.* **innocentis**), guiltless, innocent.
inopia, ae, scarcity, want.
inquam, I say, I said; **inquit,** he says, he said; **inquiunt,** they say, they said. *(Used with direct quotations only; usually placed after the first word or phrase in the quotation.)*
īnscrībō, īnscrībere, īnscrīpsī, īnscrīptus, *3, tr.,* write on, inscribe.
īnsidiae, īnsidiārum, ambush, plot, snare.
īnsidior, *1, intr.; w. dat.,* waylay, plot.
īnsigne, īnsignis, word, sign, insignia.
īnsimulō, *1, tr.; w. gen. of the charge,* charge, allege.
īnstituō, īnstituere, īnstituī, īnstitūtus, *3, tr.; w. infin.,* set up, train, undertake.
īnstitūtum, ī, institution, design, practice, device.
īnstruō, īnstruere, īnstrūxī, īnstrūctus, *3, tr.,* draw up, equip.
integer, integra, integrum, fresh, uninjured, whole, honest.
intellegō, intellegere, intellēxī, intellēctus, *3, tr.; acc. w. infin.,* understand, perceive.

intendō, intendere, intendī, intentus, *3, tr.; **ad** or **in** w. acc.*, stretch to, am bound for.
inter, *prep. w. acc.*, between, among; **inter falcāriōs,** in the section of the scythe makers; **inter sē dō, dare, dedī, datus,** *1, tr.*, exchange.
intereā, *adv.*, meanwhile.
interficiō, interficere, interfēcī, interfectus, *3, tr.*, kill.
interim, *adv.*, meanwhile.
interitus, ūs, death, destruction.
interpōnō, interpōnere, interposuī, interpositus, *3, tr.*, put between, interpose, cause.
interrogō, *1, tr.*, ask, question.
intersum, interesse, interfuī, interfutūrus, *irreg., intr.; w. dat.*, am between, am among, take part in, am present at.
intrā, *prep. w. acc.*, within.
intrōdūcō, intrōdūcere, intrōduxī, intrōductus, *3, tr.*, bring in, introduce.
intueor, intuērī, intuitus sum, *2, tr.*, fix my gaze on, fasten my eyes on.
inveniō, invenīre, invēnī, inventus, *4, tr.; acc. w. infin.*, come upon, find (out), discover.
invēstīgō, *1, tr.*, detect, search out.
inveterāscō, inveterāscere, inveterāvī, *3, intr.*, grow old, become established.
invidia, ae, envy, hatred, unpopularity.
invidus, a, um, envious, hostile.
invīsibilis, e, invisible.
invītō, *1, tr.*, invite, summon.
involūtus, a, um, covered.
ipse, ipsa, ipsum, self (Gr. 138; 808-812).
is, ea, id, he, she, it, that (Gr. 128-129, 135; 796-797); **ējus modī,** of this kind, of this sort.
Israēl, Israēlis, *m.*, Israel.
iste, ista, istud, that, this (Gr. 136; 799).
ita, *adv.*, so, in such a manner, thus.
Italia, ae, Italy.
itaque, *conj.*, therefore, and so.
item, *adv.*, likewise, in like manner, also.
iter, itineris, *n.*, journey, march, route; **iter faciō, facere, fēcī, factus,** *3, tr.*, march, make a journey.
iterum, *adv.*, again.

jaciō, jacere, jēcī, jactus, *3, tr.*, throw, hurl.
jactō, *1, tr.*, toss about, discuss.
jam, *adv.*, already, now; **jam diū,** long ago, long since, now for a long time *(w. pres. indicative)*; **jam dūdum,** long ago, long since, already, now for a long time *(w. pres. indicative)*, then for a long time *(w. imperfect indicative)*; **jam prīdem,** long ago, long since, then for a long time *(w. imperfect indicative)*.
Jerosolyma, ae (*or* **Jerosolymōrum**), Jerusalem.
Jērūsālem, *indecl. noun,* Jerusalem.
Jēsūs, ū (*declined:* **Jēsūs, Jēsū, Jēsū, Jēsum, Jēsū**), Jesus.
Jōannēs, Jōannis, John.
Jōsēphus, ī, Joseph.
Jovis. *See* **Juppiter.**
jubeō, jubēre, jussī, jussus, *2, tr.; acc. w. pres. infin.*, order, command.
jūcundus, a, um, pleasant.
Jūdaeus, ī, a Jew.
Jūdas, ae, *m.*, Judas.
jūdex, jūdicis, judge, juror; **jūdicēs** *(voc. pl.)*, gentlemen of the jury.
jūdicium, ī, judgment, trial, law court.
jūdicō, *1, tr.; acc. w. infin.*, judge, decide, think.
jungō, jungere, jūnxī, jūnctus, *3, tr.*, join, unite.
junior, junius, younger.
Juppiter, Jovis, Jupiter, *the principal god of the Romans.*
jūre, *adv.*, justly, rightly.
jūs, jūris, *n.*, right, justice, law.
jūsjūrandum, jūrisjūrandī, oath.

jussus, ūs, bidding, command.
jūstitia, ae, justice, fair dealing.
jūstus, a, um, just, lawful.
juvenis, e, young.

labor, labōris, effort, toil, work, distress.
labōrō, *1, intr.*, toil, am in difficulty.
lacrima, ae, tear.
Laeca (ae), Mārcus (ī), Marcus Laeca, *one of Catiline's confederates.*
laetitia, ae, joy, gladness.
lātē, *adv.*, widely.
Latīnē, *adv.*, in Latin.
latrō, latrōnis, bandit, robber.
latrōcinium, ī, robbery, brigandage.
lātus, a, um, wide, broad.
laudātor, laudātōris, a praiser, eulogizer.
laudō, *1, tr.*, praise.
laus, laudis, praise.
Lautumiae, Lautumiārum, the Stone Quarry, *a prison at Syracuse.*
lēctissimus, a, um, excellent.
lēgātus, ī, envoy, lieutenant.
legiō, legiōnis, *f.*, legion.
legō, legere, lēgī, lēctus, *3, tr.*, read.
Lentulus (ī), Pūblius (ī), Publius Lentulus, *a conspirator.*
Lepidus (ī), Mārcus (ī), Marcus Lepidus.
leve, *adv.*, lightly, mildly.
levis, e, light, light-minded.
lēx, lēgis, law.
libenter, *adv.*, willingly, readily.
līber, lībera, līberum, free.
līberāliter, *adv.*, generously.
līberī, līberōrum, children.
līberō, *1, tr.*, free, liberate.
lībertās, lībertātis, liberty.
libīdō, libīdinis, desire, passion, lust.
licet, *conj.*, although, granted that.
licet, licēre, licuit, *2, intr.; w. dat. of person; acc. w. infin.*, it is allowed, it is permitted.
Licinius, ī, Licinius, *coemperor with Constantine.*
līctor, līctōris, lictor.
lingua, ae, tongue, language.
litterae, litterārum, letter *(an epistle)*, dispatch, literature.
locus, ī (*pl.*, **loca, locōrum**), place.
longē, *adv.*, far, by far.
longus, a, um, long.
loquor, loquī, locūtus sum, *3, tr. and intr.*, talk, speak.
lūdus, ī, game.
lūmen, lūminis, light.
lūx, lūcis, light; **prīmā lūce,** at dawn.

māchinātor, māchinātōris, contriver, schemer, plotter.
māchinor, *1, tr.*, plot, devise.
mactō, *1, tr.*, destroy, execute.
magis, *comparative adv.*, more, rather, in a higher degree.
magistrātus, ūs, magistrate, magistracy.
magnī, of great value, highly (Gr. 701).
magnitūdō, magnitūdinis, size, greatness, extent.
magnōpere, *adv.*, greatly, especially, exceedingly.
magnus, a, um, great, large; **magnī,** of great value, highly (Gr. 701).
mājor, mājus, greater, larger.
mājōrēs, mājōrum, *m.*, ancestors, forefathers.
male, *adv.*, badly, poorly, scarcely.
mālō, mālle, māluī, *tr.; acc. w. infin.*, prefer.
malus, a, um, bad, wicked, evil.
Māmertīnī, Māmertīnōrum, the inhabitants of Messina, the Mamertines.
Māmertīnus, a, um, Mamertine, of Messina.
mandātum, ī, instruction, order.
mandō, *1, tr.; w. dat. of person;* ***ut (nē)***, commit, entrust, command.
māne, *adv.*, in the morning, early.
maneō, manēre, mānsī, mānsūrus, *2, intr.*, remain.

manifestō, *adv.*, clearly.
manifestus, a, um, clear, evident, palpable.
Mānliānus, a, um, of Manlius.
Mānlius (ī), Gājus (ī), Gaius Manlius, *radical leader and revolutionary.*
manus, ūs, *f.*, hand, band.
mare, maris, sea (Gr. 64, 1); **terrā marīque,** on land and sea.
Marīa, ae, Mary.
Marius (ī), Gājus (ī), Gaius Marius, *a consul.*
martyr, martyris, *c.*, martyr.
māter, mātris (mātrum), mother.
mātūrē, *adv.*, early.
mātūritās, mātūritātis, ripeness, full development.
maximē, *adv.*, especially, mostly, mainly.
maximus, a, um, greatest, largest; **maximī,** of highest value, very highly (Gr. 701).
Maximus (ī), Galērius (ī), Galerius Maximus, *a proconsul.*
medius, a, um, middle.
melior, melius, better.
melius, *comparative adv.*, better.
meminī, meminisse, *tr.; w. gen. of persons, gen. or acc. of things, acc. of neuter pronouns or adjs.; acc. w. infin.*, remember, bear in mind.
memoria, ae, memory; **memoriā teneō, tenēre, tenuī, tentus,** *2, tr.; acc. w. infin.*, keep in memory, remember.
mēns, mentis, mind, intellect; **mente captus (a, um),** beside oneself, out of one's mind, insane.
mercātor, mercātōris, merchant.
meritō, *adv.*, rightly, justly.
meritum, ī, kindness, favor, merit, desert.
merx, mercis, merchandise.
Messāna, ae, Messina, *a city in eastern Sicily.*
-met, *enclitic emphasizing word to which it is joined.*
Metellus (ī), Mārcus (ī), Marcus Metellus, *a conspirator.*
metuō, metuere, metuī, *3, tr.; **nē (nē nōn, ut)**; w. infin.*, fear (to).
metus, ūs, fear.
meus, a, um, my, mine; **meā sponte,** of my own accord.
mīles, mīlitis, soldier; **tribūnus (ī) mīlitum,** military tribune.
mīlle, *indecl. adj. (pl.,* **mīlia, mīlium,** *n.)*, thousand; **mīlle passūs** (*pl.,* **mīlia passuum**), a mile.
minimus, a, um, smallest; **minimī,** of smallest value, very little (Gr. 701).
minor, minus, smaller, younger; **minōris,** of less value, less highly (Gr. 701).
minus, *comparative adv.*, less, too little; **sīn minus,** but if not.
miser, misera, miserum, wretched, unfortunate, miserable.
miserēre; *w. dat. or gen.*, have mercy (on).
misericordia, ae, mercy, compassion.
Missa, ae, the Mass.
mittō, mittere, mīsī, missus, *3, tr.*, send.
modo, *adv.*, only, just now, at least; **sī modo,** if only.
modus, ī, manner, kind, measure; **ējus modī (ējusmodī),** of this kind, of this sort; **hūjus modī,** of this kind, of this sort.
moenia, moenium, walls, fortifications.
mōlēs, mōlis, burden, weight, mass.
mōlior, mōlīrī, mōlītus sum, *4, tr.*, undertake, build.
moneō, *2, tr.; **ut (nē)**,* warn, advise.
mōns, montis, *m.*, mountain.
monumentum, ī, monument, memorial.
mora, ae, delay.
mōrēs, mōrum, *m.*, character, customs.
morior, morī, mortuus sum, *3, intr.*, die.
mors, mortis, death.
mortuus, a, um, dead.

mōs, mōris, manner, custom; *pl.*, character.

moveō, movēre, mōvī, mōtus, *2, tr.*, move.

multitūdō, multitūdinis, crowd, multitude.

multō, *abl. of degree of difference*, much, by much (GR. 771).

multō, *1, tr.*, punish.

multum, *adv.*, much, greatly.

multus, a, um, much; *pl.*, many; **ad multam noctem,** far into the night.

Mulvius, a, um, Mulvian.

mundus, ī, world.

mūniceps, mūnicipis, *m.*, burgess, citizen, fellow citizen.

mūniō, *4, tr.*, fortify, construct *(w. viam or viās).*

mūnus, mūneris, *n.*, function, duty, gift, offering.

mūrus, ī, wall.

mūtō, *1, tr.*, change.

mūtus, a, um, silent, mute.

nactus, a, um (*perfect participle of* **nancīscor**), having obtained possession of, having met with, having found, having obtained.

nam, *conj.*, for.

nancīscor, nancīsī, nactus sum, *3, tr.*, obtain, fall in with, get.

nāscor, nāscī, nātus sum, *3, intr.*, am born.

nātiō, nātiōnis, tribe, nation.

nātūra, ae, nature.

nātus, a, um, born.

nauta, ae, sailor.

nāvigō, *1, intr.*, sail, navigate.

nāvis, nāvis (*abl.* **nāvī** *or* **nāve**), ship; **nāvem solvō, solvere, solvī, solūtus,** *3, tr.*, set sail.

nē, *conj.*, that . . . not *(in negative purpose clauses and noun clauses after verbs of 'willing');* in order that not *(in negative purpose clauses);* granted that . . . not *(in concessive subjunctive);* lest, from *(after verbs of hindering and preventing);* may not, would that not *(with volitive subjunctive).*

-ne, *particle used in asking questions (added to emphatic word—generally the verb—and put first in sentence).*

nē quid, that nothing (GR. 549).

nē . . . quidem, not even.

nē quis, that no one (GR. 549).

nē umquam, that never (GR. 549).

nec (neque), *conj.*, and not, nor.

necessāriō, *adv.*, unavoidably, necessarily.

necessārius, ī, connection *(business associates and persons of that sort as well as friends).*

necesse, *indecl. adj.*, necessary.

necesse est, esse, fuit, *intr.; w. infin.*, it is necessary (GR. 641, 892).

necō, *1, tr.*, kill, murder.

nēcubi, that nowhere (GR. 549).

nefārius, a, um, wicked, impious.

neglegō, neglegere, neglēxī, neglēctus, *3, tr.*, disregard, neglect.

negō, *1, tr.; acc. w. infin.*, deny, say . . . not.

negōtiātor, negōtiātōris, wholesale merchant, businessman.

negōtior, *1, intr.*, carry on business, engage in trade.

negōtium, ī, business.

nēmō, nēminis (**nūllīus, nūllō,** *and* **nūllā** *usually used in place of* **nēminis** *and* **nēmine**), no one, no.

neque (nec), *conj.*, nor, and . . . not; **neque . . . neque,** *conjs.*, neither . . . nor.

nēquitia, ae, criminal negligence, wickedness.

nesciō, *4, tr.; acc. w. infin.*, do not know, am ignorant.

nesciōquī, nesciōqua, nesciōquod, some (GR. 819).

nesciōquis, nesciōquid, someone, something (GR. 819).

nēvē (neu), *conj.*, and in order that . . . not (GR. 548).

nex, necis, violent death, slaughter, killing.

nihil, *adv.*, not, not at all.

nihil (**nīl**), *n., indecl. noun,* nothing.

nihilum, ī, nothing; **nihilī,** *gen. of indefinite value;* **nihilō,** *abl. of price.*

nimium, *adv.*, too, excessively.

nimius, a, um, too much, excessive.

nisi, *conj.*, if not, unless, except.

nōbilis, e, noble, renowned.

nocēns (*gen.* **nocentis**), guilty.

noceō, nocēre, nocuī, nocitūrus, *2, intr.; w. dat.*, harm, injure.

noctū, *adv.*, by night.

nocturnus, a, um, nocturnal, nightly.

nōlō, nōlle, nōluī, *tr.; w. infin.; acc. w. infin.; ut (nē),* am unwilling, do not wish; **nōlī, nōlīte;** *w. pres. infin.*, don't (Gr. 516).

nōmen, nōminis, name.

nōminātim, *adv.*, by name.

nōminō, *1, tr.; w. two accs.*, call, name.

nōn, *adv.*, not; **nōn modo . . . sed** (**etiam**), not only . . . but (also); **nōn modo . . . vērum** (**etiam**), not only . . . but (also); **nōn quod** (**nōn quō**), not because (Gr. 574-575); **sī . . . nōn,** if not; **ut . . . nōn,** that . . . not *(in negative result clauses and noun clauses).*

nōndum, *adv.*, not yet.

nōnne, *particle used in asking questions expecting an affirmative answer.*

nōnnūllī, ae, a, some.

nōs, nostrī, we.

noster, nostra, nostrum, our, ours, our own.

nota, ae, mark, brand.

notō, *1, tr.*, mark down, note down.

nōtus, a, um, known, well-known.

novem, *indecl. numeral,* nine.

novus, a, um, new; **rēs** (**rērum**) **novae** (**novārum**), revolution.

nox, noctis, night; **ad multam noctem,** far into the night; **noctū,** *adv.*, by night.

nūdus, a, um, stripped, bare.

nūllus, a, um, no, none.

num, *interrogative particle implying a negative answer;* whether, if (*in indirect question,* Gr. 661-662).

numerus, ī, number.

Numitōrius (**ī**), **Gājus** (**ī**), Gaius Numitorius, *a Roman knight.*

numquam, *adv.*, never.

nunc, *adv.*, now.

nuntiō, *1, tr.; acc. w. infin.*, announce, report.

nuntius, ī, messenger, message.

nūper, *adv.*, recently.

nūtus, ūs, nod, consent, will.

ob, *prep. w. acc.*, on account of, for, because of; **quam ob rem,** wherefore.

obeō, obīre, obiī, obitus, *irreg., tr.*, undergo, traverse.

oblīvīscor, oblīvīscī, oblītus sum, *3, tr.; w. gen. of persons, gen. or acc. of things, acc. of neuter pronouns or adjs.; acc. w. infin.*, forget.

obscūrē, *adv.*, darkly, obscurely.

obscūrus, a, um, obscure, dark, unknown, humble.

obses, obsidis, *c.*, hostage.

obsideō, obsidēre, obsēdī, obsessus, *2, tr.*, obstruct, blockade, besiege.

obsistō, obsistere, obstitī, *3, intr.; w. dat.*, block, oppose, counter.

obstō, obstāre, obstitī, *1, intr.; w. dat.*, resist, stand in the way, prevent.

obsum, obesse, obfuī, obfutūrus, *irreg., intr.; w. dat.*, am harmful.

obtineō, obtinēre, obtinuī, obtentus, *2, tr.*, hold, occupy, gain.

occīdō, occīdere, occīdī, occīsus, *3, tr.*, kill, cut down.

occultē, *adv.*, secretly.

occupō, *1, tr.*, seize.

occurrō, occurrere, occurrī, occursum, *3, intr.; w. dat.*, go to meet, happen upon, run in the way of.

oculus, ī, eye; **sub oculīs omnium,** in the sight of all.
ōdī, ōdisse, *tr.*, hate.
odium, ī, hatred.
offēnsiō, offēnsiōnis, disfavor, dislike, disapproval.
offēnsus, a, um, annoying.
offerō, offerre, obtulī, oblātus, *irreg., tr.*, present, offer, expose.
officium, ī, duty, loyalty, service, allegiance.
omittō, omittere, omīsī, omissus, *3, tr.*, dismiss, omit, interrupt, let go.
omnīnō, *adv.*, altogether, at all, entirely.
omnipotēns (*gen.* **omnipotentis**), almighty.
omnis, e, all, every; **praeter omnium opīniōnem,** contrary to the expectation of everyone; **sub oculīs omnium,** in the sight of all.
onus, oneris, *n.*, burden, cargo.
opera, ae, services, pains, efforts; **operam dō, dare, dedī, datus,** *1, tr.*, pay attention to, take care that.
opēs, opum, *f.*, wealth, resources.
opīniō, opīniōnis, belief, reputation, opinion; **praeter omnium opīniōnem,** contrary to the expectation of everyone.
opīnor, *1, tr.*, think.
oportet, oportēre, oportuit, *2, intr.; acc. w. pres. infin.*, it behooves, it is necessary.
oppidum, ī, town.
opprimō, opprimere, oppressī, oppressus, *3, tr.*, overwhelm, surprise.
oppugnō, *1, tr.*, attack, assault, storm.
ops, opis, power, help, assistance.
optimē, *adv.*, best.
optimus, a, um, best.
optō, *1, tr.; w. infin.; ut (nē),* desire, pray for, hope for.
opus, operis, *n.*, work, fortification; **tantō opere,** so much, so greatly.
ōrātiō, ōrātiōnis, speech, prayer; **ōrātiōnem habeō,** *2, tr.*, deliver a speech.
ōrātor, ōrātōris, orator, speaker.
ōrātōrius, a, um, oratorical.
orbis, orbis, *m.*, ring, circle, the world; **orbis (orbis) terrārum** (*sometimes* **terrae**), the world.
Ordinārius, ī, Ordinary *(of the Mass)*.
ōrdō, ōrdinis, *m.*, rank, order.
orior, orīrī, ortus sum, *4, intr.*, rise, arise, start.
ōrō, *1, tr.; ut (nē),* beg, pray, plead.
ōs, ōris, *n.*, mouth, face, expression.
ostendō, ostendere, ostendī, ostentus (ostēnsus), *3, tr.; acc. w. infin.*, show, tell, point out.
ostentō, *1, tr.*, display, show, exhibit.

pācō, *1, tr.*, pacify.
pactum, ī, way, manner, agreement.
paene, *adv.*, almost, nearly.
palam, *adv.*, openly.
Panhormus, ī, *f.*, Panhormus, *a city.*
pāpa, ae, *m.*, Pope.
parātus, a, um; *w. pres. infin. or* **ad** *w. acc.*, prepared (for), ready (for).
pārēns, pārentis, *c.*, parent, father.
parietēs, parietum, *m.*, walls *(of a room)*.
pariō, parere, peperī, partus, *3, tr.*, bring forth, bear, gain.
parō, *1, tr.; w. pres. infin.*, prepare, get ready.
parricīdium, ī, murder, murder of a parent, high treason.
pars, partis, part, direction.
partim . . . partim, *advs.*, partly . . . partly.
partus, a, um, gained.
parum, *indecl. noun; w. gen.*, too little, not enough.
parum, *adv.*, little, too little.
parvus, a, um, small, little, insignificant.
passus, ūs, a pace; **mīlle passūs** (*pl.*, **mīlia passuum**), a mile.
patefaciō, patefacere, patefēcī, patefactus (*passive,* **patefīō**), *3, tr.*, open, disclose.

pateō, patēre, patuī, *2, intr.*, lie open, am open, extend.

pater, patris (patrum), father; **patrēs (patrum) cōnscrīptī (cōnscrīptōrum),** senators, gentlemen of the Senate.

paternus, a, um, paternal.

patientia, ae, patience, endurance.

patior, patī, passus sum, *3, tr.; acc. w. infin.*, suffer, allow, permit, endure.

patrēs (patrum) cōnscrīptī (cōnscrīptōrum), senators, gentlemen of the Senate.

patria, ae, fatherland, native land, country.

patrōnus, ī, patron, advocate, lawyer.

paucī, ae, a, few.

paulisper, *adv.*, for a short time, for a little while.

paulō, *abl. of degree of difference,* (by) a little *(modifying* ***ante, post,*** *or a comparative)*; **paulō anteā,** shortly before.

paulum, *adv. or noun w. gen.*, a little.

Paulus, ī, Paul.

pāx, pācis, peace.

peccātor, peccātōris, sinner.

peccātum, ī, crime, mistake, sin *(in Christian Latin)*.

pecūnia, ae, money, wealth; **dē pecūniīs repetundīs,** concerning extortion.

pecūniōsus, a, um, wealthy, rich.

pedester, pedestris, pedestre, of infantry, by land.

pējor, pējus, worse.

pējus, *comparative adv.*, worse.

pellō, pellere, pepulī, pulsus, *3, tr.*, drive, repulse, rout.

penitus, *adv.*, deep down, deeply, utterly.

per, *prep. w. acc.*, through, throughout, by, owing to; **per indicium,** through informers; **per omnia saecula saeculōrum,** forever and ever; **per saecula,** forever.

percipiō, percipere, percēpī, perceptus, *3, tr.; acc. w. infin.*, learn of, perceive, gain, acquire.

perditus, a, um, desperate, abandoned, ruined.

perdūcō, perdūcere, perdūxī, perductus, *3, tr.*, lead through, conduct, win over, influence, prolong.

perendinō diē, on the day after tomorrow.

perficiō, perficere, perfēcī, perfectus, *3, tr.*, perform, complete, finish.

perfringō, perfringere, perfrēgī, perfrāctus, *3, tr.*, break through, burst through.

perfruor, perfruī, perfrūctus sum, *3, intr.; w. abl.*, enjoy.

pergō, pergere, perrēxī, perrēctum, *3, intr.; w. infin.*, keep straight, go straight, proceed.

perīclitor, *1, tr.*, risk, endanger, try, test.

perīculōsus, a, um, dangerous.

perīculum, ī, danger.

permagnī, of very great value, very highly (Gr. 701).

permittō, permittere, permīsī, permissus, *3, tr.; w. dat. of person; acc. of thing;* ***ut (nē),*** give over, entrust, yield, permit.

permoveō, permovēre, permōvī, permōtus, *2, tr.*, arouse, influence, excite, alarm.

perniciēs, perniciēī, destruction, disaster.

perniciōsus, a, um, dangerous, destructive.

perpetuus, a, um, unbroken, perpetual; **in perpetuum,** forever.

persaepe, *adv.*, very often.

persequor, persequī, persecūtus sum, *3, tr.*, follow through, pursue, press hard, avenge, persecute.

perspiciō, perspicere, perspexī, perspectus, *3, tr.; acc. w. infin.*, view, inspect, perceive, see clearly, ascertain.

persuādeō, persuādēre, persuāsī, persuāsum, *2, intr.; w. dat.;* ***ut (nē),*** persuade.

perterreō, *2, tr.,* terrify greatly, frighten thoroughly.

pertimēscō, pertimēscere, pertimuī, *3, tr.,* become thoroughly frightened, fear exceedingly.

pertineō, pertinēre, pertinuī, *2, intr.;* ***ad*** *w. acc.,* pertain to, stretch to.

perturbō, *1, tr.,* confuse, disturb.

perveniō, pervenīre, pervēnī, perventum, *4, intr.;* ***in*** *or* ***ad*** *w. acc.,* arrive.

pēs, pedis, *m.,* foot; **pedem referō, referre, rettulī, relātus,** *irreg., tr.,* retreat, fall back.

pessimē, *adv.,* worst.

pessimus, a, um, worst.

pestis, pestis, plague, ruin.

petō, petere, petīvī, petītus, *3, tr.;* ***ut (nē),*** seek, beg, request, ask for, attack, beseech.

Petrus, ī, Peter.

Pīlātus (ī), **Pontius** (ī), Pontius Pilate.

pīlum, ī, javelin.

pīrāta, ae, *m.,* pirate.

pius, a, um, pious.

Pius, ī, Pius, *name of several popes.*

placet, placēre, placuit, placitum, *2, intr.; w. dat.; w. infin.; acc. w. infin.;* ***ut (nē),*** it pleases, it seems good.

plācō, *1, tr.,* calm, appease, pacify.

plaga, ae, blow, net.

plānē, *adv.,* clearly, plainly.

plānus, a, um, clear, plain.

plēbs, plēbis, the common people, the masses; **tribūnus** (ī) **plēbis,** tribune of the people.

plēnus, a, um; *w. gen. or abl.,* full.

plūrēs, plūra, more.

plūrimus, a, um, very many, the greatest number; *pl.,* the most; **plūrimī,** of highest value, very highly; **plūrimum possum, posse, potuī,** *irreg., intr.,* am very influential; **plūrimum valeō, valēre, valuī,** *2, intr.,* am very powerful.

plūs, *comparative adv.,* more.

plūs, plūris, *n.; w. gen.,* more; **plūris,** of higher value, more highly (Gr. 701).

poena, ae, punishment, penalty.

polliceor, *2, tr.; acc. w. infin. (usually future),* promise.

Pomptīnus (ī), **Gājus** (ī), Gaius Pomptinis, *a praetor.*

pōnō, pōnere, posuī, positus, *3, tr.,* put, place, set, pitch *(w.* ***castra****).*

pōns, pontis, *m.,* bridge.

pontifex, pontificis, chief priest, pope.

populus, ī, people, nation.

porta, ae, gate.

portō, *1, tr.,* carry.

portus, ūs, harbor, port.

poscō, poscere, poposcī, *3, tr.;* ***ab (ā)*** *w. abl. of person; acc. of thing;* ***ut (nē),*** demand.

possum, posse, potuī, *irreg., intr.; w. pres. infin.,* am able, can; **plūrimum posse,** to be very influential.

post, *adv.,* afterwards *(time).*

post, *prep. w. acc.,* after, behind.

posteā, *adv.,* afterwards.

posterī, posterōrum, descendants.

posteritās, posteritātis, future generations, posterity.

posthāc, *adv.,* after this.

postquam, *conj.,* after.

postulō, *1, tr.;* ***ab (ā)*** *w. abl. of person; acc. of thing;* ***ut (nē)****; acc. w. infin.,* demand.

potentia, ae, might, force, power.

potestās, potestātis, power, control, opportunity.

potior, *4, intr.; w. abl. or gen.,* get possession of, become master of.

potius, *adv.,* rather.

prae, *prep. w. abl.,* for, on account of *(preventing cause),* before *(of place).*

praecipuē, *adv.,* especially, particularly.

praeclārē, *adv.*, excellently, remarkably.

praeclārus, a, um, famous, renowned.

praedicō, *1, tr.*, openly declare, proclaim.

praedīcō, praedīcere, praedīxī, praedictus, *3, tr.; acc. w. infin.*, say, foretell.

praedō, praedōnis, *m.*, pirate, robber.

praeferō, praeferre, praetulī, praelātus, *irreg.*, *tr.*, carry in front of, offer, present, hold out, bear before.

praeficiō, praeficere, praefēcī, praefectus, *3, tr.; w. dat. of thing of which*, put in command of.

praemittō, praemittere, praemīsī, praemissus, *3, tr.*, send ahead.

praemium, ī, reward.

praescrībō, praescrībere, praescrīpsī, praescrīptus, *3, tr.*, prescribe, dictate.

praesēns (*gen.* **praesentis**), present, propitious.

praesentia, ae, presence.

praesertim, *adv.*, especially, particularly.

praesidium, ī, garrison, protection.

praestō, *adv.*, at hand.

praestō, praestāre, praestitī, praestitus, *1, tr.*, exhibit, furnish, excel.

praesum, praeesse, praefuī, praefutūrus, *irreg.*, *intr.; w. dat.*, am over, am in command of, am in charge of.

praeter, *prep. w. acc.*, except, past, contrary to, beyond, besides; **praeter omnium opīniōnem**, contrary to the expectation of everyone.

praetor, praetōris, praetor.

praetōrius, a, um, of *or* belonging to praetors, praetorian.

praetūra, ae, the praetorship, the office of praetor.

precēs, precum, *f.*, prayers, entreaties.

premō, premere, pressī, pressus, *3, tr.*, press, press hard, overwhelm.

prīdem, *adv.*, long ago, long since (*used especially with jam*).

prīdiē, *adv.*, on the day before.

prīmum, *adv.*, first; **cum prīmum, ubi prīmum, ut prīmum**, *conjs.*, as soon as.

prīmus, a, um, first; **prīmā lūce**, at dawn; **in prīmīs**, especially.

prīnceps, prīncipis, chief, leading man.

prīncipium, ī, beginning; **in prīncipiō**, in the beginning, in the first place.

prior, prius, former.

priusquam, *conj.*, before.

prīvātus, a, um, private, personal, personally, apart.

prō, *prep. w. abl.*, in front of, on behalf of, in place of, in proportion to.

probō, *1, tr.; acc. w. infin.; w. infin.*, approve, prove.

prōcēdō, prōcēdere, prōcessī, prōcessum, *3, intr.*, go forth, proceed, advance from.

prōcōnsul, prōcōnsulis, proconsul.

prōdūcō, prōdūcere, prōdūxī, prōductus, *3, tr.*, lead forth, protract, bring forth.

proelium, ī, battle; **proelium committō, committere, commīsī, commissus**, *3, tr.*, join battle, begin battle.

profectiō, profectiōnis, a setting out, departure.

profectō, *adv.*, actually, truly, indeed.

prōferō, prōferre, prōtulī, prōlātus, *irreg.*, *tr.*, bring forward, extend, produce.

prōficiō, prōficere, prōfēcī, prōfectus, *3, tr.; ut (nē)*, effect, accomplish.

proficīscor, proficīscī, profectus sum, *3, intr.*, set out, depart.

profiteor, profitērī, professus sum, *2, tr.; acc. w. infin.*, avow openly, profess, admit.

profugiō, profugere, profūgī, profugitum, *3, intr.*, flee from, run away, escape from.

prōgredior, prōgredī, prōgressus sum, *3, intr.*, go forward, advance, proceed.

prohibeō, *2, tr.*, ward off (from), prevent, keep away from.
prope, *adv.*, almost, nearly.
prophēta, ae, *m.*, prophet.
propinquus, a, um, near, close, neighboring.
propior, propius, nearer.
propitius, a, um, gracious, favorable.
prōpōnō, prōpōnere, prōposuī, prōpositus, *3, tr.*, put forward, propose, explain.
Prōprium, ī, Proper *(of the Mass).*
propter, *prep. w. acc.*, on account of, because.
prōsequor, prōsequī, prōsecūtus sum, *3, tr.*, attend, pursue, prosecute.
prōsum, prōdesse, prōfuī, prōfutūrus sum, *irreg., intr.; w. dat.*, profit, benefit, am useful.
prōvidentia, ae, preparation, foresight.
prōvideō, prōvidēre, prōvīdī, prōvīsus, *2, tr.; ut (nē),* see ahead, provide, take care.
prōvincia, ae, province.
proximus, a, um; *w. dat.*, nearest, next.
pūblicē, *adv.*, publicly.
pūblicus, a, um, public; **rēs (reī) pūblica (ae),** state, government, republic.
pudor, pudōris, sense of shame, propriety, honor.
puer, puerī, boy.
pugna, ae, fight.
pugnō, *1, intr.*, fight.
pulcher, pulchra, pulchrum, beautiful, noble, glorious.
pūniō, *4, tr.*, punish.
pūrgō, *1, tr.*, clean, purify, free from blame.
putō, *1, tr.; acc. w. infin.*, think.

quā, *adv.*, where.
quaerō, quaerere, quaesīvī, quaesītus, *3, tr.; ut (nē),* seek, ask, examine judicially, investigate.
quaesō, I beg (you), I ask (you), please; **quaesumus,** we beg (you) (Gr. 459).
quaestiō, quaestiōnis, inquiry, investigation, law court.
quālis, e, of such a sort, of such a kind, such as, of what kind; **tālis, e . . . quālis, e,** such . . . as.
quam, *adv.*, how, as, than; *w. superlative,* as . . . as possible; **quam ob rem,** wherefore; **quam prīmum,** as soon as possible; **tam . . . quam,** so . . . as, both . . . and, as well . . . as, as much . . . as.
quamdiū, *conj.*, as long as (Gr. 571).
quamquam, *conj.*, although, and yet; **quamquam quid,** and yet why.
quamvīs, *adv. and conj.*, as you will, ever so much, however, although.
quantus, a, um, how much, how large; **quantī,** of what value, how highly (Gr. 701); **tantus, a, um . . . quantus, a, um,** as great . . . as, as large . . . as; **tantō . . . quantō,** *used in comparing comparatives* (Gr. 607).
quārē, *adv.*, wherefore, why.
quasi, *adv. and conj.*, as if, just as, nearly.
quattuor, *indecl. numeral,* four.
-que, *conj.*, and.
quemadmodum, *adv.*, as, how.
querimōnia, ae, complaint.
queror, querī, questus sum, *3, tr.*, complain of, lament.
quī, quae, quod, *relative pronoun and adj., interrogative adj.*, who, what, which, that, any; **īdem, eadem, idem . . . quī, quae, quod,** the same . . . as; **sunt quī;** *w. subj.*, there are some who.
quia, *conj.*, because, that *(introducing a noun clause in Christian Latin).*
quīcumque, quaecumque, quodcumque, whoever, whatever.
quīdam, quaedam, quoddam, certain, some (Gr. 820).
quīdam, quiddam, one, a certain one, a certain thing (Gr. 820).

quidem, *adv.*, indeed, at least, truly; **nē . . . quidem**, not even.
quīn, *conj.*, that not, that, from (Gr. 650-654).
quīnque, *indecl. numeral*, five.
quīntus, a, um, fifth.
Quirītēs, Quirītium, Roman citizens *(in their strictly civil capacity).*
quis, quid, *interrogative and indefinite pronoun*, what, anyone, anything; **nē quis, nē quid**, that no one, that nothing (Gr. 549).
quisquam, quidquam, anyone, anything (Gr. 843).
quisque, quaeque, quodque, each, every (Gr. 831-835).
quisque, quidque, each one, every one (Gr. 831-835).
quō, *adv.*, whither, where *(of motion).*
quō, *conj.*, that, in order that *(in purpose clauses containing a comparative adverb or adjective)*; **quō . . . eō**, *used in comparing comparative adjectives and adverbs* (Gr. 607).
quod, *conj.*, because (Gr. 572-576).
quodsī, *conj.*, but if.
quōminus, *conj.*, from, that . . . not (Gr. 646).
quōmodo, *adv.*, how.
quondam, *adv.*, formerly, once upon a time.
quoniam, *conj.*, because, since, whereas, that *(introducing a noun clause in Christian Latin).*
quoque, *adv.*, also.
quot, *indecl. adj.*, how many; **tot . . . quot**, as many . . . as.
quotiēns, *interrogative adv.*, how often.
quotiēs (quot), *adv.*, how often; **totiēs . . . quotiēs**, as often . . . as.

Raecius (ī), Lūcius (ī), Lucius Raecius, *a prominent Roman.*
rapiō, rapere, rapuī, raptus, *3, tr.*, snatch, seize.
ratiō, ratiōnis, method, reason, plan, way.
recēns (*gen.* **recentis**), fresh, new.
recipiō, recipere, recēpī, receptus, *3, tr.*, take back, receive, accept; *w. reflexive pronoun*, withdraw, recover.
recitō, *1, tr.*, read aloud.
recognōscō, recognōscere, recognōvī, recognitus, *3, tr.*, review, recall.
recreō, *1, tr.*, revive, restore, recover, refresh.
rēctā (viā), straightway.
rēctē, *adv.*, rightly, correctly.
redeō, redīre, rediī, reditum, *irreg., intr.*, return.
redūcō, redūcere, redūxī, reductus, *3, tr.*, lead back, draw back.
referō, referre, rettulī, relātus, *irreg., tr.*, bring back, report, refer; **grātiam referre**, to show gratitude; **pedem referre**, to retreat, to fall back.
regiō, regiōnis, boundary, limit, direction, region.
rēgnō, *1, tr.*, reign.
rēgnum, ī, kingdom, royal power.
rejectiō, rejectiōnis, challenging.
rejiciō, rejicere, rejēcī, rejectus, *3, tr.*, hurl back, drive back, repel, challenge.
relevō, *1, tr.*, lift up, raise, relieve.
religiō, religiōnis, scruple, conscientiousness; *in Christian Latin*, reverence for God, religion, sacred rites.
relinquō, relinquere, relīquī, relictus, *3, tr.*, leave, leave behind.
reliquus, a, um, remaining, the rest of.
remaneō, remanēre, remānsī, remānsūrus, *2, intr.*, remain behind.
remissiō, remissiōnis, relaxation, forgiveness.
remittō, remittere, remīsī, remissus, *3, tr.*, send back, return, release.
removeō, removēre, remōvī, remōtus, *2, tr.*, move back, remove.
repellō, repellere, reppulī, repulsus, *3, tr.*, beat back, drive back.
repente, *adv.*, suddenly.

reperiō, reperīre, repperī, repertus, *4, tr.; acc. w. infin.,* find (out).
repetō, repetere, repetīvī, repetītus, *3, tr.,* seek back, demand, recollect; **dē pecūniīs repetundīs,** concerning extortion.
reprimō, reprimere, repressī, repressus, *3, tr.,* press back, check, restrain.
requīrō, requīrere, requīsīvī, requīsītus, *3, tr.,* seek again, search for, demand, miss, need.
rēs, reī, thing, affair; **rēs (rērum) gestae (gestārum),** exploits, achievements; **rēs (rērum) novae (novārum),** revolution; **rēs (reī) pūblica (ae),** state, government, republic; **quam ob rem,** wherefore.
reservō, *1, tr.,* reserve, keep back.
resideō, residēre, resēdī, *2, intr.,* settle down, remain, abate, subside.
resistō, resistere, restitī, *3, intr.; w. dat.,* remain behind, resist, withstand.
respondeō, respondēre, respondī, respōnsus, *2, tr.; acc. w. infin.,* answer, reply.
respōnsum, ī, answer.
restituō, restituere, restitī, restitūtus, *3, tr.,* restore.
restō, restāre, restitī, *1, intr.,* remain.
resurgō, resurgere, resurrēxī, resurrēctum, *3, intr.,* arise.
resurrēctiō, resurrēctiōnis, resurrection.
retineō, retinēre, retinuī, retentus, *2, tr.,* hold back, keep.
reus, ī, defendant, the accused (person).
revertor, revertī, revertī *or* **reversus sum,** *3, intr.,* return.
revocō, *1, tr.,* call back, recall.
rēx, rēgis, king.
Rhēgīnī, Rhēgīnōrum, the inhabitants of Rhegium, *a city in southern Italy.*
rogō, *1, tr.; **ut (nē)**,* ask, request.
Rōma, ae, Rome.
Rōmānus, a, um, Roman.
Rōmānus, ī, a Roman.
Rōmulus, ī, Romulus, *the mythical founder of Rome.*
rūrsus, *adv.,* again, on the other hand.

sacer, sacra, sacrum, holy.
sacerdōs, sacerdōtis, priest.
sacrātus, a, um, holy.
sacrilegus, a, um, impious.
saeculum, ī, age, world; **in saecula saeculōrum,** world without end, forever; **per omnia saecula saeculōrum,** forever, and ever; **per saecula,** forever.
saepe, *adv.,* often.
sagāx (*gen.* **sagācis**), shrewd.
salūs, salūtis, safety, welfare, salvation.
salve (salvēte), *imperative,* hail.
salvus, a, um, safe.
sānctus, a, um, holy, saint.
sānctus, ī (sāncta, ae), a saint.
sānē, *adv.,* indeed, truly, of course.
sanguis, sanguinis, *m.,* blood.
sapiēns (*gen.* **sapientis**), wise.
satis, *indecl. noun; w. gen.,* enough, sufficient.
satis, *adv.,* sufficiently.
scelerātē, *adv.,* criminally.
scelerātus, a, um, criminal.
scelus, sceleris, *n.,* crime.
scientia, ae, knowledge, science, skill.
sciō, *4, tr.; acc. w. infin.,* know.
Scīpiō (Scīpiōnis) Āfricānus (ī), Pūblius (ī), Publius Scipio Africanus, *a famous Roman general.*
scrībō, scrībere, scrīpsī, scrīptus, *3, tr.; acc. w. infin.,* write.
Scrīptūrae, Scrīptūrārum, the Holy Scriptures.
sēcernō, sēcernere, sēcrēvī, sēcrētus, *3, tr.,* separate.
secundum, *prep. w. acc.,* according to, along.
secundus, a, um, second, favorable, successful.

secūris, secūris, axe.
sed, *conj.*, but.
sedeō, sedēre, sēdī, *2, intr.*, sit.
sēdēs, sēdis, seat, abode, habitation.
sēdō, *1, tr.*, stop, quiet, mitigate.
sēmen, sēminis, seed.
semper, *adv.*, always.
sempiternus, a, um, everlasting.
senātor, senātōris, senator.
senātōrius, a, um, senatorial.
senātus, ūs, senate.
senex (*gen.* **senis**), old.
senior, senius, elder.
sēnsus, ūs, sense, emotion, feeling, understanding.
sententia, ae, opinion, vote.
sentiō, sentīre, sēnsī, sēnsus, *4, tr.; acc. w. infin.*, feel, perceive, think.
septem, *indecl. numeral*, seven.
sequor, sequī, secūtus sum, *3, tr.*, follow, pursue.
sērius, *adv.*, too late.
sermō, sermōnis, *m.*, talk, conversation, word, saying.
Servīlius (ī), Gājus (ī), Gaius Servilius, *a Roman businessman.*
serviō, *4, intr.; w. dat.*, serve, do service to.
servitūs, servitūtis, *f.*, slavery.
servō, *1, tr.*, guard, keep.
servus, ī, slave, servant.
sevēritās, sevēritātis, strictness, sternness.
sex, *indecl. numeral*, six.
sextus, a, um, sixth.
sī, *conj.*, if; **sī modo,** *conj.*, if only; **sī . . . nōn,** if not, but if not.
Sibyllīnus, a, um, Sibylline.
sīc, *adv.*, so, in such a manner; **sīc . . . ut,** *conj.*, just . . . as.
sīca, ae, dagger.
Sicilia, ae, Sicily.
Siciliēnsis, e, Sicilian.
Siculī, Siculōrum, Sicilians.
sīcut, *conj.*, as.
signum, ī, standard, signal, sign, seal.
silentium, ī, silence, stillness.
sileō, silēre, siluī, *2, intr.*, am silent, keep silent.
silva, ae, forest.
similis, e; *w. gen. or dat.*, like, similar.
simul, *adv.*, together, at the same time; **simul atque,** *conj.*, as soon as.
simulō, *1, tr.*, pretend.
sīn, but if, if however; **sīn aliter,** but if not; **sīn autem,** but if; **sīn minus,** but if not (Gr. 587-588).
sine, *prep. w. abl.*, without.
singulāris, e, remarkable, distinguished, outstanding, alone.
singulī, ae, a, each, one at a time.
societās, societātis, fellowship, companionship.
socius, ī, companion, ally.
soleō, solēre, solitus sum, *2, intr.; w. infin.*, am accustomed.
sōlitūdō, sōlitūdinis, solitude.
sollicitātiō, sollicitātiōnis, an inciting, an alluring, a tempting.
sollicitō, *1, tr.*, stir up, tempt, instigate.
sōlum, *adv.*, only.
sōlus, a, um, alone, only.
solvō, solvere, solvī, solūtus, *3, tr.*; **nāvem solvere,** to set sail.
spectō, *1, tr.*, look at, look towards.
speculātor, speculātōris, spy.
spērō, *1, tr.; acc. w. infin.*, hope.
spēs, speī, hope.
spīritus, ūs, breath, spirit; **Spīritus (ūs) Sānctus (ī),** Holy Spirit.
spoliō, *1, tr.*, plunder, despoil.
sponte, meā (tuā, suā), of my (your, his, her, their) own accord.
Statilius (ī), Lūcius (ī), Lucius Statilius, *one of Catiline's confederates.*
statim, *adv.*, at once, immediately.
Stator, Statōris, the Stayer *(Protector)*, Mainstay.
statuō, statuere, statuī, statūtus, *3, tr.; w. infin.*, set up, place, determine.
stō, stāre, stetī, statum, *1, intr.*, stand.
strepitus, ūs, noise.

studeō, studēre, studuī, *2, intr.; w. dat. or pres. infin.*, am eager (for), strive (after), am devoted (to).

studiōsus, a, um; *w. gen.*, fond of, eager for; *as a noun*, collector, connoisseur.

studium, ī, zeal, eagerness, devotion, desire, study.

stultus, a, um, stupid, dull.

suādeō, suādēre, suāsī, suāsus, *2, tr.; w. dat. of person; acc. of thing; acc. w. infin.;* ***ut (nē)***, advise, urge.

sub, *prep. w. abl.*, under, at the foot of; *prep. w. acc.*, under, beneath, up to, about, toward *(of time)*; **sub oculīs omnium,** in the sight of all.

subitō, *adv.*, suddenly.

subjiciō, subjicere, subjēcī, subjectus, *3, tr.; w. acc. and dat.*, throw under, expose to.

subterfugiō, subterfugere, subterfūgī, *3, tr.*, escape, avoid.

suī, himself (him), herself (her), itself (it).

Sulla (ae), **Lūcius** (ī) **Cornēlius** (ī), Lucius Cornelius Sulla, *a Roman dictator.*

sum, esse, fuī, futūrus, *irreg., intr.*, am; **bonō animō esse,** to be of good cheer; **sunt quī;** *w. subj.*, there are those who, there are some who.

summus, a, um, highest.

sūmō, sūmere, sūmpsī, sūmptus, *3, tr.*, take, assume, claim.

super, *prep. w. acc.*, over, on, above.

superior, superius, higher, former.

superō, *1, tr.*, overcome, conquer, surpass.

supersum, superesse, superfuī, superfutūrus, *irreg., intr.; w. dat.*, survive, am left.

supplicātiō, supplicātiōnis, public thanksgiving, day of prayer.

supplicium, ī, punishment, penalty.

surgō, surgere, surrēxī, surrēctum, *3, intr.*, rise, stand up.

suscipiō, suscipere, suscēpī, susceptus, *3, tr.*, undertake, take (upon oneself), receive.

suspectus, a, um, suspected.

suspīciō, suspīciōnis, suspicion, indication.

suspicor, *1, tr.; acc. w. infin.*, suspect.

sustineō, sustinēre, sustinuī, sustentus, *2, tr.*, sustain, withstand.

suus, a, um, his (own), her (own), its (own), their (own); **suā sponte,** of his (her, their) own accord.

Syrācūsae, Syrācūsārum, Syracuse, *one of the principal cities of Sicily.*

Syrācūsānī, Syrācūsānōrum, the Syracusans, the inhabitants of Syracuse.

Syria, ae, Syria.

tabella, ae, tablet.

tabula, ae, tablet, list, record.

taceō, *2, tr. and intr.*, am silent, pass over in silence.

taciturnitās, taciturnitātis, silence.

tacitus, a, um, silent, silently, quiet.

tālis, e, such, of such a kind; **tālis, e . . . quālis, e,** such . . . as.

tam, *adv.*, so, to such a degree; **tam . . . quam,** so . . . as, both . . . and, as well . . . as, as much . . . as; *w. negative,* not so much . . . as.

tamen, *adv.*, nevertheless, still, yet.

tametsī, *conj.*, and yet, although, though (Gr. 598).

tamquam, *adv.*, as if, just as if, as though (Gr. 611).

tandem, *adv.*, at last, at length, finally.

tantum, *adv.*, so much, only.

tantus, a, um, so great; **tantī,** of such a value, so much (Gr. 701); **tantō opere,** so much, so greatly; **tantus, a, um . . . quantus, a, um,** as great . . . as, as large . . . as; **tantō . . . quantō,** *used in comparing comparative adjectives and adverbs* (Gr. 607).

tardus, a, um, slow.

tēctum, ī, roof, house, building.

tēlum, ī, dart, weapon.

temere, *adv.,* recklessly, rashly, without good reason.
temeritās, temeritātis, rashness.
tempestās, tempestātis, storm, weather.
templum, ī, temple, shrine.
temptō, *1, tr.,* make an attempt, try, test, try to win over.
tempus, temporis, *n.,* time.
tenebrae, tenebrārum, darkness.
teneō, tenēre, tenuī, tentus, *2, tr.,* hold; **memoriā tenēre;** *w. acc. or acc. w. infin.,* to remember.
tenuis, e, fine, thin, slender.
terminō, *1, tr.,* bound, limit.
terra, ae, earth, land; **orbis (orbis) terrārum** (*or* **terrae**), the world; **terrā marīque,** on land and sea.
terreō, *2, tr.,* terrify, frighten.
tertius, a, um, third.
testimōnium, ī, proof, testimony, witness.
testis, testis, *m.,* witness.
Tiberis, Tiberis, *m.,* the Tiber, *a river.*
timeō, timēre, timuī, *2, tr.; nē (nē nōn, ut); w. pres. infin.,* fear (to).
timidus, a, um, timorous, fearful.
timor, timōris, fear.
togātus, a, um, clothed in the toga.
tollō, tollere, sustulī, sublātus, *3, tr.,* lift up, take away; *passive,* am elated.
tot, *indecl. adj.,* so many; **tot . . . quot,** as many . . . as.
totiēns, *adv.,* so often, so many times.
totiēs . . . quotiēs, *advs.,* as often . . . as.
tōtus, a, um, whole, all of, the whole of.
trāctō, *1, tr.,* conduct, treat.
trādō, trādere, trādidī, trāditus, *3, tr.,* hand over.
trādūcō, trādūcere, trādūxī, trāductus, *3, tr.; w. two accs. or acc. and trāns w. acc.,* lead across, lead over.
trāns, *prep. w. acc.,* across.
trānseō, trānsīre, trānsiī(-īvī), trānsitus, *irreg., tr.,* go across, cross, pass.
trānsferō, trānsferre, trānstulī, trānslātus, *irreg., tr.,* carry over, transfer.
trēs, tria, three (Gr. 116).
tribūnal, tribūnālis, tribunal, judgment seat.
tribūnīcius, a, um, of tribunes.
tribūnus, ī, tribune; **tribūnus (ī) mīlitum,** military tribune; **tribūnus (ī) plēbis,** tribune of the people.
triennium, ī, a space of three years.
trucīdō, *1, tr.,* slaughter, kill fiercely.
tū, tuī, you *(sing.).*
tueor, tuērī, tuitus sum, *2, tr.,* look at, protect.
Tullus, ī, Tullus, *a Roman name.*
tum, *adv.,* then, at that time; **tum . . . cum,** *advs.,* at the time when (Gr. 560).
tumultus, ūs, uproar, disorder, confusion.
tunc, *adv.,* then.
turpis, e, shameful, base.
turpitūdō, turpitūdinis, shame, disgrace.
tūtō, *adv.,* safely, securely.
tūtus, a, um, safe.
tuus, a, um, your, yours, your own *(referring to one person);* **tuā sponte,** of your own accord.

ubi, *adv.,* where, in what place; *conj.,* when; **ubi prīmum,** *conj.,* as soon as (Gr. 556).
ubinam, *adv.,* when; **ubinam gentium,** where in the world.
ubīque, *adv.,* everywhere.
ūllus, a, um, any, anyone.
ulterior, ulterius, farther.
ultimus, a, um, farthest, last.
ultrō, *adv.,* unasked, unprovoked, of one's own accord.
umquam, *adv.,* ever, at any time; **nē umquam,** that never (Gr. 549).
ūnā, *adv.,* along (with), together.
unde, *adv.,* whence, from where.
undique, *adv.,* from all sides, on all sides, everywhere.

ūnigenitus, a, um, only-begotten.
ūnitās, ūnitātis, unity.
ūniversus, a, um, entire, all together.
ūnus, a, um, one; **ad ūnum,** to a man, without exception *(generally with omnēs).*
ūnusquisque, ūnaquisque, ūnumquidque, each, each one (Gr. 836).
urbānus, a, um, belonging to the city, of the city.
urbs, urbis, city.
usque, *adv.*, all the way (to), even (to), up (to); **usque eō,** to such an extent.
ūsus, ūs, use, advantage, experience.
ut, *conj.*, that *(in noun, purpose, and result clauses),* in order that *(in purpose clauses),* as *(in comparative clauses),* granted that *(in concessive subjunctive);* **sīc . . . ut,** just as; **ut . . . nōn,** that . . . not *(in negative result clauses and noun clauses);* **ut prīmum,** as soon as.
uterque, utraque, utrumque (*gen.* **utrīusque**), each, both *(of two).*
utilis, e; *ad w. acc.*, useful (for).
utinam, may, would that *(particle used with volitive subjunctive).*
ūtor, ūtī, ūsus sum, *3, intr.; w. abl.*, use, employ, exercise.
utrum . . . an, whether . . . or *(used in double questions,* Gr. 505).
uxor, uxōris, wife.

vacuēfaciō, vacuēfacere, vacuēfēcī, vacuēfactus, *3, tr.*, empty.
valeō, valēre, valuī, *2, intr.; w. infin.*, am strong, am influential, am well; **plūrimum valēre,** to be very powerful.
Valeriānus, ī, Valerian, *a Roman emperor.*
Valerius, ī, Valerius, *a Roman name.*
vallum, ī, wall, rampart.
varietās, varietātis, diversity, variety.
vastitās, vastitātis, desolation, ruin.
vastō, *1, tr.*, lay waste, ravage, destroy.
vehemēns (*gen.* **vehementis**), violent, impetuous, strong.
vehementer, *adv.*, greatly, violently.
vel, *conj.*, or; **vel . . . vel,** *conjs.*, either . . . or.
vēndō, vēndere, vēndidī, vēnditus, *3, tr.*, sell.
veneror, *1, tr.*, reverence, venerate.
veniō, venīre, vēnī, ventum, *4, intr.*, come.
ventus, ī, wind.
verbera, verberum, *n.*, stripes, whipping, flogging, blows.
verberō, *1, tr.*, beat, flog.
verbum, ī, word.
vērē, *adv.*, indeed, truly.
vereor, *2, tr.; w. pres. infin.;* ***nē (nē nōn, ut),*** fear (to).
vēritās, vēritātis, truth.
vērō, *adv. and conj., postp.*, in truth, but, of course; **immō vērō,** *adv.*, nay, on the contrary.
Verrēs (Verris), Gājus (ī), Gaius Verres.
versor, *1, intr.*, move about, dwell, engage in, remain, depend on, turn on.
versus, *adv. and prep. w. acc.*, towards *(usually follows word to which joined).*
vertō, vertere, vertī, versus, *3, tr.*, turn.
vērum, *adv.*, but, yet; **nōn modo . . . vērum (etiam),** not only . . . but (also).
vērum, ī, truth, reality.
vērus, a, um, true, real.
vester, vestra, vestrum, your, yours, your own *(referring to more than one person).*
veterrimus, a, um, oldest.
vetō, vetāre, vetuī, vetitus, *1, tr.; acc. w. pres. infin.*, forbid.
vetus (*gen.* **veteris**), old.
vexātiō, vexātiōnis, harassing, troubling.
vexō, *1, tr.*, harass, ravage.
vī (***abl. of*** **vīs**), violently, by force.

via, ae, road, way; **viam mūniō,** *4, tr.,* construct a road.
vīcēsimus, a, um, twentieth.
victōria, ae, victory.
vidēlicet, *adv.,* clearly, of course.
videō, vidēre, vīdī, vīsus, *2, tr.; acc. w. infin.,* see.
videor, vidērī, vīsus sum, *2, intr.; w. infin.,* am seen, seem, appear.
vigilia, ae, night watch, guard.
vigilō, *1, intr.,* am awake, am on guard.
vinciō, vincīre, vīnxī, vīnctus, *4, tr.,* bind, bind in prison.
vincō, vincere, vīcī, victus, *3, tr.,* conquer.
vinculum, ī, bond; *pl.,* chains, prison; **in vincula conjiciō, conjicere, conjēcī, conjectus,** *3, tr.,* throw into prison.
vindicō, *1, tr.,* punish, deliver, set free.
violō, *1, tr.,* injure, outrage.
vir, virī, man, husband.
vīrēs, vīrium, *f.,* strength, force.
virga, ae, twig, bough, rod *(for flogging),* wand.
virgo, virginis, virgin.
virtūs, virtūtis, courage, virtue, value, merit, manliness.
vīs (*gen.* **vis** [*rare*]; *acc.* **vim**; *abl.* **vī**; *pl.,* **vīrēs, vīrium**), power, force, violence; **vim faciō, facere, fēcī, factus,** *3, tr.,* use force.
vīta, ae, life.
vitium, ī, fault, crime.
vītō, *1, tr.,* avoid, shun, escape.
vīvō, vīvere, vīxī, vīctūrus, *3, intr.,* live.
vīvus, a, um, alive, living.
vix, *adv.,* hardly, barely, with difficulty, scarcely.
vōciferātiō, vōciferātiōnis, outcry.
vocō, *1, tr.; w. two accs.,* call.
volō, velle, voluī, *tr.; w. pres. infin.; acc. w. infin.; **ut (nē)**,* am willing, wish.
Volturcius (ī), **Titus** (ī), Titus Volturcius, *one of Catiline's agents.*
voluntās, voluntātis, will, desire, consent.
voluptās, voluptātis, pleasure.
vōs, vestrī, you *(pl.).*
vōx, vōcis, voice, cry.
vulnerō, *1, tr.,* wound.
vulnus, vulneris, *n.,* wound.
vultus, ūs, look, expression, face, countenance.

ENGLISH-LATIN VOCABULARY

abandoned, perditus, a, um.
able, am, possum, posse, potuī, *irreg., intr.; w. pres. infin.*
abode, domicilium, ī.
about (= **concerning**), dē, *prep. w. abl.*
about, bring, efficiō, efficere, effēcī, effectus, *3, tr.; ut (ut nōn or nē).*
about, turn, convertō, convertere, convertī, conversus, *3, tr.*
absent, absēns (*gen.* absentis).
absent, am, absum, abesse, āfuī, āfutūrus, *irreg., intr.; ab (ā) w. abl.;* dēsum, deesse, dēfuī, dēfutūrus, *irreg., intr.; w. dat.*
abundance, cōpia, ae.
accept, accipiō, accipere, accēpī, acceptus, *3, tr.;* recipiō, recipere, recēpī, receptus, *3, tr.*
accomplish, cōnficiō, cōnficere, cōnfēcī, cōnfectus, *3, tr.;* prōficiō, prōficere, prōfēcī, prōfectus, *3, tr.; ut (nē).*
accord, of my (your, his, her, their) own, meā (tuā, suā) sponte.
according to, dē, *prep. w. abl.*
account of, on, propter, *prep. w. acc.*
accusation, crīmen, crīminis.
accuse, accūsō, *1, tr.; w. gen. of the charge;* indicō, *1, tr.*
accused (person), reus, ī.
accustomed, am (have accustomed, have become accustomed), cōnsuēvī, cōnsuētus, *3, tr. and intr.; w. pres. infin.;* soleō, solēre, solitus sum, *2, intr.; w. infin.*
across, trāns, *prep. w. acc.*
across, go, trānseō, trānsīre, trānsiī(-īvī), trānsitus, *irreg., tr.*
across, lead, trādūcō, trādūcere, trādūxī, trāductus, *3, tr.; w. two accs. or acc. and trāns w. acc.*
act, agō, agere, ēgī, āctus, *3, tr.*
act, catch in the, dēprehendō, dēprehendere, dēprehendī, dēprehēnsus, *3, tr.*
address, appellō, *1, tr.*
admit, cōnfiteor, cōnfitērī, cōnfessus sum, *2, tr.; acc. w. infin.*
advance, prōgredior, prōgredī, prōgressus sum, *3, intr.*
advance to, aggredior, aggredī, aggressus sum, *3, tr.*
advise, moneō, *2, tr.; ut (nē).*
affair, rēs, reī.
affirm, cōnfirmō, *1, tr.; acc. w. infin.*
aflame, am, ārdeō, ārdēre, ārsī, ārsum, *2, intr.; w. infin.*
afraid, am, timeō, timēre, timuī, *2, tr.; w. infin.*
after, post, *prep. w. acc.;* postquam, *conj.*
afterwards, post, *adv.;* posteā, *adv.*
against, contrā, *prep. w. acc.;* in, *prep. w. acc.*
against, send, immittō, immittere, immīsī, immissus, *3, tr.*
aged, senex (*gen.* senis).
agent = guard.
ago, abhinc, *adv.* (Gr. 923); **long ago,** jam prīdem; jam diū; jam dūdum.
ahead, see, prōvideō, prōvidēre, prōvīdī, prōvīsus, *2, tr.; ut (nē).*
ahead, send, praemittō, praemittere, praemīsī, praemissus, *3, tr.*
aid, adjuvō, adjuvāre, adjūvī, adjūtus, *1, tr.*
aid, auxilium, ī.
alarm, commoveō, commovēre, commōvī, commōtus, *2, tr.*
all, omnis, e.
all of, tōtus, a, um (Gr. 84).
all sides, from, undique, *adv.;* **on all sides,** undique, *adv.*
all the way (to), usque, *adv.*

all together, ūniversī, ae, a.
allow, committō, committere, commīsī, commissus, *3, tr.;* patior, patī, passus sum, *3, tr.; w. pres. infin.; acc. w. infin.*
ally, socius, ī.
almost, ferē, *adv.;* prope, *adv.*
alone, sōlus, a, um (Gr. 84).
aloud, cry, clāmō, *1, tr.; acc. w. infin.*
aloud, read, recitō, *1, tr.*
Alps, Alpēs, Alpium, *f.*
already, jam, *adv.*
also, etiam, *adv.;* **not only . . . but also**, nōn modo . . . sed etiam.
although, quamquam; cum; licet; etsi, *conjs.* (Gr. 595-598).
altogether, omnīnō, *adv.*
always, semper, *adv.*
am, sum, esse, fuī, futūrus, *irreg., intr.*
am able, possum, posse, potuī, *irreg., intr.; w. pres. infin.*
am absent, absum, abesse, āfuī, āfutūrus, *irreg., intr.; ab (ā) w. abl.;* dēsum, deesse, dēfuī, dēfutūrus, *irreg., intr.; w. dat.*
am accustomed, cōnsuēvī, cōnsuētus, *3, intr.; w. pres. infin.;* soleō, solēre, solitus sum, *2, intr.; w. infin.*
am aflame, ārdeō, ārdēre, ārsī, ārsum, *2, intr.; w. infin.*
am afraid, timeō, timēre, timuī, *2, tr., w. infin.*
am away, absum, abesse, āfuī, āfutūrus, *irreg., intr.; ab (ā) w. abl.*
am bound for, intendō, intendere, intendī, intentus, *3, tr.; ad or in w. acc.*
am devoted (to), studeō, studēre, studuī, *2, intr.; w. dat.*
am distant, absum, abesse, āfuī, āfutūrus, *irreg., intr.; ab (ā) w. abl.*
am done, fīō, fierī, factus sum, *irreg., intr.*
am eager (for), studeō, studēre, studuī, *2, intr.; w. dat. or pres. infin.*
am elated. *Use passive of* tollō, tollere, sustulī, sublātus, *3, tr.*
am glad, gaudeō, gaudēre, gāvīsus sum, *2, intr.*
am ignorant, nesciō, *4, tr.; acc. w. infin.*
am in charge of, praesum, praeesse, praefuī, praefutūrus, *irreg., intr.; w. dat.*
am in command of, praesum, praeesse, praefuī, praefutūrus, *irreg., intr.; w. dat.*
am influential, valeō, valēre, valuī, *2, intr.; w. infin.*
am lacking, dēsum, deesse, dēfuī, dēfutūrus, *irreg., intr.; w. dat.*
am made, fīō, fierī, factus sum, *irreg., intr.*
am of the opinion, cēnseō, cēnsēre, cēnsuī, cēnsus, *2, tr.; acc. w. infin.; ut (nē).*
am on fire, cōnflagrō, *1, tr.*
am open, pateō, patēre, patuī, *2, intr.*
am over (= **am in charge of**), praesum, praeesse, praefuī, praefutūrus, *irreg., intr.; w. dat.*
am present, adsum, adesse, adfuī, adfutūrus, *irreg., intr.; w. dat.*
am silent, sileō, silēre, siluī, *2, intr;* taceō, *2, tr. and intr.*
am strong, valeō, valēre, valuī, *2, intr.; w. infin.*
am surprised at, admīror, *1, tr.*
am unable, nōn possum, posse, potuī, *irreg., intr.; w. infin.*
am unaware, ignōrō, *1, tr.; acc. w. infin.*
am unwilling, nōlō, nōlle, nōluī, *tr.; w. infin.; acc. w. infin.; ut (nē).*
am well, valeō, valēre, valuī, *2, intr.; w. infin.*
am willing, volō, velle, voluī, *tr.; w. pres. infin.; acc. w. infin.; ut (nē).*
am without, careō, carēre, caruī, caritūrus, *2, intr.; w. abl.*
ambush, īnsidiae, īnsidiārum.
America, America, ae.
American *(noun)*, Americānus, ī; *(adj.)*, Americānus, a, um.
among, apud; inter, *preps. w. acc.*

ancestors, mājōrēs, mājōrum, ***m.***
ancient, antīquus, a, um.
and, et, *conj.;* atque (ac), *conj.;* -que, *conj.;* **and . . . not,** neque, *conj.*
and so, itaque, *conj.*
and yet, quamquam, *conj.*
announce, nuntiō, *1, tr.; acc. w. infin.*
another, alius, alia, aliud (Gr. 85-86).
another's, aliēnus, a, um.
answer, respondeō, respondēre, respondī, respōnsus, *2, tr.; acc. w. infin.*
any, ūllus, a, um (Gr. 84); **at any time,** umquam, *adv.*
appearance, aspectus, ūs.
approach, adeō, adīre, adiī(-īvī), aditus, *irreg., tr.;* appropinquō, *1, intr.; w. dat. or ad w. acc.*
arm, armō, *1, tr.*
arms, arma, armōrum.
army, exercitus, ūs; ***(on the march),*** agmen, agminis.
arouse, commoveō, commovēre, commōvī, commōtus, *2, tr.;* incitō, *1, tr.;* permoveō, permovēre, permōvī, permōtus, *2, tr.*
arrest, comprehendō, comprehendere, comprehendī, comprehēnsus, *3, tr.*
arrival, adventus, ūs.
arrive, perveniō, pervenīre, pervēnī, perventum, *4, intr.; in or ad w. acc.*
as, ut, sīcut, velut, quemadmodum, *conjs.;* **as . . . as,** tam . . . quam; **just as,** quasi, *adv. and conj.;* sīc . . . ut, *conj.;* **so . . . as,** tam . . . quam; **such . . . as,** tālis, e . . . quālis, e.
as great . . . as, tantus, a, um . . . quantus, a, um.
as if, quasi, *adv. and conj.*
as large . . . as, tantus, a, um . . . quantus, a, um.
as long as, dummodo, *conj.* (Gr. 594).
as many . . . as, tot . . . quot.
as often . . . as, totiēs . . . quotiēs.
as soon as, ut prīmum, *conj.;* cum prīmum, *conj.*

ask, quaerō, quaerere, quaesīvī, quaesītus, *3, tr.; **ut (nē);*** rogō, *1, tr.; **ut (nē).***
ask for, petō, petere, petīvī, petītus, *3, tr.; **ut (nē).***
assault, oppugnō, *1, tr.*
assemble, conveniō, convenīre, convēnī, conventum, *4, intr.*
assembly, comitia, comitiōrum.
assume, sūmō, sūmere, sūmpsī, sūmptus, *3, tr.*
at, ad, *prep. w. acc.*
at any time, umquam, *adv.*
at dawn, prīmā lūce.
at home, domī.
at last, dēnique, *adv.;* tandem, *adv.*
at least, quidem, *adv.*
at length, aliquandō, *adv.*
at once, statim, *adv.*
at some time, aliquandō, *adv.*
at that time, tum, *adv.*
at the foot of, sub, *prep. w. abl.*
attack, aggredior, aggredī, aggressus sum, *3, tr.;* oppugnō, *1, tr.*
attack, impetus, ūs.
attempt, cōnor, *1, tr.; w. pres. infin.*
attend to, administrō, *1, tr.;* animadvertō, animadvertere, animadvertī, animadversus, *3, tr.; acc. w. infin.*
Augustus, Augustus, ī.
author, auctor, auctōris.
authority, auctōritās, auctōritātis.
avoid, vītō, *1, tr.*
away, am, absum, abesse, āfuī, āfutūrus, *irreg., intr.; ab (ā) w. abl.*
away, carry, dēferō, dēferre, dētulī, dēlātus, *irreg., tr.*
away, drive, dēpellō, dēpellere, dēpulī, dēpulsus, *3, tr.*
away, lead, dēdūcō, dēdūcere, dēdūxī, dēductus, *3, tr.*
away, run, profugiō, profugere, profūgī, profugitum, *3, intr.*
away, send, dīmittō, dīmittere, dīmīsī, dīmissus, *3, tr.*
away, slip, ēlābor, ēlābī, ēlāpsus sum, *3, intr.*

away, take, ēripiō, ēripere, ēripuī, ēreptus, *3, tr.; w. dat. of person or thing from which; ab (ā), ex (ē) w. abl.;* tollō, tollere, sustulī, sublātus, *3, tr.*

away from, ab (ā), *prep. w. abl.*

back, beat, repellō, repellere, reppulī, repulsus, *3, tr.*

back, bring, referō, referre, rettulī, relātus, *irreg., tr.*

back, call, revocō, *1, tr.*

back, draw, redūcō, redūcere, redūxī, reductus, *3, tr.*

back, drive, rejiciō, rejicere, rejēcī, rejectus, *3, tr.;* repellō, repellere, reppulī, repulsus, *3, tr.*

back, fall, pedem referō, referre, rettulī, relātus, *irreg., tr.*

back, hold, retineō, retinēre, retinuī, retentus, *2, tr.*

back, hurl, rejiciō, rejicere, rejēcī, rejectus, *3, tr.*

back, lead, redūcō, redūcere, redūxī, reductus, *3, tr.*

back, press, reprimō, reprimere, repressī, repressus, *3, tr.*

back, send, remittō, remittere, remīsī, remissus, *3, tr.*

back, take, recipiō, recipere, recēpī, receptus, *3, tr.*

bad, malus, a, um.

badly, male, *adv.*

baggage (train), impedīmenta, impedīmentōrum.

band, manus, ūs, *f.*

barbarian ***(noun),*** barbarus, ī; ***(adj.),*** barbarus, a, um.

barely, vix, *adv.*

battle, proelium, ī; **join (begin) battle,** proelium committō, committere, commīsī, commissus, *3, tr.*

battle line, aciēs, aciēī.

be. *See* **am.**

be unwilling, nōlī, nōlite (*imperative of* nōlō) ; *w. pres. infin.*

bear, ferō, ferre, tulī, lātus, *irreg., tr.;* pariō, parere, peperī, partus, *3, tr.*

bear in mind, meminī, meminisse, *tr.; w. gen. of persons, gen. or acc. of things, acc. of neuter pronouns or adjs.; acc. w. infin.*

beat back, repellō, repellere, reppulī, repulsus, *3, tr.*

beautiful, pulcher, pulchra, pulchrum.

because, quia, *conj.;* quod, *conj.;* quoniam, *conj.*

because of, propter, *prep. w. acc.*

become, fīō, fierī, factus sum, *irreg., intr.;* ***ut (ut nōn).***

become accustomed, have, cōnsuēvī, cōnsuētus, *3, intr.; w. pres. infin.*

become master of, potior, *4, intr.; w. abl. or gen.*

before, ante, *prep. w. acc.;* prō, *prep. w. abl.;* anteā, *adv.*

beg, ōrō, *1, tr.;* ***ut (nē);*** petō, petere, petīvī, petitus, *3, tr.;* ***ut (nē).***

began, coepī, coepisse, coeptus sum, *tr.; w. pres. infin.* (Gr. page 82, footnote 1).

begin battle, proelium committō, committere, commīsī, commissus, *3, tr.*

beginning, in the, in prīncipiō.

begun, have, coepī, coepisse, coeptus sum, *tr.; w. pres. infin.* (Gr. page 82, footnote 1).

behalf of, on, prō, *prep. w. abl.*

behind, post, *prep. w. acc.*

behind, leave, relinquō, relinquere, relīquī, relictus, *3, tr.*

behind, remain, resistō, resistere, restitī, *3, intr.; w. dat.*

behooves, it, oportet, oportēre, oportuit, *2, intr.; acc. w. pres. infin.*

believe, crēdō, crēdere, crēdidī, crēditus, *3, tr. and intr.; w. dat. of person in whom; acc. w. infin.*

beneath, sub, *prep. w. acc.*

best, optimus, a, um.

betake oneself, mē (tē, sē) cōnferō, cōnferre, contulī, collātus, *irreg., tr.*

better ***(adj.),*** melior, melius; ***(adv.),*** melius.

between, inter, *prep. w. acc.*

beyond, extrā, *prep. w. acc.*
bitterly, ācriter, *adv.*
blaze, ārdeō, ārdēre, ārsī, ārsum, *2, intr.; w. infin.*
blood, sanguis, sanguinis, *m.*
body, corpus, corporis, *n.*
bold, audāx (*gen.* audācis).
boldness, audācia, ae.
bond, vinculum, ī.
both *(of two),* uterque, utraque, utrumque (*gen. sing.* utrīusque, *dat. sing.* utrīque).
both . . . and, et . . . et, *conjs.*
bound for, am, intendō, intendere, intendī, intentus, *3, tr.; ad w. acc.*
boy, puer, puerī.
brave, fortis, e.
bravely, fortiter, *adv.*
bravery, fortitūdō, fortitūdinis.
break, frangō, frangere, frēgī, frāctus, *3, tr.*
breath, spīritus, ūs.
bridge, pōns, pontis, *m.*
brief, brevis, e.
briefly, breviter, *adv.*
brigandage, latrōcinium, ī.
bring, ferō, ferre, tulī, lātus, *irreg., tr.*
bring about, efficiō, efficere, effēcī, effectus, *3, tr.; ut (ut nōn or nē).*
bring back, referō, referre, retulī, relātus, *irreg., tr.*
bring forth, pariō, parere, peperī, partus, *3, tr.*
bring in, intrōdūcō, intrōdūcere, intrōdūxī, intrōductus, *3, tr.*
bring to, afferō, afferre, attulī, allātus, *irreg., tr.*
bring together, cōgō, cōgere, coēgī, coāctus, *3, tr.; acc. w. pres. infin.;* colligō, colligere, collēgī, collēctus, *3, tr.;* cōnferō, cōnferre, contulī, collātus, *irreg., tr.*
bring (upon), īnfero, īnferre, īntulī, illātus, *irreg., tr.; w. dat. of person.*
British, Britannī, Britannōrum.
Briton, Britannus, ī.
brother, frāter, frātris (frātrum).
Brutus, Brūtus, ī.
build, condō, condere, condidī, conditus, *3, tr.;* mōlior, mōlīrī, mōlītus sum, *4, tr.*
burn, cōnflagrō, *1, intr.;* incendō, incendere, incendī, incēnsus, *3, tr.*
burst forth, ērumpō, ērumpere, ērūpī, ēruptum, *3, intr.; ex (ē) w. abl.*
but, sed, *conj.;* at, *conj.;* vērō, *adv. and conj., postp.*
but if, quodsī; sīn; sīn autem, *conjs.*
but if not, sīn aliter; sīn minus.
buy, emō, emere, ēmī, emptus, *3, tr.*
by, ab (ā), *prep. w. abl.*
by a little, paulō (Gr. 771).
by far, longē, *adv.*
by force, vī.
by much, multō (Gr. 771).
by name, nōmine.

Caesar, Caesar, Caesaris.
call, appellō, *1, tr.; w. two accs.;* vocō, *1, tr.; w. two accs.*
call back, revocō, *1, tr.*
call together, convocō, *1, tr.*
call upon, appellō, *1, tr.*
camp, castra, castrōrum; **pitch camp,** castra pōnō, pōnere, posuī, positus, *3, tr.*
can, possum, posse, potuī, *irreg., intr.; w. pres. infin.*
capture, capiō, capere, cēpī, captus, *3, tr.*
care, dīligentia, ae; **take care,** prōvideō, prōvidēre, prōvīdī, prōvīsus, *2, tr.; ut (nē).*
care for, cūrō, *1, tr.; ut (nē).*
careful, dīligēns (*gen.* dīligentis).
carefully, dīligenter, *adv.*
carefulness, dīligentia, ae.
carry, ferō, ferre, tulī, lātus, *irreg., tr.;* gerō, gerere, gessī, gestus, *3, tr.;* portō, *1, tr.*
carry away, dēferō, dēferre, dētulī, dēlātus, *irreg., tr.; ad w. acc.*
carry on, exerceō, *2, tr.;* gerō, gerere, gessī, gestus, *3, tr.*

carry over, trānsferō, trānsferre, trānstulī, trānslātus, *irreg., tr.*
cast down, dējiciō, dējicere, dējēcī, dējectus, *3, tr.*
cast out, ējiciō, ējicere, ējēcī, ējectus, *3, tr.*
catch, dēprehendō, dēprehendere, dēprehendī, dēprehēnsus, *3, tr.*
catch in the act, dēprehendō, dēprehendere, dēprehendī, dēprehēnsus, *3, tr.*
catch sight of, cōnspiciō, cōnspicere, cōnspexī, cōnspectus, *3, tr.*
catch sound of, exaudiō, *4, tr.*
Catholic *(noun),* Catholicus, ī; *(adj.),* Catholicus, a, um.
Catiline, Catilīna, ae, *m.*
cause, efficiō, efficere, effēcī, effectus, *3, tr.; ut (ut nōn or nē).*
cause, causa, ae.
cavalry, equitātus, ūs; equitēs, equitum.
centurion, centuriō, centuriōnis.
certain, certus, a, um; quīdam, quaedam, quoddam.
certain, discover as, comperiō, comperīre, comperī, compertus, *4, tr.; acc. w. infin.*
certain, it is, cōnstat, cōnstāre, cōnstitit, *1, intr.; acc. w. infin.*
certain one, quīdam, quiddam.
certain thing, quīdam, quiddam.
certainly, certē, *adv.*
Cethegus, Cethēgus, ī.
chains, vincula, vinculōrum.
change, mūtō, *1, tr.*
character, mōrēs, mōrum, *m.*
charge, crīmen, crīminis.
charge of, am in, praesum, praeesse, praefuī, praefutūrus, *irreg., intr.; w. dat.*
charity, cāritās, cāritātis.
check, comprimō, comprimere, compressī, compressus, *3, tr.;* reprimō, reprimere, repressī, repressus, *3, tr.*
chief, prīnceps, prīncipis; **commander in chief,** imperātor, imperātōris.
children, līberī, līberōrum.
choose, dēligō, dēligere, dēlēgī, dēlēctus, *3, tr.*
Christ, Chrīstus, ī.
Christian *(noun),* Chrīstiānus, ī; *(adj.),* Chrīstiānus, a, um.
Cicero, Cicerō, Cicerōnis.
citizen, cīvis, cīvis, *m.;* **fellow citizen,** cīvis, cīvis, *m.*
city, urbs, urbis.
clear, clārus, a, um; manifestus, a, um.
clearly, plānē, *adv.*
cohort, cohors, cohortis.
collect, cōgō, cōgere, coēgī, coāctus, *3, tr.; acc. w. pres. infin.*
Columbus, Columbus, ī.
column *(of soldiers),* agmen, agminis.
come, veniō, venīre, vēnī, ventum, *4, intr.*
come (to), adveniō, advenīre, advēnī, adventum, *4, intr.*
come together, conveniō, convenīre, convēnī, conventum, *4, intr.*
come upon, inveniō, invenīre, invēnī, inventus, *4, tr.*
coming, adventus, ūs.
command, imperō, *1, tr.; w. dat. of person; ut (nē);* jubeō, jubēre, jussī, jussus, *2, tr.; acc. w. pres. infin.;* mandō, *1, tr.; w. dat. of person; ut (nē).*
command, imperium, ī.
command of, am in, praesum, praeesse, praefuī, praefutūrus, *irreg., intr.; w. dat. of person.*
command of, put in, praeficiō, praeficere, praefēcī, praefectus, *3, tr.; w. dat. of thing of which.*
commander in chief, imperātor, imperātōris.
commit, committō, committere, commīsī, commissus, *3, tr.;* mandō, *1, tr.; w. dat. of person.*
common, commūnis, e.
companion, socius, ī.
company, coetus, ūs.

compare, cōnferō, cōnferre, contulī, collātus, *irreg., tr.*
conceal, abdō, abdere, abdidī, abditus, *3, tr. (Always takes an object.)*
concerning, dē, *prep. w. abl.*
condemn, condemnō, *1, tr.; w. gen. of the charge;* damnō, *1, tr.; w. acc. of person; gen. or abl. of thing.*
condition, condiciō, condiciōnis.
confess, cōnfiteor, cōnfitērī, cōnfessus sum, *2, tr.; acc. w. infin.*
conflagration, incendium, ī.
confuse, perturbō, *1, tr.*
conquer, superō, *1, tr.;* vincō, vincere, vīcī, victus, *3, tr.*
consider, arbitror, *1, tr.; acc. w. infin.*
conspiracy, conjūrātiō, conjūrātiōnis.
conspiracy, form a, conjūrō, *1, intr.*
conspirators, conjūrātī, conjūrātōrum.
conspire, conjūrō, *1, intr.*
construct, mūniō, *4, tr. (w.* ***viam*** *or* ***viās****).*
consul, cōnsul, cōnsulis, *m.*
consular rank, of, cōnsulāris, e.
contemplate, cōgitō, *1, tr. and intr.; acc. w. infin.*
contend, contendō, contendere, contendī, *3, intr.; w. pres. infin.*
continually, continenter, *adv.*
contrary to, praeter, *prep. w. acc.*
convenient, idōneus, a, um; *w. dat. or* ***ad*** *w. acc.*
cost, cōnstō, cōnstāre, cōnstitī, cōnstātum, *1, intr.; w. abl. or gen.*
council, concilium, ī.
counsel, cōnsilium, ī.
country, patria, ae.
courage, fortitūdō, fortitūdinis; virtūs, virtūtis.
courageous, audāx (*gen.* audācis); fortis, e.
court, law, quaestiō, quaestiōnis.
crime, crīmen, crīminis; scelus, sceleris, *n.*
criminal = wicked, bad.
criminal negligence, nēquitia, ae.
crops, frūmenta, frūmentōrum.
cross, trānseō, trānsīre, trānsiī(-īvī), trānsitus, *irreg., tr.*
cross, crux, crucis.
crowd, frequentia, ae.
crowded, frequēns (*gen.* frequentis).
cruel, crūdēlis, e.
cry, vōx, vōcis.
cry aloud, clāmō, *1, tr.; acc. w. infin.*
custody, custōdia, ae.
custom, mōs, mōris, *m.*

daily, cotīdiē, *adv.*
danger, perīculum, ī.
dangerous, perniciōsus, a, um.
dare, audeō, audēre, ausus sum, *2, intr.; w. infin.*
daring ***(noun),*** audācia, ae; ***(adj.),*** audāx (*gen.* audācis).
dark, obscūrus, a, um; **deal in the dark,** obscūrē agō, agere, ēgī, āctus, *3, tr.*
dart, tēlum, ī.
dawn, at, prīmā lūce.
day, diēs, diēī, *m. (f.);* **spend days in,** diēs cōnsūmō, cōnsūmere, cōnsūmpsī, cōnsūmptus, *3, tr.;* ***in*** *w. abl.*
deal in the dark, obscūrē agō, agere, ēgī, āctus, *3, tr.*
dear, cārus, a, um.
death, mors, mortis; **sentence to death,** capite damnō, *1, tr.*
deathless, immortālis, e.
decide, cōnstituō, cōnstituere, cōnstituī, cōnstitūtus, *3, tr.; w. pres. infin.;* dēcernō, dēcernere, dēcrēvī, dēcrētus, *3, tr.; w. infin. if subject is the same;* ***ut (nē)*** *if subject is different.*
decree, dēcernō, dēcernere, dēcrēvī, dēcrētus, *3, tr.; w. infin. if subject is the same;* ***ut (nē)*** *if subject is different.*
decree, cōnsultum, ī.
deed, facinus, facinoris, *n.*
deep, altus, a, um.
defend, dēfendō, dēfendere, dēfendī, dēfēnsus, *3, tr.*

defendant, reus, ī.
defile, angustiae, angustiārum.
definite, certus, a, um.
degree, to such a, adeō, *adv.;* tam, *adv.*
delay, mora, ae.
delight, gaudium, ī.
deliver, vindicō, *1, tr.*
demand, postulō, *1, tr.; ab (ā) w. abl. of person; acc. of thing; ut (nē); acc. w. infin.*
deny, negō, *1, tr.; acc. w. infin.*
depart, discēdō, discēdere, discessī, discessum, *3, intr.; ab (ā), ex (ē), or dē w. abl.;* proficīscor, proficīscī, profectus sum, *3, intr.*
depraved, improbus, a, um.
desire, cupiō, cupere, cupīvī, cupītus, *3, tr.; w. pres. infin.;* optō, *1, tr.; w. infin.; ut (nē).*
desirous, cupidus, a, um; *w. gen.*
desperate, perditus, a, um.
destroy, frangō, frangere, frēgī, frāctus, *3, tr.;* vastō, *1, tr.*
destruction, exitium, ī; perniciēs, perniciēī.
destructive, perniciōsus, a, um.
determine, cōnstituō, cōnstituere, cōnstituī, cōnstitūtus, *3, tr.; w. pres. infin.;* dēcernō, dēcernere, dēcrēvī, dēcrētus, *3, tr.; w. infin. if subject is the same; ut (nē) if subject is different;* statuō, statuere, statuī, statūtus, *3, tr.; w. infin.*
devote, dēdō, dēdere, dēdidī, dēditus, *3, tr. (Always takes an object.)*
devoted (to), am, studeō, studēre, studuī, *2, intr.; w. dat.*
devotion, studium, ī.
die, morior, morī, mortuus sum, *3, intr.*
differ, differō, differre, distulī, dīlātus, *irreg., tr.*
difficult, difficilis, e; impedītus, a, um.
difficulties, angustiae, angustiārum.
difficulty, difficultās, difficultātis; **with difficulty,** vix, *adv.*
diligence, dīligentia, ae.
direction, pars, partis.
disaster, calamitās, calamitātis; perniciēs, perniciēī.
disclose, patefaciō, patefacere, patefēcī, patefactus, *3, tr. (passive,* patefīō).
discover, inveniō, invenīre, invēnī, inventus, *4, tr.; acc. w. infin.*
discover (as certain), comperiō, comperīre, comperī, compertus, *4, tr.; acc. w. infin.*
disembark, expōnō, expōnere, exposuī, expositus, *3, tr.*
disgrace, īnfāmia, ae; turpitūdō, turpitūdinis.
dishonor, īnfāmia, ae.
dismiss, dīmittō, dīmittere, dīmīsī, dīmissus, *3, tr.*
disorder, tumultus, ūs.
dispatch, litterae, litterārum.
dissension, dissēnsiō, dissēnsiōnis.
distant, am, absum, abesse, āfuī, āfutūrus, *irreg., intr.; ab (ā) w. abl.*
distribute, dispōnō, dispōnere, disposuī, dispositus, *3, tr.*
disturb, perturbō, *1, tr.*
ditch, fossa, ae.
divide, dīvidō, dīvidere, dīvīsī, dīvīsus, *3, tr.*
do, faciō, facere, fēcī, factus, *3, tr.* (*passive,* fīō, fierī, factus sum); agō, agere, ēgī, āctus, *3, tr.;* committō, committere, commīsī, commissus, *3, tr.*
do harm to, noceō, nocēre, nocuī, nocitūrus, *2, intr.; w. dat.*
do not wish, nōlō, nōlle, nōluī, *tr.; w. infin.; acc. w. infin.; ut (nē).*
domestic, domesticus, a, um.
domicile, domicilium, ī.
done, am, fīō, fierī, factus sum, *irreg., intr.*
doom, fātum, ī.
doubt, dubitō, *1, tr. and intr.; w. infin.; dē w. abl.*
doubtful, dubius, a, um.

down, cast, dējiciō, dējicere, dējēcī, dējectus, *3, tr.*
down, hurl, dējiciō, dējicere, dējēcī, dējectus, *3, tr.*
down, lay, dēpōnō, dēpōnere, dēposuī, dēpositus, *3, tr.*
down from, dē, *prep. w. abl.*
draw back, redūcō, redūcere, redūxī, reductus, *3, tr.*
draw near to, appropinquō, *1, intr.; w. dat. or ad w. acc.*
draw up, īnstruō, īnstruere, īnstrūxī, īnstrūctus, *3, tr.*
drive, agō, agere, ēgī, āctus, *3, tr.;* pellō, pellere, pepulī, pulsus, *3, tr.*
drive away, dēpellō, dēpellere, dēpulī, dēpulsus, *3, tr.*
drive back, rejiciō, rejicere, rejēcī, rejectus, *3, tr.;* repellō, repellere, reppulī, repulsus, *3, tr.*
duty of. *Use genitive of nouns, neuter nominative of possessive pronouns.*
dwell, habitō, *1, tr.*
dwell in, incolō, incolere, incoluī, *3, tr.*

each *(of two),* uterque, utraque, utrumque (*gen. sing.* utrīusque, *dat. sing.* utrīque).
eager, ācer, ācris, ācre.
eager (for), cupidus, a, um; *w. gen.;* studiōsus, a, um; *w. gen.*
eager (for), am, studeō, studēre, studuī, *2, intr.; w. dat. or pres. infin.*
eagerly, ācriter, *adv.*
eagerness, studium, ī.
earth, terra, ae.
easily, facile, *adv.;* **more easily,** facilius, *comparative adv.*
easy, facilis, e.
effect, prōficiō, prōficere, prōfēcī, prōfectus, *3, tr.; ut (nē).*
effect, to the same, in eandem sententiam.
effort, labor, labōris.
efforts, opera, ae.
eight, octō, *indecl. numeral.*
eighth, octāvus, a, um.

either . . . or, aut . . . aut, *conjs.*
elated, am. *Use passive of* tollō, tollere, sustulī, sublātus, *3, tr.*
elder, senior, senius.
elections, comitia, comitiōrum.
eloquence, ēloquentia, ae.
emperor, imperātor, imperātōris.
empire, imperium, ī.
employ, adhibeō, *2, tr.; ad w. acc.;* ūtor, ūtī, ūsus sum, *3, intr.; w. abl.*
encourage, cohortor, *1, tr.; ut (nē);* cōnfirmō, *1, tr.;* hortor, *1, tr.; ut (nē).*
encumbered, impedītus, a, um.
end, fīnis, fīnis, *m.;* **world without end,** in saecula saeculōrum.
endless, īnfīnītus, a, um.
endure, patior, patī, passus sum, *3, tr.; acc. w. infin.*
enemy *(in war),* hostis, hostis, *m.; (personal),* inimīcus, ī.
energy, industria, ae.
enjoy, perfruor, perfruī, perfrūctus sum, *3, intr.; w. abl.*
enough, satis, *adv. and indecl. noun; w. gen;* **not enough,** parum, *indecl. noun; w. gen.*
enroll, cōnscrībō, cōnscrībere, cōnscrīpsī, cōnscrīptus, *3, tr.; acc. w. infin.*
enter upon, ineō, inīre, iniī(-īvī), initus, *irreg., tr.*
entrust, crēdō, crēdere, crēdidī, crēditus, *3, tr.; w. dat. of person to whom;* mandō, *1, tr.; w. dat. of person;* permittō, permittere, permīsī, permissus, *3, tr.; w. dat. of person; acc. of thing; ut (nē).*
envoy, lēgātus, ī.
envy, invidia, ae.
equip, armō, *1, tr.;* īnstruō, īnstruere, īnstrūxī, īnstrūctus, *3, tr.*
escape, effugiō, effugere, effūgī, *3, tr. and intr.;* ēlābor, ēlābī, ēlāpsus sum, *3, intr.*
especially, maximē, *adv.;* potissimum, *adv.*

eternal, aeternus, a, um.
even, etiam, *adv.*
even if, tametsī, *conj.* (Gr. 598).
even (to), usque (ad), *adv.*
ever, umquam, *adv.*
everlasting = eternal.
every, omnis, e.
evident, manifestus, a, um.
evil, malus, a, um.
exact, dīligēns (*gen.* dīligentis).
exactly as = just as.
excellent, optimus, a, um.
except, praeter, *prep. w. acc.*
exchange, inter sē dō, dare, dedī, datus, *1, tr.*
ex-consul, cōnsulāris, cōnsulāris.
exercise, ūtor, ūtī, ūsus sum, *3, intr.; w. abl.*
exertion, industria, ae.
exhaust, cōnficiō, cōnficere, cōnfēcī, cōnfectus, *3, tr.*
exhort, hortor, *1, tr.; ut (nē).*
exile, exilium, ī.
expel, dēpellō, dēpellere, dēpulī, dēpulsus, *3, tr.*
explain, expōnō, expōnere, exposuī, expositus, *3, tr.; acc. w. infin.*
expose, aperiō, aperīre, aperuī, apertus, *4, tr.*
extend, pateō, patēre, patuī, *2, intr.*
extensive, īnfīnītus, a, um.
extraordinary, incrēdibilis, e.
eye, oculus, ī.

fail, dēsum, deesse, dēfuī, dēfutūrus, *irreg., intr.; w. dat.*
faith, fidēs, fideī.
faithfulness, fidēs, fideī.
fall back, pedem referō, referre, rettulī, relātus, *irreg., tr.*
false, falsus, a, um.
fame, fāma, ae; glōria, ae.
famous, clārus, a, um; ille, illa, illud.
far, longē, *adv.;* **by far,** longē, *adv.*
farther, ulterior, ulterius.
Farther Gaul, Gallia (ae) **Ulterior** (Ulteriōris).
farthest, extrēmus, a, um; ultimus, a, um.
fate, fātum, ī.
father, pater, patris (patrum).
fatherland, patria, ae.
favor, grātia, ae.
favorable, secundus, a, um.
fear, metus, ūs; timor, timōris.
fear (that), metuō, metuere, metuī, *3, tr.; nē (nē nōn, ut);* timeō, *2, tr.; nē (nē nōn, ut);* vereor, *2, tr.; nē (nē nōn, ut).*
fear (to), timeō, *2, tr.; w. infin.;* vereor, *2, tr.; w. pres. infin.;* metuō, metuere, metuī, *3, tr.; w. infin.*
feel, sentiō, sentīre, sēnsī, sēnsus, *4, tr.; acc. w. infin.*
feelings, animus, ī.
fellow citizen, cīvis, cīvis, *m.*
few, paucī, ae, a.
field, ager, agrī.
fierce, ācer, ācris, ācre; **atrōx** (*gen.* atrōcis).
fight, pugnō, *1, intr.*
fill (with), compleō, complēre, complēvī, complētus, *2, tr.; w. abl.*
finally, dēnique, *adv.*
find, inveniō, invenīre, invēnī, inventus, *4, tr.; acc. w. infin.;* reperiō, reperīre, repperī, repertus, *4, tr.; acc. w. infin.;* **having found,** nactus, a, um.
find out, cognōscō, cognōscere, cognōvī, cognitus, *3, tr.; acc. w. infin.;* comperiō, comperīre, comperī, compertus, *4, tr.; acc. w. infin.;* explōrō, *1, tr.;* inveniō, invenīre, invēnī, inventus, *4, tr.; acc. w. infin.;* reperiō, reperīre, repperī, repertus, *4, tr.; acc. w. infin.*
finish, cōnficiō, cōnficere, cōnfēcī, cōnfectus, *3, tr.*
fire, ignis, ignis, *m.;* incendium, ī.
fire, am on, cōnflagrō, *1, intr.*
fire, set on, īnflammō, *1, tr.*
fire to, set, incendō, incendere, incendī, incēnsus, *3, tr.*

first ***(adj.)***, prīmus, a, um; ***(adv.)***, prīmum.
fitted for (to), aptus, a, um; *w. dat.; ad w. acc.*
five, quīnque, *indecl. numeral.*
fixed, certus, a, um.
Flaccus, Flaccus, ī.
flee, fugiō, fugere, fūgī, fugitūrus, *3, intr.*
flee from, effugiō, effugere, effūgī, *3, tr. and intr.;* profugiō, profugere, profūgī, profugitum, *3, intr.*
fleet, classis, classis (*abl.* -ī *or* -e).
flight, fuga, ae; **put to flight,** in fugam dō, dare, dedī, datus, *1, tr.*
flock, gather into a, congregō, *1, tr.*
follow, sequor, sequī, secūtus sum, *3, tr.*
follow up, cōnsequor, cōnsequī, cōnsecūtus sum, *3, tr.*
fond of, studiōsus, a, um; *w. gen.*
foot ***(of an animal, mountain, etc., or a unit of measure)***, pēs, pedis, *m.*
foot of, at the, sub, *prep. w. abl.*
for ***(prep.)***, ad, *prep. w. acc. (with adjectives, and with gerund and gerundive to express purpose);* dē, *prep. w. abl.;* prō, *prep. w. abl.*
for ***(conj.)***, enim, *postp.;* nam *(when* **for** *means* **because** *and introduces a REASON).*
for a short time, paulisper, *adv.*
for the sake of, causā; *w. gen.*
forbid, vetō, vetāre, vetuī, vetitus, *1, tr.; acc. w. pres. infin.*
force, cōgō, cōgere, coēgī, coāctus, *3, tr.; acc. w. pres. infin.*
force, vīs (*acc.* vim, *abl.* vī); vīrēs, vīrium, *f.;* **by force,** vī.
forces ***(a military term)***, cōpiae, cōpiārum.
forefathers, mājōrēs, mājōrum, *m.*
foreign, aliēnus, a, um; barbarus, a, um; externus, a, um.
foresee, prōvideō, prōvidēre, prōvīdī, prōvīsus, *2, tr.; ut (nē).*
forest, silva, ae.
foretell, praedīcō, praedīcere, praedīxī, praedictus, *3, tr.; acc. w. infin.*
forever, in perpetuum; in saecula saeculōrum.
forget, oblīvīscor, oblīvīscī, oblītus sum, *3, tr.; w. gen. of person, gen. or acc. of things, acc. of neuter pronouns or adjs.; acc. w. infin.*
form a conspiracy, conjūrō, *1, intr.*
former, antīquus, a, um; ille, illa, illud; prior, prius; superior, superius.
forth, bring, pariō, parere, peperī, partus, *3, tr.*
forth, burst, ērumpō, ērumpere, ērūpī, ēruptum, *3, intr.; ex (ē) w. abl.*
forth, rush, ērumpō, ērumpere, ērūpī, ēruptum, *3, intr.; ex (ē) w. abl.*
forth, send, ēmittō, ēmittere, ēmīsī, ēmissus, *3, tr.*
forthwith = immediately.
fortifications, moenia, moenium.
fortify, mūniō, *4, tr.*
fortitude, fortitūdō, fortitūdinis.
fortunate, it is, bene accidit, accidere, accidit, *3, intr.;* bene fit, fierī, factum est, *intr.* (GR. 659).
fortune, fortūna, ae.
forward, go, prōgredior, prōgredī, prōgressus sum, *3, intr.*
found (= **establish**), condō, condere, condidī, conditus, *3, tr.*
found, having (= **having obtained**), nactus, a, um.
four, quattuor, *indecl. numeral.*
France. *Use* Gallia, ae.
free, līberō, *1, tr.;* **set free,** vindicō, *1, tr.*
free, līber, lībera, līberum.
Frenchman, Gallus, ī.
frenzy, furor, furōris.
fresh, integer, integra, integrum.
fresher, recentior, recentius.
friend, amīcus, ī.
friendship, amīcitia, ae.
from ***(prep.)***, ab (ā), *w. abl.;* dē, *w abl.;* ex (ē), *w. abl.*

from *(conj.)*, quōminus (Gr. 646).
from all sides, undique, *adv.*
front of, in, ante, *prep. w. acc.;* prō, *prep. w. abl.*
full, plēnus, a, um; *w. gen. or abl.*

gain, cōnsequor, cōnsequī, cōnsecūtus sum, *3, tr.*
garrison, praesidium, ī.
gate, porta, ae.
gather into a flock, congregō, *1, tr.*
gather together, congregō, *1, tr.*
gathering, coetus, ūs.
Gaul *(an inhabitant of Gaul)*, Gallus, ī; *(the country)*, Gallia, ae; **Farther Gaul,** Gallia (ae) Ulterior (Ulteriōris); **Hither Gaul,** Gallia (ae) Citerior (Citeriōris).
general, imperātor, imperātōris.
gentlemen of the jury, jūdicēs *(voc.)*
gentlemen of the Senate, patrēs (patrum) cōnscrīptī (cōnscrīptōrum).
German *(noun)*, Germānus, ī; *(adj.)*, Germānus, a, um.
Germany, Germānia, ae.
get, comparō, *1, tr.*
get possession of, potior, *4, intr.; w. abl. or gen.*
get ready, comparō, *1, tr.;* parō, *1, tr.; w. pres. infin.*
Ghost, Holy, Spīritus (ūs) Sānctus (ī).
give, dō, dare, dedī, datus, *1, tr.*
give over, permittō, permittere, permīsī, permissus, *3, tr.; w. dat. of person; acc. of thing;* ***ut (nē).***
give thanks, grātiās agō, agere, ēgī, āctus, *3, tr.*
give up, dēdō, dēdere, dēdidī, dēditus, *3, tr. (always takes an object);* dēpōnō, dēpōnere, dēposuī, dēpositus, *3, tr.*
give way, cēdō, cēdere, cessī, cessūrus, *3, intr.*
glad, am, gaudeō, gaudēre, gāvīsus sum, *2, intr.*
gladness, laetitia, ae.
glory, glōria, ae.
go, eō, īre, īvī (iī), itum, *irreg., intr.*
go across, trānseō, trānsīre, trānsiī(-īvī), trānsitus, *irreg., tr.*
go forward, prōgredior, prōgredī, prōgressus sum, *3, intr.*
go into, ineō, inīre, iniī(-īvī), initus, *irreg., tr.*
go out, ēgredior, ēgredī, ēgressus sum, *3, intr.;* exeō, exīre, exiī(-īvī), exitum, *irreg., intr.*
go to, adeō, adīre, adiī(-īvī), aditus, *irreg., tr.*
go to meet, occurrō, occurrere, occurrī, occursum, *3, intr.; w. dat.*
God, Deus, ī (*voc.* Deus, *nom. pl.* dī *or* diī, *abl. and dat. pl.* dīs *or* diīs).
good, bonus, a, um.
good, it seems, placet, placēre, placuit, placitum, *2, intr.; w. dat.; w. infin.; acc. w. infin.;* ***ut (nē).***
government = state.
grace *(in Christian Latin)*, grātia, ae.
grain, frūmentum, ī.
grandfather, avus, ī.
granted that. *Use* ut *with subjunctive* (Gr. 519).
grasp, comprehendō, comprehendere, comprehendī, comprehēnsus, *3, tr.*
grave = serious.
great, magnus, a, um; **so great,** tantus, a, um; **very great,** summus, a, um.
greater, mājor, mājus.
greatest, maximus, a, um; summus, a, um.
greatest number, plūrimus, a, um.
greatly, magnōpere, *adv.;* multum, *adv.;* vehementer, *adv.*
greatness, magnitūdō, magnitūdinis.
grief, dolor, dolōris.
grow, crēscō, crēscere, crēvī, crētum, *3, intr.*
guard, custōdiō, *4, tr.;* servō, *1, tr.*
guard, custōdia, ae; custōs, custōdis; vigilia, ae.
guide, dūcō, dūcere, dūxī, ductus, *3, tr.*

Haedui, Haeduī, Haeduōrum.
hail, avē, *interjection.*
hand, manus, ūs, *f.*
hand over, trādō, trādere, trādidī, trāditus, *3, tr.*
handwriting, manus, ūs; **in his own handwriting**, ipsīus manū scrīptus (a, um).
happen, fīō, fierī, factus sum, *irreg., intr.; ut (ut nōn).*
harbor, portus, ūs.
hard, press, premō, premere, pressī, pressus, *3, tr.*
hard work, industria, ae.
hardly, vix, *adv.*
harm, damnō, *1, tr.; w. acc. of person; gen. or abl. of thing;* noceō, nocēre, nocuī, nocitūrus, *2, intr.; w. dat.*
hasten, contendō, contendere, contendī, *3, intr.; w. pres. infin.*
hate, ōdī, ōdisse, *tr.* (Gr. 443-448, 451).
hatred, invidia, ae; odium, ī.
have, habeō, *2, tr.*
have accustomed (have become accustomed), cōnsuēvī, cōnsuētus, *3, tr. and intr.; w. pres. infin.*
have begun, coepī, coepisse, coeptus sum, *tr.; w. pres. infin.* (Gr. page 82, footnote 1).
have mercy (on), miserēre; *w. dat. or gen.*
having found, nactus, a, um (*perfect participle of* nancīscor).
having obtained, nactus, a, um (*perfect participle of* nancīscor).
having obtained possession of, nactus, a, um (*perfect participle of* nancīscor).
he, *masc. of* is, ea, id *or of* ille, illa, illud.
he (she, it) said (says), inquit. *(Used with direct quotations only; usually placed after the first word or phrase of the quotation.)*
head, caput, capitis.
hear, audiō, *4, tr.; acc. w. infin.;* exaudiō, *4, tr.; acc. w. infin.*
heaven, caelum, ī.
heavy, gravis, e.
help, adjuvō, adjuvāre, adjūvī, adjūtus, *1, tr.*
help, auxilium, ī.
Helvetians, Helvētiī, Helvētiōrum.
her (herself), suī.
her (own), suus, a, um; **of her own accord**, suā sponte.
here, hīc, *adv.*
hesitate, dubitō, *1, tr. and intr.; w. infin.; dē w. abl.*
hide, abdō, abdere, abdidī, abditus, *3, tr. (Always takes an object.)*
high, altus, a, um.
higher, superior, superius.
highest, summus, a, um; suprēmus, a, um.
hill, collis, collis, *m.*
him (himself), suī.
hinder, impediō, *4, tr.*
his (own), suus, a, um; **in his own handwriting**, ipsīus manū scrīptus (a, um); **of his own accord**, suā sponte.
Hither Gaul, Gallia (ae) Citerior (Citeriōris).
hold, obtineō, obtinēre, obtinuī, obtentus, *2, tr.;* teneō, tenēre, tenuī, tentus, *2, tr.*
hold back, retineō, retinēre, retinuī, retentus, *2, tr.*
hold in, contineō, continēre, continuī, contentus, *2, tr.*
holy, sānctus, a, um.
Holy Spirit, Spīritus (ūs) Sānctus (ī).
home, domus, ūs, *f.;* **from home**, domō; **(to) home**, domum; **of the home**, domesticus, a, um.
honor, honor, honōris.
honorable, honestus, a, um.
hope, spēs, speī.
hope for, optō, *1, tr.; w. infin.; ut (nē).*

horseman, eques, equitis.
Hortensius, Hortēnsius, ī.
hostage, obses, obsidis, *c.*
hostile, īnfestus, a, um.
hour, hōra, ae.
house, domus, ūs, *f.; tēctum*, ī.
how, quam, *adv.;* quōmodo, *adv.*
how large, quantus, a, um.
how many, quot, *indecl. adj.*
how much, quantus, a, um.
however, autem, *conj., postp.;* quamvīs, *conj.* (Gr. 596).
hundred, one, centum, *indecl. numeral.*
hurl, jaciō, jacere, jēcī, jactus, *3, tr.*
hurl back, rejiciō, rejicere, rejēcī, rejectus, *3, tr.*
hurl down, dējiciō, dējicere, dējēcī, dējectus, *3, tr.*

I, ego, meī.
if, sī, *conj.;* **as if**, quasi, *conj.;* **but if**, quodsī, *conj.;* sīn, *conj.;* sīn autem, *conj.;* **but if not**, sīn aliter; sīn minus; **even if**, tametsī, *conj.;* **if . . . or if**, sīve (seu) . . . sīve (seu).
if not, nisi, *conj.;* sī . . . nōn.
if only, dummodo, *conj.*
ignorant, am, nesciō, *4, tr.*
illustrious, illūstris, e.
immediately, statim, *adv.*
immortal, immortālis, e.
impede, impediō, *4, tr.*
impious, impius, a, um; nefārius, a, um.
in, in, *prep. w. abl.;* in, *prep. w. acc.*
in front of, ante, *prep. w. acc.;* prō, *prep. w. abl.*
in his own handwriting, ipsīus manū scrīptus (a, um).
in large numbers, frequēns (*gen.* frequentis).
in order that, ut, *conj. (in purpose clauses);* quō, *conj. (in purpose clauses containing a comparative adverb or adjective).*
in order that not, nē, *conj. (in negative purpose clauses).*
in secret = secretly.
in such a manner, ita, *adv.;* sīc, *adv.*
in such a way, ita, *adv.*
in the beginning, in prīncipiō.
in the presence of, apud, *prep. w. acc.*
in truth, vērō, *adv. and conj., postp.*
incite, incitō, *1, tr.*
increase, crēscō, crēscere, crēvī, crētum, *3, intr.*
indeed, quidem, *adv.;* vērē, *adv.*
Indies, Indī, Indōrum.
induce, addūcō, addūcere, addūxī, adductus, *3, tr.; ut (nē).*
inexperienced (in), imperītus, a, um; *w. gen.*
inflict (upon), īnferō, īnferre, intulī, illātus, *irreg., tr.; w. dat. of person.*
influence, addūcō, addūcere, addūxī, adductus, *3, tr.; ut (nē);* indūcō, indūcere, indūxī, inductus, *3, tr.; ut (nē);* permoveō, permovēre, permōvī, permōtus, *2, tr.*
influence, auctōritās, auctōritātis; grātia, ae.
influential, am, valeō, valēre, valuī, *2, intr.; w. infin.*
inform, certiōrem (-ēs) faciō, facere, fēcī, factus, *3, tr.; acc. w. infin.*
information, indicium, ī.
inhabit, incolō, incolere, incoluī, *3, tr.*
injure, noceō, nocēre, nocuī, nocitūrus, *2, intr.; w. dat.*
injustice, injūria, ae.
inquiry, quaestiō, quaestiōnis.
inscribe, īnscrībō, īnscrībere, īnscrīpsī, īnscrīptus, *3, tr.*
inspect, perspiciō, perspicere, perspexī, perspectus, *3, tr.; acc. w. infin.*
inspire (in), īnferō, īnferre, intulī, illātus, *irreg., tr.; w. dat. of person.*
instigate, concitō, *1, tr.*
instigator, auctor, auctōris.
instruction, mandātum, ī.
intellect, animus, ī; mēns, mentis.
into, in, *prep. w. acc.*
into, go, ineō, inīre, iniī(-īvī), initus, *irreg., tr.*

into, send, immittō, immittere, immīsī, immissus, *3, tr.*
investigation, quaestiō, quaestiōnis.
invite, invītō, *1, tr.*
it, is, ea, id; ille, illa, illud; suī.
it behooves, oportet, oportēre, oportuit, *2, intr.; acc. w. pres. infin.*
it happens, accidit, accidere, accidit, *3, intr.; w. dat. of person;* ***ut (ut nōn).***
it is certain, cōnstat, cōnstāre, cōnstitit, *1, intr.; acc. w. infin.*
it is fortunate, bene accidit, accidere, accidit, *3, intr.;* bene fit, fierī, factum est, *intr.* (Gr. 659).
it is necessary, oportet, oportēre, oportuit, *2, intr.; acc. w. pres. infin.;* necesse est, esse, fuit, *intr.;* ***ut (nē);*** *w. infin.*
it pleases, placet, placēre, placuit, placitum, *2, intr.; w. dat.; w. infin.; acc. w. infin.;* ***ut (nē).***
it seems good, placet, placēre, placuit, placitum, *2, intr.; w. dat.; w. infin.; acc. w. infin.;* ***ut (nē).***
Italy, Italia, ae.
its (own), suus, a, um.
itself, suī.

jail = prison.
javelin, pīlum, ī.
Jesus, Jēsūs, ū (*declined:* Jēsūs, Jēsū, Jēsū, Jēsum, Jēsū).
Jew, Jūdaeus, ī.
John, Jōannēs, Jōannis.
join, jungō, jungere, jūnxī, jūnctus, *3, tr.*
join battle, proelium committō, committere, commīsī, commissus, *3, tr.*
join together, conjungō, conjungere, conjūnxī, conjūnctus, *3, tr.*
journey, iter, itineris, *n.;* **make a journey,** iter faciō, facere, fēcī, factus, *3, tr.*
joy, gaudium, ī; laetitia, ae.
Judas, Jūdas, ae.
judge, jūdicō, *1, tr.; acc. w. infin.*
judge, jūdex, jūdicis.
judgment, jūdicium, ī.
juror, jūdex, jūdicis.
jury, gentlemen of the, jūdicēs *(voc.).*
just, jūstus, a, um.
just as, quasi, *conj.;* sīc . . . ut, *conj.*
just now, modo, *adv.*
justice, jūs, jūris, *n.*
justly, jūre, *adv.;* meritō, *adv.*

keen, ācer, ācris, ācre.
keep, retineō, retinēre, retinuī, retentus, *2, tr.;* servō, *1, tr.*
keep in memory, memoriā teneō, tenēre, tenuī, tentus, *2, tr.; w. acc. or acc. w. infin.*
keep silent, sileō, silēre, siluī, *2, intr.*
kill, interficiō, interficere, interfēcī, interfectus, *3, tr.;* occīdō, occīdere, occīdī, occīsus, *3, tr.*
kind, genus, generis, *n.;* modus, ī; **of such a kind,** tālis, e; **of this kind,** ējus modī; hūjus modī.
king, rēx, rēgis.
kingdom, rēgnum, ī.
know, sciō, *4, tr.; acc. w. infin.;* **do not know,** ignōrō, *1, tr.; acc. w. infin.;* nesciō, *4, tr.; acc. w. infin.*
knowledge, scientia, ae.
known, nōtus, a, um.

lack, careō, carēre, caruī, caritūrus, *2, intr.; w. abl.*
lacking, am, dēsum, deesse, dēfuī, dēfutūrus, *irreg., intr.; w. dat.*
Laeca, Laeca, ae.
land, terra, ae; **native land,** patria, ae; **on land and sea,** terrā marīque.
language, lingua, ae.
large, magnus, a, um; **how large,** quantus, a, um; **in large numbers,** frequēns (*gen.* frequentis).
last, extrēmus, a, um; ultimus, a, um; **at last,** dēnique, *adv.;* tandem, *adv.*
last night, proximā nocte.
lately, nūper, *adv.*
later, posteā, *adv.*

latter, hic, haec, hoc (Gr. 795).
law, lēx, lēgis; jūs, jūris, *n.*
law court, quaestiō, quaestiōnis.
lawful, jūstus, a, um.
lay down, dēpōnō, dēpōnere, dēposuī, dēpositus, *3, tr.*
lay waste, vastō, *1, tr.*
lead, dūcō, dūcere, dūxī, ductus, *3, tr.;* dēdūcō, dēdūcere, dēdūxī, dēductus, *3, tr.*
lead across, trādūcō, trādūcere, trādūxī, trāductus, *3, tr.; w. two accs. or acc. and **trāns** w. acc.*
lead away, dēdūcō, dēdūcere, dēdūxī, dēductus, *3, tr.*
lead back, redūcō, redūcere, redūxī, reductus, *3, tr.*
lead in, indūcō, indūcere, indūxī, inductus, *3, tr.; **ut (nē)**.*
lead on, addūcō, addūcere, addūxī, adductus, *3, tr.; **ut (nē)**;* indūcō, indūcere, indūxī, inductus, *3, tr.; **ut (nē)**.*
lead out, ēdūcō, ēdūcere, ēdūxī, ēductus, *3, tr.*
lead over, trādūcō, trādūcere, trādūxī, trāductus, *3, tr.; w. two accs. or acc. and **trāns** w. acc.*
lead to, addūcō, addūcere, addūxī, adductus, *3, tr.; **ut (nē)**.*
leader, dux, ducis.
leading man, prīnceps, prīncipis.
learn, cognōscō, cognōscere, cognōvī, cognitus, *3, tr.; acc. w. infin.*
learn of, percipiō, percipere, percēpī, perceptus, *3, tr.; acc. w. infin.*
least *(adj.),* minimus, a, um; *(**adv.**),* minimē; **at least,** quidem, *adv.*
leave, discēdō, discēdere, discessī, discessum, *3, intr.; **ab (ā), ex (ē),** or **dē** w. abl.;* relinquō, relinquere, relīquī, relictus, *3, tr.*
leave behind, relinquō, relinquere, relīquī, relictus, *3, tr.*
legion, legiō, legiōnis, *f.*
length, at, aliquandō, *adv.*
Lentulus, Lentulus, ī.
less *(adj.),* minor, minus; *(**adv.**),* minus; **none the less,** tamen, *adv.*
lest, nē, *conj. (in negative purpose clauses).*
letter, litterae, litterārum.
levy (on), imperō, *1, tr.; w. dat. of person.*
liberate, līberō, *1, tr.*
liberty, lībertās, lībertātis.
lie open, pateō, patēre, patuī, *2, intr.*
lieutenant, lēgātus, ī.
life, vīta, ae.
lift up, tollō, tollere, sustulī, sublātus, *3, tr.*
light, lūx, lūcis.
like, similis, e; *w. gen. or dat.*
likewise, I said, dīxī ego īdem.
line, battle, aciēs, aciēī.
line up, expōnō, expōnere, exposuī, expositus, *3, tr.*
listen to, audiō, *4, tr.*
little *(adj.),* parvus, a, um; *(**adv.**),* parum; paulum, *adv. or noun w. gen.;* **(by) a little,** paulō, *abl. of degree of difference;* **too little,** parum, *indecl. noun; w. gen.;* minus, *adv.;* parum, *adv.*
live, vīvō, vīvere, vīxī, victūrus, *3, intr.;* habitō, *1, tr.*
long *(adj.),* longus, a, um.
long *(of time),* diū, *adv.;* **a long time,** diū, *adv.;* **as long as,** dummodo, *conj.* (Gr. 594).
long (ago), jam prīdem; jam diū; jam dūdum.
long for, dēsiderō, *1, tr.*
long (since), jam prīdem; jam diū; jam dūdum.
longer, diūtius, *comparative adv.*
longest, diūtissimē, *adv.*
look, aspectus, ūs.
lord, dominus, ī.
loud, clārus, a, um.
love, dīligō, dīligere, dīlēxī, dīlēctus, *3, tr.;* amō, *1, tr.*
love, cāritās, cāritātis; amor, amōris.
Lucius, Lūcius, ī.

made, am, fīō, fierī, factus sum, *irreg., intr.*
madness, furor, furōris.
mainly, maximē, *adv.*
make, faciō, facere, fēcī, factus, *3, tr.;* **to make a journey,** iter facere; **make a plan,** cōnsilium capiō, capere, cēpī, captus, *3, tr.;* **make war on,** bellum īnferō, īnferre, intulī, illātus, *irreg., tr.*
man, homō, hominis; vir, virī; **leading man,** prīnceps, prīncipis; **young man,** adulēscēns, adulēscentis.
manage, administrō, *1, tr.*
manliness, virtūs, virtūtis.
manner, modus, ī; mōs, mōris, *m.;* ratiō, ratiōnis; **in such a manner,** ita, *adv.;* sīc, *adv.*
many, complūrēs, complūra; multī, ae, a; **how many,** quot, *indecl. adj.;* **so many,** tot, *indecl. adj.;* **very many,** plūrimus, a, um.
march, iter, itineris, *n.;* **to march,** iter facere.
Mary, Marīa, ae.
master, dominus, ī.
master of, become, potior, *4, intr.; w. abl. or gen.*
matter, rēs, reī.
may not, nē, *conj. (with volitive subjunctive).*
meanwhile, interim, *adv.*
meet, go to, occurrō, occurrere, occurrī, occursum, *3, intr.; w. dat.*
meeting, coetus, ūs.
memorial, monumentum, ī.
memory, memoria, ae; **keep in memory,** memoriā teneō, tenēre, tenuī, tentus, *2, tr.; w. acc. or acc. w. infin.*
merchant, mercātor, mercātōris.
mercy (on), have, miserēre; *w. dat. or gen.*
message, nuntius, ī.
messenger, nuntius, ī.
method, ratiō, ratiōnis.
middle, medius, a, um.
mile (*lit.,* **a thousand paces**), mīlle passūs; **miles,** mīlia (mīlium) passuum.
military tribune, tribūnus (ī) mīlitum.
mind, animus, ī; mēns, mentis; **bear in mind,** meminī, meminisse, *tr.; w. gen. of persons, gen. or acc. of things, acc. of neuter pronouns or adjs.; acc. w. infin.*
mine, meus, a, um.
misdeed, facinus, facinoris, *n.*
misfortune, calamitās, calamitātis.
miss, dēsīderō, *1, tr.*
mistake, peccātum, ī.
money, pecūnia, ae.
monument, monumentum, ī.
more *(noun),* plūs, plūris, *n.; w. gen.; (adj.),* plūrēs, plūra (Gr. page 22, footnote 2); ***(adv.),*** magis; plūs.
more easily, facilius, *comparative adv.*
most *(adj.),* plūrimus, a, um; ***(adv.),*** maximē; plūrimum.
most recently, nūperrimē, *adv.*
mostly, maximē, *adv.*
mother, māter, mātris (mātrum).
mountain, mōns, montis, *m.*
move, moveō, movēre, mōvī, mōtus, *2, tr.*
much *(adj.),* multus, a, um; ***(adv.),*** multum; multō, *abl. of degree of difference* (Gr. 771); **how much,** quantus, a, um.
my, meus, a, um; **of my own accord,** meā sponte.

name, nōmen, nōminis; **by name** (**named**), nōmine.
narrow, angustus, a, um.
narrow place, angustiae, angustiārum.
nation, nātiō, nātiōnis; populus, ī.
native land, patria, ae.
nature, nātūra, ae.
near, propinquus, a, um.
near to, draw, appropinquō, *1, intr.; w. dat. or ad w. acc.*
nearer *(adj.),* propior, propius; ***(adv.),*** propius.
nearest, proximus, a, um; *w. dat.*

nearly, prope, *adv.;* quasi, *adv. and conj.*

necessary, it is, oportet, oportēre, oportuit, *2, intr.; acc. w. pres. infin.;* necesse est, esse, fuit, *intr.; ut (nē); w. infin.*

negligence, criminal, nēquitia, ae.

neighboring, fīnitimus, a, um; *w. dat.*

neither . . . nor, neque . . . neque, *conjs.*

never, numquam, *adv.;* **that . . . never,** nē . . . umquam *(in negative purpose clauses).*

nevertheless, tamen, *adv.*

new, novus, a, um.

next *(adj.),* fīnitimus, a, um; *w. dat.;* proximus, a, um; *w. dat.; (adv.),* deinde; proximē.

night, nox, noctis; **last night,** proximā nocte; **night before,** superiōre nocte.

night watch, vigilia, ae.

nightly, nocturnus, a, um.

no, nūllus, a, um (Gr. 84); nēmō, nēminis.

no one, nēmō, nēminis (nūllīus, nūllō, nūllā *usually used in place of* nēminis *and* nēmine); **that . . . no one,** nē . . . quis *(in negative purpose clauses).*

noble, nōbilis, e.

nocturnal, nocturnus, a, um.

none, nūllus, a, um (Gr. 84).

none the less, tamen, *adv.*

nor, neque, *conj.*

not, nōn, *adv.;* nihil, *adv.;* nē, *conj. (with commands, wishes, and hortatory subjunctive);* **if not,** nisi, *conj.;* **that . . . not,** nē *(in purpose clauses);* ut nōn *(in result clauses).*

not at all, minimē, *adv.;* nihil, *adv.*

not enough, parum, *indecl. noun; w. gen.*

not know, ignōrō, *1, tr.; acc. w. infin.;* nesciō, *4, tr.; acc. w. infin.*

not only . . . but (also), nōn modo . . . sed (etiam); nōn modo . . . vērum (etiam).

not yet, nōndum, *adv.*

nothing, nihil (nīl), *n., indecl. noun;* nihilum, ī; **that . . . nothing,** nē . . . quid *(in negative purpose clauses).*

notice, animadvertō, animadvertere, animadvertī, animadversus, *3, tr.; acc. w. infin.*

now, nunc, *adv.;* jam, *adv.;* **just now,** modo, *adv.*

nowhere, that, nēcubi *(in negative purpose clauses).*

number, numerus, ī; **greatest number,** plūrimus, a, um; **in large numbers,** frequēns (*gen.* frequentis).

obscure, obscūrus, a, um.

observe, cōnspiciō, cōnspicere, cōnspexī, cōnspectus, *3, tr.; acc. w. infin.;* cōnspicor, *1, tr.; acc. w. infin.*

obtain *(by asking),* impetrō, *1, tr.; ab (ā) w. abl. of person; acc. of thing; ut (nē).*

obtained (possession of), having, nactus, a, um *(perfect participle of* nancīscor).

occupy, obtineō, obtinēre, obtinuī, obtentus, *2, tr.*

of consular rank, cōnsulāris, e.

of course, vērō, *adv. and conj., postp.*

of my (your, his, her, their) own accord, meā (tuā, suā) sponte.

of such a kind, tālis, e.

of the home, domesticus, a, um.

of this kind, ējus modī; hūjus modī.

of this sort, ējus modī; hūjus modī.

offer, offerō, offerre, obtulī, oblātus, *irreg., tr.*

often, saepe, *adv.*

oftener, saepius, *adv.*

oftenest, saepissimē, *adv.*

old, vetus (*gen.* veteris).

old-time, antīquus, a, um.

on, in, *prep. w. abl.;* in, *prep. w. acc.*

on account of, propter, *prep. w. acc.*

on all sides, undique, *adv.*

on behalf of, prō, *prep. w. abl.*

on the right, dexter, dext(e)ra, dext(e)rum.
once, at, statim, *adv.*
one, ūnus, a, um; *(of two),* alter, altera, alterum (Gr. 87).
one, a certain, quīdam, quiddam (Gr. 820).
one, no, nēmō, nēminis (nūllīus, nūllō, nūllā *usually used in place of* nēminis *and* nēmine).
one hundred, centum, *indecl. numeral.*
oneself, betake, mē (tē, sē) cōnferō, cōnferre, contulī, collātus, *irreg., tr.;* **take upon oneself,** suscipiō, suscipere, suscēpī, susceptus, *3, tr.*
only *(adj.),* sōlus, a, um (Gr. 84); *(adv.),* modo; **if only,** dummodo, *conj.;* **provided only,** dummodo, *conj.* (Gr. 594).
onto, in, *prep. w. acc.*
open, aperiō, aperīre, aperuī, apertus, *4, tr.;* patefaciō, patefacere, patefēcī, patefactus (*passive,* patefīō), *3, tr.*
open, am, pateō, patēre, patuī, *2, intr.*
open, lie, pateō, patēre, patuī, *2, intr.*
openly, apertē, *adv.;* palam, *adv.*
opinion, am of the, cēnseō, cēnsēre, cēnsuī, cēnsus, *2, tr.; acc. w. infin.; ut (nē).*
opposite, contrā, *prep. w. acc.*
or, aut, *conj.;* **either . . . or,** aut . . . aut, *conjs.;* **if . . . or if,** sīve (seu) . . . sīve (seu), *conjs.*
order, imperō, *1, tr.; w. dat. of person; ut (nē);* jubeō, jubēre, jussī, jussus, *2, tr.; acc. w. pres. infin.*
order, mandātum, ī.
order that, in, ut, *conj. (in purpose clauses);* quō, *conj. (in purpose clauses containing a comparative);* **in order that not,** nē, *conj. (in negative purpose clauses).*
originator, auctor, auctōris.
other, alius, alia, aliud (Gr. 85-86); *(of two),* alter, altera, alterum (Gr. 87).
ought, dēbeō, *2, tr.; w. pres. infin.; gerundive with sum* (Gr. 878).
our (own), noster, nostra, nostrum.
ours, noster, nostra, nostrum.
out of, dē, *prep. w. abl.;* ex (ē), *prep. w. abl.*
outer, exterior, exterius.
outermost, extrēmus, a, um.
outrage, facinus, facinoris, *n.*
outside (of), extrā, *prep. w. acc.*
over, am (= am in charge of), praesum, praeesse, praefuī, praefutūrus, *irreg., intr.; w. dat.*
over, carry, trānsferō, trānsferre, trānstulī, trānslātus, *irreg., tr.*
over, give, permittō, permittere, permīsī, permissus, *3, tr.; w. dat. of person; acc. of thing; ut (nē).*
over, hand, trādō, trādere, trādidī, trāditus, *3, tr.*
over, lead, trādūcō, trādūcere, trādūxī, trāductus, *3, tr.; w. two accs. or acc. and trāns w. acc.*
overcome, superō, *1, tr.*
overhang, impendeō, impendēre, *2, intr.; w. dat.*
overlook, ignōrō, *1, tr.; acc. w. infin.*
overtake, cōnsequor, cōnsequī, cōnsecūtus sum, *3, tr.*
overwhelm, opprimō, opprimere, oppressī, oppressus, *3, tr.*
owe, dēbeō, *2, tr.; w. dat. of person.*
own, his (her, its, their), suus, a, um; **in his own handwriting,** ipsīus manū scrīptus (a, um); **of his own accord,** suā sponte.
own, my, meus, a, um; **our own,** noster, nostra, nostrum.
own, your, tuus, a, um *(one person);* vester, vestra, vestrum *(more than one).*

pace, passus, ūs.
pacify, pācō, *1, tr.*
pain, dolor, dolōris.
pains, opera, ae.
parent, pārēns, pārentis, *c.*

part, pars, partis.
pass, trānseō, trānsīre, trānsiī(-īvī), trānsitus, *irreg., tr.*
pass over in silence, taceō, *2, tr.*
past, praeter, *prep. w. acc.*
patience, patientia, ae.
patriot, amāns (amantis) patriae.
patriotism = love of country.
Paul, Paulus, ī.
peace, pāx, pācis.
penalty, poena, ae; supplicium, ī.
people, populus, ī.
perceive, cōnspiciō, cōnspicere, cōnspexī, cōnspectus, *3, tr.; acc. w. infin.;* cōnspicor, *1, tr.; acc. w. infin.;* intellegō, intellegere, intellēxī, intellectus, *3, tr.; acc. w. infin.;* percipiō, percipere, percēpī, perceptus, *3, tr.; acc. w. infin.;* perspiciō, perspicere, perspexī, perspectus, *3, tr.; acc. w. infin.;* sentiō, sentīre, sēnsī, sēnsus, *4, tr.; acc. w. infin.*
personal, prīvātus, a, um.
personal enemy, inimīcus, ī.
persuade, persuādeō, persuādēre, persuāsī, persuāsum, *2, intr.; w. dat.; ut (nē).*
pertain to, pertineō, pertinēre, pertinuī, *2, intr.; ad w. acc.*
pest, pestis, pestis.
Peter, Petrus, ī.
pick out, dēligō, dēligere, dēlēgī, dēlēctus, *3, tr.*
Pilate, Pīlātus, ī.
pitch camp, castra pōnō, pōnere, posuī, positus, *3, tr.*
place, collocō, *1, tr.;* cōnstituō, cōnstituere, cōnstituī, cōnstitūtus, *3, tr.;* pōnō, pōnere, posuī, positus, *3, tr.;* statuō, statuere, statuī, statūtus, *3, tr.*
place, locus, ī (*pl.*, loca, locōrum); **narrow place**, angustiae, angustiārum.
plague, pestis, pestis.
plainly, apertē, *adv.;* plānē, *adv.*
plan, cōnsilium, ī; ratiō, ratiōnis; **make a plan**, cōnsilium capiō, capere, cēpī, captus, *3, tr.*
pleases, it, placet, placēre, placuit, placitum, *2, intr.; w. dat.; w. infin.; acc. w. infin.; ut (nē).*
pleasure, gaudium, ī; voluptās, voluptātis.
plot, īnsidior, *1, intr.; w. dat.*
plot, conjūrātiō, conjūrātiōnis; īnsidiae, īnsidiārum.
point out, dēmōnstrō, *1, tr.; acc. w. infin.;* indicō, *1, tr.; acc. w. infin.*
Pompey, Pompējus, ī.
ponder, cōgitō, *1, tr. and intr.; acc. w. infin.*
poorly, male, *adv.*
portrait, imāgō, imāginis.
possession of, get, potior, *4, intr.; w. abl. or gen.*
possession of, having obtained, nactus, a, um.
power, imperium, ī; vīs (*acc.* vim, *abl.* vī); potestās, potestātis; **royal power**, rēgnum, ī.
praetor, praetor, praetōris.
praise, laudō, *1, tr.*
praise, laus, laudis.
pray, ōrō, *1, tr.; ut (nē).*
pray for, optō, *1, tr.; w. infin.; ut (nē).*
prayer, ōrātiō, ōrātiōnis.
prefer, mālō, mālle, māluī, *tr.; acc. w. infin.* (Gr. 408-410, 425-429).
prepare, comparō, *1, tr.;* parō, *1, tr.; w. pres. infin.*
prepared (for), parātus, a, um; *w. infin. or ad w. acc.*
presence of, in the, apud, *prep. w. acc.*
present, offerō, offerre, obtulī, oblātus, *irreg., tr.*
present, praesēns (*gen.* praesentis).
present, am, adsum, adesse, adfuī, adfutūrus, *irreg., intr.; w. dat.*
preserve, cōnservō, *1, tr.*
press, premō, premere, pressī, pressus, *3, tr.*

press back, reprimō, reprimere, repressī, repressus, *3, tr.*
press hard, premō, premere, pressī, pressus, *3, tr.*
prevent, prohibeō, *2, tr.*
prison, carcer, carceris; vincula, vinculōrum.
private, prīvātus, a, um.
proceed, prōgredior, prōgredī, prōgressus sum, *3, intr.*
promise, polliceor, *2, tr.; acc. w. infin. (usually future).*
proof, indicium, ī.
proper, idōneus, a, um; *w. dat. or ad w. acc.*
prophetic utterance, fātum, ī.
protection, praesidium, ī.
provide, prōvideō, prōvidēre, prōvīdī, prōvīsus, *2, tr.; ut (nē).*
provided only, dum, dummodo, *conjs.* (Gr. 594).
province, prōvincia, ae.
public, pūblicus, a, um.
punish, pūniō, *4, tr.;* vindicō, *1, tr.*
punishment, poena, ae; supplicium, ī.
pursue, sequor, sequī, secūtus sum, *3, tr.*
put, pōnō, pōnere, posuī, positus, *3, tr.*
put in command of, praeficiō, praeficere, praefēcī, praefectus, *3, tr.; w. dat. of thing of which.*
put off, differō, differre, distulī, dīlātus, *irreg., tr.*
put to death = kill, slaughter, lead to death.
put to flight, in fugam dō, dare, dedī, datus, *1, tr.*
put up with = bear, endure.

quickly, celeriter, *adv.*
quiet, tacitus, a, um.

race, genus, generis, *n.*
rage, furor, furōris.
rampart, vallum, ī.
rank *(of soldiers),* ōrdō, ōrdinis, *m.;* **of consular rank,** cōnsulāris, e.
rather, potius.
ravage, vastō, *1, tr.*
read, legō, legere, lēgī, lēctus, *3, tr.*
read aloud, recitō, *1, tr.*
ready, get, comparō, *1, tr.;* parō, *1, tr.; w. pres. infin.*
ready (for), parātus, a, um; *w. infin. or ad w. acc.*
real, vērus, a, um.
reality, vērum, ī.
reason, causa, ae; ratiō, ratiōnis.
recall, revocō, *1, tr.*
receive, accipiō, accipere, accēpī, acceptus, *3, tr.;* recipiō, recipere, recēpī, receptus, *3, tr.*
recently, nūper, *adv.*
recklessness, audācia, ae.
recognize, cognōscō, cognōscere, cognōvī, cognitus, *3, tr.*
reconnoiter, explōrō, *1, tr.*
recover, mē (tē, sē) recipiō, recipere, recēpī, receptus, *3, tr.*
refer, referō, referre, rettulī, relātus, *irreg., tr.*
reinforcements, auxilia, auxiliōrum.
rejoice, gaudeō, gaudēre, gāvīsus sum, *2, intr.*
release, remittō, remittere, remīsī, remissus, *3, tr.*
reliability, fidēs, fideī.
rely on, cōnfīdō, cōnfīdere, cōnfīsus sum, *3, intr.; w. dat. of person; abl. of thing; acc. w. infin.*
remain, maneō, manēre, mānsī, mānsūrus, *2, intr.;* restō, restāre, restitī, *1, intr.*
remain behind, resistō, resistere, restitī, *3, intr.; w. dat.*
remainder, cēterī, ae, a.
remaining, reliquus, a, um.
remember, memoriā teneō, tenēre, tenuī, tentus, *2, tr.; w. acc. or acc. w. infin.;* meminī, meminisse, *tr.; w. gen. of persons, gen. or acc. of things, acc. of neuter pronouns or adjs.; acc. w. infin.* (Gr. 436-442).
renown = glory.

renowned, nōbilis, e.

repel, rejiciō, rejicere, rejēcī, rejectus, *3, tr.*

reply, respondeō, respondēre, respondī, respōnsus, *2, tr.; acc. w. infin.*

report, afferō, afferre, attulī, allātus, *irreg., tr.*; nuntiō, *1, tr.; acc. w. infin.;* referō, referre, rettulī, relātus, *irreg., tr.*

report to, dēferō, dēferre, dētulī, dēlātus, *irreg., tr.; ad w. acc.*

repress, comprimō, comprimere, compressī, compressus, *3, tr.*

repulse, pellō, pellere, pepulī, pulsus, *3, tr.*

reputation, fāma, ae.

request, petō, petere, petīvī, petītus, *3, tr.; **ut (nē)**;* rogō, *1, tr.; **ut (nē)**.*

rescue = save.

resist, resistō, resistere, restitī, *3, intr.; w. dat.*

resolution, cōnsultum, ī.

rest (of), the, cēterī, ae, a; reliquus, a, um.

restrain, contineō, continēre, continuī, contentus, *2, tr.;* reprimō, reprimere, repressī, repressus, *3, tr.*

retreat, pedem referō, referre, rettulī, relātus, *irreg., tr.*

return, remittō, remittere, remīsī, remissus, *3, tr.;* revertor, revertī, revertī *or* reversus sum, *3, intr.*

reverence, veneror, *1, tr.*

revolution, rēs (rērum) novae (novārum).

reward, praemium, ī.

Rhine, Rhēnus, ī.

right *(noun),* jūs, jūris, *n.; (adj.),* dexter, dext(e)ra, dext(e)rum.

rightly, jūre, *adv.;* meritō, *adv.*

rise, orior, orīrī, ortus sum, *4, intr.*

river, flūmen, flūminis.

road, via, ae.

robbery, latrōcinium, ī.

Roman *(noun),* Rōmānus, ī; *(adj.),* Rōmānus, a, um.

Rome, Rōma, ae.

roof, tēctum, ī.

rout, pellō, pellere, pepulī, pulsus, *3, tr.*

route, iter, itineris, *n.*

royal power, rēgnum, ī.

ruin, exitium, ī; pestis, pestis.

rumor, fāma, ae.

run away, profugiō, profugere, profūgī, profugitum, *3, intr.*

rush forth, ērumpō, ērumpere, ērūpī, ēruptum, *3, intr.; **ex (ē)** w. abl.*

safe, salvus, a, um; tūtus, a, um.

safely, tūtō, *adv.*

safety, salūs, salūtis.

said, he (she, it), inquit *(with direct quotations);* **I also said, I said likewise,** dīxī ego īdem.

sail, nāvigō, *1, intr.*

sailor, nauta, ae.

saint *(noun),* sānctus, ī; sāncta, ae; *(adj.),* sānctus, a, um.

sake of, for the, causā; *w. gen.*

salvation, salūs, salūtis.

same, īdem, eadem, idem; **the same . . . as,** īdem, eadem, idem . . . quī, quae, quod (ac, atque); **to the same effect,** in eandem sententiam.

savage, atrōx (*gen.* atrōcis).

save, cōnservō, *1, tr.*

save from, ēripiō, ēripere, ēripuī, ēreptus, *3, tr.; w. dat. of person or thing from which; **ab (ā)** or **ex (ē)** w. abl.*

say, dīcō, dīcere, dīxī, dictus, *3, tr.; acc. w. infin.;* praedīcō, praedīcere, praedīxī, praedictus, *3, tr.; acc. w. infin.;* **he, she, it said (says),** inquit. *(Used with direct quotations only.)*

say . . . not, negō, *1, tr.; acc. w. infin.*

scarcely, vix, *adv.*

scarcity, inopia, ae.

scatter, differō, differe, distulī, dīlātus, *irreg., tr.*

science, scientia, ae.

Scipio, Scīpiō, Scīpiōnis.

seal, signum, ī.

second, alter, altera, alterum (Gr. 87); secundus, a, um.
secretly, clam, *adv.*
see, cōnspiciō, cōnspicere, cōnspexī, cōnspectus, *3, tr.; acc. w. infin.;* videō, vidēre, vīdī, vīsus, *2, tr.; acc. w. infin.*
see ahead, prōvideō, prōvidēre, prōvīdī, prōvīsus, *2, tr.; ut (nē).*
seek, petō, petere, petīvī, petītus, *3, tr.; ut (nē);* quaerō, quaerere, quaesīvī, quaesītus, *3, tr.*
seems good, it, placet, placēre, placuit, placitum, *2, intr.; w. dat.; w. infin.; acc. w. infin.; ut (nē).*
seize, comprehendō, comprehendere, comprehendī, comprehēnsus, *3, tr.;* occupō, *1, tr.;* rapiō, rapere, rapuī, raptus, *3, tr.*
self, ipse, ipsa, ipsum.
sell, vēndō, vēndere, vēndidī, vēnditus, *3, tr.*
senate, senātus, ūs; **gentlemen of the Senate,** patrēs (patrum) cōnscrīptī (cōnscrīptōrum).
senator, senātor, senātōris.
send, mittō, mittere, mīsī, missus, *3, tr.*
send against, immittō, immittere, immīsī, immissus, *3, tr.*
send ahead, praemittō, praemittere, praemīsī, praemissus, *3, tr.*
send away, dīmittō, dīmittere, dīmīsī, dīmissus, *3, tr.*
send back, remittō, remittere, remīsī, remissus, *3, tr.*
send forth, ēmittō, ēmittere, ēmīsī, ēmissus, *3, tr.*
send into, immittō, immittere, immīsī, immissus, *3, tr.*
send out, ēmittō, ēmittere, ēmīsī, ēmissus, *3, tr.*
sentence, damnō, *1, tr.; acc. of person; gen. or abl. of thing.*
sentence to death, capite damnō, *1, tr.*
separate, dīvidō, dīvidere, dīvīsī, dīvīsus, *3, tr.*
serious, gravis, e.
servant, servus, ī.
serve, serviō, *4, intr.; w. dat.*
services, opera, ae.
set, pōnō, pōnere, posuī, positus, *3, tr.*
set fire to, incendō, incendere, incendī, incēnsus, *3, tr.*
set free, vindicō, *1, tr.*
set on fire, īnflammō, *1, tr.*
set out, proficīscor, proficīscī, profectus sum, *3, intr.; ad w. acc.*
set up, cōnstituō, cōnstituere, cōnstituī, cōnstitūtus, *3, tr.;* statuō, statuere, statuī, statūtus, *3, tr.*
seven, septem, *indecl. numeral.*
several, complūrēs, complūra.
severe, gravis, e.
shame, turpitūdō, turpitūdinis.
sharp, ācer, ācris, ācre.
she, *fem. of* is, ea, id *or of* ille, illa, illud.
ship, nāvis, nāvis (*abl.* nāvī *or* nāve).
short, brevis, e.
short time, for a, paulisper, *adv.*
shout, clāmō, *1, tr.; acc. w. infin.*
shout, clāmor, clāmōris.
shouting, clāmor, clāmōris.
show, dēmōnstrō, *1, tr.; acc. w. infin.;* ostendō, ostendere, ostendī, ostentus (ostēnsus), *3, tr.; acc. w. infin.*
shrine, templum, ī.
shun, vītō, *1, tr.*
Sicily, Sicilia, ae.
sides, from all, undique, *adv.;* **on all sides,** undique, *adv.*
sight, aspectus, ūs.
sight of, catch, cōnspiciō, cōnspicere, cōnspexī, cōnspectus, *3, tr.*
sign, signum, ī.
signal, signum, ī.
silence, pass over in, taceō, *2, tr. and intr.*
silent, tacitus, a, um.
silent, am, sileō, silēre, siluī, *2, intr.;* taceō, *2, tr. and intr.*
silent, keep, sileō, silēre, siluī, *2, intr.*
similar, similis, e; *w. gen. or dat.*

sin *(in Christian Latin)*, peccātum, ī.
since, cum, *conj.*; **long since,** jam prīdem; jam diū; jam dūdum.
six, sex, *indecl. numeral.*
sixth, sextus, a, um.
size, magnitūdō, magnitūdinis.
sky, caelum, ī.
slaughter = kill.
slaughter, caedēs, caedis.
slave, servus, ī.
slavery, servitūs, servitūtis.
slip away, ēlābor, ēlābī, ēlāpsus sum, *3, intr.*
small, parvus, a, um.
smaller, minor, minus.
smallest, minimus, a, um.
snare, īnsidiae, īnsidiārum.
snatch, ēripiō, ēripere, ēripuī, ēreptus, *3, tr.; w. dat. of person or thing from which; ab (ā) or ex (ē) w. abl.;* rapiō, rapere, rapuī, raptus, *3, tr.*
so, adeō, tam *(degree)*, sīc *(manner)*, ita, *advs.;* **so . . . as,** tam (ita) . . . quam; **and so,** itaque, *conj.*
so great, tantus, a, um.
so many, tot, *indecl. adj.*
soldier, mīles, mīlitis.
solicit = tempt.
some, aliquis, aliqua, aliquod (Gr. 815); nōnnūllī, ae, a; **there are some who,** sunt quī; *w. subjunctive.*
some time, at, aliquandō, *adv.*
someone, aliquis, aliquid (Gr. 815).
something, aliquis, aliquid (Gr. 815).
son, fīlius, ī.
soon as, as, ut prīmum; cum prīmum, *conjs.*
sorrow, dolor, dolōris.
sort, of this, hūjus modī; ējus modī.
soul, animus, ī.
sound of, catch, exaudiō, *4, tr.*
spare, cōnservō, *1, tr.*
speak, loquor, loquī, locūtus sum, *3, tr. and intr.*
speech, ōrātiō, ōrātiōnis.
spend days in, diēs cōnsūmō, cōnsūmere, cōnsūmpsī, cōnsūmptus, *3, tr.; in w. abl.*
spirit, animus, ī; spīritus, ūs; **Holy Spirit,** Spīritus (ūs) Sānctus (ī).
splendid. *Use* bonus *or* optimus.
stand, stō, stāre, stetī, statum, *1, intr.*
standard, signum, ī.
start, orior, orīrī, ortus sum, *4, intr.*
state, cīvitās, cīvitātis; rēs (reī) pūblica (ae); (= **condition**), condiciō, condiciōnis.
station, collocō, *1, tr.;* dēpōnō, dēpōnere, dēposuī, dēpositus, *3, tr.;* dispōnō, dispōnere, disposuī, dispositus, *3, tr.*
sternness, sevēritās, sevēritātis.
still, tamen, *adv.*
stir up, concitō, *1, tr.;* sollicitō, *1, tr.*
storm, expugnō, *1, tr.;* oppugnō, *1, tr.;* **take by storm,** expugnō, *1, tr.*
storm, tempestās, tempestātis.
strength, vīrēs, vīrium, *f.*
strengthen, cōnfirmō, *1, tr.*
stretch to, pertineō, pertinēre, pertinuī, *2, intr.; ad w. acc.;* intendō, intendere, intendī, intentus, *3, tr.; ad or in w. acc.*
strictness, sevēritās, sevēritātis.
strive, contendō, contendere, contendī, *3, intr.; w. pres. infin.*
strive (after), studeō, studēre, studuī, *2, intr.; w. dat. or pres. infin.*
strong, firmus, a, um; fortis, e; **am strong,** valeō, valēre, valuī, *2, intr.*
such, tālis, e; **such . . . as,** tālis, e . . . quālis, e; **of such a kind,** tālis, e; **in such a manner,** ita, *adv.;* sīc, *adv.;* **in such a way,** ita, *adv.*
suddenly, subitō, *adv.*
suffer, patior, patī, passus sum, *3, tr.; w. pres. infin.; acc. w. infin.*
sufficiently, satis, *adv.*
suitable, idōneus, a, um; *w. dat. or ad w. acc.*
Sulpicius, Sulpicius, ī.
summon together, convocō, *1, tr.*
supply, cōpia, ae.

support, adsum, adesse, adfuī, adfutūrus, *irreg., intr.; w. dat.*
supposing that, ut, *conj.* (Gr. 596).
sure, certus, a, um.
surely *(in questions asked in surprise)*, num (Gr. 503).
surpass, superō, *1, tr.*
surprise, dēprehendō, dēprehendere, dēprehendī, dēprehēnsus, *3, tr.;* opprimō, opprimere, oppressī, oppressus, *3, tr.*
surprised at, am, admīror, *1, tr.*
surrender, dēdō, dēdere, dēdidī, dēditus, *3, tr. (Always takes an object.)*
suspect, suspicor, *1, tr.; acc. w. infin.*
sustain, sustineō, sustinēre, sustinuī, sustentus, *2, tr.*
swift, celer, celeris, celere.
sword, gladius, ī.

take, capiō, capere, cēpī, captus, *3, tr.;* sūmō, sūmere, sūmpsī, sūmptus, *3, tr.;* accipiō, accipere, accēpī, acceptus, *3, tr.*
take away, ēripiō, ēripere, ēripuī, ēreptus, *3, tr.; w. dat. of person or thing from which; ab (ā) or ex (ē) w. abl.;* tollō, tollere, sustulī, sublātus, *3, tr.*
take back, recipiō, recipere, recēpī, receptus, *3, tr.*
take by storm, expugnō, *1, tr.*
take care, cūrō, *1, tr.; ut (nē);* prōvideō, prōvidēre, prōvīdī, prōvīsus, *2, tr.; ut (nē).*
take my word for it, mihi crēde.
take (upon oneself), suscipiō, suscipere, suscēpī, susceptus, *3, tr.*
talk, loquor, loquī, locūtus sum, *3, tr. and intr.*
tell, dīcō, dīcere, dīxī, dictus, *3, tr.; acc. w. infin.;* ostendō, ostendere, ostendī, ostentus, *3, tr.; acc. w. infin.*
temple, templum, ī.
tempt, sollicitō, *1, tr.*
ten, decem, *indecl. numeral.*
tenth, decimus, a, um.
termination, fīnis, fīnis, *m.*
terms, condiciōnēs, condiciōnum.
terrify, terreō, *2, tr.*
territory, fīnēs, fīnium, *m.*
than, quam, *adv.;* **rather than**, potius quam.
thank, grātiās agō, agere, ēgī, āctus, *3, tr.*
thanks, grātiae, grātiārum; **give thanks**, grātiās agō, agere, ēgī, āctus, *3, tr.*
that *(demonstrative pronoun)*, is, ea, id; ille, illa, illud; *(relative pronoun)*, quī, quae, quod.
that *(conj.)*, ut; quō *(in purpose clauses containing a comparative adverb or adjective).*
that . . . never, nē umquam *(in negative purpose clauses).*
that . . . no one, nē quis *(in negative purpose clauses).*
that . . . not, nē, *conj. (in negative purpose clauses and some noun clauses);* ut nōn *(in result clauses and some noun clauses);* quōminus *(after verbs of hindering, preventing, etc.).*
that . . . nothing, nē quid *(in negative purpose clauses).*
that . . . nowhere, nēcubi *(in negative purpose clauses).*
their *(reflexive)*, suus, a, um.
their own, suus, a, um; **of their own accord**, suā sponte.
them (themselves), suī.
then, tum, *adv.*
there, ibi, *adv.*
therefore, itaque, *conj.*
thereupon, deinde, *adv.*
they, eī, eae, ea.
thing, rēs, reī; **certain thing**, quīdam, quiddam (Gr. 820).
think, arbitror, *1, tr.; acc. w. infin.;* cēnseō, cēnsēre, cēnsuī, cēnsus, *2, tr.; acc. w. infin.; ut (nē);* cōgitō, *1, tr. and intr.; acc. w. infin.;* exīstimō, *1, tr.; acc. w. infin.;* putō, *1, tr.; acc.*

w. infin.; sentiō, sentīre, sēnsī, sēnsus, *4, tr.; acc. w. infin.*
third, tertius, a, um.
this, hic, haec, hoc; **of this kind (sort)**, hūjus modī; ējus modī.
thousand, mīlle, *indecl. adj.* (*pl.*, mīlia, mīlium, *n.*).
threaten, impendeō, impendēre, *2, intr.; w. dat.*
threatening, īnfestus, a, um.
three, trēs, tria. (*Declined like the plural of* gravis.)
throng, frequentia, ae.
through, per, *prep. w. acc.*
throw, jaciō, jacere, jēcī, jactus, *3, tr.*
throw out, ējiciō, ējicere, ējēcī, ējectus, *3, tr.*
thus, ita, *adv.;* sīc, *adv.*
time, tempus, temporis, *n.;* **a long time**, diū, *adv.;* **at any time**, umquam, *adv.;* **at some time**, aliquandō, *adv.;* **at that time**, tum, *adv.;* **for a short time**, paulisper, *adv.*
to, ad, *prep. w. acc.*
to such a degree, adeō, *adv.;* tam, *adv.*
to the same effect, in eandem sententiam.
together, bring, cōgō, cōgere, coēgī, coāctus, *3, tr.; acc. w. pres. infin.;* cōnferō, cōnferre, contulī, collātus, *irreg., tr.;* colligō, colligere, collēgī, collēctus, *3, tr.*
together, call, convocō, *1, tr.*
together, come, conveniō, convenīre, convēnī, conventum, *4, intr.*
together, gather, congregō, *1, tr.*
together, join, conjungō, conjungere, conjūnxī, conjūnctus, *3, tr.*
together, summon, convocō, *1, tr.*
toil, labor, labōris.
too little, parum, *indecl. noun; w. gen.;* minus, *adv.;* parum, *adv.*
toward, sub, *prep. w. acc.*
towards, in, *prep. w. acc.*
town, oppidum, ī.
train, exerceō, *2, tr.*
transfer, trānsferō, trānsferre, trānstulī, trānslātus, *irreg., tr.*
treat, agō, agere, ēgī, āctus, *3, tr.*
trial, jūdicium, ī.
tribe, gēns, gentis; nātiō, nātiōnis.
tribune, tribūnus, ī; **military tribune**, tribūnus (ī) mīlitum.
troop, manus, ūs, *f.*
troops, cōpiae, cōpiārum.
trouble, difficultās, difficultātis.
true, vērus, a, um.
truly, vērē, *adv.*
trust, crēdō, crēdere, crēdidī, crēditus, *3, tr. and intr.; w. dat. of person to whom or in whom; acc. w. infin.;* cōnfīdō, cōnfīdere, cōnfīsus sum, *3, intr.; w. dat. of person; abl. of thing; acc. w. infin.*
truth, vēritās, vēritātis; vērum, ī; **in truth**, vērō, *adv. and conj., postp.*
try, cōnor, *1, tr.; w. pres. infin.*
turn about, convertō, convertere, convertī, conversus, *3, tr.*
twentieth, vīcēsimus, a, um.
two, duo, duae, duo (Gr. 115).
type, of this, ējus modī; hūjus modī.

unable, am, nōn possum, posse, potuī, *irreg., intr.; w. infin.*
unasked, ultrō, *adv.*
unaware, am, ignōrō, *1, tr.; acc. w. infin.*
unbelievable, incrēdibilis, e.
uncertain, dubius, a, um.
uncover, aperiō, aperīre, aperuī, apertus, *4, tr.*
under, sub, *prep. w. abl.;* sub, *prep. w. acc.*
undergo, obeō, obīre, obiī, obitus, *irreg., tr.*
understand, intellegō, intellegere, intellēxī, intellēctus, *3, tr.; acc. w. infin.*
undertake, suscipiō, suscipere, suscēpī, susceptus, *3, tr.;* mōlior, mōlīrī, mōlītus sum, *4, tr.*
undutiful, impius, a, um.

unfavorable, aliēnus, a, um.
uninjured, integer, integra, integrum.
unite, conjungō, conjungere, conjūnxī, conjūnctus, *3, tr.;* jungō, jungere, jūnxī, jūnctus, *3, tr.*
unpopularity, invidia, ae.
unprovoked, ultrō, *adv.*
unpunished, impūnītus, a, um.
unsigned = without a name.
unskilled (in), imperītus, a, um; *w. gen.*
until, ad, *prep. w. acc.*
unwilling, am, nōlō, nōlle, nōluī, *tr.; w. infin.; acc. w. infin.;* ***ut (nē).***
up (to), usque, *adv.*
up to, sub, *prep. w. acc.*
upon, in, *prep. w. acc.*
upright, honestus, a, um.
uproar, tumultus, ūs.
urge, hortor, *1, tr.;* ***ut (nē).***
use, ūtor, ūtī, ūsus sum, *3, intr.; w. abl.;* adhibeō, *2, tr.;* ***ad*** *w. acc.*
useful (for), ūtilis, e; ***ad*** *w. acc.*
utterance, prophetic, fātum, ī.

very great, summus, a, um.
very many, plūrimus, a, um.
victory, victōria, ae.
view, perspiciō, perspicere, perspexī, perspectus, *3, tr.; acc. w. infin.*
vigorous, firmus, a, um.
violence, vīs (*acc.* vim, *abl.* vī).
violent, vehemēns (*gen.* vehementis).
violently, vehementer, *adv.;* vī.
virtue, virtūs, virtūtis.
visit, adeō, adīre, adiī(-īvī), aditus, *irreg., tr.*
voice, vōx, vōcis.

wage war, bellum gerō, gerere, gessī, gestus, *3, tr.*
wait, exspectō, *1, tr.*
wait for, exspectō, *1, tr.*
wall, mūrus, ī; vallum, ī.
walls, moenia, moenium.
want, careō, carēre, caruī, caritūrus, *2, intr.; w. abl. See also* **wish, desire.**
want, inopia, ae.
war, bellum, ī; **wage war,** bellum gerō. gerere, gessī, gestus, *3, tr.;* **make war on,** bellum īnferō, īnferre, intulī, illātus, *irreg., tr.*
ward off (from), prohibeō, *2, tr.*
warn, moneō, *2, tr.;* ***ut (nē).***
Washington (George), Washingtonius, ī.
Washington *(the city). Use the English form unchanged in Latin.*
waste, lay, vastō, *1, tr.*
watch, night, vigilia, ae.
way, ratiō, ratiōnis; via, ae.
way, give, cēdō, cēdere, cessī, cessūrus, *3, intr.*
way, in such a, ita, *adv.*
way (to), all the, usque (ad), *adv.*
waylay, īnsidior, *1, intr.; w. dat.*
we, nōs, nostrī.
weapons, arma, armōrum; tēla, tēlōrum.
wear out, cōnficiō, cōnficere, cōnfēcī, cōnfectus, *3, tr.*
weather, tempestās, tempestātis.
welfare, salūs, salūtis.
well, bene, *adv.*
well, am, valeō, valēre, valuī, *2, intr.; w. infin.*
well-known, nōtus, a, um.
what ***(interrogative pronoun),*** quis, quid; ***(interrogative adj.),*** quī, quae, quod; ***(relative pronoun),*** quī, quae, quod.
when, cum, *conj.;* ubi, *conj.*
where, ubi, *adv.;* ***(of motion),*** quō, *adv.*
wherefore, quārē, *adv.*
which ***(interrogative and relative),*** quī, quae, quod.
whither, quō, *adv.*
who ***(relative pronoun),*** quī, quae, quod; ***(interrogative pronoun),*** quis, quid.
whole, integer, integra, integrum; tōtus, a, um (Gr. 84); **the whole of,** tōtus, a, um (Gr. 84).

why, cūr, *adv.*
wicked, improbus, a, um; nefārius, a, um.
wickedness, nēquitia, ae.
wide, lātus, a, um.
widely, lātē, *adv.*
will, voluntās, voluntātis.
willing, am, volō, velle, voluī, *tr.; w. pres. infin.; acc. w. infin.; **ut (nē)**;* **am not willing,** nōlō, nōlle, nōluī, *tr.; w. infin.; acc. w. infin.; **ut (nē)**.*
wind, ventus, ī.
winter quarters, hīberna, hībernōrum.
wish, volō, velle, voluī, *tr.; w. pres. infin.; acc. w. infin.; **ut (nē)**;* **do not wish,** nōlō, nōlle, nōluī, *tr.; w. infin.; acc. w. infin.; **ut (nē)**.*
with, cum, *prep. w. abl.*
with difficulty, vix, *adv.*
withdraw, concēdō, concēdere, concessī, concessus, *3, tr. and intr.;* discēdō, discēdere, discessī, discessum, *3, intr.; **ab (ā), ex (ē), dē** w. abl.;* mē (tē, sē) recipiō, recipere, recēpī, receptus, *3, tr.*
without, sine, *prep. w. abl.*
without, am, careō, carēre, caruī, caritūrus, *2, intr.; w. abl.*
withstand, resistō, resistere, restitī, *3, intr.; w. dat.;* sustineō, sustinēre, sustinuī, sustentus, *2, tr.*
witness, testis, testis, *m.*
wonder at, admīror, *1, tr.*
word, verbum, ī; **take my word for it,** mihi crēde.
work, hard, industria, ae.
world, mundus, ī; orbis (orbis) terrārum (*sometimes* terrae).
world without end, in saecula saeculōrum.
worse *(adj.)*, pējor, pējus; *(adv.)*, pējus.
worst *(adj.)*, pessimus, a, um; *(adv.)*, pessimē.
worthy (**of**), dignus, a, um; *w. abl.*
would that, utinam *(particle used with volitive subjunctive).*
would that not, nē, *conj. (with volitive subjunctive).*
wound, vulnerō, *1, tr.*
wound, vulnus, vulneris, *n.*
wretched, miser, misera, miserum.
write, scrībō, scrībere, scrīpsī, scrīptus, *3, tr.; acc. w. infin.,* cōnscrībō, cōnscrībere, cōnscrīpsī, cōnscrīptus, *3, tr.; acc. w. infin.*
write on, īnscrībō, īnscrībere, īnscrīpsī, īnscrīptus, *3, tr.*
wrong, injūria, ae.

year, annus, ī.
yet, adhūc, *adv.;* tamen, *adv.;* **not yet,** nōndum, *adv.*
yield, cēdō, cēdere, cessī, cessūrus, *3, intr.;* concēdō, concēdere, concessī, concessus, *3, tr. and intr.*
you *(sing.)*, tū, tuī; *(pl.)*, vōs, vestrī.
young, juvenis, e.
young man, adulēscēns, adulēscentis.
younger, junior, junius.
your (**own**), tuus, a, um *(when referring to one person);* vester, vestra, vestrum *(when referring to more than one person);* **of your own accord,** tuā sponte.
yours, tuus, a, um *(when referring to one person);* vester, vestra, vestrum *(when referring to more than one).*

zeal, studium, ī.